Global Perspectives on Value Education in Primary School

Aytekin Demircioğlu
Kastamonu University, Turkey

A volume in the Advances in Early Childhood and
K-12 Education (AECKE) Book Series

Published in the United States of America by
    IGI Global
    Information Science Reference (an imprint of IGI Global)
    701 E. Chocolate Avenue
    Hershey PA, USA 17033
    Tel: 717-533-8845
    Fax: 717-533-8661
    E-mail: cust@igi-global.com
    Web site: http://www.igi-global.com

Library of Congress Cataloging-in-Publication Data

Names: Demircioğlu, Aytekin, 1977- editor.
Title: Global perspectives on value education in primary school / edited by
  Aytekin Demircioğlu.
Description: Hershey, PA : Information Science Reference, [2023] | Includes
  bibliographical references and index. | Summary: "Teaching values is an
  important issue at the level of basic education, pre-school education
  and primary school all over the world. The values to be transferred to
  children and young people may vary according to countries, cultures and
  time. However, every culture and society wish to teach its own values to
  its citizens. Primary schools are the most important places where this
  aim is realized. For this reason, the main objective of this book is to
  examine and introduce values education studies at primary school
  level"-- Provided by publisher.
Identifiers: LCCN 2023029636 (print) | LCCN 2023029637 (ebook) | ISBN
  9781668492956 (h/c) | ISBN 9781668492994 (s/c) | ISBN 9781668492963
  (eISBN)
Subjects: LCSH: Moral education. | Values--Study and teaching (Elementary)
Classification: LCC LC268 .G527 2023 (print) | LCC LC268 (ebook) | DDC
  370.11/4--dc23/eng/20230718
LC record available at https://lccn.loc.gov/2023029636
LC ebook record available at https://lccn.loc.gov/2023029637

This book is published in the IGI Global book series Advances in Early Childhood and K-12 Education (AECKE) (ISSN: 2329-5929; eISSN: 2329-5937)

British Cataloguing in Publication Data
A Cataloguing in Publication record for this book is available from the British Library.

For electronic access to this publication, please contact: eresources@igi-global.com.

Advances in Early Childhood and K-12 Education (AECKE) Book Series

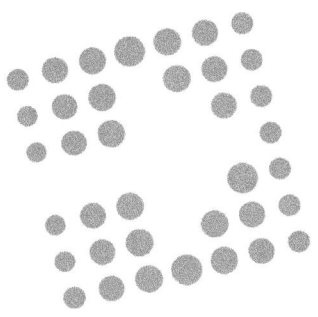

Jared Keengwe
University of North Dakota, USA

ISSN:2329-5929
EISSN:2329-5937

MISSION

Early childhood and K-12 education is always evolving as new methods and tools are developed through which to shape the minds of today's youth. Globally, educational approaches vary allowing for new discussions on the best methods to not only educate, but also measure and analyze the learning process as well as an individual's intellectual development. New research in these fields is necessary to improve the current state of education and ensure that future generations are presented with quality learning opportunities.

The **Advances in Early Childhood and K-12 Education (AECKE)** series aims to present the latest research on trends, pedagogies, tools, and methodologies regarding all facets of early childhood and K-12 education.

COVERAGE

- K-12 Education
- Urban K-12 Education
- Diverse Learners
- Standardized Testing
- Reading and Writing
- Poverty and Education
- Performance Assessment
- STEM Education
- Learning Outcomes
- Literacy Development

IGI Global is currently accepting manuscripts for publication within this series. To submit a proposal for a volume in this series, please contact our Acquisition Editors at Acquisitions@igi-global.com or visit: http://www.igi-global.com/publish/.

Titles in this Series

For a list of additional titles in this series, please visit: www.igi-global.com/book-series

701 East Chocolate Avenue, Hershey, PA 17033, USA
Tel: 717-533-8845 x100 • Fax: 717-533-8661
E-Mail: cust@igi-global.com • www.igi-global.com

Table of Contents

Detailed Table of Contents

Chapter 1

Turgay Öntaş, Tekirdag Namik Kemal University, Turkey
Okan Çoban, Ministry of National Education, Turkey

In this study, social and democratic participation skills were associated in the context of values education. Since the construction of values is the focus of many different social science disciplines, analyses were carried out by establishing a connection between the concepts. Basically, connections were established between concepts through child and childhood. The prevailing view of childhood often portrays children as innocent and disinterested in political matters, suggesting that they should be raised as apolitical beings. However, children are exposed to political content through both formal and informal education processes. Primary educational institutions have the aim of developing social and democratic participation skills in children. In the global context, the construction of values in children is regarded as essential for cultivating citizenship skills.

Chapter 2

Antonio Daniel Juan Rubio, Universidad de Granada, Spain

Reading encouragement is a transversal subject present throughout the entire educational stage of any student from early childhood education through primary education to Secondary Education and higher education. In this chapter, the authors intersperse the pleasure of reading in another language (English) and the reflection on the values transmitted by each of the selected stories. The main purpose is to teach a list of values to students in primary education but using this selection of stories as a basis to reach the internalization of these values. We cannot forget that they are still children and that we have to adapt the contents and learning channels to their evolutionary stage. By using fantastic characters, the concepts are extrapolated in a different way, making it easier for children to internalize the values. Therefore, the main objective of this work is to implement a didactic proposal based on the use of stories in English for values education in a group of children in the fifth grade of primary school.

Chapter 3

Md Ikhtiar Uddin Bhuiyan, Jahangirnagar University, Bangladesh
Md Meshkat Mollik, Jahangirnagar University, Bangladesh

This chapter examines the opportunities and challenges of leveraging technology to enhance quality education in primary schools in Bangladesh. A qualitative approach is employed, collecting data from primary schools in Turkey, the United States, and China through interviews, observations, and analysis of curricular materials. Thematic analysis is conducted using NVivo and SPSS software. The study investigates the concept of value education across cultures, presents comparative analyses of different approaches, and highlights challenges faced by educators in culturally diverse classrooms. It also explores the state of primary education in Bangladesh, identifies reasons for the lack of quality education, and proposes strategies for improvement. Emphasizing the crucial role of the government, the research assesses opportunities for effective implementation of quality education and provides solutions to prevailing problems.

Chapter 4

Fatmanur Özen, Giresun University, Turkey

Values education aims to cultivate learners' values, discipline them according to established rules, and positively transform their characters by contributing to their moral development. This education, encompassing both cognitive and affective dimensions of teaching, represents one of the most significant goals of education systems. The objective of this section is to analyze research trends related to values education in Türkiye and the outcomes of these studies at the basic education level, alongside a systematic examination of doctoral dissertations. To achieve this, doctoral dissertations registered and available in the Thesis Center of the Turkish Council of Higher Education were reviewed using keywords such as value/ values education, character education, moral education, and citizenship education. This study examines 102 doctoral dissertations, categorizing them based on the subject of values education, exploring how values education is defined within the dissertations, examining the research methods, and evaluating the findings at the basic education level.

Chapter 5

Gülcan Demir, Sinop University, Turkey
Esra Savaş, Boyabat Mevlana Vocational and Technical Anatolian High School, Turkey
Lütfiye Hilal Özcebe, Hacettepe University, Turkey

Individual and societal values, which are the reasons behind decisions and choices, guide thoughts and behaviors. Values also shape an individual's actions regarding their health, contributing to health improvement. Our values play a crucial role in enhancing the quality of life, encompassing physical, social, environmental, emotional, and mental well-being. The periods of elementary school, childhood, and adolescence are stages where health risks can pose threats. During this time, children may be influenced by new social relationships and their environment, which can lead to undesired changes in existing values. Health-based values education provides school-aged children with opportunities to develop knowledge and skills for healthy growth and disease prevention. This education conveys health-related values to children, encouraging them to adopt a healthy lifestyle. Furthermore, values education, commencing from an early age and progressing gradually, can play a protective role against risks that may arise during adolescence.

Chapter 6

Muhammad Waseem Bari, Government College University, Faisalabad, Pakistan
Faiza Baig, Government College University Faisalabad, Pakistan
Irum Shahzadi, Government College University, Faisalabad, Pakistan

Primary education is the earliest level of formal education that serves as a center for developing young brains and providing the fundamentals of education. Workplace bullying is a ubiquitous issue that affects workers all over the world, including in the education sector. Educators, staff, and students may experience the negative effects of workplace bullying. Physical aggression, verbal abuse, and social isolation are just a few examples. Bullying can occur in a variety of contexts, including face-to-face interactions, online communication, and indirect forms such as gossip and rumor spreading, and it can make it harder for educationalists to provide a supportive learning environment for their students. It can have a negative impact on educators' well-being and job satisfaction and promotes stress, anxiety, burnout, or other deviant behaviors, which eventually impede students' education. Therefore, an exploratory study is vital that investigates the antecedents and consequences of workplace bullying in primary education.

Chapter 7

Isabel María García, Centro Universitario de la Defensa de San Javier, Spain

Education in values is an issue of great relevance in today's society. That is why the chapter focuses on highlighting several points. The subject of values has been, is, and will always be a fundamental, transcendent, and a permanently topical issue in education. Values are constantly present in our lives and that is why we must emphasize the work and empowerment of these, inside and outside the classroom and in any subject, in a playful and motivating way for our children, that is, using the activity that is present in all human beings, the game. Therefore, the main objective of this chapter will be to know the relevance of games, not only for recreational purposes, but also for learning, and to highlight the need to work on education in values for the personal development of children.

Chapter 8

Bekir Tastan, Kastamonu University, Turkey

Disasters cause great damage worldwide every year. A conscious and scientific strategy should be used to reduce the damage. Disaster management ensures the successful completion of the process. If people want to manage disasters properly, they must act diligently at every stage of disaster management. These tasks can be fulfilled by vigilant, responsible, and educated individuals. Disaster awareness can be increased with the support of education. Primary school is the most memorable period of education. In this period, disaster education is not included in the curriculum. Teaching values in the curriculum can play an important role in increasing disaster awareness in this period. This study shows how values education and disaster awareness are integrated in primary schools. In the first part of the study, disasters are mentioned. In the following sections, the contribution of disaster education and values education to disaster awareness is discussed.

Values education is carried out in many countries with different names and systems. Although differences are observed according to the social, political, religious, and economic structure of each country, value education aims to provide an ideal structure for the individual and society by transferring cultural, moral, national, and universal values to individuals. In this study, values education in Germany, one of the important countries of Europe, was examined, and the situation of values education applied in the state of North Rhine-Westphalia was revealed as well as general values education in Germany. In Germany, values education is mainly given in Ethics and Religion courses. The data in the research were obtained by using the literature review technique, one of the qualitative research methods. As a result of the research, it has been understood that the values education in the Values and Norms course in primary schools in the state of North Rhine-Westphalia is not given at a sufficient level, and this course is only a specific course.

The purpose of this chapter is to highlight the significance and processes involved in conducting shared reflections to nurture value development in children in primary schools. The chapter describes the characteristics and application of the value-based reflection framework (VBRF), which was devised specifically for this study and employed as a reflective instrument for classroom reflections. Additionally, to facilitate children's reflections, value scenarios were also used to prompt children to relate value practices to real-world contexts. This chapter serves as a guide for teachers, empowering them with guidelines for conducting reflection sessions during moral education classes, as well as informing educators, curriculum designers, and policymakers about incorporating reflective practices for children's value development.

According to Mustafa Kemal, salvation is possible only through national education. The consciousness of freedom should be taught in schools. Teachers also had duties on the path to national awakening and organization. After the Grand National Assembly was established in Ankara, the government gave the students and teachers the task of enlightening Turkish people. The idea was that future generations should be raised with a national, scientific, and secular education to protect Türkiye's independence and strengthen the republic regime. The feelings of virtue, self-sacrifice, order, discipline, and self-confidence should be reinforced in the new generation. The "citizenship education at primary school," which the intellectuals of constitutionalism focused on within the scope of the "new man-new society" project, constituted an important dimension of nation-building. In this study, citizenship education courses with different names such as Citizenship, Homeland, Malumat-ı Vataniye, etc. will be evaluated by using official course books from the 1920s to 1950s in the Republic of Türkiye.

This chapter looks at value-based education and its implications on reflections in English language teaching of primary and secondary school children. The chapter considers the classification, methods, theoretical framework, advantages, and disadvantages of value education and using reflections. Constructivist learning and reflection theories were used to explain links and effects of reflective experiences and integrating value-based education principles in young learner education. It further examined values students were expected to develop and exhibit, and implications on English language teaching. Published books, articles, research findings, institutional reports, and personal observation when teaching and training ELT students were the main sources of information. Value-based education and reflective practices are emphasized to ensure effective English language teaching in Turkish schools. Thus, it is recommended that educators be exposed to value-based education and teach values and reflective tools when teaching contextual language.

This study aims to highlight the place and significance of visual arts in values education at the primary school level. Using a literature review method, one of the qualitative research approaches, the research concludes that visual arts serve as an effective tool for fostering values education in primary schools. Visual arts hold great importance in values education due to their ability to facilitate originality through diverse activities and practices. They provide an effective platform for developing values such as self-confidence, self-respect, sensitivity, awareness, empathy, respect, love, responsibility, cooperation, justice, respect for differences, and tolerance, both in individual achievements and group work. Visual arts are believed to play a vital role in values education by embodying abstract concepts.

The concept of value, which is included in sciences such as philosophy, sociology, and psychology, is a term that questions what and what is important for individuals or groups and includes concepts such as independence, trust, wisdom, success, kindness, etc. Tawakkul means that an individual leaves the course and outcome of a job to Allah after showing his determination and determination. In this respect, the present study consists of evaluations on Turkish words such as köŋül ba-, köŋül ur-, etc., which are expanded from the concept of köŋül 'gönül' used for the first time in Turkish Qur'an translations and other Islamic texts for the concept of 'tawakkül'. In the study, firstly, the concept of 'tawakkul' as an Islamic value is mentioned and then linguistic analyses are made on the expressions derived from the word köŋül 'gönül', which is one of the important concepts in term derivation in both pre-Islamic and Islamic period Turkish religious vocabulary.

    Leila Soudani, Ibn Khaldoun University, Tiaret, Algeria
    Meriem Chafaa, Ibn Khaldoun University, Tiaret, Algeria
    Moulkheir Selmani, Ibn Khaldoun University, Tiaret, Algeria

The Algerian educational system of today is different from that of years ago; more approaches are included, more teaching techniques are combined, and the emphasis on language learning has grown. Primary, middle, and high schools offer classes in Arabic, French, and Tamazight. It would be vital to incorporate English into primary schools in light of the government's plan to designate it as a second language in addition to French. This produces a generation that can advance in linguistic proficiency. Of course, switching from French to English, a language that has been used as a second language for hundreds of years, is difficult. The most important weapon for change is education. Such a change obviously meets numerous hurdles and difficulties; for instance, there needs to be an adequate number of teachers and instructors who can spread the language at all levels. This chapter focuses on the methods, requirements, and challenges of introducing English to the Algerian primary school and the potential obstacles that policymakers and educators may face when teaching English.

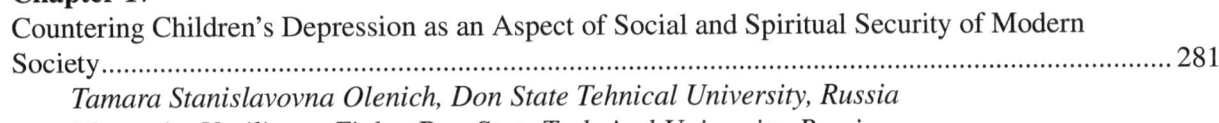

    Monica Mastrantonio, Justus Liebig, Germany

In the survey Imaginable Futures conducted worldwide in the year of 2022, which had 311 responders across the globe, kindness was mentioned as the one core skill for the future. Together with the importance of education for peace, mental health, and the development of survival skills in case of disasters, kindness is listed as the core skill to social bonds. Children school education and school curriculums are mostly based on content acquisition, whereas research data points to what the new generations will need in the near future. Kindness is connected to happiness, well-being, empathy, and sociability, and it can generate physical benefits, like low blood pressure. However, how can these skills be integrated in the school curriculum? How prepared are the teachers to implement this new acquisition? This research concludes that kindness and hope should be far and firstly implemented as key educational figures at this critical time of Anthropocene.

    Tamara Stanislavovna Olenich, Don State Tehnical University, Russia
    Margarita Vasilievna Finko, Don State Technical University, Russia

The chapter examines the peculiarities of the problem of depression among school children in the context of ensuring social and spiritual security. The chapter describes the problem of depression and its most negative consequence, suicide, and the reasons that push children to these social actions, among which the authors have identified the following: the social hierarchy of postmodern society, apathy and indifference of parents, the activities of religious cults and "death groups." The activities of death groups are one of the main causes that lead to a violation of social security and have an impact on the younger generation, committing children to suicide. The mechanism of work of such groups, basic techniques, and mechanisms of their work are described. The authors conduct a sociological study in local secondary schools located in the Don region to identify the level of depression among school children. The authors propose a number of educational innovations and other methods aimed at identifying and preventing depression in the younger generation.

Chapter 18

Value education is the teaching and learning of values as empathy, respect, responsibility, etc. in schools. It aims to feed moral development and ethical advances to array students and equip them with the skills to navigate complex social situation. As an important part of education, value education is interested in developing moral values and ethics of the students. It also helps these students develop understanding and evaluating of the importance of these values like respect, honesty, empathy, and the like. They understand how to manage and live satisfactory quality lives.

Chapter 19

Values play a key role in order to exist in social life practices and to ensure the continuity of culture. As a matter of fact, values are a system of beliefs consisting of the experiences of the individual through socialization. In this context, in the study, sample activities were presented in the worksheets supported by nine values in the 4th grade social studies curriculum (SSLC). Literary genres such as epics, stories, poems, proverbs, quotations, comics, and biography were used in the worksheets. As a matter of fact, it is known that the use of literary works in the learning and teaching process serves permanent learning. For this reason, literary works were used in the worksheets prepared on value transfer in the study. Literary works appear as a reflector and transmitter of culture. These works are seen as important works in reflecting the social life, social relations, moral, and religious values of the period. This is important in order to ensure that values are internalized correctly. In this context, it is thought that the study will guide educators.

Preface

As editor of *Global Perspectives on Value Education in Primary School*, it is with great enthusiasm that I present this comprehensive reference book exploring the pivotal role of values education in shaping young minds across the world. At the core of our societies lies the shared aspiration to instill fundamental values in the next generation, fostering a foundation of ethical consciousness, empathy, and social responsibility.

In the fast-paced and interconnected world we inhabit, the significance of values education has never been more pronounced. As I state, the values to be imparted may vary across countries, cultures, and epochs, yet the overarching aim remains the same - to inculcate virtues that will serve as guiding lights for the children and youth of today, as they mature into responsible and compassionate adults of tomorrow.

Primary schools occupy a crucial position in this noble endeavor, serving as the fertile ground where seeds of values are sown and nurtured. The purpose of this compilation is to present a comprehensive survey of values education studies, with a particular focus on the primary school level, from diverse corners of the globe. By examining a rich tapestry of practices and approaches, we aspire to kindle inspiration for future value studies that will fortify the moral fabric of society.

Within these pages, esteemed researchers, scientists, educators, and practitioners from all walks of life will find a treasure trove of insights, analysis, and exemplary instances of values education. By showcasing country and culture-specific value studies, we celebrate the richness and diversity of human experience, while also revealing the universal themes that transcend geographical boundaries.

From case studies elucidating successful values education programs to discussions on the nuanced differentiation of values to be taught, this book encompasses a broad spectrum of themes. By offering comparisons on value education methodologies, we encourage a global exchange of ideas, paving the way for a harmonious and collaborative approach to nurturing values in the young generation.

Chapter 1 delves into the association of social and democratic participation skills within the context of values education. By establishing connections between concepts through child and childhood, the prevailing view of children as disinterested in political matters is challenged. The chapter explores how primary educational institutions play a pivotal role in developing social and democratic participation skills in children, emphasizing the significance of values education in cultivating citizenship skills on a global scale.

Chapter 2 focuses on the transversal subject of reading encouragement throughout different educational stages, from Early Childhood Education to Secondary Education. The main objective is to teach a list of values to primary school students through the use of selected stories. By using fantastic characters and creative storytelling, the chapter aims to help children internalize these values, recognizing the need to adapt content and learning channels to their developmental stage.

In Chapter 3, the utilization of technology to enhance quality education in primary schools in Bangladesh is examined. The chapter employs a qualitative approach, gathering data from schools in Turkey, the United States, and China to compare different approaches to value education. Challenges faced by educators in culturally diverse classrooms are highlighted, alongside proposed strategies for improvement. Emphasizing the role of the government, the research assesses opportunities for effective implementation of quality education and presents solutions to prevailing problems.

Chapter 4 delves into research trends related to values education in Türkiye, specifically at the basic education level. The study reviews 102 doctoral dissertations to categorize them based on the subject of values education, examine research methods, and evaluate findings. The chapter offers insights into how values education is defined and practiced within these dissertations, contributing to a better understanding of values education in the Türkiye context.

In Chapter 5, the relationship between values and health improvement is explored. The chapter highlights the role of values in enhancing physical, social, environmental, emotional, and mental well-being. It underscores the importance of values education for school-aged children, providing them with knowledge and skills for healthy growth and disease prevention. The chapter emphasizes the protective role of values education against risks that may arise during adolescence.

Chapter 6 focuses on the critical issue of workplace bullying in the education sector, particularly in primary schools. The chapter explores how bullying affects educators, staff, and students, leading to negative impacts on well-being, job satisfaction, and student education. An exploratory study is presented to investigate the antecedents and consequences of workplace bullying in primary education, shedding light on potential solutions.

Chapter 7 highlights the relevance of games in teaching values, particularly freedom, solidarity, health, justice, responsibility, and others. The chapter underscores the importance of integrating values education into different subjects through playful and motivating activities. The primary objective is to promote personal development and empower children through Education in Values.

Chapter 8 addresses the significance of disaster education and values education integration in primary schools. The chapter explores how disaster awareness can be increased by incorporating values education in the curriculum, helping children develop knowledge and skills for disaster prevention and response. The study emphasizes the need for a conscious and scientific strategy to reduce the damage caused by disasters.

Chapter 9 examines values education in Germany, focusing on the state of North Rhine-Westphalia. The study reveals that values education in the state is mainly given in Ethics and Religion courses. The chapter emphasizes the need for more comprehensive values education and highlights areas for improvement in the existing curriculum.

Chapter 10 highlights the significance of conducting shared reflections to nurture value development in primary school children. The Value-Based Reflection Framework (VBRF) is presented as an effective reflective instrument for classroom reflections, and value scenarios are used to prompt children to relate value practices to real-world contexts. The chapter serves as a guide for teachers and educators in incorporating reflective practices for children's value development.

Chapter 11 explores the role of citizenship education in primary schools during the early years of the Republic of Türkiye. The chapter evaluates citizenship education courses and their impact on nation-building and national awakening. The research assesses various courses offered from the 1920s to the 1950s, shedding light on the development of national values in the new generation.

Chapter 12 delves into the implications of Value-Based Education and reflections in English Language Teaching at Primary and Secondary school levels. The study examines the classification, methods, theoretical framework, and advantages of value education, emphasizing the importance of reflective experiences and integrating Value-Based Education principles in young learner education. Practical recommendations for effective English Language Teaching in Turkish schools are provided.

Chapter 13 explores the significance of visual arts in values education at the primary school level. The chapter highlights how visual arts can effectively foster values such as self-confidence, empathy, respect, love, cooperation, and tolerance through diverse activities and practices. Visual arts are seen as a valuable tool for embodying abstract concepts and promoting values in children.

Chapter 14 examines the linguistic analysis of Turkish words related to the concept of 'tawakkul' (trust in Allah) derived from the word 'köŋül' (heart). The study explores the expansion of this concept in Turkish Qur'an translations and Islamic texts, emphasizing the importance of 'tawakkul' as an Islamic value.

Chapter 15 addresses the introduction of English language education in Algerian primary schools alongside French. The chapter explores the challenges and requirements of incorporating English as a second language and the potential obstacles faced by policymakers and educators in teaching English.

Chapter 16 presents a survey on Imaginable Futures conducted worldwide, which identifies kindness as a core skill for the future. The chapter emphasizes the importance of nurturing kindness in children as a means to strengthen social bonds and contribute to their well-being and happiness.

Chapter 17 focuses on depression among school children and its negative consequences, such as suicide. The chapter examines the reasons behind depression, including social hierarchy, parental apathy, religious cults, and "death groups." Sociological studies are conducted in local secondary schools to identify the level of depression among school children and propose prevention strategies.

Chapter 18 emphasizes the importance of value education in schools, highlighting the role it plays in moral development, ethical advancement, and the fostering of social skills among students.

Chapter 19 presents sample activities in worksheets supported by 9 values in the 4th-grade Social Studies Curriculum. The chapter uses literary genres to transfer values and stresses the significance of using literary works in values education for internalizing values correctly.

The intended readership encompasses a wide spectrum of individuals, ranging from seasoned researchers seeking to expand their understanding of values education, to teachers seeking to enhance their pedagogical strategies in the classroom. University students, parents, and all those with an interest in values will also find this book a valuable resource, guiding them in shaping a brighter future for our world.

I express my profound gratitude to all the esteemed contributors who have enriched this volume with their expertise and dedication. It is our sincerest hope that *Global Perspectives on Value Education in Primary School* will inspire and ignite a collective commitment to cultivating a more compassionate, just, and enlightened society through the medium of value-based education.

With unwavering optimism and the spirit of global cooperation,

Aytekin Demircioğlu
Kastamonu University, Turkey

Chapter 1
Building Values in Primary Education Enhancing Social and Democratic Participation

Turgay Öntaş
 https://orcid.org/0000-0003-2258-0862
Tekirdag Namik Kemal University, Turkey

Okan Çoban
Ministry of National Education, Turkey

ABSTRACT

In this study, social and democratic participation skills were associated in the context of values education. Since the construction of values is the focus of many different social science disciplines, analyses were carried out by establishing a connection between the concepts. Basically, connections were established between concepts through child and childhood. The prevailing view of childhood often portrays children as innocent and disinterested in political matters, suggesting that they should be raised as apolitical beings. However, children are exposed to political content through both formal and informal education processes. Primary educational institutions have the aim of developing social and democratic participation skills in children. In the global context, the construction of values in children is regarded as essential for cultivating citizenship skills.

INTRODUCTION

Regarding developmental periods, the primary school period coincides with the "middle childhood" period (between the ages of 6-12). Middle childhood is the period of life that begins when children start school and lasts until adolescence (Özgen, 2021). Primary schools generally educate children between the ages of 6-11. Primary school education can be in different age ranges. The time spent in primary school may vary in different countries. Middle childhood years contribute substantially to a child's adolescence and adulthood. During middle childhood, children move into expanding roles and different

DOI: 10.4018/978-1-6684-9295-6.ch001

environments. They begin to spend more time in school and other activities. While adjusting to school life, they experience more of the world around them and gain new achievements. They become more flexible in their thinking and develop self-awareness and empathy. They achieve new academic skills (such as arithmetic, reading, and writing) and learn the rules of their culture or society. Thus, they begin to develop their own identity.

In the middle childhood development stage, personality, moral, and social development are some of the milestones for children. Children develop patterns of behaviors based on their social interactions, learn from the guidance of their caregivers and their observation, and reflect on the morals of the people with whom they interact at this stage of development.

Generally, primary school children go through various stages of development, both physically and mentally. Physical, cognitive, social, emotional, language and moral development areas contain a process that primary school children experience quickly. During primary school, when social groups gain importance for children in terms of social and emotional development and emotional regulation skills develop, children's awareness of moral values and rules is also formed. While students learn basic moral principles in primary school, moral values, and behaviors are also related to their social and emotional learning (Özteke-Kozan, 2021).

Moral development deals with the multi-faceted manifestations of ideas, issues, and evaluation processes in morality. It also means reaching a goal (Schrader, 2018). Parents and teachers are among the most essential factors in the moral development of students. Especially in primary school, students are affected by the model behaviors of their teachers. For the moral development of students in primary school, teachers can develop and reinforce values such as respect, cooperation, honesty, and responsibility among students. The Moral Development of students in primary school is related to many factors, such as teachers' model behavior, practical communication skills, social and emotional learning, and student participation. Education and training design should be done by considering the developmental characteristics of primary school students. Learning environments can be created to contribute to the multi-faceted development of students. Considering the developmental characteristics of primary school students, active learning and the development of social skills should be supported with a student-centered approach, and a sense of achievement and self-confidence should be encouraged.

Regarding the nature of teaching and learning, effective teaching practices are essential in developing individuals and society. Learning is also a social process. In this context, values, morals, character, and citizenship education have an essential place, significantly because they contribute to young generations' social, cultural, and moral development. Schooling and education contribute to the development of values in young people. Because teaching, above all, has content that considers the multi-faceted well-being of students (Arthur, 2011).

While examining the nature of teaching and learning, the concepts of "child" and "childhood" should also be addressed. Childhood refers to the period in human life from language acquisition (age 1 or 2) to puberty at 12 or 13. In other words, it is the period of the human lifespan between infancy and adolescence. When the meanings attributed to childhood are examined from a historical perspective, it is seen that there are transitions from a miniature adult to an individual on its own. Regarding the new sociology of childhood, the child is a living creature living in reality. When approaching teaching and the nature of learning, it should not be forgotten that children are individuals. The child should be approached by reviewing whether the contents that are tried to be indoctrinated are suitable for the nature of the child.

Citizenship values are the primary content among the subjects being tried to be indoctrinated into children. Social and democratic participation is directly related to citizenship education. Those who approach the concept of the child as a political subject claim that children could participate actively in political processes. They also argue that children are aware of social issues early on. Children are, by nature, curious, creative, and critical thinkers. The main argument of those who approach children as political subjects is that enhancing children's social and political awareness could contribute to developing a democratic society.

Citizenship education in primary school includes teaching children about democratic values, social responsibilities, human rights, laws, and other citizenship issues. Citizenship education in primary school is usually given within the social studies course. In social studies courses, students are guided on social responsibility, human rights, and compliance with the law. In addition to fulfilling their civic duties, children are taught the importance of living harmoniously with people with different opinions by participating in democratic processes. Citizenship education in primary school also aims to increase student's awareness of social and political issues.

This text will mention many concepts related to the construction of citizenship values. Inclusive concepts will be included while addressing citizenship values in primary school education. To deal with the subject inclusively while discussing the construction of values in primary school education, it will be tried to establish a connection with social and democratic participation skills.

Method

In this study, social and democratic participation skills were associated with values education. The study was prepared by reviewing the literature. While reviewing the literature, essential sources were reached through the concepts mentioned in the title. The conceptual construction processes of the authors created an original work. In the conceptual construction process, associations were made in line with the contexts of the concepts. Since the study is a general review, an additional literature review section did not add.

The study has tried to explain the developmental characteristics of children in the primary school period, general approaches to values education, identity formation as the main element of citizenship education and values education, the formation of social and democratic participation values as well as primary school teachers' role in the formation of values. Identity formation emerges as a pivotal element in citizenship and values education. We examine how children's sense of self and belonging develops and how this process influences their understanding of citizenship and the adoption of values. Exploring identity formation provides insights into how children perceive themselves within the broader social and cultural contexts and how this shapes their attitudes and behaviors toward others. By exploring the developmental characteristics of children, examining general approaches to values education, understanding the role of identity formation, exploring the formation of social and democratic participation values, and highlighting the critical role of primary school teachers, this study provides a comprehensive framework for promoting values education and citizenship development among primary school students.

Developmental Characteristics of Children in Primary School

Primary school is a critical educational stage for the development of children. Children gain different experiences at school and in the family environment during this educational stage. Their experiences form the basis for their social and emotional development for their life after primary school. Children's perceptions of social interactions in their environment profoundly affect the development of their sense of belonging (Howard, 2006). In the primary school stage, regarding social development, children acquire the behaviors of making new friends, cooperating, developing empathy, and obeying the rules. Regarding emotional development, they develop abilities and skills such as self-knowledge, emotion control, stress management, self-esteem, and responsibility. These skills and abilities enable children to be successful socially, academically, and emotionally and live harmoniously in the society they belong.

In addition to primary school children's social and emotional development, moral and identity development processes are also critical. Many factors affect the moral development processes of children: genetics, family, school, and social environment. Although children's moral development is too complex to be explained by just one theory, many theories are put forward to explain moral development in children. For this reason, approaching the developmental processes of children with the ecosystem approach is necessary to understand the subject in a holistic way. In addition to social and emotional development, moral and identity development are conditions that must be considered for children to develop healthy attitudes.

Primary education should also support children's academic, social, emotional, and moral development. In addition to teaching academic skills, primary education provides opportunities for students to develop social and emotional skills. Through social interactions, students learn social skills such as cooperation and empathy. Primary education should ensure that students have a safe and supportive learning environment.

Primary school is a stage that needs to be supported in terms of the developmental characteristics of children, especially in terms of social and emotional development. As an educational institution, there are applications that primary schools have developed for these needs of children. In this study, associating social and emotional development, which is generally considered in the context of values education, with citizenship values reveals the need to review approaches to values education.

Approaches to Values Education

Values education is the collective name given to the processes used in educational institutions or other institutions to make children aware of the importance of values in society (Halstead, 2018, 151). Values education is an educational practice based on moral and/or political values and the development of norms, dispositions, and skills related to these values (Linköping University). As an essential element of whole-person education values, education aims to foster students' positive values and attitudes (Education Bureau, 2022). Regarding values education, it is necessary to establish a connection between virtues, moral education, and character education. Value clarification, values analysis, and character education are essential and controversial approaches to values education (Sunal & Haas, 2011). Since the 1980s, interest in character education programs supporting essential virtues has increased (Hunt & Mullins, 2018).

While analyzing the subject of values education, explaining the subject of virtue is also necessary. Arthur et al. (2015; 2017) classified virtues as:

- Moral virtues: Virtues that enable us to respond in ethically sound ways to situations in any field of experience: Courage, self-discipline, compassion, gratitude, justice, humility, and honesty.
- Civic virtues: These are necessary for participatory and responsible citizenship. These virtues help each thrive and promote society's common good.
- Performance virtues: The most frequently mentioned in this category is the ability to bounce back from negative experiences. Others include determination, confidence, and teamwork.

- Intellectual virtues: Right thinking, autonomy, judgment, and perseverance emerge. Intellectual virtues are necessary to pursue knowledge, truth, and truth.

Each virtue field has its values. A value related to moral virtues can be supportive of values of civic virtue. The virtues that should be taught to children in primary school contribute to the character development of children. When the virtues that should be gained in primary school relate to values education, it is seen that values education is the broadest term. These values could be aesthetic, religious, political, environmental, etc. Under the general heading of moral education, several courses are offered in schools worldwide: moral education, human rights education, peace education, citizenship education, life skills education, etc. (Arthur, 2017, 20). These nomenclatures have slight differences (Kaymakcan & Meydan, 2014: 141). The concept of value is also the subject of study in religious education and the tradition of religious thought (Demircioğlu, 2020).

Character education, a subset of moral education, deals with developing positive character traits called virtues. The primary purpose of character education is to build a strong nation with noble character, tolerance, and morals (Retnesar et al., 2021). These three types of education serve a common purpose: Contributing to individuals to lead a life under their values, moral principles, and character traits. Developmental psychologist Thomas Lickona (1991), one of the critical theorists of character education, considered the family institution to be damaged and the disturbing levels of the program contents published in the mass media as a problem, especially with the depression in youth culture in the USA. For this reason, he wanted the development of respect and responsibility among the fundamental values. A formation called the character education movement appealed to the teaching of fundamental values, especially in literature, social studies, and social science courses (Hunt & Muhlis, 2018).

Relationship Between Values Education and Citizenship Education

There is a complex relationship between moral education and citizenship education. In many respects, it is accepted that there is a common feature between these two fields (Halstead, 2019). Values education helps children develop values and moral principles. It is in question that children gain universal values through values education, which also aims to teach the values accepted in society and to gain the ability to behave by these values. Values that are stated to be universal such as honesty, respect, responsibility, justice, and tolerance, have an essential place in reaching the common good. Hoge (2002:106) compared character education and citizenship education from different perspectives in his article titled "Character Education, Citizenship Education, and the Social Studies":

Different approaches to citizenship education have come to the fore. Mc Laughin's (1992) conceptualization, which examines citizenship education minimally and maximally, becomes prominent (Kaymakcan & Meydan, 2010). Trying to give an identity to the individual through education is a form of relationship between the state and the citizen. The importance of political participation in the context of the roles attributed to education and the desire to bring various virtues to children determine the place of citizenship education in the construction of identity. Minimal and maximal citizenship concepts refer to different citizenship rights and responsibilities levels. While minimal citizenship expresses those citizens who have fundamental rights and fulfilling society's expectations, maximal citizenship emphasizes the participation of individuals in society in a more active and participatory manner.

Table 1. Comparison of character education and citizenship education

Comparison Focus	Character Education	Citizenship Education
Central Concern Content Taught	Improved people's character traits and values	Improved government Knowledge of government, law, and politics
Pre-eminent Values	Responsibility; respect for self and others; honesty; kindness/caring; fairness; cooperation	Freedom; equality; legal rights; justice; citizen participation; patriotism; respect for diversity, authority, property, and privacy
Fears	Bad people; loss of traditional moral standards	Bad government; loss of freedom and rights
Instructional Concern	The internalization of established prosocial values	The acquisition of citizenship knowledge and skills
Instructional Focus	Individuals; personal behavior	Society; social problems
Areas of Implementation and Advocates	Implemented primarily in elementary, advocates are a diverse group of educators who embrace the need for character education.	Implemented chiefly in middle and high schools, advocates are social studies educators who have assumed citizenship education responsibilities.
Dominant Instructional Methods	Trait-of-the-week instruction; slogans; instructive biography; rewards programs	Direct instruction on government, law, and politics; issues-based discussions; mock trials and field trips

Source: Hoge (2002, p. 106)

Citizenship education aims to equip students with the knowledge, skills, and values necessary to become active and responsible citizens in a democratic society. The objectives of citizenship education can be broadly divided into three main areas: civic knowledge, civic skills, and civic values. Civics aims to provide students with an understanding of the history, institutions, and principles of democracy. Students learn about the fundamental rights and freedoms guaranteed by democratic societies, such as freedom of expression, freedom of the press, and the right to vote. They also learn about the role of government and the importance of civic participation in maintaining a healthy democracy. Citizenship values aim to promote the development of positive attitudes and behaviors that contribute to the well-being of individuals and society. These values include respect for diversity, social responsibility, empathy, and tolerance. Students learn about the importance of these values and how they can be applied in their daily lives to foster positive social change.

Based on the idea that good citizens have good character virtues, it can be ensured that children can be contributed to their development in line with the relevant goals. Citizenship allows the explicit teaching of virtue, knowledge, reasoning, and practice. Thus, citizenship education becomes a supporting element for strengthening social and democratic participation with skills such as political literacy and involvement in the political process (Arthur et al., 2017, 20).

The idea of citizenship is about membership in a political community. Although civic education is also called political education in contemporary US society, the latter phrase is generally avoided. Political participation in any society indicates vitality in a democratic society. It is possible to consider citizenship education practices in schools in terms of inequality, discussion-oriented pedagogy, and the role of non-governmental organizations (Parker, 2014).

In terms of practice, citizenship education, and values education often overlap. Schools can integrate both approaches into their curricula while using civic education to teach students about civic duties and responsibilities while promoting the development of personal values and ethical behaviors. In this way, citizenship education can provide a context for values education as students learn how to apply their values and ethics to civic life.

Motivation and action to do the right thing come to the fore when considering the fundamental dimensions of morality and citizenship education. In the first stage, interpretation, judgment, knowledge, and understanding of complex issues and institutions and a sophisticated understanding of ethical rules and democratic principles. In the second stage, interests, commitments, belief, and perseverance in the face of difficulties; in the third stage, effective citizenship skills, including moral and political participation, including discourse, political participation, and the ability to communicate and interact effectively with people who are different from themselves (Colby, 2014: 369-370).

Both areas have common goals, such as adapting children to society, developing awareness of social responsibility, and respecting human rights. On the other hand, citizenship education can also contribute positively to the student's behaviors in the social and democratic participation processes of the universal values they learn in values education. As children gain civic skills, they learn more than just the ability to obey the law. To be a good citizen, one must obey the law and be equipped with moral values (Carr, 2006).

The Main Element of Citizenship Education, Identity Formation, and Values Education

Identity development is fundamentally linked to one's understanding of the psychological, physiological, and social development that takes place throughout one's life and to one's participation in the process that takes place throughout one's life. There are psychosocial, sociocultural, and narrative approaches to identity development. Regardless of which of these different approaches in identity development are determined, identity can be accepted as a personal and social phenomenon that transforms throughout human life (Hall, 2018, 321-322).

In some countries, character education is strengthened mainly through religious education and nationalism. However, independence, cooperation, and honesty are the fundamental values that should be given (Muttaqin et al., 2018). On the one hand, these values, which fulfill the purpose of identity construction, have also become the subject of theories that examine how children develop their social, cultural, and individual identities and how education is effective in this process. Educators should focus on identity formation theories while providing information about different social, cultural, and individual identities through education. Teachers can follow various strategies based on the theories of identity formation in education. Educators should recognize that students know different identities, approach the subjects critically, encourage inclusivity, and gain skills such as empathy. İdentity formation theories in education show how children develop their social, cultural, and individual identities and that education plays an active role in identity formation processes.

Citizenship education provides the acquisition of knowledge, skills, and tendencies to live in a democratic society (Mullins, 2018). Officially conducted citizenship education studies in schools can also be enriched with implicit or extra-curricular curriculum studies. It is possible to influence students with explicit and implicit programs for character development (Kaymakcan & Meydan, 2016). Citizenship education, which also tries to gain citizenship virtues, emphasizes active social participation. Indicators of active participation in society also depend on the relationship established with social and democratic participation values.

There may be differences between the values revealed by citizenship education and moral values. The main difference is that while moral values are individual, citizenship values have social characteristics. As an influential citizen, one must internalize behaviors that include citizenship skills, being a good person, and moral values (Ersoy, 2016).

Developing Social and Democratic Participation Values

A shared sense of citizenship creates a diversity-encompassing framework and emphasizes core values that all citizens can share. These values can be universal and democratic, such as democracy, human rights, equality, justice, tolerance, respect, and cooperation. These values unite individuals from different cultural and religious backgrounds and help create a common citizenship identity. Creating a shared sense of citizenship in a multicultural society requires a process based on mutual understanding, communication, and dialogue. In this process, it is crucial for individuals to understand different cultural values and perspectives and to emphasize the common points of values along with mutual respect and tolerance. Education is crucial in promoting a shared sense of citizenship in multicultural societies.

Schools provide a platform to teach students democratic values, human rights, equality, and tolerance through citizenship education. The education system encourages students from different cultural, religious, and ethnic groups to understand each other, work together and agree on shared values. However, there may be difficulties in establishing a shared sense of citizenship in multicultural societies. Differences between different values and beliefs can sometimes cause tension. In this case, dialogue, understanding, and negotiation skills become essential. Community leaders, educators, and nonprofit organizations can help meet these challenges by developing and promoting policies, programs, and activities that support this process.

Justice, equality, responsibility, freedom, difference, privacy, and the rule of law stand out as democratic values (Howard, 2018, 157). Value education is crucial for the development of democratic societies. For value educators, teaching citizenship and moral values and limiting people's relations with the state in the lessons that will teach moral values are among the topics discussed (Akbas, 2008). In most Western countries, the compulsory education system is crucial in integrating into social life (Hovdelien, 2015).

Social cohesion is encouraged in democratic schools. Efforts are made to ensure that disadvantaged children are successful by integrating them into the school community. Democratic schools are one of the measures against the transmission of poverty from one family to another (Edelstein & Krettenauer, 2014). Social and democratic participation skills for primary school students are abilities and attitudes that enable them to participate in social life effectively and responsibly. Some social and democratic participation skills for primary school students can be listed as follows:

- Communication skills: Primary school students' ability to express their ideas clearly and effectively, listen, and provide feedback is essential.
- Collaboration and teamwork: It gives primary school students experience in valuing the opinions of others and finding standard solutions.
- Empathy and tolerance: Primary school students' ability to understand and respect the feelings and perspectives of others supports participation in social and democratic life.
- Consciousness of responsibility: The awareness of primary school students to bear responsibility for the consequences of their actions and decisions and to fulfill their duties towards society is necessary for participation in social and democratic life.

Values that support democracy have both political and social dimensions (Howard, 2018). Democratic values are essential for individuals to live freely in society and for the government to manage by protecting the rights and freedoms of individuals. The values standing out in the context of democratic values - such as respect, justice, equality, secularism, freedom, fraternity, rejection of all kinds of discrimination, and solidarity/cooperation - are included in the curriculum of different countries (Bektaş & Zabun, 2019).

Developing social and democratic participation values in children is essential for them to grow up as concerned and responsible citizens. By encouraging active participation, teaching respect for diversity, developing critical thinking and communication skills, encouraging responsible decision-making, and providing leadership opportunities, children can develop the skills and values necessary to participate and contribute to democratic societies. The development of social and democratic values of participation requires incorporating moral and political dimensions in the context of global citizenship education. Global citizenship education programs include respecting differences by raising children's awareness of different cultures and values (Veugelers, 2011).

A concept that should be addressed while talking about global citizenship education is global moral education. Especially the moral problems of war and peace, ecological problems, demographic problems, and economic problems are among the essential problems of the global world (Köylü, 2013). Global moral education can also support initiatives to solve these problems to reach the common good.

The values desired to be gained through political education or values education ultimately aim to improve something (Dunlop, 2005). Education is often associated with political competence, although there is little evidence that citizenship courses appear to improve political knowledge. (Kołczyńska, 2020: 5). Democratic political values education is critical to promoting active and responsible citizenship in a democratic society. Democratic political values promote individual freedom, equal rights, social justice, and civic responsibility. These values are essential to creating a democratic and inclusive society where everyone can participate and thrive.

The Role of the Primary School Teacher in the Construction of Values

Primary school teachers spend the most time with students at the primary school level. Primary school teachers contribute to the development of students in different years depending on the countries education systems. Considering that primary school is at the compulsory education level, teachers who contribute to the development of children in their multi-dimensional development have an important role. Looking at responsibilities of classroom teachers in general, they have legal, administrative, educational, and ethical responsibilities (Özen & Çakır, 2021). Especially the instructional and educational responsibilities of classroom teachers are related to the acquisition of values and virtues as affective characteristics.

The attitudes and behaviors that teachers should reflect in values or character education can be summarized as follows, based on Ekşi and Katmış's (2011, 127-128) study: "Even if the teachers themselves are not examples of virtue, they should exhibit good character examples, not impose their own opinions by revealing their positions in class discussions, create a moral climate in the classroom and set themselves an example."

While educational institutions care about students' cognitive development, they also aim to contribute to their being individuals who will fulfill various political and social functions and their citizenship roles (Kaymakcan & Meydan, 2016). Leaving the necessary responsibility for the moral development of students only to the family and religious institutions negatively affects the holistic development of the subject (Schwartz, 2018). Schools and teachers have responsibilities in terms of moral development.

For this reason, expectations from teachers increase every semester. The role attributed to teachers has continuously increased due to parents and society's changing expectations and interests. In addition to the academic teaching roles of teachers, they are given a formative responsibility as a model for young people. There are findings that teachers can affect how students understand by addressing complex moral and social issues (Arthur, 2011, 185). Teachers have a critical role in the implementation of democratic values, tolerance, respect, responsibility, and justice in daily life by increasing the awareness of children in the processes of values education and citizenship education.

According to Arthur's research (2011), especially from the perspective of children aged 10-12, the following roles of teachers come to the forefront:

- helping to develop positive attitudes.
- helping to develop good behaviors.
- helping to develop good character.
- helping students to know how to be a good person.
- helping students behave like good people.

The role of the teacher in values education is based on showing how to apply the relevant values in students' personal and social lives. In addition, it is one of the roles of the teacher to create suitable environments for values to live in. Increasing awareness of values, gaining inquiry skills, creating a values-based learning environment, organizing activities, cooperating, and communicating with families are among the roles attributed to the teacher. The leading role of the teacher in values education is to explain the importance and applicability of values to students and to create a learning environment that respects values. Teachers' undertaking these roles enables students to contribute to their ethical and moral development by adopting and integrating values into their lives. Teachers can support children by modeling, discussing, and thought-provoking activities, community service practices, integrated teaching, continuous assessment, and feedback, considering the relationships between values, morality, and character education.

Developing social and democratic participation skills in primary school students helps them actively and responsibly participate in social life and respect democratic values. Teachers can consider the following suggestions to improve the social and democratic participation skills of primary school students:

- The opportunity to participate in democratic processes can be given to the students while making decisions and solving problems in the classroom. This opportunity develops students' decision-making, problem-solving, and critical-thinking skills.
- Social responsibility projects and community service activities can be organized. This can be ensured that they gain awareness about social justice and are sensitive to social problems.
- Teachers can contribute to developing an inclusive understanding by working on cultural and social awareness.
- While teaching citizenship education and democratic values, teachers can enable them to be implemented in daily life.

Developing social and democratic participation skills is essential for the future lives of primary school students. Individuals who are sensitive to democratic values and social justice issues are more likely to contribute to the construction of a more just and egalitarian society. When the essential competencies for participation in democratic forms of social life are examined, especially in multicultural societies, the ability to interact in heterogeneous groups, the ability to act autonomously and to use tools (using language, symbols, and texts; using information and information technologies interactively and collaboratively) come to the fore (Edelstein & Krettenauer, 2014). Building common values in multicultural societies is vital in terms of creating an environment where different cultural, ethnic, and religious groups of society can live together.

The principles of values education are based on the idea that values are learned and developed through socialization, education, and experience. Values education aims to promote positive attitudes and behaviors that contribute to the well-being of individuals and society. Values education also emphasizes the importance of critical thinking and reflection. Students should be encouraged to think critically about their values and reflect on how their values affect their behaviors and interactions with others. By developing their critical thinking skills, students can become more aware of their values and how they relate to the values of others. Values education is a critical component of personal and Social Development. By integrating values into education, modeling positive values, encouraging critical thinking and reflection, fostering a sense of community, and committing to continuing professional development, we can foster positive values and behaviors in students and contribute to the well-being of society.

Context of Turkey

Values education in Turkey is carried out in the context of root values. Root values are the fundamental values of the society and form the basis of Turkish culture and national unity. These values are transferred to students through the curricula and programs determined by the Ministry of National Education, and their adoption is encouraged. Teaching and adopting the core values aims to strengthen Turkey's social integrity and national identity. Through values education, students learn to understand, internalize, and apply these root values daily. Thus, values education in Turkey helps to ensure that root values are preserved, transmitted, and passed on to future generations. Citizenship education and values education in Turkey are complementary and intertwined concepts.

Values education enables individuals to adopt moral values, support character development and strengthen their social skills. On the other hand, citizenship education aims for individuals to participate in society as active and responsible citizens and teaches them to adopt democratic values. Social studies course in Turkey is an essential component of citizenship education. This course enables students to understand the social structure, adopt democratic values, and raise awareness of citizenship rights and responsibilities.

CONCLUSION

Values education for children should be age-appropriate, interactive, and attractive. Teachers and parents can be good role models, use real-life scenarios, encourage critical thinking, and emphasize positive reinforcement to support the development of positive values and behaviors in children.

The importance of democratic values in primary school can increase as students learn about social responsibility, human rights, obeying the law, equality, justice, cooperation, tolerance, and other citizenship issues. Primary school students should understand the importance of these values and apply them effectively in their lives. Learning democratic values in primary school helps students become active citizens, participate in democratic processes, and gain social awareness. It can enable them to participate in democratic processes by increasing their awareness of social and political issues.

Building values in primary school is integral to raising responsible and caring citizens. Values such as social and democratic participation, respect for diversity, and responsible decision-making are critical to students' development as individuals and members of their communities. A values-based curriculum is one of primary school's most important ways to build values. This type of curriculum focuses on the acquisition of knowledge and skills as well as the development of personal and social values. By incorporating values such as empathy, respect, and responsibility into the curriculum, teachers can help students develop the skills and values necessary for social and democratic participation.

Creating values in primary school requires a collaborative effort between teachers, parents, and the community. By working together, teachers and parents can reinforce the values taught in the classroom, provide opportunities for students to practice these values, and encourage community participation. This collaboration can also create a supportive and inclusive learning environment where all students feel valued and respected. A values-based curriculum, modeling, active learning experiences, collaboration, and continuing professional development for teachers are essential to creating values in primary education. By prioritizing values education, we can help students develop the skills and values necessary for social and democratic participation, respect for diversity, and responsible decision-making.

The citizens of tomorrow will face a rapidly changing world with new technologies, global challenges, and diverse communities. In this context, citizenship values will play a critical role in shaping the development of responsible and engaged citizens who can overcome these challenges and make positive contributions to their communities and the world. It is important to note that civic values are not fixed or static but rather evolve and change over time. The citizens of tomorrow must adapt to new challenges and changing social norms while maintaining core values such as respect for diversity, social responsibility, critical thinking, active participation, and ethical behaviors. Education plays a critical role in developing these civic values. Schools and other educational institutions can promote civic values through extra-curricular and extra-curricular activities, modeling, and community partnerships. By prioritizing citizenship values in education, we can help prepare tomorrow's citizens to face the challenges of a changing world and to become responsible and engaged members of their communities and the world.

Strengthening character education based on school culture is essential for promoting positive character traits in students. School culture, which includes the values, beliefs, and attitudes of the school community, plays a crucial role in shaping students' character development. One way to strengthen character education based on school culture is modeling. Teachers and staff should model positive character traits such as respect, responsibility, honesty, and empathy in their interactions with students and each other. Teachers and staff can inspire students to develop similar values and behaviors by modeling positive character traits. Strengthening character education based on school culture is crucial for developing positive character traits in students. Through modeling, curricular integration, extra-curricular activities, continuing professional development, and community involvement, schools can create a positive school culture that supports the development of responsible and engaged citizens.

REFERENCES

Akbaş, O. (2008). Sosyal bilgilerde değerler ve öğretimi [Values and teaching in social studies]. In B. Tay & A. Öcal (Eds.), *Sosyal bilgiler öğretimi* [Social studies teaching] (pp. 335–360). Pegem Akademi.

Arthur, J. (2011). Personal character and tomorrow's citizens: Student expectations of their teachers. *International Journal of Educational Research, 50*(3), 184–189. doi:10.1016/j.ijer.2011.07.001

Arthur, J., Harrison, T., & Taylor, E. (2015). *Building Character through Youth Social Action.* Research report. University of Birmingham, Jubilee Centre for Character and Virtues. https://www.jubileecentre. ac.uk/userfiles/jubileecentre/pdf/Research%20Reports/Building_Character_Through_Youth_Social_Action.pdf

Arthur, J., Kristjánsson, K., Harrison, T., Sanderse, W., & Wright, D. (2017). *Teaching character and virtue in schools.* Routledge. doi:10.4324/9781315695013

Bektaş, Ö., & Zabun, E. (2019). Vatandaşlık eğitiminde değerler karşılaştırması: Türkiye ve Fransa [Comparison of values in citizenship education: Turkey and France]. *Değerler Eğitimi Dergisi, 17*(37), 247-289. doi:10.34234/ded.512221

Carr, D. (2006). The moral roots of citizenship: Reconciling principle and character in citizenship education. *Journal of Moral Education, 35*(4), 443–456. doi:10.1080/03057240601012212

Colby, A. (2014). Fostering The Moral and Civic Development of College Students. In L. Nucci, D. Narvaez, & T. Krettenauer (Eds.), *Handbook of Moral and Character Education* (pp. 368–385). Routledge.

Demircioğlu, A. (2020). İbn Sina ve Gazali'nin bazı değer kavramları yönünden karşılaştırılması [Comparison of Avicenna and Ghazali for some value concepts]. *OPUS–Uluslararası Toplum Araştırmaları Dergisi, 16*(28), 1562–1584. doi:10.26466/opus.684445

Dunlop, F. (2005). Democratic values and the foundations of political education. J. M. Halstead & M. J. Taylor (Eds.), Values in education and education in values (pp.66–76). Taylor & Francis.

Edelstein, W., & Krettenauer, T. (2014). Citizenship and democracy education in a diverse Europe. In L. Nucci, D. Narvaez, & T. Krettenauer (Eds.), *Handbook of moral and character education* (pp. 386–400). Routledge.

Education Bureau, The Government of Hong Kong Special Administrative Region of the People's Republic of China. (2022). *Values Education.* https://www.edb.gov.hk/en/curriculum-development/4-key-tasks/moral-civic/index.html

Ekşi, H., & Katılmış, H. (2011). *Karakter eğitimi el kitabı* [Handbook of character education]. Nobel.

Ersoy, A. F. (2016). Sosyal bilgiler dersi ve vatandaşlık eğitimi [Social studies course and citizenship education]. In R. Turan & T. Yıldırım (Eds.), *Sosyal bilgilerin temelleri* [Foundations of social studies] (pp. 143–164). Anı Publishing.

Hall, S. E. (2018). Kimlik [Identity]. In Değerler eğitimi ansiklopedisi [Moral education/A Handbook] (pp. 320–322). EDAM.

Halstead, J. M. (2018). Değerler eğitimi [Value Education]. In *Değerler eğitimi ansiklopedisi* [Moral Education/A Handbook] (pp. 151-152). EDAM.

Halstead, J. M. (2019). Ahlak eğitimi ve yurttaşlık eğitimi [Moral education and civic education]. In R. Bailey, R. Barrow, D. Carr, & C. McCarthy (Eds.), *Eğitim felsefesi kılavuzu* [The SAGE Handbook of philisophy of education] (pp. 249–264). Pegem Akademi.

Hoge, J. D. (2002). Character education, citizenship education, and the social studies. *Social Studies, 93*(3), 103–108. doi:10.1080/00377990209599891

Hovdelien, O. (2015). Education and common values in a multicultural society – The Norwegian Case. *Journal of Intercultural Studies (Melbourne, Vic.), 36*(3), 306–319. doi:10.1080/07256868.2015.1029887

Howard, R. W. (2018). Demokratik değerler [Democratic values]. In *Değerler eğitimi ansiklopedisi* [Moral education/A Handbook] (pp. 157–159). EDAM.

Howard, S. (2006). What is Waldorf early childhood education? Waldorf Early Childhood Education Association.

Hunt, T. C., & Mullins, M. M. (2018). Giriş [Introduction]. In Değerler eğitimi ansiklopedisi [Moral Education/A Handbook] (pp. vi-xxvi). EDAM.

Kaymakcan, R., & Meydan, H. (2010). Democratic citizenship and religious education: New approaches and an evaluation in the context of DKAB courses in Turkey. İnönü University. *Journal of Theology Faculty., 1*(1), 29–53.

Kaymakcan, R., & Meydan, H. (2014). *Ahlak, değerler ve eğitimi* [Morals, values and education]. DEM.

Kołczyńska, M. (2020). Democratic values, education, and political trust. *International Journal of Comparative Sociology, 61*(1), 3–26. doi:10.1177/0020715220909881

Köylü, M. (2013). *Küresel ahlak eğitimi* [Global moral education]. DEM.

Lickona, T. (1991). *Educating for Character: How our schools can teach respect and responsibility.* Bantam House. https://liu.se/en/research/values-education

McLaughlin, T. H. (1992). Citizenship, diversity and education: A philosophical perspective. *Journal of Moral Education, 21*(3), 235–250. doi:10.1080/0305724920210307

Mullins, M. M. (2018). Vatandaşlık eğitimi [Citizenship education]. In *Değerler eğitimi ansiklopedisi* [Moral education/A Handbook] (pp. 500–502). EDAM.

Muttaqin, M., Raharjo, T., & Masturi, M. (2018). The implementation of main values of character education reinforcement in elementary school. *Journal of Primary Education, 7*(1), 103–112. doi:10.15294/jpe.v7i1.22766

Özen, F., & Çakır, R. (2021). İlkokulda öğretmenin sorumlulukları [Teacher's responsibilities in primary school]. In I. Korkmaz (Ed.), *İlkokulda öğretim: Öğretmen el kitabı* [Teaching in primary school: Teacher's handbook] (pp. 587–610). Pegem Akademi.

Özgen, G. (2021). *Kuşaklararası annelik bağlamında ehil annelik: Orta çocukluk döneminde çocuğu olan annelerin annelik süreçleri ve deneyimleri üzerine bir araştırma* [Expertise in motherhood in the context of intergenerational transmisson of motherhood: A study on the motherhood processes and experiences of mothers with children in the middle childhood] [Unpublished doctoral dissertation]. Marmara Üniversitesi Eğitim Bilimleri Enstitüsü, İstanbul.

Özteke-Kozan, H. İ. (2021). İlkokul öğrencisinin gelişim özellikleri [Developmental characteristics of primary school students]. In I. Korkmaz (Ed.), *İlkokulda öğretim: Öğretmen el kitabı* [Teaching in primary school: teacher's handbook] (pp. 17–39). Pegem Akademi.

Parker, W. C. (2014). Citizenship education in the United States: Regime type, foundational questions, and classroom practice. In L. Nucci, D. Narvaez, & T. Krettenauer (Eds.), *Handbook of moral and character education* (pp. 347–367). Routledge.

Retnasari, L., Hidayah, Y., & Prasetyo, D. (2021). Reinforcement of character education based on school culture to enhance elementary school students' citizenship character. *Jurnal Ilmiah Sekolah Dasar, 5*(2), 351–358. doi:10.23887/jisd.v5i2.38072

Schrader, D. E. (2018). Ahlaki gelişim [Moral development]. In *Değerler eğitimi ansiklopedisi* [Moral education/A Handbook] (pp. 26-28). EDAM.

Schwartz, M. J. (2018). Ahlak eğitiminde öğretmenin rolü [The role of the teacher in moral education]. In *Değerler eğitimi ansiklopedisi* [Moral education/A Handbook] (pp. 11-13). EDAM.

Sunal, C. Y., & Haas, M. E. (2011). *Social studies for the elementary and middle grades. A constructivist approach*. Pearson.

Veugelers, W. (2011). The moral and the political in global citizenship: Appreciating differences in education. *Globalisation, Societies and Education, 9*(3-4), 3–4, 473–485. doi:10.1080/14767724.2011.605329

KEY TERMS AND DEFINITIONS

Character Education: "Character education" is an educational approach that aims to teach children and young people mature character qualities such as ethical and moral values, positive behavior, responsibility, honesty, and empathy.

Citizenship Education: Citizenship education is an educational approach that aims to prepare individuals to become informed, responsible, and active citizens in their societies. It involves teaching knowledge, skills, and values related to civic rights and responsibilities, democratic principles, social justice, participation in public affairs, and respect for diversity. Citizenship education empowers individuals to contribute positively to their communities and engage in democratic processes.

Identity Formation: Identity formation is an essential process in which the child discovers his/her self and determines his/her values, beliefs, and social identity. This process forms the basis for the child's identity development, lasting throughout life.

Moral Development: "Moral development" refers to how children develop their knowledge and understanding of social and personal values, right and wrong, ethical norms, and social behavior. This is a social and personal process in which children learn how to behave in society and adopt these values.

Primary Education: Primary education refers to the initial phase of formal education that children receive, typically between the ages of 6 and 12. The foundational level of education focuses on basic literacy, numeracy, and the development of fundamental skills and knowledge across various subjects.

Social and Democratic Participation: Social and democratic participation refers to the active involvement of individuals in social, political, and civic processes within their communities and societies. It entails engaging in activities promoting social justice, equality, inclusivity and exercising democratic rights and responsibilities. Social and democratic participation involves volunteering, community service, advocacy, voting, and engaging in dialogue and decision-making processes. It aims to foster active citizenship, collective action, and the promotion of the common good.

Value Education: Value education imparts moral, ethical, and social values to individuals. It aims to develop positive attitudes, beliefs, and behaviors that align with core values such as honesty, respect, responsibility, empathy, and justice. Value education promotes character development, ethical decision-making, and the integration of values into daily life.

Chapter 2
The Use of Stories in English to Educate in Values in Primary Education

Antonio Daniel Juan Rubio

https://orcid.org/0000-0003-3416-0021

Universidad de Granada, Spain

ABSTRACT

Reading encouragement is a transversal subject present throughout the entire educational stage of any student from early childhood education through primary education to Secondary Education and higher education. In this chapter, the authors intersperse the pleasure of reading in another language (English) and the reflection on the values transmitted by each of the selected stories. The main purpose is to teach a list of values to students in primary education but using this selection of stories as a basis to reach the internalization of these values. We cannot forget that they are still children and that we have to adapt the contents and learning channels to their evolutionary stage. By using fantastic characters, the concepts are extrapolated in a different way, making it easier for children to internalize the values. Therefore, the main objective of this work is to implement a didactic proposal based on the use of stories in English for values education in a group of children in the fifth grade of primary school.

INTRODUCTION

When we are young, stories are an essential part of our lives. Adults entertain us with stories of various kinds, with characters we want to be like or, on the contrary, avoid being like. Real or fantastic stories deal with a wide range of subjects. Generally, these short stories are used to lull us to sleep, distract us. At the same time, we eat, take us away from the television or modern electronic devices, and keep us quiet and attentive, even if only to the voice of the person reading or narrating them to us (Adela Johan, 2013).

DOI: 10.4018/978-1-6684-9295-6.ch002

However, can stories have more uses, and can we learn from them? There is no right or wrong answer, everything is correct if well-founded, justified, and contextualized. Hence, following this maxim, we will make the most of the usefulness of stories. This activity, if we promote it, can become one of humans' most pleasurable habits, according to Heathfield (2014).

In this chapter we will use the story as a didactic and motivating tool for the pupils in 5th-grade Primary Education. English children's literature will be used to justify teaching/learning English and the development of the critical competencies established by the legislation regulating the Primary Education stage in Spain. To do this, we will put on parallel paths the transmission of values to inculcate in a very heterogeneous group on the one hand and the pleasure of reading as an attractive and motivating activity even in a foreign language on the other.

They aim to converge in the objective of learning English differently and achieve the integral formation of people, making them enjoy the stories that are read. The main objective of this chapter is to implement a didactic proposal based on the use of stories in English for the education in values in a group of children in the fifth year of Primary Education. To achieve this general objective, a pair of specific objectives will be specified: to compile the observations and data of interest in the practice diary throughout the implementation of the didactic proposal that will serve to exemplify the descriptions and observations made and to observe the possibilities of reflection and the capacity of the group of students who make up the population of the group studied.

THEORETICAL FRAMEWORK

Benefits of Literature for Second Language Learning

The use of literary texts, as a source of authentic language in the English classroom, is a resource that has been revalued in recent years. This has only sometimes been the case, partly because these texts have been considered too complex to use in the foreign language classroom (Sun, 2016). In this chapter we want to vindicate the usefulness and necessity of using actual literary texts in their different genres and formats, due to their great benefits and advantages to the teaching/learning process. Here, the teacher's skills and knowledge come into play in choosing a literary resource. It will be accessible and relevant, considering the learners' interests, abilities, and needs and making learning possible, even if they do not have advanced language skills (Ray & Seely, 2018).

The foreign language (FL) teacher must provide the necessary tools to enable learners to deal with a literary text. Considering the communicative approach, the FL classroom becomes an interactive learning space centered on the learner and their interests, promoting "authentic" texts, such as literary texts (Bernal & García, 2020).

Collie & Slater (2012) offer the following reasons why literature can be considered beneficial in language learning:

- Literature is valuable 'authentic' material not produced to teach a language. As a result, it enables the reader to get to know the written language of the target language in a natural context.
- It not only helps students to achieve a higher level of communication but also to understand other cultures and societies.

- It enriches language knowledge by using a wide variety of registers.
- It leads to greater involvement of learners, who can connect their personal experience with the text, enjoying and engaging with the reading.

Through English and literature, it is evident that students will acquire competence in linguistic communication in that language as they process and produce texts in English and establish communicative actions generated by their reading. However, we must take advantage of the opportunity to work on other competencies.

Basic language skills can be quickly developed using literary texts. Written texts offer us a style, structure, and a way of connecting ideas that we do not usually find in spoken language. Therefore, reading and writing skills will be significantly enriched. The reading competence developed by the students is evident since they must put into practice their ability to infer and deduce the meaning of the text through the context (Mourao, 2019).

Ghosn (2012) said that literature promoted oral language because good stories generated enthusiasm and conversation among students (rather than the usual artificial texts found in a textbook). This view was reaffirmed by Collie & Slater (2012), who said that a literary text is an excellent aid to oral work, which will encourage learners to use the language. Listening comprehension is also practiced through conversations and debates arising from the text.

In conclusion, literature will enrich the students' language (both in the mother tongue and in the FL) while facilitating the practice and development of the four fundamental language skills and the acquisition of critical competencies.

Definitions of a Story

López Díaz (2019, 5) commented, "The short story is a brief narration of imaginary events, starring a small group of characters and with a simple plot. The story's structure is of the following type: introduction, middle, and denouement".

Stories are introduced in schools and form part of the school curriculum. They are intended to cover all areas of a child's education (Daniel, 2012). The story is literature, where a language is used better to assimilate the moral values typically implicit in it.

Moreover, it plays a significant role in the development and education of children, as it helps them in their language learning, in the structuring of their minds, in the development of their memory, and the development of their critical sense (Smorgorzewska, 2014).

With all this, they establish a reasonable basis for their later training and development as individuals. According to Grugeon & Gardner (2010), the short story is a brief narrative with a simple and linear plot characterized by an intense concentration of action, time, and space. Molina Prieto (2008, p. 2) adds: "The short story is a brief oral or written narration of an imaginary event."

Benítez Grande-Caballero (2019, p. 86) believed that "stories have always been used as an important pedagogical resource for learning values and beliefs, not only by educational bodies but even by spiritual traditions, where teachers often speak of parables." Today, stories are increasingly used as an essential way of practicing personal development by us autonomously (Dunst et al., 2012). Stories have an empathic quality because no matter how distant the story's setting or how fantastic it is when we enter a story, it always seems to us that the story is possible and can happen to us (Berkowitz, 2021).

Based on the idea of López Díaz (2019), stories are essential for educating in values. The ability of a story to impart values is an excellent advantage for education. Most of the values that shape our personality come to us through stories, according to Morgan & Rinvolucri (2019). All stories have a logical plot that links all the parts and makes it easier for us to remember them. What we retain best from the story is that it is moral, according to Huff (2022).

Finally, we will justify the benefits of the story when it is used as a pedagogical resource based on the consequences it can have when taken to the classroom. According to Ellis & Brewster (2014), the pedagogical function of stories is the following:

- Children's stories provide pupils with language enrichment and the opportunity to translate their fantasies and are the first contact with literary language.
- Stories prepare for life by contributing to the accumulation of ideas and feelings, overcoming fears and anxieties.
- They facilitate the structuring of time in the child's mind and empathy with the characters in the story.
- They allow pupils to have the opportunity to live with their imagination, to satisfy their desire to know and to get to know other environments and cultures.
- They discover kindness, generosity, and fantasy. They will strengthen their ability to concentrate and are suitable transmitters of values to help them cope with life in society.

Ferreira Pinto & Soares (2012) provided five criteria for the selection of stories for children which serve to overcome any obstacles or challenges that teachers may face:

1. Upholds & cultivates values. There are too many "worthy" books out there to waste your time on those that do not mesh with the goals and standards you have. Select stories that help children choose virtue over evil, model godly character, and encourage integrity.
2. Appeals to the child's age, maturity &/or intellectual levels. Consider where the children are intellectually, emotionally, and maturity-wise, and pick books relevant to their experiences. Also, consider the story's length, number of illustrations, length of chapters, and vocabulary.
3. Stimulates the mind & imagination. Good books encourage a child's self-education. That is, they should foster conversation about what is happening in the story and stir up questions about why the characters act a certain way.
4. Provides useful information. Spoon-feeding our children exactly what we know limits their knowledge of a subject. Good stories can fill our gaps and give them all they need to understand the topic.
5. It can be read over and over. Good books have stood the test of time and are still enjoyed today, even though many were written long ago. A classic piece of literature is such because of its dynamic writing, universal themes, and engaging storyline.

It is also worth mentioning digital storytelling's role in education nowadays. Digital Storytelling is a short form of digital media production that allows people to share experiences and stories. Digital stories are often present in compelling interactive formats. According to Davis et al. (2019), digital storytelling has been widely used as a participatory approach to enable people from various backgrounds to create and share short audio-visual narratives. They argue that it is essential for diverse communities to create digital stories in creative, meaningful ways, and it is essential for them to have the skills and technology to do so in safe spaces where they feel comfortable.

Finally, we should also consider the potential limitations or drawbacks of using stories in English. According to Satriani (2019), some of the most serious are the following:

- Passivity: Less use of the storytelling method can lead the learners to become passive listeners.
- Less Questioning: Learners may not be able to question much and hence, will not understand the lesson much better.
- Less Active Participation: Learners become less active participants when they become passive listeners.
- Lack of Learning by Doing: Learning by doing needs to be implemented in this method.
- Monotonous: Excessive use of this method can make the lesson more varied and varied.

Values as a Concept

According to Arufe Giraldés (2021), the term value is a polysemic and complex term to define. Depending on the technical or scientific field from which we study this word, its definition will differ to a greater or lesser extent.

According to Ortega Ruiz & Mínguez Vallejos (2021, p. 64), "values are those normative principles that regulate the behavior of the person at any time, situation or circumstance, being characterized by norms." According to García Campos (2018, p. 62), values are the following: "Values are the criteria or decisions that make it possible to clarify and accept what should be promoted in a culture as educational so that the human being develops or is educated."

Values according to Díaz (2015, 92) are: "Those unreal qualities, independent of the subject and of an absolute character, such as, the truth or the desire for something, which, because of the appreciation that is given to it, confers it the category of value. Moreover, according to Acosta (2017), values have three dimensions: an objective one of being and worth in themselves; a subjective one, they are valued insofar as they represent an interest in the subject; and a social character insofar as they are the aspiration of a non-determined human collective.

The value will determine human conduct and attitudes, occupying the central part of the individual's personality. In turn, it is related to motivation since human behavior is conditioned and stimulated by the needs and interests that the person has, not only on an individual level but also on a collective level, so that each social group forms a set of norms, beliefs, and aspirations which transmits to its members (Gervilla, 2012).

Values have a social origin because each society has a specific system of values and a double dimension, individual and social. Since one of the objectives of education is to reconcile the individual aspirations of the subject with those of the society to which they belong, the teaching function appears as a task of particular relevance since the attitude and disposition of its professionals foster the necessary climate in the classroom for the transmission of specific values (Anaut, 2012).

Benítez Grande-Caballero (2019) argues that values are the rules of conduct according to which we behave and which are under what we consider to be correct. They designate states we attach importance to and have a particular hierarchy within the things we like. Therefore, value as a human quality is the reasoned and firm conviction that something is good or bad and that it is good for us. Every human being internalizes what satisfies his or her needs and, on this basis, has interests, forms convictions, specifies his or her future aspirations, and comes to analyze possibilities of achieving them: this is how values are manifested (Trujillo, 2020).

After analyzing all these definitions that complete the meaning of the word "value," we can summarise that values are qualities or decisions marked by a set of rules of conduct that belong to a specific culture, which are complemented and strengthened as the individual grows and matures (Cortina, 2020).

Stories teach children about life, about us, and others. Stories are a unique way for students to develop an understanding, respect, and appreciation for other cultures. It can promote a positive attitude toward people from different lands, races, and religions. Storytelling is critical to the child's overall development by enhancing their imagination and creatively promoting language learning. Stories bring the process of language learning to life since it enables language development and promotes early literacy skills in the child.

The Importance of Value Education

Once we have understood what values are, we will now justify why value education is important, not only in the school context but throughout a person's life. Ortega Ruiz & Hernández Prados (2018, p.1) indicate that "education is nothing other than a process of transmission by which someone, on the one hand, transmits or delivers to another their experience or keys to the interpretation of existence. On the other hand, the receiver recreates, reinterprets, in a new context, what has been given to him/her, bequeathed by the educator".

According to Martínez Martin & Hoyos Vásquez, G. (2014, p. 17), "Educating in values is participating in an authentic process of personal development and construction. Educating in values is programming and articulating in social relations and institutions what we have been told from moral, political, and legal philosophy". Educating in values means creating conditions so that students learn to value specific values as such, learn to reject counter-values and learn to construct their matrix of values in the face of socially controversial issues in plural contexts when establishing a hierarchy between values or interpreting them according to the cultural context and personal biography (López, 2021).

Secondly, value education is about creating social conditions that provide good opportunities for certain citizenship practices. Such practices should make it possible to appreciate and value coexistence in plural and heterogeneous societies, favor involvement in collective projects, support a model of society based on inclusion, and propose a way of life that of active citizenship in which each person assumes responsibility and takes charge of the world in which they live and is responsible for their actions and its consequences (Touriñán, 2015).

Let us consider the information provided by these authors. It stands out that the importance of working with the appropriate pedagogical material, having knowledge of intervention strategies in the classroom, and designing curricular activities is necessary. For this to happen, teachers must create conditions and a series of rules that help to regulate socialization so that students feel comfortable being the way they are so that the moment comes when they no longer need our involvement in their behavior because the atmosphere will always be good (Carreras et al., 2018).

Elexpuru Albizuri & Medrano Samaniego (2022) also agree, arguing that educating in values is a continuum that cannot be approached from one or several didactic units. The values initiated in each programming unit are the first contact, which will necessarily have to continue throughout the course if we want the children to develop and make their intended attitudes.

According to Ortega Ruiz and Hernández Prados (2018, 4), "Learning values is not so much a question of intelligence as of imitation of models of experience, of testimony of value. Values are apprehended in their concept or idea, but they are appropriated by imitation, by osmosis". Alonso (2018) stated that educating in values meant finding spaces for both individual and collective reflection so that students could elaborate rationally and autonomously on the principles of value. These principles would allow them to face reality critically.

The aim is for students to construct their values and criteria based on exciting experiences and previous knowledge provided by the teacher (Corominas, 2022). Values are vital at the Primary Education stage as this is the time of maturity when pupils' personalities are forged, which is why teachers play an essential role.

METHOD

Description of the Reference Group

Getting to know each of the children in the group is vital, as their characteristics and personalities, especially those related to their reading habits, will help us understand their involvement and their way of acting in the specific activities more clearly. The reference group is made up of 25 children aged between 10 and 12, of whom 13 are girls and 12 are boys, in 5th Primary Education. The group is very varied academically speaking.

Another vital factor to consider is the learning pace of the pupils, since the fact that there are pupils from different origins and that they live in different personal and family contexts, in addition to their possible difficulties in the classroom - ADHD, developmental delays, behavioral problems - will influence the development of the proposal.

On a second basis, we have considered the learning pace and conceptual level, in which we have pointed out, more concretely, their habits in the field of reading. Finally, the social level is briefly addressed, understanding it as the relationships with the rest of their classmates and other school groups.

Description of the Research Method

The Primary Education stage has a very peculiar characteristic: the whole weekly school timetable is based on very well-marked sessions. Anyone who observes it may think that every day they do the same thing week after week, but this is the best way to create work and study habits and establish the contents to be worked on. Subjects are scheduled in one-hour periods, except for the last session of the day, which is half an hour.

After we observed the timetable and routines of the group, we agreed that the storytelling sessions presented in this chapter would take place in the last half-hour session on Wednesdays. In addition, some of the lessons could be complemented on Mondays, before going to the library if necessary. The storytelling sessions would begin in April and occur every Wednesday until the beginning of May.

We have established the following routines to encourage the reading habits of the group. Every Monday, they go to the library and borrow books. Each student can stay with the same book for a maximum of two weeks, which is enough time as each book's length is adapted to each user's reading capacity. When they choose a book, they pick it up and leave a yew tree in the shape of a puma in its place. These strategies help in the management and tidiness of the library. After reading the book, they must make a reading card that does not consist of a summary of the book, but they must elaborate on an argued opinion of it, connecting it with the synopsis of the text.

RESULTS

The first question that had to be resolved to be able to implement this proposal was which stories we choose. The market for children's stories is growing by leaps and bounds, offering many different types of stories, both externally and internally. The search for stories was broken down into minor themes based on which values to work on in the classroom.

In addition, two other characteristics that were also taken into account and made the list of possible candidates decrease the age group to be worked with: 10 - 12 years old and the language; since being a bilingual school, we looked for books in English that they could understand without difficulty and that would not divert them too much from the objectives and contents to be achieved with each of the programmed sessions. After a period of research and investigation, these were the five stories selected to work on in the classroom:

Table 1. Choice of stories

Title	Author	Value
Susan laughs	Jane Willis	Courage Perseverance Autonomy
Elmer the Elephant	David McKee	Self-control Self-esteem Self-respect
The Rainbow Fish	Marcus Pfizer	Loyalty Sincerity Co-operation
My Friend Whale	Simon James	Civic awareness Responsibility Solidarity
And Tango makes three	Justin Richardson & Peter Parnell	Tolerance Justice Respect for difference

Source: Own elaboration

The sessions always begin with a short motor wedge to help them disconnect from the previous session and reconnect in the session that is about to begin. This is necessary because we need them to be concentrated for almost the entire session. These wedges are simple and basic: move a little at a slow pace and breathe in and out profoundly to calm them down.

After a couple of sessions following this ritual, the pupils no longer needed information about what we would do, but when they finished the previous class, they were ready to go on their own. They were ready to pick up their tables autonomously, leaving only the pencil case and getting ready for storytime.

Once the story is over, the following questions are asked in English: "What did you think of the story?"; "Why do you think this story is interesting?". These first two questions initiate the subsequent reflection session, as without knowing what comes next, they can make small hypotheses about what will be worked on next. This is followed by the first block of reflection, entitled "time to think," in which more specific questions are proposed that relate the story read to the value or values that will be worked on in each session.

The next block, "time to play," begins, where a game or activity is proposed, depending on the story, in which they put into practice the value or values worked on. These activities are approached differently as they must be short, concrete, and offer a clear result for the subsequent conclusions and reflections. They consist of two parts, one to be carried out in the classroom and the other to be completed at home. The objective is that it is necessary to have a period in which they can think in a relaxed way about what they have extracted from the story, and the most beneficial thing for this is the change of context. In addition, the answers they bring from home are also interesting.

After the activity, the session ends with a sentence or a picture that makes them go away thinking about it. This is why it is read aloud, repeated a couple of times, and paraphrased so that they understand why this sentence has been chosen to close the session.

Table 2. Story 1: Susan laughs

Title: Susan Laughs Author: Willis, Jeanne Themes: personal abilities, different skills, self-image. Publication date: 2000 Publisher: Henry Holt and Co. (2000), 32 pages
Susan is an ordinary girl who does ordinary things like any other girl. Susan jumps, sings, plays, screams... and even does a little mischief. Is she different?
OBJECTIVES: - To discover and reflect on the abilities that a person with a disability has. - To observe that everyone can do anything if they have aids and adaptations. - To include people with disabilities in their context and not treat them as different people.
REFLECTION QUESTIONS: - What do you think of Susan's story? - Can you do all the things Susan does? - Do you think Susan is different because she can do everything she does from her wheelchair?
ACTIVITY/GAME: 1 / Get into pairs and have a blank piece of paper and a pencil for each pair. 2 / One will cover the other partner's eyes with the hands. 3 / The person with their eyes covered should draw something that the person with their eyes open will describe. 4 / When you are done, the person with his/her eyes open will have to write what he/she wanted his/her partner to draw next to each drawing. 5/ When the game is over, you will have to write on the back of the paper what each of you felt while doing the activity. 6/ At the end of the activity, you will have to reflect on whether you think that people like Susan can do anything and whether she has the same abilities as a person who does not need a wheelchair.
SENTENCE TO REFLECT ON: You can do anything you want. Break through the obstacles and go for your dreams.
OBSERVATION CRITERIA FOR THE SESSION: - The students' faces will be observed throughout the reading of the story, as the end is the most striking part, and the facial expression with its corresponding non-verbal language will provide the most information. - The contributions of those pupils who are more reluctant to do activities with people less skilled or capable than themselves will be collected. - Wait for the pairs to form; if a pair is more interesting to observe, have one person draw and the other describes. These pairs will be observed more closely to pick up on their movements and non-verbal language.

Source: Own elaboration

Table 3. Story 2: Elmer the Elephant

Title: Elmer the Elephant Author: David McKee Themes: Self-image, acceptance of differences, prejudice, and stereotypes. Publication date: 1989 Publisher: Ediciones Beascoa, S.A (1989), 32 pages
Elmer is not grey like the other elephants in his herd; he has skin of many colors. All the elephants love Elmer because he makes jokes and laughs a lot, but Elmer does not know if they are laughing at him or with him, so one day, he disguises himself and hides in his herd without anyone recognizing him.
OBJECTIVES: - To accept the different capacities and abilities that each one of us has. - To reflect on whether being different is good or bad. - To observe that each of us has abilities and personalities that make us unique and irreplaceable. - To include all people regardless of their abilities, skills, and personality.
REFLECTION QUESTIONS: - What do you think of Elmer's story? - Do you think the other elephants were laughing at Elmer or with Elmer? - How do we feel when someone laughs at us? - How do you think a classmate feels when others laugh at him or her? - Can you remember a situation similar to Elmer's?
ACTIVITY/GAME: 1 / You need a piece of paper on which you must write your name. 2/ Underneath, you must write one quality that makes you unique. 3/ Then you must explain why that quality makes you different from others and why it is your remarkable quality. 4/ We will write on the posters the list of qualities we have in our class. 5/ At the end of the activity, you must reflect on whether you think we all must be the same or whether the qualities that make us each special are good or bad.
SENTENCE TO REFLECT ON: A matter of attitude: All different abilities are our strengths.
OBSERVATION CRITERIA FOR THE SESSION: - The students' faces will be observed throughout the reading of the story, and the facial expression with their corresponding non-verbal language will provide the most information. - Contributions from students who cannot accept the differences between their classmates or who feel self-conscious about not being able to be the way they are will be collected. - Read out the individual qualities before writing them on the list in case they need to understand the purpose of the activity. - The group's responses will be observed to see if the qualities they provide are related to their personality or skills.

Source: Own elaboration

DISCUSSION

Story 1: Susan Laughs

The story is simple. At first, the children thought it was a text more focused on Early Childhood Education, as each page was composed of a simple sentence with the main character's name, the activity she was doing, and a drawing explaining the action. Their faces started showing curiosity for the session as this was a new activity. When the last picture appeared on the whiteboard, followed by the sentence "I am Susan," all their faces changed, totally perplexed.

After the activity of drawing in pairs, we could see that the duos expected were formed, so it was easy to adapt them to what we wanted. We were mainly looking for students who were reluctant to make physical contact or who did not allow to be guided by their classmates to play the role of blind people so that they would have to comply with the descriptions of the other person. On the other hand, we also wanted students who were quiet or not very participative to guide their classmates who played the role of the blind person by describing something specific.

Table 4. Story 3: My Friend Whale

Title: My Friend Whale Author: Simon James Themes: Ecology, species protection, respect for the animal world. Publication date: 2004 Publisher: Candlewick Press (2004), 32 pages.
This is the story of a boy with a blue whale as a friend. Every night when the moon rises, he meets her at the beach. The boy swims with her until the sun rises, and they say goodbye. What will happen if one day the whale stops appearing?
OBJECTIVES: - To care for the environment and biodiversity. - To raise awareness of the danger of senseless mass hunting. - To seek solutions for endangered species.
REFLECTION QUESTIONS: - What do you think of the whale story? - Where do you think the whale has gone? - What do you think happens when a species of animal becomes extinct or endangered? - How can we protect animals?
ACTIVITY/GAME: 1 / You need a piece of paper on which you must write your name. 2/ Underneath, you must write an alternative ending for this story, as it has been left with an open ending. 3/ Then, explain where you think the whale has gone. 4/ At the end of the activity you will have to write your opinion about the story and reflect on why taking care of our planet is essential.
SENTENCE TO REFLECT ON: Let us always try to ensure that our actions leave a green footprint on our path.
OBSERVATION CRITERIA FOR THE SESSION: - The students' faces will be observed throughout the reading of the story, and the facial expression with their corresponding non-verbal language will provide the most information. - Contributions from students who do not understand or favor caring for the planet and animals will be collected. - The group's alternative endings will be read to see if they understand the story.

Source: Own elaboration

After the drawing activity, when it was their turn to see if the drawings matched the descriptions, we could see how many children's heads showed the typical comic book sketches. Little by little, the children whispered and compared the drawings of some with those of others.

The fact that this was the first class to use the proposal provided novelty and intrigue throughout the story session. The simplicity of the storyline made it easy to understand, allowing the students to focus on the story without concentrating too much on the foreign language meanings.

The children's disbelief when they discovered Susan's disability was evident on their faces, which implied that they did not identify with Susan when they discovered her limitations. This has led to a long period of input from different pupils regarding people's abilities to cope with the challenges of everyday life. It could be concluded that the children have accepted and understood that any person, regardless of whether they are disabled, can face the challenges they set themselves; they need the necessary resources and adaptations to do so.

Story 2: Elmer the Elephant

The presented story is familiar to the pupils as it is a title that is widely used and worked on in different situations. Therefore, the language and the plot, despite being in English, were clear to their understanding. Elmer is one of those stories that has been worked on so much that it no longer surprises them.

Table 5. Story 4: The Rainbow Fish

Title: The Rainbow Fish Author: Marcus Pfister. Themes: self-image, friendship, selfishness, sharing, cooperating Publication Date: 1992 Publisher: Ediciones Norte-Sur, 1994, 24 pages
The rainbow fish was the envy of the whole ocean for his precious shiny scales, and he knew it. One day a little fish asked him for one of his scales because he had so many, but the rainbow fish disagreed, which provoked criticism and rumors of his selfishness throughout the ocean. Suddenly the rainbow fish was alone and went to an old octopus for advice, who told him to share his scales. The rainbow fish took the advice and shared his colored scales with all the fish and thus became happier but less pretty.
OBJECTIVES: - To reflect on the importance of friendship and social relationships. - To instil the value of sharing things with your peers. - To think about the importance of cooperating to achieve specific objectives.
REFLECTION QUESTIONS: - What do you think about the story of the rainbow fish? - How do you think the rainbow fish feels? - Why do you think he feels that way?
ACTIVITY/GAME: 1 / You have a picture of the unpainted goldfish and this box of paints with a different color for each of you. 2/ You must work as a team to paint the goldfish. Each of you will have to paint at least one scale. 3/ To achieve the objective, you have 15 minutes and only have to organize yourselves. 4/ When the time is up, and we have observed the result of the activity, they will have to go to the other DIN A3, where there is a grid with their individualized name, and write down how they thought the activity was going to turn out, how it turned out, why you think it turned out this way and finally, a proposal for improvement.
SENTENCE TO REFLECT ON: You feel you belong to very few people; your country is your friends and you miss that...
OBSERVATION CRITERIA FOR THE SESSION: - The students' faces will be observed throughout the reading of the story, and the facial expression with their corresponding non-verbal language will provide the most information. - The contributions of the students who tend to be more selfish and individualistic in the group will be collected, contrasting them with those of the students who are more cooperative and work well as a team, seeking to generate a debate in the classroom. - The way the class organizes itself when carrying out the activity of painting the fish will be observed. - Students' contributions on the individual grid will be read out.

Source: Own elaboration

Some difficulty was observed when it came to an understanding of what was sought with the word "quality," as the answers of some children did not correspond to what we were looking for in them. The activity had to be paraphrased to direct it toward the objective we wanted to achieve. Elmer's story required little concentration from the students, as they knew the story's plot. Therefore, the story and the language were an excellent influence on their understanding. After writing down the qualities that make each pupil unique on the papers, we could see the variety of "differences" in the class.

Among the children's contributions, their qualities were more related to the area of friendship, where those who considered themselves funny because they always knew how to make others laugh or those who considered themselves skilled in a particular field and related this skill to the quality of learning quickly and overcoming new challenges in their lives stood out. Girls, on the other hand, focused more on social skills and peer-to-peer interaction, as their best qualities were listening and giving advice to each other.

Overall, the answers given by the group were within their maturity level, with peaks of difference between the youngest pupils in the class and the repeaters from previous years who were one year older than the age of the reference year.

Table 6. Story 5: And Tango Makes Three

Title: And Tango Makes Three Authors: Richardson Justin and Parnell, Peter Themes: family diversity, homosexuality, families. Publication date: 2016 Publishing house: Kalandraka Editora, 2016, 32 pages
This is the story of a unique pair of chinstrap penguins who were given the opportunity by the keeper of the Central Park Zoo in New York, Rob Gramzay, by depositing an egg in their nest, to have a baby after observing that they were unsuccessfully hatching a stone. Thus, Tango was born the first penguin to have two parents.
OBJECTIVES: - To reflect on the importance of the family. - To observe the different types of families that exist today. - To think about the meaning of family for each of us.
REFLECTION QUESTIONS: - What do you think of Tango's family story? - What does being a family mean to you? - How many types of families do you know?
ACTIVITY/GAME: 1 / You have a sheet of paper divided into three parts. 2 / On the left side of the sheet of paper, in the part where it says DRAW, you have to draw YOUR FAMILY. 3 / On the right-hand side, in the box above, you must describe your family. In other words, you must describe your drawing. 4 / On the right, in the box below, you must reflect and write WHAT IS FAMILY FOR YOU? WHY IS IT IMPORTANT? 5 / On the other side of the sheet of paper, you will find another box where you must write your opinion about today's story and why it made you think.
SENTENCE TO REFLECT ON: OHANA means family, and family means we will always be together and never leave each other.
OBSERVATION CRITERIA FOR THE SESSION: - The students' faces will be observed throughout the reading of the story, and the facial expression with their corresponding non-verbal language will provide us with the most information. - We will collect the contributions of the pupils who do not understand perfectly the types of families that exist or perhaps, due to the family context, do not accept them respectfully, seeking to generate a debate in the classroom. - The way the class reacts when listening to their classmates' contributions will be observed. - Drawings and answers about the family will be observed.

Source: Own elaboration

Story 3: My Friend the Whale

On the celebration of Earth Day at school, the students could include story time in the activities that were taking place that week at started faster started at a faster pace than the two previous sessions, as they included the story time at the end of Wednesdays in their routine timetable.

The children's expressions towards the story of the whale brought intrigue, even a bit of sadness on the part of some girls, above all. The story's ending was left open, which generated a range of comments and diverse contributions within the group. Asking students to create their endings was sometimes not accepted with pleasure. This activity involved thinking and giving their opinion, but they had to use their imagination and creativity to create a nice ending that the teacher liked.

The reflections aloud were most enriching for some of the students, these contributions gave much information about situations they had to live through and the contexts they came from. The students got into a debate with each other, the answers of those who advocated practices to care for the planet and protect animals crossed with the answers of the more "practical" students, who thought that if you had to survive you would not stop to think about whether that animal might become extinct.

The fact that the story was related to a specific celebration, such as Earth Day, helped the students to settle into the activity more quickly. Once the students knew what would happen, they could predispose their movements and actions to the session. The children's facial expressions, together with their non-verbal language, while the story was being read, were not unfamiliar.

The activity of writing an alternative ending did not go down well with all the classmates, as having to write a story required them to think and be creative, which not all of them were motivated to do. Seeing that the essays were not going as well as we had hoped, as motivation was low since it was the last hour of the day, it was decided to offer them the opportunity to write it quietly at home after reflecting a little on what they had worked on in class.

Story 4: The Rainbow Fish

As with the story of Elmer the Elephant, the story of The Rainbow Fish was not new to them. They had worked on it before n languages but limited themselves to reading and understanding it.

The Rainbow Fish story is one of those stories that have been exploited *ad nauseam*, leaving little room for imaginative new activities and resources. The most remarkable thing about this story is the complexity of its comprehension since, despite having worked with it and knowing the story before, we had to play the video twice and read it out loud a third time and even make a summary in Spanish for 100% of the class to understand its plot.

The rule was that each student had to paint at least several parts of the fish, and this was the only guideline. Everything started well, but a leadership conflict arose between the two pupils. They both scold each other for always being in charge and doing what they said. On the other hand, "satellite children" orbited around the decision-making area to find out what needed to be done but did not contribute any decisions.

At the end of the time the level of frustration in the class was widespread, as they started with a simple task they had been unable to achieve. After the reflection question as to whether they had been cooperative or competitive, there was a wide range of opinions, as those who had been cooperative or competitive had a wide range of opinions, with those who had been able to paint claiming that they had been cooperative, as opposed to the vast majority who had not even had time to get close to the drawing, who claimed that the classmates who had painted had been most competitive.

The first conclusion drawn from the story of Rainbow Fish was that the pupils already knew the story and worked on it in their mother tongue meaning they had no difficulty understanding it. However, when it was read in a foreign language, the first obstacle appeared, as it is a dense story, and they needed help to follow it in English.

Finally, they need very well-defined rules, as leaving them free in such a large group without specifying the roles of each team member was disconcerting for them, and they did not concentrate on the objective to be achieved. They sought support from the more "capable" pupils, but as they did not have the teacher's approval of their decisions, they did not have the confidence to carry them out.

In this age group and the school context, the teacher and clear and concrete guidelines are necessary to achieve success and provide the pupils with confidence so they feel capable of achieving the objective.

Reading the students' opinions grid, we could observe that they were not frustrated or angry for not having painted the fish in its entirety. On the contrary, they were reflective and methodical, even self-critical, giving solutions of the most praiseworthy to paint the whole fish in the established time without problems.

Story 5: And Tango Makes Three

The last story presented is justifiably placed at the end, as at first glance, it may seem simple, but it is one of the most complex to work on at this age, as family diversity is something that is still a somewhat taboo subject and is not seen 100% in society. Added to this is that these are specific contexts the pupils have never even attempted to observe.

In the class, there are different types of families, as several children come from dysfunctional families where they only live with one parent and have a visiting arrangement with the other parent, even single mothers with no father figure—even restructured families with a married couple who provide children on both sides.

The plot of the story was very new for the pupils. This novelty was evident in their facial expressions and non-verbal language. They began to accept the story as the mUsingre animals. Using ls in the stories was a valuable resource, so it was simple to extrapolate to real life and their close contexts. However, in this case, the extraction of content and its adaptation to real life must be entirely caught on.

The debate and the contributions were very enriching. There was a moment when they discussed that families could break up because something did not work. In the faces of children from families with separated parents, one could see identification with these comments and contributions. Later, looking at the children's drawings, one drew particular attention to the drawing of a girl whose parents are separated and who lives far away. In the space where she had to draw her family, the girl divided the space vertically, drawing her mother with her on one side and herself again with her father on the other. In addition to this, another drawing that attracted attention was that of the refugee girl. She handed in the grid with a sheet of paper attached, as her family was immense. After analyzing the drawing, the student provided a color pattern to understand third parties.

It is very complex for pupils of this age to understand that the concept of family may not include offspring or the need for two people to be united in marriage. They know cases of people who have decided to have children alone or even couples with no offspring for various reasons. On the other hand, they also accept that some people live alone and have a balanced life without a partner or children. All these examples of families exist, and they know them but cannot relate them or name them with the corresponding nomenclature.

CONCLUSION

Days go by and you educate your gaze; you know where to focus your eyes at any given moment, and from what initially seemed to you that anything goes, now you select according to precise criteria. Depending on the story you are using, you look for the opinions and contributions of particular students, given the diversity of the students in the classroom. You may be surprised by some unexpected contribution that helps you to conclude, or, on the contrary, specific pupils from whom you expected and wanted a specific contribution that does not appear.

When we carried out the planned lessons, the most challenging part began; sitting down to conclude everything, we had our field diary full of notes, with various colors to differentiate the objective from subjective opinions and the observations made. On the other hand, we had the activities that the children did to exemplify further what we have seen.

Within these conclusions, we observed that the questions we had asked at the beginning were being achieved. You give coherent explanations as to why certain pupils make specific contributions to certain values or others, and their reactions to the stories can be positive or negative depending on which argument and which child. We found a close relationship between the contributions made by the students during the session and their subsequent responses to the reflection activities we asked them to do at home.

The implementation time was short regarding the evolution in the competencies related to the values worked on and the habit of reading. However, it was only short due to our limited implementation time. We would have loved to be able to implement more than five stories. One of the aims was achieved as the children included "story time" at the end of the day on Wednesdays in their timetable routines. Therefore, we would have been delighted if this proposal could have been carried out for a whole school year.

The proposal, its implementation, and reflections were completed. However, we were not satisfied and thought about proposing a personal application based on everything that happened during the five sessions we carried out. The question is straightforward: If you were the teacher, how would you make this activity last a full academic year? You never think about improving the situation because there are no good or bad models; our only intention is to contribute your grain of sand to the educational process.

REFERENCES

Acosta, M. (2017). Estrategias didácticas para educar en valores. *Revista Educación en Valores*, 2(8), 59–60.

Adela Kohan, S. (2013). *Escribir es para niños. Todas las claves para escribir lo que los niños quieren leer*. Ediciones Alba.

Alonso, J. M. (2018). *La educación en valores en la institución escolar: Planteamiento y programación*. Editorial Plaza y Valdés.

Anaut, L. (2012). *Valores escolares y educación para la ciudadanía*. Editorial Graó.

Arufe Graldés, V. (2021). La educación en valores en el aula de educación física. ¿Mito o Realidad? *Revista digital de Educación física*, 9.

Benítez Grande-Caballero, L. J. (2019). *Actividades y recursos para educar en valores*. PPC.

Berkowitz, D. (2021). Oral storytelling: Building community through dialogue, engagement, and problem solving. *NAEYC Young Children*, 2(3), 36–41.

Bernal, G., & García, M. (2020). Storytelling: A key to speaking fluently in English. *Cuadernos de Lingüística Hispánica*, 15, 151–162.

Carreras, L., Eijo, P., Estany, A., Gómez, M. T., Guich, R., Mir, V., Ojeda, F., Planas, T., & Serrats, M. G. (2018). *Cómo educar en valores*. Ediciones Narcea.

Collie, J., & Slater, S. (2012). *Literature in the Language Classroom: A resource book of ideas and activities*. Cambridge University Press.

Corominas, F. (2012). *Educar hoy*. Editorial Palabra.

Cortina, A. (2020). *La educación y los valores*. Biblioteca Nueva.

Daniel, A. K. (2012). *Storytelling across the Primary classroom*. Routledge.

Davis, H., Waycott, J., & Schleser, M. (2019). Digital storytelling. In Managing Complexity and Creating Innovation through Design (pp.15–24). doi:10.4324/9780429022746-3

Díaz, C. (2015). *Educar en valores: Guía para padres y maestros*. Editorial Trillas.

Dunst, C. J., Simkus, A., & Hamby, D. W. (2012). Children's story retelling for teachers and pupils. *CELL Reviews*, *5*(2), 1–14.

Elexpuru Albizuri, I., & Medrano Samaniego, C. (2022). *Desarrollo de los valores en las instituciones educativas*. Ediciones Mensajero.

Ellis, G., & Brewster, J. (2014). *Tell it again: The storytelling handbook for Primary English Language Teachers*. British Council.

Ferreira Pinto, C., & Soares, H. (2012). Using children's literature in ELT: A story-based approach. *Sensos*, *2*, 23–39.

García Campos, V. (2018). Escuela de Valores. *Revista Digital Enfoques Educativos*, *16*, 60–70.

Gervilla, E. (2012). Educadores del future, valores de hoy. *Revista de educación de la Universidad de Granada*, *15*, 7-25.

Ghosn, I. (2012). Four good reasons to use literature in primary school ELT. *ELT Journal*, *56*, 2.

Grugeon, E., & Gardner, P. (2010). *The art of storytelling for teachers and pupils*. David Fulton Publishing.

Heathfield, D. (2014). *Storytelling with our students*. Delta Publishing.

Huff, M. J. (2022). *Storytelling with puppets, props, and playful tales*. Curriculum Corporation.

López, R. (2021). *Educar en valores*. Adice Ediciones.

López Díaz, C. (2019). *El valor de los cuentos como parte de la educación en valores*. Central Sindical Independiente y de Funcionarios.

Martínez Martin, M., & Hoyos Vásquez, G. (2014). *Educar en valores es crear condiciones. ¿Qué significa educar en valores hoy?* Octaedro.

Molina Prieto, R. (2018). *Los cuentos ayudan a crecer*. Central Sindical Independiente y de Funcionarios.

Morgan, J., & Rinvolucri, M. (2014). *Using stories in the language classroom*. Cambridge University Press.

Mourao, S. (2019). *Using stories in the Primary classroom*. APAC.

Ortega Ruiz, P., & Hernández Prados, M. (2018). Lectura, narración y experiencia en la educación en valores. *Revista iberoamericana de educación, 45*, 1-5.

Ortega Ruiz, P., & Mínguez Vallejos, R. (2021). *Los valores en la educación*. Editorial Ariel.

Ray, B., & Seely, C. (2018). *Fluency through TPR Storytelling: Achieving natural language acquisition in school*. Command Performance Language Institute.

Satriani, I. (2019). Storytelling in teaching literacy: Benefits and challenges. English Review. *Journal of English Education*, *8*(1), 113–120. doi:10.25134/erjee.v8i1.1924

Smorgorzewska, J. (2014). Developing children's language creativity through telling stories: An experimental study. *Thinking Skills and Creativity*, *13*, 20–31. doi:10.1016/j.tsc.2014.02.005

Sun, P. Y. (2016). *Using drama and theatre to promote literacy development*. ERIC.

Touriñán, J. M. (2015). Educación en valores, educación intercultural y formación para la convivencia pacífica. *Revista Galega do Ensino*, 47.

Trujillo Trujillo, J. A. (2020). La Educación en Valores. *Cuadernos de Educación y Desarrollo*, *2*, 14.

KEY TERMS AND DEFINITIONS

Children's Literature: The genre encompasses a wide range of works, including acknowledged classics of world literature, picture books and easy-to-read stories written exclusively for children, and fairy tales, lullabies, fables, folk songs, and other primarily orally transmitted materials.

Education in Values: Values education refers to the aspect of the educational practice which entails that moral or political values, as well as norms, dispositions, and skills grounded in those values, are mediated to or developed among students.

Foreign Language: A foreign language is a language that is not an official language of, nor typically spoken in a specific country. Native speakers from that country usually need to acquire it through conscious learning, such as language lessons at school, self-teaching, or attending language understanding and engaging include the ability to understand and engage in a discipline's discourses and rhetorical situations by delivering expressing and interpreting or performances and to express and interpret ideas—both their own and those of others—in clear oral presentations or performances.

Primary Education: Primary education is compulsory and free. This stage of education is divided into six academic years, generally for those aged between 6 and 12.

Second Language Learning: Second language learning (SLL) is concerned with the process and study of how people acquire a second language, often referred to as L2 or target language, as opposed to L1 (the native language).

Values: Values are individual beliefs that motivate people to act one way or another. They serve as a guide for human behavior. Generally, people are predisposed to adopt the values they were raised with. People also tend to believe those values are "right" because they are the values of their culture.

Written Skills: You use writing skills to write effectively and succinctly. A good writer can communicate their point to their audience without using too much fluff and in a way that the other person can understand.

Chapter 3
Leveraging Technology to Enhance Quality Education in Primary Schools:
Opportunities and Challenges in Bangladesh

Md Ikhtiar Uddin Bhuiyan
Jahangirnagar University, Bangladesh

Md Meshkat Mollik
(iD) https://orcid.org/0000-0001-8541-3717
Jahangirnagar University, Bangladesh

ABSTRACT

This chapter examines the opportunities and challenges of leveraging technology to enhance quality education in primary schools in Bangladesh. A qualitative approach is employed, collecting data from primary schools in Turkey, the United States, and China through interviews, observations, and analysis of curricular materials. Thematic analysis is conducted using NVivo and SPSS software. The study investigates the concept of value education across cultures, presents comparative analyses of different approaches, and highlights challenges faced by educators in culturally diverse classrooms. It also explores the state of primary education in Bangladesh, identifies reasons for the lack of quality education, and proposes strategies for improvement. Emphasizing the crucial role of the government, the research assesses opportunities for effective implementation of quality education and provides solutions to prevailing problems.

DOI: 10.4018/978-1-6684-9295-6.ch003

INTRODUCTION

Quality primary education is crucial for the growth and development of children, as well as for creating ideal citizens who contribute to keeping society peaceful. In Bangladesh, the government has made extensive efforts to achieve Education for All, increasing the gross enrolment rate and gender parity index. However, the quality of education remains a huge concern, with evidence suggesting a deterioration in learning achievement. The chapter aims to focus on the current state of primary education in Bangladesh, explore the concept of quality education in the primary school system, and provide recommendations for policymakers, educators, and stakeholders to overcome the challenges and seize the opportunities to improve the quality of education with leveraging technology in primary schools.

It is crucial to recognize the significance of primary education in the overall development of a nation. The foundational skills and knowledge acquired during this stage lay the groundwork for the entire population, irrespective of socio-economic status, physical or mental limitations, and geographical location. The state has a constitutional responsibility to ensure equal opportunities for quality primary education for all children. This demand is further intensified by many individuals beginning their professional careers after completing their primary education.

Bangladesh follows a centralized primary education system, one of the largest in the world. The government established the Directorate of Independent Primary Education in 1981 to strengthen this system and legislated compulsory primary education in 1990. Subsequently, the Department of Primary and Mass Education was formed in 1992 to expedite primary and mass education programs. In 2003, the government elevated it to the Ministry of Primary and Mass Education, highlighting its commitment to fulfilling minimum education requirements (Ahmmed & Mullick, 2014).

The National Education Policy of 2010 recommended extending primary education up to class VIII to ensure the quality of primary education, and implementation efforts have commenced. The government nationalized approximately 25,240 private primary schools in 2013 (Alam et al., 2021b). Moreover, significant investments, amounting to 58 thousand crore rupees, have been made through the Primary Education Development-3 program. Additional measures include the introduction of satellite and community schools, Anand Schools for education and upgrading primary education, providing meals, curriculum reform, and teacher training. These steps collectively aim to improve the quality of primary education in Bangladesh, involving active participation from parents and local community members (Sommers, 2013).

METHODOLOGY

This methodology outlines the research approach for investigating the utilization of technology to enhance the quality of education in primary schools. The study aims to determine the impact of technology integration on student learning outcomes and identify the factors influencing its successful implementation. This methodology provides an overview of the research type, data collection procedures, and data analysis tools employed throughout the study.

The researchers use a qualitative approach to gather data from primary schools in different countries to examine the challenges and opportunities of achieving quality education in Bangladesh. Data is being collected through semi-structured interviews with teachers and administrators, classroom observations, and analysis of curricular materials. After data collection, the research topic is addressed through thematic analysis using AntConc, NVivo, and SPSS software. Additionally, the study examines the possibilities and barriers to leveraging technology in primary schools in Bangladesh.

a. Research Type: This research adopts a mixed-methods approach, combining both exploratory and descriptive research methods. The exploratory phase involves an in-depth literature review to understand the existing practices, challenges, and potential benefits of leveraging technology in primary education. The descriptive phase involves collecting and analyzing data to understand the current state of technology integration in primary schools and its impact on educational outcomes.

b. Data Type and Sample Selection Procedure: The research collects primary and secondary data. Primary data is collected through surveys, interviews, and observations among primary school teachers, administrators, and students. Secondary data is obtained from academic journals, government reports, and other relevant publications.

To ensure a representative sample, a multistage sampling procedure is employed. Firstly, a list of primary schools is obtained, and then a random sampling technique is used to select a certain number of schools. Within each selected school, teachers, administrators, and students are chosen through stratified random sampling to ensure diverse perspectives and a balanced representation.

c. Data Analysis Tools: The collected data is analyzed using various tools and techniques to address the research objectives. The following steps are being followed for data analysis:

1. Data Cleaning: The collected data is carefully examined for completeness, accuracy, and consistency. Any missing or erroneous data is rectified or excluded from the analysis.

2. Quantitative Analysis: Descriptive statistics, such as mean, standard deviation, and frequency distribution, summarize the quantitative data from surveys and observations. Inferential statistics, including correlation and regression analyses, are conducted to identify relationships between variables and test hypotheses.

3. Qualitative Analysis: The qualitative data gathered from interviews and open-ended survey questions are analyzed using thematic analysis. Themes and patterns are identified, and the data is coded accordingly to reveal insights and recurring themes related to the research objectives.

4. Integration of Quantitative and Qualitative Findings: The results from the quantitative and qualitative analyses are synthesized to provide a comprehensive understanding of the impact of technology integration on primary education. Triangulation compares and contrasts the findings from both data sources, enabling a more robust interpretation of the results.

5. Formation of Hypotheses: Based on the research objectives, hypotheses are formulated to establish the relationships between the dependent variables (e.g., student learning outcomes) and independent variables (e.g., technology integration methods, teacher training, and infrastructure availability). Econometric models and financial ratios are developed to test these hypotheses using the collected data.

By employing a mixed-methods approach, this research methodology aims to gather comprehensive and reliable data to examine the utilization of technology in primary schools. The combination of quantitative and qualitative analyses enables a deeper understanding of the impact of technology integration on student learning outcomes. The research findings can provide insights and recommendations for policymakers, educators, and other stakeholders to enhance the quality of education.

LITERATURE REVIEW

Technology integration in primary school education has gained significant attention in recent years due to its potential to enhance the quality of learning experiences. Rohaan (2009) found that technology integration positively influences student engagement, motivation, and learning outcomes (Rohaan et al., 2009). Similarly, Buchanan (2019) observed improved collaboration, critical thinking skills, and increased creativity due to technology integration in U.S. primary schools (Buchanan et al., 2019). Moltudal (2022) emphasized that technology integration enhances problem-solving skills, information literacy, and overall academic performance (Moltudal et al., 2022).

Elmira et al. (2022) conducted an empirical study and found that teachers who effectively integrate technology positively influence student achievement and engagement (Elmira et al., 2022). Fernández-Batanero et al. (2022) highlighted the positive impact of educational robotics on student motivation, interest, and self-efficacy in STEM subjects (Fernández-Batanero et al., 2022). Pinto-Llorente & Sánchez-Gómez (2020), in a meta-analysis, demonstrated the positive effects of online learning on student achievement, engagement, and critical thinking skills in primary education (Pinto-Llorente & Sánchez-Gómez, 2020).

Domingo & Garganté (2016) explored how technology can foster culturally responsive instruction and promote equity in primary schools(Domingo & Garganté, 2016). Schuck (2016) reviewed mobile learning applications, showing that it improves student engagement, collaboration, and problem-solving skills (Schuck, 2016). Gee et al. (2017) emphasized promoting critical thinking, problem-solving, and collaboration through educational games. Rohaan et al. (2010) found that augmented reality enhances student engagement, motivation, and content comprehension (Rohaan et al., 2010).

Volpe & Gori (2019) highlighted how technology promotes productive inquiry-based learning in primary science education (Volpe & Gori, 2019). Islam (2019) emphasized the importance of providing equal access to technology to ensure equitable educational opportunities (Md. M. Islam, 2019). Lee and Tsai (2018) observed that digital storytelling improves writing skills, creativity, and positive attitudes toward writing. Ambia & Rahman (2021) reviewed the positive impact of digital learning on student achievement, engagement, and critical thinking skills (Ambia & Rahman, 2021).

Yasmin & Rumi (2020) discussed how digital fabrication and making in education foster creativity, problem-solving skills, and the democratization of invention(Yasmin & Rumi, 2020). Al-Fraihat et al. (2017) found that educational robotics improves understanding, problem-solving, and spatial reasoning skills in primary school mathematics. Abusaleh & Haque (2022) highlighted the positive effects of mobile learning on student engagement, academic achievement, and self-directed learning skills (Abusaleh & Haque, 2022).

Shohel & Howes (2011) emphasized the importance of pedagogical approaches, teacher training, and technological infrastructure for successful technology integration (Shohel & Howes, 2011). Alam et al. (2021a) discussed the benefits of open educational resources (OER) in expanding access to quality educational materials and promoting collaboration among educators (Alam et al. 2021a). Monia (2020) conducted a meta-analysis showing that digital technologies enhance literacy skills in primary education, including reading comprehension, vocabulary development, and writing proficiency (Monia, 2020).

The reviewed literature demonstrates that technology integration in primary education can enhance the quality of learning experiences. Various studies indicate that technology integration positively influences student engagement, motivation, collaboration, critical thinking skills, and academic achievement. Educational robotics, mobile learning, augmented reality, digital storytelling, and other digital tools have shown promising results in promoting student learning outcomes and fostering 21st-century skills.

Additionally, the literature emphasizes the importance of equitable access to technology, teacher training, pedagogical approaches, and the sustainability of educational resources in ensuring the successful integration of technology in primary schools (Obaydullah, 2019).

As primary education continues to evolve, educators, policymakers, and researchers must leverage the findings from these studies to inform the effective implementation of technology in primary classrooms. By embracing technology and leveraging its potential, primary schools can create engaging, inclusive, and learner-centered environments that enhance the quality of education and prepare students for the challenges and opportunities of the digital age.

BACKGROUND

During the British period in the Indian subcontinent, the indigenous education system was primarily focused on spiritual and philosophical teachings. The introduction of modern education in the country can be attributed to the British. In 1835, William Adam presented a detailed report recommending the implementation of education plans, using the mother tongue in textbooks, teacher training, and establishing regular schools (Haque, 2013). In 1854, Wood's Education Despatches further shaped the education system under government oversight, leading to the Education Department's establishment and the Inspector role under the Director of Public Education. Lord Curzon played a role in expanding primary education, and Gopalkrishna Gokhale introduced a bill for compulsory primary education in 1910, which was later rejected (Roy, 2017).

The Compulsory Primary Education Act was passed in 1919, initially applicable only to municipal areas. The Bengal (Rural) Primary Education Act was enacted in 1930 for rural areas, but its implementation was limited. 1939 this act made primary education free and universal, and district-level school boards were established for administration and control. The Sergeant Commission Report 1944 recognized the importance of pre-primary education (T. Islam et al., 2019).

After the partition of India in 1947, a resolution was presented at the Education Conference advocating for nationalized universal compulsory, and free primary education.

In conclusion, the British period in the Indian subcontinent significantly changed the education system. The introduction of modern education, the establishment of education departments, and the implementation of acts and commissions played crucial roles in shaping primary education. The strive for compulsory and free primary education continued during the Pakistan period.

Theoretical Framework

Primary education, as defined by the International Dictionary of Primary Education, refers to a phase of study where no differentiation is introduced, either through optional subjects or the streaming of pupils into different types of institutions or education. The World Book Encyclopedia emphasizes that primary education extends from the beginning of compulsory education, typically starting at the age of 6 to 11+. Children may transition to secondary education at the ages of 10, 12, or 14 or continue in the same school after completing their formal education. Progressive countries recognize primary education as a crucial stage in a child's educational journey, emphasizing its importance before transitioning to secondary education, which should be accessible to all children.

In Bangladesh, primary education spans five years, from first to fifth grade, catering to students aged 6 to 11+. The academic year runs from January to December, with most primary schools operating in two shifts: the first shift from 9:30 am to 12 pm and the second from 12:00 pm to 4:15 pm. The first and second grades are taught in the first shift, while classes from third to fifth are taught in the second. The same teachers provide education in both shifts. Notably, according to the National Education Policy 2010, primary education extends to the eighth grade. In recent years, additional grades have been introduced in some primary schools, with 764 schools offering up to the sixth grade in 2016 (Yunus & Shahana, 2018).

Primary education in Bangladesh is predominantly free, and the government has taken significant steps to ensure universal access. In 1973, primary education was nationalized, resulting in 36,015 schools becoming public. Subsequently, in 2013, the government nationalized 25,240 registered primary schools. The government has emphasized primary education through the Primary Education Development Program, allocating a substantial budget of 58 thousand crores for its implementation. The passage of the "Primary Education (Compulsory) Act" in 1990 made primary education compulsory for children aged 6 to 10 years, and committees at the ward, union, upazila, and district levels were formed to oversee its implementation. Ebtedayi madrasas and the cooperative madrasa education system provide religious education alongside the standard primary school curriculum, covering subjects such as Bengali, Mathematics, English, and Science and religious texts like the Quran and Hadith (Islam, 2019).

Structure, Aims, and Objectives of Primary Education

In 1974, Bangladesh passed an Act to provide free primary education to all children between the ages of 6 and 10. This aimed to ensure access to education for every child in the country. 1990 primary education was made compulsory through the 'Primary Education (Compulsory) Act.' Implementing this act involved forming ward, union, upazila, and district committees. Additionally, each ward has a 6-member 'Compulsory Primary Education Committee.' The primary education system includes primary (ebtedayi) madrasas and a cooperative madrasa education system, offering a 5-year course (Schuck, 2016).

The objectives of primary education, as outlined in the National Education Policy of 2010, include developing humane values, fostering a child-friendly environment, implementing a standardized curriculum across all types of primary schools, cultivating moral and spiritual qualities, promoting patriotism and nation-building, equipping students with necessary skills for higher education, and encouraging vocational education. The policy also emphasizes mother tongue education for minorities and exceptional attention to developing education in backward areas.

One of the goals is to provide equal opportunities for underprivileged children, including those with disabilities. The policy seeks to create an inclusive environment and support the development of marginalized students. It also aims to promote manual labor and pre-vocational education to instill an appreciation for vocational skills. Additionally, the policy focuses on increasing opportunities for tribal children and giving special attention to the education system in backward areas.

In conclusion, Bangladesh has taken significant steps to ensure free and compulsory primary education for all children. The objectives include holistic development, standardized curriculum, moral values, patriotism, skill-building, and equal opportunities. Implementing these objectives and addressing the challenges will contribute to the overall improvement of primary education in the country.

Evaluation of National Education Policy 2010

National Education Policy 2010 lays out a comprehensive plan for primary education in Bangladesh. The policy recognizes the critical importance of primary education nationally. It aims to ensure equal opportunities for all children, regardless of their socio-economic background, physical-mental limitations, or geographical location. It is the constitutional responsibility of the state to create these opportunities. The policy emphasizes the need to provide high-quality primary education as it forms the foundation for subsequent levels of education and dramatically benefits individuals in their future careers (Fernández-Batanero et al., 2022).

The challenges and issues in primary education include disparities in facilities across locations and schools, infrastructure problems, teacher shortages, and inadequate training. The policy aims to address these problems and strengthen the overall education system by making primary education public, compulsory, unpaid, and standardized for all. While achieving 100% enrollment is challenging due to economic, regional, and geographical constraints, efforts are underway to increase enrollment to 100% by 2010-11. Additionally, the policy emphasizes the establishment of primary schools in villages that lack such facilities (Islam, 2019).

The implementation of primary education is the total responsibility of the state, and the policy prohibits the transfer of this responsibility to the private or NGO sectors. To improve the quality and duration of primary education, the policy proposes extending the primary education period from five to eight years up to class VIII. This includes the formulation of new curricula, textbooks, and teacher guidelines, expanding infrastructure, providing teacher training, and restructuring education administration and management.

The policy also aims to introduce a non-discriminatory education system by implementing a uniform curriculum and syllabus for all types of primary schools, including public and private schools, kindergartens, and Madrasahs (including Ibtedayi). The curriculum will include prescribed subjects such as Bengali, English, Moral Education, Bangladesh Studies, Mathematics, Social Environment and Climate, and Information Technology, possibly incorporating additional subjects with the appropriate permissions.

Table 1. Number of teachers in Ebtedayee Madrasah 2020

Division	Ebtedayee Madrasah			
	Male	Female	Total	% of Female
Barishal	1338	656	1994	32.9
Chattogram	2217	665	2882	23.1
Dhaka	1122	528	1650	32
Khulna	1187	488	1675	29.1
Mymensingh	2184	1079	3263	33.1
Rajshahi	2262	773	3035	25.5
Rangpur	2744	1164	3908	29.8
Sylhet	457	127	584	21.7
Total	13511	5480	18991	28.9

Source: DPE (APSC, 2020)

To improve the quality of education and students' skills, permanent primary education will be introduced in all types of Madrasahs, including Ibtedayi, along with new integrated education programs. Efforts will be made to eliminate disparities in facilities between different types of primary schools, and mandatory registration will be required for all primary schools, including general, kindergarten, English medium, and Madrasahs.

The curriculum and syllabus will be prepared by an expert committee, ensuring specific subjects for all students at the primary level. Infrastructure development, provision of computer education, appointment of computer teachers, and emphasis on English language skills will be implemented. Co-curricular subjects may be introduced from the first class onwards to enhance the learning experience. These measures aim to enhance the quality and effectiveness of primary education in Bangladesh.

1. Section: Aboriginal Children

To cater to the educational needs of Aboriginal children, special provisions will be made, including the arrangement of Aboriginal teachers and textbooks that allow them to learn their language. Tribal communities will be actively involved in the preparation of these textbooks. Furthermore, marginalized Aboriginal children will receive specific assistance. In areas predominantly inhabited by tribal communities, primary schools will be established to ensure access to education. Considering the sparse population in some areas, residential arrangements will be made for students and teachers if necessary.

2. Section: Disabled Children

Schools will have disability-friendly facilities, such as accessible toilets and transportation, to accommodate students with various disabilities. Special attention will be given to addressing the specific needs of disabled children. Each Primary Teacher's Institute (PTI) will have at least one instructor trained in teaching methods for students with disabilities.

3. Section: Street Children and Underprivileged Children

Efforts will be made to provide free admission, educational materials, supplies, lunch arrangements, and scholarships to street children and other underprivileged children to encourage their enrollment and retention in primary schools. Adequate measures will be implemented to ensure their protection within the school environment. Disparities among different types and locations of primary schools will be gradually reduced, focusing on providing special assistance to schools in relatively backward and rural areas, aiming to achieve significant progress in reducing inequality.

4. Section: Teaching Method

An active learning approach will be adopted, providing opportunities for individual and group tasks to develop student's creative thinking and skills. Research on effective teaching methods will be encouraged, and support will be provided for their development, testing, and implementation.

Figure 1. Disabled child in primary education level
Source: DPE (APSC, 2020)

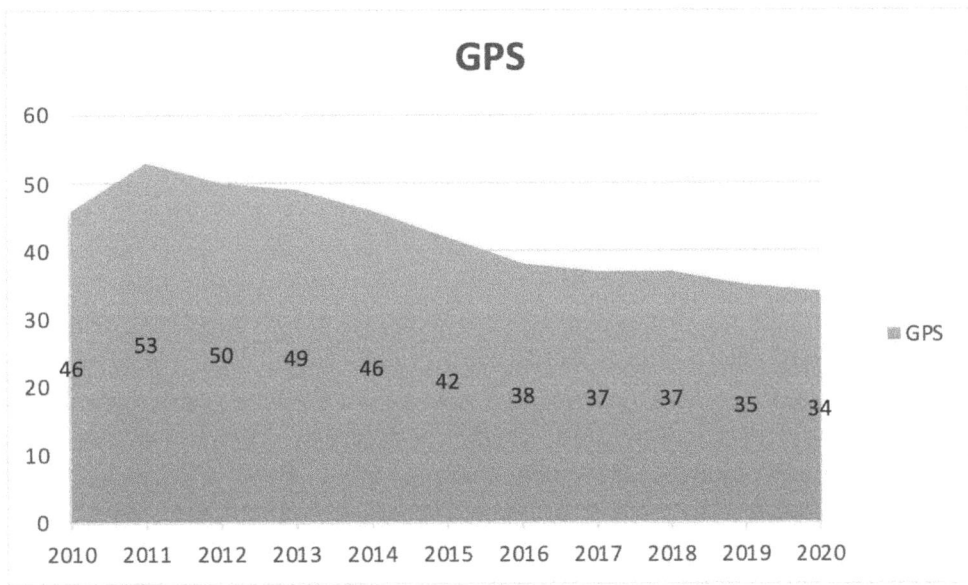

Figure 2. Student-teacher ratio (STR) by year and type of schools 2010-2020
Source: DPE (APSC, 2020)

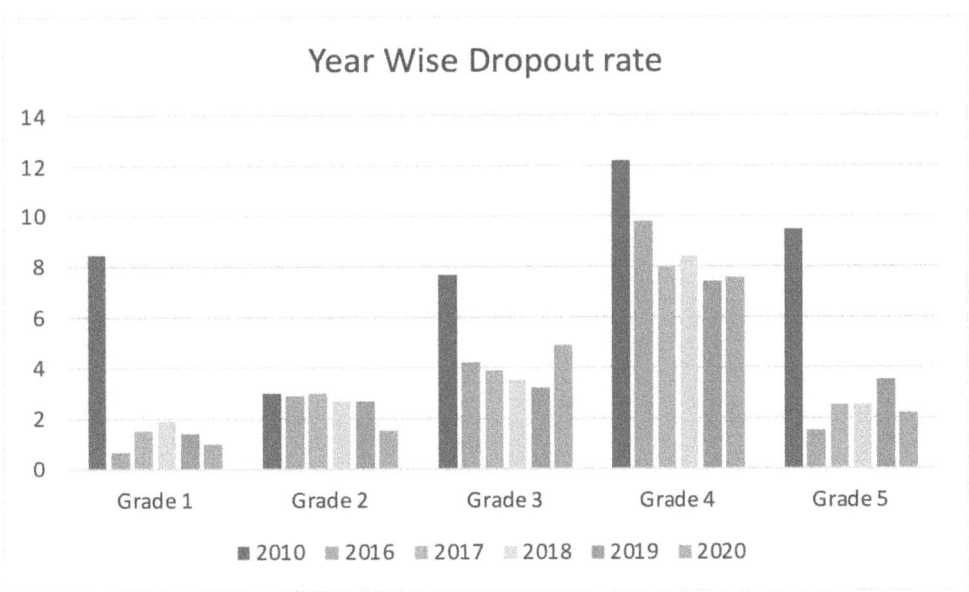

5. Section: Student Assessment

Continuous assessment will be conducted in grades 1 and 2, followed by quarterly, half-yearly, and annual examinations from grades 3 to 8. At the end of the 5th grade, a common question paper-based final examination will be held at the Upazila/Municipality/Thana (larger cities) level. At the end of the 8th grade, the relevant Education Board will conduct a public examination called the Junior School Certificate Examination.

6. Recruitment and Promotion of Teachers

The minimum qualification for recruiting teachers for classes I to V will be an HSC with a second division or a Bachelor's degree with a second division or its equivalent. Female candidates will be given preference for lower classes. Teachers must undergo training within three years of joining and obtain a C-in-Ed/B.D. degree. Similarly, for the recruitment of Headmasters, a minimum second-division graduation or equivalent degree is required, followed by obtaining a C-in-Ed/BEd (Primary) degree within a year. Suitable arrangements will be made to promote teachers through different levels and pay scales, and opportunities for professional growth will be provided. Salaries and allowances will be set accordingly, considering teachers' importance and dignity in shaping the nation's economic reality and future. Additionally, accountability measures will be implemented to ensure the quality of teaching.

These provisions and strategies for Aboriginal children, disabled children, street children, underprivileged children, teaching methods, student assessment, recruitment, and promotion of teachers are all outlined in the National Education Policy to ensure quality primary education in Bangladesh.

Table 2. C-inEd trained teachers by gender and division in GPS and NNPS 2020

Division	GPS				NNPS			
	Male	Female	Total	% of Female	Male	Female	Total	% of Female
Barishal	4607	8759	13366	65.5	3860	4936	8796	56.1
Chattogram	11039	21981	33020	66.6	4498	6063	10561	57.4
Dhaka	8751	22108	30859	71.6	3590	5705	9295	61.4
Khulna	6716	13175	19891	66.2	6144	6253	12397	50.4
Mymensingh	3317	7052	10369	68.0	3020	3383	6403	52.8
Rajshahi	7671	14556	22227	65.5	5872	5154	11026	46.7
Rangpur	6340	11994	18334	65.4	7917	7436	15353	48.4
Sylhet	3325	8097	11422	70.9	1750	2556	4306	59.4
Total	**51766**	**107722**	**159488**	**67.5**	**36651**	**41486**	**78137**	**53.1**

Source: DPE (APSC, 2020)

ISSUES AND CHALLENGES IN PRIMARY EDUCATION

Primary education in Bangladesh faces various issues and challenges. These following challenges call for urgent attention and require comprehensive solutions to ensure quality primary education for all children in Bangladesh.

1. Upgradation of Primary Education Up to Class VIII

One of the significant goals outlined in the National Education Policy is the extension of primary education from five years to eight years. However, implementing this expansion faces challenges related to infrastructure and the availability of competent teachers. Despite the announcement in the policy, the government has been unable to initiate primary education from 6th to 8th grade as planned in the 2011-12 financial year. In the existing circumstances, the responsibility for education in these grades remains with the Ministry of Primary and Mass Education, and the need for schools and teachers remains unchanged. To ensure the provision of necessary facilities for primary education, the burden of regulation lies with the Ministry of Primary and Mass Education. At the same time, measures can be taken to address teacher shortages and infrastructural issues in secondary schools.

2. Quality Matters of Education

The quality of primary education still needs to be at the desired level, and there are several reasons for this. According to the 7th Five Year Plan (2015/16 - 2019/20) and studies conducted in 2016, the following factors contribute to the quality challenges:

A. Capacity of Teachers: Although there has been an increase in the proportion of trained teachers, a significant number of teachers still need to be trained. Additionally, teachers' training often needs to be improved to enhance their performance. The minimum educational qualification for female teachers, ranging from SSC to Higher Secondary, must be revised.

B. Absenteeism and Idleness of Teachers: Studies indicate that around 13-17% of teachers are absent, and 30% are idle. Teacher absenteeism and tardiness create barriers to learning and disrupt students' progress.

C. Inadequacy of Curriculum: Teaching quality, curriculum, and textbooks help achieve set goals. Modernization and unification of the curriculum across different educational institutions have been suggested, but these efforts have primarily focused on the basics. Combining the three streams of education (Bangla et al.) to yield better results has been challenging and often perpetuates existing disparities.

Figure 3. Student absenteeism (percentage)
Source: DPE (APSC, 2020)

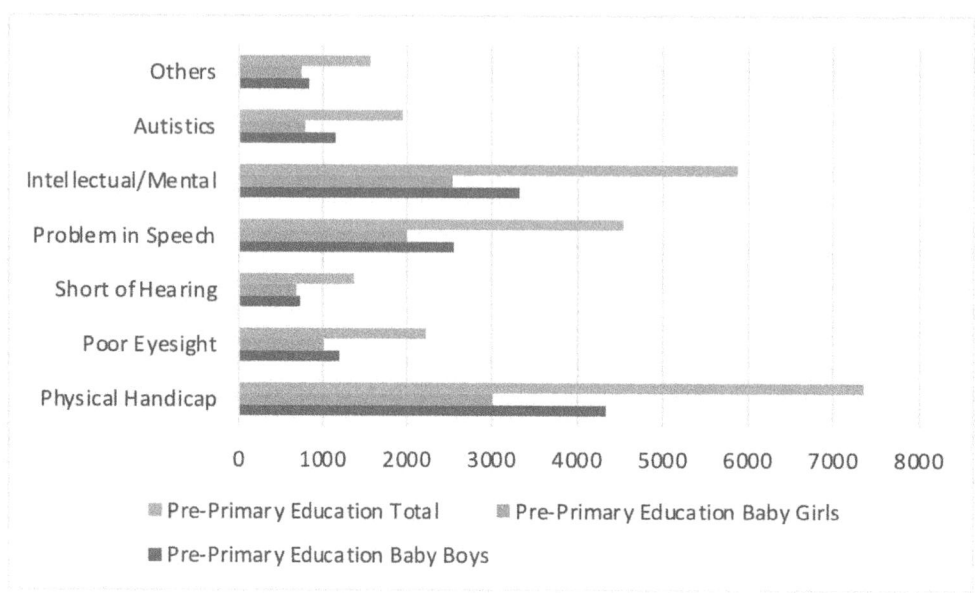

Table 3. The scenario of passing the examination

Year	No of Inst.	Descriptive Roll			Appeared in the Exam			Passed the Exam		
		Boy	**Girl**	**Total**	**Boy**	**Girl**	**Total**	**Boy**	**Girl**	**Total**
		46.02 %	53.98 %		45.6 7%	54.33 %	95.54 %	45.62 %	54.3 %	97.59 %
2019	98811	1178146	1376918	2555064	1124225	1329926	2454151	1072154	1271589	2343743
		46.11%	53.89%		95.42%	96.59%	96.05%	95.4%	95.6%	95.5%

Source: DPE (APSC, 2020)

D. Lack of Physical Infrastructural Facilities: The poor physical infrastructure of schools, especially in remote regions, hampers the overall educational experience. These schools often need to meet minimum acceptable standards, thereby limiting the attainment of desired equality. Girls, in particular, face limitations due to inadequate facilities, which discourages their attendance. Surveys have revealed a need for more separate facilities for girls, access to soap and water in toilets, and proper sanitary waste disposal in schools. Moreover, the Ministry of Primary and Mass Education has identified a shortage of primary schools in 1,500 villages where the population exceeds 2,000 and no school is within a 2 km radius. These areas, such as coastal and hilly regions, typically have limited educational opportunities and are isolated.

3. Foreign Language Learning at the Elementary Level

The question of foreign language learning at the primary level has sparked various opinions. Some argue that it is unnecessary to introduce foreign languages at this stage and emphasize focusing on the mother tongue. Others advocate for the early introduction of English, while some suggest teaching English from class III onwards. Additionally, there are proponents of teaching languages aligned with specific religions, such as Arabic, Sanskrit, or Pali.

4. Introduction of Trade Education at the Primary Level

Currently, trade education is not available at the primary education level. However, there have been discussions and support for introducing at least one trade course at the primary level within education commissions.

Figure 4. Repetition rate (EFA 12)
Source: DPE (APSC, 2020)

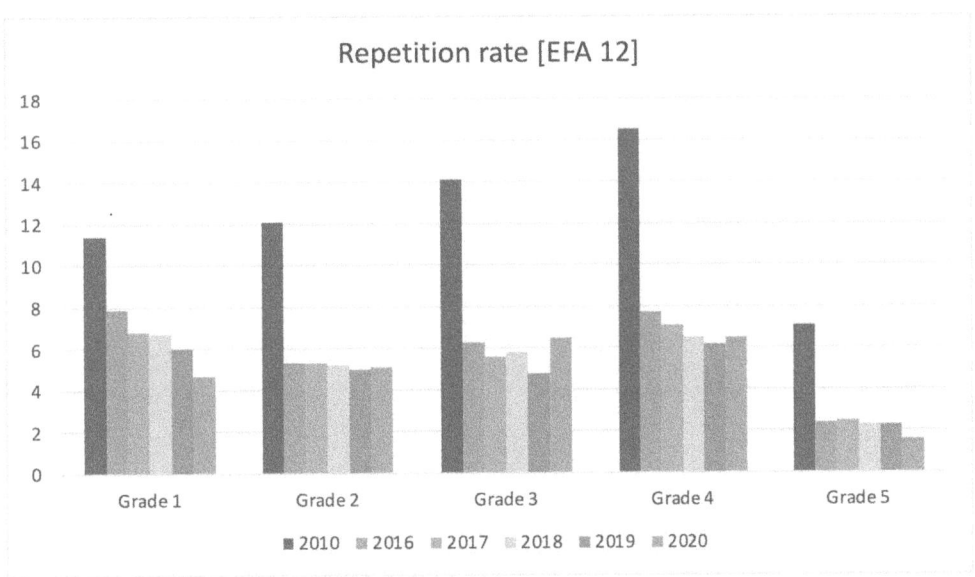

5. Introduction of Uniform Education and Elimination of Discrimination

In Bangladesh, primary education encompasses various streams, including public and private primary schools, Kindergarten (Bangla and English medium), and Ibtedayi. Establishing a uniform education system at the primary level is crucial. Dr. Mohammad Shahidullah's quote sheds light on the issue, criticizing the fragmentation caused by multiple education systems and its impact on Muslim society. The constitution of Bangladesh emphasizes the commitment to a non-discriminatory education system, and the National Education Policy of 2010 aims to introduce a uniform curriculum and syllabus for all primary-level educational institutions, including government and private schools, kindergartens, and various types of madrasas, including Ibtedayi. Efforts are underway to address the disparities in facilities between different types of primary schools and ensure equality.

6. Creating Educational Opportunities and Preventing Dropouts

Despite guaranteeing compulsory primary education for all children, poverty, parental ignorance, religious factors, and geographical challenges prevent many children from accessing education. Child marriage, child labor, and social factors also contribute to high dropout rates. Urban slums, in particular, face limited access to education, with children from poor slum families experiencing low enrollment rates. While there has been some progress in reducing dropout rates, it remains a significant issue. In hilly areas, the geographical terrain poses challenges, and children have to cross small and large mountain streams daily, especially during the monsoon season, which is laborious and risky. Extreme poverty further hinders access to education, with a substantial percentage of families living below the poverty line. Inconsistencies in curricula and the lack of holiday arrangements during the summer season also disrupt school attendance for many children. Addressing these issues and ensuring access to primary education is crucial for the country's overall development.

Figure 5. Year wise dropout rate
Source: DPE (APSC, 2020)

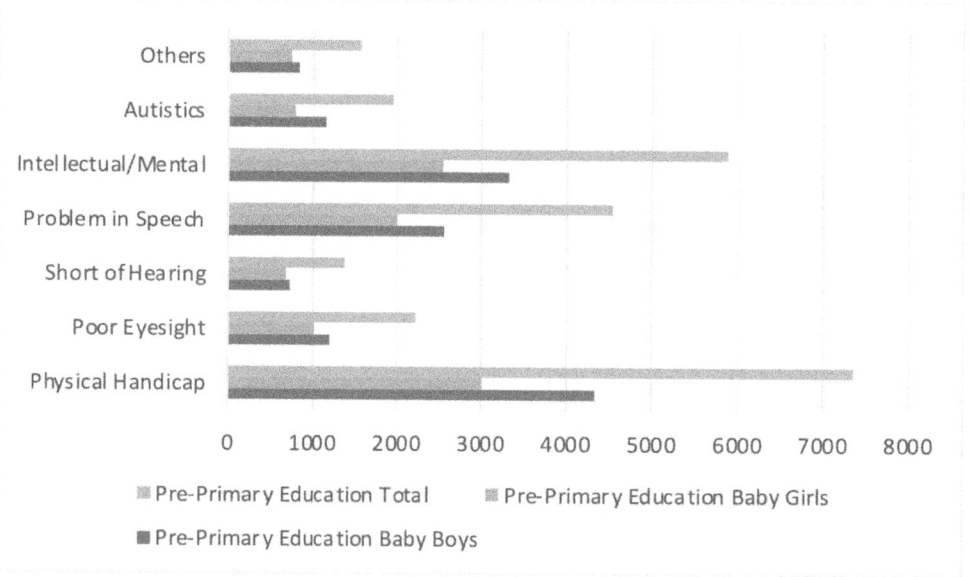

7. Gender Discrimination

Gender discrimination remains a significant obstacle to women's education, particularly at the primary level. This disparity is prevalent in underdeveloped villages and urban slums. Many prioritize boys' education while neglecting girls, assuming that boys will support them in the future, whereas girls will leave after marriage. Consequently, limited resources are allocated to boys, while girls are expected to focus on household chores. This mindset deprives many girls of educational opportunities, leading to high dropout rates. It is crucial to raise public awareness and take steps to eradicate gender discrimination, fostering a skilled workforce.

8. Management, Capacity, and Financing

Another set of challenges in the education system pertains to management, capacity, and funding. There needs to be coordination among the various sectors and sub-sectors of primary education. Enhancing coordination in the allocation of educational resources is necessary. The current educational budget is significantly lower than other South Asian countries. To achieve the objectives outlined in the Seventh Five Year Plan, efforts must be made to reach the 20% budget allocation target set by UNESCO, equivalent to about 6% of the GDP.

9. School Timings in Areas Affected by Natural Calamities

Natural calamities disrupt students' studies in different regions of Bangladesh. In disaster-prone areas, there should be flexibility in school timetables to accommodate such situations. The National Education Policy 2010 acknowledges this need, stating that schools in Haor, Char, and other disaster-affected areas can modify schedules and holidays based on local recommendations and monitoring systems.

10. Increasing Access to Primary Education for Tribal Children

At the primary education level, provisions should be made to accommodate the use of mother tongues for indigenous children, providing indigenous teachers and textbooks for their learning needs. The involvement of indigenous communities is crucial in developing textbooks. Additionally, special assistance should be provided to marginalized tribal children. Primary schools should be established in all areas inhabited by tribal communities, whether in hilly or plain regions.

11. Children With Learning Disabilities

Currently, our schools lack an education system tailored to the needs of disabled students. However, it is imperative to create educational opportunities for individuals with disabilities, aligning with the demands of the present era. The National Education Policy 2010 emphasizes the need for disability-friendly school facilities, including accessible toilets and mobility aids. Particular attention should be given to the needs of disabled individuals, and training on teaching methods for differently-abled students should be provided in teacher training institutes.

12. Creating Educational Opportunities for Street Children and Underprivileged Children

The presence of street children and underprivileged children in our society necessitates the creation of educational opportunities as a constitutional responsibility. The National Education Policy of 2010 calls for free admission to primary schools, provision of free educational materials, mid-day meals, and special arrangements such as scholarships to ensure their access to education. Schools are urged to implement effective measures to protect and support these children.

Table 4. Enrolment of special needs children in private primary schools 2020

Type of Disabilities	Grade 1		Grade 2		Grade 3		Grade 4		Grade 5		Total		
	Boys	Girls	Boys	Girls	Boys	Girls	Boys	Girls	Boys	Girls	Boys	Girls	All
Physical Handicap	109	81	81	67	47	47	71	44	47	38	355	277	632
Poor Eyesight	19	11	17	10	13	14	8	5	5	4	62	44	106
Short of Hearing	10	7	13	9	8	4	4	-	5	1	40	21	61
Problem in Speech	17	8	17	13	25	16	7	10	2	2	68	49	117
Intellectual/ Mental	39	37	36	33	33	30	26	27	15	10	149	137	286
Autistics	21	18	16	12	7	4	10	5	4	3	58	42	100
Others	21	21	12	12	2	4	7	2	4	3	46	42	88
Total	236	183	192	156	135	119	133	93	82	61	778	612	1390

Source: DPE (APSC, 2020)

Technology to Enhance Quality Education in Primary Schools

Leveraging technology to enhance the quality of education in primary schools presents significant opportunities for Bangladesh. However, to fully realize these opportunities, increasing the budget allocated to this sector is crucial. Investing in technology-enabled education can have a transformative impact on primary school students' learning outcomes, providing them access to a more engaging, interactive, and personalized learning experience.

Integrating technology in primary education can bridge the digital divide and provide equal learning opportunities for all children. It enables access to digital content, online resources, and educational platforms that can supplement traditional teaching methods. Technology can facilitate interactive learning experiences and promote critical thinking, creativity, and problem-solving skills among students. Moreover, it can help teachers enhance their instructional practices, access professional development resources, and track students' progress effectively.

While the potential benefits of leveraging technology in primary education are immense, several challenges must be addressed. One key challenge is the need for more infrastructure, including reliable internet connectivity, computers, and digital devices in many primary schools, especially in rural areas. Another significant hurdle is insufficient training and capacity-building opportunities for teachers to integrate technology into their teaching practices effectively. Additionally, ensuring the availability of quality digital content, localized educational resources, and appropriate software applications aligned with the national curriculum could be improved.

Increasing the budget allocated to leveraging technology in primary education is essential to address the challenges mentioned above and seize the opportunities presented by digital learning. Adequate funding can be allocated to upgrading school infrastructure, providing internet connectivity, and procuring necessary hardware and software. Moreover, investing in comprehensive teacher training programs, professional development initiatives, and capacity-building workshops can empower educators to use technology in the classroom effectively. Additionally, budgetary provisions can be made to develop localized digital content and educational resources aligned with the national curriculum.

1. Total Allocation for the Education Sector

In the financial year 2016-17, a significant allocation was made to the education sector, emphasizing the development of skilled human resources. The proposed budget allocated a total of Tk 53,134 crore for the education sector, encompassing the Ministry of Primary and Mass Education and the Ministry of Education. This allocation represents a substantial increase compared to the previous year. In the financial year 2015-16, the allocation for the education sector was Tk 31,605 crore, accounting for 10.71 percent of the total budget. However, in 2016-17, the allocation increased to Tk 53,134 crore, constituting 15.6 percent of the total budget. This represents a growth of approximately 68.12 percent compared to the revised allocation for the previous fiscal year.

2. Review of ADP Allocation

The proposed allocation for the Annual Development Program (ADP) in the education sector for FY 2016-17 is Tk 13,877 crore, 46.02 percent higher than the revised allocation in 2014-15. The ADP allocation for the education sector has gradually increased in numerical and percentage terms, indicating a positive trend compared to previous financial years. In the last fiscal year, 110 development projects in the education sector combined investment, technical, and self-financing. Of these, five projects were newly initiated. However, in the financial year 2016-17, there were 96 projects in this sector, with 90 being investment projects, five technical projects, and one self-financed project. This year, three projects are newly initiated, including establishing Shahid Kamruzzaman Textile Institute, Chittagong Veterinary and Animal Sciences University 2nd Campus, and the augmentation of physical and academic facilities at Noakhali University of Science and Technology.

Increasing the budget for leveraging technology in primary education is crucial for Bangladesh to unlock the full potential of digital learning. By allocating sufficient funds, the government can address infrastructure gaps, provide necessary training to teachers, develop localized educational resources, and ensure equitable access to technology-enabled learning for all primary school students. This investment will enhance the quality of education and equip the younger generation with the digital skills and knowledge necessary for their future success in an increasingly technology-driven world.

RESULTS

Five hundred forty-six primary school teachers and office staff received ICT training from various organizations. The Ministry of Education, along with the Ministry of ICT, serves as the primary provider of ICT training in the country. The training programs mainly focus on equipping teachers with basic ICT skills, teaching strategies using ICT in the classroom, and creating PowerPoint presentations. The majority of the training programs emphasize internet browsing and email usage.

In terms of ICT infrastructure, all primary schools located in metropolitan areas have computers and laptops available for use. However, the availability of computers is lower in urban and rural primary schools, with less than half of the urban schools and around one-fourth of the rural schools having computers. Approximately 16.7% of metropolitan schools have fewer than five computers, compared to 5.7% in urban schools and 11.4% in rural schools. Around 20% of metropolitan schools have 5-10 computers, while the exact number is available in 34.3% of urban schools and 25.7% of rural schools.

Regarding laptops, their availability could be higher across all areas. Approximately one-third of rural primary schools have only one laptop, while nearly half (42.9%) of urban primary schools have two laptops. Most primary schools in metropolitan areas have three laptops. Regarding computer availability, all secondary schools in metropolitan and urban areas have computers in the Head Teacher's room, while 42.9% of rural primary schools have computers in the Head Teacher's room.

In terms of classroom infrastructure, all secondary classrooms in metropolitan areas have electric connections, computers, laptops, internet lines, overhead projectors, and multimedia projectors. Most rural and urban secondary classrooms have electric lines. Most (76.7%) of metropolitan secondary classrooms have whiteboards, and 62.8% have electric boards. However, the use of computers for classroom teaching is limited, with Head Teachers primarily using computers for official purposes. Computer and general assistant teachers also use computers for administrative tasks, while Science and Mathematics teachers use them less frequently. Overall, ICT training has helped secondary teachers develop their skills and improve the quality of teaching in classrooms.

The training programs also focus on developing ICT and video materials for secondary schools, with trainers emphasizing the positive impact of ICT training on teachers' skills. Regardless of location, almost all ICT teachers in secondary schools utilize ICT during their classes. The common challenges schools face in all areas include more ICT teacher training, a shortage of skilled teachers, and limited opportunities for students to use ICT in the classroom. ICT trainers highlight the scarcity of training opportunities, skilled teachers, inadequate ICT materials, and infrastructural limitations as the major challenges faced by secondary schools in effectively utilizing ICT.

Recommendations

In this chapter, we have explored the concept of value education and its implementation across different cultures. Our study has presented a comparative analysis of various approaches to value education and highlighted the challenges educators face in culturally diverse classrooms. We have also investigated the state of primary education in Bangladesh, identified the reasons for the lack of quality education, and proposed strategies to achieve quality education. Furthermore, the study has emphasized the importance of the effective role of the government in ensuring quality teaching and learning in primary schools in Bangladesh. Our research has assessed the opportunities for effective execution of quality education in primary schools in Bangladesh and identified solutions to the problems in ensuring quality education. This study will play a significant role in formulating and implementing primary education policy of the Bangladesh government and will stimulate strategic discussions among policymakers and practitioners to overcome the prevailing challenges of the schools and improve children's outcomes.

There are solid recommendations for leveraging technology to enhance quality education in primary schools. Based on the analysis and understanding of the Upazila Resource Centers (URCs) and sub-cluster training, the following recommendations are proposed:

1. Increase Budget Allocation: To ensure the effective functioning of Upazila Resource Centers (URCs) and support their responsibilities, it is crucial to increase the budget allocated to them. Adequate funding will enable the expansion of URC infrastructure, enhance the quality and accessibility of training programs, update resources, and strengthen their capacity to provide valuable services to primary school teachers.
2. Technology Integration: Recognizing the potential of technology in enhancing the quality of education, it is recommended to further leverage technology in URCs and sub-cluster training programs. By integrating digital tools, e-learning platforms, and online resources, teachers can access online training modules, participate in webinars and virtual workshops, and utilize educational apps and software to support their professional development and classroom instruction.
3. Collaboration with Stakeholders: Foster collaboration among key stakeholders such as the Directorate of Primary Education, District Primary Education Officer (DPEO), headmasters, Assistant Upazila Education Officer (AUEO), School Management Committees (SMCs), and Parent-Teacher Associations (PTAs). Collaboration and coordination will ensure effective planning, implementation, and monitoring of training programs and allocating resources and support for URCs and sub-cluster training.
4. Continuous Evaluation and Improvement: Establish a system for continuous evaluation and improvement of URCs and sub-cluster training programs. Regular assessment of training needs, impact evaluation, and feedback from teachers and participants will enable the identification of strengths and areas for improvement. This feedback should inform the design and delivery of future training programs to ensure they meet the evolving needs of primary school teachers.

5. Scaling and Replication: Based on the success and positive outcomes observed in the existing URCs and sub-cluster training programs, consider scaling up and replicating these models in other regions and upazilas across the country. This expansion will require careful planning, allocation of resources, and collaboration with local authorities to ensure effective implementation and sustainability.

6. Research and Innovation: Encourage research and innovation in the field of primary education to identify new approaches, strategies, and best practices. Foster partnerships with educational institutions, research organizations, and experts to explore innovative solutions for enhancing the quality of education and professional development of primary school teachers.

By implementing these recommendations, the establishment of Upazila Resource Centers (URCs) and the expansion of sub-cluster training programs can contribute significantly to the professional development of teachers, improvement of primary education quality, and preparation of students for the challenges of the digital age.

Additional Recommendations on Leveraging Technology to Enhance Quality Education in Primary Schools: Opportunities and Challenges in Bangladesh:

1. Infrastructure Development: Invest in developing robust technological infrastructure in primary schools, including access to reliable internet connectivity, sufficient computer labs, and appropriate hardware and software resources. This will create an enabling environment for the effective integration of technology into classroom instruction.

2. Teacher Training and Capacity Building: Provide comprehensive training programs to enhance their digital literacy skills, pedagogical knowledge, and ability to integrate technology into their teaching practices. Continuous professional development opportunities should be offered to ensure teachers stay updated with the latest advancements in educational technology.

3. Content Localization: Develop and promote locally relevant digital educational content that aligns with the national curriculum. This content should be available in local languages to cater to the diverse linguistic backgrounds of students in Bangladesh. Collaborate with educational content developers, publishers, and local stakeholders to create high-quality, context-specific digital resources.

4. Accessible and Inclusive Technology: Ensure that the technology used in primary schools is accessible and inclusive for all students, including those with disabilities or special learning needs. Provide assistive technologies, software, and tools that support inclusive education practices and enable equal access to educational resources for all students.

5. Public-Private Partnerships: Foster partnerships between the government, private sector, and civil society organizations to leverage their expertise, resources, and innovation in advancing educational technology initiatives. Encourage collaboration in the development of digital content, provision of technology infrastructure, and implementation of teacher training programs.

6. Monitoring and Evaluation: Establish a robust monitoring and evaluation framework to assess the effectiveness and impact of technology integration in primary schools. Regularly evaluate the implementation of technology initiatives, collect feedback from teachers, students, and other stakeholders, and use the findings to make informed decisions and improvements.

7. Digital Citizenship and Online Safety: Integrate digital citizenship and online safety education into the curriculum to empower students with the knowledge and skills necessary to navigate the digital world responsibly. Teach them about online privacy, digital etiquette, critical thinking, and cyberbullying prevention to ensure their safe and responsible use of technology.

8. Research and Innovation Funding: Allocate funding for research and innovation in educational technology to support the development of evidence-based practices and explore emerging technologies that have the potential to enhance learning outcomes. Encourage collaboration between researchers, educators, and technology experts to drive innovation in the field.
9. Community Engagement and Awareness: Engage parents, community members, and local leaders in leveraging technology for quality education. Conduct awareness campaigns, workshops, and community events to promote the benefits of technology integration and encourage active involvement and support from the community.
10. Sustainable Funding Models: Develop sustainable funding models to support the long-term implementation and maintenance of educational technology initiatives. Explore public-private partnerships, corporate social responsibility programs, and innovative financing mechanisms to ensure the continuous availability and upgradation of technology infrastructure and resources.

Implementing these recommendations will help Bangladesh harness the full potential of technology to enhance the quality of education in primary schools, address existing challenges, and create a conducive environment for the holistic development of students in the digital era.

CONCLUSION

The study challenges the conventional thinking that the teacher-student ratio and proper enabling conditions are the main detrimental factors in classroom educational quality. Instead, the study finds that the current classroom teaching-learning education approaches need to be improved in making the subject matter understood by students. Leveraging technology is identified as a potential solution to enhance quality education in primary schools in Bangladesh. Furthermore, the study proposes strategies to overcome challenges in implementing value education programs in culturally diverse classrooms. The study concludes by emphasizing the need for policymakers and practitioners to address the prevailing challenges and improve the outcomes of primary education in Bangladesh. By implementing the findings and recommendations of this study, Bangladesh can ensure that it meets its goal of 2041 and the Sustainable Development Goals of providing quality education for all.

REFERENCES

Abusaleh, K., & Haque, N. (2022). *The Impact of the COVID-19 Outbreak on Primary Education in Bangladesh.* doi:10.4018/978-1-7998-8402-6.ch016

Ahmmed, M., & Mullick, J. (2014). Implementing inclusive education in primary schools in Bangladesh: Recommended strategies. *Educational Research for Policy and Practice, 13*(2), 167–180. Advance online publication. doi:10.100710671-013-9156-2

Alam, M. J., & Islam, S. R. (2021a). Discrete Primary Education Curriculum in Bangladesh. doi:10.4018/978-1-7998-7271-9.ch036

Alam, M. J., Islam, S. R. B., & Ogawa, K. (2021b). Discrete Primary Education Curriculum in Bangladesh: Implications of Gamification for Quality Education. In Handbook of Research on Acquiring 21st Century Literacy Skills Through Game-Based Learning (Vol. 1). doi:10.4018/978-1-7998-7271-9.ch036

Ambia, S. J. M. U., & Rahman, M. (2021). Challenges in Primary Level Inclusive Education in Bangladesh. *International Journal for Innovation Education and Research*, *9*(11), 14–20. Advance online publication. doi:10.31686/ijier.vol9.iss11.3453

Buchanan, J., Pressick-Kilborn, K., & Maher, D. (2019). Promoting environmental education for primary school-aged students using digital technologies. *Eurasia Journal of Mathematics, Science and Technology Education*, *15*(2). Advance online publication. doi:10.29333/ejmste/100639

Domingo, M. G., & Garganté, A. B. (2016). Exploring the use of educational technology in primary education: Teachers' perception of mobile technology learning impacts and applications' use in the classroom. *Computers in Human Behavior*, *56*, 21–28. Advance online publication. doi:10.1016/j.chb.2015.11.023

Elmira, U., Abay, D., Shaimahanovna, D. A., Erzhenbaikyzy, M. A., Aigul, A., & Rabikha, K. (2022). The importance of game technology in primary education. *World Journal on Educational Technology: Current Issues*, *14*(4), 996–1004. Advance online publication. doi:10.18844/wjet.v14i4.7652

Fernández-Batanero, J. M., Montenegro-Rueda, M., & Fernández-Cerero, J. (2022). Are primary education teachers trained for the use of the technology with disabled students? *Research and Practice in Technology Enhanced Learning*, *17*(1), 19. Advance online publication. doi:10.118641039-022-00195-x

Haque, F. (2013). Education for Sustainable Development: An Evaluation of the New Curriculum of the Formal Primary Education in Bangladesh. *European Scientific Journal*, *1*, 1857–7881.

Islam, M. (2019). Quality of Primary Education Management System of Bangladesh: A Case Study on Jhenaidaj Upazila Education Office. *International Journal for Research in Applied Science and Engineering Technology*, *7*(2), 78–96. Advance online publication. doi:10.22214/ijraset.2019.2014

Islam, T., Rashel, A., Lim, Y. T., & Sang-Gyun, N. (2019). The role of management and monitoring in achieving quality primary education at char area in Bangladesh. *International Journal of Learning. Teaching and Educational Research*, *18*(7), 245–260. Advance online publication. doi:10.26803/ijlter.18.7.16

Moltudal, S. H., Krumsvik, R. J., & Høydal, K. L. (2022). Adaptive Learning Technology in Primary Education: Implications for Professional Teacher Knowledge and Classroom Management. *Frontiers in Education*, *7*, 830536. Advance online publication. doi:10.3389/feduc.2022.830536

Monia, S. H. (2020). Towards a normative legal mechanism of a unitary primary education in bangladesh. *Education. Sustainability Science*, *3*(2), 65–68. Advance online publication. doi:10.26480/ess.02.2020.65.68

Obaydullah, H. M. A. and Dr. A. K. M. (2019). Inclusive Practice and Barriers in the Primary Education of Bangladesh. *International Journal of Advance Research and Innovative Ideas in Education, 5*(4).

Pinto-Llorente, A. M., & Sánchez-Gómez, M. C. (2020). Perceptions and attitudes of future primary education teachers on technology and inclusive education: A mixed methods research. *Journal of Information Technology Research*, *13*(3), 37–57. Advance online publication. doi:10.4018/JITR.2020070103

Rohaan, E. J., Taconis, R., & Jochems, W. M. G. (2009). Measuring teachers' pedagogical content knowledge in primary technology education. *Research in Science & Technological Education*, *27*(3), 327–338. Advance online publication. doi:10.1080/02635140903162652

Rohaan, E. J., Taconis, R., & Jochems, W. M. G. (2010). Reviewing the relations between teachers' knowledge and pupils' attitude in the field of primary technology education. In International Journal of Technology and Design Education (Vol. 20, Issue 1). doi:10.100710798-008-9055-7

Roy, G. (2017). Competency-Based Assessment in Primary Education in Bangladesh - A Review. SSRN *Electronic Journal*. doi:10.2139/ssrn.2899109

Schuck, S. (2016). Enhancing teacher education in primary mathematics with mobile technologies. *The Australian Journal of Teacher Education*, *41*(3), 126–139. Advance online publication. doi:10.14221/ajte.2016v41n3.8

Shohel, M. M. C., & Howes, A. J. (2011). Models of Education for Sustainable Development and Non-formal Primary Education in Bangladesh. *Journal of Education for Sustainable Development*, *5*(1), 129–139. Advance online publication. doi:10.1177/097340821000500115

Sommers, C. (2013). *Primary education in rural Bangladesh: Degrees of access, choice and participation of the poorest.* ESP Working Paper Special Series on the Privatisation in Education Research Initiative, No. 52.

Volpe, G., & Gori, M. (2019). Multisensory interactive technologies for primary education: From science to technology. *Frontiers in Psychology*, *10*, 1076. Advance online publication. doi:10.3389/fpsyg.2019.01076 PMID:31316410

Yasmin, S., & Rumi, M. A. (2020). Impact of pre-primary education on children in Bangladesh: A study on government primary schools in Sylhet City. *American Journal of Educational Research*, *8*(5).

Yunus, M., & Shahana, S. (2018). New Evidence on Outcomes of Primary Education Stipend Programme in Bangladesh. *Bangladesh Development Studies*, *41*(4).

KEY TERMS AND DEFINITIONS

APSC: Annual primary school census.

BANBEIS: Bangladesh Bureau of Educational Information and Statistics. The national agency for collecting, processing, and disseminating educational information and statistics.

BBS: Bangladesh Bureau of Statistics. The national statistical organization is responsible for collecting, compiling, and disseminating statistical data of all the sectors of the economy.

DPE: Directorate of Primary Education.

HSC: Higher Secondary School Certificate.

JSC: Junior School Certificate examination.

MICS: Multiple Indicator Cluster Survey. A household survey program was developed by UNICEF to provide data on the situation of children and women in countries.

NCTB: National Curriculum and Textbook Board.

SSC: Secondary School Certificate.

Chapter 4
At the Basic Education Level:
Values Education Research and Their Results – Turkey Example

Fatmanur Özen

Giresun University, Turkey

ABSTRACT

Values education aims to cultivate learners' values, discipline them according to established rules, and positively transform their characters by contributing to their moral development. This education, encompassing both cognitive and affective dimensions of teaching, represents one of the most significant goals of education systems. The objective of this section is to analyze research trends related to values education in Türkiye and the outcomes of these studies at the basic education level, alongside a systematic examination of doctoral dissertations. To achieve this, doctoral dissertations registered and available in the Thesis Center of the Turkish Council of Higher Education were reviewed using keywords such as value/values education, character education, moral education, and citizenship education. This study examines 102 doctoral dissertations, categorizing them based on the subject of values education, exploring how values education is defined within the dissertations, examining the research methods, and evaluating the findings at the basic education level.

INTRODUCTION

Education aims to develop individuals in all aspects, including clarifying their collective duties, roles, and responsibilities within society. Individual behaviors can be seen as a product of the social environment and may be influenced by the culture of the community and the pressure to conform to societal norms (Myers, 2011). The desired behaviors endorsed by educational systems can be considered the outcome of national values, principles, and virtues to shape individuals' character. Akbaş (2008) emphasizes that teaching values, disciplining learners according to established rules, and contributing to their moral development and character formation are critical goals of education.

DOI: 10.4018/978-1-6684-9295-6.ch004

This educational objective, which targets the attitudes of individuals/learners, encompasses both the cognitive and affective dimensions of teaching (Clement, 2009: 19). Values education, including character education, moral education, and citizenship education, is a multifaceted concept with applications in areas such as multicultural education, gender education, religious education, ethics education, legal education, critical thinking, empathy development, cooperation skills, decision-making skills, moral reasoning, life skills, sexuality education, drug education (Kirschenbaum, 1994), and more.

In this section, the focus is on evaluating values education as it is addressed in Türkiye. The analysis revolves around the content of values education in doctoral dissertations produced within the country. In Türkiye, values education is integrated not only with values education itself but also with citizenship, character, and moral education.

In this section, the focus is on evaluating values education as it is addressed in Türkiye. The analysis revolves around the content of values education in doctoral dissertations produced within the country. In Türkiye, values education is integrated not only with values education itself but also with citizenship, character, and moral education. In this section, the focus is on evaluating values education as it is addressed in Türkiye. The analysis revolves around the content of values education found in doctoral dissertations produced within the country. In Türkiye, values education is integrated not only with values education itself but also with citizenship, character, and moral education.

BACKGROUND: VALUES AND VALUE EDUCATION

The concept of value can be defined in various ways depending on the context. In general, value refers to the worth, significance, or importance assigned to something, whether it is an object, a concept, a belief, or an action (Scholarly Community Encyclopedia, n.d.). For individuals or groups, values are the moral principles and ideas they consider essential in life and guide their actions and decisions (Sinclair, 1990: 1615).

There are several common interpretations of value. Moral values are concerned with principles of right and wrong, guiding ethical judgments and behaviors. They often stem from philosophical or religious frameworks and help individuals determine what is morally acceptable or unacceptable (Yudkin, Gantman, Hofmann & Quoidbach, 2021).

Personal values are deeply held beliefs and principles that shape an individual's attitudes, choices, and behaviors. They reflect what individuals consider important and meaningful in their lives, such as honesty, integrity, freedom, compassion, or personal growth (Sagiv, Roccas, Cieciuch & Schwartz, 2017).

Cultural values are shared beliefs, norms, and ideals that characterize a particular society or community. They influence collective behavior, social interactions, and decision-making within that culture. Cultural values include respect for elders, cooperation, individualism, and environmental stewardship (Von Suchodoletz & Hepach, 2021).

In addition to individual and cultural values, emotional, economic, and functional values are relevant within the business context (Lee, Lee & Choi, 2010). These different interpretations of value highlight its multifaceted nature and the various dimensions in which it can be understood and applied.

It is essential to acknowledge that value is subjective and can vary among individuals and cultures. What holds value for one person or group may not have the exact understanding of the notion of value requires taking into account the specific context and perspective involved (İşisağ, 2010; Özen, 2022). However, despite these variations, Schwartz (1992) argues that specifics tend to become standard across societies over time. Schwartz developed a theoretical framework called the circumplex model of human values in 1992, which aims to understand and categorize universal values that guide human behavior. This model organizes values into a circular structure, known as the circumplex, based on their underlying dimensions and motivational goals.

In Schwartz's circumplex model, values are considered beliefs and goals individuals deem essential. They represent broad, abstract concepts that guide our behavior and influence our choices. Values serve as motivational goals, directing our actions and shaping our attitudes. They represent the desired end-states that people strive to achieve. The circumplex model proposes two underlying dimensions that categorize values:

a. Self-transcendence versus self-enhancement: This dimension reflects the motivation to transcend self-interest and promote the welfare of others (self-transcendence) versus the motivation to pursue and enhance one's interests and achievements (self-enhancement).
b. Openness to change versus conservation: This dimension represents the motivation to embrace change, novelty, and self-direction (Openness to change) versus the incentive to preserve tradition, maintain stability, and conform to societal norms (conservation).

These dimensions help categorize values within the circumplex model and provide insights into individuals' and societies' motivations and priorities.

As proposed by Schwartz (1992, 2012), the circumplex model identifies ten value types that are clusters of closely related values positioned within the circumplex. These value types are as follows:

Self-direction: Independent thought and action, creativity, freedom. Stimulation: Excitement, novelty, challenge. Hedonism: Pleasure, enjoyment, self-indulgence. Achievement: Personal success, competence, ambition. Power: Social status, dominance, control. Security: Safety, stability, harmony. Conformity: Obedience, restraint, compliance. Tradition: Respect for customs and preservation of the past. Benevolence: Concern for others' welfare, compassion, and helping. Universalism: Equality, social justice, environmental concern.

The circumplex model allows for the examination of value conflicts and compatibilities. Values positioned closer together on the circumplex are more compatible, while values farther apart are more likely to conflict (Schwartz, 1992, 2012). This model provides a framework for understanding the relationships and dynamics between different values and their impact on individuals and societies.

In a study conducted by Schwartz in 2013, it was found that interpersonal value similarities are achieved through institutional education. Value education refers to the education provided to individuals to learn and embrace values respected, accepted, and essential in society. It is crucial in helping individuals develop their character and become valuable community members by acquiring fundamental values that shape their lives. Value education holds significance for several reasons. Firstly, it aids in developing a solid moral and ethical foundation in individuals. Individuals become more compassionate, responsible, and ethical in their actions by understanding and internalizing values such as honesty, empathy, respect, responsibility, and integrity. This, in turn, fosters personal growth and a sense of purpose. Values serve as the building blocks of character, and value education plays a pivotal role in shaping individuals' character by instilling virtues and guiding principles. It helps individuals make ethical decisions, develop a firm sense of right and wrong, and cultivate virtues that contribute to positive character traits like honesty, fairness, and empathy.

Individuals face numerous choices and decisions in a complex and rapidly changing world. Value education equips individuals with the necessary skills and ethical frameworks to make informed and responsible choices. It enables individuals to consider the consequences of their actions, prioritize the well-being of others, and align their choices with moral principles. Living a life aligned with one's values promotes a sense of fulfillment, meaning, and well-being. When individuals act by held values, they experience greater satisfaction, purpose, and happiness. Value education assists individuals in identifying their core values and encourages them to live harmoniously with those values, leading to a more fulfilling and meaningful existence.

Values are crucial in promoting social cohesion and harmony within communities and societies. When individuals share common values, it fosters a sense of unity, understanding, and cooperation. Value education has the potential to teach individuals to respect diversity, appreciate different perspectives, and engage in constructive dialogue, which can bridge social divides and promote inclusivity among people (Nowack & Schoderer, 2020). Moreover, value education nurtures responsible citizenship by encouraging active participation in the community and fostering a sense of social responsibility. It motivates individuals to contribute positively to society, address social issues, and work toward improving their communities. By instilling values such as civic duty, environmental consciousness, and respect for human rights, value education cultivates engaged and responsible citizens who actively contribute to the welfare of society (Karasu Avcı, Faiz & Turan, 2020). Values such as tolerance, forgiveness, and empathy are essential in resolving conflicts and promoting peace. Value education equips individuals with the skills to manage conflicts peacefully, respect diverse opinions, and find common ground. By promoting dialogue, understanding, and empathy, value education can create a more peaceful and harmonious society (Özkan, 2011; Tinker, 2016).

In summary, value education is important because it fosters personal development, builds character, promotes social cohesion, guides ethical decision-making, nurtures responsible citizenship, contributes to conflict resolution, and enhances overall well-being and happiness in individuals and societies.

Value education holds particular significance in the character development of children, as they learn and adopt values primarily within their family and school environments. It is hoped that values education provided in schools will positively contribute to children's character development. Not only does value education help individuals learn and adopt values, but it also helps society uphold and develop its shared values, contributing to a peaceful and harmonious life. However, values education has faced criticisms that should be acknowledged and addressed for effective implementation. One major criticism is the potential for subjectivity and bias in determining which values should be taught. Cultural, religious, and societal perspectives often influence values adding to diverse interpretations and preferences. Critics argue that values education can be manipulated to promote specific ideologies or agendas, undermining the goal of fostering critical thinking and moral development. Another criticism is the lack of consensus on teaching and prioritizing values. Stakeholders, including parents, educators, and policymakers, may hold varying opinions on essential or appropriate educational values. This lack of agreement can result in confusion and inconsistency in implementing values education programs (Çelik Yılmaz & Argon, 2020).

Implementation challenges are also prevalent in values education. These challenges may include inadequate teacher training and resources, limited instructional time, and difficulties assessing the effectiveness of values education initiatives. With proper support and help, values education can significantly impact students' moral development (Brighouse, Ladd, Loeb & Swift, 2015).

Ethical dilemmas can arise when teaching values, mainly when a society has conflicting values. Balancing individual freedom and responsibility with communal well-being can be complex. Critics argue that values education should encourage open dialogue and critical thinking to navigate these ethical dilemmas rather than imposing specific values or moral frameworks (Mathur & Corley, 2014).

Lastly, critics question the effectiveness of values education in shaping students' behavior and character. They argue that simply teaching values in a classroom setting may not be sufficient to instill long-lasting moral development. Family environment, social influences, and personal experiences also play crucial roles in shaping values and behavior. To address these criticisms constructively, it is essential to continuously refine values education programs, ensuring they are inclusive, balanced, and responsive to the diverse needs and perspectives of students (Forghani, Keshtiaray & Yousefy, 2015; OECD, 2009; Özcan, 2023). By addressing these concerns, value education can better fulfill its goal of fostering ethical and responsible individuals who contribute positively to society.

METHOD

This study, which includes the systematic analysis of doctoral dissertations on values education, moral education, character education, and citizenship education prepared in Türkiye, first systematic review and then meta-synthesis used. Systematic analysis is a methodical approach to examining and understanding complex problems or phenomena (Duverger, 2020: 223). It involves a rigorous process of gathering, organizing, evaluating, and interpreting data or information to draw meaningful insights and conclusions (Tawfik, Dila, Mohamed, et al., 2019). The critical characteristics of systematic analysis include objectivity: It strives to minimize bias and personal opinions by employing a systematic and logical framework. For comprehensive data collection, relevant information is gathered from various sources to understand the problem or phenomenon under study thoroughly. In this context, doctoral dissertations prepared on the subject and known as scientific and original were reviewed in this study. Structured approach: The analysis follows a predetermined set of steps or procedures to ensure consistency and reproducibility. In this context, the words value education, moral education, character education, and citizenship education were searched in the Türkiye Council of Higher Education Thesis Center, and the doctorate theses reached were classified under these headings. In this context, 102 doctoral dissertations were reviewed. Within the scope of the purpose of this research, doctoral dissertations were analyzed according to the year they were completed, the title of the dissertations, the university/institute/branch of science in which they were produced, method, data collection group, data collection tool, definitions, and related topics. Thus, doctoral dissertations prepared in Türkiye were classified under these headings and made ready to facilitate analysis and interpretation. The data is critically evaluated and synthesized to identify patterns, relationships, and trends. Based on the analysis, conclusions are drawn, and recommendations may be made to address the problem or inform decision-making.

Systematic analysis can involve various methods and techniques, such as quantitative analysis, qualitative analysis, statistical modeling, literature reviews, case studies, and others. The specific approach depends on the nature of the problem and the available data (Bellibaş, 2018: 520; Gümüş, 2018: 542). Of these methods, quantitative and qualitative analysis were used in this study.

FINDINGS

Since establishing the Türkiye Council of Higher Education Thesis Center in 2001, doctoral dissertations have been made available electronically. For this research, the dataset for doctoral dissertations was compiled from the theses published until December 30, 2022. Table 1 presents the classification of the doctoral dissertations included in the research according to the year of completion and their respective subjects.

Table 1 indicates that since 2001, primarily values education and citizenship education have been studied in doctoral dissertations. On the other hand, there are relatively fewer studies on character and moral education.

Table 1. Distribution of doctoral dissertations by years and subjects

Subject	Years (2007 - 2023, December 30), 20...																		
	01	04	07	08	09	10	11	12	13	14	15	16	17	18	19	20	21	22	Total
Value education			2	1	2	2	1	2	3	3	8	1	2	6	8	3	6	6	56
Moral education	1	1				2						2		1	1		1		9
Character education			2			2	2	1		1		1			2	1		1	13
Citizenship education			1		1	1	3	1		2	3	1	3	2		1	2	3	24
Total	1	1	5	1	3	7	6	4	3	6	11	5	5	9	11	5	9	10	102

Table 2 shows the institutes and programs in Türkiye where dissertations on values, morals, character, and citizenship education are studied. Table 2 indicates that different dissertations have been made within the scope of doctoral programs at other universities in Türkiye. It was understood that more theses were prepared, especially at Marmara, Gazi, and Atatürk Universities. When the programs in which doctoral dissertations are completed are evaluated, it is understood that social studies and Turkish teaching programs come to the fore. It is seen that the subject is also researched in primary education doctoral programs. Also, it is understood that moral and character education is studied in religious education postgraduate programs.

Table 3 shows that mostly experimental approaches, case studies, and document analysis approaches are used in doctoral dissertations with value education; it also indicates that the explanatory sequential pattern is used as a mixed method. While partly the document analysis approach comes to the fore in moral and character education, case study with descriptive, sequential patterns was used more frequently in citizenship education research. The cross-sectional survey is also a research standard method in character education research.

Table 2. Distribution of doctoral dissertations by the university institute/branch of science

University	Institute	Branch of Science	Total
VALUE EDUCATION			
Anadolu	Education Science	Department of Classroom Teaching Department	1
Atatürk	Social Science	Department of Social Studies Education Department	2
	Education Science	Department of Turkish Education	3
		Department of Turkish Language and Literature Education	1
Aydın A Menderes	Social Science	Education Science	1
		Department of Curriculum and Instruction	1
Bursa Uludağ	Social Science	Department of Religious Education	2
	Education Science	Department of Primary Education	1
		Department of Preschool Education Department	1
Çanakkale OM	Education Science	Education Science Department	1
	Postgraduate Education	Department of Turkish Education	1
Dokuz Eylül	Education Science	Department of Turkish Education	2
Erciyes	Education Science	Department of Turkish Education	1
Fırat	Education Science	Department of Curriculum and Instruction	1
Gazi	Education Science	Department of Classroom Education	3
		Department of Preschool Education	3
		Department of Physical Education and Sports	1
		Department of Turkish Language and Literature Education	1
Gaziantep	Social Science	Education Science	1
	Education Science	Education Science	1
Giresun	Social Science	Department of Social Studies Education	1
Hacettepe	Social Science	Department of Education Programs and Curriculum	1
		Department of Classroom Education	1
Hitit	Postgraduate Edu.	Department of Philosophy and Religious Studies	1
İnönü	Education Science	Curriculum and Instruction	1
		Classroom Education Department	1
		Department of Turkish Education	1
İstanbul	Education Science	Department of Social Studies Education	1
İstanbul Cerrahpaşa	Postgraduate Education	Department of Classroom Education	1
Konya N.Erbakan	Education Science	Department of Curriculum and Instruction	1
		Department of Primary Education	1
Kütahya Dumlupınar	Postgraduate Education	Department of Classroom Education	1
Marmara	Education Science	Department of Social Studies Education	2
	Social Science	Department of Religious Education	1
Mersin	Social Science	Department of Curriculum and Instruction	1
	Education Science	Department of Curriculum and Instruction	1
Ondokuz Mayıs	Education Science	Department Classroom Education	1

continues on following page

Table 2. Continued

University	Institute	Branch of Science	Total
Rize RT Erdoğan	Social Science	Department of Philosophy and Religious Studies	1
Sakarya	Social Science	Department of Philosophy and Religious Studies	1
	Education Science	Department of Turkish Education	2
		Department of Social Studies Education	1
Selçuk	Education Science	Department of Guidance and Psychological Counseling	1
	Social Science	Department of Child Development and Education	2
Yüzüncü Yıl	Education Science	Department of Curriculum and Instruction	1
MORAL EDUCATION			
Ankara	Social Science	Department of Religious Education	2
	Education Science	Department of Educational Philosophy Program	1
Erciyes	Social Science	Department of Religious Education	1
Marmara	Social Science	Department of Religious Education	2
Ondokuz Mayıs	Postgraduate Education	Department of Religious Education	1
	Education Science	Department of Classroom Education	1
	Social Science	Department of Religious Education	1
Sakarya	Social Science	Department of Religious Education	1
CHARACTER EDUCATION			
Ankara	Education Science	Department of Educational Administration and Supervision Program	1
	Social Science	Department of Basic Islamic Sciences (Tafsir)	1
Atatürk	Education Science	Department of Curriculum and Instruction	1
		Department of Classroom Education Department	1
Gazi	Education Science	Department of Social Studies Teaching Program	1
		Department of Preschool Education	1
Kütahya Dumlupınar	Education Science	Department Social Studies Teaching Program	1
	Postgraduate education	Department of Social Studies Education Program	1
Marmara	Social Science	Department of Religious Education	1
		Department of Social Studies Education Department	1
		Educational Administration and Supervision Department	1
Sakarya	Social Science	Department of Religious Education	1
Yıldız Teknik	Social Science	Department of Curriculum and Instruction	1
CITIZENSHIP EDUCATION			
Anadolu	Education Science	Department of Classroom Teaching	2
Ankara	Education Science	Department of Preschool Education Program	1
Atatürk	Social Science	Department of Social Studies Education	1
Gazi	Education Science	Department of Classroom Teaching	1
		Department of Social Studies Education	1
		Department of English Language Education	1
Gaziantep	Education Science	Department of Curriculum and Instruction	1

continues on following page

Table 2. Continued

University	Institute	Branch of Science	Total
Erzurum B. Yıldırım	Social Science	Department of Primary Education	1
Kütahya Dumlupınar	Education Science	Department of Social Studies Teaching	1
Marmara	Education Science	Department of Social Studies Education	10
Ondokuz Mayıs	Social Science	Department of Philosophy and Religious Sciences	1
	Education Science	Department of Classroom Teaching	1
Sakarya	Education Science	Department of Social Studies Education Department	1
Collage London*	Education Science		1*
Total			102

*This thesis was written by a Turkish academician in a foreign university and was published by the Türkiye Council of Higher Education Thesis Center.

Table 3. Distribution of doctoral dissertations by method information

Method		Education			
		Value	Moral	Character	Citizenship
Quantitative	Cross-sectional survey	2		3	1
	Longitudinal survey				1
	Relational survey		1		
	Experimental pattern	15		1	1
	Semi-experimental pattern	2		1	
Qualitative	Case study	11		2	5
	Phenomenology				3
	Grounded theory	1			
	Narrative research	1			
Document analysis		9	8	3	3
Action research		2		1	3
Mixed	Convergence research	2			2
	Explanatory sequential patterns	6		2	5
	Confirmatory sequential pattern	5			
Total: 102		56	9	13	24

Although the subject of this analysis is doctoral dissertation studies on the value, moral, character, and citizenship education at the primary education level, all studies with the same topic completed with different groups have been included in the analysis. This is because all doctoral thesis studies related to value, morals, character, and citizenship education proposes early initiation of these aspects in early childhood. However, out of the 102 doctoral dissertations included in this research, 24 of them were completed with data collected from groups other than primary education (secondary school students, higher education students, secondary school teachers, faculty members, civil, administrative authorities, adults belonging to different religious groups living in Türkiye, etc.). Nine studies completed with prospective teachers studying in education faculties were included in this research about the research conducted at the primary education level. This is because the groups from which data were collected are those continuing their education in programs that train teachers for primary education.

Table 4. Distribution of doctoral dissertations by data collection tool, data collected group/document information

Data Collection Toll	Education			
	Value	Moral	Character	Citizenship
Scale	26	1	5	4
Questionnaire	7		1	6
Open-ended questions	7			
Structured/semi-structured interview form	17	1	6	16
Structured observation form, course evaluation form, vignettes, worksheet, completed fable, letter, and video recordings	13		1	7
Researcher or participant diaries	3		1	4
Achievement test (multiple choice)	4			2
Text/work analysis form/control list	15	3	3	6
Curriculum/educational activities prepared by the researcher	24	1	4	4
Data collected group/document				
Children of unspecified age	1			
Children in need of protection staying in kindergarten	1			
Students of Turkish origin living in different countries				1
Syrian refugee children receiving preschool education	1			
Preschool students	7			1
Primary school student	15	1	3	7
Secondary school student	6			
Higher education student	1		1	
Pre-Primary school teacher	15		6	15
Secondary school teacher	8			1
Student of faculty of education	4		2	3
Member of the Board of Education				1
University lecturer	2		1	1
Parent	5		2	
School counselor				1
Program development specialist			1	1
Civil and administrative authorities	1			
Non-Muslim (Orthodox, Greek, Armenian, and Jewish) citizen		1		1

continues on following page

Table 2. Continued

Data Collection Toll	Education			
	Value	Moral	Character	Citizenship
Religious books / Religious identities		1	2	
Literary figures and their works	9	2	1	
Literary periodical/newspaper/book/course book/educational book series/ internet source/Social media	5	3	1	6
Official curricula prepared for the primary education level in Türkiye	5		2	8
Official curricula prepared for the primary education level in Germany/ the United States of America/France/England	4	1		4
Official curricula prepared for the secondary education level in Türkiye	2	1		
The content of the ethical values education given to the civil administrators at the higher education level	1			
The songs in the music textbooks used at the basic education level in Türkiye	1			
Life science books used at the basic education level	1			
The social science books used at the basic education level in Türkiye and Germany	1			
Cartoons	2			
Religious and value education programs in schools where Montessori, Reggio Emilia, and International Baccalaureate models are applied in Türkiye and the United States of America	1			

When examining Table 4, it can be understood that the data sets for doctoral studies on values education are generally composed of primary school and preschool students. At this point, researchers have collected data from students and teachers, and parents of the student groups they collected data from. Although Table 4 indicates that previously developed scales or scales prepared explicitly for the relevant research, whose validity and reliability have been proven, are frequently used as data collection instruments in studies on values education, in almost all studies, researchers have used multiple data collection tools together (such as open-ended questions, semi-structured interviews, checklists, structured observation forms, etc.). It can be inferred from the values education doctoral dissertations studies that researchers often investigate the impact of their prepared curriculum or activities on students' learning. In this context, it was found that 24 different teaching programs or activities prepared in this regard had a positive impact on students' knowledge and attitudes regarding the subject. In another group of doctoral dissertations on values education, an evaluation is made on the content of values education programs prepared in Türkiye or different countries and on the reflections of these programs on in-class practices.

Similar to values education, it can be observed from Table 4 that similar results are found in doctoral dissertations on character education. In doctoral dissertations on citizenship education, researchers preferred data collection through surveys or structured observation forms rather than scales. They generally associated their research with social studies or citizenship knowledge course contents. They used student achievements included in the official curriculum of these courses or the contents of textbooks and other teaching materials (such as literary periodicals/newspapers/books/course books/educational book series/

internet sources/social media) as criteria for evaluation. Similarly to values education dissertations, researchers also prepared teaching programs or lesson activities for social studies teacher candidates or primary/secondary school students. They analyzed their impact on learners using experimental designs. In doctoral dissertations on citizenship education, examining educational programs from different countries and making inferences or comparisons for the programs implemented in Türkiye are also common. In the early years, citizenship education doctoral dissertations focused more on instilling national values. In contrast, in recent years, postgraduate theses have included international or supranational citizenship values such as digital citizenship, global citizenship, and sustainability policies.

Unlike the theses on values, character, and citizenship education, theses on moral education differ in data collection from specific groups. Only one dissertataion collected data from a group of elementary school students, and another collected data from adults from different religions for analysis. The common denominator of moral education dissertataion is the analysis of religious book contents in the context of moral life or studying sacred or literary figures' moral teachings or lifestyles. In this context, the researchers evaluate the Qur'an, the life of Prophet Muhammad (PBUH), and Abdülkerim Kuşeyrî's Risâle or Mevlâna's work called Mesnevî, which includes an approach to moral education. Based on these relevant works, recommendations are made for moral life and choices.

Literary identities and works related to character education are also discussed in doctoral dissertations on value education. In this context, Ahmet Hamdi Tanpınar's Saatleri Ayarlama Enstitüsü (The Time Regulation Institute) and Oğuz Atay's Tutunamayanlar (The Disconnected) are mentioned as literary works. Values education Supported by Mesnevi, Cengiz Aytmatov's works, Hüseyin Nihâl Atsız's works, sample texts from Kutadgu Bilig, 166 stories by Ömer Seyfettin, the book Kızlara Mahsus Kıraat Muallimi (Recitation Teacher for Girls) prepared by Ebu'l-Muammer Fuad, Yusuf and Züleyha Mesnevis, Ali Ulvi Elöve's Çocuklara Neşideler (Songs to the Children), İbrahim Alâattin Gövsa's Çocuk Şiirleri (Children's Poetry), İbrahim Aşkî (Tanık)'s Çocukların Şiir Defteri (Children's Poetry Notebook), Sabri Cemil (Yalkut)'s Çocuklara Mahsus Küçük Şiirler (Little Poems for Children), and Tevfik Fikret's works titled Şermin... have been examined by researchers within the scope of doctoral dissertations in terms of national and moral values that are intended to be transmitted to the Turkish nation, especially the younger generation.

Table 5 compiles the definitions provided in the dissertation for value, value education, morality, moral education, character, character education, citizenship education, and other concepts associated with these educations. When the common aspects in the definitions of value and value education found in doctoral dissertations in Table 5 are evaluated, it is observed that value definitions encompass individual and societal dimensions. Value definitions with a unique dimension emphasize personal preferences, awareness, satisfaction, and behaviors of being a good person. In value definitions with a societal context, common goals, moral rules, societal continuity, cultural elements, and acceptance are emphasized. Regarding value education, some notions consider the individual an active and passive agent. Value education is an education that includes learning experiences aimed at empowering the individual by developing their personality. On the other hand, it is also an education provided to control individual preferences that may threaten peace for the continuity of social harmony.

Table 5. Distribution of doctoral dissertations by common emphases in definitions and related topics

	Common Emphases in Definitions	Related Topics
Value Education	**Value definitions:** *Individual dimension:* personal preference; things like beauty, truth, love, honesty, and loyalty; anything that emerges as a standard in the thoughts, attitudes, and actions of individuals; the individual's awareness of abilities, striving to be a good person, being at peace with herself and the society, and achieving material and spiritual satisfaction. *Social dimension:* A common thought, purpose, basic moral principle or belief accepted by the majority; necessary things in order to ensure and maintain the existence, unity, and functioning of a social group or society; cultural elements (truthfulness, individuality, cooperation, etc.); all kinds of feelings, thoughts, behaviors, rules or values of social, humane, ideological or divine origin that are accepted, adopted and kept alive within a society, a belief, an ideology or among people. **Value education definitions:** *Individual dimension (individual active):* Bringing out the best in people and enabling them to develop their personality and achieve human perfection fully; the process of acquiring and transferring our moral, human, social, and spiritual values; character development, including spiritual, moral, social and cultural, and the development of virtues, attitudes, and personal qualities; it is a pedagogical practice that enables people to learn values and morals, to gain knowledge about other people in this field, to gain the ability and tendency to apply values and rules together. *Social dimension (individual passive):* Connecting individuals, providing development, happiness, and peace, protecting them from risks and threats; bringing local and universal values to the individual through means such as family, social environment, educational institutions, and the media; civic education; it is an education program that aims to develop and teach the values of peace, responsibility, sharing and cooperation to individuals.	**Related to education:** human values education, moral education, character education, values education program, creative drama, discipline-based art education **Related to the individual:** morality, moral judgment, moral development, attitude, norm, character, benevolence, aesthetics, aesthetic value, cognitive level, affective level, social development, emotional development, behavior, social skill **Related to society:** universality, ethics, social and universal values, undesirable behavior, democratic behavior
Moral Education	**Moral definitions:** free will, balanced character; model of the perfect human being, self-acceptance, self-control, inwardness, self-determination, wisdom; caring for goodness, refraining from evil. **Moral education definitions:** raising the individual in belief, worship, and moral values towards Allah and Prophet; appropriately directing the temperaments that may differ from person to person; education of the soul; The perfect human education model is a person-centered morality based on Islamic morality.	**Related to education:** religious education, self, and nafs education, skill-centered approach, moral-conscience education, moral-personality character education, theories of moral and value education, principles related to moral education, socialization education **Related to the individual:** happiness, virtue, moral judgment development, morality-individuation
Character Education	**Character definitions:** a unique collection of various spiritual abilities in one person; an individual's unique structure, the main symptom that distinguishes him from others, and the main feature that determines the individual's behavior patterns, core structure, character; temperament, respect, responsibility, honesty, reliability, self-discipline, sportsmanship, being fair, being at peace with oneself, being tolerant, being sensitive to the environment and living things. **Character education definitions:** deliberate practices to enable learners to know good, desire good, and do good; will envelop and activate in the dimension of emotion, thought, and behavior; by doing and active learning opportunities; bringing positive character traits to learners in the dimensions of thought, emotion, and behavior.	**Related to education:** the life of the Prophet Muhammad, moral education, moral classroom environment, democratic classroom environment, **Related to the individual:** self-efficacy, self-respect, patience, peace, righteousness, patriotism
Citizenship Education	**Citizenship definitions (nationality dimension):** The legal bond that determines the mutual rights, duties, and obligations between a particular state and a person; a social and political phenomenon expressing one's position and characteristics in the state and the world; an active person who has the knowledge, skills, and attitudes to contribute to the development and welfare of the society. **Citizenship education (nationality dimension):** educational activities aiming to equip the individuals who are subject to the political will (state) that is dominant in a country with the principles it has determined; didactic transmission of political knowledge: provide learners with adequate knowledge and understanding of national history, the structure, and processes of the state and political life; developing learners' political, social and scientific participation skills at the most basic level for scientific and technological developments and risks that affect individual and social life. **Citizenship education (international dimension):** Have knowledge, skills, and attitudes in a global context in areas such as social justice, identity, diversity, human rights, and self-esteem.	**Related to the nation:** education policy, socio-scientific issue, active citizen, minority **International:** global citizen, global citizenship education, sustainable development, environmental citizenship, global morality, diaspora, diasporic identity, belonging, integration, political literacy, digital citizen, intercultural communication ability

When the definitions analyzed in Table 5 are examined, it is understood that the individual dimension is frequently emphasized in moral and moral education. In the definitions, it is understood that moral education is a source of character education and that religious beliefs accompany morality. Similarly, in the descriptions of character and character education, emphasis is placed on the individual dimension, spiritual dimension, individual good behaviors, and individual moral choices. While citizenship definitions emphasize the national dimension, citizenship education definitions are associated with national and international dimensions. In this context, citizenship education is approached with the aspect of forming a national identity and nurturing global citizens.

DISCUSSION

Values education is a topic of great significance in Türkiye, where the educational system plays a pivotal role in shaping the values and character of its citizens. Scholars in the country have been actively studying and promoting values education, recognizing its potential to foster responsible and ethical individuals in a diverse and rapidly changing society (Sünney, 2019).

Value education aims to "reveal the best side of the individual, to ensure the development of her personality in all aspects, to help reach perfection, to protect and save the individual and society from bad morals… and to ensure the continuity of all these" (Aydın & Akyol Gürler, 2014: 15). Value education is precious for the recovery of the individual's personality and learning her responsibilities towards the society and even the whole world. Individuals "integrate into the society they live in, socialize and internalize the sense of belonging thanks to value education" (Ulusoy & Arslan, 2014: 7). Many rules about living together and behavioral expectations of democratic life are internalized by values education (Cogan & Derricot, 1998). Thus, it can be evaluated that the selection of the good ones from the innate characteristics of the person is identified with the character education dimension of value education, the acquisition of ethical values, adaptation to social life with moral education, and the dimension of knowing and applying the administrative policies of the country in which they live and internalizing the rules produced by these policies… in summary the acquisition of social life knowledge, skills, and behavior are identified with the citizenship education dimension of values education.

Value education refers to imparting core values, ethics, and principles to individuals to help shape their character and behavior (Ekşi, 2003). A solid sense of values is essential for building strong, compassionate, and socially responsible citizens. Thus, values education is one of the essential responsibilities of the families of individuals from an early age, the education systems in the country they live in, the education programs developed to be implemented throughout this system, and finally, the schools and teachers who implement these programs (Acat & Aslan, 2011; Kocayiğit & Sağnak, 2012). This definition indicates that there are different value education practices in the world, as much as the number of cultures, countries, or even more. Thus cultural diversity, family and social structures, religious and philosophical traditions, political and governmental influence, historical background of the country, and globalization and westernization socioeconomic context, even the learner's moral maturity and human values in the learner context affect the knowledge, skills, and behaviors that are tried to be gained during values education (Akan, 2021; Yazıcıoğlu & Aktepe, 2022).

Cultures worldwide have unique values, beliefs, and norms that historical, religious, and social influences have shaped. What is considered necessary in one culture may hold a different significance in another. For example, American scholars highlight the significance of values education in promoting diversity and inclusion. They believe students should learn to appreciate different cultures, backgrounds, and perspectives to create a more harmonious and cohesive society (Berkowitz & Bustamante, 2013). Scholars in the United Kingdom acknowledge the diverse and multicultural society in which values education operates. They explore the challenges of moral relativism and pluralism, seeking to strike a balance between teaching universal values and respecting cultural differences (Arthur et al., 2015). In Japan, values education strongly emphasizes virtues such as respect, humility, and harmony. The "Wa" (harmony) concept is deeply ingrained in Japanese society, promoting cooperation and unity. In schools, students participate in various activities like cleaning classrooms together (called "osouji"), promoting a sense of responsibility and teamwork. The practice of bowing as a sign of respect is also taught from an early age, reflecting the value of deference to others (Ellington, 1990; Matvienko1, Kudina & Kuzmina, 2022). In India, values education is closely linked to the rich tapestry of its diverse religions and philosophies. The concept of "Ahimsa" (non-violence) from Jainism, "Dharma" (righteousness) from Hinduism, and "Seva" (selfless service) from Sikhism are integral to values education. Stories from epics like the Ramayana and the Mahabharata are used to teach moral lessons, emphasizing virtues such as truth, honesty, and compassion (Du Val d'Epremesnil, 2021; Patil & Patil, 2021).

The behaviors individuals are expected to learn and implement within the scope of values education also differ depending on the culture. African cultures emphasize communalism, respect for elders, and a strong sense of identity and belonging, promoting virtues like hard work, integrity, and unity (Etta, Esowe & Asukwo, 2016). Western cultures value education often focuses on individualism, critical thinking, and personal responsibility (Cortina, Arel & Smith-Darden, 2017). In the United States, values education may involve teaching the importance of freedom of speech, equality, and the pursuit of happiness. The concept of "giving back to the community" is emphasized, and students may be encouraged to volunteer for charitable causes (Alvarez & Kemmelmeier, 2017; Nagashima, 2020: 80). Values education in Islamic culture centers around the teachings of the Quran and the life of Prophet Muhammad. For example, in Arab countries, children are taught the importance of "Sadaqah" (charity) and "Sabr" (patience) from a young age (Abu-Nimer, 2000). For Confucian cultures like China and Korea, values education is deeply influenced by Confucian teachings, emphasizing concepts like "Filial Piety" (respect for parents and elders) and "Ren" (benevolence). Students are taught to respect authority and adhere to social hierarchies. Confucian values also promote the importance of education and moral self-cultivation (Assadullayev, 2018). In conclusion, values education is a diverse and dynamic field shaped by the unique cultural backgrounds of different societies. Similarly, it was seen that the cultural and social factors affecting the values education approach were analyzed in the doctoral dissertations made in Türkiye, and the role of religion, traditions, and cultural values were taken into consideration in the dissertations prepared in the context of values education and character development in the country.

The diverse nature of value education across different countries and cultures results from the interplay between historical, cultural, religious, political, and societal factors. Each society strives to instill values aligning with its citizens' identity, beliefs, and vision. Character education in the United States has been the subject of extensive research and academic study. Scholars emphasize the development of positive character traits such as integrity, responsibility, empathy, and perseverance. Various programs and curricula, like the "Six Pillars of Character" and "Social-Emotional Learning," have been developed and implemented in schools. The focus is often on fostering students' social and emotional skills alongside academic achievement, aiming to cultivate well-rounded individuals capable of making ethical decisions (Bones, 2010; Denham & Brown, 2010). Character education is integrated into personal, social, health, and economic education in the United Kingdom. It emphasizes the development of character traits like resilience, respect, and tolerance. Schools often engage students in discussions about moral dilemmas and encourage them to reflect on their values and actions.

Scholars in the UK emphasize the role of teachers as role models and advocates for character education, emphasizing the importance of teacher training and professional development in this area (UK Department for Education, 2017). Character education in Finland is often embedded in its holistic approach to education. Finland emphasizes fostering students' well-being, self-esteem, and interpersonal skills. While not explicitly termed "character education," the focus on promoting positive values and social competencies is crucial to Finland's educational philosophy. Teachers emphasize cooperation, empathy, and inclusivity to create a positive learning environment (Suwalska, 2021). Character education in Nigeria is influenced by its multicultural society. Values like respect for elders, community engagement, and perseverance are emphasized. Traditional values and beliefs are often integrated with modern educational practices to develop well-rounded individuals with strong moral character (Alutu & Adubale, 2020).

In conclusion, character education varies across countries, reflecting unique cultural, philosophical, and educational perspectives. While some countries have well-defined programs and curricula, others incorporate character education more holistically. Nonetheless, the common goal across these diverse approaches is to foster positive character traits and ethical behavior in the next generation of citizens. Although scholars emphasize the integration of values education throughout the curriculum, rather than treating it as a separate subject (Chowdhury, 2016) in Türkiye, moral and character education is often included in religious education; in citizenship education, social studies and basic education programs; it has been seen that value education is handled within the scope of Turkish, social studies education and basic education programs. Moral education is often integrated into the broader values education curriculum. Scholars focus on teaching students about honesty, respect for elders, community engagement, and the importance of personal integrity. Religious values and traditional beliefs play a significant role in shaping moral education in Türkiye.

Türkiye's citizenship education emphasizes specific values that are considered essential for fostering a sense of national identity and promoting active citizenship (İnce, 2012). As stated in doctoral dissertations, educational priorities and values in citizenship education change over time. While the subjects of nationalism and patriotism, unity and integrity of the nation, democratic values, human rights and tolerance, and history and national heritage preserve their indispensable values in citizenship education, With globalization, it is seen that subjects such as multiculturalism and tolerance, digital citizenship, migration, and refugees, international cooperation are included in citizenship education studies, albeit limited.

CONCLUSION

In Türkiye, values education is essential to the primary education curriculum. The Turkish National Education System promotes universal human values like respect, tolerance, empathy, honesty, and responsibility. These values are integrated into different subjects and activities across grade levels to foster students' moral development. Moral education in Türkiye aims to instill ethical principles and moral reasoning in students. The Turkish curriculum emphasizes the development of moral character, social responsibility, and ethical decision-making skills. Moral values are often taught through subjects like social studies, religious culture, and ethics.

Character education focuses on developing positive character traits, virtues, and life skills in students. Turkish education emphasizes cultivating integrity, resilience, self-discipline, empathy, and teamwork. Character education is typically integrated into various subjects, extracurricular activities, and school initiatives.

Citizenship education in Türkiye aims to foster active, responsible, and informed citizens who contribute to their communities and society. It promotes democratic values, human rights, social justice, and civic participation. Citizenship education is included in the curriculum through subjects like social studies, history, and democracy courses. While values, morals, character, and citizenship education are prioritized in the Turkish education system, there can be challenges in effective implementation and assessment. These challenges include varying interpretations among educators, limited resources, and the need for ongoing teacher training. There is a growing recognition of the importance of holistic and participatory approaches to character and citizenship education.

Efforts are being made to further enhance values, morals, character, and citizenship education in Türkiye. This includes updating curriculum frameworks, developing educational resources, promoting inclusive and democratic practices, and fostering partnerships between schools, families, and communities. Ongoing research and collaboration among educators and stakeholders play a crucial role in improving the quality and impact of these educational initiatives. When considering what kind of values education the country's education systems should provide, it is essential to focus on holistic development and equipping students with the necessary knowledge, skills, attitudes, and values to navigate a complex and interconnected world. In this context, education systems should promote universal values for fostering positive relationships, tolerance, empathy, respect, and understanding among individuals. These values include honesty, integrity, compassion, fairness, responsibility, and environmental consciousness.

Education should emphasize ethical principles and moral reasoning, encouraging students to develop a strong sense of right and wrong. It should promote integrity, justice, empathy, accountability, and a commitment to social responsibility. Values education should foster cultural understanding, respect for diversity, and appreciation for different perspectives, beliefs, and backgrounds. It should promote inclusivity, combating discrimination, prejudice, and stereotypes. Education should foster social and emotional skills, including empathy, self-awareness, self-management, and interpersonal communication. These skills enable students to build positive relationships, resolve conflicts constructively, and navigate challenges effectively.

Education systems should instill a sense of active citizenship, encouraging students to participate responsibly in their communities, democracy, and social issues. This includes promoting democratic values, human rights, social justice, equality, and civic engagement. Given the pressing global challenges related to the environment, education systems should emphasize environmental values, sustainability, and ecological awareness. Students should develop a sense of responsibility towards nature, fostering a sustainable and environmentally conscious mindset. With the rapid advancement of technology, values education should address digital citizenship. This includes promoting ethical and responsible use of technology, digital literacy, online safety, and combating cyberbullying and misinformation.

Finally, education systems should nurture a love for learning and a growth mindset, encouraging students to become lifelong learners. This includes fostering curiosity, creativity, critical thinking, and adaptability. Collaboration between schools, families, and communities is crucial for values education. Education systems should actively involve parents, guardians, and community members to reinforce shared values and provide a supportive environment for students holistic development.

It is important to note that values education should be integrated across the curriculum and implemented through various teaching methodologies, including experiential learning, role modeling, and participatory activities. Professional development opportunities for educators and ongoing evaluation of values education programs are also essential for their effectiveness.

REFERENCES

Abu-Nimer, M. (2000). A framework for non-violence and peacebuilding in Islam. *The Journal of Law and Religion, 15*(1/2), 217–265. doi:10.2307/1051519

Acat, M. B., & Aslan, M. (2011). Okulların karakter eğitimi yetkinliği ölçeği (OKEYÖ). *Değerler Eğitimi Dergisi, 9*(21), 7-27. https://dergipark.org.tr/en/pub/ded/issue/29179/312453

Akan, Y. (2021). An analysis of the impact of the values education class over the university students' levels of acquisition of moral maturity and human values. *International Journal of Psychology and Educational Studies, 8*(2), 38–50. doi:10.52380/ijpes.2021.8.2.294

Akbaş, O. (2008). Değer eğitimi akımlarına genel bir bakış. *Değerler Eğitimi Dergisi, 6*(16), 9–27.

Alutu, A. N. G., & Adubale, A. A. (2020). Effective character education for undergraduates students: A case study of the University of Benin. *International Journal of Educational Research, 7*(1), 120–128.

Alvarez, M. J., & Kemmelmeier, M. (2017). Free speech as a cultural value in the United States. *Journal of Social and Political Psychology, 5*(2), 707–735. doi:10.5964/jspp.v5i2.590

Arthur, J., Kristjánsson, K., Walker, D. I., Sanderse, W., Jones, C., Thoma, S., Curren, R., & Roberts, M. (2015). *Character education in UK schools research report*. University of Birmingham Jubilee Centre for Character and Virtues. https://www.jubileecentre.ac.uk/userfiles/jubileecentre/pdf/Research%20 Reports/Character_Education_in_UK_Schools.pdf

Assadullayev, E. (2018). Bureaucratic tradition of China: Confucianism and legalism. *Journal of Civilization Studies, 3*(6), 133–148. https://dergipark.org.tr/tr/download/article-file/612819

Aydın, M. Z., & Akyol Gürler, Ş. (2014). *Okulda değerler eğitimi*. Nobel.

Bellibaş, M. Ş. (2018). Sistematik derleme çalışmalarında betimsel içerik analizi. In K. Beycioğlu, N. Özer, & Y. Kondakçı (Eds.), *Eğitim yönetiminde araştırma* (pp. 511–529). Pegem Akademi.

Berkowitz, M. W., & Bustamante, A. (2013). Using research to set priorities for character education in schools: A global perspective. *KEDI Journal of Educational Policy, 10*(3), 7–20.

Bones, G. N. (2010). *The six pillars of character in 21st-century Newbery award books* [Doctoral dissertation, Liberty University]. ProQuest Dissertataion Publishing. https://www.proquest.com/docview/743818398

Brighouse, H., Ladd, H. F., Loeb, S., & Swift, A. (2015). Educational goods and values: A framework for decision-makers. *Theory and Research in Education, 14*(1), 3–25. doi:10.1177/1477878515620887

Çelik Yılmaz, Ç., & Argon, T. (2020). Prejudice, discrimination, and alienation in educational environments. In S. Polat & G. Günçavdı (Eds.), *Empowering multiculturalism and peacebuilding in schools* (pp. 35–60). IGI Global. doi:10.4018/978-1-7998-2827-3.ch002

Chowdhury, M. (2016). Emphasizing morals, values, ethics, and character education in science education and science teaching. *The Malaysian Online Journal of Educational Science, 4*(2), 1–16.

Clement, N. (2009). Perspectives from research and practice in values education. In T. Lovat & R. Tomey (Eds.), *Values education and quality teaching the double helix effect* (pp. 13–25). Springer Dordrecht. doi:10.1007/978-1-4020-9962-5_2

Cogan, J. J., & Derricot, R. (1998). *Citizenship for the 21st Century: an international perspective on education.* Cogan Page.

Cortina, K. S., Arel, S., & Smith-Darden, J. P. (2017). School belonging in different cultures: The effects of individualism and power distance. *Frontiers in Education, 2,* 56. Advance online publication. doi:10.3389/feduc.2017.00056

Denham, S. A., & Brown, C. (2010). "Plays nice with others": Social–emotional learning and academic success. *Early Education and Development, 21*(5), 652–680. doi:10.1080/10409289.2010.497450

Du Val d'Epremesnil, D. (2021). Integrating life in education: An Indian perspective. *Religious Education (Chicago, Ill.), 116*(3), 239–251. doi:10.1080/00344087.2021.1892996

Duverger, M. (2020). *Introduction to the social sciences (RLE Social Theory).* Routledge. doi:10.4324/9781003074458

Ekşi, H. (2003). Temel insani değerlerin kazandırılmasında bir yaklaşım: karakter eğitimi programları. *Değerler Eğitimi Dergisi, 1*(1), 79-96. https://dergipark.org.tr/en/pub/ded/issue/29200/312609

Ellington, L. (1990). Dominant values in Japanese education. *Comparative Education Review, 34*(3), 405–410. doi:10.1086/446958

Etta, E. E., Esowe, D. D., & Asukwo, O. O. (2016). African communalism and globalization. *African Research Review, 10*(3), 302–316. doi:10.4314/afrrev.v10i3.20

Forghani, N., Keshtiaray, N., & Yousefy, A. (2015). A critical examination of postmodernism based on religious and moral values education. *International Education Studies, 8*(9). Advance online publication. doi:10.5539/ies.v8n9p98

Gümüş, S. (2018). Nitel araştırmaların sistematik derlenmesi. In K. Beycioğlu, N. Özer, & Y. Kondakçı (Eds.), *Eğitim yönetiminde araştırma* (pp. 533–550). Pegem Akademi.

İnce, B. (2012). Citizenship education in Turkey: Inclusive or exclusive. *Oxford Review of Education, 38*(2), 115–131. doi:10.1080/03054985.2011.651314

İşisağ, K. U. (2010). The acceptance and recognition of cultural diversity in foreign language teaching. *Gazi Akademik Bakış, 4*(7), 251-260. https://dergipark.org.tr/en/pub/gav/issue/6524/86512

Karasu Avcı, E., Faiz, M., & Turan, S. (2020). Etkili vatandaşlık eğitiminde değerler eğitimi: Sosyal bilgiler öğretmenlerinin düşünceleri. *Değerler Eğitimi Dergisi, 18*(39), 263–296. doi:10.34234/ded.655916

Kirschenbaum, H. (1994). *100 ways to enhance values and morality in schools and youth settings.* Allyn and Bacon.

Kocayiğit, A., & Sağnak, M. (2012). İlköğretim okullarında etik iklimin çeşitli değişkenler açısından incelenmesi. *Değerler Eğitimi Dergisi, 10*(23), 183-197. https://dergipark.org.tr/en/pub/ded/issue/29177/312444

Lee, J.-S., Lee, C.-K., & Choi, Y. (2010). Examining the role of emotional and functional values in festival evaluation. *Journal of Travel Research, 50*(6), 685–696. doi:10.1177/0047287510385465

Mathur, S. R., & Corley, K. M. (2014). Bringing ethics into the classroom: Making a case for frameworks, multiple perspectives and narrative sharing. *International Education Studies, 7*(9). Advance online publication. doi:10.5539/ies.v7n9p136

Matvienko1, O. V., Kudina, V. V., & Kuzmina, S. A. (2022). *Values education and teaching zest for life: Japanese experience and New Ukrainian school reform.* 8th International Conference on Higher Education Advances (HEAd'22), Valencia, Spain. http://dx.doi.org/ doi:10.4995/HEAd22.2022.14626

Myers, D. G. (2011). *Social psychology* (10th ed.). McGraw Hill Companies, Inc.

Nowack, D., & Schoderer, S. (2020). *The role of values for social cohesion: theoretical explication and empirical exploration.* Deutsches Institut für Entwicklungspolitik., . doi:10.23661/dp6.2020

Nzıadam, L. (2020). Education in a democratic and multicultural Nigerian State: an assessment. *Afro Eurasian Studies, 9*(2), 102-112. https://do.org/10.33722/afes.1099684

OECD. (2009). *Creating effective teaching and learning environments: first results from TALIS.* https://www.oecd.org/education/school/43023606.pdf

Özcan, S. (2023). Opinions of classroom teachers on values education in primary school curriculum. *Journal for the Education of Gifted Young Scientists, 11*(2), 129–136. doi:10.17478/jegys.1300101

Özen, F. (2022). Kültürlerarası farklılaşma, eğitim ve öğrenme. In M. Güçlü (Ed.), *Eğitim antropolojisi* (pp. 80–96). Pegem Akademi.

Özkan, R. (2011). Toplumsal yapı, değerler ve eğitim ilişkisi. *Kastamonu Eğitim Fakültesi Dergisi, 9*(1), 333-344. https://dergipark.org.tr/tr/pub/kefdergi/issue/49053/625844

Patil, V. K., & Patil, K. D. (2021). Traditional Indian education values and new national education policy adopted by India. *Journal of Education, 203*(1), 242–245. doi:10.1177/00220574211016404

Sabancı, O., & Altıkulaç, A. (2020). Values and value education according to students of education faculty. *International Journal of Education Technology and Scientific Researches, 13*(13), 1881–1932. doi:10.35826/ijetsar.273

Sagiv, L., Roccas, S., Cieciuch, J., & Schwartz, S. H. (2017). Personal values in human life. *Nature Human Behaviour, 1*(9), 630–639. doi:10.103841562-017-0185-3 PMID:31024134

Scholarly Community Encyclopedia. (n.d.). *Value (ethics).* https://encyclopedia.pub/entry/28294

Schwartz, S. H. (1992). Universals in the content and structure of values: Theoretical advances and empirical tests in 20 countries. *Advances in Experimental Social Psychology*, *25*, 1–65. doi:10.1016/S0065-2601(08)60281-6

Schwartz, S. H. (2012). An overview of the Schwartz Theory of the Basic Values. *Online Readings in Psychology and Culture*, *2*(1), 1–12. doi:10.9707/2307-0919.1116

Sinclair, J. (Chief Ed.) (1990). Value. In Collins Cobuild English Language Dictionary (5th ed.). William Collins Sons & Co Ltd.

Suherman, A. (2018). Implementing character education values in integrated physical education subject in elementary school. *SHS Web of Conferences, 42*, 45. https://doi.org/10.1051hsconf/20184200045

Sünney, F. H. (2019). Eğitim felsefesi ve hedefleri yönünden karakter ve değer eğitimi. In M. Kağan & N. Yılmaz (Eds.), *Karakter ve değer eğitimi* (pp. 175–186). Pegem Akademi. doi:10.14527/9786050370133.10

Suwalska, A. (2021). Values and their influence on learning in primary education in Finland selected aspects. *Roczniki Pedagogiczne*, *13*(2), 141–154. doi:10.18290/rped21132.10

Tawfik, G. M., Dila, K. A. S., Mohamed, M. Y. F., Tam, D. N. H., Kien, N. D., Ahmed, A. M., & Huy, N. T. (2019). A step-by-step guide for conducting a systematic review and meta-analysis with simulation data. *Tropical Medicine and Health*, *47*(1), 46. doi:10.118641182-019-0165-6 PMID:31388330

Tinker, V. (2016). Peace education as a post-conflict peacebuilding tool. *All Azimuth: A Journal of Foreign Policy and Peace, 5*, 27-42. https://doi.org/ doi:10.20991/allazimuth.167339

Ulusoy, K., & Arslan, A. (2014). Değerli bir kavram olarak "değer ve değerler eğitimi". In R. Turan & K. Ulusoy (Eds.), *Farklı yönleri ile değerler eğitimi* (pp. 1–16). Pegem Akademi. doi:10.14527/9786053648222.01

United Kingdom Department for Education. (2017). *Developing character skills in schools qualitative case Studies final report - August 2017.* https://assets.publishing.service.gov.uk/government/uploads/system/uploads/attachment_data/file/634712/Developing_Character_skills-Case_study_report.pdf

Von Suchodoletz, A., & Hepach, R. (2021). Cultural values shape the expression of self-evaluative social emotions. *Scientific Reports*, *11*(1), 13169. doi:10.103841598-021-92652-8 PMID:34162979

Yap, S. F. (2014). Beliefs, values, ethics and moral reasoning in socio-scientific education. *Issues in Educational Research*, *24*(3), 299–319.

Yazicioglu, T., & Aktepe, V. (2022). Identifying the values to be acquired by the students in inclusive classrooms based on the views of the classroom teachers. *International Journal of Progressive Education*, *18*(1), 52–64. doi:10.29329/ijpe.2022.426.4

Yudkin, D. A., Gantman, A. P., Hofmann, W., & Quoidbach, J. (2021). Binding moral values gain importance in the presence of close others. *Nature Communications*, *12*(1), 2718. Advance online publication. doi:10.103841467-021-22566-6 PMID:33976160

KEY TERMS AND DEFINITIONS

Character Education: An approach to education that focuses on developing positive character traits and values in individuals. It aims to foster students' moral, ethical, and social-emotional development, equipping them with the necessary skills and qualities to become responsible, respectful, and compassionate individuals. Character education goes beyond academic learning and emphasizes cultivating virtues such as honesty, integrity, empathy, fairness, perseverance, responsibility, respect, and citizenship. It seeks to instill these values in students, helping them develop a solid moral character and guiding their behavior in various situations.

Citizenship Education: Refers to educating individuals about their rights, responsibilities, and roles as active and engaged members of a democratic society. It aims to develop a sense of civic identity, promote democratic values, and prepare individuals to participate responsibly in their communities and society. Citizenship education encompasses the knowledge, skills, and attitudes necessary for individuals to become informed, responsible, and active citizens. It teaches individuals about their country's political, social, and legal systems and the principles of democracy, human rights, social justice, and global citizenship. The objectives of citizenship education include promoting an understanding of the rights and freedoms granted to citizens, encouraging respect for diversity and inclusion, fostering critical thinking and informed decision-making, and developing skills for civic participation and social action.

Moral Education: The process of teaching individuals about moral values, ethical principles, and responsible behavior. It aims to develop an individual's understanding of right and wrong and guide them in making ethical decisions and engaging in moral reasoning. Moral education aims to develop a solid moral character, integrity, and a commitment to ethical conduct. It involves imparting knowledge about various moral values such as honesty, empathy, fairness, compassion, justice, respect, and responsibility. Moral education encompasses teaching individuals about the consequences of their actions, empathy and consideration for others, and the significance of personal integrity. It encourages individuals to reflect on ethical dilemmas, make informed decisions, and take responsibility for the consequences of their choices.

Value Education: Imparting moral, ethical, and social values to individuals. It aims to develop a sense of integrity, empathy, respect, responsibility, and other positive qualities in individuals. Value education goes beyond the academic curriculum and focuses on nurturing the overall personality of individuals, helping them become responsible and well-rounded citizens. The primary objective of value education is to instill core values and principles that guide individuals in making ethical decisions, behaving responsibly, and contributing positively to society.

Chapter 5
Values Education in Health

Gülcan Demir
https://orcid.org/0000-0003-4639-399X
Sinop University, Turkey

Esra Savaş
https://orcid.org/0000-0003-4539-638X
Boyabat Mevlana Vocational and Technical Anatolian High School, Turkey

Lütfiye Hilal Özcebe
https://orcid.org/0000-0002-0918-8519
Hacettepe University, Turkey

ABSTRACT

Individual and societal values, which are the reasons behind decisions and choices, guide thoughts and behaviors. Values also shape an individual's actions regarding their health, contributing to health improvement. Our values play a crucial role in enhancing the quality of life, encompassing physical, social, environmental, emotional, and mental well-being. The periods of elementary school, childhood, and adolescence are stages where health risks can pose threats. During this time, children may be influenced by new social relationships and their environment, which can lead to undesired changes in existing values. Health-based values education provides school-aged children with opportunities to develop knowledge and skills for healthy growth and disease prevention. This education conveys health-related values to children, encouraging them to adopt a healthy lifestyle. Furthermore, values education, commencing from an early age and progressing gradually, can play a protective role against risks that may arise during adolescence.

INTRODUCTION

Individuals differentiate themselves from one another not only through their physical appearance but also through their beliefs, thoughts, and actions. Values are crucial in shaping our interactions with the social environment and influencing our behaviors. They guide our attitudes and actions, helping us determine

DOI: 10.4018/978-1-6684-9295-6.ch005

what is right and good. Our values significantly determine how we communicate in our relationships with society (Mintz, 2018). As a result, values and the core beliefs that influence our behaviors emerge as the most important factors guiding our attitudes.

Values also shape our preferences, habits, and attitudes related to health, thus closely influencing our health behaviors. Individuals who value health may prioritize their well-being by engaging in regular physical activity, adopting balanced eating habits, and sharing health-related information and resources with others. If a person's values are based on virtues such as prioritizing health, helping others, and sharing, they will likely be inclined to assist in health emergencies or when others face health problems. Conversely, if an individual's values focus on individual success and competition rather than health, they may adopt a competitive approach to their health behaviors. Such individuals may focus on optimizing their health and compete by setting health-related goals. They may adopt a competitive attitude while taking steps related to their health and try to succeed in sports or exercise (Cass et al., 2020). Individuals' health behaviors are shaped by decisions and actions based on their values.

The cultural patterns of society influence values and can evolve, develop, and be reinforced over time within the prevailing environment (Ratnawat, 2018). The cultural patterns of society have a significant impact on individuals' attitudes, beliefs, preferences, and values. The visible aspect of this relationship is reflected in individuals' choices and behaviors. However, individuals' internalized values, beliefs, and norms influence the formation of these behaviors and preferences. Bertsch (2009) suggests that attitudes and behaviors resulting from cultural variances essentially manifest internalized values in the context of addressing problems. Consequently, values themselves are not directly observable; instead, their significance is derived from the choices and actions of individuals (see Figure 1).

Figure 1. Culture's cycle
Source: Bertsch (2009)

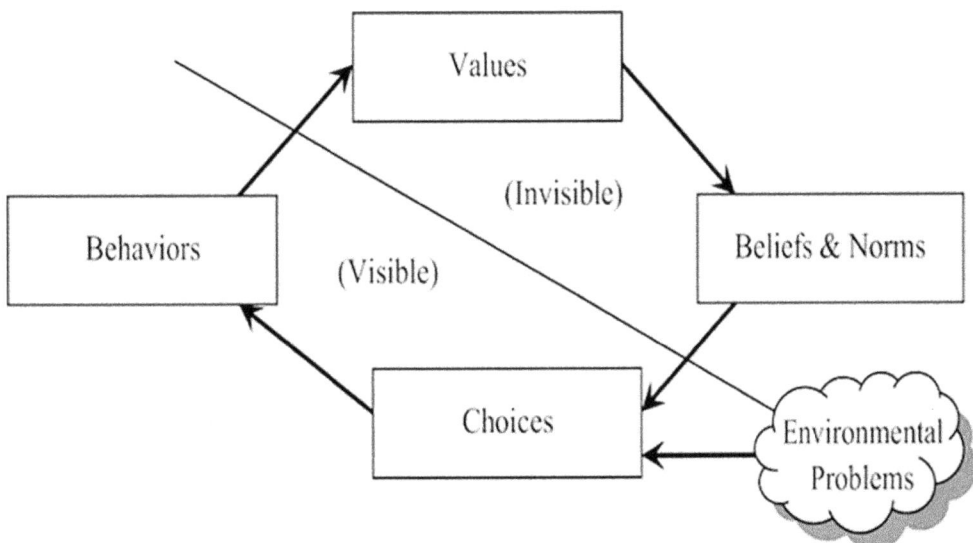

According to the World Health Organization (WHO), health is defined as "a state of complete physical, mental, and social well-being, rather than merely the absence of disease or infirmity" (WHO, 2023a). This definition highlights the multidimensional nature of health, with particular dimensions that cannot be fully measured. An individual's health status is influenced by various factors, including their physical, social, and economic environment and their characteristics and values. Consequently, some health factors are within individuals' control, while others are beyond their control. Gender, genetic traits, education level, employment status, working conditions, and cultural background are among the factors that determine an individual's health status (Committee, 1998; WHO, 2017).

Cultural factors, such as customs, traditions, and the beliefs and values of individuals, families, and communities, significantly shape decision-making and practices related to health. Different cultural groups may assign distinct meanings and values to health. When individuals face circumstances beyond their control, whether socially, environmentally, or culturally, addressing societal expectations and needs can involve providing opportunities for individuals to take responsibility and modify their behavior (Gonzalez & Birnbaum-Weitzman, 2020; Nurse Key, 2017).

This section offers suggestions for behavior changes related to oral health, physical activity, healthy eating, substance use, sexual health, mental health, and other topics. It takes into consideration the role of values in influencing health behaviors.

LITERATURE REVIEW

Hofstede defines "values" as the tendency to prefer certain situations over others (Bertsch, 2009). Everyone in society consciously or unconsciously makes decisions about their health to be accepted in their environment. Shaping these decisions are unseen factors such as personal norms and values. For example, when a teenager is consistently informed about the harms of smoking by their family but simultaneously encouraged to smoke by their peers, their behavior will depend on which health values have a more substantial influence (Kulig, 2023). Therefore, establishing a value system based on health is necessary to enable individuals to choose options in their best interest. Particularly from a young age, this system should be integrated into educational institutions to promote positive health outcomes.

The education process encompasses transmitting dynamic values that ensure social continuity through various settings and methods throughout a person's life. Education is a societal intervention that supports an individual's biological, psychological, social, and moral development. Its purpose is not only to complete an individual's personality development but also to internalize the values of the social group to which they belong (van Delden & van der Graaf, 2021). The objectives of education are determined by the cultural structure of society (Eroğlu, 2012). Therefore, the content and scope of education should be as flexible as possible, as educational needs can vary from country to country, region to region, and even city to city. In addition to meeting these needs, educational policies should support the societal value system and contribute to forming personal health values. Personal values can develop through intentional or unintentional social interactions and education. Education not only acquires scientific knowledge but also questions the purpose of acquiring that knowledge. Individuals' awareness of this transfer process is crucial for making sense of their lives, exercising self-control, promoting autonomy, and constructing their identities (Çetin & Balanuye, 2015).

Schools play a significant role in students' spiritual, moral, social, and cultural development, providing them with social skills and instilling values (Halstead & Taylor, 2000). Adolescence, spanning from ages 10 to 18, is a crucial phase for identity development, and when values education is effectively implemented in schools, it can yield positive outcomes. Values education encompasses moral, citizenship, personal, social, cultural, spiritual, and religious development and should be tailored to individual characteristics (Broadbent & Boyle, 2014). The correct and effective delivery of values education in schools can support students in taking care of their physical, emotional, and social well-being and making sound decisions. Additionally, it can foster behaviors that align with personal values, such as understanding, respect, honesty, empathy, and promotion of equality (T. Janelle, 2023). Providing values education related to health to school-age children can assist them in assessing their health status and making positive behavior changes for their well-being. Comprehensive values education should be an integral part of the school curriculum to prevent risky behaviors and promote the preservation of students' health. Students must develop self-regulation and self-management skills to be aware of their physical, mental, emotional, and cognitive well-being (Gamage et al., 2021).

Schools also provide suitable environments for developing life skills based on health. Life skills encompass ten essential skills categorized as personal, social, academic, and vocational skills. Self-awareness, empathy, critical thinking, creative thinking, decision-making, problem-solving, effective communication, interpersonal relationships, stress management, and coping skills with emotions significantly influence children's and adolescents' well-being and health outcomes (Ulfatin & Mukhadis, 2017). The right to receive a quality education applies to everyone when acquiring life skills. The Incheon Declaration emphasizes the importance of acquiring relevant values, attitudes, knowledge, and skills through quality education to enable individuals to lead healthy life, make sound decisions, and develop problem-solving abilities for local and global issues (UNESCO, 2015). Alongside scientific knowledge, students must develop skills such as error recognition, avoidance of risky behaviors, resistance to peer pressure, and making appropriate choices for their health while enhancing their life skills.

The Influence of Our Values on Health Behavior and Skills

Health behaviors encompass actions undertaken to safeguard, improve, and enhance one's well-being. Individual characteristics, beliefs, expectations, motivations, values, perceptions, and other cognitive factors significantly shape our health behaviors and skills (Glanz et al., 2008).

Values are subjective judgments that direct human behavior and exhibit variations among individuals and social groups. Although values are abstract concepts, they become evident through tangible indicators manifested in human actions. Therefore, observed behaviors can provide valuable insights into an individual's values, beliefs, perceptions, and attitudes (Gamage et al., 2021). Individuals draw upon their preexisting conscious or unconscious knowledge when faced with multiple options or reacting to a situation. These assessments form attitudes that coexist with values and beliefs (OECD, 2018).

The impact of our values on health behaviors and skills is of utmost importance. Our values shape our thoughts, emotions, and actions, while health behaviors encompass the measures we take to safeguard, improve, and restore our health. The influence of our values on health behaviors and skills encompasses several aspects: enhancing motivation, influencing the decision-making process, fostering a sense of responsibility, facilitating internal harmony, and strengthening social connections and relationships (Cepni et al., 2021). For instance, an individual's value on health can bolster their motivation to adopt a healthy lifestyle. This value can encourage them to maintain healthy behaviors such as healthy eating, regular physical activity, and stress management. Furthermore, our values guide us in selecting options that preserve our health instead of engaging in compromised behaviors. Our values significantly impact our fulfillment of responsibilities, including regular health check-ups, consistent medication use, and maintaining a healthy diet to preserve and enhance our well-being (Zhelanov et al., 2021).

When it comes to internal harmony, exhibiting health behaviors that contradict our values can result in internal conflict and discomfort. Aligning our values with appropriate health behaviors enhances our inner peace and happiness (Bożek et al., 2020). Furthermore, our values play a role in shaping societal norms. If we reside in an environment that embraces health-related values, it becomes easier to manifest healthy behaviors. Additionally, engaging in health behaviors that align with our values provides an opportunity to connect with like-minded individuals and strengthen relationships (Hanel et al., 2020).

During the transition from childhood to adulthood, commonly called adolescence, individuals are predisposed to explore themselves and their surroundings, understand their values, shape them, and infuse their lives with purpose. How they shape these value systems can yield positive or negative outcomes depending on their environment and experiences, and it can even lead to identity confusion (Backes & Bonnie, 2019; MentalHelp, 2023). Negative value judgments can impede adolescents' acceptance within peer groups and be associated with unhealthy situations such as social isolation.

Our values have a significant impact on our health behaviors and skills. Having values that prioritize our health, adopting a healthy lifestyle, making health-related decisions following our values, and fulfilling our health responsibilities are crucial. By doing so, we can maintain a healthier life and enhance our overall quality of life.

Values Education for Health

One of the most crucial values individuals prioritize is their health and well-being. Leading a healthy life is considered a fundamental human right for everyone. To safeguard, maintain, and enhance health, it is essential to have knowledge of and internalize healthy lifestyle behaviors (Amin et al., 2021). According to Schwartz's model of human values, personal values are shaped by environmental opportunities, social sanctions, internal conflicts, and shared realities. Internal conflict emerges when there is a discrepancy between an individual's and societal values. In such circumstances, individuals may experience a sense of failure, and their sense of belonging may be compromised. This inconsistency can lead to fluctuations in an individual's overall well-being (Hanel et al., 2020). Numerous risky health-related behaviors are strongly associated with the values held by individuals and the community. For instance, the value of achievement has been linked to more stress-inducing behaviors, hedonism to excessive eating behaviors (Young & West, 2010), and sensation-seeking among adolescents to substance use and risky sexual behaviors (Liu et al., 2007) (Figure 2).

Childhood and adolescence can threaten individuals' health due to the risks they take, which can have long-term consequences throughout their lives. Children and adolescents worldwide encounter similar health issues and risk factors. Unhealthy eating habits, sedentary lifestyles, substance abuse, and engagement in risky sexual behaviors among school-aged children and adolescents can lead to mental health problems, disruptions in physiological and biological development, injuries, unintended pregnancies, sexually transmitted infections, and non-communicable diseases, all of which pose threats to their well-being. Personal hygiene, environmental behaviors, and other choices and actions related to a healthy lifestyle significantly impact individuals' health (Kulig, 2023; Reiner et al., 2019). Therefore, schools are ideal and supportive environments for promoting health-related values to safeguard and improve children and adolescents' physical, emotional, social, and mental well-being. Schools can reach a diverse range of individuals from different sociodemographic backgrounds. To ensure the well-being of future generations, schools must possess health-related resources and knowledge (UNICEF, 2022). Consequently, comprehensive health education programs should be implemented in schools, focusing on nurturing students' knowledge, skills, attitudes, and values concerning preserving and enhancing individual and societal health.

Figure 2. Model of human values
Source: Halstead and Taylor (2000)

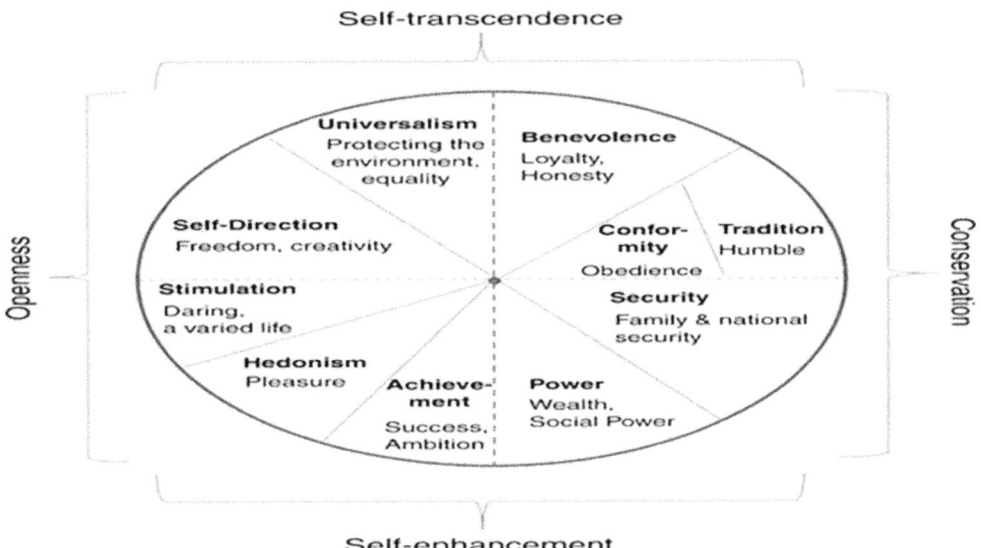

Values education plays a crucial role in guiding students to cultivate personal, familial, and societal levels of health throughout their lives (M. Janelle, 2023). Schools offer a significant opportunity to impart knowledge on leading a healthy lifestyle, given their accessibility to all school-aged children. Gradual provision of health education in schools can be a vital protective measure, reducing students' health risks and fostering resilience (Pulimeno et al., 2020).

To summarize, values education for health enhances health awareness, shapes health-related behaviors, nurtures responsibility and self-management skills, fosters healthy relationships and social connections, and ultimately improves the overall quality of life. Therefore, individuals must embrace values that prioritize health and receive values education.

Health Literacy in Values Education

Health literacy refers to individuals' ability to access, comprehend, evaluate, and utilize health-related information to make informed decisions about their health (WHO, 2023b, 2023c). Values education is a significant component of health literacy and aims to equip individuals with the skills to internalize and embrace values associated with health alongside health knowledge and competencies. These values encompass adopting a healthy lifestyle, maintaining personal well-being, demonstrating self-respect and respect for others, cultivating a sense of responsibility, engaging in scientific thinking, and making health-related decisions based on core values (Sørensen & Paakkari, 2023).

Health literacy provides a solid foundation for individuals to comprehend healthcare services, monitor their health status, actively participate in health-related decision-making, and apply practical skills for a healthy life. It plays a pivotal role in accurately understanding health information and effectively navigating the processes of accessing and utilizing healthcare services (Özdenk et al., 2019; WHO, 2023c). Values education supports health literacy by empowering individuals with health-related knowledge and skills. Internalizing health-related values enables individuals to approach health information and resources critically, make informed decisions regarding their health, and apply healthy life skills in their daily routines (Vamos et al., 2020).

In conclusion, values education for health and health literacy are mutually reinforcing concepts. Values education contributes to the development of health literacy by enhancing individuals' understanding of health-related knowledge and skills. Consequently, individuals gain the capacity to make informed decisions, embrace healthy lifestyles, and actively contribute to promoting health awareness at the societal level.

Primary education, which refers to the elementary education period, is a critical stage where fundamental values are formed, and behaviors are shaped. When values education for health and health literacy are addressed together during the school years, the aim is to provide students with knowledge and skills for a healthy life and instill values associated with healthy behaviors. This way, students can make informed decisions regarding a healthy lifestyle, access health-related information, evaluate it, and contribute to promoting health awareness at the societal level (Vamos et al., 2020). Therefore, values education for health holds significant importance in both primary and secondary education since health literacy is a process that focuses on equipping students with health-related knowledge and skills.

In this educational approach, which aims to provide knowledge and awareness about the fundamentals of a healthy life, fundamental concepts related to health, such as body functioning, nutrition, hygiene, and physical activity, are addressed. Health literacy aims to foster students' comprehension and evaluation skills concerning information related to healthcare, helping them acquire health-related knowledge while building awareness to incorporate into daily living practices. Students begin developing the ability to make educated health-related decisions during primary education by receiving knowledge and skills relevant to leading a healthy lifestyle. Students gain knowledge on proper nutrition, regular physical activity, and personal hygiene behaviors and incorporate these behaviors into their lives. They also acquire the capability to obtain dependable and precise information by critically analyzing health-related data. As a result, they can make health decisions based on accurate information without being exposed to false or misleading information (Bröder et al., 2017; Nielsen-Bohlman et al., 2004). Finally, it is essential to emphasize students' participation in societal health issues and the significance of leading a healthy life within the community. Students can actively promote healthy behaviors, raise awareness about health-related issues, and improve access to healthcare services. This contributes to the development of health consciousness at the societal level (Roberts, 2015).

In this process, teachers and parents play a crucial role. Educational programs should be designed to support values education for health and health literacy, and teachers should receive the necessary training in these areas. Parents should engage in conversations about health-related topics with their children, serve as role models for healthy behaviors, and guide them toward reliable sources. Values education for health and health literacy lay the foundation for a future healthy society by equipping students with the knowledge, skills, and values necessary for leading a healthy life.

The following sections present strategies for acquiring health behaviors and their associated values.

METHODOLOGY

Individual and societal values, which are the reasons behind decisions and choices, guide thoughts and behaviors. Values also shape an individual's actions regarding their health, contributing to health improvement. Our values play a crucial role in enhancing the quality of life, encompassing physical, social, environmental, emotional, and mental well-being.

In elementary school, childhood, and adolescence, health risks can pose threats. During this time, children may be influenced by new social relationships and their environment, which can lead to undesired changes in existing values. However, values education emphasizing health literacy in elementary schools facilitates the transmission of positive values.

Health-based values education provides school-aged children opportunities to develop knowledge and skills for healthy growth and disease prevention. This education conveys health-related values to children, encouraging them to adopt a healthy lifestyle. Furthermore, values education, commencing early and progressing gradually, can protect against risks that may arise during adolescence.

Values education in health, emphasizing health literacy in elementary schools, shapes children's thoughts and behaviors concerning health while promoting the conscious adoption of values. As a result, children become better equipped to choose a healthy lifestyle, safeguard themselves from health risks, and make informed decisions about their well-being.

The qualitative research is based on a literature review conducted both nationally and internationally. This study aims to determine the role of health literacy in the health-related behaviors of school-going children, examine the influence of health-related values, beliefs, traditions, and customs, and identify different aspects through which health values can be developed with health literacy. The research hypothesis examined whether values education in health can be applied to health-related topics through health literacy. Furthermore, the study aims to propose solutions that can instill healthy behaviors. In addition, a detailed examination of national and international health organizations' public health policies has been conducted to evaluate their effectiveness.

RESULTS

The results obtained based on the literature review are presented below.

Oral and Dental Health

Personal hygiene serves as the foundation for a healthy life. Many health issues among school-age children and adolescents arise from their need for more knowledge about personal hygiene practices. Therefore, students require adequate information. As they interact closely with large groups in schools, students should pay attention to clothing, body, oral, dental, eye, nose, skin, and nail hygiene to safeguard their health. This responsibility falls under their obligations (Anggara & Negara, 2022). The poor health status of school-age children is attributed to their limited awareness of the health benefits associated with personal hygiene. A healthy childhood paves the way for healthy adulthood and is pivotal for cultivating positive values related to health and the utilization of healthcare services. A lifelong commitment to maintaining personal hygiene is established during childhood (Pérez Pico et al., 2022).

Tooth decay, fractures, and cavities are among children's prevalent and troublesome conditions. Children with poor oral health may experience tooth swelling and pain due to infections during school, play, eating, and speaking. Dental decay affects at least one tooth in children and adolescents (CDC, 2022a). The oral health status of children may vary based on the economic level of their families. Tooth decay can detrimentally impact their quality of life by impairing learning performance. Preventable tooth decay can be addressed by implementing school oral and dental health programs. Collaborative efforts between schools and dentists should facilitate regular check-ups. Students should be equipped with adequate information about oral and dental care.

Moreover, teachers, school staff, and parents should receive information about school health services. Students and school staff should receive adequate oral and dental health information. Teachers, school staff, and parents should also receive crucial details regarding school health services for promoting and maintaining oral and dental hygiene. Students should also be encouraged to develop oral and dental health skills by adopting healthy eating practices and drinking enough water. Likewise, schools must create safe environments to prevent injuries while making available essential resources needed in case of personal care emergencies (CDC, 2023a).

Recommendations have also been put forth regarding integrating oral and dental health into school health programs (WHO, 2003):

Healthy school environment: School policies directly impact students' oral and dental health, and the location and structural features of the school can also influence changes in students' behavior. Access to clean and safe water is essential for successfully implementing oral and dental health practices in schools. School cafeterias, vending machines, and nearby markets should offer appropriate food choices that promote healthy eating and enhance oral and dental health.

Oral and dental health education: Health education should prioritize improving students' oral health, providing knowledge, shaping their attitudes, beliefs, and values, and enabling them to apply these skills in personal and social contexts while taking responsibility. Oral and dental health education should be integrated with other health topics such as tobacco and alcohol use, healthy nutrition, and non-communicable diseases.

Health services: Schools require oral and dental health services to monitor, screen, and prevent diseases related to poor oral hygiene and examine students' oral health status. Dependent upon a school's resources, oral health facilities may be established with an on-staff dental hygiene team providing needed services to students.

Student involvement: Active student participation is crucial for effective oral and dental health programs in schools. Peer education has proven to be effective in enhancing oral health capacities. Peer education programs, supported by knowledgeable and experienced teachers, should be integrated into comprehensive oral health programs.

The health of school personnel: To encourage students to maintain oral health, it is essential for teachers and all school personnel to have good oral health themselves. Having teachers who value oral health and possess knowledge about effective toothbrushing techniques is essential as they serve as role models. Guidelines should be developed to assist teachers in monitoring students' oral health.

Physical Activity

Physical activity encompasses all movements that require energy expenditure and engage the skeletal-muscular system, such as performing household chores, walking to work or school, playing games, and using stairs in daily life. Regular physical activity helps prevent hypertension, diabetes, and obesity and contributes to maintaining heart health. It also fosters social connections, improves psychosocial well-being, and aids in preserving mental health. Physical activity is crucial to children's and adolescents' development process (CDC, 2022b). The WHO recommends that children aged 5-17 engage in at least 60 minutes of moderate to vigorous-intensity aerobic and muscle-strengthening activities per week (WHO, 2020b).

Due to technological advancements, there has been an increase in physical inactivity and sedentary behavior, leading to a higher risk of developing chronic diseases, also known as non-communicable diseases. The Global Physical Activity Report (2022) reveals that 19% of children aged 11-17 engage in sufficient physical activity, with girls being less active than boys. This disparity further highlights the inequality among various socio-economic groups (WHO, 2022a). Educating children about the importance of physical activity from an early age and raising awareness about its benefits is crucial. Failing to do so may reduce physical activity levels among individuals who lack awareness later in life.

Physical activity reduces the risk of stress and depression in school-age children, contributes to brain development, and helps maintain healthy body weight by boosting metabolism. It promotes children's overall health and can lead to improved academic performance (CDC, 2022b). Schools have been proven to be the most suitable and effective environments for increasing adolescent physical activity. Therefore, inclusive physical activity education programs can be developed in schools to help students develop daily active habits. Within the capacities of schools, strategies should be implemented to encourage students' physical activity, such as in-school physical activities (e.g., recess, physical activity breaks), walking or cycling programs to school, and involving school staff, families, and the community (CDC, 2022b; WHO, 2020b). Students can enhance their knowledge and skills and develop regular physical activity habits outside school.

The WHO provides the following physical activity recommendations for children and adolescents aged 5-17 (WHO, 2020b, 2022d):

- Engage in at least 60 minutes of moderate to vigorous intensity aerobic and physical activities every day.
- Include muscle-strengthening activities at least three days per week.
- Activities can be made more enjoyable for those who do not meet the recommendations, and lighter exercises can be started for shorter durations.
- Ensure access to physical activity for all children and adolescents, provide equal opportunities, and gradually increase activities based on age.
- Minimize sedentary time and limit screen time for children and adolescents as much as possible.

Comprehensive school-based physical education programs prevent students from remaining sedentary for extended periods by promoting their understanding of the importance of maintaining good health. Evidence-based interventions aimed at increasing physical activity levels include the following (WHO, 2022c):

Providing all students with high-quality school curricula and comprehensive physical activity education: The curriculum for physical activity education should focus on developing knowledge, skills, and attitudes related to physical fitness and motor skills while ensuring the active participation of all students.

Facilitating opportunities to enhance physical activity within the school setting: Following awareness studies on physical activity, it is imperative to establish an environment enabling students to apply their acquired knowledge. This entails ensuring access to essential equipment, organizing competitions to boost their motivation, and implementing measures such as facilitating bike commuting to and from school.

Developing strategies to promote sustainability: It is imperative to formulate strategies aimed at enhancing students' physical activity levels, fostering sustainability, and tackling the challenges and needs experienced by students. This could include implementing bike lanes, providing sports equipment in schools, and creating recreational areas, among other measures.

Embracing inclusive approaches to physical activity: Physical activity plans should be tailored to suit each age group and individual student, ensuring all students have equal opportunities to participate.

Healthy Nutrition

Healthy nutrition involves the sufficient and balanced consumption of nutrients to maintain, enhance, and prevent diseases in individuals. Food choices are influenced by various factors, including age, gender, genetic makeup, lifestyle, and cultural, environmental, and economic aspects. The intake of macronutrients (carbohydrates, proteins, and fats) and micronutrients (vitamins and minerals) according to age and developmental requirements plays a vital role in promoting an active lifestyle and productivity (Pekcan et al., 2019; Wetherill et al., 2010). The WHO recommends avoiding products high in fat, salt, and artificial sugars, while emphasizing the daily consumption of fruits and vegetables and regular engagement in physical activity to maintain and improve overall health (WHO, 2010).

School-aged children and adolescents (aged 5-19) are recognized as a critical period for ensuring proper nutrition to support healthy growth and development (UNICEF, 2021). Nutritional habits established during childhood contribute to fostering awareness of healthy eating practices during the rapid growth period of adolescence. School-based nutrition education can significantly shape healthy lifestyle habits among school-aged children and adolescents, promoting positive behavioral changes. School nutrition programs actively contribute to improving children's health. Promoting healthy eating behaviors can be achieved through inclusive nutrition education that incorporates a curriculum focusing on knowledge and skills related to proper nutrition, a school environment that fosters healthy eating practices, and easy access to nutritious food for students. Increased motivation for healthy nutrition in school-aged children has been linked to improved school attendance, academic performance, and higher levels of attention and perception (CDC, 2023b).

Nutrition recommendations for children aged 5-9 during the growth and development stage (UNICEF, 2021) include the following:

- Avoid consuming low-quality foods and limit the intake of excessive sugar, fat, and salt.
- Start the day with a nutritious breakfast and avoid prolonged periods without eating.
- Ensure that vegetables and fruits are consumed daily.
- Stay away from processed snacks high in fat and carbonated drinks.

- Engage in sufficient physical activity to reduce the risk of overweight and obesity.

In addition to the above recommendations, adolescents aged 10-19, who experience rapid growth and increased peer influence, should consider the following:

- Ensure adequate micronutrients such as iron and folic acid intake, particularly for adolescent girls.
- Provide support to adolescents with eating disorders related to body image.
- Prevent fast food consumption, which tends to increase with growing autonomy and disposable income.
- Pay attention to the nutritional needs of adolescent girls after unprotected sexual intercourse to support pregnancy health.

To promote students' knowledge of healthy nutrition and encourage healthy eating habits, schools can implement the following policies (WFP, 2020):

Establish supportive school feeding programs: Develop age-appropriate and progressive nutrition education curricula for students. Schools should foster a culture of healthy eating to promote nutritional values.

Implement school meals and nutrition guidelines: Develop and update nutrition guidelines for school-aged children. Additionally, school cafeterias should offer foods that support healthy growth and development. Products high in fat, salt, and sugar should be limited.

Provide parent monitoring and education: Organize regular healthy nutrition seminars for parents to assist them in developing and monitoring their children's healthy eating habits.

Ensure access to safe food and water: Ensure students have access to safe food and water within the school premises.

Offer service provision and referral: School management and staff should provide the necessary support to offer appropriate counseling and guidance services to children and adolescents with eating disorders.

Substance Use

The transition from childhood to adolescence brings about differentiation and autonomy in biological, psychological, and social aspects. During this rapid period of change, adolescents tend to engage in risky behaviors due to their increased search for excitement, curiosity, and aspirations for growth. The causes of preventable diseases such as tobacco, alcohol, and drug use emerge during childhood and adolescence. Initiating substance use at an early age increases the likelihood of developing problematic behaviors in children. Substance addiction tends to escalate during adolescence and youth (Frobel et al., 2022). When considering gender differences, it is believed that male adolescents, influenced by societal gender norms and roles, prioritize power and achievement values and are more prone to taking risks. In contrast, female adolescents exhibit distinct behaviors to conform to societal expectations (Liu et al., 2007). Evidence suggests that smoking adolescents value pleasure, thrilling life experiences, independence, and self-direction, whereas nonsmoking adolescents tend to embrace more conventional values (Grube et al., 1990).

Factors underlying youth substance use include mental health issues, family history of substance use, peer group influence, lack of parental supervision, easy access to substances, socio-economic conditions, academic failure, and negative life experiences. These risk factors heighten the likelihood of substance use during early childhood (O'Connell et al., 2009). Recognizing the presence of potential adverse circumstances and the susceptibility of every adolescent to substance use, it is crucial to address protective factors to prevent substance addiction. Collaboration with families, schools, and the broader community is paramount. Strengthening the resilience of vulnerable groups against substance use is essential. Therefore, adopting a multisectoral approach and ensuring the participation of the entire population would be appropriate (Renstrom et al., 2017).

To prevent substance use in schools, effective public health policies that can be implemented within the framework of health values education are as follows (UN, 2020):

Awareness and education programs: Comprehensive and impactful education programs about the dangers and risks of substance use should be implemented in schools. Students should be equipped with knowledge and awareness about combating substance addiction, healthy lifestyle choices, and avoiding risky behaviors. Values education should convey to students that substance use contradicts essential values such as respect, responsibility, self-regulation, and self-control and threatens their health.

School policies and peer support programs: Schools should impose stringent policies to discourage student substance use. These policies should address substance use at school through regulations prohibiting it, disciplinary measures against substance abusers within the school environment, as well as regulations concerning behaviors associated with substance use and risks involved with its consumption. Peer support programs must build unity, encourage healthy friendships and activities among peers, and inculcate resistance against substance use among their student participants.

Family engagement and early intervention: Raising family awareness about substance use while encouraging collaboration between families and schools are two crucial strategies in combatting substance use disorders. Schools should provide parents and guardians with information and education about drug and substance use risks, maintain regular communication with them and direct them toward support programs. Furthermore, counseling services may help identify early problems related to substance abuse and provide early interventions when needed. Support, counseling, and rehabilitation services relating to substance use should be made accessible for students and their families alike.

Regulation of environmental factors and collaboration: Schools should develop policies to regulate environmental factors to prevent substance use. For instance, security measures can be implemented to restrict access to substances within the school environment, and control over substance-related advertisements can be enforced. Schools should collaborate with local health organizations, authorities, civil society organizations, and other stakeholders to implement joint projects and programs to prevent substance use.

Continuous support, monitoring, and role models: Health values education should teach students strategies to avoid substance use. Students should acquire resistance, stress management, problem-solving, decision-making, and communication skills. Values education can utilize the stories of teachers, healthcare professionals, families, and successful young individuals as role models.

This multifaceted approach provides an effective strategy for preventing substance use in schools. However, it is crucial to consider local conditions, available resources, and community needs while implementing these policies and measures.

Sexual Health

Sexuality is an integral aspect of life, approached from a holistic perspective on health. It is a complex process that varies from person to person, influenced by biological, sociocultural, and personal experiences. Individuals take emotional steps in their sexual development when they begin to notice their relationship with their parents and become aware of their gender during the early years of life. Exploring their bodies during childhood and engaging in social relationships contribute to their sexual well-being. Social interactions and societal roles are crucial during adolescence in promoting healthy sexual maturation. Adolescents who have experienced adverse incidents like sexual violence, abuse, or incest, and lack knowledge about sexual health, may engage in unprotected sexual relationships. This can lead to outcomes such as early pregnancies, unsafe abortions, and sexually transmitted infections (Kayır, 2011). The issues that arise stem from a lack of awareness and knowledge about the sexual and reproductive health rights of children and adolescents.

The concept of sexual values refers to the underlying principles behind the rules established for appropriate emotions, thoughts, and behaviors related to sexual health. To educate individuals about sexual values, it is crucial first to teach them what these values encompass (T. Janelle, 2023). Parent-child and peer interactions during childhood lay the groundwork for the formation of sexual identity, perceptions, and attitudes about sexuality during adolescence. Parents' conservative attitudes toward sexuality can influence how individuals perceive sexual values and behave (Wetherill et al., 2010). Sexual health education provided to students enables them to respect their values as well as those of others when making decisions regarding sexuality. A comprehensive and high-quality sexual health education program should provide age-appropriate information and skills that focus on behavioral outcomes, foster healthy sexual relationships, and consider cultural values. This program should empower students to make informed decisions about their sexual health (CDC, 2023c). Awareness of sexual and reproductive health rights can significantly enhance physical, mental, and social well-being. Individuals aware of their rights can make informed decisions about sexuality, access accurate information and services, experience a sense of freedom and self-management, express themselves on matters of sexual and reproductive health, and possess skills to protect themselves against sexual violence and abuse.

Effective public health policies and considerations for sexual health within the framework of health values in schools are as follows (WHO, 2019):

Comprehensive sexual health education: Schools should develop and implement comprehensive sexual health education programs. These programs should provide age-appropriate information and cover various topics related to sexual health. It is essential to provide students with accurate information, discuss the risks and prevention methods related to sexual health, and address issues of sexual abuse and violence.

Professional educators: For optimal sexual health education, qualified health professionals or educators with up-to-date knowledge of sexuality should be appointed. Furthermore, this educator must empathize with young people when communicating their message openly and compassionately.

Access to sexual health services: Schools should develop a system to facilitate access for their students to sexual health services such as contraceptive methods, testing and treating for sexually transmitted infections, pregnancy counseling services, etc.

Service delivery comply with confidentiality principles: It is vitally important that these services adhere to confidentiality principles when providing them.

Prevention of sexual violence and abuse: Schools should implement effective policies to stop sexual violence and abuse in school settings. Students should receive information regarding sexual violence, its definition and prevention methods, as well as available resources and support systems. Furthermore, procedures should be in place for reporting violence or abuse and initiating appropriate intervention strategies.

Gender equality: Schools should raise awareness and foster acceptance of egalitarian values through raising awareness by creating programs that challenge gender roles and stereotyping, as well as including topics regarding gender equality in curriculum plans.

Teaching sexual values: Educating students regarding proper values related to sexual health is vitally important. They should learn that mutual consent, honesty, respect, equality, and responsibility are fundamental to sexual relationships. Students should receive education about respecting sexual identity, orientation diversity, and gender equality values in society and social gender roles.

Raising awareness of risk factors: Students should receive information regarding potential consequences of sexual health risks such as STDs, unintended pregnancies, violence against women, or abuse by men. Students should acquire knowledge and develop skills to protect themselves from these risks.

Developing correct information and communication skills: Students should learn how to access reliable sources of sexual health-related data. Critical thinking skills must be developed to challenge misinformation and base decisions on scientific evidence. Furthermore, healthy communication techniques, setting boundaries, and understanding consent should also be learned and practiced regularly.

Emphasizing sexual rights and freedoms: Students should be informed about their sexual health rights and freedoms, and respecting these rights should be emphasized. They should be taught that sexual violence, forced marriage, and sexual discrimination are wrong and violate these rights.

Inclusive and diversity-oriented approach: Students must be educated about respecting different sexual orientations, gender identities, and bodies. Sexual health education programs should reflect the diversity within society and address the needs of everyone.

School-family collaboration: Sexual health education will be more effective with the support of families and parents. Schools should inform families about sexual health topics, encourage participation, and promote discussions at home.

Implementing effective sexual health policies and education programs in schools, these strategies will enable students to have accurate information about sexual health, make informed decisions, protect themselves from risks, and safeguard their sexual rights. They will contribute to the conscious and healthy development of young people regarding sexual health.

Mental Health

Mental health is often overshadowed in comparison to physical health. However, conditions such as depression, anxiety, stress disorders, eating disorders, self-harm, behavioral disorders, and other mental health problems can harm physical and social well-being. Mental well-being encompasses acknowledging one's abilities, contributing to society, and enhancing one's potential for self-fulfillment. Mental health problems can arise at any stage of life and manifest in various ways. However, they are particularly vulnerable during early childhood, and adverse life experiences can impact them more significantly than others (WHO, 2020a, 2022b). Unfortunately, children's mental health problems often go unnoticed and are frequently overlooked due to their limited ability to express themselves clearly. Improving and enhancing the mental health of children who do not exhibit observable behavioral symptoms can be challenging. Issues such as difficulties adjusting to school, lack of concentration, attention problems, challenges in social relationships, and even early school dropout may emerge. Adolescents with poor mental health, commonly called the "storm and stress period," may engage in risky behaviors that jeopardize their well-being. Effective school mental health programs aim to enhance the well-being of both teachers and students. School mental health emphasizes the development of social and emotional learning, building resilience, preventing behavioral, emotional, and social problems, and promoting family, community, and policy initiatives (Cavioni et al., 2020).

Mental health holds significant importance within health values education in schools. In this context, there are adequate public health policies and considerations that can be implemented to protect, support, and enhance mental health (WHO, 2020a, 2022b):

Mental health education programs should be developed in schools to provide students with information about mental health and teach them protective skills. These programs should cover emotional well-being, stress management, problem-solving, and relationship skills. This way, students become aware of and empowered to maintain their mental health.

Establishing an effective system within schools that enables students to seek *psychological assistance* is essential in meeting psychological support services needs. Psychologists, guidance counselors, or advisors must offer students individual or group therapy, counseling, or psychological support so that they may learn to address any challenges by seeking psychological aid when necessary. Doing this allows for effective problem resolution as students can enlist help when necessary to cope effectively with problems they encounter in school and life.

Mental health awareness in schools is integral to student life and should be treated as such. Activities, seminars, or panels that address mental health can provide students with valuable information while dispelling stigmata associated with seeking help for mental illness and encouraging help-seeking behaviors. By creating an environment conducive to mental well-being, students gain awareness and foster an atmosphere supportive of mental well-being in school.

An ideal *school atmosphere* supporting mental wellness can be accomplished when school management and staff take measures necessary for student well-being. Steps such as creating a positive school climate, fostering student solidarity and empathy, preventing bullying, and emphasizing diversity and tolerance are taken.

Monitoring and evaluating mental health is crucial in schools to track and assess students' mental well-being. This process can be done using surveys, assessment tools, or interviews. The collected data can be used to evaluate the effectiveness of policies and plan necessary interventions.

Parental support highlights the importance of schools supporting parents on mental health issues. Parenting skills can be strengthened through educational programs or workshops that support children's mental health and provide emotional support.

The significance given to mental health within the scope of health values education in schools positively affects students' overall well-being, learning process, social relationships, stress management, reduced stigma, and long-term health. Policies and programs related to mental health enable schools to effectively work towards protecting, supporting, and enhancing students' mental health (Fazel et al., 2014). These goals can be achieved by collaborating with school management, teachers, psychologists, and parents.

In addition to providing knowledge about individuals' well-being, values can be instilled to promote healthy behaviors for maintaining good health.

CONCLUSION AND RECOMMENDATIONS

Individuals are influenced by the health-based values of their family members, environment, and the communities they belong to. These existing values, whether positive or negative, unknowingly shape their lives. Children who are susceptible to adopting health-threatening behaviors and are unaware of the extent of their impact are more likely to be at risk of contracting diseases. Moreover, the potential negative consequences on their health can significantly impact various aspects of their lives. Educational institutions are responsible for intervening and initiating behavioral changes concerning values that could jeopardize their health. Schools provide the most suitable environment for reaching children. Comprehensive value-based education can be achieved through a well-structured curriculum encompassing topics related to children's erroneous health decisions, health issues they may suffer from, and their inclination towards certain health behaviors. Health-based values education can assist school-age children in minimizing potential risks and attaining beneficial outcomes. By implementing practices that enhance health, school health education programs will support students in maintaining well-being throughout their lives. Additionally, inclusive educational programs encompass the entire community and can enhance motivation and instill lasting values in children. This approach will guide them toward prioritizing their health and engaging in positive health behaviors.

REFERENCES

Amin, A., Zubaedi, Z., Siregar, A., & Alimni, A. (2021). The Relationship of Education on Healthy Living Values of Multicultural Islamic Perspective with Healthy Lifestyle Behavior of Junior High School Students in Bengkulu, Indonesia. doi:10.21203/rs.3.rs-895737/v1

Anggara, N., & Negara, C. K. (2022). Health Education on Personal Hygiene of Students. *Journal of Education, 1*(1).

Backes, E. P., & Bonnie, R. J. (2019). *The Promise of Adolescence: Realizing Opportunity for All Youth.* Academic Press.

Bertsch, A. (2009). *Exploring perceptions of values in US managers: interstate cross-cultural differences and similarities within the USA.* University of Reading.

Bożek, A., Nowak, P. F., & Blukacz, M. (2020). The Relationship Between Spirituality, Health-Related Behavior, and Psychological Well-Being. *Frontiers in Psychology, 11*, 1997. Advance online publication. doi:10.3389/fpsyg.2020.01997 PMID:32922340

Broadbent, C., & Boyle, M. (2014). Promoting positive education, resilience, and student well-being through values education—*The European Journal of Social & Behavioral Sciences.*

Bröder, J., Okan, O., Bauer, U., Bruland, D., Schlupp, S., Bollweg, T. M., Saboga-Nunes, L., Bond, E., Sørensen, K., Bitzer, E. M., Jordan, S., Domanska, O., Firnges, C., Carvalho, G. S., Bittlingmayer, U. H., Levin-Zamir, D., Pelikan, J., Sahrai, D., Lenz, A., ... Pinheiro, P. (2017). Health literacy in childhood and youth: A systematic review of definitions and models. *BMC Public Health, 17*(1), 361. doi:10.118612889-017-4267-y PMID:28441934

Cass, A. L., Holt, E. W., Criss, S., Hunt, E. R., & Reed, R. (2020). Health-Related Priorities, Perceptions, and Values of University Students: Implications for Wellness Education. *American Journal of Health Education, 52*(1), 37–47. doi:10.1080/19325037.2020.1844103

Cavioni, V., Grazzani, I., & Ornaghi, V. (2020). *Mental health promotion in schools: A comprehensive theoretical framework.* Academic Press.

CDC. (2022a). *Children's Oral Health.* Centers for Disease Control and Prevention. Retrieved 17/06/2023 from https://www.cdc.gov/oralhealth/basics/childrens-oral-health/index.html

CDC. (2022b). *Health Benefits of Physical Activity for Children.* Centers for Disease Control and Prevention. https://www.cdc.gov/physicalactivity/basics/adults/health-benefits-of-physical-activity-for-children.html

CDC. (2023a). *Dental Sealants Can Improve Students' Oral Health.* Centers for Disease Control and Prevention. Retrieved 15 June from https://www.cdc.gov/healthyschools/features/dental_health.htm

CDC. (2023b). *Healthy Eating Learning Opportunities and Nutrition Education.* Centers for Disease Control and Prevention. Retrieved 15 June from https://www.cdc.gov/healthyschools/nutrition/school_nutrition_education.htm

CDC. (2023c). *What Works In Schools: Sexual Health Education.* Centers for Disease Control and Prevention. Retrieved 15 June from https://www.cdc.gov/healthyyouth/whatworks/what-works-sexual-health-education.htm#:~:text=What%20is%20sexual%20health%20education,(STI)%20and%20unintended%20pregnancy

Cepni, A. B., Hatem, C., Ledoux, T. A., & Johnston, C. A. (2021). The Importance of Health Values Among Health Care Providers. *American Journal of Lifestyle Medicine, 15*(3), 224–226. doi:10.1177/1559827621992271 PMID:34025310

Çetin, N., & Balanuye, Ç. (2015). Değerler ve eğitim ilişkisi üzerine. *Kaygı. Bursa Uludağ Üniversitesi Fen-Edebiyat Fakültesi Felsefe Dergisi*, (24), 191–203.

Committee, N. H. (1998). *The social, cultural and economic determinants of health in New Zealand: action to improve health.* National Advisory Committee on Health and Disability.

Eroğlu, S. E. (2012). Values: Great challenge for the construction of social structure with social institutions. *Journal of Human Sciences, 9*(2), 82–90.

Fazel, M., Hoagwood, K., Stephan, S., & Ford, T. (2014). Mental health interventions in schools in high-income countries. *The Lancet. Psychiatry, 1*(5), 377–387. doi:10.1016/S2215-0366(14)70312-8 PMID:26114092

Frobel, W., Grafe, N., Meigen, C., Vogel, M., Hiemisch, A., Kiess, W., & Poulain, T. (2022). Substance use in childhood and adolescence and its associations with quality of life and behavioral strengths and difficulties. *BMC Public Health, 22*(1), 275. doi:10.118612889-022-12586-2 PMID:35144574

Gamage, K. A. A., Dehideniya, D., & Ekanayake, S. Y. (2021). The Role of Personal Values in Learning Approaches and Student Achievements. *Behavioral Sciences (Basel, Switzerland), 11*(7), 102. Advance online publication. doi:10.3390/bs11070102 PMID:34356719

Glanz, K., Rimer, B. K., & Viswanath, K. (2008). *Health behavior and health education: Theory, research, and practice* (4th ed.). Jossey-Bass.

Gonzalez, P., & Birnbaum-Weitzman, O. (2020). Sociocultural. In M. D. Gellman (Ed.), *Encyclopedia of Behavioral Medicine* (pp. 2105–2107). Springer International Publishing. doi:10.1007/978-3-030-39903-0_1511

Grube, J. W., Rokeach, M., & Getzlaf, S. B. (1990). Adolescents value images of smokers, ex-smokers, and nonsmokers. *Addictive Behaviors*, *15*(1), 81–88. doi:10.1016/0306-4603(90)90010-U PMID:2316415

Halstead, J. M., & Taylor, M. J. (2000). *The Development of Values, Attitudes and Personel Qualities*. National Foundation for Educational Research.

Hanel, P. H., Wolfradt, U., Wolf, L. J., Coelho, G. L. H., & Maio, G. R. (2020). Well-being as a function of person-country fit in human values. *Nature Communications*, *11*(1), 5150. doi:10.103841467-020-18831-9 PMID:33051452

Janelle, M. (2023). *Teaching Values to Students in Health Education*. Project School Welness, PSW. Retrieved 12 June from https://www.projectschoolwellness.com/teaching-values-to-students-in-health-education/

Janelle, T. (2023). *Understanding Sexual Values and the Fundamental Role Values Play in Raising Sexually Healthy Children*. Western Oregon University. Retrieved 19 April from https://wou.edu/health/resources/student-health-101/spiritual-wellness/personal-values/

Kayır, A. (2011). Cinsellik ve Cinsel Eğitim. In *Gria Reklam Ltd.Şti.: Turkey Family Health and Planning Foundation*. CETAD.

Kulig, J. C. (2023). *Values In Health Education*. Encyclopedia of Public Health. Retrieved 15 June from https://www.encyclopedia.com/education/encyclopedias-almanacs-transcripts-and-maps/values-health-education

Liu, H., Yu, S., Cottrell, L., Lunn, S., Deveaux, L., Brathwaite, N. V., Marshall, S., Li, X., & Stanton, B. (2007). Personal values and involvement in problem behaviors among Bahamian early adolescents: A cross-sectional study. *BMC Public Health*, *7*(1), 135. doi:10.1186/1471-2458-7-135 PMID:17605792

MentalHelp. (2023). *Self-Identity and Values*. Supermind Platforms, Inc. Retrieved 15 June from https://www.mentalhelp.net/adolescent-development/self-identity-and-values/

Mintz, S. (2018). *What are values?* Ethics Sage. Retrieved 15 June from https://www.ethicssage.com/2018/08/what-are-values.html

Nielsen-Bohlman, L., Panzer, A. M., & Kindig, D. A. (2004). Health Literacy: A Prescription to End Confusion. National Academies Press. doi:10.17226/10883

Nurse Key, F. (2017). *Concepts and values in health promotion*. Retrieved 15 June from https://nursekey.com/concepts-and-values-in-health-promotion/

O'Connell, M. E., Boat, T., & Warner, K. E. (2009). *Risk and Protective Factors for Youth*. youth.Gov. Retrieved 3 June from https://youth.gov/youth-topics/youth-mental-health/risk-and-protective-factors-youth

OECD. (2018). *The future of education and skills: Education 2030*. OECD Publishing. https://www.oecd.org/education/2030-project/

Özdenk, S., Demir Özdenk, G., Özcebe, L. H., & Üner, S. (2019). Bir üniversitenin 4. sınıf öğrencilerinin sağlık okuryazarlığı ve ilişkili bazı faktörlerin incelenmesi. *Mersin Üniversitesi Saglik Bilimleri Dergisi*, *12*(1), 48–59. doi:10.26559/mersinsbd.412666

Pekcan, G., Şanlıer, N., & Baş, M. (2019). *The Turkish Dietary Guidelines*. M. o. H. o. Turkey.

Pérez Pico, A. M., Mingorance Álvarez, E., Villar Rodríguez, J., & Mayordomo Acevedo, R. (2022). Differences in Hygiene Habits among Children Aged 8 to 11 Years by Type of Schooling. *Children (Basel, Switzerland)*, *9*(2), 129. Advance online publication. doi:10.3390/children9020129 PMID:35204850

Pulimeno, M., Piscitelli, P., Colazzo, S., Colao, A., & Miani, A. (2020). School is an ideal setting to promote health and well-being among young people. *Health Promotion Perspectives*, *10*(4), 316–324. doi:10.34172/hpp.2020.50 PMID:33312927

Ratnawat, R. G. (2018). *Understanding values and their role in human life*. Retrieved 11 June from https://www.hrkatha.com/opinion/understanding-values-and-their-role-in-human-life/

Reiner, R. C. Jr, Olsen, H. E., Ikeda, C. T., Echko, M. M., Ballestreros, K. E., Manguerra, H., Martopullo, I., Millear, A., Shields, C., Smith, A., Strub, B., Abebe, M., Abebe, Z., Adhena, B. M., Adhikari, T. B., Akibu, M., Al-Raddadi, R. M., Alvis-Guzman, N., Antonio, C. A. T., ... Kassebaum, N. J. (2019). Diseases, Injuries, and Risk Factors in Child and Adolescent Health, 1990 to 2017: Findings From the Global Burden of Diseases, Injuries, and Risk Factors 2017 Study. *JAMA Pediatrics*, *173*(6), e190337. doi:10.1001/jamapediatrics.2019.0337 PMID:31034019

Renstrom, M., Ferri, M., & Mandil, A. (2017). Substance use prevention: Evidence-based intervention. *Eastern Mediterranean Health Journal*, *23*(3), 198–205. doi:10.26719/2017.23.3.198 PMID:28493267

Roberts, J. (2015). *Local action on health inequalities: improving health literacy*. https://assets.publishing.service.gov.uk/government/uploads/system/uploads/attachment_data/file/460710/4b_Health_Literacy-Briefing.pdf

Sørensen, K., & Paakkari, L. (2023). *Guide to Health Literacy Contributing to Trust Building and Equitable Access to Healthcare*. Academic Press.

Ulfatin, N., & Mukhadis, A. (2017). Personal values and social skills student MTS and its development in curriculum and school program. *Advances in Economics, 45*, 218-222. https://doi.org/https://doi.org/10.2991/coema-17.2017.39

UN. (2020). *UNODC/WHO International Standards on Drug Use Prevention*. Retrieved 12 June from https://www.unodc.org/unodc/en/prevention/prevention-standards.html

UNESCO. (2015). *Education 2030 Incheon Declaration*. WHO, UNICEF, UNESCO. Retrieved 10 June from https://uis.unesco.org/sites/default/files/documents/education-2030-incheon-framework-for-action-implementation-of-sdg4-2016-en_2.pdf

UNICEF. (2021). *Nutrition in Middle Childhood and Adolescence*. UNICEF. Retrieved 11 June from https://www.unicef.org/nutrition/middle-childhood-and-adolescence

UNICEF. (2022). *Promoting and protecting mental health in schools and learning environments*. https://healtheducationresources.unesco.org/library/documents/five-essential-pillars-promoting-and-protecting-mental-health-and-psychosocial

Vamos, S., Okan, O., Sentell, T., & Rootman, I. (2020). Making a Case for "Education for Health Literacy": An International Perspective. *International Journal of Environmental Research and Public Health*, *17*(4), 1436. Advance online publication. doi:10.3390/ijerph17041436 PMID:32102271

van Delden, J. J. M., & van der Graaf, R. (2021). Social Value. In A. Ganguli-Mitra, A. Sorbie, C. McMillan, E. Dove, E. Postan, G. Laurie, & N. Sethi (Eds.), *The Cambridge Handbook of Health Research Regulation* (pp. 46–55). Cambridge University Press. doi:10.1017/9781108620024.007

Wetherill, R. R., Neal, D. J., & Fromme, K. (2010). Parents, peers, and sexual values influence sexual behavior during the transition to college. *Archives of Sexual Behavior*, *39*(3), 682–694. doi:10.100710508-009-9476-8 PMID:19291385

WFP. (2020). *The global and strategic role of WFP in school health and nutrition*. W. F. Pro.

WHO. (2003). *Oral health promotion: an essential element of a health-promoting school* (1727-2335). https://apps.who.int/iris/handle/10665/70207C

WHO. (2010). *A healthy lifestyle - WHO recommendations*. Regional Office For Europe. https://www.who.int/europe/news-room/fact-sheets/item/a-healthy-lifestyle---who-recommendations

WHO. (2017). *Determinants of health*. World Health Organization. Retrieved 13 June from https://www.who.int/news-room/questions-and-answers/item/determinants-of-health

WHO. (2019). *Translating community research into global policy reform for national action*. https://www.who.int/publications/i/item/9789241515627

WHO. (2020a). *Guidelines on mental health promotive and preventive interventions for adolescents: Helping adolescents thrive*. W. H. Organization. https://www.who.int/publications/i/item/9789240011854

WHO. (2020b). *WHO guidelines on physical activity and sedentary behavior* (Geneva: World Health Organization, Issue. https://apps.who.int/iris/handle/10665/336656

WHO. (2022a). *Global status report on physical activity 2022*. W. H. Organization. https://apps.who.int/iris/handle/10665/363607

WHO. (2022b). *Mental disorders*. World Health Organization. Retrieved 10 June from https://www.who.int/news-room/fact-sheets/mental-disorders

WHO. (2022c). *Physical activity*. World Health Organization. Retrieved 11 June from https://www.who.int/news-room/fact-sheets/detail/physical-activity

WHO. (2022d). *Promoting physical activity through schools: policy brief.* W. H. Organization. https://www.who.int/publications/i/item/9789240049567

WHO. (2023a). *Constitution.* World Health Organization. Retrieved 1 June from https://www.who.int/about/governance/constitution

WHO. (2023b). *Improving health literacy.* World Health Organization. Retrieved 9 June from https://www.who.int/activities/improving-health-literacy

WHO. (2023c). *The mandate for health literacy.* World Health Organization. Retrieved 10 June from https://www.who.int/teams/health-promotion/enhanced-wellbeing/ninth-global-conference/health-literacy

Young, R., & West, P. (2010). Do 'good values' lead to 'good' health behaviors? Longitudinal associations between young people's values and later substance use. *BMC Public Health*, *10*(1), 165. doi:10.1186/1471-2458-10-165 PMID:20346109

Zhelanov, D. V., Palamar, B. I., Gruzieva, T. S., Zhelanova, V. V., Leontieva, I. V., & Yepikhina, M. A. (2021). Value-Motivational Component of a Healthy Lifestyle of Modern University Students: The Real State and Logic of Formation. *Wiadomosci Lekarskie (Warsaw, Poland)*, *74*(5), 1079–1085. doi:10.36740/WLek202105106 PMID:34090268

KEY TERMS AND DEFINITIONS

Adequate and Balanced Nutrition: It refers to the consumption of an adequate amount and variety of nutrients to provide the necessary energy for the proper functioning of the body in a healthy manner.

Adequate Nutrition: It involves the consumption of the necessary amount of nutrients by an individual to meet and maintain the demands of daily life activities.

Balanced Nutrition: Balanced nutrition involves consuming essential nutrients from each food group in a well-balanced manner, which is necessary for growth, development, and the body's renewal.

Drug Substance: These are addictive chemical substances that adversely affect an individual's nervous system.

Health Literacy: An individual can access, understand, critically evaluate, and apply accurate health-related information to control their health and make the most appropriate health decisions.

Healthy Nutrition: Healthy nutrition entails the preparation and consumption of essential nutrients in adequate and balanced proportions, using healthy cooking techniques to meet the individual's daily activity requirements and considering factors such as age, sex, and lifestyle.

Physical Activity: Physical activity refers to daily movements that involve engaging the muscular and skeletal systems and expending energy to maintain and sustain overall bodily health and prevent diseases.

Sedentary: Sedentary is a term used to describe the state in which a person remains immobile in the same position for an extended period.

Chapter 6
Antecedents and Consequences of Workplace Bullying in Primary Education:
An Exploratory Study

Muhammad Waseem Bari

ⓘ https://orcid.org/0000-0003-2329-3857

Government College University, Faisalabad, Pakistan

Faiza Baig

Government College University Faisalabad, Pakistan

Irum Shahzadi

Government College University, Faisalabad, Pakistan

ABSTRACT

Primary education is the earliest level of formal education that serves as a center for developing young brains and providing the fundamentals of education. Workplace bullying is a ubiquitous issue that affects workers all over the world, including in the education sector. Educators, staff, and students may experience the negative effects of workplace bullying. Physical aggression, verbal abuse, and social isolation are just a few examples. Bullying can occur in a variety of contexts, including face-to-face interactions, online communication, and indirect forms such as gossip and rumor spreading, and it can make it harder for educationalists to provide a supportive learning environment for their students. It can have a negative impact on educators' well-being and job satisfaction and promotes stress, anxiety, burnout, or other deviant behaviors, which eventually impede students' education. Therefore, an exploratory study is vital that investigates the antecedents and consequences of workplace bullying in primary education.

DOI: 10.4018/978-1-6684-9295-6.ch006

INTRODUCTION AND BACKGROUND

Education psychologists are concerned about bullying in primary schools, as millions of children worldwide experience violence and bullying at school (Meehan et al., 2023). Bullying is linked to physical and psychological problems and poor academic outcomes (Zych, 2021). One must understand how bullying affects students' development to prevent and intervene. However, most studies have focused on bullying in urban schools in European-American contexts, leaving rural schools in underdeveloped nations unexplored (Cunningham, 2022). Workplace bullying is a ubiquitous issue affecting workers worldwide, including in the education sector (Cowan, 2012). In the context of primary education, workplace bullying can have similar harmful impacts on educators, staff, and students (Cruz et al., 2021).

Bullying is defined as "a pattern of repeated harmful behavior that involves a power imbalance between the perpetrator(s) and the victim(s). It can manifest in various ways, including physical aggression, verbal abuse, and social marginalization. Individuals or groups can perpetrate bullying. It can occur in various contexts, including face-to-face interactions, online communication, and indirect forms such as gossip and rumor spreading. Even though bullying occurs in workplaces and schools, it has not received much attention until recent years. Employers keep workplace bullying covert for fear of tarnishing their company's reputation and profitability.

Workplace bullying and harassment are distinct terms. Bullying is the repeated, unwanted exercise of physical, social, or emotional power against an individual, resulting in physical or emotional harm (Saunders et al., 2007). It is associated with adverse outcomes such as anger, aggression, violence, hyperactivity, and externalizing problems that further lead to delinquent and antisocial behaviors (D. Olweus, 1994). Harassment, on the other hand, includes unwanted and hurtful interactions specific to one's race, color, religion, sex, age, disability, or national origin and affects one's working conditions or decisions related to one's job. Workplace harassment is studied using several terminologies, such as bullying, incivility, social undermining, and abusive supervision. Despite these differences, they all share a common feature of negative workplace interactions that cause harm to the target individual. "Bullying" is used instead of "harassment" for historical and cultural reasons. Bullying is commonly used in research, awareness campaigns, and interventions targeting such situations (Smith & Brain, 2000). Thus, "bullying" has gained increased public recognition.

Bullying is fundamentally an abuse of power not limited to physical violence but also includes verbal intimidation and professional undermining. This mistreatment can come from anyone, not necessarily a manager or superior. It can be linked to antisocial personality disorder and/or childhood abuse. Ostracism and excessive supervision are also common signs of bullying behavior. However, many fail to recognize these characteristics and view them as an inevitable personality clash that must be tolerated. Several factors, such as personality traits, organizational structure, and work environment, influence the prevalence of bullying in primary schools. Studies suggest that individuals with low self-esteem and high neuroticism are more likely to be bullied (Glambek et al., 2014). In addition, organizational factors, such as poor leadership, a lack of supportive policies and procedures, and a toxic organizational culture, can foster an environment conducive to bullying. Workplace bullying can be exacerbated by occupational characteristics such as a heavy workload and an uncomfortable working environment.

Bullying affects students' academic performance, social life, and mental health, increasing their risk of anxiety, depression, and other issues in adulthood. Students who frequently bully others are more likely to engage in criminal activities and have negative consequences. Despite anti-bullying laws and prevention programs, the problem of bullying persists. Addressing this issue requires a comprehensive character-building approach to foster positive values such as compassion and respect, which can deter bullying behaviors (Bosworth & Judkins, 2014). This approach entails implementing strategies at the school and classroom levels to cultivate a positive peer culture. Research supports this approach as a solution to the problem of bullying in schools.

Tragically, 11-year-old Carl, unable to endure the continued harassment, took his own life (Lickona, n.d.). This heartbreaking incident underscores the seriousness of the bullying, which received widespread attention after a series of school shootings in the 1990s, including the infamous Columbine High School massacre in 1999. A Secret Service study found that 71% of high school students who committed shootings experienced bullying (Borum et al., 2015). The following decade saw a wave of student suicides related to bullying and other factors, such as family troubles and depression. In September 2009 alone, nine bullying-related student deaths (Vossekuil; Bryan RobertA. Fein, ph.D; Marisa Reddy ph.D & Randy Borum, Psy.D, 2002). The chapter focuses on investigating the antecedents of workplace bullying in primary education. In particular, we will review the existing literature on individual, organizational, and environmental factors that contribute to workplace bullying in this context. We will also discuss the consequences of workplace bullying for victims, bystanders, and the organization, as well as prevention and intervention strategies that can be used to address the problem. This chapter seeks to promote awareness of workplace bullying in primary education and educate educators, policymakers, and researchers on its causes, effects, and solutions.

The Antecedents of Workplace Bullying

Bullying is a severe problem in primary education and can considerably impact student learning and academic performance. Workplace bullying in academic settings can impair student learning and reduce the effectiveness of educators in primary education. Workplace bullying is a prevalent issue that has been observed in several nations. Leymann (1996) asserts that hostile work environments and a lack of coping mechanisms among innocent victims are the root causes of workplace bullying. Workplace bullying has been linked to traits of organizational dysfunction, such as an unproductive information flow, an authoritarian approach to resolving conflicts, a lack of mutual discussion about the tasks and goals of the work unit, and insufficient opportunities to influence personal matters. Studies indicate that bullying is highly prevalent among Pakistan's primary school employees. Pakistan. Anjum & Shoukat (2013) surveyed employees from four elementary institutions and found that 78 percent had experienced workplace bullying. Antecedents of bullying in primary education can be categorized into individual, organizational factors, and environmental basis.

Individual Factors

Individual variables are personal traits and characteristics that can increase a person's propensity to engage in bullying. According to research, aggressiveness, impulsivity, and a lack of empathy have all been linked to an increased risk of bullying behavior (O'Driscoll et al., 2011). Additionally, individuals who exhibit low self-esteem, have low social standing, or have a history of bullying/abuse may be more likely to engage in bullying (Glambek et al., 2014). According to O'Driscoll et al. (2011), individuals whose personalities tended towards aggression were more likely to be bullies. These individuals typically tend to be hostile, irritable, and impulsive, and they may be unable to control their aggressive urges. Low empathy is another personality attribute linked to bullying behavior (O'Driscoll et al., 2011). Individuals with low empathy may be less likely to regard the sentiments and viewpoints of others, making bullying more straightforward.

Individuals with low self-esteem are also more prone to be bullied because bullying can help them feel better by making others feel bad (Glambek et al., 2014). Additionally, individuals with low social standing may feel compelled to assert themselves through intimidation. Finally, individuals who have previously been bullied or abused are more inclined to employ bullying to deal with their trauma. Overall, individual characteristics play a big role in the development of bullying behavior. In order to avoid and combat bullying in primary education, educators and administrators need to be aware of these aspects.

Organizational Factors

Organizational factors relate to the organization's policies, practices, and culture that can contribute to or prevent workplace bullying. For instance, studies found that a lack of clear communication and conflict resolution mechanisms within an organization might contribute to the emergence of a bullying culture. Organizational factors play a crucial role in the emergence and prevention of workplace bullying. Lutgen-Sandvik et al. (2007) identified the role of organizational culture in the development of workplace bullying. They found that organizations that tolerate or encourage aggressive and competitive behavior can create an environment conducive to bullying. According to research conducted by Gupta et al. (2017), additional organizational elements such as job instability, extreme stress, and poor leadership have been found to contribute to workplace bullying.

Job insecurity has been positively associated with workplace bullying, with employees who reported feeling uncertain/ insecure about their job are more likely to be victims of bullying behavior in the workplace. Similar findings were made by Qureshi et al. (2014), who found that poor leadership, such as a lack of encouragement and direction from superiors, is a significant predictor of bullying in the workplace. Organizations can also play a role in preventing workplace bullying. Research has suggested that interventions such as training programs, clear policies and procedures, and supportive leadership can reduce the incidence of workplace bullying. These interventions help create a culture of respect and courtesy within the organization, making bullying more challenging.

Environmental Factors

These are factors external to the organization that can contribute to workplace bullying. The socio-cultural environment in which the organization functions is one factor that comes into play. Bullying may rise, for instance, in a society that values assertiveness and competition. Those who exhibit similar traits may be viewed as more successful and rewarded with promotions and other benefits, thereby increasing bullying behavior (Sloan et al., 2010). Furthermore, Economic and political factors beyond the workplace can also contribute to a bullying work environment. For example, economic pressures can raise job instability and competition, contributing to a more hostile work environment and increasing bullying incidents.

The physical working environment, such as noise levels, lighting, and the availability of private spaces for employees, are other environmental elements that may contribute to workplace bullying. A lack of privacy or personal space can increase stress and amplify employee disagreements, potentially leading to bullying behavior (Puni et al., 2018). Overall, it is critical for organizations to consider the broader environmental factors that may contribute to workplace bullying and to develop strategies to address these factors in order to create a safer and more respectful workplace for all employees. The other physical surroundings of the workplace can exacerbate bullying. For instance, bullying behavior may go undetected if teachers and students are not being watched over and monitored.

Furthermore, bullying can also be facilitated by the physical layout of the school, such as any isolated sections where it might go unreported the physical layout of the school, such as any isolated sections where it might go unreported. Research suggests that environmental factors play a significant role in workplace bullying in primary education. For instance, the research found that the cultural norms and expectations regarding assertiveness and competition in the region influenced bullying behavior among teachers in primary education. Since these environmental issues affect both staff and students, primary educational institutions must be aware of them and take measures to establish a safe and supportive environment for both staff and students.

Consequences of Workplace Bullying

Bullying in primary education has serious consequences for both the victim and the bully. These include lower self-esteem and academic performance, increased absenteeism, a higher risk of mental health issues like anxiety and depression, and physical symptoms such as headaches, abdominal problems, and sleeping disorders (Donegan, 2012). The perpetrators face disciplinary action, academic consequences, and social isolation. Bullying has long-lasting impacts that continue into adulthood, impacting the victim's and the bully's personal and professional lives. Researchers have explained the consequences of workplace bullying (Fahie & Devine, 2014), depicted in Figure 1.

Individual Consequences

Individuals' physical and psychological health suffers from workplace bullying, which causes psychological stress, isolation, mental fatigue, self-doubt, embarrassment, and humiliation (Hauge & Skogstad, 2010). Bullying is a vital risk factor for developing depressive symptoms, as evidenced by (Agervold & Mikkelsen, 2006) and a study of over 7,500 French workers (Sloan et al., 2010). Moreover, it causes a rise in the victim's anxiety and anger, insomnia, and other mental health issues. Workplace bullying leads to losing identity, altering the victim's self-perception and worldview.

Bullying in primary education negatively affects children's mental health and well-being (Arseneault et al., 2013). Children who experienced bullying in primary school were at a higher risk of developing mental health issues in adulthood, such as anxiety, depression, and suicidal thoughts. Smith & Brain (2000) found a correlation between bullying, poor academic performance, and increased absenteeism among elementary school students. It was also associated with an elevated risk of substance abuse and criminal behavior in adulthood (Espelage, 2014).

Workplace bullying in the context of primary education also has severe consequences for teachers. It causes emotional distress, reduced job satisfaction, decreased commitment, and can lead teachers to leave the profession (Hauge et al., 2009). Bullying victims and witnesses are more likely to experience anxiety, despair, and low self-esteem. It also disturbs the learning environment and harms students' academic performance (Nguyen et al., 2017). Moreover, it harms teacher-student relationships, resulting in communication breakdown and loss of trust (Gupta et al., 2017). These findings emphasize the need to address bullying in primary education to prevent long-term negative consequences.

Physical Consequences

Bullying at work in primary education has harmful physical effects. It causes headaches, fatigue, and insomnia (Goodboy et al., 2016). Bullying victims are more likely to experience stress-related ailments, such as cardiovascular disease and digestive issues (Park & Ono, 2017). These physical symptoms may harm the victim's general health and well-being, increasing absenteeism and impairing productivity. There are other additional physical consequences. For example, poor workplace organization and unfavorable social dynamics can lead to colleague conflicts (Africa et al., 2003). It negatively impacts employee relationships, performance, career growth, job security, and other organizational elements such as workplace structure and politics (Einarsen et al., 2007).

Workplace bullying in primary schools is often associated with abuse of power. Academic bullying can also occur, where teachers or administrators bully their peers to gain a career advantage, leading to a hostile academic culture and negatively impacting the quality of education (Gumbus & Meglich, 2012; Giorgi, 2012). This lowers job satisfaction, morale, and productivity among targets. Workplace bullying causes significant staff turnover in elementary education because victims may quit, losing valuable skills and experience. Workplace bullying increases the risk of musculoskeletal disorders, for example, back and neck pain (Hauge & Skogstad, 2010). Schools and educational institutions must recognize and address this issue to protect their staff's health and well-being.

Psychological Consequences

Bullying in the workplace has severe psychological consequences, including depression, anxiety, and post-traumatic stress disorder. Children bullied in school or other places of employment are at an increased risk of developing psychiatric problems in later life. According to the findings of a study conducted by Buonomo et al. (2020), it was found that children who were bullied in elementary school had a greater probability of suffering anxiety, sadness, and post-traumatic stress disorder when they were in their teenage years. Moreover, workplace bullying also leads to a loss of self-esteem, a negative self-image, and a sense of worthlessness (Einarsen et al., 2007). In primary school contexts, children who endure bullying struggle with low self-esteem, a negative self-image, and self-doubt. This can lead to academic underachievement, social isolation, and emotional problems (Niedhammer et al., 2006; Hinduja et al., 2010).

Workplace bullying disrupts student learning and diminishes the intellectual effectiveness of primary education. It contributed to a toxic school climate and impacted students' emotional and psychological health and well-being (Glambek et al., 2015). Bystanders who observe bullying suffer from feelings of remorse, powerlessness, and fear (Gumbus & Meglich, 2012). Such students may find it challenging to focus on their studies and experience lower academic achievement due to the stress of witnessing bullying (Glambek et al., 2015). Therefore, addressing workplace bullying in primary education is crucial to foster a healthy learning environment for all children.

Economic Consequences

Workplace bullying not only harms the victim's health and well-being, but it can also have economic consequences (Giorgi et al., 2015; Fahie & Devine, 2014). Victims of workplace bullying may experience higher absenteeism, decreased productivity, and high turnover rates, resulting in significant economic costs for institutions and organizations (Robert, 2018). A Scandinavian (2016) study found that bullied employees took more sick leave than non-bullied employees. This reduces productivity and increases the organization's healthcare costs for the organization.

A study by Sherrow & Ph (2014) found that workplace bullying has strongly predicted turnover intentions and that bullied employees are more likely to leave their positions. Employee turnover can result in significant expenses associated with hiring, training, and lost output during the changeover. Bullying at work also lowers employee morale and job satisfaction, which results in high turnover rates (Li et al., 2020). Turnover of experienced and hardworking employees has always negatively impacted educational quality and institutional performance. Workplace bullying damages the school's and its staff's reputation, resulting in a negative perception among the public, parents, and other stakeholders. Preventing and addressing workplace bullying benefits employees' health and well-being, fosters a positive work environment, and boosts the organization's economic sustainability (Schulte et al., 2015).

Figure 1. Consequences of workplace bullying
Source: Fahie and Devine (2014)

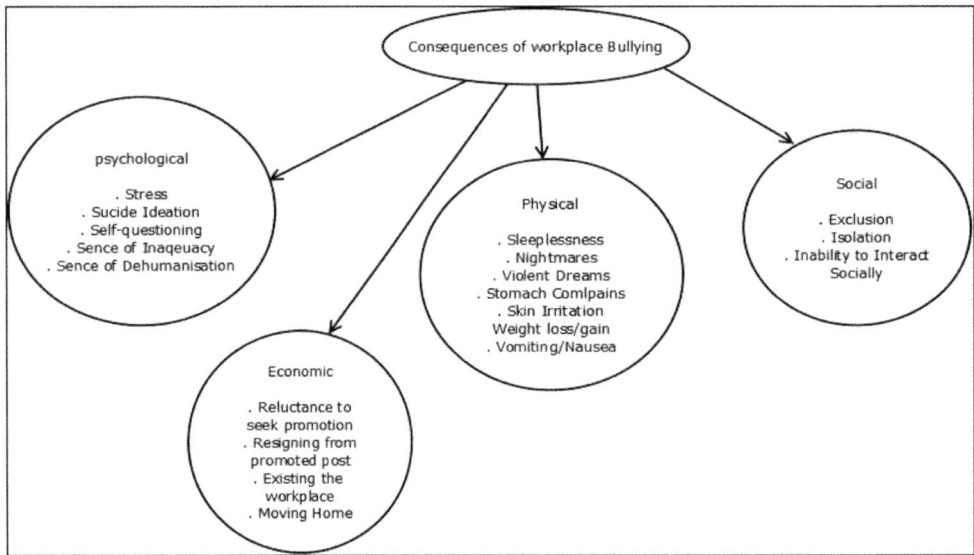

Prevention and Intervention Strategies

To prevent bullying in primary education, it is crucial to employ effective techniques to establish a safe and inclusive workplace environment for all students and staff. The following are strategies and preventive measures that can be used to address bullying in educational settings.

School-Wide Anti-Bullying Policies

By instituting school-wide anti-bullying rules, elementary schools can play a significant role in combating bullying. These policies should be explicit, exhaustive, and effectively communicated to all students, faculty, and parents. Schools can foster a safe and respectful learning environment by explicitly identifying and defining bullying and explaining the repercussions of such behavior. In comparison to schools without such policies, Smith et al. (2008) found that schools with well-developed anti-bullying policies and procedures had reduced rates of bullying occurrences. A zero-tolerance policy against bullying can convey that abusive behavior will not be tolerated. Bullies can face repercussions and interventions under this strategy (Espelage et al., 2013). Schools need to establish a system for reporting and investigating bullying incidents. This allows students to report bullying confidentially and ensures appropriate measures are taken. Schools can also support victims by offering counseling services, peer support programs, and conflict resolution strategies. These regulations can help prevent and successfully manage bullying behavior, fostering healthy social relationships and improving students' overall well-being.

Education and Awareness-Raising

Education and awareness-raising are critical strategies for preventing workplace bullying in primary education. Schools can provide students, parents, and staff with the knowledge and understanding necessary to recognize, prevent, and respond to bullying effectively through education and awareness. This strategy seeks to instill a culture of respect, empathy, and inclusiveness in the school community.

Schools can organize a variety of educational and awareness-raising activities to combat bullying. For instance, school assemblies can address the entire student body, allowing for lectures on the causes and effects of bullying from school counselors or guest speakers (Ttofi & Farrington, 2011). Classroom discussions can also be conducted to facilitate open conversations about bullying, encouraging students to share their experiences and understand the impact of their actions on others (Kallestad, 2010). Schools can also display posters and distribute booklets highlighting the significance of kindness, respect, and the negative impacts of bullying (Younan & Younan, 2018).

Engaging external experts, such as anti-bullying specialists or psychologists, can provide valuable insights and guidance during awareness-raising activities. These specialists can provide workshops or training sessions for students, parents, and staff, providing practical techniques for detecting and dealing with bullying behaviors (Johann & Martinez, 2016). Schools must stay updated with the latest research and evidence-based practices when implementing education and awareness programs. This ensures that the strategies employed align with primary education's most effective methods for addressing workplace bullying.

There is another study by Swearer et al. (2010) indicated that educating students and staff about bullying can help increase awareness and understanding of the issue, leading to a decrease in bullying behaviors. Research by Salmivalli & Poskiparta (2012) suggests that promoting empathy and encouraging students to stand up for their peers can effectively reduce bullying behaviors. By educating students about the impact of their actions and promoting a culture of kindness and empathy, schools can create a safer and more supportive environment for all students.

Encourage Positive Behavior

Positive student behavior promotes a desirable school atmosphere that prevents bullying (Ttofi & Farrington, 2011). Positive reinforcement and role-modeling help in creating a bullying-free school environment. This can be achieved through promoting kindness, empathy, and respect. According to a study by Waasdorp et al. (2021), schools with Positive Behavioral Interventions and Supports (PBIS) programs had substantially fewer bullying incidents in comparison to schools that did not have such programs.

According to research, teachers can also promote positive behavior by fostering a pleasant learning environment where students feel valued and respected (Ttofi & Farrington, 2011). This can be done by encouraging students who demonstrate positive behaviors and providing corrective feedback to those who engage in negative behaviors such as bullying. Positive reinforcement has been demonstrated to be an effective strategy in reducing bullying incidents in elementary schools. Ttofi & Farrington (2011) conducted a meta-analysis of 89 studies and discovered that school-based initiatives that encourage positive behaviors effectively reduce student bullying. These findings highlight the significance of promoting positive behavior to curb bullying in elementary schools.

Establish Clear Rules and Consequences

Establishing clear rules and consequences for bullying behavior is an effective prevention strategy for managing workplace bullying in the context of primary education. According to Gredler (2003), setting rules against bullying and making it clear to students that bullying is unacceptable can help prevent bullying behavior. Disciplinary proceedings or counseling can curb bullying and show that the school takes it seriously.

Clear rules and punishments can make learning safe and supportive. Students are more likely to feel safe and supported if they know what is expected of them and what will happen if they do not follow the rules. Thus, it promotes positive behavior and discourages bullying (Espelage, 2014). Enforcing anti-bullying policies consistently can instill a sense of duty and accountability in children.

Provide Support to Students Involved in Bullying

An efficient prevention and intervention technique for bullying is to offer support to all students affected by it, including both the victim and the bully. Research has shown that students who bully others frequently struggle with underlying social and emotional problems such as a lack of empathy, difficulties with peer relationships, and anger management problems (Espelage & Swearer, 2019). Providing these students support, and resources they need to address these difficulties can reduce the likelihood of future bullying incidents.

It is also crucial to the victim's recovery and well-being to support them after being bullied. Swearer et al. (2010) found that victims of bullying frequently suffer from anxiety, depression, and low self-esteem. They can better deal with the repercussions of bullying and avoid becoming victims again if they have access to counseling, peer support groups, and other forms of emotional assistance. An integral part of any anti-bullying strategy is ensuring that the bully and the victim receive the help they need. Schools may provide a safe and supportive learning environment for all students by addressing the underlying problems contributing to bullying behavior and providing tools for recovery and well-being (Espelage & Swearer, 2019; Swearer et al., 2010).

Parent-Community Involvement

Involving parents and the community in bullying prevention programs help in broadening the approach, as they can provide additional resources and support to the school. Parents and community members can support the school's anti-bullying initiatives by modeling and encouraging prosocial behaviors and presenting a unified front against bullying.

Studies demonstrate that integrating parents and the community in bullying prevention reduces bullying. For instance, Gage et al. (2014) conducted a study in which they discovered that a community-wide effort to eliminate bullying involving parents, teachers, and other influential community members resulted in a considerable reduction in bullying behavior among middle school kids. Similarly, another study by Domitrovich (2010) indicated that incorporating parents in a school-based social-emotional development program reduced student aggression. By collaborating, schools, parents, and community members can promote positive behavior and reduce bullying in schools.

Coping Strategies

Previous studies have demonstrated that victims of bullying are not necessarily powerless or passive in the face of bullying (Hoel & Cooper, 2010). Various researchers have uncovered a variety of coping mechanisms. Aquino & Thau (2009) suggest that victims may adopt problem-focused coping strategies, such as directly confronting the bully, reaching out for social support, or even seeking revenge. On the other hand, victims may also utilize emotion-focused coping strategies, such as humor, substance abuse, suppressing emotional responses, or even forgiveness.

It was observed in a study carried out by Blase & Blase (2011) that teachers often cope with bullying situations by discussing them with colleagues and family members. The participants in this study were from multiple nations. Similarly, a survey by the Association of Secondary Teachers Ireland Fahie & Devine (2014) revealed that teachers frequently sought support from their professional networks and personal relationships. These findings imply that bullied individuals may use various coping strategies to deal with their experiences. to address the impacts of bullying on students' well-being and academic progress, educators, parents, and professionals must recognize and support those who have been victimized by offering the appropriate resources, guidance, and intervention measures.

Figure 2.
Source: Adapted from Fahie and Devine (2014)

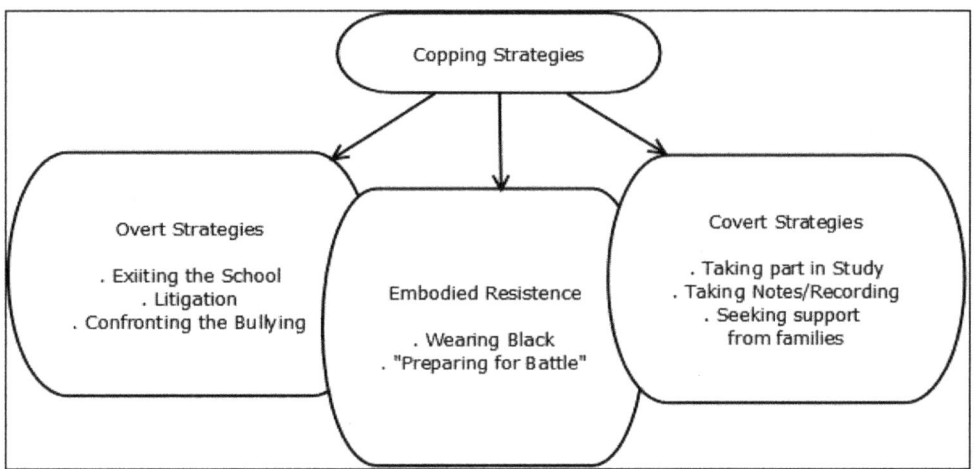

Researchers have classified coping strategies as overt, covert, or embodied, as seen in Figure 2 (Fahie & Devine, 2014). Overt strategies refer to visible or explicit actions taken by victims to cope with bullying. It directly confronts the bully, seeking support from others and even seeking revenge (Sokol et al., 2016). Covert strategies, on the other hand, are more subtle or concealed ways of coping with bullying. They may involve internal processes or actions that are not immediately apparent to others. Embodied coping methods include those that draw on a person's physical and sensory capabilities. It could entail doing physical work, breathing exercises, or sensory activities like watching television or being outside (Horton, 2019). These strategies emphasize the connection between the body and mind in coping with bullying. Figure 2 shows a functional visual representation of the different coping approaches used by victims of bullying.

Anti-Bullying Strategy

An anti-bullying strategy is a comprehensive and coordinated approach a school community takes to prevent and address bullying effectively (Sherer & Nickerson, 2010). It entails implementing several regulations, initiatives, and interventions to safeguard all students and foster a learning environment. According to Jessiman et al. (2022), the strategy is defined by the active participation of school administration, staff, students, parents, and the larger community in eliminating bullying behaviors and promoting positive relationships within the school. An anti-bullying strategy is a community-wide, coordinated effort that is designed and implemented strategically. It is based on the recognition that bullying is a complex issue that requires a multifaceted approach to prevention and intervention (Branch et al., 2013). The strategy aims to reduce bullying incidents and ensure that appropriate responses are in place when bullying occurs.

The whole school approach, as described by the National Centre Against Bullying (Meier, 2008), emphasizes the importance of involving all school community members in implementing anti-bullying strategies. This includes students, teachers, school staff, parents, and even external stakeholders such as community organizations and local authorities. By working collaboratively, sharing responsibilities, and promoting a culture of respect and empathy, the whole-school approach aims to create a cohesive and supportive environment that actively prevents and addresses bullying (Short et al., 2018).

RECOMMENDATIONS

Preventions by Government

Policymakers and practitioners should rely on well-established evidence-based initiatives that have been proven effective in addressing bullying. It is important to learn from existing successful programs and adapt them based on the key elements that have proven effective. it is recommended to set up a mechanism that accredits effective anti-bullying programs. The system in England and Wales in 1996, where efficient programs in prison and probation were approved based on precise criteria informed by research on deterrence, is a notable example of such a system (McGuire, 2001). Only accredited programs are permitted for use in England and Wales, and similar systems have been adopted in other countries like Scotland and Canada. Governments enact laws and develop policies that explicitly address bullying in schools and other settings. These regulations provide guidelines for schools, organizations, and communities to follow in preventing and responding to bullying incidents.

Disciplinary Measures for Reducing Bullying

To ensure the effectiveness of anti-bullying programs in schools, it is crucial to develop a similar accreditation system that incorporates proven elements identified through rigorous evaluations. One potential approach could involve organizing this accreditation system by an international entity such as the International Observatory on Violence in Schools. Additionally, implementing firm disciplinary methods for addressing bullying has been a significant factor in reducing bullying and victimization. The effectiveness of such disciplinary approaches is exemplified by the Olweus program (D. Olweus, 1994), which incorporates various firm sanctions. These may include engaging in serious discussions with bullies, involving the principal in addressing the issue, assigning closer supervision to bullies during recess, and implementing consequences such as removing privileges. Additionally, it has been demonstrated that using strict disciplinary measures to deal with bullying is crucial in reducing bullying and victimization.

Olweus Program

The effectiveness of such disciplinary approaches is exemplified by the Olweus program (D. Olweus, 1994), which incorporates various strong sanctions. These may include engaging in serious discussions with bullies, involving the principal in addressing the issue, assigning closer supervision to bullies during recess, and implementing consequences such as removing privileges. Schools can effectively prevent bullying by adopting and enforcing these strict disciplinary measures. Additionally, it is essential to train and educate staff members, particularly teachers, and administrators, about workplace bullying so they can create prevention initiatives. Further research is required to understand better the nature and effects of workplace bullying in primary school education and to develop effective prevention and intervention techniques.

CONCLUSION

Bullying poses a significant threat not only to those who are directly involved but also to the educational environment. as a whole. With approximately 30% of children reporting their involvement in bullying situations, it is evident that this is a pressing issue affecting the lives of many children (Olweus, 2014). Bullying has short-term and long-term implications for both the victim and the bully. Victims may experience low self-esteem, loneliness, depression, anxiety, increased absenteeism, and poor academic performance. Bullying in primary education has significant implications and severe consequences for victims and bullies. Some victims may turn to violence or self-harm, while bullies may struggle academically and face long-term mental health difficulties and substance abuse. Additionally, witnessing bullying can make other students feel unsafe, impacting their ability to learn and grow. School psychologists and social workers in primary education need to implement effective interventions and create a safe and respectful environment that supports the well-being of all students.

REFERENCES

Africa, S., Psychology, O., Science, P., Hoel, H., Zapf, D., Psychology, O., Cooper, C. L., Psychology, O., & Activities, E. (2003). *Bullying and Emotional Abuse in the Workplace*. Academic Press.

Agervold, M., & Mikkelsen, E. G. (2006). *Relationships between bullying, psychosocial work environment, and individual stress reactions*. doi:10.1080/02678370412331319794

Anjum, A., & Shoukat, A. (2013). Workplace Bullying: Prevalence and Risk Groups in a Pakistani Sample. *Journal of Public Administration and Governance*, *3*(2), 226. doi:10.5296/jpag.v3i2.3985

Aquino, K., & Thau, S. (2009). Workplace Victimization: Aggression from the Target's Perspective. *Annual Review of Psychology*, *60*(1), 717–741. Advance online publication. doi:10.1146/annurev.psych.60.110707.163703 PMID:19035831

Arseneault, L., Bowes, L., & Shakoor, S. (2013). *Bullying victimization in youths and mental health problems : 'Much ado about nothing'?* doi:10.1017/S0033291709991383

Blase, J., & Blase, J. (2011). *The mistreated teacher : a national study*. doi:10.1108/09578230810869257

Borum, R., Cornell, D. G., Modzeleski, W., & Jimerson, S. R. (2015). *What Can Be Done About School Shootings? A Review of the Evidence. February 2010*. doi:10.3102/0013189X09357620

Bosworth, K., & Judkins, M. (2014). *Tapping Into the Power of School Climate to Prevent Bullying : One Application of School-wide Positive Behavior Interventions and Supports*. doi:10.1080/00405841.2014.947224

Branch, S., Ramsay, S., & Barker, M. (2013). Workplace bullying, mobbing, and general harassment: A review. *International Journal of Management Reviews*, *15*(3), 280–299. doi:10.1111/j.1468-2370.2012.00339.x

Buonomo, I., Fiorilli, C., Romano, L., & Benevene, P. (2020). The Roles of Work-Life Conflict and Gender in the Relationship between Workplace Bullying and Personal Burnout. A Study on Italian School Principals. *International Journal of Environmental Research and Public Health*, *17*(23), 1–17. doi:10.3390/ijerph17238745 PMID:33255556

Cowan, R. L. (2012). *It's Complicated: Defining Workplace Bullying From the Human Resource Professional's Perspective*. doi:10.1177/0893318912439474

Cruz, P. D., Noronha, E., & Editors, S. T. (2021). *Special Topics and Particular Occupations*. Professions, and Sectors. doi:10.1007/978-981-10-5308-5

Cunningham, L. R. (2022). *Intra-Racial Bullying Among African American Female Students in Middle School From*. Academic Press.

Domitrovich, C. E. (2010). *Integrated models of school-based prevention: logic and theory*. https://doi.org/ doi:10.1002/pits

Donegan, R. (2012). Bullying and Cyberbullying: History, Statistics, Law, Prevention and Analysis. *The Elon Journal of Undergraduate Research in Communications*, *3*(1), 33–42.

Einarsen, S., Aasland, M. S., & Skogstad, A. (2007). Destructive leadership behavior: A definition and conceptual model. *The Leadership Quarterly*, *18*(3), 207–216. doi:10.1016/j.leaqua.2007.03.002

Espelage, D. L. (2014). *Ecological Theory : Preventing Youth Bullying, Aggression, and Victimization.* doi:10.1080/00405841.2014.947216

Espelage, D. L., Ph, D., Low, S., Ph, D., & Polanin, J. R. (2013). The Impact of a Middle School Program to Reduce Aggression, Victimization, and Sexual Violence. *The Journal of Adolescent Health*, *53*(2), 180–186. doi:10.1016/j.jadohealth.2013.02.021 PMID:23643338

Espelage, D. L., & Swearer, S. M. (2019). *Research on School Bullying and Victimization: What Have We Learned and Where Do We Go From Here?* Academic Press. doi:10.1080/00313831.2012.725099

Fahie, D., & Devine, D. (2014). The Impact of Workplace Bullying on Primary School Teachers and Principals. *Scandinavian Journal of Educational Research*, *58*(2), 235–252. doi:10.1080/00313831.2 012.725099

Gage, N. A., Prykanowski, D. A., & Larson, A. (2014). *School Climate and Bullying Victimization : A Latent Class Growth Model Analysis.* Academic Press.

Giorgi, G., Leon-Perez, J. M., & Arenas, A. (2015). Are Bullying Behaviors Tolerated in Some Cultures? Evidence for a Curvilinear Relationship Between Workplace Bullying and Job Satisfaction Among Italian Workers. *Journal of Business Ethics*, *131*(1), 227–237. doi:10.100710551-014-2266-9

Glambek, M., Matthiesen, S. B., Hetland, J., & Einarsen, S. (2014). Workplace bullying as an antecedent to job insecurity and intention to leave: A 6-month prospective study. *Human Resource Management Journal*, *24*(3), 255–268. doi:10.1111/1748-8583.12035

Glambek, M., Skogstad, A., & Einarsen, S. (2015). *Take it or leave a five-year prospective study of workplace bullying and indicators of expulsion in working life.* Academic Press.

Goodboy, A. K., Martin, M. M., Brown, E., Goodboy, A. K., Martin, M. M., Bullying, E. B., Goodboy, A. K., Martin, M. M., & Brown, E. (2016). *Bullying on the school bus : deleterious effects on public school bus drivers.* doi:10.1080/00909882.2016.1225161

Gumbus, A., & Meglich, P. (2012). Lean and Mean: Workplace Culture and the Prevention of Workplace Bullying. *Journal of Applied Business and Economics*, *13*(5), 11–20. http://search.proquest.com.library. capella.edu/docview/1315304221

Gupta, R., Bakhshi, A., & Einarsen, S. (2017). Investigating Workplace Bullying in India: Psychometric Properties, Validity, and Cutoff Scores of Negative Acts Questionnaire–Revised. *SAGE Open*, *7*(2). Advance online publication. doi:10.1177/2158244017715674

Hauge, L. J., & Skogstad, A. (2010). *Personality and Social Sciences The relative impact of workplace bullying as a social stressor at work.* doi:10.1111/j.1467-9450.2010.00813.x

Hauge, L. J., Skogstad, A., & Einarsen, S. (2009). *Work & Stress : An International Journal of Work, Health & Organisations Individual and situational predictors of workplace bullying : Why do perpetrators engage in the bullying of others ?* doi:10.1080/02678370903395568

Hinduja, S., Patchin, J. W., Justice, C., & Atlantic, F. (2010). *Archives of Suicide Research Bullying, Cyberbullying.* doi:10.1080/13811118.2010.494133

Hoel, H., & Cooper, C. L. (2010). *The experience of bullying in Great Britain : The impact of organizational status.* doi:10.1080/13594320143000780

Horton, P. (2019). The bullied boy: Masculinity, embodiment, and the gendered social-ecology of Vietnamese school bullying. *Gender and Education*, *31*(3), 394–407. doi:10.1080/09540253.2018.1458076

Jessiman, P., Kidger, J., Spencer, L., Simpson, E. G., Kaluzeviciute, G., Burn, A. M., Leonard, N., & Limmer, M. (2022). School culture and student mental health : A qualitative study in UK secondary schools. *BMC Public Health*, *22*(1), 1–18. doi:10.118612889-022-13034-x PMID:35351062

Johann, A., & Martinez, S. (2016). *Managing workplace violence with Evidence-Based Interventions.* Academic Press.

Kallestad, J. H. (2010). Changes in School Climate in a Long-Term Perspective. *Scandinavian Journal of Educational Research*, *54*(1), 1–14. doi:10.1080/00313830903488429

Leymann, H. (1996). The content and development of mobbing at work. *European Journal of Work and Organizational Psychology*, *5*(2), 165–184. doi:10.1080/13594329608414853

Li, N., Zhang, L., Xiao, G., Chen, Z. J., & Lu, Q. (2020). Effects of organizational commitment, job satisfaction, and workplace violence on turnover intention of emergency nurses: A cross-sectional study. *International Journal of Nursing Practice*, *26*(6), 1–9. doi:10.1111/ijn.12854 PMID:32529786

Lutgen-Sandvik, P., Tracy, S. J., & Alberts, J. K. (2007). Burned by bullying in the American workplace: Prevalence, perception, degree, and impact. *Journal of Management Studies*, *44*(6), 837–862. doi:10.1111/j.1467-6486.2007.00715.x

McGuire, J. (2001). *What works in correctional intervention? Evidence and practical implications Offender rehabilitation in practice: Implementing and evaluating effective programs.* Academic Press.

Meehan, Z. M., Hubbard, J. A., Bookhout, M. K., Swift, L. E., Docimo, M., & Grassetti, S. N. (2023). School Absenteeism and In-class Avoidant Behaviors Mediate the Link Between Peer Victimization and Academic Outcomes. *School Mental Health*, *2010*(2), 519–527. Advance online publication. doi:10.100712310-023-09566-1

Meier, M. (2008). *Cyber Bullying: Overview and Strategies for School Counsellors, Guidance Officers, and All School Personnel.* Academic Press.

Nguyen, D. T. N., Teo, S. T. T., Grover, S. L., Phong, N., & Grover, S. L. (2017). Psychological safety climate and workplace bullying in Vietnam s public sector. *Public Management Review*, *00*(00), 1–22. doi:10.1080/14719037.2016.1272712

Niedhammer, I., David, S., & Degioanni, S. (2006). *Association between workplace bullying and depressive symptoms in the French working population.* doi:10.1016/j.jpsychores.2006.03.051

O'Driscoll, M. P., Cooper-Thomas, H. D., Bentley, T., Catley, B. E., Gardner, D. H., & Trenberth, L. (2011). Workplace bullying in new zealand: A survey of employee perceptions and attitudes. *Asia Pacific Journal of Human Resources, 49*(4), 390–408. doi:10.1177/1038411111422140

Olweus, D. (1994). Bullying at school: Basic facts and an effective intervention program. *Promotion & Education, 1*(4), 27–31.

Olweus, D. A. (2014). *Bullying in schools : facts and intervention.* Academic Press.

Park, J. H., & Ono, M. (2017). Effects of workplace bullying on work engagement and health : The mediating role of job insecurity. *International Journal of Human Resource Management, 5192*(22), 1–24. doi:10.1080/09585192.2016.1155164

Puni, A., Mohammed, I., & Asamoah, E. (2018). Transformational leadership and job satisfaction: The moderating effect of contingent reward. *Leadership and Organization Development Journal, 39*(4), 522–537. doi:10.1108/LODJ-11-2017-0358

Robert, F. (2018). Impact of Workplace Bullying on Job Performance and Job Stress. *Journal of Management Info, 5*(3), 12–15. doi:10.31580/jmi.v5i3.123

Salmivalli, C., & Poskiparta, E. (2012). *Making bullying prevention a priority in Finnish schools: The KiVa anti-bullying program.* https://doi.org/ doi:10.1002/yd

Saunders, P., Huynh, A., & Goodman-Delahunty, J. (2007). Defining workplace bullying behavior, professionals lay definitions of workplace bullying. *International Journal of Law and Psychiatry, 30*(4–5), 340–354. doi:10.1016/j.ijlp.2007.06.007 PMID:17692375

Scandinavian, S. (2016). Workplace bullying and sickness absence : a systematic review and meta-analysis of the research literature. *Scandinavian Journal of Work, Environment & Heal, 42.*

Schulte, P. A., Guerin, R. J., Schill, A. L., Bhattacharya, A., Cunningham, T. R., Pandalai, S. P., Eggerth, D., & Stephenson, C. M. (2015). Considerations for incorporating "well-being" in public policy for workers and workplaces. *American Journal of Public Health, 105*(8), e31–e44. doi:10.2105/AJPH.2015.302616 PMID:26066933

Sherer, Y. C., & Nickerson, A. B. (2010). *Anti-bullying practices in American schools: perspectives of school psychologists.* https://doi.org/ doi:10.1002/pits

Sherrow, H. M., & Ph.D. (2014). *The Origins of Bullying.* Academic Press.

Short, R., Case, G., & McKenzie, K. (2018). The long-term impact of a whole school approach of restorative practice: The views of secondary school teachers. *Pastoral Care in Education, 36*(4), 313–324. doi:10.1080/02643944.2018.1528625

Sloan, L., Matyók, T., Schmitz, C., & Short, G. (2010). A story to tell: Bullying and mobbing in the workplace. *International Journal of Business and Social Science, 1*(3), 87–98.

Smith, P. K., & Brain, P. (2000). *Bullying in Schools : Lessons From Two Decades of Research.* Academic Press.

Smith, P. K., Smith, C., & Osborn, R. (2008). *Educational Psychology in Practice : Theory, research, and Practice in Educational Psychology A content analysis of school anti-bullying policies : Progress and limitations.* doi:10.1080/02667360701661165

Sokol, N., Bussey, K., & Rapee, R. M. (2016). Teachers' perspectives on effective responses to overt bullying. *British Educational Research Journal, 42*(5), 851–870. doi:10.1002/berj.3237

Swearer, S. M., Espelage, D. L., Vaillancourt, T., Hymel, S., Swearer, S. M., Espelage, D. L., Vaillancourt, T., & Hymel, S. (2010). What Can Be Done About School Bullying? *Educational Researcher, 39*(1), 38–47. Advance online publication. doi:10.3102/0013189X09357622

Ttofi, M. M., & Farrington, D. P. (2011). *Effectiveness of school-based programs to reduce bullying : a systematic and meta-analytic review.* doi:10.1007/s11292-010-9109-1

Vossekuil, Fein, Reddy, & Borum. (2002). *The Final Report And Findings Of The Safe School Initiative : Implications For The Prevention Of School Attacks In Of The Safe School Initiative.* https://static1. squarespace.com/static/55674542e4b074aad07152ba/t/5733a5f8c2ea51ad0fa1f82a/1463002617464/ssi_final_report.pdf

Waasdorp, T. E., Fu, R., Perepezko, A. L., Bradshaw, C. P., Evian, T., Fu, R., Perepezko, A. L., & Bradshaw, C. P. (2021). The role of bullying-related policies : Understanding how school staff respond to bullying situations The role of bullying-related policies . *European Journal of Developmental Psychology, 00*(00), 1–16. doi:10.1080/17405629.2021.1889503 PMID:34899942

Younan, B., & Younan, B. (2018). *A systematic review of bullying definitions : how definition and format affect study outcome.* doi:10.1108/JACPR-02-2018-0347

Zych, I. (2021). *Childhood Risk and Protective Factors as Predictors of Adolescent Bullying Roles.* Academic Press.

KEY TERMS AND DEFINITIONS

Anti-Bullying Strategy: An anti-bullying strategy refers to a planned and systematic approach aimed at preventing and addressing bullying behaviors.

Bully: A bully repeatedly and intentionally hurts, threatens, or frightens another person.

Bullying: Bullying is a form of aggressive behavior that involves the repeated use of power or force, either physically, verbally, or emotionally, to intimidate, harm, or dominate another person who is perceived as vulnerable.

Coping Strategy: Coping strategies are individuals' techniques or behaviors to manage and deal with challenging or stressful situations.

Parent-Community Involvement: Parent-community involvement refers to the active participation and collaboration between parents and the broader community in supporting and promoting the well-being and education of children.

Positive Behavior: Positive behavior refers to actions, and attitudes considered beneficial, respect-ful, and constructive. It involves behaving in a way that promotes kindness, cooperation, and empathy toward others.

Workplace Bullying in Primary Education: It refers to the persistent mistreatment or harassment of teachers or staff members by their colleagues or superiors within the school environment.

Chapter 7
Teaching Education in Values Through Games in Primary Education

Isabel María García
ⓘ https://orcid.org/0000-0001-7005-2509
Centro Universitario de la Defensa de San Javier, Spain

ABSTRACT

Education in values is an issue of great relevance in today's society. That is why the chapter focuses on highlighting several points. The subject of values has been, is, and will always be a fundamental, transcendent, and a permanently topical issue in education. Values are constantly present in our lives and that is why we must emphasize the work and empowerment of these, inside and outside the classroom and in any subject, in a playful and motivating way for our children, that is, using the activity that is present in all human beings, the game. Therefore, the main objective of this chapter will be to know the relevance of games, not only for recreational purposes, but also for learning, and to highlight the need to work on education in values for the personal development of children.

INTRODUCTION

The primary aim of school education, fundamentally in its compulsory stages of Primary and Secondary Education, is to contribute to the development of pupils of those skills considered necessary for them to develop as citizens with full rights and duties in the society in which they live. Values have been, are, and always will be a fundamental, transcendent, and topical issue in education (Aktepe & Yel, 2019). For this reason, we want to address the subject and show that values can be taught in any area, at any time, and almost in any place.

We usually deal with education in values in tutoring hours or the subject "Education for Citizenship." However, we must bear in mind that values are constantly present in our lives, in each of our actions, and that is why we must emphasize the work and promotion of these values, inside and outside the

DOI: 10.4018/978-1-6684-9295-6.ch007

classroom and in any subject, in a playful and motivating way for our children, that is, using the activity that is present in all human beings, play (Escámez et al., 2017). There is not much recent research on the advantages of play in the development of children. However, we know that from birth, within the family environment, play is something they actively develop, and it causes them pleasure. Besides, games can promote countless values of interest to the education of the youngest children from Early Childhood to Primary Education. For the sake of clarity, throughout the chapter, we will use interchangeably the terms "play" and "game" since both are synonyms.

Based on a theoretical foundation, "Education in Values" is the process that helps people construct their values rationally and autonomously (Cortina, 2020). In other words, to provide human beings with the cognitive and affective mechanisms that help them to live together with the fairness and necessary understanding to integrate as social individuals and as unique persons in the world around us.

Nevertheless, why does this need to educate in values? The school emphasizes the continuous cultural, social, and educational changes that affect the development of students. The current crisis of values, the increase in violence, social changes, and technological changes demand educational systems that promote the person's integral development in all areas. And this requires rethinking the work of teachers, analyzing, and reflecting on what is for and not so much on what and how. Education in values responds to these demands by promoting the training of future critical, responsible, autonomous, and democratic citizens (Benitez Grande, 2021).

In order to achieve these approaches, we find in the "Democratic School" the reference framework, whose main principles are based on the objective that we intend to achieve with this research: to promote, not only in the students but also in the entire educational community, the participation of all the agents involved in the different learning communities. According to Louis (2023), one commonality shared by the educational systems in all countries is heated discussions about democratic values and education.

This diversity of culture, age, gender, ethnic origin, socio-economic class, abilities, etc., must be seen from a positive point of view rather than a negative one and in which values such as respect, solidarity, cooperation, collaboration, and equal opportunities, both in terms of access and educational success, are worked on (Parra, 2018). The commitment of this type of school is based on ensuring that there are no individual, group, or social differences, making the most of its organizational and curricular possibilities so that there are no difficulties in accessing the culture offered by the compulsory curriculum.

From another point of view, it is also essential to consider the "School Coexistence Plan," which must be drawn up in all public educational centers, as it considers the characteristics and circumstances of both the center and its pupils. Promoting a positive climate in the school environment for students is the daily task of the teacher. However, giving a voice to families and students in order to encourage participation, debate, and reflection, and work with them on various aspects such as the culture of peace, mediation, and conflict resolution is a profound step forward in the complicated task of educating in values according to Díaz Torres & Rodríguez Gómez (2018).

Also related to this chapter is the subject "Education for Citizenship" in Primary Education, which aims to work on pupils' autonomy, critical spirit, self-esteem, desire to excel, and dialogue... through 3 different blocks of content that develop values related to the individual and interpersonal and social relations, community life and living in society. Remember that "Education for Citizenship" aims to develop the knowledge, skills, and understanding students need to participate in society as active and responsible citizens fully.

The main objectives we seek to foster with the chapter are the following: to know the meaning and importance of values in our society; to know the relevance of play, both for children and adults, not only for recreational purposes but also for learning; to highlight the need to work on Education in Values for personal development in order to integrate the children into the society in which they live; and to provide educational practices through play, including the Education in Values.

THEORETICAL FRAMEWORK

The Concept of the Term "Values"

Values are words. Unfortunately, entirely too often, they are just that. However, there is no doubt that the words identified as values have an extraordinary power to give meaning and direction to human endeavors, as Ortega and Mínguez pointed out (2019).

The term "axiology" refers to the study of these potent words, called values, and comes from the Greek "Axios," meaning that which is valuable, estimable, or worthy of honor. The term "value" is related to a person's existence, affecting his or her behavior, shaping and modeling his or her ideas, and conditioning his or her feelings. It is something changing and dynamic, which we have chosen freely among various alternatives. It depends, to a large extent, on what has been internalized throughout the socialization process. According to Panev (2020), the acquisition of primary values in young people increases the possibility for the favorable development of other values and forming of a complete personality.

In a first attempt to define "value," Camps et al. (2018, p. 45) would define it as: "The reasoned conviction that something is good or bad in order to become more human." Consequently, we would understand counter-value as everything that would make it difficult for a man to become more of a person and detract him from his humanity. Therefore, the person - as a social being - adds value to the natural condition of things. Things are what they are, but they have value according to the value attributed to them. In general, the value of a thing (be it an object, a situation, or a behavior) is what makes it wanted or sought after. A thing is valuable when it possesses specific qualities that we consider essential (Sahin, 2019).

According to Lovat and Clement (2018), there are specific characteristics that define values:

- Values are transcendent: they are not in objects or among facts; they are not properties like, for example, color or weight. They are added to facts from the outside; hence, we say they transcend them.
- They are mental, i.e., non-material, appreciations. Values exist differently from the way objects and facts of the world exist. Goodness or beauty cannot be touched, but we can consider that they exist.
- Values are both individual and collective. They are individual in that a subject always internalizes them; they become part of a person's way of being. However, they are collective because a community of individuals shares values.
- Values are social-historical, i.e., they are attributed to a particular time and in a particular society. The individual who values cannot disregard the conditioning factors that have marked his or her life at a given time. For example, the events of war and the experiences of that war influence the values and the way of valuing a whole generation.

For Buxarrais & Martínez Martín (2019), values are organized in a hierarchy. According to these authors, some of the criteria that determine the position of a given value are:

- Durability: Durable goods are preferred to ephemeral or changeable ones.
- Greater or lesser divisibility: Higher values are broad and indivisible; lower values can be easily diluted and satisfied in several concrete interests. Higher values, such as justice, freedom, and beauty, unite people, while material values, such as money or success, separate people because they create conflicts.
- Foundation: Many personal values are based on supreme ideals from the religious sphere, from tradition.
- Depth of satisfaction in fulfilling them: The intensity of the experience of values is also a factor that can influence the hierarchical position given to each person.

Generally, the values held by an individual or a whole community are organized hierarchically; they form an ordered set, often called a scale of values. Thanks to these scales or tables, our attitudes have a certain coherence. Thus, an individual's intellectual and sentimental personality, which influences all his actions, depends on the composition and internal organization of the scale of values he possesses (Thornberg, 2018).

Values can be defined as those things that someone values. In other words, values are considered 'important' by an individual or an organization. Examples include courage, honesty, freedom, innovation, Etc. According to Oyserman, values are internalized cognitive structures that guide choices by evoking a sense of basic principles of right and wrong, a sense of priorities, and a willingness to make meaning and see patterns. Like other cognitive constructs, values can be studied at the individual level or the group level. That is societies, cultures, and other social groups have value-based norms, priorities, and guidelines, which describe what people ought to do if they are to do the 'right,' 'moral,' and 'valued' thing.

Educative Regulations and Implications

In the latest Spanish educative regulation, Organic Law (3/2020 of 29 December, LOMLOE) on Education, we find numerous references to Education in Values in different aspects regulated in Early Childhood and Primary education. Concerning the principles of education, the following elements occupy a relevant place:

- The transmission of those values that favor personal freedom, responsibility, democratic citizenship, solidarity, tolerance, equality, respect, and justice, constitute the basis of life in common.
- The need to include citizenship education in the curriculum. Its purpose is to offer all students a space for reflection, analysis, and study of the fundamental characteristics and functioning of a democratic regime, of the principles and rights established in the Spanish Constitution and in universal human rights treaties and declarations, as well as of the shared values that constitute the substratum of democratic citizenship in a global context.

In developing this new educative law, we find teachers' aims, objectives, and functions in relation to education in values. For example, Article 2 references the achievement of aims for transmitting and implementing values and training for peace, respect, social cohesion, cooperation, and solidarity among peoples, as well as respect for living beings and the environment.

On the other hand, Article 17 lists the objectives of Primary Education about this education in values:

- To know and appreciate the values and rules of coexistence, to learn to act by them, to prepare for the active exercise of citizenship, and to respect human rights.
- To develop habits of individual and teamwork, effort, and responsibility in study, as well as attitudes of self-confidence, critical sense, personal initiative, curiosity, interest, and creativity in learning.
- To acquire skills for preventing and peacefully resolving conflicts, enabling them to function independently in the family environment and in the social groups with which they interact.
- To know, understand and respect different cultures and the differences between people, equal rights and opportunities for men and women, and non-discrimination of people with disabilities.

Education in values seems to be the essential response to democratic and non-denominational education. Educational activity is not a neutral activity. We must assume that there is no such thing as instruction as such, but that education takes place at school. In other words, any educational intention, however "aseptic" it may be, is always intentional and must be based on an ethical conception. Teacher education must provide the knowledge and skills necessary for integration and influence attitudes and beliefs. More research needs to be conducted on how knowledge, beliefs, and attitudes predict teachers' intentions (Luik & Taimalu, 2021).

Values give meaning to education. We must ask ourselves what people we want to educate so that they can face the reality of today's world and its problems. Depending on the person we want, we will work for a school that builds people who reproduce the current society and its values or one that forms critical people capable of transforming society into a fairer and more caring society, according to Brown et al. (2016).

The school community must be democratic and participatory, where commitment is individual and collective and where projects, rights, and duties of coexistence are negotiated cooperatively. Mosley & Baltazar (2019) use the metaphor of "fried snow" to argue why it is impossible to build a true school democracy from the old paradigm of the traditional hierarchical, rational, technological, and heteronomous school.

This school model is riddled with contradictions between what is "said" and what is "done" in schools. Building a genuinely democratic school would be possible if the institutional, curricular, teacher training and school management dimensions were challenged. According to Inglehart (2016), this type of school is characterized by certain aspects:

1. Equality of opportunities: of access and success.
2. Flexible organization of the curriculum.
3. Compensation of inequalities.
4. Participation in decision-making.

Everyone directly involved in the school (school committees, councils, professional educators, young people, their parents, and other school community members) has a participatory right to the decision-making process. In classrooms, students and teachers collaborate in planning and reaching decisions that respond to the concerns, aspirations, and interests of both.

Value education aims at transforming a mind into a healthy, innocent, natural, and attentive one capable of higher levels of sensitivity and perception. It develops moral, spiritual, aesthetic, and social values in a person. It teaches us to preserve whatever is good and worthwhile in the culture we inherited. It helps us accept and respect the attitudes and behaviors of those who differ from us (Surendranath & Lavanya, 2021).

They emphasize cooperation and collaboration rather than competition and structural equity in which all young people have the right to access school programs and outcomes that the school values. Therefore, those working in democratic schools try to ensure that the school does not include institutional barriers, thus improving the climate and increasing students' self-esteem. Suppose we want to turn our students into moral human beings. In that case, the school curriculum is one of the best ways to serve this purpose because moral values can be inculcated among our students through a value-based school curriculum (Aneja, 2021).

A planned and open democratic curriculum emphasizes access to a wide range of information and the right of those with different opinions to have their views heard. Educators must help young people to seek out diverse ideas and to express their views. This curriculum teaches students to be "critical interpreters" of their society (Ritchie, 2018). In this way, they help students acquire knowledge and skills in many different aspects.

In this sense, the teacher must educate on different terms, not socialize or instruct. This is not only achieved by carrying out a democratic school but also by living values inside and outside the classroom, with plans, programs, or areas that promote such education, such as the Coexistence Plan. This plan seeks to collect and specify the values, objectives, and priorities of action of the educational project that orient and guide the coexistence of the center, as well as the actions planned to achieve the objectives, considering the characteristics and circumstances of the center and the educational community to educate for coexistence.

Although teachers usually prefer positive interventions over punishment to manage classroom behavior, many classrooms are not positive learning environments (Banks, 2018). Therefore, the teaching staff will promote a positive classroom climate in which the participation of students is encouraged and positive relationships are established between students and teachers, dealing with aspects such as the following:

- Culture of peace.
- Democratic participation.
- Effective equality between men and women.
- Mediation and peaceful conflict resolution.

For the development of this plan, as in all aspects of education, it is essential to count on the participation and collaboration of families. The school must establish practical information tools and strategies for all aspects of its functioning and organization (Hurtado et al., 2018). For this reason, the teaching staff will provide information about the rules of coexistence, the activities that promote a favorable climate, and the resources to regulate this climate.

A supportive and equitable environment in all classrooms serves as a platform for all academic, social, and emotional learning. At the core of a supportive classroom is a caring, engaging teacher who establishes authentic, trusting relationships with each student. Around this issue, in 5th Primary, the area of "Education for Citizenship and Human Rights" will be dealt with, as it is set out in Royal Decree 157/2022, whose task will be based on educating in democracy in a shared way, without excluding families, public institutions, educational centers and society itself.

This subject will be divided into three content blocks related to developing outstanding aspects of several competencies. However, it is directly related to social and citizenship competence, promoting social skills to live in society, encouraging respect, tolerance, solidarity, justice, equality, mutual help, and cooperation, and proposing the knowledge of rules and principles of coexistence established by the Constitution. Furthermore, it develops in students the construction of dignified and integral persons, reinforcing their autonomy, their self-esteem, and their desire for self-improvement, favoring a critical spirit, and improving interpersonal relations through dialogue.

We must bear in mind that values are constantly transmitted, consciously or unconsciously, in all the activities (tone of voice, games we propose, programmed activities we carry out, at lunchtime, Etc.) that are proposed to the pupils or in the relationship with them. It is essential to establish some fundamental values for life, agreed upon based on the legitimacy of participation in the development of educational goals, as well as from the Regulations of Organisation and Operation of the center, which is included in the Universal Declaration of Human Rights and the Spanish Constitution: freedom, justice, equality, respect, solidarity, responsibility, commitment, tolerance, peace, participation-cooperation, honesty, health. To these values considered minimum and essential, each educational community may add those necessary to respond to the problems detected and prioritized in the center.

We understand that inevitably one value leads to another, that many necessarily encompass others, and that they all begin to include each other. There are some that appear to be higher in the hierarchy than others and underlie the possibility of developing the rest of them. These values must be pointed out and taught first (Haydon, 2021).

- Liberty: that natural faculty possessed by human beings of being able to act according to their own will. It began to be linked to other faculties, such as justice and equality. It includes reflecting on what we do with our freedom, what it is for and how to protect it, and knowing the limits.
- Justice: What should be done according to what is reasonable, equitable, or indicated by law. It knows what is fair or not. Justice depends on a society's values and each person's individual beliefs.
- Equality: Social equality to the context or situation where people have the same rights and opportunities in a particular aspect or at a general level.
- Respect: enables us to recognize, accept, appreciate, and value the qualities of others and their rights. In other words, recognition of one's worth and the rights of individuals and society. Respect is closely related to tolerance and equality. Besides, it also encourages respect for the environment in ecological terms.
- Solidarity: helping someone without receiving anything in return and without anyone knowing about it. This value goes hand in hand with generosity and empathy, indispensable pillars of coexistence. Realizing that the other person is as important as I am, respect, nobility, responsibility, love, sensitivity, and compassion are integrated, to give some examples.

- Responsibility: A person characterized by responsibility has the virtue not only of making a series of decisions consciously but also of assuming the consequences of these decisions and of being accountable to whoever is responsible for them at any given moment. An element that must be present and without which it is impossible to speak of responsibility is that of freedom.
- Commitment: This implies being consistent with one's convictions, exercising one's conduct, and collaborating with oneself and the environment.
- Tolerance: respect for the thoughts and actions of others when they are opposed to or different from one's own. It also implies another value, such as respect.
- Peace is not understood as the absence of conflict, since it is permanent in daily differences, but as an attitude to analyze and resolve them. Peace as a social value achieves the fruits of balance, justice, and equality.
- Participation-cooperation: Involvement of people to achieve achievements and benefits in the educational or social sphere. No one wants to win individually but to benefit as a whole society.
- Honesty: Consists of behaving and expressing oneself with sincerity and coherence, respecting the values of justice and truth.
- Health: The state in which a person usually exercises his or her functions. A good state of health conditions the quality of life. A person needs to feed himself, educate, work, share with friends and family, participate in community life, and enjoy the landscape.

In this way, many more virtues are awakened to be taught, strengthening and building a way of being. Thus, in the integration of more values, which emerge almost naturally, we find patience, joy, kindness, gratitude, optimism, simplicity, forgiveness, understanding, faith, hope, sensitivity, trust, sacrifice, self-improvement, loyalty, altruism, order, wisdom and an almost endless list of values and virtues wholly intertwined with each other. Each one of them deserves and needs to be taught (with definitions and examples), individually understood, and integrated to be transmitted to the way of living together in the classroom and the school in general (Albizuri et al., 2018).

O play a game is to engage in activity directed toward bringing about a specific state of affairs, using only means permitted by specific rules, where the means permitted by the rules are more limited in scope than they would be in the absence of the rules, and where the sole reason for accepting such limitation is to make possible such activity o play a game is to engage in activity directed toward bringing about a specific state of affairs, using only means permitted by specific rules, where the means permitted by the rules are more limited in scope than they would be in the absence of the rules, and where the sole reason for accepting such limitation is to make possible such activity o play a game is to engage in activity directed toward bringing about a specific state of affairs, using only means permitted by specific rules, where the means permitted by the rules are more limited in scope than they would be in the absence of the rules, and where the sole reason for accepting such limitation is to make possible such activity o play a game is to engage in activity directed toward bringing about a specific state of affairs, using only means permitted by specific rules, where the means permitted by the rules are more limited in scope than they would be in the absence of the rules, and where the sole reason for accepting such limitation is to make possible such activity.

The Importance of Games in the Teaching-Learning Process

One exemplary definition of a game is the one Arjoranta offers (2019). She affirmed that to play a game is to engage in an activity directed toward bringing about a specific situation, using only means permitted by specific rules, where the means permitted by the rules are more limited in scope than they would be in the absence of the rules, and where the sole reason for accepting such limitation is to make possible such activity.

Most authors place the origin of games in animal play, which evolved in man towards a superior integrated structure. Many theories have been formulated in order to try to explain why man plays. A new approach to learning in the form of educational games has been adopted in recent years, especially in English language teaching. The educational game-learning approach used to teach English to non-native English speakers who use English as a second or foreign language has recorded tremendous success (Adipat et al., 2021).

According to Gozcu & Caganaga (2021), the paths of observation and research can be divided into two main lines:

a) Efficient cause theory: They try to search for and analyze the causes that determine play activity in children. The aim is to find out why the child plays. Among them, we highlight:
    ◦   Rest or recreation: activity in which it is not a question of satisfying purely human needs. Play is regarded as a distraction, an element of recreation, and pleasurable relaxation, utilizing a compensatory activity instead of work. Play serves as a recreation and rest for adults but does not explain children's play since life is often a continuous game for them.
    ◦   Superfluous energy: Play aims to release surplus energies not expended during utilitarian practices. Play is a simulation, a parody of serious life in which surplus energy is used.
    ◦   Recapitulation or atavism: Play serves as a stimulus and a means to achieve development and reach higher stages.
    ◦   Cathartic: Playful activities channel human activities and are the means to release tensions and frustrations. Anti-social tendencies are sublimated and discharged through play. Most authors state that the cathartic function does not manifest itself in children.
b) Theories of final cause: They try to explain the purpose that the human being pursues when carrying out a playful activity:
    ◦   Preparatory exercise considers play a preparatory exercise for adult life and an instrument of natural self-affirmation of the child. Through the activities played, the child rehearses and develops skills and serves as a mechanism for stimulating development and learning.
    ◦   Evasion: Through play, dreams or desires that cannot be achieved in real life can be realized. When children play, they experience the roles they assume as their own, not differentiating between fiction and reality. It is modeled on symbolic play (imitation play, the ability to symbolize to create mental representations that will be useful to teach the child how to cope in his future life).

There are other theories, but they need to be sufficiently accurate to cover the broad spectrum of play. Play does not obey a unique but differentiated behavior but with common aspects that make the reality of play significant for a man at all stages of his life (Dichev & Dicheva, 2017). Play is an activity present in all human beings. It is usually associated with childhood, but the truth is that it manifests itself throughout man's life, even into old age. It is commonly identified with fun, satisfaction, and leisure. However, its transcendence is much greater since, through play, values and rules of conduct are transmitted, conflicts are resolved, and many facets of the personality are developed (Grace, 2019).

There are many authors, such as Kucher (2021), Syafii et al. (2021), and Yolageldili & Arikan (2021), who, from different points of view, have considered play as an essential factor that enhances both the physical and psychological development of human beings. The child's development is fully linked to play because it is a natural and spontaneous activity to which the child devotes as much time as possible. It also develops his personality and social skills, his intellectual and motor skills. It provides him with experiences that teach him to live in society, to know his possibilities and limitations, and to grow and mature. A child's abilities develop more effectively in play than outside of it. They will discover the pleasure of doing things and being with others. It is one of the most important means of expressing feelings, interests, and hobbies. It is linked to creativity, problem-solving, language development, or social roles.

According to Kula (2021), the play has a clear educational function. She proved that teachers usually play mind games with students in the Free Activities course, mainly for 2 hours per week, strategy games were played most, memory games were the least played games, and mind games contributed to communication, creativity, problem-solving, mathematical and logical thinking, and academic skills. In addition, classroom teachers experienced some problems related to classroom management, physical conditions, and student characteristics while playing mind games. Some standard features that can be observed are the following:

- Play is a process, not necessarily with an outcome but capable of having one if the participant wishes.
- Play is necessary for both children and adults.
- Play is not the antithesis of work: both are part of the totality of our lives.
- Play is always structured by the environment, materials, or contexts in which it occurs.
- Exploration is a preliminary step to more challenging forms of play, which, in the school environment, are likely to be teacher-directed.
- Appropriately directed play ensures that children learn from their current knowledge and skills.
- Parents have a right to expect play in schools to be organized meaningfully and differently from that practiced at home and elsewhere. If they can see that this is the case, they are more likely to attach value and importance to it.
- Play is an excellent medium for learning.

These characteristics require teachers to be mediators of play, making it a constructive activity essential to the holistic growth of our students. This idea encompasses changing the teacher's profile from an instructor to a guide/ tutor. For this reason, play is a good strategy for the new challenges teachers face today. According to Trasobares & Valdivieso (2019), teachers must intervene in the game from three different perspectives:

- According to the moment when the play takes place.
- According to the type of play that children develop.
- According to the structure of the play activity.

Strategies are needed to encourage play in the educational stage and to facilitate the acquisition of meaningful and functional learning. According to Sáez López et al. (2019), they are the following:

a) They are preparing the right environment for children to play (having a space suitable for play, dedicating specific time for play, and selecting and maintaining materials in good conditions).
b) State the basic rules of play.
c) Witness children's play.
d) Teach traditional games.
e) Help to resolve conflicts that arise during play. In other words, the aim is also to teach the children how to resolve conflicts by teaching them to reach agreements, negotiate, or share.
f) Respect the play preferences of each child.
g) Encourage families to take an interest in play.
h) Observe children's play. Through this observation, the educator can follow the evolution of the children, their new acquisitions, their relationships with their peers, adults, behavior, Etc.

According to Grace (2019), games have certain advantages concerning social and emotional development, among others. Her book provides a contemporary foundation for designing social-impact games. It is structured in 3 parts: understanding, application, and implementation. The book serves as a guide to designing social impact games, mainly focused on the needs of media professionals, indie game designers, and college students. It serves as a guide for people looking to create social impact play, informed by heuristics in game design. It also improves certain aspects that are worth mentioning, as we can see in the following table:

Table 1.

Social development	symbolic games: processes of cooperation and communication with others; knowledge of the adult world; preoccupation with working life. Cooperative games: favor communication and self-confidence; decrease aggressive and passive behavior.
Emotional development	produces emotional satisfaction; controls anxiety; controls symbolic expression of aggression; facilitates conflict resolution

Source: Own elaboration

Types of Games Related to Education in Values

They are usually classified according to their contents or the number of participants, individual, collective, or social games. The different typologies proposed to describe games depend significantly on the theoretical framework from which they are studied. This paper will focus on the classification proposed by Dimitra et al. (2020), who established a standard sequence for developing play behaviors following a hierarchical order. Their report aims to identify the main types, benefits, and drawbacks of game-based learning approaches in education and also to explore their implementation:

- Exercise games (0-2 years): During the first months, children repeat all kinds of movements and gestures for pure pleasure, consolidating what has been acquired. These are simple exercises such as releasing and retrieving a dummy, shaking a noisy object, opening and closing a door, Etc. They act with natural objects for the pleasure of getting immediate results.
- Symbolic games: representation of one object by another. The language will help in this representation. Objects are transformed to symbolize others that are not present (fictional games); for instance, a wooden bucket can become a lorry. They simulate imagined events by acting out scenes through fictional or real roles or characters. At the end of this stage (4-7 years), symbolism gradually loses ground in favor of more socialized fantasy games, bringing the child closer to accepting social rules.
- Construction or assembly games: These mark an intermediate position between the levels of play and adapted behavior. If a piece of wood was used to represent a lorry, now it can be used to build it through the magic of playful forms, combining several elements to make a whole.
- Games with rules: Their beginning depends on the environment in which the child moves. They tend to occur mainly between 7 and 11 years of age. These games continue and can develop in adolescents and adults, taking on a more elaborate form (chess, cards, strategy games, draughts). They develop social action strategies, learn to control aggressiveness, and exercise responsibility and democracy; the rules also force them to trust the group and cooperate with themselves.

The game, which contributed to the acquisition of vital skills in the history of humanity, is gaining an increasingly important role in modern information society. Moreover, Wiselia et al. (2019) point out that modern humanity assumed his life to be a role-playing game in which participation does not require any responsibility and shall deliver only pleasure.

Zheng (2017), based on the analysis of more than 60 definitions, identifies several key characteristics of the game: rules, purpose and function, artifact, or activity, separate yet connected, role of the player, (un)productive, competition and conflict, goals and end conditions. Nevertheless, the issue of the effectiveness of using games in education remains open. The broadest study on the effectiveness of games diagnoses that the most frequently occurring outcomes were knowledge acquisition/content understanding and affective and motivational outcomes (Bylieva & Sastre, 2018).

Game-based learning incorporates game characteristics and principles into learning activities. Learning activities inspire student engagement and enthusiasm to learn. Points systems, badges, leaderboards, discussion boards, quizzes, and classroom response systems are all components of game-based learning. There are many benefits of game-based learning in helping children's cognitive development. One of its most significant benefits is the development of active learning among children.

The games can be easily modified based on the preferred instructional plans. Several games have student-monitoring tools attached to them. These tools are highly beneficial, as they allow the instructors to monitor the student's performance and promptly make the desired changes. Karakoc et al. (2022) distinguish the following types of games.

1. Real-Life Games: Real-life games, based on real scenarios, have proven to be highly motivating but can also cause stress in some situations. Children are required to make body movements and use their brains. These games engage learners in almost every aspect of their education.

2. Game-Based Learning In A Hybrid Space: Hybrid learning spaces can be filled with various resources. You can use digital resources in various ways, such as multimedia games and physical spaces as creative spaces to engage with the resources.
3. Board Games. "Monopoly" can be thought of as an educational game. It contains all the necessary elements, including a story, characters, points, competition, and many other features.

Game-based learning is a great way to improve young learners' creativity, critical thinking, and problem-solving skills. It is based on the use of imagination. Instructors can give students the freedom to develop solutions and ideas that boost their creativity.

ANALYSIS OF RESULTS

Including values education through games in the teaching-learning process in tutorial-teaching practice is not only possible but desirable. By way of example, we intend to show how the development of these four games promotes education in values, but, in addition, they respond to the objectives prescribed in the curriculum, responding to different competencies as well as to the objectives determined in the different school plans.

We have chosen four games to broaden the range of action and the target groups (diversity of ages, objectives, plans, and spaces), setting out in each one the objectives to be achieved. The materials to be used to develop these games will be the following:

*   Ideas and activities in the family: Infant and Primary Education. Responsible education.
*   Traditional trivia board.
*   Cardboard
*   Paintings
*   Computers

Game 1: "Let Us Go Shopping" (4th Grade of Primary Education)

Students will work in groups. Each team, guided by the teacher, will shop online in different supermarkets. This game aims to solve a real problem and implement values such as responsibility, cooperation, eating habits, and respect for their classmates. In addition to the area of mathematics, they will work around environmental knowledge and language, promoting in all of them the various basic skills: mathematical competence; competence in learning to learn; competence in linguistic communication; competence in knowledge and interaction with the physical world; social and citizenship competence; cultural and artistic competence; autonomy and personal initiative competence; information processing and digital competence. Once each purchase has been calculated, they will share the difference in prices between one establishment and another, and they will see how it is possible to save depending on the food they buy and the brands of each one.

Numbers And Operations

*   Perform operations with whole numbers and decimals to solve an actual situation: How much will it cost to buy something?

- Use of mental calculation strategies and standard algorithms.
- Approximation of the final price in euros.

Measurement: Magnitudes

- Know the magnitudes with which different foods are measured: kg, g, l, ml, Etc.
- Differentiate one magnitude from another and know which measures they belong to: length, mass, and capacity.

Geometry

- Each student must bring a food item to differentiate geometric bodies by the shape of the food (for instance, a soda can, cylindrical shape).
- Work in groups on making food with different geometric shapes to build a small supermarket and simulate different situations.

Information processing, chance, and probability.

- Making a table (with Microsoft Word or Excel) dividing food according to the food pyramid studied around Knowledge of the Environment.
- Drawing up a graph according to the number of pupils who eat one food or another. We will comment on this graph in class, and a small debate will be facilitated.

Game 2: "To Live Together Is to Live" (5ᵗʰ Grade of Primary Education)

This game aims to work on self-concept and values related to coexistence and friendship: solidarity, respect, tolerance, cooperation, equality, and honesty. It will begin individually, where each child must describe him/herself in writing to later carry out a dynamic of getting to know each other, commenting to his/her classmates how he/she thinks he/she behaves with his/her peers. Once this round of presentation has been completed, as a group, they will invent a story according to the values assigned by the teacher, the theme of which will continue to deal with "friendship." This will encourage reading, and they will be able to go to other classrooms in lower grades to tell their compositions and show the other children in the school that respect for others and companionship is a fundamental basis for positive coexistence, both in the school classroom and in society. We will mainly work on linguistic communication and social and civic competencies.

Listening, Speaking, And Conversing

- Oral presentation of descriptions of oneself in order to show their classmates how they are with others.
- Please participate in the story-telling activity in lower classrooms, representing the compositions they have made.
- Respect each pupil's turn to speak in their presentation and in the debate that will take place on the importance of positive coexistence in school/classroom/society.

Literary Education

- Composition of a story, in groups of 4-5 pupils, following guidelines given by the teacher.
- Reading of the stories composed about friendship, where they deal with values related to solidarity, tolerance, and honesty.

Knowledge Of The Language
They must locate both the descriptions and the stories:

- Common and proper nouns.
- Adjectives.
- Structure of narrative and descriptive texts.
- Application of spelling rules in the correction of texts.

Reading Competence

- Use of reading strategies for good representation and presentation to classmates.
- Use of ICT to upload different compositions to the school blog.
- Use the library to look for other stories related to those already written.

Game 3: "The Goose of Emotions" (1st Cycle of Primary Education)

It consists of expressing joy, fear, anger, sadness, disgust, or surprise, using the goose game as an excuse. The game follows the same rules as the traditional game. The only difference is that when we fall into a goose, instead of the classic "I shoot because it is my turn," the shot will only be repeated if the person who has fallen into the goose expresses with his or her body and face the emotion that another participant will propose. The rest of the game will be the same. It is also goose oriented to the Nansa Valley so that they work on their competence in knowledge and interaction with the physical world while developing mathematical competence. The game also aims to develop social and citizenship skills and linguistic communication skills. We will work on this game concerning the plans that are immersed in each center, in this case, related to the Reading Plan, the Diversity Attention Plan, the Tutorial Action Plan, and the Coexistence Plan, from which many values of great relevance are derived such as solidarity, cooperation, respect, equality, responsibility, empathy, Etc.

Reading Plan

- By reading the instructions of the game, they will be able to promote the development of the reading habit, improving reading skills so that, playfully, it becomes a priority element both in schools and families.

Plan Of Attention To Diversity

- With this game, we can promote the creation of a suitable space for all students, regardless of their country or disability, considering the needs of each one.

Coexistence Plan

- Strategies will be developed in the game to resolve possible conflicts, thus promoting the achievement of non-violence in the family, social and personal spheres. The teacher will foster a positive atmosphere among peers, creating a coexistence of respect, dialogue, collaboration, cooperation, and freedom, making it compatible with compliance with the rules of the center-classroom playground.

Tutorial Action Plan

- Favors the reception and integration of pupils, promoting personal and emotional development and improving relations between peers. Furthermore, it is a game that can incorporate families into the educational community. In this way, they will work with their children on emotions and skills of great importance for developing the teaching-learning process. On the other hand, learning strategies are integrated and strengthened.

Game 4: "Class Trivia" (Any Grade of Primary Education)

This game will be played in pairs or small groups (3-4 people). The teacher-tutor will create a series of questions related to 4 blocks: Mathematics, Spanish language, and literature, knowledge of the natural and social environment and general culture about things dealt with in class related to different cultures and ethnic groups from which other classmates come from, as well as problems that have to do with real life so that they can look for the most appropriate solution. Each question will have three answer options, only one of which will be correct. They will be able to create their board or use the same one used in the traditional game, where the younger ones will earn "congratulations" and "positives" in the marks for the older ones for each question they get right. They will have to learn to respect the turn of the game and the rules (the teacher will hand them out on a piece of paper for each group or student) and learn that it is not a playful activity to compete but to enjoy with their classmates, to live together, to socialize, to learn from each other, respecting each member of the groups that participate and collaborating at all times. It will be related to the different areas of Primary Education mentioned above, the Coexistence Plan, the Plan for Attention to Diversity, the Tutorial Action Plan, and the Reading Plan.

Reading Plan

- By reading the rules for carrying out the game and the questions that will be asked to each group, together with the answers, the pupils will encourage the reading habit. They will also be able to visit the libraries to help the teacher create questions or consult questions they need to learn how to answer.

Plan of Attention to Diversity (PAD)

- This game serves as a resource to develop the PAD, promoting school integration and social inclusion, favoring cooperation between students, teachers, and families, who can participate whenever they want in this game, helping each group to solve questions or teachers to ask questions.

Tutorial Action Plan (TAP)

- The TAP will be promoted from several aspects: promoting the personal and emotional development of each student; integrating learning strategies and study techniques in the classroom, as it is a game, they will learn in a more motivating way and will pay more attention to each aspect; improving the sense of group-class and peer relationships; and promoting the intervention of families in the school, an aspect that positively influences the teaching-learning process of the student.

Coexistence Plan

- Through this game, many relevant values will be developed, immersed in the questions, to promote good coexistence among peers, spreading the exercise of tolerance, respect, solidarity, freedom, autonomy, health habits, equality, and cooperation and fostering a positive climate among all members of the educational community. In addition, by respecting rules, strategies for the peaceful resolution of conflicts will also be developed.

CONCLUSION

We all know that in addition to the explicit curriculum developed in schools, there is another hidden curriculum that acts effectively in the teaching-learning process of students but affects not only them but also the teaching staff, learning conceptions, attitudes, and forms of behavior. According to Karaman et al. (2022), this curriculum could be defined as the set of norms, beliefs, customs, languages, and symbols that are manifested in the structure and functioning of an institution. The question posed is the following: Is it possible to educate in democracy, respect, solidarity, and cooperation, in all that encompasses education in values, from an institution that is competitive and authoritarian? The educational process plays a significant role in helping children perform their duties according to their nature and achieve their desired goals. In this case, "game" is one of the indispensables at the beginning of the primary points where children's unique structures intersect.

The main feature of games appeared in societies, including the characteristics of the society, and carrying cultural traces in this way. In this situation, games have become part of daily social life and an important field of interest in human life. The game reduces the environment of the world we live in into the world of the child. A child provides opportunities to himself according to suitable games for his age to find answers to questions about the real world.

Thanks to games, children have different perspectives on many issues. In addition to this, the game is essential in helping the child reflect on his thoughts, develop his vocabulary, and learn cultural values. The game allows the child to show interest in many situations and to be confident and active in different environments.

The elements that come to the fore in the views of social studies teachers on the definition of the educational game are mostly consolidation of knowledge, learning with fun, and other factors that make learning effective in diverse ways. This result shows that teachers see educational games as a part of teaching and learning. They can be evaluated as they perceive it as an essential source that helps them learn. The game-based learning technique, depending on the lesson achievements, allows the children to learn in the environment created by the teacher. It is an essential element of learning. At the same time, the diversity in the definitions of teachers can be interpreted in such a way that educational games can be beneficial from many different angles. The critical point here is not game-oriented but game usage in the context of its positive effect on students. Games are one of the most basic learning methods, especially for children. Each game can affect each student differently, allowing for different learning and achievements.

This chapter provides an answer to the question posed. From our point of view, it is possible to educate students under this conception as long as the school changes in several aspects: promoting the democratic school that acts under the development of multiple values constantly mentioned in this research and training teachers to promote education in values inside and outside the classroom (Ding, 2019). These values should not only be explained but they should also be preached in some way. One of the best options is to deal with them through a natural and motivating activity such as play since children develop meaningful, creative, and motivating learning, leaving aside the memoiristic one, which is only used in the short term and cannot be used in the future in the society in which they are immersed.

We have started from the need to highlight education in values for its intrinsic value, analyzing the concept of value, its characteristics, and organization and highlighting the extensive legal regulations that refer to this demand. These regulations respond to the principles of the Democratic School on which our current educational system is based.

Secondly, after this theoretical and legal overview, we focused on play as a natural way of learning, motivating the pupil, referring to its origin, concept, and reasons for its use. For this, we proposed activities both inside the classroom and outside so that they can explore different experiences that make them reflect.

In addition, we have continuously mentioned the essential role of families as a critical nucleus for personal development and growth. Finally, we concluded with a practical presentation of how a game dynamic responds to the education of values and, in turn to the objectives of the educational plans of the centers and the development of competencies in all subjects.

REFERENCES

Adipat, S., Laksana, K., Busayanan, K., Asawasowan, A. & Adipat, B. (2021). Engaging students in the learning process with game-based learning. *Journal of Technology in Education, 4*(3), 542-552. . doi:10.46328/ijte.169

Aktepe, V., & Yel, S. (2019). Describing the value judgments of primary teachers. *Turkish Journal of Educational Sciences*, *7*(3), 607–622. doi:10.29329/ijpe.2019.203.19

Albizuri, I. E., Samaniego, C. M., & Torrientes, E. Q. (2018). Desarrollo de los valores en las instituciones educativas. *El Mensajero.*

Aneja, N. (2021). The importance of value education in the present education system. *International Journal of Social Science and Humanities Research*, *2*(3), 230–243.

Arjoranta, J. (2019). How to define games and why we need to. *The Computer Games Journal, 8*(1), 109–120. doi:10.100740869-019-00080-6

Banks, T. (2018). Creating positive learning environments: Antecedent strategies for managing the classroom environment and student behavior. *Creative Education*, 5(7), 519–524. doi:10.4236/ce.2014.57061

Benítez Grande-Caballero, L. J. (2021). *Actividades y recursos para educar en valores*. PPC.

Brown, H., Woods, A., Hirst, E., & Heck, D. (2016). *The public construction of values in education*. Australian Association for Research in Education.

Buxarrais, M. R., & Martínez Martín, M. (2019). Educación en valores y educación emocional: Propuestas para la acción pedagógica. *Teoría de la Educación*, *10*(2), 263–275. doi:10.14201/eks.7519

Bylieva, D. & Sastre, M. (2018). Classification of Educational Games according to their complexity and the player's skills. *The European Proceedings of Social & Behavioural Sciences*, 438-446. DOI: doi:1 0154058epshs.2018.12.02.47

Camps, V., García, J., Gil, R., & Ruiz, J. (2018). *Educar en valores: Un reto educativo actual*. Servicio de Publicaciones de la Universidad de Deusto.

Cortina, A. (2020). *La educación y los valores*. Biblioteca Nueva.

Díaz Torres, J.M. & Rodríguez Gómez, J.M. (2018). La educación en valores como estrategia de desarrollo y consolidación personal moral. *Estudios sobre educación*, *15*, 159-169. doi:10.15581/004.15.23441

Dicher, C., & Dichera, D. (2017). Gamifying education: What is known, what is believed, and what remains uncertain. *International Journal of Educational Technology in Higher Education*, *14*(1), 1–9. doi:10.118641239-017-0042-5

Dimitra, K., Kousris, K., Zafeiriou, C., & Tzafilkas, K. (2020). Types of Game-Based Learning in Education. *The European Educational Researcher*, *3*(2), 87–100. doi:10.31757/euer.324

Ding, L. (2019). Applying gamification to asynchronous online discussions: A mixed methods study. *Computers in Human Behavior*, *91*, 1–11. doi:10.1016/j.chb.2018.09.022

Escámez, J., García, R., Pérez, C., & Llopis, A. (2017). *El aprendizaje de valores y actitudes: Teoría y práctica*. Octaedro.

Gozcu, E. & Caganaga, L. (2021). The importance of using games in ELF classrooms. *Cypriot Journal of Educational Science, 11*(3), 126-135.

Grace, L. (2019). *Doing things with games: Social impact through play*. Routledge. doi:10.1201/9780429429880

Haydon, G. (2021). *Enseñar valores: un nuevo enfoque*. Ediciones Morata.

Hurtado, S., Alvarez, C. I., Guillermo-Wann, C., Cuellar, M., & Arellano, L. (2018). *A model for diverse learning environments*. Springer.

Inglehart, R. (2016). Mapping global values. *Comparative Sociology*, *5*(2), 115–136. doi:10.1163/156913306778667401

Karakoc, B., Eryilmaz, K., Ozpolat, E. T., & Yildirim, I. (2022). The effect of game-based learning on student achievement: A meta-analysis study. *Technology. Knowledge and Learning, 27*(1), 1–16. doi:10.100710758-020-09471-5

Karaman, B., Er, H., & Karadeniz, O. (2022). Teaching with educational games in social studies: A teacher's perspective. *The Turkish Online Journal of Educational Technology, 21*(1), 124–137.

Kucher, T. (2021). Principles and best practices of designing digital game-based learning environments. *International Journal of Technology in Education and Science, 5*(2), 213-223. . doi:10.46328/ijtes.190

Kula, S. S. (2021). Mind games with the views of classroom teachers. *International Journal of Research in Education and Science, 7*(3), 747–766. doi:10.46328/ijres.1471

Louis, K. S. (2023). Democratic Schools, Democratic Communities. *Leadership and Policy in Schools, 2*(2), 93–108. doi:10.1076/lpos.2.2.93.15544

Lovat, T., & Clement, N. (2018). The pedagogical imperative of values education. *Journal of Beliefs & Values, 29*(3), 273–285. doi:10.1080/13617670802465821

Luik, P., & Taimalu, M. (2021). Predicting the intention to use technology in education among student teachers: A path analysis. *Education Sciences, 11*(9), 1–14. doi:10.3390/educsci11090564

Mosley, A. & Baltazar, E. (n.d.). *An introduction to logic: from everyday life to formal systems.* Smith College.

Ortega, P., & Mínguez, R. (2019). *Los valores en la educación.* Ariel Ediciones.

Oysterman, D. (2018). *Psychology of Values.* Elsevier.

Panev, V. (2020). Theoretical basis and models for developing students' values in Primary Education. *International Journal of Cognitive Research in Science, Engineering, and Education, 8*(1), 81–91. doi:10.5937/IJCRSEE2001081P

Parra, J. M. (2018). Educación en valores y su práctica en el aula. *Revista Tendencias Pedagógicas, 8,* 69–71.

Ritchie, L. (2018). Opening the curriculum through open educational practices: International experience. *Open Praxis, 10*(2), 201–208. doi:10.5944/openpraxis.10.2.821

Sáez López, J. M., Sevillano García, M. L., & Pascual Sevillano, M. A. (2019). Aplicación del juego ubicuo con realidad aumentada en Educación Primaria. *Comunicar, 61,* 71–82. doi:10.3916/C61-2019-06

Sahin, U. (2019). Values and Values Education as Perceived by Primary School Teacher Candidates. *International Journal of Progressive Education, 15*(3), 74–90. doi:10.29329/ijpe.2019.193.6

Surendranath, R., & Lavanya, M. (2021). *Value Education.* Charulatha Publications.

Syafii, L., Kusnawan, W., & Syukroni, A. (2020). Enhancing listening skills using games. *International Journal on Studies in Education, 2*(2), 78–107. doi:10.46328/ijonse.21

Thornberg, R. (2018). The lack of professional knowledge in values education. *Teaching and Teacher Education, 24*(7), 1791–1798. doi:10.1016/j.tate.2008.04.004

Trasobares, P., & Valdivieso, L. (2019). *Aprendizaje del inglés a través del juego en Educación Primaria.* Servicio de Publicaciones de la Universidad de Valladolid.

Wiselia, D., Tanusetiawana, R., & Purnomoa, F. (2019). Simulation Game as a Reference to Smart City Management. *Procedia Computer Science, 116,* 468–475. doi:10.1016/j.procs.2017.10.053

Yolageldili, G., & Arikan, A. (2021). Effectiveness of using games in teaching grammar to young learners. *Elementary Education Online, 10*(1), 219–229.

Zheng, R., & Gardner, M. K. (2017). *Handbook of Research on Serious Games for Educational Application.* IGI Publishing. doi:10.4018/978-1-5225-0513-6

KEY TERMS AND DEFINITIONS

Child Development: Child development can be defined as the process by which a child changes over time. It covers the whole period from conception to an individual becoming a fully functioning adult. It is a journey from total dependence to complete independence.

Curriculum: The term curriculum refers to the lessons and academic content taught in a school or a specific course or program. The curriculum is a standards-based sequence of planned experiences where students practice and achieve proficiency in content and applied learning skills.

Education in Values: Values education refers to the aspect of the educational practice which entails that moral or political values, as well as norms, dispositions, and skills grounded in those values, are mediated to or developed among students.

Educational Games: All games may be used in an educational environment. However, educational games are designed to help people learn about certain subjects, expand concepts, reinforce development, understand a historical event or culture, or assist them in learning a skill as they play.

Game: A game is an activity or sport usually involving skill, knowledge, or chance, in which you follow fixed rules and try to win against an opponent or solve a puzzle.

Primary Education: It is the education phase for children from 6 to 12 years old. Each year corresponds to a grade from first grade (6 years old) to sixth grade (12 years old).

Teaching-Learning Process: The teaching-learning process, or the education process, has been defined as a systematic, sequential, planned course of action on the part of both the teacher and learner to achieve the outcomes of teaching and learning.

Value: A value is a conception, implicit or explicit, distinctive of an individual or characteristic of a group, of the desirable, which influences the selection from available modes, means, and ends of action.

Chapter 8
The Contribution of Values Education to Increasing Disaster Awareness of Primary School Students

Bekir Tastan

Kastamonu University, Turkey

ABSTRACT

Disasters cause great damage worldwide every year. A conscious and scientific strategy should be used to reduce the damage. Disaster management ensures the successful completion of the process. If people want to manage disasters properly, they must act diligently at every stage of disaster management. These tasks can be fulfilled by vigilant, responsible, and educated individuals. Disaster awareness can be increased with the support of education. Primary school is the most memorable period of education. In this period, disaster education is not included in the curriculum. Teaching values in the curriculum can play an important role in increasing disaster awareness in this period. This study shows how values education and disaster awareness are integrated in primary schools. In the first part of the study, disasters are mentioned. In the following sections, the contribution of disaster education and values education to disaster awareness is discussed.

INTRODUCTION

Today, one of the most frequently discussed topics is disasters. Disasters cause damage to thousands of people and their property almost every year. Disasters also cause significant assets losses. The occurrence of disasters depends on the geological, geophysical, climatic, meteorological and biological characteristics of the earth. At the same time, various activities of people also cause disasters. They are caused by the interaction of two different factors. Disaster hazard is one of them and vulnerability is another. Hazard is a dangerous event or phenomenon that leads to a disaster. Many disaster hazards

DOI: 10.4018/978-1-6684-9295-6.ch008

cannot be eliminated. For example, it may be possible to predict the location of an earthquake. However, with today's technology it is difficult to predict exactly when an earthquake will occur. Some disaster hazards occur very quickly. Others, however, may take some time to materialise. For example, it is very difficult to track the occurrence of hazards such as drought, climate change and desertification because they take time to emerge. Vulnerability is a secondary component that causes disasters. It indicates the extent to which risk elements are vulnerable to disaster hazards. Infrastructure components and environmental elements can all be damaged by hazards or buildings can collapse. Disasters also damage the socio-economic structure of societies. With these features, vulnerability is seen as the most important component in disasters. Although many disaster hazards cannot be prevented, it is theoretically possible to determine vulnerability and propose mitigation solutions. Therefore, it is safer and easier to reduce undesirable situations after disasters with vulnerability studies.

Disaster management activities are a kind of management model that outlines the steps to be taken in a system to cope with adverse events that may occur before or after a disaster. It covers the tasks to be completed before, during and after the disaster. Mitigation works are carried out before the disaster as a part of disaster risk works. Modern disaster management emphasises the importance of the steps to be taken before the disaster. If mitigation measures are implemented timely, disaster damage can be reduced largely. If disaster management activities are carried out meticulously, damages caused by disasters can be minimised. Losses of life and property can be reduced.

Disasters cause thousands of deaths worldwide every year. The negative effects of disasters last for years and many people face economic difficulties or job losses due to disasters. The economic costs of disasters are quite high. According to estimates, the two earthquakes that hit southern Turkey on 6 February 2023 could have an economic impact of $100 billion or more on the country. In previous years, earthquakes in many parts of the world have caused huge economic losses. Less developed countries are more likely to experience such losses. On the other hand, industrialised countries are less damaged and adversely affected by such disasters because they are better equipped to cope with disasters.

There are many factors contributing to the greater damage caused by disasters in less developed countries, including inadequate disaster preparedness, failure to comply with certain engineering regulations in the construction of buildings and use of low quality materials, defects in the organisation of disaster management activities and lack of public awareness on disasters. A high level of awareness despite disasters can be demonstrated, for example, by not building houses along fault lines and stream beds and not residing in houses at risk of earthquakes. Similarly, complying with engineering regulations when designing structures and taking into account all the tragedies that can occur in residential areas represents both the nature of the individual duty and the responsibility for society.

The phenomenon of education has a very important place in people's lives. Through education a person begins to see permanent behavioural changes. Education offers a more comprehensive approach than teaching, but at the same time it has more challenging methods for detecting changes in attitudes and behaviour. One of the most important ages for schooling is when children start primary school. During this critical period the young person leaves home, makes new friends and continues to socialise. Although pre-school education is just as important, it has a greater impact on the minds of primary school pupils because primary school education lasts longer. In primary school, children learn to respect their environment and the rights of their friends, to keep their promises, to follow the rules at school, to appreciate nature and to develop a sense of citizenship. Giving and accepting value education begins in this sense in the first years of school. If a young person can have positive thoughts about his/her environment during this time, respect the rights of his/her peers and be aware of his/her obligations, he/she can increase his/her positive feelings in the future. On the other hand, children who do not learn to feel good during this period have difficulties in interacting with their friends and environment in later ages. In this context, providing values education at an early age plays an important role in preparing children for life.

Values education has a great effect on the acquisition of disaster awareness. For example, a manager who works by taking into account all possible disasters in the settlement area in his/her management activities will both fulfil his/her professional obligations and do the right thing for the society. It is possible to raise a good manager, engineer or contractor by including disaster awareness in the values education given at primary school age. As a result, it is possible to take important steps to raise awareness against disasters and reduce disaster damages. In this context, in this study, topics such as disasters, disaster management, and disaster awareness in values education are discussed. It is tried to raise awareness about the importance of the subject by giving examples on how to handle disaster awareness in values education. As a result, it is aimed to produce a road map for the activities to be carried out to increase the level of awareness in children in order to be prepared for disasters in the work of teachers and administrators.

DISASTERS

Almost every year, hundreds of disasters occur in different countries of the world. Thousands of people have lost their lives and billions of dollars of economic losses have occurred due to disasters. The occurrence of so much damage in disasters is due to the fact that disasters affect many areas and the society is vulnerable to disasters. When a disaster occurs, many problems arise. These problems cause long term problems. From past to present, various types of disasters have occurred worldwide. The number and frequency of disasters have increased in recent years. The 2004 Indian Ocean earthquake and tsunami, the 2008 Cyclone Nargis and the 2010 Haiti earthquake caused 200,000 deaths (Ritchie and Hoser, 2020). The 2011 Japan earthquake and subsequent tsunami caused destruction at the Fukushima power plant and affected 60,000 people (Matanle, 2011). The beginning of the pandemic was in 2020. On 12 April 2023, the COVID-19 pandemic killed 6,897,025 people and infected 755,894,127 people (WHO, 2023). In 2022, the Emergency Incident Database recorded 387 natural disasters worldwide. In these disasters, 30,704 people lost their lives, but 185 million people were indirectly affected. The economic damage from these disasters amounted to USD 223.8 billion. A heat wave killed more than 16,000 people in Europe, while drought affected 88.9 million people in Africa. The total of 387 disaster events is slightly higher than the average number of disasters between 2002 and 2021 (CRED, 2023). On 6 February 2023, two consecutive earthquakes of magnitude 7.8 and 7.5 occurred in Elbistan and Pazarcık districts of Kahramanmaraş province in Turkey. More than 48,000 people lost their lives and more than 500,000 buildings were damaged. The number of people indirectly affected by the earthquake was estimated at 14,013,196 (Republic of Turkey Strategy and Budget Directorate, 2023). These earthquakes were among the disasters that caused the highest loss of life and property in the history of Turkey.

Can disasters, despite their terrible impact, be prevented or mitigated? This question concerns two different issues: Recognising the causes of disasters and reducing their impact. In order to understand disasters, research is ongoing to identify the risks that lead to disasters and to determine the susceptibility of society to them. These research projects focus on risk and vulnerability. Identification of disaster risk is the first step in disaster characterisation. Many terrible disasters occur in the world. They have quite different characteristics from each other. Some natural disasters are caused by the physical properties of the earth, while others are caused by weather conditions. For example, earth movements cause earthquakes, while floods are the result of extreme weather features. The speed at which a disaster develops can also be used to categorise risk. For example, disasters such as landslides, avalanches and floods happen very quickly. They happen unexpectedly. Some disasters take longer. Some of these disasters are even difficult to feel. One of these gradual disasters is, for example, climate change. Extensive observation is needed to recognise the impact. Drought, like climate change, is a long-term disaster. We have to wait for the consequences.

A secondary factor causing disasters is the vulnerability of society. The house you live in, your surroundings and your economic situation affect the damage caused by a disaster. Vulnerability is the total of the conditions and characteristics of a community, system or property exposed to the harmful effects of a hazard (UNISDR, 2009). Understanding hazards requires identifying the vulnerability levels and hazard characteristics of different social groups (Cannon et al., 2003). Vulnerability to disasters is a complex concept. Vulnerability varies due to changes in both social and physical conditions around the world (Birkmann, 2006). There are many factors affecting vulnerability. Diseases, urbanisation, wars, foreign debts and some structural adjustment programmes are some of these factors (Cannon et al., 2003).

Disasters cause significant damage to societies. Although vulnerability plays an important role in this situation, it is difficult to estimate vulnerability because of the way disaster hazards interact. Sometimes two disaster hazards peacefully coexist, while at other times more than one disaster hazard may interact and cause multiple disasters to occur in the same place at the same time. Compound hazards are such disaster risks. Some of their names are chains, ongoing risks, domino effects, and interactions, hitting risks, multiple risks or trigger risks (Kappes et al., 2012). In these situations, one hazard can change the frequency and magnitude of another. If an avalanche removes the protective forest layer in winter, a greater frequency and magnitude of rockfall can be observed at the same location in spring (Papathoma-Köhle et al., 2011). In most cases, trigger hazards occur during disasters. Depending on how the triggering process develops differently, the strength of the impact chain may increase. In this case, vulnerability can change and emerge depending on the presence of critical infrastructure (Pescaroli & Alexander, 2015). The vast majority of disaster studies only address the links between natural disasters and try to identify the interactions between hazards. However, the number of studies on situations where natural disasters cause technological disasters is still quite small.

Various hazard interactions can occur when hazards trigger each other. For example, earthquakes can cause ground shaking and liquefaction. Tsunamis, rockfalls, avalanches, debris flows and shallow, slow-moving landslides can occur. Such hazard relationships may also include other hazards unrelated to these hazards. For example, a strong thunderstorm may occur during an earthquake. Such hazards occur independently of the first hazard and aggravate the damage caused by the first hazard. Moreover, it is very difficult to estimate the extent of the damage it can cause, as it is often unpredictable.

When disasters trigger each other or when different disasters occur independently, the damage caused by disasters increases. The actions to counteract them are carried out in a certain systematic process. This management system is called disaster management. Disaster management process defines and applies the technical, managerial and legal framework of the activities to be carried out before, during and after the disaster (Deniz, 2012). In the past, disaster management studies mainly focussed on post-disaster activities, but now they also focus on pre-disaster activities. In this context, disaster management systems deal with multiple risk situations and focus on integrated hazards from multiple sources.

DISASTER EDUCATION

Disasters are caused by two factors. One of them is vulnerability and the other is hazard. Some hazards are inevitable. For example, earthquakes occur near fault lines. Extreme rainfall cannot be prevented at present. Especially climate change has increased the frequency of extreme precipitation. Some measures can be taken to prevent the occurrence of such catastrophic risks. As vulnerabilities reflect different characteristics of the society, different prevention strategies can be developed. Pre-disaster management research includes disaster activities. Some of these activities are related to the determination of vulnerability to disasters. These studies are called vulnerability reduction studies. In addition to vulnerability reduction studies, risk assessment studies are also among the activities carried out in the pre-disaster period. Risk assessment research includes activities to determine disaster hazards, vulnerabilities and risk situations. Risk is a combination of disaster hazard and vulnerability. High probability of disaster hazard and vulnerability means high risk. Risk is a normalised value between zero and one. Zero risk means that there is no possibility of disaster, one risk or risk close to 1 means that there is a possibility of disaster.

The purpose of all these disaster definitions and explanations is to provide a better understanding of disasters. In order to ensure sustainable development, education plays a key role in minimising disaster damages and ensuring the safety of people during disasters. Previous disasters have demonstrated the beneficial effects of education on disaster management systems. During the 2004 tsunami disaster in India, a child who was aware of the nature of disasters and knew how to respond quickly and appropriately helped reduce fatalities. Tilly Smith, a 10-year-old British student, had to leave the beach immediately during the 2004 Indian Ocean tsunami because it was a tourist beach. As a result, the lives of more than 100 tourists were saved. As far as she understood from her geography lessons, she had recognised the warning signs of the approaching tsunami (Shaw et al., 2011). Such cases show us how important education is in human life. Education not only develops the individual's ability to adapt to the natural environment, but also teaches respect. The term education actually refers to the permanent establishment of certain behaviour patterns in the individual's mind. These patterns of behaviour are certain rules developed by society and may refer to universal norms. Education takes place within a certain framework in every society. However, educational content and frameworks that develop competences for adaptation to age-related conditions are probably largely provided by modern societies.

Until recently, disaster management was considered as a whole of post-disaster activities. However, later developments have shown that pre and post disaster researches are at least as important. Some of the researches on disaster management include measures for disaster risk reduction. In this sense, training activities are also important. Every member of the society has a job to do within this framework. Learning, which educates all members of the society about disasters, is at the centre of our educational activities. However, activities that leave lasting effects on children's disaster behaviour are more important. Early education on disaster avoidance helps children to adapt to life, environment and disasters.

Studies conducted in many countries, including Japan, show a direct correlation between education and students' perceptions of disaster risk and risk reduction. Disaster-focused early childhood education has many benefits. These include (Torani et al., 2019);

- Children explain what they learnt from their parents. As a result, providing education to children will increase disaster awareness in the society.
- Being familiar with the concepts of disaster risk and disaster from an early age will enable you to respond quickly when disaster occurs.

- What is learnt from childhood is not easily forgotten.
- In many countries, children are an important part of the society.
- Childhood disaster education encourages children to learn about disaster-related topics such as resilience and risk reduction.

As mentioned before, it is very important that children are familiarised with the terms, facts and explanations related to disasters at a young age. However, how and in what form this education is to be provided and at which level which topic is to be taught are not explained in sufficient detail in the teaching materials. Moreover, most people are not sufficiently aware of concepts such as climate change, carbon footprint, trigger hazards, disaster sensitivity, disaster management and integrated risk, and education programmes do not provide explanations about these ideas.

Children who learn these virtues correctly and completely will be better equipped to act responsibly in future situations such as disaster prevention and building disaster-resistant structures. Individuals learn from an early age how dangerous events such as earthquakes, floods and landslides are characterised as disasters on television and in the media. The occurrence of these dangerous events does not necessarily mean that a tragedy will occur. It is important to ensure that children do not develop phobias towards these risky situations. As a result, it is possible to take effective preventive measures against these events. Just because the first of two equally dangerous situations causes an accident in one country does not guarantee that it will occur in another country. Therefore, the distinction between the concepts of risk and disaster should be taken into account in training programmes.

VALUES EDUCATION

Education plays an important role in the discovery of new things and the dissemination of knowledge in developing and developed societies. It is remarkable that all these find meaning in a qualified educational environment. In almost all societies, education is a service provided by the state to citizens. However, the content and scope of this service is influenced by cultural, economic, family structure and social values. While education plans in underdeveloped countries change frequently, plans in rich countries are based on long-term and permanent improvements. Changes in education are therefore temporary. The wealth gap has a detrimental effect on the educational environment in such cultures. Not everyone benefits equally from educational opportunities. Education is the sum total of all efforts to change behaviour permanently. Education makes people better citizens. It shows us how to do our work better, but it also shows us how to act in the interests of society. Education has a meaningful impact on the life of every individual. It leads to permanent behavioural changes at every stage of life, from childhood to adulthood. According to the Turkish Education Association Dictionary (Turkish Language Association, 2023), education equips children and young people with the knowledge, skills and understanding they need to participate in society and develop their personalities. It is defined as social welfare activities carried out inside and outside the school. Today, thanks to technological developments in this field and the contribution of online education activities, education has become accessible to everyone. The target group has not remained the same; the sphere of influence has also developed.

The sum of the material and immaterial qualities that constitute the social, cultural, economic and scientific value of a society is called value (Turkish Language Association, 2023). Values provide social order. Law alone cannot provide peace and order in society. In some cases, the law does not prohibit things that are considered socially bad. For example, although smoking is not tolerated by the society, it is legal. Values such as helping those in need (fire, earthquake, and financial difficulties), sharing, hospitality may not be accepted by law (Kirmizi, 2014). It is a set of ideas whose roots are found in traditions and historical perspectives, and whose trunk and branches expand towards the future by taking strength from these roots. In reality, the way people adopt and adhere to values determines how society will develop in the future. The education system is responsible for instilling in people not only defined skills and behaviours but also core values. The core values of the programme are justice, honesty, self-discipline, patience, respect, love, responsibility, patriotism and usefulness (Republic of Turkey Ministry of National Education, 2015).

Individuals can take a healthy step in the process of adopting the value of educational products not only through formal education institutions, but also by including all members of the society in the educational process. Family is the first place where educational values are given. Innovations and technological changes lead to a decrease in the value of family education. Other factors affecting this situation include the participation of women in working life and the increase in divorce rates. Although value education has been included in the literature in recent years, it has also been a problem of the past. It is also called moral or moral education (Tosun, 2021). The importance of each individual in society, their preferences and how they should live are represented by a set of values. When the general aims of educational institutions are evaluated, it can be seen that they mostly include values such as patriotism, cleanliness, health, organisation, justice, creativity and entrepreneurial spirit (Akbaş, 2008). In addition to providing basic knowledge in schools, it is aimed to give each educated individual the opportunity to make appropriate moral decisions and to show them in their behaviour. The education system concretises its function in the context of imparting values through educational programmes, which include curricula. In the Turkish education system, values can be defined as individual programmes, learning areas, unit subjects, etc. They are present in all units of the curriculum throughout the entire learning process (Republic of Turkey Ministry of National Education, 2015). For example, it is seen that 18 values are included in the social sciences curriculum. These are (Republic of Turkey Ministry of National Education, 2015):

1. Justice 10. Aesthetic
2. Giving importance to family unit 11. Equality
3. Independence 12. Freedom
4. Peace 13. Respect
5. Science 14. Affection
6. Diligence 15. Responsibility
7. Solidarity 16. Saving
8. Sensitivity 17. Patriotism
9. Integrity 18. Helpfulness

Values education is implemented in different countries of the world. These practices are evaluated using different programmes that vary according to the needs of the country and the age group. Most values education programmes focus on social and emotional development. A values education programme is implemented in more than 60 countries, including Europe, Asia, Africa, the Middle East and the Americas. Starting in the United States of America and spreading to many countries around the world, character education partnerships are in place from pre-school to senior high school. It is implemented in school-based classes in different countries from preschool to high school (Dönmez & Uyanık, 2022).

VALUES EDUCATION AND DISASTER AWARENESS

Every person from seven to seventy, especially the socially vulnerable, is affected by disasters. Within the scope of disaster prevention, actions are taken to reduce the damage caused by such events. These processes include some mitigation activities which are pre-disaster measures. Activities for mitigation of disaster damages include actions carried out before the effects of the disaster such as creation of early warning systems, hazards, vulnerabilities and risk assessments. One of the most important efforts of this period is educational research. Much of the damage caused by a tragedy can be prevented through education. Primary school students are one of the focus groups of these trainings. Disaster response efforts are greatly supported by children's early disaster awareness. Future education initiatives for children will stem from the realisation that learning can stop disasters. Pupils in primary school begin the concrete operational phase. The transmission of basic ideas and knowledge during this period is facilitated by a more comprehensive study and dissemination of disaster education through case studies and drills.

Today's groundbreaking discoveries and technological advances, the widespread use of personal computers, the creation of 3D displays and simple data transmission have led to various breakthroughs in the education sector. Today, 3D diagrams, pictures, animations and tables on the internet can represent complex ideas and methods. The use of various technological media in education and training environments will significantly improve students' understanding of disasters due to the complexity of disaster structures and vocabulary. Early childhood education needs clearer explanations and visuals.

There are various reasons why disasters occur. Any situation that can cause destruction is dangerous. Earthquakes, floods, fires, avalanches, landslides and explosions are a few examples of such dangerous situations. Simulated experiments can show how these events work. Such an event is extremely favourable for disaster pedagogy. Textbooks, smart boards, internet, bookshops, stories, online courses, online atlases and electronic games are used in disaster education. In addition, schools in many countries, through informal teaching traditions, train children on how to defend themselves and others in emergencies. (Değirmenci et al., 2019) Children from kindergarten to first grade are particularly familiar with concerns related to risk management culture. Teachers should use games and hands-on activities to teach children about environmental hazards and apply different scientific disciplines to conduct classroom activities in a cognitive and physical way to encourage this interest. Furthermore, seminars and other activities should be organised to increase students' interest in disasters. However, in many schools there are not enough teachers to do this (Kekic & Milenkovic, 2015). In-service training can help to fill this teacher gap. These courses for science, social studies and classroom teachers enable students to learn disaster terms, types of disasters, how to protect against disasters and many other skills related to disasters.

Activities can significantly improve children's understanding of disasters. The lack of sufficient activities in this area is one of the main challenges faced by teachers in disaster education. Teachers say that there are several problems related to disaster education. These are; students do not show much interest in disaster education. Research on disasters is primarily focussed on earthquake related issues. There are only a few tasks to be completed in this regard (Kırıkkaya et al., 2011). Despite the large number of earthquake-related trainings offered, it has been observed that there are gaps in children's seismic understanding. Şimşek's (2007) research on 40 primary school children showed that despite some awareness of earthquakes among children, many of them did not have sufficient knowledge about earthquake protection. To address this problem, it is now necessary to distinguish between the content of education and the method of delivery. Values are the sum of principles that form the perspective of leadership programmes.

The core values in the curriculum are justice, friendship, honesty, self-control, patience, love, responsibility, patriotism, and enmity. The Turkish Social Sciences curriculum respects justice and emphasises family unity, sensitivity, peace, knowledge, diligence, solidarity, sensitivity, honesty, aesthetics, freedom, respect, love, responsibility, thrift, patriotism and compassion (Republic of Turkey Ministry of National Education, 2015). As part of the life science curriculum, students are trained in basic knowledge, skills and values and develop fundamental family, social, national, spiritual and human values. They love their homeland, learn history, are motivated to preserve cultural values, and are sensitive to nature and the environment. They are aware of national and cultural values. While implementing lifelong learning programmes, care should be taken to transfer values to students (Republic of Turkey Ministry of National Education, 2018). When these principles are considered together, it becomes clear that they aim to develop the national and spiritual aspects of society, to provide honesty and justice education, to develop a sense of responsibility and to shape the social behaviours that children will exhibit when they grow up. In fact, these values are characteristic traits of all societies and are intended to be passed on to future generations. Early learning is more permanent and forms the basis of the child's future behaviour patterns. Disaster education is great importance in terms of increasing the ability to respond to disasters in countries like Turkey where disasters are frequently experienced.

The training programmes offered in schools can be evaluated in two parts: internal and external. The comprehensive evaluation of these programmes highlighted the lack of disaster management education in schools. However, in countries with high disaster risk, it is an important requirement to include disaster preparedness courses in primary school curricula. In addition, disaster education activities should be carried out as activities independent of the programme. It can be said that club activities are more effective in raising awareness of children about disasters (Shaw et al., 2011). Since disaster education is not taught as a unit in primary school classes, it can be taught by using various techniques. Value education is one of them. It tries to ensure that people are morally honest, aware of their obligations, obey the laws and internalise moral principles. We can see that there is a great overlap between the broad objectives of value education and resilience education. Disaster-causing variables are frequently seen in developing cultures. The level of education is low in developing societies. In a society with such a fragile economy, it is not possible to adequately transfer the knowledge and experience needed in old age through education. Therefore, when these uneducated people get a job, they will not be able to do that job well. For example, most buildings are not disaster resistant due to inadequate building materials and lack of proper construction methods. During the disaster, many of the survivors are trapped under the wreckage when the buildings collapse due to building behaviour. The environment and infrastructure components are more vulnerable because they are not disaster resilient. This is a contributing factor to the hazards of natural or man-made disasters.

Responsibility is a value that should be taught in primary school. This idea is part of the core value. Responsibility is the ability to accept all the consequences associated with any task or event. Various institutions decide on settlements, construction projects and urbanisation. Employees of these institutions are responsible for these works. When disasters occur, the number of deaths increases, so it is very important to identify the person in charge for this activity. Responsibility refers to the ability to transmit through early value education. Teachers can make sense of their responsibilities in the fields of life sciences, social sciences and science education by making connections between the factors that are effective during disasters. In fact, life science helps people to feel positive about life and to control it. Its aim is to help people learn about life. For example, life safety units in life science lessons cover how to live safely at school, at home and outside school. The structure of buildings, their durability and resistance to disasters are important parts of personal safety. Teachers should be concerned about disasters and emphasise the importance of safe buildings for disaster preparedness. Responsibility and values are very important for safety. The person in charge has a sense of responsibility for these workings. He ensures that these works are carried out carefully. As a result, they strengthen buildings and ensure the safety of living spaces.

The life process, the living unit includes natural events and natural disasters in nature. Disasters are not a separate process, but dealing with natural disasters can help raise awareness of this issue. However, presenting this topic only on the basis of existing knowledge does not guarantee that the topic will be protected. When discussing this topic, it is important to include the causes of the disaster. However, disaster-related deaths, injuries, environmental damages and financial losses are of great importance. According to the widespread belief, disasters can be caused only by the natural features of the Earth. However, the main factors causing disasters are the physical and socio-economic vulnerabilities of the society. When talking about disasters, it is necessary to express the causes of disasters as dangerous events, as well as poor construction of buildings, lack of management, poor orientation of building materials and settlements where dangerous events cause disasters. We should also mention construction and similar issues. Especially it is necessary to mention that dishonest payment activity is very important for disaster detection. Values such as responsibility, patriotism, honesty, and diligence are associated with the unit. One of the most important measures to avoid tragedies is to protect these ideals.

CONCLUSION

Disasters affect thousands of people every year and cause numerous losses of life and property. Disasters occur when a dangerous event and a risk factor coincide. Most of the dangerous events that cause disasters cannot be prevented. However, the measures to be taken can reduce the damage caused by dangerous events. Activities to reduce disaster damages and cope with disasters are carried out in a systematic process. This process is called disaster management. Disaster management includes activities carried out before, during and after the disaster. These activities should be implemented in coordination. Education is very important for successful disaster management. Informal disaster education starts in the family. It should be given officially in kindergartens and primary schools. However, when school education programmes are evaluated, there is no guiding series for disaster education. Life Science and Social Studies basic education courses provide information about disasters, but not detailed information. Similarly, it has been observed that there is no directive for teachers on how to conduct disaster education.

In primary school, disasters are taught using various methods and resources. In this context, value-based education can be very important. Honesty, responsibility, commitment to duty, not lying and many other socially acceptable characteristics are among the virtues that are in the focus of value education. According to research, many sentences and situations describing disasters in primary schools are quickly forgotten. For example, when asked about different earthquakes, most children cannot remember the answers. This shows how quickly theoretical knowledge can be forgotten. However, disaster-specific education will be more effective and permanent. Disasters actually occur due to unfavourable consequences arising from events. Teaching people about disasters should focus on events rather than terms. For example, in the case of building collapses in earthquakes, it should be mentioned that buildings must be durable. Here, accountability and integrity should be the values connected to the earthquake event.

Earthquakes cause deaths when buildings fail. Therefore, a robust structure is required for buildings. The importance of "doing one's duty" can also be matched with the goal of building residential areas and disaster-resistant cities. Instead of using terminology and verbal information, teachers can use pictures of disasters and descriptions of atmospheric conditions to show students why these disasters occur. It should be emphasised that the creation of colonies and the development of structures serve to protect human life and provide them with permanent habitats.

One of the values taught in primary schools is patriotism. Patriotism involves the desire to sacrifice time and effort to serve the country in the best possible way. Disasters have caused great loss of life and property. There are steps that can be taken before disasters to prevent this. A disaster management framework is used to take these actions. Intensive efforts should be made to take measures to prevent risky situations from turning into disasters. When talking about patriotism, in addition to the economic damage and destruction caused by disasters, it is important to demonstrate that the fight against disasters is carried out in the context of loving the country and fulfilling the responsibility of citizenship.

Science is an important value emphasised in primary education. It tries to understand the nature of disasters, reduce the damage they cause and prevent them. Science has enabled us to learn where disasters occur, how terrible they are, how often they occur and how big they are. The link between science and disasters and the idea that science can prevent disasters should be discussed in primary schools to increase the importance of science. Our life is surrounded by science. Building construction, site selection, communication, determination of disaster damage, and the identification of disaster zones are largely based on Geographic Information Systems (GIS) and Remote Sensing (RS). Disaster monitoring and rescue operations are largely based on GIS and remote sensing research. Developments in satellite technology and computer science have facilitated the development of these professions. The importance of science and examples of solutions from various scientific fields can be included in scientific awareness in the context of disasters.

The study shows how teaching core values can increase disaster awareness and how disaster education can be linked to value education. Although disaster education is not taught in primary schools, this approach can increase awareness of disasters among the public. The earlier disaster education is adopted, the greater its impact and permanence. If we want our children to live joyful, calm, healthy and safe lives, we must ensure that their environment is free from natural disaster risks. After all, our children are the developers of our future. This can only be realised by providing comprehensive disaster education and linking this knowledge with our values. In this context, initiatives to raise awareness about disasters should be the focal point in the creation of disaster education content, visual materials and school textbooks. This information will be used instead of verbal expressions in disaster education, which will help to ensure consistency and emphasise inconsistencies.

Two different types of events can cause disasters: the presence of a harmful event and vulnerability. It is often believed that disasters are caused solely by harmful events. The occurrence of natural disasters is just one of many contributing factors. These events depend on the natural processes that exist in the world. If individuals do not take measures against the occurrence of these disasters and their harmful effects, disasters will occur in addition to these features. It is therefore important to recognise that other factors play a role here besides the threats that cause accidents. Science should be combined with the concepts of disaster education and value education to remove the conceptual ambiguity in this regard. Another problem with disaster terminology is that disasters are seen as fate. In most societies, disasters are seen as fate. There are various explanations that post-disaster events can never be prevented. However, most of the damage that may occur can be prevented by taking precautions before a disaster occurs. For this reason, it should not be forgotten that these events can be prevented with disaster training and science has great support in this regard.

REFERENCES

Akbaş, O. (2008). Değer eğitimi akımlarına genel bir bakış. *Değerler Eğitimi Dergisi, 6*(16), 9–27.

Birkmann, J. (2006). Indicators and criteria for measuring vulnerability: Theoretical bases and requirements. *Measuring Vulnerability to Natural Hazards: Towards Disaster Resilient Societies*, 55–77.

Cannon, T., Davis, I., & Wisner, B. (2003). *At Risk: Natural Hazards, People's Vulnerability and Disasters*. Taylor & Francis.

CRED. (2023). *Disasters Year in Review 2022*. https://www.cred.be/publications

Değirmenci, Y., Kuzey, M., & Yetişensoy, O. (2019). Sosyal bilgiler ders kitaplarında afet bilinci ve eğitimi. *E-Kafkas Journal of Educational Research, 6*(2), 33–46.

Dönmez, Ö., & Uyanık, G. (2022). Farklı Ülkelerde Değerler Eğitimi ve Değer Eğitimi Programlarından Örnekler. *Temel Eğitim Araştırmaları Dergisi, 2*(1), 74–88. doi:10.55008/te-ad.1099697

Kappes, M. S., Keiler, M., von Elverfeldt, K., & Glade, T. (2012). Challenges of analyzing multi-hazard risk: A review. In Natural Hazards (Vol. 64, Issue 2, pp. 1925–1958). doi:10.100711069-012-0294-2

Kekic, D., & Milenkovic, M. (2015). *Disaster risk reduction through education*. https://www.researchgate.net/publication/309728178_Disaster_risk_reduction_through_education

Kırıkkaya, E. B., Ünver, A. O., & Çakın, O. (2011). Teachers views on the topic of disaster education at the field on elementary science and technology curriculum. *Necatibey Eğitim Fakültesi Elektronik Fen ve Matematik Eğitimi Dergisi, 5*(1), 24–42.

Kirmizi, F. S. (2014). 4. sınıf Türkçe ders kitabı metinlerinde yer alan değerler. *Değerler Eğitimi Dergisi, 12*(27), 217–259.

Matanle, P. (2011). The Great East Japan Earthquake, tsunami, and nuclear meltdown: Towards the (re) construction of a safe, sustainable, and compassionate society in Japan's shrinking regions. *Local Environment, 16*(9), 823–847. doi:10.1080/13549839.2011.607160

Papathoma-Köhle, M., Kappes, M., Keiler, M., & Glade, T. (2011). Physical vulnerability assessment for alpine hazards: State of the art and future needs. In Natural Hazards (Vol. 58, Issue 2, pp. 645–680). doi:10.100711069-010-9632-4

Pescaroli, G., & Alexander, D. (2015). A definition of cascading disasters and cascading effects: Going beyond the "toppling dominos" metaphor. *Planet@ Risk, 3*(1), 58–67.

Ritchie, H., & Hoser, M. (2020). *Natural Disasters*. https://ourworldindata.org/naturaldisasters

Shaw, R., Shiwaku, K., & Takeuchi, Y. (2011). *Disaster education*. Emerald Group Publishing. doi:10.1108/S2040-7262(2011)7

Simsek, C. L. (2007). Children's Ideas about Earthquakes. *International Journal of Environmental and Science Education*, 2(1), 14–19.

TDK. (2023). *TDK (Turkish Language Institution)*. https://sozluk.gov.tr/

Torani, S., Majd, P. M., Maroufi, S. S., Dowlati, M., & Sheikhi, R. A. (2019). The importance of education on disasters and emergencies: A review article. *Journal of Education and Health Promotion*, 8. PMID:31143802

Tosun, Y. (2021). *Sınıf öğretmenlerinin değerler eğitimini zorlaştıran faktörlere ilişkin görüşleri ve değerler eğitimine yönelik uygulamaları*. Van Yüzüncü Yıl Üniversitesi Eğitim Bilimleri Enstitüsü / Eğitim Bilimleri Ana Bilim Dalı / Eğitim Programları ve Öğretim Bilim Dalı.

Turkish Ministry of National Education. (2015). *Sosyal bilgiler dersi 4, 5, 6 ve 7. sınıflar öğretim programı*. Ankara: Milli Eğitim Basımevi. http://mufredat.meb.gov.tr/Dosyalar/201812103847686-SosyalBilgilerÖğretimProgramı.pdf

Turkish Ministry of National Education. (2018). *Hayat Bilgisi Dersi Öğretim Programı*. http://mufredat.meb.gov.tr/Dosyalar/2018122171428547-hayatbilgisiöğretimprogrami.pdf

Turkish Republic Strategy and Budget Presidency. (2023). *Kahramanmaras and Hatay earthquake report*. https://www.sbb.gov.tr/2023-kahramanmaras-ve-hatay-depremleri-raporu/

UNISDR. (2009). *2009 UNISDR Terminology on Disaster Risk Reduction. International Stratergy for Disaster Reduction*. ISDR.

WHO. (2023). *WHO Coronavirus (COVID-19) Dashboard*. https://covid19.who.int/

Chapter 9
Values Education in Primary Schools in Germany:
The Example of North Rhine–Westphalia

Ferah İzgi
Cyprus Science University, Cyprus

ABSTRACT

Values education is carried out in many countries with different names and systems. Although differences are observed according to the social, political, religious, and economic structure of each country, value education aims to provide an ideal structure for the individual and society by transferring cultural, moral, national, and universal values to individuals. In this study, values education in Germany, one of the important countries of Europe, was examined, and the situation of values education applied in the state of North Rhine-Westphalia was revealed as well as general values education in Germany. In Germany, values education is mainly given in Ethics and Religion courses. The data in the research were obtained by using the literature review technique, one of the qualitative research methods. As a result of the research, it has been understood that the values education in the Values and Norms course in primary schools in the state of North Rhine-Westphalia is not given at a sufficient level, and this course is only a specific course.

INTRODUCTION

Children learn values from their families and peers, social media, playgroups, the local community, and other institutions early in life. There is evidence that children probably develop a sense of morality during the first two years of their lives (Kagan & Lamb, 1987; Buzelli, 1992), which is closely linked to their emotional and social development (Dunn, 1988; Kuebli, 1994).

Therefore, children come to school with different values from their preschool experiences. The role of the school is twofold: to build on and complement the values that children are already beginning to develop by offering more significant exposure to a set of values that prevail in society (such as equality

DOI: 10.4018/978-1-6684-9295-6.ch009

of opportunity and respect for diversity); and helping children reflect on, make sense of and apply their own evolving values. The first of these tasks has received increasing official attention in the UK since the Education Act 1988 through discussion papers (OFSTED, 1994a; School Curriculum and Assessment Agency, 1995) and the shared values statement produced by the National Forum. On Values in Education and Society (School Curriculum and Assessment Authority, 1996b; cf. Smith & Standish,1997.)

In 2014, UNICEF Monitoring Values for Children asked, "Who best teaches children values." The results show that children rank third after parents and grandparents, well ahead of teachers, friends, the media, or social networks (UNICEF, 2014). This result is due to the increasing importance of teachers in imparting values education: While only 50 percent of children found teachers necessary for their values in 2006, this figure was 80 percent in 2014. Thus, from the children's point of view, teachers showed that they attach importance to the transfer of values more clearly than in previous years. In addition to the increasing importance of teachers in forming values from the student's point of view, values become more important against the background of social changes with issues such as digitalization, globalization, and migration (Mandl, 2016). In particular, the issue of migration has become more critical in the context of school in recent years, and with it, in the study of values from different religions and cultures.

METHOD

In this study, the qualitative research method was used. In order to obtain data in the research, curricula of various courses within the scope of value education in Germany were examined using the literature review technique within the scope of the qualitative research method. The document analysis technique is the third basic data collection technique used in qualitative research (Merriam, 2013). It is a technique for obtaining, systematically examining, and evaluating official or unofficial records (Ekiz, 2003). All articles, books, statistics, and biographies related to the subject to be researched can be examined with this technique (Türkbal, 2003). In addition, document analysis in educational research can be a data source in the examination of textbooks and curriculum documents (as cited in Yıldırım & Şimşek, 2011). Literature search technique; It consists of the stages of reaching the documents, checking whether the documents are original, and analyzing the data obtained by understanding the documents. The curricula of "Ethics" and "Religion" courses, in which values education is predominantly given in Germany, were first examined, and the values included in these curricula were tabulated based on education and state.

LITERATUR REVIEW

The Importance of Values Education

Values education has become an educational phenomenon that has become increasingly important in recent years.

Values transferred to individuals in different forms and methods, which have become increasingly important in today's societies, have been seen as a problem in the historical process, and criticism has been brought about. These criticisms continue today. (Aslanargun, 2007). It is an area increasingly taking place in education programs and policies in many countries.

Various value theories have been produced by considering this field differently by morality, customs, religion, tradition-custom, law, political science, philosophy, and sociology.

Values are good-bad, pleasurable-painful, beautiful-ugly, etc. Due to its characteristics, it is also in the fields of interest of various philosophical branches. The values to be gained or gained through schools play an essential role in our lives. As a representation of the desired, it guides our behavior and influences our way of life. Shared core values form the basis of cooperation and social cohesion. Therefore, values education is essential for both the individual and the society.

Values Education from Past to Present

While the concept of "value study" or "value education" in the past was focused on the acquisition of values, this concept gradually left its place in the concept of value creation. Value creation refers to the active relationship with the environment and its scope of various, sometimes held values (Schubarth, 2010). Families often have to make decisions by considering competing values , triggering a conflict (Schwartz, 2012). Value creation occurs by considering which value is more important in the relevant situation. Thus, the process of value formation and personality development details the functioning of the individual development, development, and acquisition of values or attitudes (Franz, 2010; Multrus, 2008; Nunner-Winkler 2007; Schubarth, Speck, and von Lynen Berg, 2010; Speck, 2010; Standop, 2005).

This is important not only for the allocation of values but also for the interaction between people and the environment, but it is also essential that values change over the entire lifespan. Both processes are complex and continue throughout life (Bacon, 2010). They can occur indirectly, i.e., tacitly and incidentally, or directly, i.e., purposefully and with appropriate measures as a framework. It is not possible to directly control which values children eventually acquire and which they attach to. It is related to what they perceive and experience in large countries, how they operate, and how they reflect on their use (Heritage, 2013).

Value assessments aim to learn to evaluate and acquire moral values (Schubarth, 2010). This is also called value competence, along with the principle.

The school plays a vital role in the determination of values. As a public institution, the school is subject to the Basic Law of the Federal Republic of Germany, the relevant state law (Bavaria, Baden-Württemberg, Etc.), and school law. The central values of the Basic Law are human dignity, internal security, individual freedom, legal and social freedom, public health, and democracy (Detjen, 2012). Values including liberty, justice, freedom, greetings, and solidarity (the state constitution of North Rhine-Westphalia of 28 June 1950; the Brandenburg instrument constitution of 20 August 1992, last amended by the law of 5 December 2013; each from 1 February 2017) are enshrined in its states.

In addition, each school is committed to protecting public values through its rules. These can be experienced through the school climate, where "the appreciation and equality of individual members in their differences" (Naurath et al., 2013, p. 37) should be expressed. A climate of appreciation, fostering children's abilities and strengths and fostering teachers', 200), naturopaths, and students' negotiation abilities (200). In the classroom, knowledge acquisition by the learner supported by the teacher usually occurs in an institution such as a school or university. Teaching is seen as a communication process in which learning processes that are planned, initiated, and directed for competence, socialization, and personal development occur in the interaction between the teacher and the learner. According to Giesecke (2004), the teaching material in every school subject touches on values and norms. The formation of values at school means "to place the valuable aspects of the facts more in the center of the lesson"

(Giesecke, 2004, p. 237). This happens mainly through reflection and joint reflection, where fundamental questions of morality or ethics are discussed and debated argumentatively. For example, this is possible by confronting students with values and norms in a German literary text or subject-specific lessons (Giesecke, 2004). Its direction is entirely implicit in the linguistic and social sciences, so a more explicit discussion of values occurs in ethics or religion. Values are rarely dealt with in the natural sciences. As a result, the cognitive aspect of value formation is often emphasized in daily lessons; that is, it consists of reflections on what values and norms are being addressed. Much less often, this leads to concrete value-driven action. The teacher himself represents another possibility for the formation of values, and this serves as a role model for students. The teacher plays an essential role in the lesson as it significantly determines their personality, the lesson concept they plan, and their didactic learning process. Teachers act as role models in dealing with values in their behavior. Behaviors and attitudes of role models provide direction and support. Role models must act authentically to be believable (Riemer, 2011).

How teachers communicate with students, how they deal with conflicts, how they present themselves professionally and didactically, how they deal with the intellectual content of the subject, how they consider students' strengths and weaknesses, and how they distinguish between personal views and factual information play an important role (Giesecke, 2004, p. 238). The formation of values at school is related mainly to the quality of personal relationships (Giesecke, 2004, p. 239). In this context, reference should be made to Bandura's (1977) social-cognitive learning theory. This assumes that social learning by example occurs through observing and imitating actions in interaction. (Lokhande, 2011). To achieve this, particular preconditions and conditions are required, mainly including the personality traits of the model and the observer, as well as their relationship to each other and the situation. For a teacher to be a role model, it is important to be charming and attractive and to meet the student's needs as well as social status, power, and reputation. Self-confidence, experiences, interests, values, emotions, or moods play an essential role on the observer side. In particular, an emotionally positive relationship and perceived similarity between teacher and student increases the student's desire to imitate. The situation in which the behavior is performed and its consequences are also critical. When a behavior is rewarded and reinforced, it is more likely to be repeated.

In addition to a more implicit value formation through lessons or the teacher's role model function, there are explicit measures to promote the formation of values in schools. These include Learning by Service (Seifert & Zentner, 2010) or Just Community Scholl (Baader, 2001). This article focuses on dilemmas or dilemmas stories.

Dilemmas That Support Value Creation

A dilemma is a predicament or situation one finds himself in when he has to or has to choose between two equally disturbing alternatives (Lind, 2011). This predicament demands from the individual a moral judgment in which possible divergent values must be weighed and, if necessary, prioritized. Moral judgments and judgments differ depending on which values are given more importance. Each individual has to make a decision. Such dilemmas, or tales of dilemmas, encourage discussion, negotiation, and reflection when dealing with values. In addition to a deeper understanding of the facts, these activities reflect the hierarchy and importance of one's values. Dilemmas and dilemma stories are implemented in different approaches. Four of them are presented below:

1. Konstanz dilemma discussion method (Lind, 2009), 2. value discourse (Oser & Spycher, 2005), 3. values and knowledge education approach to combine value and subject-oriented teaching (VaKE; Patry, 2007), and 4. dilemma stories to sensitize values in the scientific context in primary schools (Kopp, Wallner & Mandl, 2017).

Konstanz Dilemma Discussion Method

Konstanz dilemma discussion method (KMDD) goes back to Kohlberg's theory of moral development (1964). Kohlberg used dilemmas to classify different levels of moral development in children and adolescents (Nunner-Winkler, 2009) and to encourage this development by presenting students with arguments one level above their moral level. The purpose of the Konstanz dilemma discussion is to promote value competence to convey an action-oriented aspect and a more cognitive aspect of excellent reflection and thinking ability (Lind, 2012). However, the main goal is to improve cognitive abilities. These include the following aspects (Lind, 2012, p. 3):

- Recognize your principles;
- to pay close attention to the circumstances and facts of a situation;
- Distinguish their principles according to their importance and relevance;
- Express their principles in a social context;
- listening to the arguments of others;
- Finding meta-principles for resolving a conflict in case of conflict of equal principles;

Lind (2012) selects three central directions for promoting value formation that has been empirically validated for effectiveness: First, side arguments are chosen that show little difference in one's moral development (Berkowitz, 1981), or counterarguments are used (Walker, 1986). A second feature is the rhythmic alternation of support and challenge phases to obtain students' optimal level of attention. The third aspect concerns the design of dilemmas: quasi-real dilemmas are preferred here. Half-truth dilemmas do not correspond to reality but are relevant to everyday life. A typical lesson is didactically prepared with the Konstanz dilemma. The discussion is as follows (see Lind, 2009; 2011):

1. Beginning of the lesson: The teacher waits until all participants pay attention.
2. Teacher's presentation of the semi-real dilemma.
3. Silent reflection by participants: Participants receive the story and can reread it and take notes in peace.
4. Clarifying the dilemma: The teacher asks the participants whether they see it as a dilemma.
5. Initial voting: The teacher votes for and against, according to the main character's decision.
6. Preparation of the discussion in small groups: Pro- and con-groups of 3-4 people each are formed; they collect their arguments and supplement them with more arguments.
7. Debate in plenary: Pro and con groups discuss their ideas—different perceptions. Two rules are essential: 1. Discussion is allowed without attacking or evaluating each child, and 2. Participants themselves call the next speaker from the opposite camp.
8. Nomination of the best counterarguments: Each participant can nominate the best argument of their respective competitor.

9. Second vote: Pros and cons are re-voted.
10. Reflection (support): The lesson regarding the joy experienced and obtained is given. Moreover, Learning success is reflected.

An exemplary dilemma is as follows (adapted from Lickona, 1989):

The Kitten Dilemma

Paula tells this story. Paula is eight years old and loves to climb trees. She is the best climber in the neighborhood. She falls from the tree one day, but it does not hurt. His father sees the fall. She gets worried and tells him to promise not to climb trees anymore. Paula makes a promise, and they both shake hands. That same day, Paula meets her friend Anna and other friends. Anna's cute kitten sits in a tree and cannot go down alone anymore. Something must be done immediately. Otherwise, the kitten may fall from the tree. Since Paula is the best climber, the kids ask her if she can climb a tree to save the kitten. However, Paula remembers the promise she made to her father. Studies on using the Konstanz dilemma argument were less conducted than with students. A longitudinal study by Lind (2015) with more than 3,000 psychology and teacher education students showed that the Konstanz dilemma discussion appropriately supports the formation of values. This effect is more pronounced in seminars than in lectures. The general orientation of the interviewees regarding values cannot be affected much.

Value Discourse (Oser, 1986)

also uses Kohlberg's stages of dilemmas to support moral development. This approach is about resolving conflicts in which moral norms are used and justified. The value discourse approach assumes that professional ethics is learned only when the teacher confronts moral issues and discusses them in the specific classroom and problem-solving situations (Öser, 1992). The joint discussion of value issues between teachers and students has particular importance in this approach (Öser, 1992). Through mutual understanding, role-playing and practical solutions to values-related issues, value discourse has a procedural concept that the teacher can adopt. Therefore, the focus of the approach is on the teacher himself. The purpose of value discourse is to encourage moral development within a moral development stage (Öser, 1992). Oser and Spychiger (2005) are concerned with promoting moral learning through insight into the possible consequences of actions. The experiences in which children experience negative values , such as injustice, serve to gain positive values , such as justice (Öser, 2005).

Values and Knowledge Education Approach (VaKE)

There are comparisons within the approach. These are designed so that a hero has to decide between two alternative courses of action that are morally incompatible. Deciding in favor of an alternative always implies that a significant value has been violated. Students are encouraged to decide on the story's hero and then justify it. This value-driven truth is linked to the truth-focused teaching content to arrive at such a decision. To achieve this, students can use all available resources (e.g., research work on the Internet and discussion with peers) (Zierer, 2010).

The aim of the approach is that students learn to present and defend the chosen point of view convincingly with arguments, evidence, and evidence, that is, to justify their ideas through discussion.

An example of a dilemma story from VaKE is as follows (Patry, Weyringer, Aichinger, & Weinberger, 2016, p. 132):

The dilemma "people of the planet Wahinu" The year is 2173. There are 15 billion people on Earth. There needs to be more water and food for that many people. That is why people are looking for a new planet. They discover a new planet and call it "Wahinu." Now people from all over the world fly there with rockets. One hundred people can start a whole new life on this planet. At first, everyone was thrilled. Everything is new and exciting. You learn a new one first. You get to know the environment and other people. All different. Most of them speak different languages and do not understand each other. There are no rules or laws. It is Chaos! People start arguing. "We need rules and a new system!" One group says: "There has to be someone who makes the rules and laws for us. That person has to decide what is right and wrong for us." The second group said, "No, we must set our rules and laws together!" What should people do? Which system should the people of the planet Wahinu choose? (Patry et al., 2016, p. 132).

Konstanz dilemma discussion method

Konstanz dilemma discussion method (KMDD) goes back to Kohlberg's theory of moral development (1964). Kohlberg used dilemmas to classify different levels of moral development in children and adolescents (Nunner-Winkler, 2009) and to encourage this development by presenting students with arguments one level above their moral level. The purpose of the Konstanz dilemma discussion is to promote value competence to convey an action-oriented aspect and a more cognitive aspect of excellent reflection and thinking ability (Lind, 2012). However, the main goal is to improve cognitive abilities. These include the following aspects (Lind, 2012, p. 3):

- Recognize your principles;
- to pay close attention to the circumstances and facts of a situation;
  - Distinguish their principles according to their importance and relevance;
- Express their principles in a social context;
- listening to the arguments of others;
  - Finding meta-principles for resolving a conflict in case of conflict of equal principles;

Lind (2012) selects three central directions for promoting value formation that has been empirically validated for effectiveness: First, side arguments are chosen that show little difference in one's moral development (Berkowitz, 1981), or counterarguments are used (Walker, 1986). A second feature is the rhythmic alternation of support and challenge phases to obtain students' optimal level of attention. The third aspect concerns the design of dilemmas: quasi-real dilemmas are preferred here. Half-truth dilemmas do not correspond to reality but are relevant to everyday life. A typical lesson is didactically prepared with the Konstanz dilemma. The discussion is as follows (see Lind, 2009; 2011):

1. Beginning of the lesson: The teacher waits until all participants pay attention.
2. Teacher's presentation of the semi-real dilemma.
3. Silent reflection by participants: Participants receive the story and can reread it and take notes in peace.
4. Clarifying the dilemma: The teacher asks the participants whether they see it as a dilemma.
5. Initial voting: The teacher votes for and against, according to the main character's decision.

6. Preparation of the discussion in small groups: Pro- and con-groups of 3-4 people each are formed; they collect their arguments and supplement them with more arguments.

7. Debate in plenary: Pro and con groups discuss their ideas—different perceptions. Two rules are essential: 1. Discussion is allowed without attacking or evaluating each child, and 2. Participants themselves call the next speaker from the opposite camp.

8. Nomination of the best counterarguments: Each participant can nominate the best argument of their respective competitor.

9. Second vote: Pros and cons are re-voted.

10. Reflection (support): Lesson, joy experienced and gained given in terms of Learning success is reflected.

An exemplary dilemma is as follows (adapted from Lickona, 1989):

The Kitten Dilemma This story is told by Paula. Paula is eight years old and loves to climb trees. She is the best climber in the neighborhood. She falls from a tree one day, but it does not hurt. His father sees the fall. She worries and tells him to promise not to climb trees anymore. Paula makes a promise, and they both shake hands. That same day, Paula meets her friend Anna and other friends. Anna's cute kitten sits in a tree and cannot go down alone anymore. Something must be done immediately. Otherwise, the kitten may fall from the tree. Since Paula is the best climber, the kids ask her if she can climb a tree to save the kitten. However, Paula remembers the promise she made to her father. Studies on using the Konstanz dilemma argument were less conducted than with students. A longitudinal study by Lind (2015) with more than 3,000 psychology and teacher education students showed that the Konstanz dilemma discussion appropriately supports the formation of values. This effect is more pronounced in seminars than in lectures. The general orientation of the interviewees regarding values cannot be affected much.

Functioning of Values Education in Primary Schools

How does values education, which is distinguished by a multitude of values, work in primary schools? How can educational institutions help children become socially competent, confident, and responsible?

The main findings can be summarized as follows: Values education is the process by which individuals develop value systems and value skills in interaction with their environment. Science sees this as a fundamental aspect of personal growth that can be facilitated in various ways. The stages where people are susceptible to values education are early childhood and youth. This makes certain age-appropriate pedagogical concepts promising for these age groups. Contemporary concepts foster development by focusing on self-directed value acquisition to shape autonomous, responsible personalities and integrate the daily experiences of children and young people.

The Importance of Family in Values Education

The key to values education is the various areas of socialization. The family, the first authority and the most significant influence in socialization, is significant here. Parents' values and values education skills have the most significant impact on children's value development. This effect depends on the structures and roles in the family, socioeconomic and sociocultural factors, parenting styles, and relationship patterns, respectively. For sustainable values education, a socially integrative, democratic, or authoritarian parenting style (e.g., emotional warmth, empathetic approach, clear communication, and sense of responsibility) is particularly beneficial. Families face new challenges regarding values education in a globalized, pluralistic society.

Family education services can offer support here. Demand is high, so expanding and promoting these services is recommended.

The Importance of School in Values Education

Beyond the family, preschool is the first pedagogical authority in the child's life. Then the primary school level is also practical. Children embedded in a community of peers have rudimentary experiences with values and learn value-oriented behaviors from each other. Values are here first, primarily through respectful communication, and as stated earlier.

It is communicated through different forms of interaction through teachers who act as role models.

Second, it can promote values education by openly discussing and reflecting on values with children. In this context, schools are the most critical environments that empower teachers in their values and education skills.

As stated before, school, as the second pedagogical authority after the family, plays a crucial role in values education, primarily since it can educate children and young people for a long time. Values education is an integral part of the education and training mission of the school. However, the legal provision and relevance of school values education are hampered by several constraints that complicate its implementation, including a lack of consensus about values, low levels of professionalism among teaching staff, and structural constraints. In principle, schools have numerous opportunities to promote values education indirectly (through the school culture) or directly, using specific methods (such as problem-solving exercises and class councils). Critical conditions for the success of the school's values education include consensus about values, a respectful school culture, and faculty's value skills. In order to strengthen the values of education in the school, it is recommended to update the curriculum and the teaching staff and tie continuity in education more firmly. As an extra-curricular learning and training space that is voluntary and distinguished by participation and openness, children's youth work, who are the youth of tomorrow, offers young people countless opportunities to embrace values and value skills. Activation and participation of young people are crucial here, as is the commitment and role of educators as "relevant and interesting" adults. In order to strengthen values education in youth work, it is recommended to include it as a topic in teaching staff training and continuing education, sensitize sponsors and institutions, and develop environments for values education in youth work. Therefore, a value discourse approach should also be adopted. (See previous pages for detailed information on value discourse.)

Family and educational institutions, as well as peers, constantly influence adolescents' values of education. However, using this influence in a pedagogical context is challenging because there is no place for peers in the classical pedagogical model, where younger generations are influenced by their elders.

Peer Projects in Values Education

In values education, peer counseling is of great importance. Peer projects and examples of practice show how this can be achieved: for example, through peer mediation, peer counseling (e.g., personal discussions about sexuality or drugs), or peer education (e.g., knowledge transfer in workshops).

These planned, pedagogically driven processes fall under the category of peer involvement. It is characterized by the exchange of information between peers, their previous education by adults, the information asymmetry between peers, and the lack of concrete interaction between adults. Peer involvement is often justified because reaching young people through their peers is more accessible regarding values issues and education. However, research into the quality and effectiveness of peer concepts is just beginning in Germany and lags far behind implementation. Developments in other countries can provide a valuable impetus for the values education debate in Germany. An international research project commissioned by Bertelsmann Stiftung highlights several development trends concerning Germany. It shows a trend towards integrative-oriented programs, that is, programs that connect the various components, for example, values education that promotes social cohesion. There is also a discernible link between skill development and prevention. Another aspect is the link between the values debate and other relevant discourses, such as the human rights debate and the integration of values.

Valuable ideas emerge from the multitude of concepts using role models and the work of organizations that support the necessary scientific evaluation and support for concepts and programs.

1. Proactive discussion on values and values education: Democratic society is based on harmony based on shared (core) values. This fundamental consensus must be continually renewed and consolidated. An ongoing, rational discussion on values and values education is a vital prerequisite here. Such discussions are especially fruitful when conducted in line with the conflicts and contradictions in society and activated in the daily lives of (young) people.

Four steps are crucial in negotiating and solving dilemmas in gaining and internalizing values in values education (Öser, 1992): First, the teacher is responsible for creating a round table inviting all students to participate. In the second step, students can express all their views, regardless of whether they offer need, justification, blame, or possible solutions. Each participant is encouraged to listen to others for the best solution. Here, the teacher acts as the leader of the discussion, on the one hand, and a carrier of knowledge, on the other hand, who adds his view to the discussion. In the third step, each participant must contribute to the solution and take responsibility for their views, i.e., justify. When these three aspects are fulfilled, the fourth step, the solution to the dilemma, occurs (Öser, 1992). An example of a possible dilemma, which is also used to measure moral value judgment, is as follows (Colby & Kohlberg, 1987).

Valjean's Dilemma

In a European country, a poor man named Valjean could not find work like his sister and brother. Penniless, he stole the food and medicine he needed. He was caught and sentenced to six years in prison. A few years later, he escaped prison and started a new life with a new name in another part of the country. He saved money and built a factory. He paid his workers the highest wages and used the factory's profits to build a hospital for those who could not afford good medical care. Twenty years pass when a tailor recognizes the company's owner as Valjean, an escaped convict still wanted by the police in his hometown. "Should the tailor tell Valjean to the police? Why or why not? Was it right for Valjean to steal food and medicine because he did it for a good cause? Should people who break the law for a good cause go to jail? Should Valjean be sent back to prison even though he is poor? Would nine hospitals help? Does a citizen have a duty to report an escaped prisoner to the authorities? Does the tailor have the right not to do this? What is the most responsible thing for a tailor to do? What would you do if you were a tailor?"

2. Supporting values education: Values education especially requires support from (educational) legislators. The need for proactive values education and the objectives, methods, and resources to achieve it should be clearly articulated, and appropriate measures initiated or encouraged. The role of pedagogical institutions in values education should be presented proactively. Value skills should be included in the curriculum equally with other core skills and should be actively promoted in education and training institutions. It should be noted that values education forms the core of the educational task, is indispensable for personal development, and forms the basis of the entire spectrum of preventive work.

3. Clarifying the aims and methods of values education: The starting point for any education The method and effectiveness in values education is a shared understanding of goals and potential. Dealing with the diversity of values in our society requires both. A shared value base needs to be recognized, and different notions of value should be respected. Based on this, it is essential to communicate through methods. Value competence and value acquisition must be promoted according to prosocial democratic value systems.

4. In the education of professionals, the fixation of continuing education in values education as a compulsory component: Qualified values education requires professional educators. Therefore, values education is a compulsory part of all pedagogical education. The essential elements of a values education curriculum are the knowledge and skills related to creating value systems and various values, concepts, and examples of good practice in values education, as well as the role model function of pedagogical professionals.

5. Empowering families as primary values education authority: Since the foundation of values education is in the family, parents need appropriate skills to support their children's values education. This requires more comprehensive and refined services within the framework of family education.

6. Recognition and dissemination of preschool education as an authority in values education: Preschool education, together with the family, has a significant impact on values education in early childhood. Therefore, more focus should be placed on the professional development of values (education) and skills in teachers. How preschool schools function in values education and how they should be developed further is necessary for researchers and preschool development.

7. Making the school a central authority, especially in primary school values education: Schools have various opportunities to promote values education in children and young people that have not been adequately realized until now. Values education should be part of the school program and overall school improvement. In the curriculum and pedagogical work, more attention should be paid to values education issues, particularly the practical adoption of value systems and skills. At the same time, the issue of "values education" is both current pedagogical concepts such as violence prevention and a valid framework for social, intercultural, and democratic learning.

8. Utilizing the hidden potential of extra-curricular youth work: Good youth work is always good for values education. Suppose this is especially true based on long-term, consistent relationship work. Touching the potential of youth work involves developing the framework within which such work takes place. It is essential to establish and develop professionalism among those working in education.

Actors and supporters should be more sensitive to the issue and called upon to develop environments for values education in youth work. Extra-curricular services are indispensable for the value of the education of children and young people. Especially the spread of all-day education brings cooperation in values education in new fields.

9. Recognizing and promoting the potential of peers in values education: Involving peers in values education (peer participation) opens up promising prospects. It is widely known that peers are more likely to reach youth than adults. The existing peer concepts in values education should be recognized more and rapidly disseminated. In addition, these concepts should be supported scientifically, and their results should be made public.

10. Increasing working with role models: Values education always takes place in interaction with reference figures. Children and young people have role models that they direct themselves to. This value-driven function should be exploited more, and more work should be done with role models. Good practice. Such examples should be publicized more widely.

11. Focus on value skills: The main objective of all activities around values education should be Cation, the ability to cope with the increasing diversity of values. Here people require individual value skills. Further education services should therefore aim, to a greater extent, at promoting value. Skills and abilities are required, such as empathy, embracing other perspectives, reflection, judgment, and handling conflict and cooperation.

12. Using developmental concepts: Constructive concepts in values education combine the daily experiences of children and young people and focus on self-worth with the goal of an autonomous, re-sponsible personality aimed at both concrete and concrete purposes. Value-driven action and reflection on that action. Concepts of this nature should be further developed.

13. Expanding concepts with an integrative orientation: Values education is a complex process that includes cognitive, emotional-emotional, motivational, and behavioral aspects. To better promote values education, further use should consist of concepts with an integrative orientation that connects multiple promotion strategies such as experiential, cognitive, social, and emotional learning, skill development, reflection, and action orientation.

14. To disseminate existing knowledge on values education, science, and practice have provided many important insights and examples supporting values education. It should consist of concepts with an integrative orientation based on insights and practical experience, linking multiple promotion strategies such as cognitive, social, and emotional learning, skill development, reflection, and action orientation.

15. Orientation to good practice examples: Current practice examples Values education represents a broad repository of ideas and concepts—Cretan values education study. Documenting examples of good practice provides new impetus for discussions around values education.

16. Promote interaction of actors and institutions: Proactive values education requires interaction between actors and institutions. Germany is relatively new in this regard. Therefore, interaction should be encouraged more actively.

17. Intensification of research, development, and quality assurance: Values education requires continuous research and (quality) development. The substantial research and development requirement includes research projects, creating value systems, and documenting concepts and projects. Scientific support and evaluation of concrete projects.

18. Promoting international exchange: Further exchanges with other countries and regions are recommended for values education in Germany. A broader perspective will increase the chances of new possibilities in research and development in Germany.

VALUES EDUCATION IN GERMANY

What is the current state of practice in values education in Germany? "Werte lernen und leben. The publication Theorie und Praxis der Wertebildung in Deutschland ("Learning and living values. The theory and practice of values education in Germany") answers these questions.

Germany consists of 16 states. "Primary school in Berlin and Brandenburg is six years; in other states, it is four years. Grundschule (primary school) lasts four or six years, depending on the state in which it is required. The states prepare education programs in Germany. "Due to the federative structure of the Federal Republic of Germany, the authority in educational affairs is shared between the federal state and the states. However, most of the educational decision-making power rests with the states. Therefore, the education program of each state has its characteristics. German, English, music, art, sports, and religion courses are among the courses taught at the primary school level. Religion is an elective course in all states and has taken its place in education programs.

Table 1. Ethics Lessons in the States of Germany

States	Lessons
Hamburg, Bremen	Philolosphy
Baden-Württemberg, Bayern,	Philosophieren mit Kindern Mecklenburg-Vorpommern (Philosophy with Children)
Mecklenburg-Vorpommern	Philosophieren mit Kindern Mecklenburg-Vorpommern (Philosophy with Children)
Saarland	Allgemeine Ethics (General Ethics
Niedersachsen (Lower Saxony	Werte und Normen (Values and Norms) Niedersachsen (Lower Saxony)
Sachsen-Anhalt	Ethikunterricht (Ethics Lesson
Brandenburg	Lebensgestaltung-Ethik-Religionskunde (living, ethics, religion)
North Rhen Westphalia	Praktische Philosophie, Religion

Source: Act. from Ethikunterricht, 2008, Bilici, 2008

There are also curricula for these ethics courses taught in many states of Germany. It is seen that there are six essential subject areas (freedom, conscience, justice, love, human dignity, and religion) in the curriculum of the "Ethics" course taught in the state of Hessen. A wide variety of individual values were also included in the program, in which individual values were predominant.

In Germany, values education is handled both directly as a separate course and with a hidden curriculum in each course. Ethics and philosophy courses and values education are provided for those who do not choose values education or religion course together with religion course according to the wishes of their families (Öztürk, Ferah Özcan, Çimen, Özkan, & Balkaş, 2016). It is emphasized that values education in Germany has two dimensions, individual and social. In the individual dimension, the process of self-confidence, the realization of self-worth, and building values are supported; it includes values such as tolerance, respect, harmonious living without conflict with society, justice, honesty, and democratic value systems in the social dimension. The primary purpose of values education practices in Germany is to maintain a harmonious life between the values of the individual and the values expected by society. Different methods such as modeling, presentations, role-playing, discussion, games, projects, and active participation of families are used in the internalization and socialization of values (Kopp, Niedermeier,

& Mandl, 2014). According to the German education system, education and the internalization of values are the shared responsibility of the family, school, and society. It is more beneficial for the child's development, valuing education as holistic instead of focusing on specific areas. In other words, values education and development areas should not be considered separately. In England and the 21st century, democracy and experimentation values are considered examples of values education and education programs in 77 countries, which are necessary for individuals to live in harmony. For this reason, these values are included starting from preschool (Moss & Urban, 2010).

It is seen that the most comprehensive religious lesson curriculum among the education programs of the states is the Christianity lesson curriculum according to the Catholic belief of the Schleswig-Holstein state. Therefore, within the scope of values education, religious education in the states' curricula should be handled in terms of various religions and sects. A point to be noted here is the congregation or communities according to which Islamic religious teaching will be given. The second course within the scope of values education in Germany is the ethics course. He emphasizes that if parents do not want their children to take religion lessons, the state offers alternatives to children who do not attend religion lessons, that elective lessons are offered for students who do not choose religion lessons. These lessons are opened under the name of ethics/morality. For example, 'Philosophy with Children' (Philosophieren) for primary schools in Mecklenburg-Vorpommern Kindern), 'Applied Philosophy (Praktische Philosophie)' for secondary education in North Rhine-Westphalia, 'Values and Norms (Werte und Normen)' in Lower Saxony, and 'Morality (Ethics)' in the states of Thuringia and others." Ethics started to take place in the curriculum as an integrative curriculum course after 1990 in Germany.

Finding a course called Ethics or Values in every state is impossible. However, these courses are mainly given at the secondary and high school levels. It can be said that ethics is seen as a values education that is taught in the integrity of education rather than a course. In Germany-Schleswig-Holstein, religion classes are elective courses for various denominations and religions. Religion lessons according to the Protestant sect,

There are three elective courses in which fundamental values are taught as a religion course according to the Catholic sect and the religion of Islam. The most comprehensive content is in the Christian teaching curriculum according to the primary school Catholicism sect.

CONCLUSION

Values education is an integral part of the educational and upbringing task of the school, as it can educate children for a long time. However, the legal provision and relevance of school values education are hampered by several constraints that complicate its implementation, including a lack of consensus about values, low levels of professionalism among teaching staff, and structural constraints. In principle, schools have numerous opportunities to promote values education indirectly (through the school culture) or directly, using specific methods (such as class councils and problem-solving exercises). Critical conditions for the success of the school's values education include consensus about values, a respectful school culture, and the value skills of the teacher-training faculty. In order to strengthen the values of education in the school, it is necessary to update and develop the curriculum and teaching staff constantly.

Family and educational institutions, as well as peers, constantly influence adolescents' values of education. However, using this influence in a pedagogical context is challenging because there is no place for peers in the classical pedagogical model, where younger generations are influenced by their elders simultaneously. Peer projects and practical examples show how this can be achieved: for example, through peer mediation, peer counseling, or peer education (e.g., knowledge transfer in workshops).

These are planned, pedagogically guided processes that fall under the category of peer involvement. It is characterized by the exchange of information between peers, their previous education by adults, the information asymmetry between peers, and the lack of concrete interaction between adults. Peer involvement is often justified because reaching young people through their peers is more manageable regarding values issues and education. However, research into the quality and effectiveness of peer concepts has just begun in Germany and lags far behind practice.

In addition, it seems to represent a suitable method for school and teaching due to the adaptability of values in terms of content in values education and dilemmas in values education. In addition to teaching children values at an early age, especially in the context of increasing global problems such as poverty, global warming, and famine, to enable them to develop values and act value-oriented actively, most importantly, it seems that the teacher himself should serve as an authentic role model for values-oriented thinking and acting.

Therefore, by applying the culture of argumentative discourse based on others' clarified self and empathetically perceived value orientations, subject teaching, implicit or planned learning in a democratic teaching style makes an indispensable contribution to democratic education.

REFERENCES

Aslanargun, E. (2007). Criticisms of modern educational administration and educated post-modern management. *Journal of Educational Administration in Theory and Practice, 50*, 195–212.

Baader, M. (2001). On the theory and practice of the just community approach in moral education. In E. Liebau (Ed.), *The formation of the subject. Contributions to the pedagogy of participation* (pp. 159–193). Juventa.

Bandura, A. (1977). *Social learning theory*. Prentice Hall.

Berkowitz, M. W. (1981). A critical appraisal of the 'plus-one' convention in moral education. [Allyn and Bacon.]. *Phi Delta Kappan,* 488–489.

Colby, A., & Kohlberg, L. (1987). The Measurement of Moral Judgement, Volume 2, Standard Issue Scoring Manual. Cambridge University Press.

Detjen, J. (2012). *Constitutional values: Which values determine the Basic Law?* Federal Agency for Civic Education.

German Red Cross. (2014). *Working aid for the project "Value formation in families." Basics a value-sensitive family formation.* http://www.Wertebildunginfamilien.de/wp-content/uploads/2014/12/Arbeitshilfe_Wertebildung.pdf

Ethics. (2015). *Lehrplan Ethik, bildungsgang Realschule Jahrgangsstufen* 5-10. Hessisches Kulturministerium.

Ethicunterricht. (2008). Zur Situation des Ethikunterrichts in der Bundesrepublik Deutschland. Kultusministerkonferenz vom. *Eric, 51*(3), 6-11.

Franz, M. (2010). *The main thing is value creation. Experiencing and developing values with children, manual for value education in kindergarten and after-school care.* Don Bosco.

Giesecke, H. (2004). What can the school contribute to value education? In S. Gruehn, G. Kluchert, & T. Koinzer (eds.), What makes schools? School, teaching and value education: Theoretical, historical, empirical. Achim Leschinsky on his 60th birthday (pp. 235-246). Beltz. 17

Kopp, B., Niedermeier, S., & Mandl, H. (2014). *Actual practical value education in Germany* (Conference Paper), ICERI 2014 (17th-19th November 2014), Seville, Spain.

Kohlberg, L. (1964). Development of moral character and moral ideology. *Review of child development research, 1,* 381-431.

Lickona, Th. (1989). *How to raise good children! The moral development of the child from Birth through adolescence and what you can do to help.*

Lind, G. (2009), Morality is teachable. Munich: Oldenbourg. Lind, G. (2011). Moral education. In: E. Zierer & K. Kiel (eds.). Basic knowledge of lesson design (p. 39-50). Schneider.

Lind, G. (2012). The method of dilemma discussion. In F. Brüggen, W. Sander, & Ch. Igelbrink (Hrsg.), Basic texts on judgment formation (judgment formation, vol. 2).

Verlag, L. I. T. Lind, G. (2015). Favorable learning environments for moral competence development. A multiple intervention study with 3,000 students in a higher education context. *International Journal of University Teaching and Faculty Development. (4)*4. https://www.novapublishers.com/catalog/product_info.php?products_id=53411

Mandl, H. (2016), Mint and Values - Formation of Values in Experimental Lessons. Interview with the Siemens Foundation. https://www.siemens-stiftung.org/de/projects/mint-und- values/insight/

Merriam, S. B. (2013). *Qualitative research* (S. Turan, Trans.). Nobel Publishing.

Moss, P. and Urban, M. (2010). *Democracy and experimentation: Two fundamental values for education.* Bertelsmann Stiftung, 1-96

Multrus, U. (2008), Values education in schools - An overview of current concepts. In the Bavarian State Ministry for Education and Culture (ed.), Values make you strong. Values Education Practice Guide (1st Edition, pp. 22-37). Brigg Pedagogy.

Naurath, E. (2013). Appreciation as a basic pedagogical attitude for the formation of values. In E. Naurath, M. Blasberg-Kuhnke, E. Gläser, R. Mokrosch, & S. Müller-Using (Eds.), *How values are formed. Interdisciplinary and subject-specific value formation* (pp. 29–42). Goettingen University Press Osnabrück., doi:10.14220/9783737001304.29

Naurath, E., Blasberg-Kuhnke, M., Gläser, E., Mokrosch, R., & Müller-Using, S. (Eds.). (2013). *How values are created. Interdisciplinary and subject-specific values.* Goettingen University Press.

Nunner-Winkler, G. (2007). Understanding Morals - Developments in Childhood. In D. Horster (ed.), *Moral Development of Children and Adolescents* (pp. 51-76). Wiesbaden: Publishing house for social sciences.

Nunner-Winkler, G. (2009). Processes of moral learning and unlearning. *Journal of Education*, *55*(2), 528–548.

Oser, F. (1986). Moral education and value education: The discourse perspective. In M. C. Wittwock (Ed.), *Handbuch der Lehrforschung* (pp. 917–941). Macmillan.

Oser, F. (1992). *Morality in professional action: A discourse approach for teaching*. In FK.

Oser, A. D., & Patry, J.-L. (Eds.), *Effective and Responsible Teaching* (pp. 109–125). Jossey Bass.

Oser, F. (2005). Negative knowledge and morality. *Journal of Education*, *49*, 171–181.

Oser, F., & Spychiger, M. (2005). *Learning is painful. On the theory of negative knowledge and the practice of error culture*. Beltz.

Öztürk, F., Ferah Özcan, A., Çimen, S., Ozkan, A., & Balkaş, S. R. (2016). Cross-cultural comparative research on values education: The case of Germany, Sweden, South Korea, and Malaysia. *Journal of Academic Social Research*, *4*(30), 629–649.

Patry, J.-L. (2007). VaKE introduction and theoretical background. In K. Tirri (Ed.), *Values and Foundations in Gifted Education* (pp. 157–169). Peter Lang.

Patry, J.-L., Weinberger, A., Weyringer, S., & Nussbaumer, M. (2012). Combination of values and knowledge transfer. In B. J. Irby, G. Brown, R. Lara-Alecio, & S. Jackson (Eds.), *The Handbook of Educational Theories* (pp. 563–577). Publishing in the Information Age.

Patry, J.-L., Weyringer, S., Aichinger, K., & Weinberger, A. (2016). Integration work with immigrant youth with VaKE (Values and Knowledge Education). *International Educational Dialogues: Past and Present*, *3*(3), 123–139.

Piaget, J. (1986). *The child's moral judgment*. Necklace. (Original work published 1932)

Religionunterricht. (2009) *Kerncurriculum für das Gymnasium Schuljahrgange 5-10*, Evangelische Religion. Niedersachsisches Kultusministerium.

Religionsunterricht. (2014) *Kern-curriculum für die Schulformen des Sekundarbereichs I schuljahrgange 5-10, Islamische Religion*. Niedersachsisches Kultusministerium.

Riemer, H. L. (2011). *Role models and role models. About the change in values and the chances of its rediscovery*. Dr. Köster.

Saglam, M. (1999). *Education systems of European countries*. Anadolu University Press.

Standup, J. (2005). *Werte-Erziehung*. Beltz Verlag.

Schubarth, W. (2010), The return of values." The debate about new values and the chances of value formation, In W. Schubarth, K. Speck and H. von Lynen Berg (eds.), Value formation in youth work, school, and community. Balance sheet and outlook (pp. 21-42). VS publishing house for social sciences.

Schubarth, W., Speck, K. & Lynen Berg, H. von (2010). *Value formation in youth work, school, and community: balance and perspectives.* VS publishing house for social sciences.

Schwartz, S. H. (2012). An overview of the Schwartz theory of core values. *Online Readings in Psychology and Culture, 2*(1). http://scholarworks.gvsu.edu/orpc/vol2/iss1/11

Seifert, A., & Zentner, S. (2010). *Service Learning – Learning through engagement: Method, quality, examples, and selected focal points.* Freudenberg Foundation.

Speck, K. (2010). *Value formation and participation of children and young people.*

Speck, K. (2010). Value formation and participation of children and young people. In: W. Schubarth, K. Speck and H. von Lynen Berg (eds.), Value formation in youth work, school, and community: Balance sheet and perspectives (pp. 61-90). VS publishing house for social sciences.

Standup, J. (2005). *Value formation: Introduction to the most important concepts of value formation.* Beltz.

Turkbal, A. (2003). *Scientific research methods and writing techniques.*

UNICEF. (2014) *Geolino UNICEF Children's Values Monitor.* https://www.unicef.de/blob/56990/a121cfd7c7acbdc2f4b97cbcdf0cc716/geolino-unicef-child Values Monitor-2014-data.pdf

Walker, L. J. (1986). Cognitive processes in moral development. In G. L. Sapp (Ed.), *Handbook of moral development* (pp. 109–145). Religious Education Press.

Weinberger, A., Patry, J.-L., & Weyringer, S. (2016). Improving professional practice through hands-on research: VaKE (Values and Knowledge Education) in university teacher education. *Professions and Learning, 9*(1), 63–84.

Zierer, K. (2010). *School value education.* Schneider.

KEY TERMS AND DEFINITIONS

Didactic Expression: The expressions of the works written to give information, moral lessons, religion, and technical information are called didactic.

Dilemma; It is a state of being forced to choose between two situations. These two situations can be desired or undesirable for the individual.:

Experimentation: A procedure carried out to support or refute a hypothesis or to determine the efficacy or probability of something that has not been tried before. Experiments provide insight into the cause-effect relationship by showing what outcome occurs when a particular factor is manipulated.

Implicit learning: It is learning that is done unconsciously, without being aware of it, without reward. The person is not aware of this learning until the state of need; she becomes aware of the knowledge when the need arises.

Peer Counseling: Includes implementing a preventive and improving program implemented by their peers for the healthy development of individuals, taking into account their developmental processes.

Role Playing: It is a technique that increases the individual's desire to learn and aims to develop the individual's versatile development by putting himself in someone else's place, taking an active role in teaching, expressing himself, being creative, perceiving life in a multifaceted way, to develop his desire and to feel for research. It is an empathy-based technique.

Proactive discussion: The tendency to initiate change rather than react to events. 2 (Psychol) expresses or denotes a mental process that affects a later process.

Value transfer: It is the cognitive transfer of these values to children, together with activities such as educational programs, stories, or social skill group work, which include concepts such as sharing, love, respect, the ability to solve problems through communication, staying away from violence, not being prejudiced.

Chapter 10
Shared Reflective Practices and Scenario-Based Learning for Values Development in Primary School Children

Priyadarshini Muthukrishnan
(iD) https://orcid.org/0000-0003-1545-0963
HELP University, Malaysia

Soon Seng Thah
Department of Education, HELP University, Malaysia

Goh Lay Huah
Academy of Future Education, Xi'an Jiaotong-Liverpool University, China

ABSTRACT

The purpose of this chapter is to highlight the significance and processes involved in conducting shared reflections to nurture value development in children in primary schools. The chapter describes the characteristics and application of the value-based reflection framework (VBRF), which was devised specifically for this study and employed as a reflective instrument for classroom reflections. Additionally, to facilitate children's reflections, value scenarios were also used to prompt children to relate value practices to real-world contexts. This chapter serves as a guide for teachers, empowering them with guidelines for conducting reflection sessions during moral education classes, as well as informing educators, curriculum designers, and policymakers about incorporating reflective practices for children's value development.

INTRODUCTION

Although there are many educational strategies to promote development in children, achieving meaningful and lasting change in sustaining moral ideals and virtues remains a challenge. Especially in the current AI era, instilling ethical and moral values and embedding these values into curricular activities

DOI: 10.4018/978-1-6684-9295-6.ch010

is vital. Furthermore, the transmission of traditional social values such as faith, ethics, morality, respect, tolerance, justice, and compassion from generation to generation may be threatened by the inevitable deterioration of traditional social relationships that begin in the family and grow through neighborhood associations, religious affiliations, and hometown associations that lead to a moral crisis in society. As a result, fundamental values such as kindness, collaboration, humility, and tolerance could start to seem strange, particularly to the younger generation. Therefore, there is a dire need for the development of value in children for a sustainable value-driven community.

This chapter discusses how reflective practices could foster values development in primary school children using a scenario-based learning approach in teacher-mediated classroom discussions that includes shared reflections, interactions, and scaffolded discussions among children. This chapter will assist teachers in designing and implementing reflective sessions in the classroom using a scenario-based teaching approach. Specifically, this research chapter discusses using the Value-Based Reflection Framework (VBRF) to carry out shared-reflective classroom sessions. VBRF is based mainly on reflection-in-action and reflection-on-action. Previous research on the framework for the formation of values in children has revealed important aspects of understanding the development of values, mainly based on the conception and motives that underpin each value. In addition, this chapter is part of a significant study conducted with 59 primary school children from an international school in Malaysia. The effectiveness of VBRF has been supported by empirical and qualitative evidence (Huah et al., 2022; Muthukrishnan & Huah, 2023). In the current chapter, key findings from the research study on the reflection exercise and selected case studies are discussed to emphasize the effectiveness of using the VBRF in fostering value development.

BACKGROUND

The value system of a society may be referred to as its character (Sahin, 2019), and it influences how individuals interact with one another (Doring et al., 2010). Values dispositions are essential for the development of self-identity and self-concept. Pomeranz et al. (2011) defined values as an individual's ethics or "concepts or ideas of what individuals consider to be good, bad, right, and wrong in their lives." As is universally recognized, curriculums must be underpinned by explicit and implicit values (Hughson & Wood, 2022). In addition, Hughson and Wood's learning compass for 2030 recognizes the need to strengthen value formation in young children by incorporating a value system into the school curriculum using a variety of approaches, particularly in the four thrust areas: personal, social, societal, and human values. However, there have been growing concerns regarding the erosion of human values among the younger generation, necessitating more significant efforts to develop shared values of citizenship at the school level to create more inclusive, equitable, and sustainable societies. Balakrishnan (2010) argued that children must be imaginative and equipped with the skills to face and overcome moral challenges. At this time, formal education must integrate implicit and explicit curricular activities that foster value development in children.

The value curriculum in schools is typically called moral, civic, or citizenship education. In the primary years, values, sociocultural beliefs and norms, life skills, and attitudes are established, and it remains challenging to develop a value-driven society, especially in the AI era. The following sections discuss the potential of using shared reflections to foster children's values development.

Reflective Practices in Values Development

Values, sociocultural beliefs and norms, life skills, and attitudes are formed in the primary years. According to Dewey's (1933) theory, reflective practice is essential to learning because not all learning experiences are functional until they are reflected upon. According to research in developmental psychology, by late childhood (ages 7 to 12), children can learn from experience through self-reflection as a self-conscious action (Zelazo, 2000). According to Schön (1983), reflective practice is a dialogue between thought and action that aids skill acquisition. Boud, Keough, and Walker (1985) viewed that reflection allows individuals to examine their past experiences to gain new insight and appreciation.

Moreover, reflection is essential for children to develop a sense of ownership over their self-development and become natural thinkers in defining themselves. It enables them to comprehend the importance of everyday experiences, retain lessons learned, and develop a sense of self-worth and accomplishment. Moreover, reflection is more than just pondering; it entails mentally recreating past experiences by recalling one's behaviors and unpacking the minor details of those experiences through introspection. It requires reflective and reflexive thought to adopt a critical stance for future actions toward personal development.

Reflection is the process of dwelling deeply into one's thoughts, emotions, and motivations to determine the "Why?" factor in reasoning and decision-making. Reflective practice is a more advanced form of learning that involves a conscious, continuous, and dynamic process of considering honestly and critically all aspects of experiences for greater clarity, future actions to refine and enhance them as necessary, and overall improvement. Primarily, reflective practice generates foresight that enables an individual to implement a set of predetermined and constructive behavioral patterns to navigate unexpected and anticipated situations more effectively.

Reflective practice in value development is viewed as a practice-based tool involving cycles of ongoing learning that allow children to pause, reflect, question, and alter their moral dispositions and attitudes toward desirable behavior. Reflections have long-lasting and incremental effects on personal development. Therefore, cultivating a habit of thought produces progressive and observable changes in children's value formation. Children acquire memory, inquiry, exploration, explanation, interpretation, collaboration, decision-making, and review skills through meditation. Reflective practices in children involve their deliberate efforts to reflect on their value practices in everyday experiences to validate their value dispositions, comprehend the context of value experiences, generate new understandings of values, and "establish a progressive pathway for long-term value formation. A wealth of research supports the benefits of reflections in young children, such as journal writing, weekly reports, teacher-led discussions, collaborative peer discussion, and concept maps to encourage reflective practices in children (Yussen, 1985).

Importance of Shared Reflection in Values Development

In daily practice, many of our actions are unconscious and unspoken. Shared reflection, as opposed to individual thinking, provides knowledge beyond the person's thoughts by gathering multiple perspectives and gaining insight from the views of others. It also facilitates identification with others to promote mutual learning and development.

John Dewey (1933) conceptualized reflection as comprising three key components: 1) a systematic manner of thinking and a means of making sense, 2) the cultivation of reflective dispositions, and 3) a dialogic component involving the use of language or communication to express views. Reflection is a slow pedagogy and requires time. According to Allan (2018), group reflection is characterized by "slow thinking." In his book "An Analysis of Daniel Kahneman's Thinking Fast and Slow, Daniel Kahneman explains how the mind functions to enhance judgment and decision-making. In classrooms, the teacher creates a shared reflective culture in which children are encouraged to reflect on their values, beliefs, and practices in a conducive learning environment that provides an unhurried time to sit, think, converse, and derive meaning through dialogue and sharing experiences. A collective or shared reflection on values offers the opportunity to bring unspoken and unconscious actions to the forefront, facilitating the identification of value practices.

Figure 1. Shared reflective practices

In a shared reflection session, individuals reflect on events individually before contributing their thoughts and ideas to a collective process of reflection, where individual opinion is valued and encouraged, and group sharing is encouraged and respected. Dialoguing or articulation during the shared reflection session is vital. The articulation process makes the 'invisible thought' of a person's 'invisible thought' explicit in a way that calls out and initiates further sharing in the group (Zhang et al., 2020). Furthermore, "thinking aloud" has been widely used in the inquiry-based learning approach.

According to Bandura (1997), if prompted, children only spontaneously explain their thinking during the learning process. Creating an interactive learning environment by scaffolding the discussions is imperative to encourage children's self-reflection. In the learning process, scaffolding refers to temporary support offered to the learners to enable them to complete a task (Vygotsky, 1977). Research studies on children's reflection primarily believed that by providing adequate information, children would reflect spontaneously (Zhang et al., 2020).

Shared reflection provides children with the opportunity and space to express their points of view and be heard regularly, and teachers care for and foster a culture of collaborative learning. We are promoting a collaborative learning culture by providing children with the opportunity and place to express their opinions and be heard. Furthermore, during reflective sessions, it is essential to pose questions and give suggestions to children to encourage them to reflect on their values and develop a meaningful understanding of values, dispositions, and behaviors. Therefore, dialogue or expression is essential during the shared reflection session (Hmelo and Lin, 2000; Valkanova, Jackson, and Watts, 2004). The process of articulation makes an individual's "invisible thought" explicit in a way that elicits and initiates further sharing in the group (Zhang et al., 2020). Piaget (1977) used terms such as "thinking over," "reflection," and "conscious of one's thoughts" to describe the inner conflicts and conversations of children. Additionally, Piaget and Inhelder (1993) imply that it is possible to induce "inner conversation" in children. Similarly, inquiry-based learning has extensively utilized " thinking aloud " (Kucan & Beck, 1997).

During the shared reflection sessions, the teacher encourages the children to share their views without judgment and to allow free expression and narration of both positive and negative aspects, especially without dwelling on the harmful elements alone. Children describe their knowledge of values, self-perception, beliefs, and practices that stimulate reflections and thinking by one or more children in the group, encouraging them to engage in meaningful dialoguing and intriguing them to evoke responses.

Roles and Responsibilities of Teachers During Shared Reflection Session

During shared reflection sessions, teachers assume the following roles and responsibilities:

- Mediator
- Facilitator
- Moderator
- Active listener
- Appreciate diversity and inclusivity
- Being reflective and reflexive
- Non-judgmental behavior
- Fostering collaborative learning
- Checking misconceptions in children that require actions
- Develop healthy identities

- Achieve personal and collective goals
- Being empathetic, sympathetic, and compassionate
- Establish and maintain supportive relationships
- Make responsible and caring decisions

Scenario-Based Learning (SBL) in Value Development

Scenario-based learning is an inquiry-based learning approach that requires the children to actively analyze hypothetical problem scenarios that mirror real-life situations and are presented through visuals and storylines that need children to understand the given concerns and propose appropriate solutions to solving the problems. Children are naturally interested in reading and listening to stories and relating them to their experiences. Furthermore, the familiarity and relevance of the depicted scenario allow the curious child to reflect on their value practices spontaneously.

The theories that support SBL are the constructivist learning approach (Vygotsky, 1997) and situated learning theory (Lave & Wenger, 1991). Situated learning theory asserts that learning occurs best in the context in which it will be used, and situated cognition claims that knowledge is comprehended more efficiently when located within its context. The scenarios designed for a specific purpose should be age-appropriate, and they need to be straightforward, ill-structured, or complex procedures, with analytical branching for decisions or that require narrative explanations. SBL allows children to understand, think, decide, and identify solutions to complicated situations. In addition, it improves thinking skills and promotes children's decision-making and problem-solving skills. SBL sessions can be carried out as an individual or a group activity that focuses on guiding and scaffolding children's understanding to achieve the intended purpose.

Presenting real-life scenarios to develop values in young children ensures a success rate of value acquisition through reflection, reorientation, and disposition to practice appropriate values. To analyze a value-based scenario, the children must immerse themselves in the context, relate it to their previous experiences, and reflect on their values and practices. It also enables the children to assess their current level of value practices, and upon realizing the need for cultivating appropriate values, they tend to recalibrate their value disposition to conform to the expected behavior.

Storifying the Scenario for Reflective Sessions for Values Development

Teachers can create value scenarios that are more relevant and age-appropriate for children if they can connect the real-world context with a specific value they intend to foster. However there are many methods to create the ideal content for scenario-based value lessons; however, the teacher must make the stories authentic and realistic. The scenarios may be structured similarly to a narrative, with characters and a storyline illustrating a positive or negative display of values by the story's main character. Teachers could extract such scenarios from textbooks, moral education books, digital images, photographs, and clippings from newspapers and magazines. When children read the designs, they will assume the role of the main character and analyses and interpret the underlying values.

Design is advantageous in achieving the desired outcomes in value development. First, identify the values children have to accomplish after the reflection session and then work backward from the learning objectives and design scenarios. Second, choose the format for a face-to-face classroom discussion or an online presentation. Teachers could utilize the affordances of digital products such as animated, cartoon, audio, videos, and digital stories to create scenarios for value reflections. In addition, teachers should be mindful in choosing and designing critical incidents and challenging situations for systems that trigger critical thinking and resolve cognitive conflicts in children. Scenarios should provide opportunities to dispel myths, generate a new understanding of values, dispel misconceptions, allow room for brainstorming, and make an appropriate decision related to the scenario discussed. The design of procedures can begin with real-life situations around daily events at home, school, on the road, in parks or play areas, school campuses, and classrooms. It is advantageous to create a storyboard before planning the scenarios. Additionally, peer review could be considered to ensure that the flow of the storyline and the visual correspond in clarity and relevance to achieve value outcomes.

Research Study on the Use of Value-Based Reflection Framework (VBRF) in Value Development

Teacher-led reflection sessions complemented by articulation and peer-group sharing are essential to develop children's values. In this study, reflection refers to children's conscious and deliberate effort to recall and reflect on their values, dispositions, and practices to improve their value practices. Reflective practice is the capacity to examine one's actions to engage in continuous learning. It involves evaluating behaviors and engaging in thoughtful and reflexive practices. In this study, reflective practices refer to children's descriptions of their knowledge of values, self-perception, beliefs, and practices that provoke reflections and thoughts by one or more children in the group, encouraging them to elicit responses by engaging in meaningful dialogues. The teacher is essential as a guide and facilitator to trigger interest in children and initiate discussion. The child is guided to reflect on what this value means to oneself and others.

Schwartz (1992) advanced values research by identifying a circular motivational continuum that underlies the structure of values. He partitioned this continuum into ten universal value types and four higher-order values. In this structure, adjacent values in the circle (e.g., universalism and benevolence) are positively related as they express compatible motivations. In contrast, opposing values (e.g., power and universalism) are negatively related as they describe conflicting motivations (Schwartz, 1992).In addition, Cheng and Fleishmann (2011) proposed 16 value concepts in their meta-inventory of human values: (1) freedom, (2) helpfulness, (3) accomplishment, (4) honesty, (5) self-respect, (6) intelligence, (7) broad-mindedness, (8) creativity, (9) equality, (10) responsibility, (11) social order, (12) wealth, (13) competence, (14) justice, (15) security, and (16) spirituality.

The notions of reflection-in-action and reflection-on-action were central to Schön's (1983) efforts and incorporated into the VBRF. The premises for using reflection-based exercise for value development is:

First, children must learn values not by mere exposure to understanding values but through conscious efforts to think, reflect, observe others, and practice values in a socially mediated system. Secondly, children expand their understanding of values and generate new insights through dialoguing in a collaborative peer-group setting during the reflection sessions. This foster values development in children.

The primary objective of the VBRF is to cultivate systematic meta-awareness and to allow children to reflect on and clarify explicitly the values underlying their attitudes and behavior. To foster value development in children, the VBRF promotes 14 values designated as primary values. Values include generosity, cooperation, courage, fairness, gratitude, perseverance, honesty and integrity, moderation, respect, responsibility, tolerance, humility, and love and affection. The VBRF comprises two layers, with the inner layer representing a reflection framework that assists teachers in generating classroom reflections and discussions. It is used to reflect on the value statement, the source of a value statement, what it means to self, and what it means for others. The peripheral layer represents the fourteen essential values that must be reinforced through reflective activities. The VBRF is illustrated in Figure 2.

The central premise of using the VBRF for values development is that children learn values through self-reflection and expression in a teacher-facilitated, scaffolded, and teacher-facilitated sharing session. Two assumptions support the current research. First, children acquire values through conscious efforts to think, reflect, observe others, and practice values in a socially mediated system rather than through passive exposure to understanding values. Second, children improve their knowledge of values and generate new insights through dialogue during peer-group reflection sessions.

Figure 2. Values Based Reflection Framework (VBRF) with 14 values

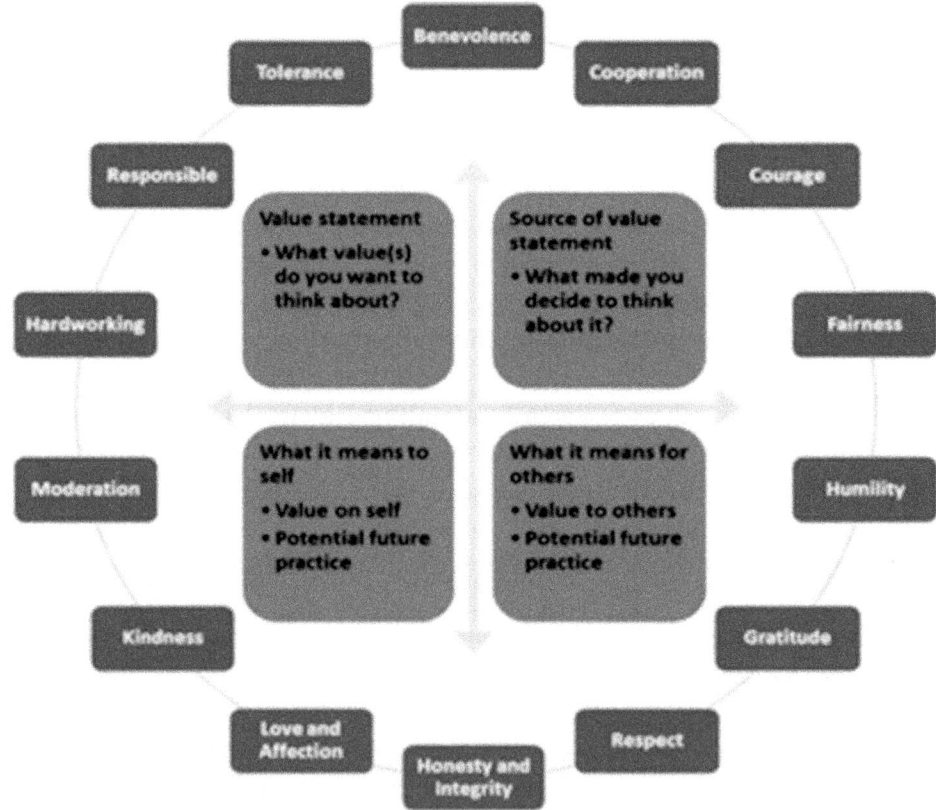

Objectives of using the VBRF in Shared Reflections

The primary objective of the VBRF is to cultivate systematic meta-awareness and to allow children to reflect on and clarify explicitly the values underlying their attitudes and behavior. Effective use of the VBRF for value reflective sessions must be coupled with real-life scenarios that must be presented in pictures and narration. Mini systems are learning situations that allow children to relate the values discussed to the real world. In this study, 56 scenarios with a brief narration for each were carefully selected and designed digitally to foster value development. A sample scenario with a short description is presented in Figure 3.

Narration: The picture shows a benevolent (kind) student. He offers his food to a friend who has less.

Teachers could create a set of value scenarios that are age appropriate and fit the specific needs of the class, the children, the curriculum, or the standards. This study, 56 real-life scenarios were used for each of the 14 values presented in the VBRF to suit primary school children. For each value, four strategies with narration make a complete set to carry out 14 weeks of reflection sessions for 14 weeks, suitable for a school term.

Figure 3. A Value Scenario (benevolence) for a reflection session

Implementation of The VBRF In Classroom for Shared Reflection Sessions

In the current investigation, fifty-nine children between the ages of eight and 11 from an international school in Selangor, Malaysia, participated in the study with parental consent. The study was conducted during the COVID-19 pandemic; therefore, due to Malaysia's restricted movement control order (RMCO), the research implementation and reflection sessions were carried out through Zoom meetings for 14 weeks, one week per week. Five classes involving Year 4 and 5 children took part in this study. With the help of the respective classroom teacher and a researcher from the research team, the reflection sessions were carried out during the homeroom teacher period for about 30 to 40 minutes. Each reflection session comprised two stages.

Stage 1 was a teacher-led discussion session that involved scenario-based learning. During this session, the teacher discussed four value-based scenarios to help reflect, take perspective, and debate among children. The teacher began each session with greetings followed by a meeting of the four values using real-life examples and experiences, allowing children to share and reflect on their value practices. This was followed by a wrap-up of the discussion and a statement of appreciation. Finally, the children were prepared for the stage 2 session on reflective writing.

In stage 2, a reflective writing session, children were given 10 to 15 minutes to reflect on their understanding and practices of the values discussed in response to the four open questions: 1. *What value(s) do you want to write about today?* 2. *What are your thoughts about this value(s)?* 3. *What do(es) the value(s) mean to you*? and 4. *How will you show your values to your family, friends, and others?* Subsequently, the children were encouraged to choose at least one or more values of the day and journal their thoughts for the four questions in the Google form. The children were encouraged to seek clarification through chat or audio throughout the virtual session.

Processes Involved in Shared Reflection Sessions

The following steps may guide the teacher who is interested in carrying out the shared reflection sessions:

Step 1: The teacher selects four values for the children to consider during reflection. The teacher can create a schedule for reflection sessions on the 14 values presented in the VBRF. The values can be introduced in cycles, targeting four values per week.

Step 2: The teacher introduces the four values to the children at the beginning of the week, preferably on Monday, the first working day. The teacher concisely describes the values and puts the scenarios and values on the classroom bulletin board (in physical classes).

Step 3: The children are instructed to practice the week's four values consciously and observe them practiced by themselves and others. Children are also encouraged to comprehend the concept of values and ruminate on their attitudes and actions about the four values of the week.

Step 4: Teacher and children reflect collectively and individually during the moral education/value development/homeroom class period.

Step 5: First, the teacher initiates and solicits an open discussion on value development by discussing the values represented in the 4 picture scenarios. Children are encouraged to express their opinions while the teacher facilitates and moderates the session.

Step 6: After the teacher-led discussion, children are given "silent thinking time" to reflect and record their reflections and thoughts regarding practicing and upholding values in a journal.

The teacher poses the four questions below and asks the children to write their journals.

- Which value(s) do you wish to discuss today?
- What do you think about these values?
- What significance do the value(s) have for you?
- How did you demonstrate these values to your family, friends, and acquaintances?

Step 7: The teacher collects the children's journals and concludes the session with a summary of the main points discussed and a note of thanks.

The following four value scenarios will be discussed next week, and journaling will continue weekly until all 14 values have been discussed and documented.

Key Findings from Research on Using Shared Reflections for Value Development

To understand the values children preferred to reflect upon during the 14 weeks of reflection sessions, the journal entries collected from the children were sorted, and entries were tallied for each value. The frequency table for the values that the children had chosen for reflection is presented in Figure 1. The results indicated that the most preferred value determined for consideration was *responsibility*, while other highly selected values were *kindness*, *hardworking*, *fairness*, and *respect*. Values such as *courage*, *honesty* and *integrity*, *cooperation*, *moderation*, *benevolence*, *tolerance*, and *gratitude* received preferences that ranged from moderate to low for the reflection exercise. At the same time, *humility* was identified as the least chosen value to be reflected upon. Although the 14 values were introduced over four rounds during the 14 weeks of reflection sessions, the choice of values to write as journal entries showed that the children reflected on the values familiar to them and were easy to gauge the understanding of self and others' value practices.

Figure 4. Counts for each value reflected upon by children during the 14 weeks of reflection sessions

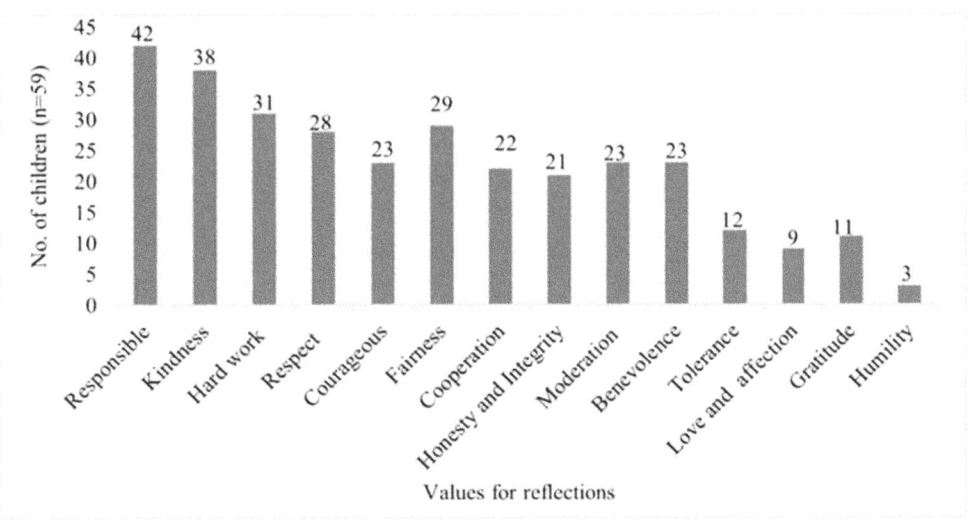

Children's Narratives from Shared Reflective Practices

Three journal entries from children collected during the 14 weeks of reflection sessions are presented in the following sections to showcase the reflections and sharing of children.

Case Study 1

Child 2 responded to the weekly reflection exercise; the journal entries are in Table 1. Child 2 shared positive remarks on the shared reflection sessions, emphasizing that the scenarios shown were exciting and relatable. Further, he learned to respect and be kind from the sessions, and he continues practicing the values in online classes and at home.

Besides, at the exit interview, the child acknowledged that the reflection sessions were fun and that he had learned many valuable practices from the session.

"I like it because it is fun, and I can learn more."

"I practice the value when I know my mom needs to work to help me."

Table 1. Excerpt from Journal entries given by Child 2

Journal entries /Timestamp	What value(s) do you want to write about today?	What are your thoughts about this value(s)?	What does the value(s) mean to you?	How will you show your values to your family, friends, and others?
6/11/2021 8:23:04	Kindness	This value is good because you are pleasant to your friends and help your friend also when they need help.	Kindness means being friendly to my friends and helping the earth to be clean and safe.	I showed kindness by helping my mum bake a cake for my dad's birthday because we could not go out to buy the cake.
9/10/2021 8:14:43	Moderation	This value is excellent because we will all fight if we do not have it.	This value means to be self-control and self-restraint.	I will show this when I get something, and my sibling does not get it. I will share it and not keep it all to myself.
9/24/2021 8:26:06	Respect	Respect is being kind and respectful.	This value means having respect for one another and being kind.	We can show respect by helping our parents, listening to our teachers, and helping older people.
6/25/2021 8:23:23	Honesty	This value is good because, in the future, more people can trust each other.	This value means to me to not lie and always be honest if you do something wrong.	I once showed honesty when I was getting a glass of water, and it accidentally slipped out of my hand. It was when my little cousins were there. My mom thought my little cousins broke something, but I told the truth, and that was when I was being honest.
10/8/2021 8:16:48	Honesty and integrity	It is good because you need to have honesty and integrity	It means to be honest and not lie a lot, and have integrity	Being open and honest when communicating with others.
7/2/2021 8:21:36	Responsible	Responsible is doing something wrong and not blaming someone else, and taking over a role in helping someone.	The value means to be responsible for your actions.	I showed responsibility by helping my sister with Mandarin because my mum did not understand it well.
10/15/2021 8:20:53	Responsible	This value is excellent because you have to be responsible.	This value means being responsible for what you have been told to do and what you have to do	I can show this to my friend when I want to borrow something, and I have to be responsible and give it back after I am done borrowing.
9/17/2021 8:23:50	Gratitude	This value is good because it teaches you to be grateful.	This value means being grateful for what you have, for example, food and shelter.	I can show this value when somebody helps clean a place and will be grateful.

Case Study 2

The excerpts taken from the journal entries submitted by Child 21 are presented in Table 2. It is evident from the responses that the child had a better understanding of the values. The child also ascertained that the reflection sessions helped them learn new values such as fairness and being *hardworking*; she also responded that she was mindfully practicing all the values known.

Table 2. Excerpt from Journal entries given by Child 21

Journal entries /Timestamp	What value(s) do you want to write about today?	What are your thoughts about this value(s)?	What do the value(s) mean to you?	How will you show your values to your family, friends, and others?
6/11/2021 8:21:42	Cooperation	It is instrumental when people are on a group project, and when they use cooperation, you can finish faster.	It means that you need to listen to your friend's ideas, and your friends listen to your ideas, then you do the project together, which is much faster.	If you get instructions from them, you can do it, which is a form of cooperation.
6/18/2021 8:25:48	Tolerance	It is perfect if you have tolerance when you get insulted	It means that if you get insulted, you accept it and do not kick up a fuss	By not showing a temper when I get insulted
6/19/2021 16:58:14	Tolerance	I think tolerance is important	It means you can tolerate insults	Do not get angry if they insult you
6/25/2021 8:21:44	Courage	This is a significant value if you do not want to lie	It means you dare to admit you did something wrong and will not lie	If I pour something on the couch, then I will not tell a lie; I will say I did it and clean up the mess
9/24/2021 8:22:14	Courage	Courage is a good thing to have when you are alone.	It means to be brave or to get brave.	Try to be courageous in a room with no one and wait until your parents come home.
7/2/2021 8:15:44	Fairness	This is a good value to have	It means if you have something gods, you have 2 of them; then you share 1 with your friend. That is fair.	If I have something good, I give it out fairly to my family
10/8/2021 8:17:02	Fairness	It is important to have it.	It means that you do not get less work, thank your friends and like that.	To be fair to them
10/15/2021 8:16:05	Responsible	I think it is a significant value to have	It means you are responsible, keeping up after yourself, and finishing your homework.	To clean up after my messes and finish my homework
9/10/2021 8:17:57	Benevolence	I think it very good to have this value	I think it means to be kind and compassionate	Always share, and do not be rude

Case study 3

Child 38 also shared positive learning experiences using shared reflection sessions, and below are the responses in the Google form during the exit survey. The journal entries from child 38 are presented in Table 3, which confirms that the child had mindfully practiced values at home, especially with her mom and brother.

"I liked attending the reflection sessions because we learned about the different values.

"I have started by practicing a bit of responsibility value."

Table 3. Excerpt from Journal entries given by Child 38

Journal entries /Timestamp	1. What value(s) do you want to write about today?	2. What are your thoughts about this value(s)?	3. What do the value(s) mean to you?	4. How will you show your values to your family, friends, and others?
6/11/2021 8:27:31	Gratitude	Being thank full for the people that help you	Saying "thank you" to the person that helped you	Whenever someone gives me something, I say, "Thank you."
6/25/2021 8:09:45	Hardworking	I think the value is something many people should do	You put all your effort into the work	Do what my mom tells me to do, and I will do it may be better
7/2/2021 8:13:30	Fairness	I think many people should do the value	To give someone a chance, like sharing	Maybe when I am watching TV, and my brother wants to watch, I will let him
6/18/2021 8:07:01	Respect	I like this value	Like caring for other people	Please and thank you to everyone.
9/10/2021 8:17:38	Benevolence	I think many people should be doing it	You should share	I will share with them if they want something I have and they don't
9/17/2021 8:24:15	Kindness	I think many people should do this	Always be nice to people	When they get me something I want, I will say thank you
9/24/2021 8:15:18	Respect	I think it is very nice to do	You need patience if someone is talking and you want to talk to them.	If my brother is talking, I will wait until they finish.
10/8/2021 8:10:52	Honesty and integrity	Many people should be honest	It means that you should always be honest	If me and my brother fight and my parents say who hit who, I will tell the truth
10/15/2021 8:18:36	Responsible	Many people should do it	If you use something and are done with it, you must return it.	When I use something, I need to put it back and not let it lie around
6/25/2021 13:11:57	Hardworking	I think the value is something many people should do	You put all your effort into the work	Do what my mom tells me to do, and I will do it. Maybe better

LIMITATIONS OF VBRF AND FUTURE RESEARCH DIRECTIONS

The VBRF, designed to promote value development in primary school children, was prepared to implement in physical classes. However, due to the COVID-19 pandemic, the research implementation was shifted to online courses, which limited the possibilities of exploring the pros and cons of using VBRF in physical classes. Another critical limitation is the difficulties associated with online interaction, such as technical difficulties, poor internet connectivity, and children's absence during the reflection sessions due to high absenteeism issues during online classes.

Therefore, it is recommended that future studies be carried out in a face-to-face setting to gather more insights into the investigation. Apart from this, the current study is a cross-sectional study. A longitudinal study could be undertaken to understand the significance of values experienced by children of varying ages on the development of values in children. In addition, it would be intriguing to comprehend the impact of the story and the maturation of values practices on the performance and happiness of children. Besides, technological advancements such as multimedia and immersive technology experiences in creating animated value scenarios and allowing children to resolve moral dilemmas could be a helpful extension of current research.

IMPLICATIONS AND RECOMMENDATIONS

Shared reflections empower children in decision-making skills and allow them to express their opinions, participate in discussions, dispel misconceptions and doubts in everyday communication and activities, and contribute to developing value-based school policies and practices. It promotes an appreciation for meaningful conversation and peer support in developing values. It is essential to integrate value-centered education into school curricula and develop age-appropriate activities, discussions, and projects that enable children to explore and reflect upon their values. Training teachers to effectively facilitate shared reflections in the classroom that promotes positive values, disposition, and culture, as well as ethical decision-making, is equally important. In addition, reflective practices in values development promote media literacy among children, enabling them to comprehend the value presented in the media and programs they watch online and to critically evaluate the people and media messages they receive through digital media. In addition, such awareness encourages a values-driven approach to dealing with moral dilemmas, online ethics, respectful communication, responsible technology use, and digital citizenship. Besides, it is essential that school curricula deliberately incorporate a value-driven approach in the design and delivery of curricula. Strengthen the national curriculum framework and guidelines for value-centered education.

CONCLUSION

In the current study, shared reflections and the Value-Based Reflection Framework (VBRF) were used to comprehend conceptions and manifestations of value practices in children and to promote children's value development. The VBRF was specially designed to encourage values development in children. No study has utilized a systematic approach to reflective practices in value enhancement in children. The VBRF developed for this study incorporated scenarios involving values, reflections, discussions, and reflective writing. It encapsulated fourteen values and, in conjunction with the values scenarios, served as a guide for teachers in conducting meditative classroom sessions. However, it should be noted that the reflection sessions were conducted online due to the pandemic. Using VBRF confirmed that reflection sessions provided children with an effective means of obtaining insights for learning new values and recalibrating their existing practices of values. The study concluded by recommending the incorporation of VBRF into the values curriculum, as it advocated a socio-constructivist approach to value development. Remarkably, this research has taken the initiative to establish a sustainable values system in children, which directly and indirectly contributes to the growth of a community based on values.

ACKNOWLEDGMENT

The authors gratefully acknowledge that this research was made possible through the

Ministry of Education Malaysia under the Fundamental Research Grant Scheme (FRGS),

Project Code FRGS/1/2019/SSI09/HELP/02/1.

REFERENCES

Allan, J. (2018). *An analysis of Daniel Kahneman's Thinking, fast and slow*. Taylor & Francis.

Balakrishnan, V. (2010). The Development of Moral Education in Malaysia. Journal of Educators & Education / Jurnal Pendidik dan Pendidikan, 25, 89-101.

Bandura, A. (1997). *Self-efficacy: The exercise of control*. W H Freeman.

Boud, D., Keogh, R., & Walker, D. (1985). *Promoting Reflection in Learning: A Model. Reflection: Turning Reflection into Learning*. Routledge.

Cheng, A., & Fleischmann, K. R. (2010). Developing a meta-inventory of human values. *Proceedings of the American Society for Information Science and Technology*, 47(1), 1–10.

Dewey, J. (1933). *How we think: A restatement of the relation of reflective thinking to the educative process*. D.C. Heath & Co Publishers.

Döring, A. K., Blauensteiner, A., Aryus, K., Drögekamp, L., & Bilsky, W. (2010). Assessing values early on: The picture-based value survey for children (PBVS–C). *Journal of Personality Assessment*, 92(5), 439–448.

Hmelo, C. E., & Lin, X. (2000). Becoming self-directed learners: Strategy development in problem-based learning. In D. H. Evensen & C. E. Hmelo (Eds.), *Problem-based learning: A research perspective on learning interactions* (pp. 227–250). Lawrence Erlbaum Associates Publishers.

Huah, G. L., Soon, S. T., Tan, J. P. S., Muthukrishnan, P., Revati, R., & Rosalind, A. (2022). A study on children's perceptions of their moral values using an online picture-based values survey. *Computer Assisted Language Learning*, 23(4), 240–262.

Hughson, T. A., & Wood, B. E. (2022). The OECD Learning Compass 2030 and the future of disciplinary learning: A Bernsteinian critique. *Journal of Education Policy*, *37*(4), 634–654.

Kucan, L., & Beck, I. L. (1997). Thinking aloud and reading comprehension research: Inquiry, instruction, and social interaction. *Review of Educational Research*, *67*(3), 271–299.

Lave, J., & Wenger, E. (1991). *Situated learning: Legitimate peripheral participation*. Cambridge University Press.

Muthukrishnan, P., & Huah, G. L. (2023). A study on children's understandings of values through reflective practices using a values-based reflection framework (VBRF). In Reimagining Innovation in Education and Social Sciences (pp. 295-304). Routledge. doi:10.1201/9781003366683-36

Piaget, J. (1977). The role of action in the development of thinking. In W. F. Overton & J. M. Gallagher (Eds.), *Knowledge and development*. Springer.

Piaget, J., & Inhelder, B. (1969). *The psychology of the child*. Basic Books.

Pommeranz, A., Detweiler, C., Wiggers, P., & Jonker, C. M. (2011, July). Self-reflection on personal values to support value-sensitive design. In *Proceedings of HCI 2011 The 25th BCS Conference on Human-Computer Interaction 25* (pp. 491-496).

Sahin, Ü. (2019). Values and values education as perceived by primary school teacher candidates. *International Journal of Progressive Education*, *15*(3), 74–90.

Schön, D. A. (1983). *The reflective practitioner: How professionals think in actions*. Basic Book.

Schwartz, S. H. (1992). Universals in the content and structure of values: Theoretical advances and empirical tests in 20 countries. In Advances in experimental social psychology, 25, 1-65. Academic Press.

Valkanova, Y., Jackson, A., & Watts, D. M. (2004). Enhancing self-reflection in children: The use of digital video in the primary science classroom. Journal of eLiteracy, 1, 42-55.

Vygotsky, L. S. (1977). *Mind in Society: The development of higher psychological processes*. Harvard University Press.

Yussen, S. R. (1985). *The growth of reflection in children*. Academic Press.

Zelazo, P. D. (2000). Self-reflection and the development of consciously controlled processing. Children's reasoning and the mind, 169-189.

Hang, Z., Bekker, T., Markopoulos, P., & Brok, P. D. (2020). Children's reflection-in-action during collaborative design-based learning. In The challenges of the digital transformation in education: Proceedings of the 21st international conference on interactive, collaborative learning (ICL2018)-Volume 1 (pp. 790-800). Springer International Publishing.

KEY TERMS AND DEFINITIONS

Children's reflection: It refers to how teachers and parents encourage children to reflect. During reflection, children compose journals and engage in reflective thinking to identify their value practices and reconcile their strengths and limitations.

Reflective Practices in Value Development: It is an act of reflecting on one's practice of values, and based on reflections, the person makes deliberate attempts to refine value practices.

Real-life scenarios: Real-life scenarios denote the daily life events and occurrences that generally occurs in children's environment, such as the family, home, friends, school, and playground. Such incidents are digitally created and presented to children during reflection sessions.

Reflection sessions: This term refers to the active participation of both teacher and student in discussing value recognition, disposition, and practices. The teacher encourages reflection and elicits responses by asking queries during this session.

Reflective writing: It is the conscious, active practice of pondering and writing in order to increase one's self-awareness.

Scenario-Based Learning: Scenario-based learning is an inquiry-based learning approach that requires children to analyze hypothetical problem scenarios that mirror real-world situations actively. These are usually presented through visuals and narratives that require children to comprehend the presented situations and propose suitable solutions for solving the problems.

Shared reflection: Shared reflection, as opposed to individual reflection, provides knowledge beyond the person's thoughts by gathering multiple perspectives and gaining insight from the views of others. It also facilitates identification with others to promote mutual learning and development.

Value-Based Reflection Framework (VBRF): The Value-Based Reflection Framework (VBRF) is a guide for educators and parents that seeks to cultivate a systematic meta-awareness towards values development in children. It consists of 14 values that must be instilled in children at a young age and questions designed to promote reflective practices. The fourteen fundamental values in VBRF are benevolence, cooperation, courage, fairness, thankfulness, perseverance, honesty and integrity, moderation, respect, responsibility, tolerance, humility, love, and affection.

Chapter 11
Citizenship Education Courses in Primary Schools in Modern Turkey (1920s–1950s)

Günseli Gümüşel
Atilim University, Turkey

Gülçin Tuğba Nurdan
Atilim University, Turkey

ABSTRACT

According to Mustafa Kemal, salvation is possible only through national education. The consciousness of freedom should be taught in schools. Teachers also had duties on the path to national awakening and organization. After the Grand National Assembly was established in Ankara, the government gave the students and teachers the task of enlightening Turkish people. The idea was that future generations should be raised with a national, scientific, and secular education to protect Türkiye's independence and strengthen the republic regime. The feelings of virtue, self-sacrifice, order, discipline, and self-confidence should be reinforced in the new generation. The "citizenship education at primary school," which the intellectuals of constitutionalism focused on within the scope of the "new man-new society" project, constituted an important dimension of nation-building. In this study, citizenship education courses with different names such as Citizenship, Homeland, Malumat-ı Vataniye, etc. will be evaluated by using official course books from the 1920s to 1950s in the Republic of Türkiye.

INTRODUCTION AND BACKGROUND

The most crucial issue of the new state and regime was the regulation of national education services and practices (Yalçın, 1985). The Turkish War of Independence profoundly affected education, and in return, education contributed to independence efforts (Akyüz, 2013).

DOI: 10.4018/978-1-6684-9295-6.ch011

When the Grand National Assembly met under the light of a single kerosene lamp in 1921, there was no seat for all the deputies in the meeting hall. While The Great Powers were invading the country and many members, including Mustafa Kemal, were sentenced to death, the first Grand National Assembly Government established the principles of an education program based on the government program (Ateş, 2007).

During the worst days of the National Struggle, the enemy forces increased their pressure to achieve a decisive victory. Thus, the Greek forces launched an attack in the Kütahya-Eskişehir region which resulted in the withdrawal of the Turkish army to Sakarya. Even though the Greek attack gained dangerous momentum, especially throughout 16-21 July 1921, Ankara Government kept its focus on the program of national education. Furthermore, during the opening speech of the third meeting of the Grand National Assembly on March 1, 1922 (when the war was still ongoing), Mustafa Kemal stated that the first goal of the education program was to give the villagers adequate information on geography, history, religion, and ethics to better their understanding on their homeland, nation and the world (*Atatürk'ün Söylev ve Demeçleri I-III*, 1997).

According to Mustafa Kemal and Turkish nationalists, salvation was only possible via national education. In addition, it was essential to inform citizens about the stages of national liberation. Mustafa Kemal reached a synthesis of ideas at the beginning of the 1920s, and he had the necessary determination and a strategy to implement them. Starting from 1923, the keywords of this strategy could be explained as *civic consciousness, civil law, and secular administration, a national education system open to universal humanist values, women's role in society, civilization, and development*. The Republic's citizenship definition was based on a human type defined by their rights and a design with obligations (*75. Yılda Tebaadan Yurttaşa Doğru*, 1998). A new republic was born under these conditions.

National education was the only alternative for the future (*Atatürk Haftası Armağanı 10 Kasım 1986*, 1986). The education Republic chose its primary goal as bringing the citizens an awareness and attitude that they became one of the elements of a democratic and modern society (Adem, 1982). Therefore, Mustafa Kemal accepted culture and education as equals and considered it one of the nation's basics (Bayer, 1997).

Single-party government's practices regarding the goal of nationalization had to accelerate the cultural change since it was difficult for democracy and good governance to go hand in hand in the country, even when there were no profound cultural changes. Most of the population was illiterate and did not have equal rights. In this sense, the reconstruction process was just starting, and poverty quickly turned into violence. Therefore, civilization, peace, and public security were inseparable. Mustafa Kemal and his administration wanted them all simultaneously (Mango, 2004).

Development was complex and slow in the early years of the Republican Era. However, as İsmet İnönü said to the members of the Teachers' Union to whom he addressed on May 5, 1925, *"they were not men who got out of their home on a spring morning and hoped for a handful of greenery among the groves in the beautiful weather"* (Turan, 2002).

Successively enacted laws on educational organization, which were facilitated by the centralization of education, accelerated the process (Gologlu, 2011). Laws on education, which were implemented to complete the Republican order, were unified with the society, and they paved the way for other innovative and beneficial practices. The planned education of the Republican era was not only limited to books.

One of the ways to understand being a Turk and the foundation of the Republic and popularize the Republic was to provide effective citizenship education to students and the public via national holidays.

The work done so far was a critical milestone and breakthrough for the nationalization process, and the Turkish national education system has finally achieved a structure that can fulfill its primary task: maintaining the existence of the Republic of Türkiye (*Atatürk Haftası Armağanı 10 Kasım 2003*, 2003). Turkish Language, History, Geography, Citizenship, Sociology, and Philosophy were among the most crucial courses of the Republic of Türkiye and citizenship education.

When we look at the education of the Republic Period in general, it is understood that the task of constructing national, secular, contemporary, and functional education on a revolutionary philosophy was loaded with policies, programs, and plans (*Devrimci Cumhuriyetin Eğitim Politikaları*, 1998). In this sense, the education history of the Republic from 1923 to 1933 is called the "Golden Age" (*Ulusal Eğitim Politikamız*, 1979). It was deemed necessary to create proud citizens with an honorable past instead of imperial subjects who kept harping on history without having any historical knowledge.

FUTURE RESEARCH AND DIRECTIONS

This study has potential limitations. All the coursebooks we analyze are from official state archives of different institutions, and it is impossible to buy them from a bookstore. Also, one must understand the atmosphere and leading ideas of the particular period of the Early Republican Era with serious background information to deconstruct the related coursebooks.

THE REFLECTIONS OF THE EARLY REPUBLICAN PERIOD NATIONALIZATION PROCESS ON EDUCATION AND CITIZENSHIP LESSONS

The Republic of Türkiye's process cannot just be called the acceleration of change as there is a fundamental total transformation behind it (Dülger, 2012). The first problem that required real population engineering was to create a society loyal to the state (Paker and Akça, 2010). The most robust way to achieve this would be a state-society relationship built on citizenship. However, it was inevitable to benefit from the society's consciousness of loyalty to the state, a remnant from the Ottoman period, while creating the bond (*Türkler Ansiklopedisi*, 2002).

The foundations of the new state, which was looking for its citizens and Republican Türkiye, were laid on the nation-state notion. The aim of the new Republic to rise on a triangle of industrialization and modern-secular national identity became the dominant element of nationalization and modernization projects. Thus, it resulted in an understanding of citizenship that had obligations to the state but could not acquire the notion of being an individual (Kılıç, 2007). The reason behind this is that the revolutionists knew that the future of Turkish citizens could only be seized through education. It could very well be the only way to hand the nation's future and the tasks of enlightening the people to the young citizens who were educated with these ideas. (Eyuboğlu, 1981). Of course, at the same time, education had to be placed under state control and supervision (Mumcu, 1992).

Citizenship education at school, which the second constitutional intellectuals focused on within the scope of the new human-new society project, provided a crucial dimension to the nation-building and nationalization project of the founding leaders of the Republic. Thanks to schools, the desired secular society and the education on the state's conscience could be controlled from one center (Üstel, 2004).

In 1924, after the proclamation of the Republic, *Malumat-ı Vataniye* was added to the curriculum of Galatasaray, a well-rooted and well-known school, to be studied in the first semesters of the first, second, third, and fourth grades (Yücel, 1994). On the other hand, another program in 1926 called the 1926 Program emphasized the role of primary education in the process of citizen building from beginning to end (*Tebliğler Dergisi*, 1926).

First Course Book Example: Citizenship Lessons from Muallim Abdülbaki (1927-1928)

Now it would be meaningful to examine the book written by Muallim Abdülbaki (Gölpınarlı) and taught in the 1927-1928 academic term to 5th-grade students.

The excerpts in the textbook explain the expectation of the state from its citizens and its cooperation with them:

As we say, every right is a reward for a duty. Turkish citizens have many duties and many rights in return. It is our right to live comfortably and work safely. However, we can only deserve this right if we help our government and protect our homeland from enemies. Our government demands taxes from us to help us. If we don't pay taxes, everything will fail. We would have neither a way to trade easily, nor the police or gendarmerie to protect us, nor the courts to separate right from wrong. Then the nation will be in confusion. We would give our enemies an opportunity. We would lose our independence, our homeland, and our nation. (Gölpınarlı, 2007)

Atatürk also touches on the same issues in his book *Knowledge of Citizenship,* however, with one difference. The citizens' most significant and sacred duty to the state is to participate in the elections (Tezcan, 1994).

In 1930, a change was made in the content of the Citizenship courses. According to the new change, the Citizenship course will be taught in all three secondary school classes, and the principles such as nation, state, democracy, Republic, and freedom will be explained in these courses. In the 1930 Primary School Curriculum, the main principle of this course was determined to explain the new democratic state to young students (1930 İlkmektep Müfredat Programı, 1930).

When the textbooks of the period are examined, it is seen that since 1933, serious attention has been paid to the books of the Citizenship and Civics courses. The books published by the state were selected through a competition in which writers and their works competed in front of a jury formed by educators.

Citizenship Textbooks of the 1930s

The first of the textbooks within the scope of this examination is the Homeland book, which was written in 1933 by the Ministry of Education for 4th-grade students in primary school (Yurt Bilgisi İlkmektep Kitapları: IV. Sınıf, 1933). In line with the nationalization approach, like all the other books of the period, the textbook's contents include national feelings, the state, the Republic, the administration before the Republic, the War of Independence, and freedom. In the same book, different forms of government, the duties of the state towards the citizen, tolerance, division of labor, work, and the duties of the citizen towards the state, elections, tax types, and the importance of tax are also explained.

There is also a textbook with the same name and date of the issue mentioned above (Yurt Bilgisi İlkmektep Kitapları: IV. Sınıf, 1933) which had the same contents but printed by a different company even though the government printing office issued it.

Figure 1. Original book cover

The textbook prepared for 4th graders of primary school starts with the subject of "nation." In this subject, the definition of being a Turk is explained through language: "Here are all the people who speak and understand the Turkish language are collectively called Turks."

Figure 2. Illustration of defeated Greeks in Smyrna (İzmir)

At the end of each topic, there are questions with the title "Questions." The questions at the end of the "Nation" topic are as follows: *Would you be happy being a Turk? Why are you proud of being a Turk?* With these questions, the self-confidence and brave behaviors desired to be given in the subject of nationalism are gradually gained by the student.

In the next part of the subject, an idealized image of the Turkish nation appears:

Turkish nation is pure and exalted. The Turkish nation knows nothing of lying; the Turkish nation is not afraid of enemies; the Turkish nation is inseparable from truth. Their morals are very pure.

The following section focuses on the concepts of the state and the Republic, summarizing these issues in a way a child can understand.

At the end of the subject, the book asks, "What does the state do?" In response to the question, the answer is given that the state does everything that benefits the people and protects the country. The state's job is to ensure the progress and well-being of the nation. It is also the pride of the state's citizens, called "our state."

The section about "Liberty" emphasizes that every Turk is independent (and, of course, this was not the case in the past during the sultanate regime). As it is repeatedly emphasized in the text, "The Turkish nation is free today," and it is not "captive or enslaved to a man called the Sultan."

An intense comparison of the old and the new is made in the section where students are informed about "Protection of Freedom. Afterward, students are presented with a simple historical explanation tailored to be understandable for young children. It is also explained that the army and navy protect the freedom of the country and the nation. It is underlined that the first duty of the Turkish state is to protect the freedom of the Turkish nation. The purpose of the establishment of the state is also explained in this task.

Likewise, the notion of "Tax" is also explained in the textbook. After briefly introducing what the state does with the collected taxes, it is emphasized that those who do not pay their taxes do not love their nation, and they are treacherous. It is focused on the idea that avoiding paying taxes and deviating from the truth to avoid paying taxes do not suit the Turks. According to the book, although people of the nation used to pay taxes, they could not ask the sultan where this money was spent. However, with the Republican administration, the people can ask where their taxes go. As stated in the aims of the Citizenship course, the goodness of the Republican regime is mentioned at every opportunity.

When we look at the other Homeland textbooks of the period, it is seen that the subjects are mainly determined according to the template of the book above (Yurt Bilgisi İlkmektep Kitapları: V. Sınıf: 1933). For this reason, a detailed understanding of this textbook while examining the similarities and differences of other books will create a more apparent scene when analyzing the effects of nationalization on education. The subjects analyzed in other books will not be told repeatedly unless there is a marked difference.

Another Homeland textbook was written for 5th graders of primary school. It is seen that the subject of "Six Arrows" was touched upon for the first time in this textbook. However, this subject was not covered in the 1935 and 1937 editions of the same book. Nevertheless, the topics covered in 1933, 1935 (Yurt Bilgisi İlkmektep Kitapları: V. Sınıf, 1935), 1937 (Yurt Bilgisi İlkmektep Kitapları: V. Sınıf, 1937) and 1938 (Yurt Bilgisi İlkmektep Kitapları: V. Sınıf, 1938) editions are the same: *Grand National Assembly, Councils, Parliament, Budget, Constitution, Civil Cases, Criminal Cases, Municipalities, Villages, and all ministries.*

The difference between the 1930s 5th-grade and 4th-grade Homeland textbooks of primary school is that the 5th-grade textbooks on the same courses touch upon much more concrete subjects than the 4th-grade textbooks.

In the 1940s, after Atatürk's death, it is seen that the published Homeland books changed in form and content. Firstly, there is more usage of images in the books, and expressions about nationalism are not as dominant as in the 1930s. There are also changes in the questions at the end of each topic. While there were previously assumed to have only one correct answer, and the answers were only repeated, it is seen that the questions in the books of the 1940s are asked in a way that encourages the students to reveal their views and experiences within a particular framework.

Homeland Textbooks of the 1940s

The 4th-grade Homeland textbook, written by Bedia Ermat and Kemal Ermat, was published in 1945 (Ermat and Ermat, 1945). There are two images at the beginning of the book. The first of these is an image of Atatürk, and the other is İsmet İnönü's painting with the subtitle "Our President of the Republic."

The topics covered in this book contain more civic and social information than the topics in the books published in the 1930s, for example, *Family, Division of Labor, School Administration, National Feeling, How We Live in the Village, Community, and Solidarity, Farming, Living in Towns and Cities, Government in Turkey.*

While defining national feeling on the subject of "National Feeling," the discourse of nationalization naturally continues to exist:

The name of the sadness or joy we feel from the good or bad that will come to our nation is the national feeling. All the nation's people feel the national feeling. The Turkish nation is most connected and loves and trusts each other the most. The Turkish nation is superior and known for its good morals, hard work, and bravery. The Turkish nation has set an example for all nations with its morality, art, and valor. Our history is older than the history of all nations in the world. (1945)

In the textbook, some advice is usually given to children or students at the end of each topic. For example, at the end of the "Division of Labor" topic, children are advised to divide their work among themselves and cooperate. Because community means power and "people are like organs of a body" (Ermat and Ermat, 1948).

Homeland books written for 5th graders were also from the same authors (Ermat and Ermat, 1943). Although the topics in this textbook may differ, the subject narration continues with the same intelligibility. The most fundamental topics in the book prepared for the 5th grades of primary school are as follows: *Duties of the State to Citizens, Freedom, Duties of Citizens the State, Taxes, Military Service, Goodness of our Republic, How the Republic of Turkey was Established, State Budget, Government, Ministries, in Turkey State Auxiliary Institutions, Red Crescent, Youth in New Turkey, Scouting.*

We see that the included topics, this time in the 5th Grade Citizenship textbook, spread over a broad scale, especially in the fields of Geography, History, Civil Sciences, and Military Service. The new Turkish youth and military service are defined in the book. The texts often mention that the young people are the trustees of the Republic. That is why Turkish youth must be strong-bodied, sound-minded, have good morals, and be hardworking and must protect their homeland. Since military services are getting more challenging, it is natural for Turkish youth to be given military training early to perform their army duties successfully. According to the authors, there is no harm in accustoming Turkish youth to military service at an early age. After all, schools are not only places that give information to students but also places that enrich their ideas and "steel" their bodies. In addition, public houses continue to work to better the physical and mental development of rural and urban youth.

There are no differences in content between the 1945 edition (Ermat and Ermat, 1945) and the 1943 edition of the same textbook.

The last book of the 5th-grade Homeland textbook for primary school, discussed within the scope of our review, is the book Citizenship Lessons by Agricultural Engineer Tarık Emin Rona. His book was selected as the winner among the twenty-two other book series in the competition (Rona, 1940). The first striking difference between this work and other Homeland books of the same degree is that the visuals in Rona's book are chosen with much more artistic content and style. Another interesting feature in terms of form is that İsmet İnönü's picture is put before Atatürk's picture at the beginning of the book.

The book Citizenship Lessons is divided into five chapters, each focusing on a different topic, which cannot be seen in other textbooks. Thus, including the "Contents" section in our study may be helpful to see the newly added topics. The subject of "Republic" is included in most of the Homeland textbooks discussed in our study. However, this subject takes the first place only in Rona's book. After giving a classical definition of the concept, it is pointed out that independence is the greatest happiness that people on earth can attain. In the textbook, enslaved people or captive nations are equated with animals.

The good sides of the Republic, which is described as the most beautiful form of government, are explained in the next section. There is no longer a need for kings that will take the nation into disaster and oppress the people. People will make their own choice. The state must protect our lives, honor, freedom, and property.

At the end of the book, the last message for the Turkish child is written in bold letters:

Turkish Boys and Girls! You are the only existence of the country, its only strength, its only support. Remember, you are a soldier. Every Turkish citizen is born a soldier and dies as a soldier. (Rona, 1940)

CONCLUSION

The emergence of citizenship as a phenomenon and institution can be attributed to the foundation of the Republic, and it is also a defensible idea that the foundations of this institution were formed by the ongoing modernization efforts starting from 1839. Due to the terms of our study, the point of convergence of both views is the same. The fact that the concepts of the homeland are expressions of the relationship between the state and the individual has caused the concept of citizenship to be born as a concept entirely related to the homeland. Suppose citizenship does not express the "legal and political" relationship between the state and the individual. In that case, the state-individual relationship cannot be called citizenship because this relationship defines the rights and freedoms of the individual. In other words, at this point, the state emerges as an institution that "legitimates and protects" the rights and freedoms of the individual. In this case, it is impossible to have rights and freedoms that the state does not grant or protect. Therefore, when citizenship is mentioned, the legal and political relationship between the inseparable state, nation, and individual should come to mind in Türkiye.

What is expected from the teachers of the Republic is to produce "national citizens" with these characteristics starting from primary school, where the enrollment rate is the highest. The most complementary features of this profile are loyalty to the state and self-sacrifice. An "ethnic-cultural" sense of belonging lies based on the official citizen understanding of the Republic, which lasted until the 1950s. This is the emphasis made in almost all textbooks, especially in the Citizenship Courses of the period. Loyalty to the state, self-sacrifice, and a sense of belonging are "naturalized" by associating them with the historical characteristics of the Turks and glorified as the most crucial indicator of patriotism and citizenship. The exaltation is done through military duty, the most sacred duty. Thus, a sense of discipline is added to the feelings aroused, and citizens are asked to surrender their right to life to the state without question, with a constantly created paranoia of external enemies and sudden attacks.

When all these are evaluated, it is understood that the Republican administration is trying to create the class in which the revolution will take place and that the concept of "identity." Just like the concept of culture, which is a phenomenon determined by certain state tendencies, the identity that the society will carry and the individual will identify with is determined in advance.

REFERENCES

Adem, M. (1982). *Kalkınma Planlarında Eğitimimizin Hedefleri ve Finansmanı.* Sevinç Publishing.

Akşin, S. (1989). *Türkiye Tarihi 4, Çağdaş Türkiye 1908- 1980.* Cem Publishing.

Akyüz, Y. (2013). *Türk Eğitim Tarihi M.Ö. 1000- M.S. 2013.* Pegem Akademi Publishing.

Ateş, T. (2007). *Türk Devrim Tarihi.* Bilgi University Publishing.

Bayer, A. (1997). *Muhtaç Olduğumuz Kudret Atatürk.* Aykırı Sanat Publishing.

Dülger, İ. (2012). *Cumhuriyet Döneminde Türk Toplumu.* Yeni Türkiye Publishing.

Ermat, B., & Ermat, K. (1943). *Yurt Bilgisi Dersleri Grade V.* Milli Eğitim Publishing.

Ermat, B., & Ermat, K. (1945). *Yurt Bilgisi Dersleri Grade IV.* Milli Eğitim Publishing.

Ermat, B., & Ermat, K. (1945). *Yurt Bilgisi Dersleri Grade V.* Milli Eğitim Publishing.

Ermat, B., & Ermat, K. (1948). *Yurt Bilgisi Dersleri Grade IV.* Milli Eğitim Publishing.

Eyuboğlu, İ. Z. (1981). *Atatürk'ten Özdeyişler.* Uygarlık Publishing.

Goloğlu, M. (2011). *Devrimler ve Tepkileri, Türkiye Cumhuriyeti Tarihi I (1924- 1930).* Türkiye İş Bankası Kültür Publishing.

Gölpınarlı, A. (2007). *Muallim Abdülbaki Gölpınarlı, Yurt Bilgisi Atatürk Dönemi Ders Kitabı.* Kaynak Publishing.

Kılıç, A. (2007). *Fedakâr Eş- Fedakâr Yurttaş, Yurttaşlık Bilgisi ve Yurttaş Eğitimi 1970- 1990.* Kitap Publishing.

Mango, A. (2004). *Atatürk Modern Türkiye'nin Kurucusu.* Remzi Publishing.

Mumcu, A. (1992). *Tarih Açısından Türk Devrimi'nin Temelleri ve Gelişimi.* İnkılap Publishing.

Özerdim, S. N. (1976). *Bilinmiyen Atatürk.* Varlık Publishing.

Paker, E. B., & Akça, İ. (2010). *Türkiye'de Ordu, Devlet ve Güvenlik Siyaseti.* İstanbul Bilgi University Publishing.

Rona, T. E. (1940). *Yurt Bilgisi Dersleri Grade V, İlkokul Kitapları.* Maarif Matbaası Publishing.

Şimşir, B. N. (2006). *Atatürk ve Cumhuriyet.* İleri Publishing.

Tezcan, N. (1994). *Atatürk'ün Yazdığı Yurttaşlık Bilgileri.* Çağdaş Publishing.

The Commission. (1926). Tebliğler Dergisi. *Maarif Vekâleti Tebliğler Mecmuası, 1.*

The Commission. (1930). *1930 İlkmektep Müfredat Programı.* Türkiye Cumhuriyeti Maarif Vekâleti Devlet Publishing.

The Commission. (1933). *Yurt Bilgisi İlkmektep Kitapları: Grade IV.* Devlet Publishing.

The Commission. (1933). *Yurt Bilgisi İlkmektep Kitapları: Grade IV*. Türk Kitapçılığı Limited Company.

The Commission. (1933). *Yurt Bilgisi İlkmektep Kitapları: Grade V*. Türk Kitapçılığı Limited Company.

The Commission. (1935). *Yurt Bilgisi İlkmektep Kitapları: Grade V*. Türk Kitapçılığı Limited Company.

The Commission. (1937). *Yurt Bilgisi İlkmektep Kitapları: Grade V*. Devlet Publishing.

The Commission. (1938). *Yurt Bilgisi İlkmektep Kitapları: Grade V*. Sühulet Publishing.

The Commission. (1979). *Ulusal Eğitim Politikamız*. Türk Eğitim Derneği Publishing.

The Commission. (1986). *Atatürk Haftası Armağanı 10 Kasım 1986*. Genelkurmay Askeri Tarih ve Stratejik Etüt Başkanlığı Publishing.

The Commission. (1997). *Atatürk'ün Söylev ve Demeçleri I- III*. Türk Tarih Kurumu Publishing.

The Commission. (1998). *75. Yılda Tebaa'dan Yurttaş'a Doğru*. Tarih Vakfı Publishing.

The Commission. (1998). *Devrimci Cumhuriyetin Eğitim Politikaları*. Kaynak Publishing.

The Commission. (2002). *Türkler Ansiklopedisi, 17*.

The Commission. (2003). *Atatürk Haftası Armağanı 10 Kasım 2003*. Genelkurmay Askeri Tarih ve Stratejik Etüt Başkanlığı Publishing.

Turan, İ. (2002). *İsmet İnönü Eğitim- Öğretim Üzerine*. Türk Eğitim Derneği İnönü Vakfı.

Üstel, F. (2004). *Makbul Vatandaşın Peşinde, II. Meşrutiyet'ten Bugüne Vatandaşlık Eğitimi*. İletişim Publishing.

Yalçın, A. (1985). *Cumhuriyetin İlk Yıllarında Eğitim Durumumuz*. Belgelerle Türk Tarihi Dün/ Bugün/ Yarın.

Yücel, H. A. (1994). *Hasan Ali Yücel, Türkiye'de Orta Öğretim*. Kültür ve Turizm Bakanlığı Publishing.

ADDITIONAL READING

Akşin, S. (1997). *Türkiye'nin Önünde Üç Model*. Telos Publishing.

Ayverdi, S. (1976). *Milli Kültür Meseleleri ve Maarif Davamız*. Bilim Publishing.

Bekata, H. O. (1960). *Birinci Cumhuriyet Biterken*. Çığır Publishing.

Hacıeminoğlu, N. (1980). *Milliyetçi Eğitim Sistemi*. Anda Publishing.

KEY TERMS AND DEFINITIONS

Citizenship: Relationship between an individual and a state to which the individual owes allegiance and, in turn, is entitled to its protection.

Culture: The ideas, customs, and social behavior of a society.

Education: The discipline concerned with teaching and learning methods in schools or school-like environments.

Homeland: A state or area set aside to be a state for a people of a particular national, cultural, or racial origin.

Idealized: Regarded or represented as perfect or better than others.

National Education System: The patterns of organization of education provision are usually approached at the country or national level, the most crucial level where formal education is regulated.

Republic: A state where political power rests with the public and their representatives.

Single-Party System: A sovereign state where only one political party has the right to form the government, usually based on the existing constitution.

Chapter 12
Using Reflection With Young Learners:
Value-Based English Language Teaching

Saziye Yaman
American University of the Middle East, Kuwait

Berke Andic
🆔 https://orcid.org/0009-0003-7595-5717
American University of the Middle East, Kuwait

ABSTRACT

This chapter looks at value-based education and its implications on reflections in English language teaching of primary and secondary school children. The chapter considers the classification, methods, theoretical framework, advantages, and disadvantages of value education and using reflections. Constructivist learning and reflection theories were used to explain links and effects of reflective experiences and integrating value-based education principles in young learner education. It further examined values students were expected to develop and exhibit, and implications on English language teaching. Published books, articles, research findings, institutional reports, and personal observation when teaching and training ELT students were the main sources of information. Value-based education and reflective practices are emphasized to ensure effective English language teaching in Turkish schools. Thus, it is recommended that educators be exposed to value-based education and teach values and reflective tools when teaching contextual language.

INTRODUCTION

Values are abstract concepts and key determiners of societal norms; they are the essential principles guiding peoples' lives in societies for judging and evaluating actions and the consequences (Knafo & Schwartz, 2004; Aspin, 2007). Values education refers to the social, moral, political, economic, intellectual, professional, aesthetic, sentimental, and material values (Ganguli et al., 1981), as well as norms,

DOI: 10.4018/978-1-6684-9295-6.ch012

practices, and skills grounded on these values. Values education is an introduction to those values and morality to convey the knowledge of the mentioned domains to children, relating those values to other people in society and acquiring the ability to apply those values and rules relatively in society and reality. Reflection becomes a key term while displaying the choices, preferences, explorations, opportunities, commitments, and responsibilities in behaviors and attitudes.

This chapter focuses on how Value Based Education can be integrated into young learner instruction. It highlights the key findings of value-based language teaching principles while singling out factors affecting how language teaching outcomes can be reflected through reflective practices and how positive values are practiced in schools to support habit formation.

The primary purpose of this paper is to deepen the understanding of value-based education for children while teaching a foreign language. The specific study objectives are to:

- Investigate the language teaching principles while teaching values,
- Determine the conceptual framework of value-based language teaching methodology,
- Propose value-based reflective practices children can perform in classes.

"Value-based education will be successful when students realize the value of persons, irrespective of their qualifications, position, or possession. This will lead to academic excellence and unfold the student's inner personality" (Nadda, 2017, p. 19). While this more recent statement by Nadda (2017) focuses on the outcome and success factors of Value Based Education, Veugelers and Vedder (2003), on the other hand, reviewed studies regarding values and education and made a conceptual clarification. They analyzed how values and communicative skills to reflect on values could be part of education and discussed school culture as part of moral education. They stated that conformity was the priority during the 1950s for values and the educational system, where the goal was to adjust to societal norms. They further elaborated on this: "The 1960s offered an impulse for self-fulfilment, social commitment and democracy in society as a whole and in education" (Veugelers & Vedder, 2003, p. 377). In chronological order, Veugelers and Vedder (2003) presented that a more technical and instrumental approach was taken in the 1980s, and values were not the priority in education. They explain this shift in approaches towards values and education: "The pedagogical mission had almost completely vanished from the thinking on education as well as from the teachers' discourse on their educational practice. This change concerned more the discourse itself than the actual practices" (p. 377).

Moving forward, teaching values is vital due to increasing mobility; people interact with varied cultures and are eager to learn more about other beliefs, food, and attractions as well as in their own countries. Becoming a more significant global village, the multicultural character of current societies also offers more experience opportunities. However, this also means there is an increased demand that all individuals can work with and accept different values. There is more room and need in societies to be able to learn about different contexts for the development of values, so young people will be able to grow in this complex nature while forming an idea about how to live together and how to practice the social rules and norms in different cultures as well. In addition, demands are placed on them for greater self-regulation concerning the development of values. Modern societies expect their members to gain this autonomy and practice learning about national and international values to decide and practice in a complicated social environment effectively. Governments, policy-makers, education parties, and practitioners are all expected to further support young learners at schools in this process of moral development, value learning, and ethical and appropriate behaviors.

BACKGROUND

Constructivism is a theory focusing on how learners construct knowledge rather than just passively receive information. It considers that individuals build their representations and perceptions and incorporate new information into their pre-existing knowledge. Learning is also considered as a social activity, which is something built together with others through interaction rather than as an abstract concept, according to Dewey (1938). This theory is grounded by the assumptions of constructivist learning principles, in which meaning is constructed through the reflective analysis of experiences (Kelly, 1955; Schon, 1987).

"Reflection is recognized as one of the most important transferable competencies in lifelong learning, and it affects continuous personal and professional development" (Colomer et al., 2020, p. 5). Therefore, reflective learning has become relevant to meet the global challenges that societies face due to the increasing technological and educational advances. It helps to develop the ability of individuals to adjust to the ever-changing and complex nature of life. As reflection allows new experiences, the new experiences based on previous experiences in various contexts and environments, it offers alternatives or ways of dealing with the new challenges, knowledge building, habit formation, and transforming behavioral and emotional well-being over time. Through practical methodological applications, reflective learning can have huge triggering effects on learners in increasing their awareness and ability, competence, and performance in different contexts. It dramatically impacts combining the theory and application through reflective practices with a considerable contribution to individuals' personal and professional lives.

All learners should acquire knowledge and skills and gain competence and performance to promote sustainable development at schools and well-being at all levels of society. Through reflections and reflective practices at schools, with a well-equipped methodology, children can gain self-confidence, awareness of their power and self-directions, critical competence, self-assured performance, and a growing motivation.

With a focus on integrating value-based education in the educational structure for children, there is an ever-increasing awareness of how values education and the language classroom overlap. In his study, Contreras (2007) reports how teachers incorporate values into Colombia's English as a Foreign Language (EFL) class. The study highlights the importance of teachers' role, especially with the new generations. "It states that language forms can be used to contribute to the fostering of values in a given society when they are taught in a learner-centered curriculum approach as well as with a cross-curriculum view" (p. 11). Moving forward with the idea, which states that "to be a citizen is to respect everybody else's rights" as well as considering the importance of social and state rules, and the "recognition of other people's rights as the basis of peaceful living together," schools are expected to promote learning experiences in which the students can grow as individuals with values and abilities to interact with others (Carreras et al., 1997 cited in Contreras, 2007). Contreras (2007) agrees with the proposed change, which is a need to change "the traditional education in citizenship and values in which the transmission of knowledge was privileged, into an educational process in which the learners develop emotional, cognitive, and communicative competencies" (p.14). For the proposed change, Contreras (2007) believes that the education parties should work on how to teach values, leaving the traditional way of teaching, but "teaching the learners how to reflect on their views of the world in order to resolve potential conflicts" (p.14).

In line with the need for teaching values in an educational context, the classroom atmosphere, the emotional climate created by the practitioners in class, and overall student engagement are other vital factors that should be considered. Brackett et al. (2011) propose the "ecological model of child development" (p. 1). Studying emotional connections of students, how that fosters in their classrooms, and the impact it has on students' school success, they focused on "Using a multimethod, multilevel approach," where they explored "the link between classroom emotional climate and academic achievement, including the role of student engagement as a mediator" (p.1). The study proposes that the interaction with the immediate environment has an effect on a child, and "the quality of interactions between the child and elements in the child's proximal environments influence developmental outcomes." Student-teacher interaction creates a primary micro context within the classroom. The emotional environment that is created in the classroom is a result of "The quality of social and emotional interactions in the classroom—between and among students and teachers (e.g., teacher and peer support, student autonomy)" (p.1).

MAIN FOCUS OF THE CHAPTER

Issues, Controversies, Solutions

Learning by doing (Piaget, 1985) and reflection on action (Schon, 1987) are the two key terms that influenced many Western nations and their preferences in education. Western societies are influenced by Piaget's proposals and initiated that children learn best through doing. Therefore, they employed high-quality programs providing young learners with a range of activities in which to take part. They are encouraged to reflect on their learning in and after the action. So, learning a foreign language has dual roles—acquiring new language rules as the system and learning about the values (international and nationwide). Learning by doing is interwoven with learners' reflections on their new learning and understanding.

Reflection is recognized as one of the most essential transferable competencies in language learning and value-based education. Reflective activities have profound effects on young learners' language learning, and therefore it has naturally become relevant to meet the challenges of a technology-related world of teaching and learning. As reflection allows for the transformation of knowledge into practice, it is directly related to the contexts and combines theory with application in the performances of young learners.

Teaching children how to reflect on their learning is essential and a need for building their personality. Reflection is how young learners being taught will also learn how to monitor their learning process. They are expected to reflect both on the results and the actions they are involved in. To make this happen, the learning environment acquires suitable conditions and the need for positive, productive learning experiences that can be used in other similar learning situations. If so, children can gradually discover the best and most effective ways of learning, imitate the roles taken, practice and master them over time, and begin to use them spontaneously. The possible ways students can reflect on their learning depend on their ever-maturing relationships with their environments, the role models and the experiences gained. This is why teachers are expected to behave as role models regarding how children need to reflect on their learning until they can do it themselves. The profound role of the teacher is also significant, as children in this age group are not yet able to engage in an internal dialogue with themselves. Teachers facilitate based on the pre-determined pedagogical activities on a learning paradigm by allocating time during lessons and using appropriate methods and tools.

During a reflective practice, in which teachers employ a process of thinking about one's practice before, during, and after the concrete activities, they present the key terms and values along with the activities in class, considering the students' developmental stages. This requires an analysis of what to teach and how to teach components of the methodology. So, based on the curriculum and the accompanying proposed tools, teachers spend time planning and thinking about what they want students to realize, what is good, and what could be better, what needs to be changed and improved. Teachers need to stop in the process of planning and think about their actions and thoughts. Such concerns and planning mark the flow of the work of reflective practitioners; thanks to the reflective practice they are involved in, they become more aware of the self and the second circle factors. Since teachers face many challenges in their practices, reflective practice in values education should only be implemented considering the context in which it takes place. Therefore, it is widely accepted that many teachers find it challenging to take advantage of reflective practices; it is not a simple process and requires time and motivation.

METHODOLOGY

Research Design

This study employed a qualitative research design to capture the complexity of the educational matter under investigation and propose solutions. This investigative method was used to review the literature to understand the nature of the issue of value-based education before proposing procedures and activities. The study enabled practitioners and researchers to record the explicit processes and unveil the implicit ways in which values could be taught in the school environment and utilized in how to reflect by the learners.

The research design focused on the outcome of an educational matter that helps reveal practitioners' cognitive behavior and perception regarding the reflection issue. The reason behind choosing a qualitative research method is that it originated in the educational sciences. Today, the educational world is advancing with such complexity that it leads to a deeper understanding concerning the nature of reflection and how it can be used as a classroom tool for students and practitioners in the classroom to practice values.

The conceptual framework highlighted the links between young learners and community practices. The study framework took the Turkish national curricula operational within the school setting, each impacting the learners. Ideally, national values are embodied in the goals and objectives of the formal curriculum and reflected in the co-curricular activities. As officially designated educators, it is expected that teachers "teach" the prescribed values in the school setting both in and outside the classroom and through co-curricular activities. Values children are exposed to are diverse and thus need to be approached with a clear structure and objective during their integration into the language classroom.

Regarding values education in Turkey, per the English Language Curriculum published by the Turkish Ministry of Education, the values associated with the learning outcomes are stated as "friendship, justice, honesty, self-control, patience, respect, love, responsibility, patriotism and altruism" (2018, p. 6). These values are highlighted to be included naturally in the syllabus when designing the lessons and materials. This chapter encompasses values of friendship, justice (fairness), honesty (trust), self-control, patience (tolerance), respect, love (family), responsibility (loyalty), patriotism (environmental values), and altruism.

Teaching Approaches and Methods for Value-Based Education

It is well-known that children learn best through active participation and concrete observation of what their peers do rather than what they say. Through multiple teaching techniques such as quizzing, question-answer, demonstration, group talks, and so on, the following reflective exercises would help them have their voices heard:

- Club activities
- Special day activities
- International day activities
- Interviews
- Newsletters, posters writing
- In-class presentations
- Portfolio

Students learn best by doing and when they are actively engaged in learning experiences rather than passively receiving information. Since reflection in value-based education promotes an interactive classroom environment for the students, it provides a valuable atmosphere for learning in values education. It feeds the pace and the quality of learning due to its reflective nature through activities. Vygotsky emphasized the importance of interaction as a crucial aspect of teaching and methodology. He believes that children can learn at two levels; first, they learn through interaction with peers, friends, Etc…, and then integrate their learning based on their experiences and interaction meaningfully into their mental structure. In line with his Zone of Proximal Development concept, he initially addresses the importance of biological factors as preconditions. Then he emphasizes the sociocultural factors as essential factors. So, he proposes that children receive knowledge through interaction and coordination with others and then process the received knowledge (digestion process) before admitting and wrapping up for personal values. The passage of the values from social to personal learning should not be underestimated; the transformation is a long journey. Interaction with others makes children's learning dynamic, with a long shelf-life.

Reflective teaching methodology introduces a set of processes and procedures in which teachers and learners reflect on their teaching/learning. This process requires information, data gathering, and interpretation of the data for teachers to make revisions and adjustments to improve students' learning and maximize the learning outcomes. While it may allow teachers to evaluate their teaching and improve their teaching practices based on feedback, observation, peer-reviewing, Etc.…, the dynamic nature of the classroom will bring more challenging activities for the students through reflective practices. It may also develop students' self-awareness; they can quickly identify gaps in their learning and areas for improvement. It is an undeniable fact that reflection in learning allows learners to monitor their learning and assess their knowledge, competence, and performance. Through involvement in reflective activities, children may:

a. Identify their weaknesses & strengths;
b. Figure out how to improve their learning
c. Sharpen their interactive skills;
d. Develop their metacognitive skills;
e. Increase autonomy and self-control
f. Monitor their learning outcomes and assess their level of learning
g. Benefit from the outcomes of their trial-error process
h. Receive-give feedback

Learners, in the process of reflective practices, can easily understand the material being taught, implement what they have learned, assess the process and the procedures, and can put theory into an application for their meaningful learning. So, values education will provide children to make ethical decisions through their interaction with others and teach them personal values and responsibilities that will promote moral integrity at personal and inter/national levels.

As young learners experience the world from pure and clean perspectives, they genuinely reflect upon those experiences; they construct their representations and incorporate new information into their pre-existing knowledge (schemas). That enables the development of children holistically for their bright and complete future. This cycle makes their learning valid and comprehensive.

The following reflective activity types and related samples are proposed to be used in classes with young learners to develop their value-based language learning.

Activity Samples for Values

Activity 1

For Activity 1, guiding information regarding the activity's use has been provided in Table 1.

Table 1. Activity 1 guide

Acquired Value(s)	Friendship and Tolerance
Target Group Age	10, 11, 12 years old
Class	Primary School Grades 4, 5, 6
Expected Knowledge	A1 (CEFR) According to Turkish Republic Ministry of Education (2018, p. 93).
Learning Outcomes	Everyday expressions Basics phrases Own likes and dislikes Others' likes and dislikes
Materials	BINGO handout Paper Student pens, pencils, crayons

In school settings for children, the following activity can be done for students to develop and reflect on *Friendship* and *Tolerance* values:

Step 1: The teacher introduces the class by presenting the target language with a story on celebrating differences, ending the story with the structure, "Today, I learned I am different from _____, but we are friends."

Step 2: Students are given BINGO cards with statements about their likes, dislikes, hobbies, personality, Etc. (provided in Table 2).

Step 3: The teacher facilitates the BINGO game.

Step 4: Once all students have at least five marks crossed out (or have five marks in vertical, horizontal, or diagonal rows), the BINGO ends.

Step 5: Students must find a classmate who has selected a BINGO mark different from theirs. The aim here is to support and emphasize the value of tolerance among peers.

For example, Paul likes winter, dislikes apples, likes cake, dislikes chocolate, and his favorite color is green. While George also likes winter, dislikes apples, likes cake, and dislikes chocolate, in contrast to Paul, his favorite color is blue. In this case, Paul and George become partners for the next activity. Students who struggle to find someone who has selected a single BINGO mark different than theirs can focus on other marks they have crossed out. For instance, Sarah and Gemma both have marks for likes painting and dislike winter. However, while Sarah said she dislikes apples, Gemma marked she likes apples. Then they can pair up too.

Step 6: For the second part of the task, the students must sit across from each other and draw their partners as they see them. This aspect of the activity is again to reinforce tolerance and help build connections between students.

Step 7: Then, in pairs, students present the likes, dislikes, hobbies, personalities, Etc. they have in common and what separates them using target language such as I like apples. _____ dislikes apples. However, we like red. I am different from _____, but we are friends.

Step 8: The final step in ending the presentation indicates the reflection on the strengthened values of friendship and tolerance.

Table 2. Bingo activity for tolerance and friendship values

Bingo				
Likes winter	Plays football	Likes pizza	Likes blue	Likes painting
Has a brother or sister	Dislikes apples	Likes dogs	Dislikes math	Dislikes winter
Likes to dance	Likes red	Likes cake	Plays video games	Likes apples
Likes pink	Likes summer	Dislikes dancing	Dislikes chocolate	Likes cats
Dislikes spiders	Likes math	Likes to read	Dislikes summer	Likes green

Activity 1: Recommendations

At the level proposed by the Turkish Ministry of Education (2018), students are expected to listen to and speak about their likes and dislikes and carry out assignments within the scope of the proposed activity. With higher grades, students expand on this knowledge with the likes and dislikes of friends and family, abilities, and hobbies. Therefore, the proposed BINGO content can be adjusted to classroom vocabulary and comprehension levels.

If this activity is applied to lower grades (grades 2 and 3), the students can draw/illustrate their likes and dislikes on a larger bingo sheet after step 2 of the activity.

Activity 1: Real Life Applications

The proposed activity enables students to identify their likes and dislikes while determining those of their classmates. This helps establish common ground, mutual understanding, and tolerance between students. Reflecting on friendship values in this activity aims to instill a sense of acceptance between peers and strengthen the awareness that shared interests bring individuals together, be they like or dislike. On a broader scale, outside of the classroom, the value of friendship and tolerance the students will have reflected on can be seen when they meet someone different. The students will likely focus on the similarities they might have that can be explored rather than focus on the differences that divide them.

Activity 2

For Activity 2, guiding information regarding the activity's use has been provided in Table 3. Required materials are shown in Figure 1 (provided in Appendix 1).

Table 3. Activity 2 guide

Acquired Value(s)	Environmental Values (Patriotism and Respect)
Target Group Age	10, 11, 12, 13 years old
Class	Primary School Grades 4, 5, 6, 7
Expected Knowledge	A1 (CEFR) According to Turkish Republic Ministry of Education (2018, p. 93).
Learning Outcomes	Everyday expressions Basics phrases Give suggestions
Materials	Target vocabulary pictures (Appendix 1) Environment word jumble and sentences (Appendix 2) Paper Student pens, pencils, crayons

Environmental values concern respect for nature, thus supporting motivation to preserve one's country and environment. The following activity proposed aims to reinforce these values and perspectives:

Step 1: The teacher starts the lesson by mentioning the weather for that day (hot, cold, warm, rainy, sunny, windy, cloudy, snowy, Etc.). Then, in short phrases, the teacher mentions that the weather is scorching in the summer or very cold in the winter. Providing a transition into the concept that "the world is getting hotter." This ultimately connects to the overarching theme of *global warming*.

Step 2: Once the teacher establishes the theme, students are shown images related to global warming causes so as to introduce vocabulary relating to rubbish, bin, electricity, light, water, paper, trees, plants, plastic bags, recycle, bicycle, and littering (Appendix 1).

Step 3: Worksheet 1 for the activity is given to the students (Appendix 2). In task A, students have to unjumble the target vocabulary. In task B, they fill in the blanks in the sentence.

Step 4: Then, the teacher creates a discussion asking students about the actions that save the planet and actions that harm the planet. The sentences are written under "Save" and "Harm" in a place visible to all students (blackboard, whiteboard, smartboard, Etc.).

Step 5: Once the teacher establishes students' comprehension of the topic and vocabulary, students are asked to think of and draw actions that save or harm the planet.

Step 6: The teacher observes the students and, while doing so, identifies the actions students are drawing. These actions are added to a neutral list on one side of the board.

Step 7: When the students complete the drawings, the teacher asks each student to come to the front of the class and act out the environmental action they have drawn. The class has to identify which action their classmate is acting out from the actions on the neutral list. When the class guesses correctly from the list, the teacher asks if this is an action that goes under "Save" or "Harm." The student(s) who have drawn this action write what the action is under their drawing.

For example, Harry shows a boy drinking from a plastic bottle. While the students are completing their drawings, the teacher sees this drawing and writes "drinking from the plastic bottle" on the board, on the neutral list side. When all drawings are complete, the teacher asks Harry to come and act out drinking from a plastic bottle. Students in the class find this action from the list. When Harry sits back down, he writes under his drawing, "drinking from the plastic bottle."

Step 8: To finalize the activity and ensure students' retention of the environmental values that were emphasized, the students' drawings, along with the sentences, are displayed in the classroom under two lists for "Save" and "Harm."

Activity 2: Recommendations

Considering student levels, for 2nd and 3rd grades, this activity can be simplified by omitting the sentence completion in Worksheet 1, task B (Appendix 2). Instead, the activity can be carried out at a single word or phrase level. Students are expected to make simple inquiries and suggestions. Therefore, "let's…" and "do not…" can be incorporated into the students' sentences. Since the theme for the 6th Grade Unit 9 in the Turkish Ministry of Education (2018) English language curriculum is "Saving the Planet," students are expected to be able to write simple suggestions to protect the environment. Therefore, the sentence under the drawing can also include "should" statements to carry the activity further.

Activity 2: Real-Life Applications

Students' application of this value is expected to influence their approach to energy and water conservation at home and in the classroom, reducing waste, increasing the use of recycled/recyclable products, and keeping the environment clean. This connects to patriotism because preserving natural resources and encouraging recycling builds a better and cleaner future. In terms of respect, students are reinforced to respect nature, the people around them, and themselves; since keeping the environment clean benefits everyone.

Activity 3

For Activity 3, information regarding the activity's use has been provided in Table 4. Required materials are shown in Figure 2 (provided in Appendix 3).

In 3rd Grade, Units 2, 3, and 4, with the themes *My Family, People I Love, Feelings*, and in 4th Grade, Units 3, 4, 7, 9, with the themes *Cartoon Characters, Free Time, Jobs, My Friends* encompass language functions and skills that provide helpful language and objectives to all cover the topics of family, love, emotions, feelings, and simple actions. Further grades build on these grade levels to possessions, descriptions, and personal information, where students can communicate in further detail.

Table 4. Activity 3 guide

Acquired Value(s)	Love (Family)
Target Group Age	8, 9, 10, 11, 12 years old
Class	Primary School Grades 3, 4, 5, 6, 7
Expected Knowledge	A1 (CEFR) According to Turkish Republic Ministry of Education (2018, p. 93).
Learning Outcomes	Everyday expressions Basics phrases Family Physical qualities
Materials	Family member picture for the teacher to show Family Love word search (Appendix 3) Paper Student pens, pencils, crayons

To reinforce these themes of the value of *Love (Family)*, proposed activity 3 suggests a thank you note for a family member that the student takes home and gives to the family member. The activity stems from children's drawings that are displayed on fridges. In the classroom:

Step 1: The teacher introduces the class activity by hiding a picture in front of them and saying to the class, "I am thinking of a family member. Can you guess who it is?" To elicit answers, the teacher asks questions regarding the person they are thinking of, their physical attributes, their interests, what they do in their free time, who they are related to, Etc. "Is s/he old?" "Is s/he young?" "Does s/he have white hair?" "Does s/he cook?" "Does s/he read books?" "Is s/he funny?" "Is s/he strong?" "Is s/he tall?" "Is s/he my mother?" Etc. Depending on the level of the students, the questions can be yes/no questions asked to the students by the teacher or asked by the students to the teacher. Furthermore, the teacher can provide family member names (mother, father, aunt, uncle, sister, brother, grandfather, grandmother, Etc.) in written form to guide the students, along with any additional vocabulary.

Step 2: Following the warmup, the teacher reveals the family member, "This is my sister. She is kind. She is strong. She likes to read and cook. I love her." This helps introduce the target activity in the next step.

Step 3: Students are given a word search (Appendix 3) with the following words: mother, father, aunt, uncle, sister, brother, grandfather, grandmother, kind, loving, funny, helpful, patient, brave, smart, strong, calm, happy.

Step 4: Students are then asked to draw a family member. Under the picture, the students should include the addressee (family member vocabulary from word search), why they appreciate them (adjectives from word search), and their feeling of love: To my _____, thank you for being so _____. I love you.

Step 5: The students are encouraged to take these drawings with the notes to the family member to be displayed in the house, either on the fridge or anywhere else the family member can see them.

Activity 3: Recommendations

To further the activity, as student proficiencies advance, students can expand on their thank you notes by opening with "Dear _____" followed by superlatives (i.e., kindest, most loving, funniest, most helpful). Suppose teachers would like to carry out this activity in the second or third grades with lower proficiency. In that case, the adjectives can be omitted, and the focus can be given to drawing the picture of the family member they love and only including "I love you _____."

If students choose two or more family members, this is allowed and encouraged to add to the activity. In this case, students can address the drawing to all members chosen but should also include an adjective for each. For example, "To my mum, dad, and grandmother, thank you for being so smart, funny, and kind. I love you."

Another variation of the activity would include a guessing game, where when the students finish their drawings, they hide their drawings from their classmates, and the class asks the students questions to find out who the chosen family member is; "Is s/he old?" "Is s/he young?" "Does s/he have white hair?" "Does s/he cook?" "Does s/he read books?" "Is s/he funny?" "Is s/he strong?" "Is s/he tall?" "Is s/he your mother?" Etc.

Activity 3: Real-Life Applications

Family love focuses on the appreciation of family members and expressing this love. The display of the student's drawing reinforces this value. Students can apply this value not only to their family members but to their friends too. Having the students draw also has a reciprocal effect in that the student can also feel their love is appreciated and valued. Strengthening the value of family love can further develop for family members to be more open to sharing their feelings for each other.

General Reflective Approaches

Language activities reinforcing value-based education can also be carried out through structured questions before, during, and after story or media-based activities. Question types from the reflective questioning framework by Rush et al. (2008) can be applied concerning questions in creating awareness, analyzing, considering alternatives, and taking action. Within this framework, Rush et al. (2008) emphasize that the framework is a tool that helps create conversation and build a person's potential. They highlight that when applying the framework for reflective questioning, rather than using close-ended questions and questions that suggest adopting a particular point of view, open-ended questions addressing analysis and action-based question types should be the focus. Although the framework targets a coaching context, its applications as a capacity-building practice in early childhood intervention are mentioned. Therefore, this framework could be adapted to be used with young learners within the English language classroom to develop their value-based language learning.

Under the curriculum, reflective open-ended questions can create an environment where students activate their background knowledge of the value covered during English classes. The questions can further examine and critically evaluate scenarios as they occur in the stories, events, or media given throughout the class. Finally, the reflective questions can be used to map a future plan for students to apply concepts they have learned to the value that was emphasized.

General Reflective Approach Recommendations

To illustrate the reflective questioning framework application, for a class where a story, event, or media emphasizing or mentioning the value of honesty (trust) will be covered, this value can be brought to the student's attention following the steps of creating awareness, carrying out an analysis, considering alternatives, and taking action.

Before the class content is mentioned or the students start their reading or viewing, the teacher can lead in with the first approach to questioning the value of honesty (trust). This stage would focus on creating awareness of the value. Questions such as "What makes a person honest?", "What makes you trust your friends?" or "How do you decide you can trust someone?" can be asked before the activity. By doing so, the students' understanding of the value of honesty (trust) can be gauged, and their standards for the value can be identified.

Following this, from a more self-reflective approach, the students can be asked questions to notice their behavior in relation to the value. This would include questions such as "How do you act honest?", "How do you feel when you act honest?", "How do you feel when someone does not act honestly with you?" These questions can help the students notice their behavior and feelings about the value.

In the subsequent approach, where alternatives are considered, students can be asked questions to identify their stance on specific experiences, scenarios, or cases where their expectations regarding the value were unmet. For instance, questions like "What do you do when someone is not honest with you?" or "What happens if you are not honest?" can be asked. With this, before the class activity, students will have activated their knowledge, shared their feelings, and pointed out their views on the value.

Finally, after the class content is covered and students have read or viewed the class material and completed exercises, they can reflect on the actions related to the value they have noticed. From the materials covered, students can be asked, "Who was/was not honest in the story/media/event?" "What can (character in story/media/event) do to be more honest?", "What can you do to be more honest?" Questions that look at the outcomes of students' actions in the class and questions that help students evaluate the value within context can support and encourage language use related to values.

Considering the expected knowledge at the students' language level within the Turkish Ministry of Education, students can provide one-word answers where applicable or act out the scenario of how they act or feel within the context of the value being covered.

FUTURE RESEARCH DIRECTIONS

All dimensions of value-based education- the values, contextual language teaching, pedagogy, and methodology for the young learners, and the accompanying evaluation and assessment techniques along with constructive feedback need to be addressed in teaching practices and publications through nationwide curricula, with the support of the schools, administrators and the teachers in classes.

CONCLUSION

Teaching language through values mainly has a dual effect on students' learning. Rather than isolating the value of learning to be learned in societies by older people, value-based language teaching increases the consciousness of young learners by providing them access to information, helping them make conscious choices, and increasing their willingness to apply them in society. There are several favorable reasons for employing value-based education. First, students learn the language either as a second (ESL) or a foreign (EFL) language in real-life contexts; second, they can learn about the values themselves. Young learners, by doing, will have the chance to practice new information in the context and improve their self-efficacy.

Under the light of constructivist learning principles and well-designed reflective practices, values education can support language teachers in fulfilling their tasks and responsibilities of teaching values and making students more reflective practitioners allowing them to enhance their critical thinking skills for life. Besides, with the help of pedagogical tools and the methodological components of teaching, value-laden issues and concepts are of greater interest and curiosity to young learners and of greater practical reference in society to them.

This chapter summarized the importance of reflective practices while teaching the values; how to use reflective practices with young learners in class; what kind of activities can be employed in class, and some proposed exercises and models.

REFERENCES

Aspin, D. N. (2007). The ontology of values and values education. In D. N. Aspin & J. D. Chapman (Eds.), *Values education and lifelong learning: Principles, policies, programs* (pp. 27–35). Springer. doi:10.1007/978-1-4020-6184-4_1

Best Sale. (2019, January 11). *Rubbish bins for recycling different types of waste garbage*. IStock. https://www.istockphoto.com/en/vector/rubbish-bins-for-recycling-different-types-of-waste-garbage-containers-vector-gm1092504754-293138771?phrase=recycle

Brackett, M. A., Reyes, R., Rivers, M., Elbertson, N., & Salovey, P. (2011). Classroom emotional climate, teacher affiliation, and student conduct. *Journal of Classroom Interaction, 45*(1), 27-36. https://www.jstor.org/stable/23870549

Colomer, J., Serra, T., Cañabate, D., & Bubnys, R. (2020). Reflective learning in higher education: Active methodologies for transformative practices. *Sustainability (Basel), 12*(3827), 3827. doi:10.3390u12093827

Contreras, O. R. (2007). Incorporating values into the English classroom. *HOW, 14*, 11-26. https://www.redalyc.org/pdf/4994/499450713002.pdf

Creative Images. (2022, February 24). *Little boy throwing ice cream wrap or plastic rubbish in the park*. IStock. https://www.istockphoto.com/en/vector/little-boy-throwing-plastic-rubbish-in-the-park-gm1372454528-441554339?phrase=littering

Dewey, J. (1933). *How we think: A restatement of the relation of reflective thinking to the educative process*. D. C. Health.

Dewey, J. (1938). *Experience and education.* Collier Books.

DoggieMonkey. (2016, November 1). *Vector illustration of shopping plastic bags with groceries products.* IStock. https://www.istockphoto.com/en/vector/grocery-shopping-gm618221966-107518513?phrase=plastic+bag

(2016). Friendship. InLonge, J. L. (Ed.), *Gale virtual reference library: The Gale encyclopedia of psychology* (3rd ed.). Gale. Credo Reference.

Ganguli, H. C., Mehrotra, G. P., & Mehlinger, H. D. (1981). Values, moral education, and social studies. In H. D. Mehlinger (Ed.), *UNESCO handbook for the teaching of social studies.* UNESCO.

Hamada, T., Shimizu, M., & Ebihara, T. (2021). Good patriotism, social consideration, environmental problem cognition, and pro-environmental attitudes and behaviors: A cross-sectional study of Chinese attitudes. *SN Applied Sciences, 3*(3), 361. Advance online publication. doi:10.100742452-021-04358-1

Ilyabolotov. (2019, January 28). *Trash can full of garbage bin filled with waste.* IStock. https://www.istockphoto.com/en/vector/trash-can-full-gm1125611454-295978809?phrase=rubbish+bin

KajaNi. (2021, August 15). *Big dump with of trash and rubbish waste recycling in city landfill.* IStock. https://www.istockphoto.com/en/vector/pile-of-garbage-isolated-on-white-background-gm1334125608-416372596?phrase=rubbish

KanKhem. (2019, March 12). *Vector illustration of happy kids riding bicycles in the park.* IStock. https://www.istockphoto.com/en/vector/vector-illustration-of-happy-kids-riding-bicycles-in-the-park-gm1135282671-301961955?phrase=bicycle+cycling+child

Kelly, G. A. (1955). *A theory of personality: The psychology of personal constructs.* Norton.

Knafo, A., & Schwartz, S. H. (2004). Identity status and parent-child value congruence in adolescence. *British Journal of Developmental Psychology, 22*(3), 439–458. doi:10.1348/0261510041552765

Lemba, J. (2020, August 13). *Paper sheets pile for paperwork and office routine: Heap of white papers.* IStock. https://www.istockphoto.com/en/vector/paper-sheets-pile-gm1266139919-371087003?phrase=paper+pile

Ogieurvil. (2018, March 6). *Funny and cute tap water - vector.* IStock. https://www.istockphoto.com/en/vector/cute-tap-water-gm927423546-254420819?phrase=water+tap

Petovarga. (2022, January 13). *Renewable energy power distribution with family house residence.* IStock. https://www.istockphoto.com/en/vector/power-distribution-transmission-of-renewable-solar-electricity-energy-grid-with-gm1364369919-435602009?phrase=electricity+tower

Piaget, J. (1985). *The equilibration of cognitive structures: The central problem of intellectual development.* University of Chicago Press.

Piliavin, J. A., & Charng, H.-W. (1990). Altruism: A review of recent theory and research. *Annual Review of Sociology, 16*(1), 27–65. doi:10.1146/annurev.so.16.080190.000331

Rush, D. D., Shelden, M. L., & Raab, M. (2008). A framework for reflective questioning when using a coaching interaction style. *CASEtools, 4*(1), 1-7. https://fipp.ncdhhs.gov/wp-content/uploads/case-tools_vol4_no1.pdf

Schön, D. (1987). *Educating the reflective practitioner*. Jossey-Bass.

Turkish Ministry of Education. (2018). *İngilizce dersi öğretim programı: İlkokul ve ortaokul 2, 3, 4, 5, 6, 7 ve 8. sınıflar* [English language curriculum: Primary and secondary school years 2, 3, 4, 5, 6, 7 and 8]. http://mufredat.meb.gov.tr/Dosyalar/201812411191321-%C4%B0NG%C4%B0L%C4%B0ZCE%20%C3%96%C4%9ERET%C4%B0M%20PROGRAMI%20Klas%C3%B6r%C3%BC.pdf

Tutti-frutti. (2019, September 23). *Ceiling lamp light bulb shine*. IStock. https://www.istockphoto.com/en/vector/ceiling-lamp-light-bulb-shine-bright-business-background-for-your-text-vector-gm1176531164-328058114?phrase=lamp

Venimo. (2017, November 26). *Vector set of icons and illustrations in flat linear style - nature*. IStock. https://www.istockphoto.com/en/vector/nature-landscapes-with-green-trees-gm879289876-245119756?phrase=trees+and+forest

Venimo. (2019, October 23). *Vector illustration in flat simple style - greenhouse with plants*. IStock. https://www.istockphoto.com/en/vector/vector-illustration-in-flat-simple-style-greenhouse-with-plants-gm1182830958-332306487?phrase=plants+indoor

Veugelers, W., & Vedder, P. (2003). Values in teaching. *Teachers and Teaching, 9*(4), 377–389. doi:10.1080/1354060032000097262

KEY TERMS AND DEFINITIONS

Altruism: Putting the needs of other people before one's own needs (Piliavin & Charng, 1990).

Friendship: The relationship between two or more people, where a shared bond of respect, trust, and care is of primary importance (Friendship, 2016).

Honesty (Trust): Being open, telling the truth, and having integrity.

Justice (Fairness): Acting fairly, and rationally and practicing equality and equity.

Love (Family): An affectionate and caring bond based on a solid and healthy attachment.

Patience (Tolerance): Staying calm by regulating negative emotions in the face of difficult or challenging situations.

Patriotism (Environmental Values): Showing respect to society and increasing social consideration for the benefit of society as a whole (Hamada, Shimizu, & Ebihara, 2021).

Reflection: Active, persistent, and careful consideration of any belief or supposed form of knowledge in the light of the grounds that support it and the further conclusions to which it tends (Dewey 1933, p.9).

Respect: Admiration or high self-regard for oneself or others based on acceptance.

Responsibility (Loyalty): Carrying out duties with accountability, considering faithfulness and devotion.

Self-Control: The ability to control or regulate emotions and behaviors depending on circumstances.

APPENDIX 1

Figure 1. Target vocabulary pictures
NOTE. Images used in Appendix 1 from iStock.

Rubbish	Bin	Light
Electricity	Water	Paper
Trees	Plants	Plastic Bag
Recycle	Bicycle	Littering

APPENDIX 2

Worksheet 1 (Environmental Values)

Task A

Look at the pictures and the words. Can you write each word correctly?
    For example: nbi = bin

1) biurbhs = _____
2) iybccel = _____
3) eestr = _____
4) rteaw = _____
5) praep = _____
6) gihlt = _____
7) ielgtinrt = _____
8) ecrylce = _____
9) ityicrlcete = _____
10) atsnlp = _____
11) isatlcp gba = _____

Answer Key: 1) rubbish, 2) bicycle, 3) trees, 4) water, 5) paper, 6) light, 7) littering, 8) recycling, 9) electricity, 10) plants, 11) plastic bag

Task B

Fill in the blanks using the words from Task A.

1) We recycle plastic.
2) DO NOT WASTE water at home.
3) DO NOT CUT trees.
4) Ride your bicycle.
5) Littering is not good for nature.
6) Save electricity.
7) Put your rubbish in the bin.
8) Plants give life.
9) Switch off the light.
10) Reuse your paper.
11) DO NOT USE plastic bagS AT THE MARKET.

APPENDIX 3

Figure 2. Family love wordsearch
NOTE. Wordsearch puzzle created using https://thewordsearch.com and available at the link: https://thewordsearch.com/puzzle/5626881/family-love/downloadable/

Family Love

F	T	G	D	B	G	R	D	P	O	R	S	C	R
R	B	G	P	R	N	Y	A	N	T	E	A	O	R
U	R	T	P	O	O	P	D	H	K	T	F	O	E
G	A	G	N	T	R	P	E	G	U	S	G	L	F
R	V	H	E	H	T	A	L	R	T	I	R	E	M
A	E	E	O	E	S	H	D	A	H	S	U	N	P
N	G	L	H	R	C	L	H	N	T	A	A	R	A
D	U	P	N	T	G	D	M	D	U	E	I	R	T
M	N	F	L	R	N	R	L	F	A	L	N	H	I
O	C	U	O	A	Y	K	K	A	T	N	U	A	E
T	L	L	V	M	N	N	I	T	E	H	N	A	N
H	E	E	I	S	N	Y	N	H	M	O	M	S	T
E	U	A	N	R	U	V	D	E	P	R	R	U	M
R	O	U	G	A	F	E	N	R	A	F	A	F	M

SISTER
HELPFUL
BROTHER
FUNNY
GRANDFATHER
DAD
PATIENT
KIND
STRONG
BRAVE
MUM
AUNT
COOL
LOVING
SMART
GRANDMOTHER
HAPPY
UNCLE

Chapter 13
Visual Arts as a Tool for Value Education in Primary School

Seda Liman Turan
Trabzon University, Turkey

ABSTRACT

This study aims to highlight the place and significance of visual arts in values education at the primary school level. Using a literature review method, one of the qualitative research approaches, the research concludes that visual arts serve as an effective tool for fostering values education in primary schools. Visual arts hold great importance in values education due to their ability to facilitate originality through diverse activities and practices. They provide an effective platform for developing values such as self-confidence, self-respect, sensitivity, awareness, empathy, respect, love, responsibility, cooperation, justice, respect for differences, and tolerance, both in individual achievements and group work. Visual arts are believed to play a vital role in values education by embodying abstract concepts.

INTRODUCTION

Education, whether planned or spontaneous, is a lifelong process that holds great significance in the growth and sustenance of society. It encompasses the transmission of factual knowledge and the crucial aspect of instilling values (Burkhardt, 1999). Values essential for the coexistence of a society can only be acquired through education. Educational institutions are responsible for preserving these values, passing them on to future generations, and ensuring their enduring impact.

Values serve as principles and beliefs that shape individuals' attitudes and actions, fostering societal cohesion and aiming to cultivate productive and responsible citizens who are in harmony with their environment. Values education occurs within the family during early childhood and later extends to formal educational settings, such as schools. Within this structured environment, visual arts play a crucial role in facilitating the effective acquisition of values education, mainly through their appeal to the affective learning domain of students. Visual arts contribute to individuals' spiritual and moral development while also promoting social and moral values essential for fostering harmonious coexistence within society. As

DOI: 10.4018/978-1-6684-9295-6.ch013

Ünver (2011) stated, "For the society that exists with its values, the accumulations of that society must continue. In the education system that aims to raise qualified people, it is possible to ensure that values are gained through art education because art education is the education of humanity" (Ünver, 2011).

Incorporating societal knowledge and values into primary education through visual arts holds significant importance within the formal educational framework, enabling their transmission to students. Edgington (1993) emphasized the imperative of utilizing every available opportunity, particularly schools, to impart specific values to students (Edgington, 1993, p. 10). Silcock and Duncan's (2001) research underscores the significance of voluntary participation, personal transformation, and consistency in formal and informal settings for students to acquire these values. Taylor (1994) identifies a range of frequently cited values, including cultural diversity, cultural identity, national consciousness, intellectual and academic values, peace, international understanding, human rights, environmental values, gender equality, anti-racism, business and economic values, health, tolerance, solidarity, and cooperation, which are shared human values.

Visual arts offer an effective means to embody and effectively teach socially significant values. According to Mercin and Diksoy (2017), visual arts provide opportunities to cultivate values such as individual thinking, emotional intelligence, trust, self-confidence, cooperation, empathy, respect, tolerance, and fairness. The visual arts education program encompasses various applications and experiences, from promoting family unity to instilling virtues like self-respect, patience, and perseverance. Consequently, visual arts hold a crucial place and significance in values education. This research aims to highlight the role of visual arts in imparting values within primary education, a crucial stage in the educational journey.

LITERATURE REVIEW

Values Education

The notion of value, introduced initially in the field of social sciences by F.W. Znaniecki, is defined by Raths, Harmin, and Simon (1966, p. 28) as "beliefs, attitudes, or feelings that an individual takes pride in, publicly endorses, carefully selects from alternatives without external influence, and consistently activates." (Halstead, 1996, p. 5). Znaniecki (1927, p. 529) identifies various concepts contributing to forming values, including social, hedonic, technical, aesthetic, religious, cognitive, symbolic, intellectual, and legal. Values, acquired and embraced through socialization, are a collection of beliefs that gradually become established within individuals or society over time (Rokeach, 1973, p. 4). Values encompass cultural elements, beliefs, tendencies, normative standards, and goals that become standardized in individuals' thoughts, attitudes, and actions as they internalize them.

Values serve as crucial mechanisms for social control and contribute to social cohesion. They influence an individual's perception of various aspects of life, and individuals learn the meaning of life through their values (Güven, 1999). Social norms, traditions, and customs enable individuals to distinguish between right and wrong, good and evil, and align their behavior with their moral principles (Beill, 2003, p. 14).

Education can be defined as deliberate activities aimed at developing the individual's knowledge, attitudes, and skills to become a competent person and a good citizen. However, education is about helping the individual to become both a competent person and a good citizen. Education, defined as developing desired behaviors in individuals, plays a vital role in understanding values. "The term values education as an overarching concept including terms such as moral education, civic education, and citizenship education" (Taylor, 1994, p. 3). Throughout history, many terms have been used to describe the values of education. These include "moral education, civic education, religious education, positive school culture, service learning, and positive youth development" (Salam, 2018, p. 316). Today, "values education, also called moral education or character education, is an attempt to create pedagogies and supportive structures in schools to promote the development of positive, ethical, pro-social dispositions and competencies in young people and to strengthen their academic focus and achievement" (Berkowitz, 2011). Any school activity where students learn or develop values and morality is called values education (Halstead, 1996; Taylor, 1994). In values education, which has maintained its existence and importance since the beginning of the history of education, values can be defined as explicit and implicit values. Explicit values education refers to the formal curriculum of schools on how and in what ways values and morality are taught, while implicit values education is related to the values implicit in school and classroom practices (Halstead, 1996; Thornberg, 2008). Education and teachers dramatically influence the transmission of values to individuals. Through education, individuals develop their character, knowledge, skills, attitudes, and values, equipping them to contribute positively to society. Taylor (1994), based on a comparative review of research covering 26 European countries, concluded that values education is complex and involves many themes, many of which overlap, closely related to each country's historical and ideological evolution. The themes identified are, for example, moral, religious, civic, democratic, national, pastoral, personal, and social goals.

Lickona (1993, p. 9) has developed a solid and compelling argument for teaching core values. According to this argument, values are related to human dignity. They promote the common good of the individual and society and protect our human rights. They seek to answer the classic ethical tests of reversibility (would you want to be treated this way?) and universalizability (would you want everyone in a similar situation to act this way?). Values define our responsibilities in a democracy, are accepted by all civilized people, and are taught by all enlightened faiths.

Values Education and Visual Arts in Primary School

The school provides the opportunity through educators to help students recognize their present situation and future role in society and to develop their active interest in the welfare of society. The school is an atmosphere in which each individual's interest in the welfare of society becomes a moral habit. Visual arts teachers, like other teachers, especially in primary schools, have an essential role in students' character development and value learning. Values education aims to develop the practical intelligence and moral understanding we need to make choices and lead a good life. Values education is about developing virtues, good habits, and dispositions that lead students to responsible and mature adulthood. Learning these habits and dispositions requires a well-planned values education. Developmental psychology theorists such as Piaget and Vygotsky emphasize the importance of the school years in developing a child's ethical values. According to them, a child's character is shaped for better or worse during school (Karatay, 2011). School values education aims to help students develop a good character that includes knowing, caring, and acting according to fundamental ethical values such as respect, justice, civic virtue, and responsibility. For values education programs to be effective, they need to involve all stakeholders in the school community and be integrated into the curriculum and culture of the school as a whole (Salam, 2018).

Values education encompasses the understanding, evaluation, and internalization of an individual's values and behaviors and active participation in learning and reflecting upon them within various settings (Robb, 1998, p. 1). Values education is a lifelong process that begins in childhood and continues throughout one's life, shaping moral development and acquisition. Early on, values education takes root in the family, and later, formal education in schools plays a significant role in imparting foundational values. "As a society, we must utilize every available opportunity, particularly schools, to transmit specific values to students" (Edgington, 1993, p. 10). For values learned in school to be integrated into students' lives, it is essential for students to willingly embrace these values, experience personal transformation, and observe consistency between formal education and real-life social situations (Silcock & Duncan, 2001).

Individuals needing help understanding and internalizing values may face uncertainty in their plans, thoughts, and ideas. When uncertainty surrounds value-based behaviors, achieving success becomes challenging in goal-setting, time management, and resource allocation (Raths, Harmin & Simon, 1966). The increasing prevalence of social issues, violence, intolerance, and the erosion of respect and fairness in our rapidly changing world (Straughan, 1999) mainly affects primary school children, resulting in adverse consequences for their well-being. "The growing social problems, violence, and intolerance worldwide increasingly impact children. Families and educators in many countries believe that an effective values education is crucial to address these issues that threaten social order" (Tillman, 2000, p. 9). Education offers the opportunity to transform these negative influences into desired behaviors and integrate values into individuals' lifestyles. By instilling universal values early on through the collaborative efforts of families, schools, and teachers, individuals can navigate their social environments with greater ease and lead peaceful and secure lives.

According to Kirschenbaum, who emphasizes the significance of character education in values education, the most effective approach is to utilize various strategies to instill desired behaviors in individuals. This includes incorporating moral and social values and elements such as citizenship within the framework of universal values. By doing so, individuals can better understand values and their application while also learning and strengthening universal values (Kirschenbaum, 2000). In addition to the influence of family, society, and the media, educational programs play a crucial role in raising individuals who recognize, understand, accept, and embrace national, spiritual, and universal values, internalizing them and transforming them into behavior. Value concepts should be incorporated into the curriculum content to be acquired by students (Cabedo-Mas, Nethsinghe & Forrest, 2017). Schools, institutions where social cohesion and individual attitudes converge, provide a fertile ground for nurturing healthy societies by instilling value elements in the younger generation (Dewey, 2008, p. 23). It is evident that when correctly and healthily educated, individuals contribute not only to their development but also to shaping society, thereby strengthening its foundation. Specific strategies for teaching values education to students within a specific program in schools exist. These strategies can be expressed as follows: (1) educate by focusing on students' knowledge, behaviors, and emotions; (2) select content that honors and rewards individual virtue in examples and encourages reflection on values content; (3) use quotes, codes, and guidelines; (4) communicate clearly, consistently, sincerely, and with high expectations without discrimination; (5) develop students' ability to resist peer pressure, maintain self-esteem and resolve conflicts in non-violent ways; (6) be a good role model through positive personal example; (7) use and enforce respectful language; (8) establish and equitably enforce fair classroom rules to teach core values; (9) reinforce students' hard work and virtuous behavior with praise and recognition; (10) correct or facilitate unethical, immoral, and disrespectful behavior; (11) enable students to work together cooperatively in heterogeneous groups; (12) involve peers, parents, and the community; (13) encourage student participation in community service; and (14) teach rather than preach (Dale, 1994). Visual arts is a very effective tool that allows all of these to be used effectively in teaching, implementing, and concretizing values education and permanently incorporating them into life skills.

One of the most effective ways to cultivate a peaceful perspective and impart values education within and beyond the school is through arts education. The key to survival and success is social understanding and collective/collaborative efforts to integrate these understandings for the common good. The role of art is to empathize, to help us understand ourselves and others, and to engage with each other in the process of making, receiving, and appropriating meanings conveyed through the elegance of aesthetic form. By developing empathy, art allows us to use our social skills more effectively. The survival value of art lies in its community-making function (Anderson, 2003). Art can teach and reconstruct values and apply these values in specific situations. The role of art and artworks in teaching our moral values can be referred to as artistic cognitivism. The imagination, which is the source of art, plays a crucial role in bringing our moral judgments into reflective balance, and through visual art, events can be presented in a visualized, i.e., embodied, way. "Effective and experiential imagination can enable us to sense the wrongness, rightness, or complete unthinkability of certain moral choices" (Gaut, 2009, s. 164). So we can make connections between events and evaluate behavior.

The visual arts have been part of the school curriculum since modern public schools in Europe began in the early nineteenth century. The fact that visual arts have been part of the school curriculum for nearly two centuries is an indication of the importance of the subject. The benefits of visual arts learning can be divided into two categories: intrinsic and instrumental. The intrinsic benefits of visual arts learning relate specifically to the unique contributions of visual art to the human experience that cannot be provided by other fields, such as the aesthetic experience that a child perceives when creating and critiquing visual artworks. The primary value of art in education lies in its unique contribution to the individual's experience of and understanding of the world. The visual arts are concerned with the aesthetic thinking of human consciousness, which is not present or addressed in any other field. The instrumental benefits of visual art learning relate to societal needs and values, such as developing collaboration skills, cultural awareness, leadership, and integrity (Salam, 2018, p. 317-318). The intrinsic and instrumental benefits that visual arts can bring to the individual should be considered as a whole and included in teaching activities.

Visual arts serves as a unique tool for expressing the ideas and emotions of the human spirit. It connects us to our history, traditions, and heritage, possessing beauty and power distinct from our culture. Art has the potential to foster intercultural understanding and improve relationships between people. It focuses on developing social competencies, promoting peace, and enhancing the ability to manage interpersonal and intercultural conflicts. Recognizing the cultural beliefs and attitudes shaped during early education is paramount (Cabedo-Mas, Nethsinghe & Forrest, 2017). Although the concept of art is challenging to define in terms of its meaning, it involves the production of products that utilize an individual's imagination to interpret, reflect, and find happiness in life (Havilland, Prins, Walrath & Mcbride, 2008, p. 691). Ultimately, art becomes one pathway that fosters continuous, conflict-free, tolerant, and peaceful human relationships (Wells, 1971, p. 190). Art plays a vital role in teaching individual, universal, moral, cultural, and social values, which are desired to be instilled from the early years of education, promoting comprehension, expression, application, and the sustainability of these behaviors. Art education, often referred to as a form of moral education (Yetkin, 1972, p. 61), encompasses the cultural element, shapes artistic perspectives within a particular culture, and contributes to the formation of that culture (Erinç, 2004, p. 12).

The function of art as an effective means of communication enables students to relate to different cultures, looking at cross-cultural art and visual culture to see how others examine life issues, experiment with their ideas and forms, and incorporate appropriate ones into their own culture. By critically examining works of art from a cross-cultural and transcultural perspective, students can access cultural understanding in their own culture and that of others, thus developing a sense of global community. Understanding others humanizes them in our eyes. By reaching beyond the narrow confines of their cultural understanding, they can see people from different cultures as human beings with human drives, emotions, and sensitivities similar to their own (Anderson, 2003). For example, in a museum visit, they can examine many artifacts from different civilizations and cultures and evaluate their cultural values and their own culture's understanding of art. Visual arts teach us the importance of art and artworks as intrinsic values, raise awareness of preserving artistic heritage from the past to the present, and cultivate sensitivity towards life. "Visual-art learning helps students understand human experiences, both past and present. It develops students' ability to value, appreciate, and criticize works from different ethnic groups and cultures" (Salam, 2018). Additionally, visual arts enable children to recognize and empathize with artworks from different cultures, expanding their understanding beyond their own. At the same time, for students, participating in cultural activities promotes awareness, loyalty, respect, and cultural appreciation.

Art education, specifically through visual arts, plays a significant role in the emotional development of individuals by providing transformative experiences that can reshape human consciousness. Visual arts create a sense of unity, foster creativity and productivity, facilitate communication of diverse ideas and cultures, and organize the educational process to enhance individuals' visual literacy, critical thinking, and problem-solving skills (MEB, 2013, p. 1). Affective learning encompasses the values, attitudes, feelings, desires, and moral principles that individuals strive to acquire, and visual arts, being cognitive, psychomotor, and predominantly affective, are instrumental in transmitting social values to individuals. "Visual arts education contributes to nurturing individuals who possess a sense of belonging in societies" (Genç, 2019, p. 83). Visual arts offer avenues for problem-solving, understanding events, fostering innovation and creativity, and cultivating an aesthetic perspective.

Visual arts, as one of the most effective approaches to comprehending and applying universal values, support the development of individuals' creative and aesthetic perspectives, character growth, self-confidence, tolerance, empathy, responsibility, respect, freedom, sharing, and order. Art education primarily encourages individuals to observe, explore, question, experiment, and draw conclusions. This cultivates their ability to establish connections between abstract and concrete images while fostering a spirit of experimentation, research, and creative development (Gökaydın, 1998, p. 3). Additionally, visual arts provide individuals with the joyful experience of creative action, maintaining this pleasure as a driving force for artistic creation. Maintaining the individual's pleasure as they engage in the creative process is another critical objective of visual arts (Kırışoğlu, 1991, p. 57). The sense of happiness derived from creating a work of art instills a desire to produce new creations, fueling further artistic endeavors.

Visual arts offer various approaches, such as observation, emotional resonance, understanding, interpretation, and aesthetic judgment. Through these approaches, art also imparts values such as self-respect, honesty, patience, friendship, industriousness, self-control, respect, tolerance, empathy, love, responsibility, patriotism, justice, self-confidence, and equality. For instance, when examining and critiquing a work of art, individuals learn values like respect, tolerance, and empathy. In group projects, they acquire values such as order, sharing, sensitivity, and equality. In addition to art practices in visual arts teaching, students will be equipped with art history knowledge about works of art.

The characteristics of artworks can increase the moral and cognitive capacity of individuals. Experiences with works of art are a source of moral learning, but the insights gained from them should be deeply considered and critically examined. It is a fact that abstract reasoning in morality is not enough; experiences and permanent formative experience are necessary for improved moral judgments. Formative experience arises from a relationship with morally relevant experiences, but it is inseparable from abstract reasoning, which also has an important role. Interaction and mutual support between the two sources of moral learning are also necessary (Baccarini, 2018). Visual arts can be used as an effective tool for this interaction.

Engaging with works of art is a powerful tool for developing moral understanding. This is because artworks can engage people more than conventional exemplifications or thought experiments and serve as good examples in place of possible real-life situations. In addition, through works of art, it is possible to recognize negative consequences and details neglected in real life (Baccarini, 2018). A work of art that will be presented to students in art criticism courses questions not only understanding the work but also making judgments at the stage of making judgments about the work. "Judgment is a functional ability that stems from understanding. For example, when we understand discrimination, we can judge one practice as appropriate and another as inappropriate. In other words, criticism is the ability to generate new true moral beliefs on our own" (Hills, 2009, p. 104). For example, when students are asked to criticize Pablo Picasso's work Guernica (1937), they will first understand and interpret the work at the stage of description and interpretation and finally make a concrete judgment about the work. Although this anti-war work does not express anything verbally, students will understand that war is a bad event through the symbols contained in the work. As a result, they will judge the concept of war.

Works of art provide experiential knowledge through semiotics; they can deepen propositional knowledge and lead to a better understanding and experience, leading the viewer to anticipate relevant knowledge. A work of art can help us classify already familiar phenomena in a new way, unifying disconnected beliefs or reorganizing the hierarchy of our moral categories and premises (Baccarini, 2018). With the exemplary artworks selected for students, the message to be conveyed and the target value to be acquired can be taught effectively. Thus, by seeing the embodied visuals of abstract information through semiotics, students can reach the right target about the subject and the message.

In addition to the art criticism activity, students will also have the opportunity to concretize and apply many abstract values through group projects. Visual art is a social field by nature. In visual arts teaching, the activity of making a mural or a large sculpture can be done in groups. Students working in groups will realize that they have a common goal and need to work together to achieve it. They will also recognize each other's different ideas and perspectives and the need to negotiate them to reach a mutual agreement. Working together to achieve a common goal by utilizing each group member's ideas is a meaningful learning process (Salam, 2018). Through activities planned in this way, individuals learn to empathize and understand the importance of empathy.

The development of empathy through visual arts is crucial as it fosters tolerance, courage, pride in displaying artistic products, collaboration in group work, and discipline. "Visual arts, with its approach and activities, can capture the attention of students of all ages, provide enjoyment, and effectively contribute to character education through values education" (Genç, 2018, p. 559). The experience of creating an image that is evaluated by students with a sense of purpose requires students to think critically. Learning how to think critically, learning to take advantage of unexpected opportunities that arise when making a painting or collage, making judgments about relationships based on one's own bodily experience, finding alternative solutions to a problem, and evaluating their intrinsic value are all central to the teaching of the visual arts. They stimulate, develop and refine the highest and most sophisticated forms of human cognition and help us learn to see and feel what we see, bringing together thought and emotion in the service of meaning (Eisner, 2001). Activities such as environmental tours, museum visits, exhibitions, and festivals organized within the scope of visual arts can instill values in students.

Additionally, various methods like educational games, drama, case studies, and role-playing can be employed to teach values. "Works of art, a powerful tool for conveying emotions, can increase our moral sensitivity and sharpen our perception of what is required of us in ways that would not otherwise be available" (Marples, 2017). In a drama activity planned with students in the visual arts course, students are asked to activate their imagination to portray an artist or a work. Our imaginary relationship with imaginary characters contributes significantly to the practical power we need to determine how we should act and feel. Creating and acting out such fiction through drama will improve students' perceptions of empathy, cooperation, harmony, and relationship building.

Visual arts can be effective in fostering the acquisition of various values that are increasingly emphasized in the school context, such as cultural diversity, cultural identity, national consciousness, intellectual and academic values, peace, international understanding, human rights, environmental values, gender equality, anti-racism, business and economic values, health, tolerance, solidarity, and cooperation (Taylor, 1994). By engaging with visual arts, students can explore their identity, develop emotionally, and actively participate in understanding and adopting these values. This benefits their educational journey and cultivates a lifelong passion for learning and exploration. Art education is essential in helping students develop relationships that enable them to understand themselves and others. Furthermore, the collaborative nature of visual arts strengthens the connection between students, teachers, and parents. Through visual arts, students acquire observational, problem-solving, innovative, and critical thinking skills and internalize democratic values supported by the knowledge, skills, and values gained through their artistic endeavors.

Art and art education play a significant role in the development of individuals and societies. As individuals become part of a society, they adopt its values and beliefs. Teachers are responsible for utilizing art as a powerful tool for fostering peaceful relationships and engaging students in aesthetic and creative activities. Teachers need to guide students in resolving conflicts peacefully and raise awareness about issues related to inequality and violence (Cabedo-Mas, Nethsinghe, & Forrest, 2017). While teachers may not explicitly present their own values, they inevitably influence students through their value judgments, as values education lies at the core of their role (Halstead & Taylor, 2000, p. 177). It is important to integrate art with students' human concerns. Although the curriculum outlines the values to be instilled in students, the teacher's knowledge, skills, and values ultimately determine the approach. Thus, the role of visual arts teachers in values education is crucial. "The topics chosen by the teacher, the teaching methods employed, classroom organization, and how students are treated all reflect the teacher's values and preferences" (Naylor & Diem, 1987, p. 347). The activities conducted by students in the classroom are influenced by the positive examples set by the teacher.

Moreover, students need to learn when and where to apply the behaviors they acquire (Mercin & Diksoy, 2017: 295). Therefore, every educational curriculum should carefully plan and manage the process of reproducing, maintaining, or changing societal values. Values education holds great significance as it is crucial in promoting positive coexistence, and art is one of the most effective means of conveying these values (Cabedo-Mas, Nethsinghe, & Forrest, 2017).

METHODOLOGY

This research sought an answer to the question, "What is the importance of visual arts in values education in primary school?". This research aims to determine how visual arts are used in teaching values education in primary school and to provide suggestions on how they can be used effectively. For this purpose, the literature review model, one of the qualitative research methods, was used in the study.

In general, qualitative analysis is to classify the information in the literature, select typical examples for reorganization and draw conclusions based on a qualitative description. Qualitative literature analysis has a unique value in distinguishing past trends and predicting future patterns (Lin, 2009, p.179). A literature review is a systematic way of collecting and synthesizing previous research (Tranfield, Denyer, & Smart, 2003). By integrating findings and perspectives from many empirical studies, a literature review can address research questions with a power that no single study has.

The literature search methodology is to read, analyze and classify literature to identify the essential qualities of the materials. It differs from other methodologies because it does not deal directly with the object under study. However, it accesses information indirectly from various works of literature, often called the "non-contact method" (Lin, 2009, p.179). In this research, sources such as various books, theses, and articles on the subject were accessed, and the information obtained from the existing research was compiled and interpreted. It tried to express how primary school education values can be concretized and transferred to students through visual arts.

CONCLUSION

Values education begins in the family and continues with the acquisition of fundamental values within the formal structure of schools. Individuals must develop values and attitudes to foster social cohesion and establish common goals. Visual arts play a significant role in nurturing individuals who possess valuable qualities aligned with the needs of society and in shaping their value systems.

During childhood, children are expected to recognize and understand individual and cultural values, exhibit appropriate behaviors both individually and within society, and carry forward the culture of their society as they grow. The primary education period offers a highly conducive environment for acquiring these behaviors. Visual arts, with their ability to impart individual, universal, moral, cultural, and social values from the early years of education, are incredibly effective in facilitating comprehension, expression, application, and the long-term integration of these behaviors. Since visual arts education concretizes abstract concepts, it is the most effective tool in transferring values education. Visual arts, one of the most effective approaches to understanding and practicing universal values, is effective in teaching values such as developing individuals' creative and aesthetic perspectives, character development, self-confidence, tolerance, responsibility, respect, freedom, sharing, and order. It encourages individuals to observe, discover, question, experiment, and draw conclusions. The visual arts foster community, creativity, and productivity, facilitate the communication of different ideas and cultures and enable individuals to develop visual literacy, critical thinking, empathy, and problem-solving skills.

While every society has its own values, many values are global and united in a way that encompasses all people, not just those who look like us or live near us. These universal values encompass the traditional sense of connection through shared beliefs, multiple narratives using visual tools, and multiple cultural perspectives.

RECOMMENDATIONS

Values education is a lifelong process that begins in childhood and continues throughout one's life, shaping moral development and acquisition. As a society, we need to use every opportunity we have to impart core values at an early age in the family and then in formal education in schools. For this, students must be willing and observe consistency. With the cooperation of family, curriculum, and teachers, negative environmental stimuli and behaviors will positively affect students. It is possible to transform negative influences into desired behaviors through education. With proper and well-planned education, it is possible to strengthen the foundation of society. In order to provide values education effectively, it is very important to include visual arts effectively in the curriculum. Planning museum visits and exhibition activities, group work and collaborative practices, transforming the subjects to be added to the curriculum for important days and weeks into artistic activities, and criticizing the works of artists within the scope of art criticism will be a practical tool in the values education of students.

For effective values education, visual arts teachers can develop social awareness among students by dedicating themselves to greater interaction with the community for positive change. Visual arts teachers should use constructivist curricula to engage their students more effectively with cultural, environmental, political, and social concerns outside the classroom walls. In well-managed classrooms, art teachers, as role models, should help students see the welfare of society as their social responsibility. In order to lead a healthier life in the changing world conditions, it is necessary to be sensitive to the environment as a social individual. Some ecological projects that will be developed with the students will significantly contribute to the development of students as individuals who are more sensitive to the environment. Projects to be implemented on waste materials for recycling in visual arts will increase students' sensitivity and environmental awareness.

To effectively realize character development through visual arts learning, an art teacher must design learning strategies comprehensively and consider the principles and rules of practice for practical values education. Although values education is evaluated within the scope of the curriculum, transferring the awareness of values to students can also be done indirectly. Good parents and a good teacher are significant for effectively transferring values to education.

REFERENCES

Baccarini, E. (2018). Art, moral understanding, radical changes. Empirical Evidence and Philosophy, 69, 40-53. doi:10.4000/estetica.3666

Berkowitz, M. W. (2011). What works in values education? *International Journal of Educational Research*, *50*(3), 153–158. doi:10.1016/j.ijer.2011.07.003

Burkhardt, J. (1999). Scientific values and moral education in the teaching of science. *Perspectives on Science*, *7*(1), 87–110. doi:10.1162/posc.1999.7.1.87

Cabedo-Mas, A., Nethsinghe, R., & Forrest, D. (2017). The role of the arts in education for peacebuilding, diversity, and intercultural understanding: A comparative study of educational policies in Australia and Spain. *International Journal of Education & the Arts*, *18*(11).

Dewey, J. (2008). *Okul ve toplum. Eğitim klasikleri dizisi-1*. Pegem Akademi.

Edgington, L. (1993). *Report of the task force on educational values and implementation of teaching values in Arizona Schools.* Arizona Department of Education.

Erinç, S. (1995). *Resmin eleştirisi üzerine.* Hil Yayınları.

Gaut, B. (2009). *Art, emotion, and ethics.* Oxford University Press.

Genç, S. (2018). Görsel sanatlar eğitiminde kök değerler. *Turkish Studies Educational Sciences, 13*(11), 543-560.

Genç, S. (2019). Görsel sanatlar eğitimi neden önemlidir? In Güzel sanatlar eğitimi araştırmaları. Akademisyen kitabevi.

Gökaydın, N. (1998). *Eğitimde tasarım ve görsel algı.* Millî eğitim basımevi.

Güven, S. (1999). *Toplum bilim.* Ezgi kitapevi.

Halstead, J. M. (1996). Values in education and education in values. In Values in education and education in values. Routledge Falmer.

Halstead, J. M. (1996). Values and values education in schools. In J. M. Halstead & M. J. Taylor (Eds.), *Values in education and education in values* (pp. 3–14). The Falmer Press.

Halstead, J. M., & Taylor, J. M. (2000). Learning and teaching about values: A review of recent research. *Cambridge Journal of Education, 30*(2), 169–202. doi:10.1080/713657146

Havilland, W., Prins, H., Walrath, D. & Mcbride, B. (2008). *Kültürel antropoloji.* Kaknüs yayınları.

Hills, A. (2009). Moral testimony and moral epistemology. *Ethics, 120*(1), 94–127. doi:10.1086/648610

Karatay, H. (2011). Transfer values in the Turkish and Western Children's literacy work Character education in Turkey. *Educational Research Review, 6*(6), 472–480.

Kırışoğlu, O. (1991). *Sanatta eğitimi.* Demircioğlu matbaası.

Kirschenbaum, H. (2000). From values clarification to character education: A personal journey. *Journal of Humanistic Counseling. Education & Development, 39*(1), 4-1.

Lickona, T. (1993). The return of character education. *Educational Leadership, 51*(3), 6–11.

Lin, G. (2009). Higher education research methodology-literature method. *International Education Studies, 2*(4), 179–181. doi:10.5539/ies.v2n4p179

Marples, R. (2017). Art, knowledge and moral understanding. *Ethics and Education, 12*(2), 243-258. doi:10.1080/17449642.2017.1323425

Mercin, L., & Diksoy, İ. (2017). Değerler eğitiminde görsel sanatların yeri. In Ö. Demirel & S. Dinçer (Eds.), *Küreselleşen dünyada eğitim.* Pegem Akademi. doi:10.14527/9786053188407.20

Michaelis, U. J. (1988). *Social studies for children (A guide to basic instruction).* Prentice Hall Inc.

Millî Eğitim Bakanlığı. (2013). *İlkokul ve ortaokul görsel sanatlar dersi öğretim programı.* Millî Eğitim Bakanlığı yayınları. http://www.eryamansanat.com/pluginfile.php/334/mod_resource/content/2/ilkokul%20ve%20ortaokul%20g%C3%B6rsel%20sanatlar%20ders%20program%C4%B1.pdf

Naylor, D. T., & Diem, R. (1987). *Elementary and middle school social studies.* Random House.

Raths, L. E., Harmin, M., & Simon, S.B. (1966). *Values and teaching: working with values in the class-room.* Charles E. Merrill Books Inc.

Robb, B. (1998). What are the values of education-and so what? *The Journal of Values Education, 1,* 1-11.

Rokeach, M. (1973). *The nature of human values.* The free press.

Salam, S. (2018). Visual-art education for character development. *Advances in Social Science, Education, and Humanities Research.* Vol. 255. *1st International Conference on Arts and Design Education (ICADE 2018),* 315-319.

Silcock, P., & Duncan, D. (2001). Values acquisition and values education: Some proposals. *British Journal of Educational Studies, 49*(3), 242–259. doi:10.1111/1467-8527.t01-1-00174

Straughan, R. (1999). *Can we teach children to be good? Basic issues in moral, personal, and social education.* Open university press.

Taylor, M. (1994). *Values education in Europe: A comparative overview of a survey of 26 countries in 1993.* Scottish Consultative Council on the Curriculum for Cidree/UNESCO.

Thornberg, R. (2008a). The lack of professional knowledge in values education. *Teaching and Teacher Education, 24*(7), 1791–1798. doi:10.1016/j.tate.2008.04.004

Tillman, D. (2000). *Living values activities for young adults.* Health Communications Inc.

Titus, D. N. (1994). *Values education in American secondary schools.* Paper presented at the Kutztown University Education Conference.

Tranfield, D., Denyer, D., & Smart, P. (2003). Towards a methodology for developing evidence-informed management knowledge by means of systematic review. *British Journal of Management, 14*(3), 207–222. doi:10.1111/1467-8551.00375

Ünver, E. (2011). *Görsel sanatlar ve eğitimi üzerine.* Detay yayıncılık.

Wells, C. (1971). *İnsan ve dünyası.* Remzi kitabevi.

Yetkin, S. K. (1972). *Estetik doctrine.* Bilgi Yayınevi.

Znaniecki, F. (1927). The object matter of sociology. *American Journal of Sociology, 32*(4), 529–584. doi:10.1086/214184

KEY TERMS AND DEFINITIONS

Aesthetic: It is a branch of philosophy that deals with the general laws of artistic creation, beauty in art, and the effects of beauty on human memory and emotions. Aesthetics is a theoretical science first used as a word and concept in 1750 by the German philosopher A. Baumgarten.

Art: Art is the creative expression of emotion, thought, and imagination through various materials or actions with an aesthetic concern.

Art Education: It is an interdisciplinary field of education based on culture and research, covering all fields and forms of fine arts, allowing individuals to express themselves creatively.

Art Criticism: Art criticism is a political, sociological, and psychological research of art in the context of the artist and the work and a process of a sensitive reaction to art.

Curriculum: Curriculum is the linking of education to a program. Curricula are standards-based planned experiences where students practice and gain proficiency in content and applied learning skills. A curriculum describes which subjects will be taught, in what order they will be taught, and how much emphasis will be placed on a subject.

Empathy: It is to understand another person's feelings, thoughts, beliefs, and desires by internalizing them.

Semiotics: Semiotics is a science based on the systematic examination of all factors, including the processes of interpreting, producing, or understanding signs.

Teaching Methods: A curriculum is a program that is formulated at the official level, in which the aim, objective, content, method, and evaluation elements are written and which stipulate that teaching is carried out according to this plan.

Visual Art: It is a field of art generally related to line, paint, and volume and appeals to our sense of sight. With changing world standards and postmodernism, different artistic actions and movements, such as conceptual art, installation, and performance art, have also been included in its scope.

Chapter 14
Tawakkul as an Islamic Morality Concept:
Based on Islamic–Turkish Texts

Sümeyra Alan
https://orcid.org/0000-0002-4406-2022
Erzurum Teknik Üniversitesi, Turkey

Hasan Isi
https://orcid.org/0000-0001-7269-3596
Trabzon University, Turkey

ABSTRACT

The concept of value, which is included in sciences such as philosophy, sociology, and psychology, is a term that questions what and what is important for individuals or groups and includes concepts such as independence, trust, wisdom, success, kindness, etc. Tawakkul means that an individual leaves the course and outcome of a job to Allah after showing his determination and determination. In this respect, the present study consists of evaluations on Turkish words such as köŋül ba-, köŋül ur-, etc., which are expanded from the concept of köŋül 'gönül' used for the first time in Turkish Qur'an translations and other Islamic texts for the concept of 'tawakkül'. In the study, firstly, the concept of 'tawakkul' as an Islamic value is mentioned and then linguistic analyses are made on the expressions derived from the word köŋül 'gönül', which is one of the important concepts in term derivation in both pre-Islamic and Islamic period Turkish religious vocabulary.

INTRODUCTION

One of the prominent concepts in the curriculum of the Turkish education system in the last 10 years is *value education*. *Value* is a concept used to express the basic principles that guide people's behaviour in general and guide their relations with other people, as well as the standards that shape attitudes (Turner, 1999: 173; Emiroğlu, 2017: 119). *Values* are agreed-upon criteria that ensure the continuity of society

DOI: 10.4018/978-1-6684-9295-6.ch014

and according to which social relations are shaped. The concept of *value* (Eng. *value*; Fr. *valeur*) is used in response to the Latin root *valere*, which means 'to be valuable, to be strong'. *Value* has been addressed by many disciplines and has different definitions depending on the discipline in which it is addressed. The common aspect of these definitions, which differ in the fields of philosophy, psychology, anthropology, sociology and theology, is that they draw attention to what its characteristics are or what *values* do (Gül, 2013: 41).

Value education is a term that serves to build a fulfilling life by helping to develop moral values. *Value education* seeks to help other individuals through the transfer of knowledge, skills, attitudes and values, which are basically created in educational institutions. *Value education* has two goals: to ensure that young individuals and all people live a more characterful life and are satisfied with their lives, to contribute to the well-being of society, and to seek compassion and kindness for people and other life groups (Kirschenbaum, 1994: 14; Ulusoy, 2010: 34). For this reason, *values education*, which foregrounds the 'socialisation' relationship between individual-society and individual-individual, emphasises moral development and critical thinking.

Values education makes education-based contributions to the concept of 'socialisation'. *Values education* in the context of socialisation is important for young people to establish harmonious relations with the society and to socialise. Because education affects people more in terms of mental aspect and this information provides attitudes and behaviours of people and then socialisation. The individual, who forms an identity with the knowledge acquired through education, establishes relationships with people and socialises with his/her identity. With the learning of social roles in education and the transfer of social culture from generation to generation, the individual can provide integrity with the society and this formation has a very important share in the individual's acquisition of healthy socialisation experiences (Emiroğlu, 2017: 117).

In the researches conducted by educational scientists, the following issues come to the fore in terms of *values education* (Çengelci et al., 2013: 47).

- *Values education* activities can be student-centred and practice-based.
- Long-term studies based on co-operation involving school, family and close environment can be planned and implemented in the field of values education.
- Opinions and suggestions of students can be taken into consideration in establishing rules in schools.
- More attention can be paid to the acquisition of the value of cleanliness in school environments.
- Studies can be carried out for the acquisition of other values that are not sufficiently emphasised in schools but are included in education programmes.

These suggestions, which are generally accepted among experts in the field of *values education*, are valuable in that they contain elements that will feed 'school' centred learning with 'family' centred learning.

Islam contains rich elements in *values education*. According to Islam, *value* is what is desired, interested and needed. The concept of *value* expresses what should be. *Value* has a practical character rather than theory. In other words, it is ideal and action orientated. *Value* is a deep-rooted belief that a person constantly demonstrates in different situations and directs its behaviour. *Values education* in the Islamic dimension is to reveal the best side of the child from birth, to ensure the development of his/her personality in every aspect, to help its reach human perfection, to protect and save the individual and society from immorality, as well as to equip him/her with a good morality and to ensure its continuity (Önder & Bulut, 2013: 18-20).

There are strong links between religion and morality. Every religion has many moral teachings and suggestions. Religion enables people to control themselves and to be virtuous. Religions, which are the most advanced of spiritual systems, are a moral system that regulates people's relations with God and other people and explains what is good and bad in these relations (Geyer & Baumeister, 2013: 242, 243; Güngör, 1995: 19). The main goal of Islam as a religion is to protect innate human values and to instil and develop them with some superior values. Damage to human values hidden in the nature of human beings deeply affects Islam.

Considering man as the most important value, Islam naturally does not want any harm to come to his physical and mental health. Because the material that Islam will work with is the human being. For this reason, it aims to first protect and then develop his natural structure (Aybakan, 2006: 404). The basic values of Islam can be characterised as essentials. *Zarûriyyât* is defined as the basic values, without which religion and world affairs depend on them. According to Islamic jurists, the so-called essential elements consist of five basic values. These are expressed as *al-darurat al-hamsa* 'five obligatory principles' and *al-usûl al-hamsa* 'five basic principles'. These basic values are protection of religion, protection of life, protection of mind, protection of generation and protection of property (Önder & Bulut, 2013: 20, 21). In this respect, one of the Islamic value concepts that reflects the relationship between the individual and God and between the individual and society is the concept of 'tawakkul', which means that the servant leaves the result of the work to God with a firm belief 'in its heart' after doing its part. The origin of the word *tawakkul* is the word *ve-ke-le*. *Vekîl*, which comes from the same root, is one of the names of Allah and means 'the one who guarantees the sustenance of His servants', while *'tawakkul'* means 'showing one's incapacity in a task and trusting someone else to do it, trusting in what is in the sight of Allah and despairing of what is in the hands of people, being a proxy, accepting to take on a task' (Solmaz, 2006: 10). In most belief systems around the world, it is ordered to believe in the sacred, but it is also recommended to trust and rely on it (Şahin, 2018: 13).

The subject of *tawakkul*, as one of the main concepts of the Qur'an, is mentioned in many verses:

- "Put your trust in Allah, who never dies and is ever living, and glorify Him with praise. Suffice it that He is aware of the sins of His servants!" (Furqan, 25/58).
- "Put your trust in Allah, the All-powerful, the All-supreme, the All-compassionate!" (Shu'ara, 26/217).
- "Put your trust in Allah, for you are on the manifest truth." (Neml, 27/79).
- "Put your trust in Allah, and Allah is sufficient as a trustee" (Ahzab, 33/3).
- "O you who believe, remember the favour of Allah upon you, when a people tried to stretch out their hands against you, but Allah repelled their hands from you. Fear and beware of Allah. Believers should put their trust in Allah alone." (Al-Ma'idah, 5/11).
- "Say: Nothing will befall us except what Allah has written for us. He is our Mawla. And the believers should put their trust in Allah alone." (Tawbah, 9/51).
- "Allah; there is no god but Him. So let the believers put their trust (only) in Allah" (Taqabun, 64/13).
- "...Say: Allah is sufficient for me. Let those who put their trust in Him." (Zumar, 39/38).
- "Consult with them about what is to be done, and when you have decided, put your trust in Allah. Surely Allah loves those who put their trust in Him." (Al-Imran, 3/159).

- "We will obey, they say. And when they leave you, a group of them plot in the night/secretly something other than what they say. Allah writes down what they plot in the night/secretly. Turn away from them and put your trust in Allah. Allah is sufficient as a trustee." (Nisâ, 81).
- "If we return to your religion after you have delivered us from it, we would be slandering Allah falsely. It is not possible for us to return to it except by the will of Allah, our Lord. Our Lord encompasses all things with His knowledge, and we put our trust in Allah alone. Our Lord, judge between us and our people in truth. You are the best of those who judge" (al-A'râf, 89).
- "The believers are only those whose hearts tremble when Allah is mentioned, and when His verses are recited, they increase their faith and put their trust in their Lord alone." (Anfal, 2).
- "Moses said: "O my people! If you have believed in Allah and submitted to Him, put your trust in Him alone." (Yûnus, 84).

The concept of 'tawakkul', which we have exemplified from various places in the Qur'an, is important in terms of showing the 'faith-based' aspect of the relationship between the individual and Allah as the cornerstone of the Islamic value system. Because the concept of 'tawakkul' reinforces the belief in tawhid. Allah wants his servants to believe in him as 'the only god' and to practise tawakkul, which is the reflection of this belief in practice (Şahin, 2018: 25). The servant who puts his trust in Allah believes that Allah has endowed him with the means and opportunities to accomplish a task and that they were created to be used; from this point of view, he thinks that neglecting the causes would lead to the idea that they were created for no reason (Çağrıcı, 2012: 2). The Islamic concept of *tawakkul* is based on the concepts of 'precaution' and 'leaving it to Allah'. According to Karaman, *tawakkul* is the Muslim's reliance on Allah to achieve the desired result after fulfilling all the material and spiritual work, precautions and reasons that are customary for the work to be done by believing that Allah Almighty is the Almighty, the Almighty is the owner of power and might. Accordingly, those who want to be protected from heat and cold should wear clothes, those who want to satisfy hunger and thirst should eat and drink, those who want to have children should marry, those who want to have children should marry, those who want to have crops should sow seeds and plough the field, those who want trees and fruits should plant saplings, and those who want to make a profit should prefer arts and trade (1996: 68). As can be seen, what is emphasised in the concept of 'tawakkul' is the state of 'taking action, doing something'. For this reason, the concept of 'tawakkul' is trust in Allah and submission to Allah by doing one's part in a task and not getting caught up in the causes.

When we look at the benefits of the concept of 'tawakkul' as an Islamic value, *tawakkul* as a mental refuge is a spiritual structure that psychologically comforts the person and prepares the ground for the person to be happy. The basic sense of trust of human beings can be damaged by internal and external threats. Consequently, he may seek to ensure his strength and sufficiency to cope with these situations. *Tawakkul* has a critical importance in situations where people face difficulties and are exposed to stress factors. *Tawakkul* is a support system that makes people free and independent, protects their mental health and gives them peace of mind. It is known that *tawakkul* facilitates acceptance, has a positive effect on anger control, makes interpersonal communication positive, provides patience, encourages optimistic thinking, gives calmness, protects from selfishness and ambition, broadens perspective and increases self-esteem (Karataş & Baloğlu, 2019: 111, 112).

In this respect, the present study consists of evaluations based on the concept of 'tawakkul', which appears for the first time in Qur'anic translations from Islamic-Turkish texts. In Islamic-Turkish texts, the concept of 'tawakkul' is represented by both Arabic تَوَكُّل *tawakkul* and the literal Turkish equivalent of the Arabic term, *köŋül ba-, köŋül baġla-, köŋül ur-* etc. In the study, the terms in the concept area of 'tawakkul' were divided into two groups in the noun and verb categories with the meanings of 'tawakkul'. The terms with the meanings of 'tawakkul, trusting (s)' in the noun category and 'to trust' in the verb category were listed as bullet points and the expressions were analysed.

LITERATURE REWIEW AND METHODOLOGY

Vocabulary on the Concept of 'Tawakkul' in Islamic-Turkish Texts

Old Turkic religious vocabulary is a terminology with rich linguistic materials through the Uighurs and Qarakhanids who adopted teachings such as Buddhism and Manichaeism etc. Although this religious vocabulary mainly aims to give Turkish equivalents to foreign terms in line with the 'Turkish' consciousness, borrowings from languages such as Chinese, Sogdian, Tocharian (A/B), Sanskrit, Tibetan, Arabic and Persian have been realised into the Turkish language. Religious terms adapted to the phonetics of Turkish were intended to be popularised by using them with Turkish equivalents in Buddhist Uyghur texts.

Old Turkic religious terminology is mainly based on religions such as Buddhism and Islam. The first branch of this vocabulary is the texts based on the Buddha religion and the vocabulary elements followed by these texts. This religious literature, which is mainly based on translation literature, contains both Turkish and foreign elements. The second branch of Old Turkish religious vocabulary is Turkish texts based on the religion of Islam. The Qur'an translations, which were introduced into the Turkish language through below-the-line translations from Persian, are known for containing many Turkish elements.

The subject of the present study includes the terms related to the concept of 'tawakkul', which were first witnessed in the Qur'an translations of the Karakhanid period and Islamic texts such as *Kutadgu Bilig* and *Nehcü'l-Feradis*. In this study, a total of 13 terms in the conceptual field of 'tawakkul' were identified, with the Turkish Qur'anic translations being predominant. These religious expressions in the noun and verb categories are mainly based on Turkish and foreign elements that correspond to the meanings of 'tawakkul, trusting, trust'. In this study, the terms identified in the noun and verb categories of the concept of 'tawakkul' in Islamic-Turkish texts are as follows:

RESULTS

In the Noun Category

In the study, a total of 7 terms in the noun category were identified in the testimony of Islamic-Turkish texts. The terms in the conceptual field of 'tawakkul' appear as examples of both literal Turkish translations and direct borrowings.

1.   **bi-niyâzlık =Ar.** تَوَكُّلْ 'indifference, trusting' (Ünlü, 2013: 419).

The expression is seen in the meanings of 'indifference; trusting' (Abik, 1993: 71). In dictionaries, the term means 'without begging, pleading; needless' (Devellioğlu, 2006: 108) and 'not in need of anyone, free, independent, contented' (Özön, 1988: 94). The word is a combination of the Arabic prefix *bi-* meaning 'Turkish -sız/-siz' and Persian *niyâz* meaning 'need, necessity, necessity, distress; object of desire, beloved thing'. The expression, which is witnessed for the first time in Chagatai Turkish texts, is within the conceptual field of 'tawakkul'. In lines T702b3-4 of *Tārīh-i Anbiyā wa Hukemā*, the expression is *bi-niyâzlık yèrige bardı, pervâ kılmadı, hem ol Ḥak ta'ālā ibadetiga meşgul èrdi* "He reached the place of indifference and caring. He did not care that he was engaged in the worship of Allah." (Abik, 1993: 107). As it can be seen, within the conceptual field of 'indifference and carelessness', the related term reflects reaching the state of 'contentment, leaving it to God and resigning to fate' (Abik, 1993: 673), which is the essence of the concept of 'tawakkul', without being obsessed with the causes and consequences. For this reason, the related term is included in the concept of 'tawakkul'.

2. **köŋül urgan** 'trusting' =Ar. مُتَوَكّلٌ (Ata, 2004: 489; Ünlü, 2012a: 579).

The term is equivalent to 'the trusting one' in Arabic (masculine) *mutawakkil/mütawakkil*, (feminine) *mütawakkilūn* and in Persian (masculine) *tekye konende/takya kunanda*, (feminine) *tekye konendegān* (Eckmann, 1976: 169; Ata, 2004: 489). The expression is defined in dictionaries as 'one who trusts, one who leaves his/her work to God or to his/her will, one who submits to fate' (Devellioğlu, 2006: 786), 'one who leaves all his/her work to God, one who shows trust; one who shows submission to fate, one who expresses trust' (Çağbayır, 2007: 3460), 'one who leaves everything to God or to the will of God' (Püsküllüoğlu, 1977: 351) and 'one who leaves everything to God, to God's will and accepts what comes from God' (Özön, 1988: 595). The term appears in the Qur'an Translation of the Rylands copy of the Karakhanid period in the Qur'an Translation of the Karakhanid period as *tap turur maŋa taŋrı anıŋ üze köŋül urur köŋül urganlar* 'Those who put their trust in God and rely on Him. This is sufficient." (RKT 31/74b1=39: 38). The expression is in the adjective category with the moulding effect of the adjective-verb suffix -gAn on the verb *köŋül ur-* meaning 'to trust in someone, to rely on' (Boeschoten, 2022: 175). The expression is the product of a literal Turkish translation.

3. **köŋül uruġlılar** 'those who trust' =Ar. مُتَوَكّلٌ (Kök, 2004: 476; Ünlü, 2012a: 579).

As in *köŋül urgan*, the term means 'those who trust'. For evaluations of the term see. **2. köŋül urgan.** The texts in which the expression occurs are as follows:

(1) *anıŋ üze köŋül urdım takı anıŋ üze köŋül ursun **köŋül uruġlılar*** "I put my trust in Allah. Again, let those who put their trust in Allah put their trust in Allah." (**KÖK TİEM 73 179r/3,** 2004: 173).
(2) *taŋrı üze köŋül ursun **köŋül uruġlılar*** "Let those who have tawakkul put their trust in Allah." (**KÖK TİEM 73 189r/4,** 2004: 183).

The term is placed in the adjective category due to the moulding effect of the adjective-verb suffix -XglI on the verb köŋül ur- meaning 'to trust, rely on someone' (Boeschoten, 2022: 175). The expression is the product of a literal Turkish translation.

4. **mütevekkil** <Ar. مُتَوَكّلٌ 'resigned' (NF Index, 2014; 306; Ünlü, 2012b: 420).

The term is the Arabic equivalent of the expressions *köŋül urgan* and *köŋül uruġlılar*. For the definitions of the expression in dictionaries, see. **2. köŋül urgan.**

The expression is found in NF 269/3, one of the Khwarezm Turkic works, in the meaning of 'those who trusted' in the example of '*Aṭā'-i Selemi (r.a.) mütevekkillerdin erdi* "He was one who trusted." (NF Text, 2014: 186).

5. **tevekkül** <**Ar.** تَوَكُّلْ 'tawakkul; resignation to fate; leaving the work to Allah and resigning to fate; sincerely surrendering to Allah, doing what is necessary for servitude and entrusting the rest to Allah' (Ünlü, 2012a: 963; Ünlü, 2012b: 588; Ünlü, 2013: 1119; Üşenmez, 2010: 598; Boeschoten, 2022: 322; NF Index, 2014: 424; Karamanlıoğlu, 2006: 120).

The term is equivalent to *tawakkul* in Arabic and *tekye kerden* in Persian (Üşenmez, 2010: 598). In dictionaries, the expression is defined as 'leaving the work to Allah and resigning to fate' (Devellioğlu, 2006: 1101), '1. Doing everything by trusting in Allah; referring the end of the work to Allah. 2. Submission to the will of Allah; resignation to fate; surrender to Allah; leaving the work to Allah. 3. Not expecting or trusting in anyone or anything other than Allah. 4. Being aware that God is the owner of all kinds of behaviour, movement and action and fully accepting His agency' (Çağbayır, 2007: 4784), 'leaving everything to God and expecting from God' (Püsküllüoğlu, 1977: 488) and 'leaving the work to God and accepting and trusting fate' (Özön, 1988: 790).

The texts in which the term occurs are as follows:

(1) *taḳı ol keminiŋ yelkenini **tevekküldin** ḳılġıl* "Also, secure the sail of that ship from trust." (**NF Text 396/3,** 2014: 275).

(2) ***tevekkül** delil ḥaḳ çınoḳ bilgüke unutma ḳıyāmet taḳı ölgüke* "Tawakkul and evidence are for true knowledge, and doomsday is for dying, remember!" (**MM 4a/9: 169,** 2006: 7).

(3) *eşitgil hakîkat **tevekkül** sözi* "Hear the word of truth and trust!" (**MM 4a/11/74,** 2006: 7).

(4) *kir **tevekkül** bile vü vehmi berbād ètkil* "Enter with tawakkul, eliminate delusion!" (**BV 373/6,** 1988: 309).

(5) ***tevekkül** ehli ki çıḳmas seferde çāredin* "The person of tawakkul does not go on an expedition out of remedy." (**BV 662/2,** 1988: 553).

(6) *ḳanā'at tevḥid **tevekkül** ve teslim ü taḥammül kim kim bu ṣıfatlar birle mevṣūf bolsa* "With conviction, tawhid, tawakkul, submission and patience, if he were characterised by these attributes" (**GT 105/4a,** 2011: 173).

(7) *yolga çun koygay ḳadem reh-rev **tevekkül** ḳımayın* "When the traveller does not trust when he steps on the road" (**FK 503/5,** 1989: 459).

As can be seen, the term has conceptual fields such as 'referring the end of the work to Allah, resigning to fate; surrendering to Allah'.

6. **tevekkül kılmak** 'trust in god' < **Ar.** تَوَكُّلْ (NF Dizin, 2014: 424).

The term is equivalent to *tawakkul* in Arabic and *tekye kerden* in Persian (Üşenmez, 2010: 598). The expression within the concept area of 'tawakkul' has become a permanent noun with the moulding of the noun-verb suffix *-mAk* on the verb *tevekkül kıl-* 'to trust'. The word occurs in the Islamic-Turkish text NF 436/2 in the example of ***tevekkül** ḳılmaḳ taḳı umunçnı ḳısḳa tutmaḳ, tèdi* "He said, to trust in God and keep hope short." (2014: 303). For the place of the term in dictionaries, see. **5. tevekkül.**

7. **tevekkül kılgan** 'one who trusts' **<Ar.** مُتَوَكّلْ (Sağol, 1993, 932, Kök, 2004: 604, Ünlü, 2012a: 963, Ünlü, 2012b: 588; Üşenmez, 2010: 598).

According to Üşenmez (2010: 598), the term is equivalent to the Arabic term *mütevekkil* and the Persian term *tevekkül konend* (2010: 598). For the place of the Arabic expression *mütevekkil* in dictionaries, see. **4. mütevekkil.**

The texts in which the expression occurs are as follows:

(1) *anıŋ üze tevekkül ḳıldım taḳı anıŋ üze tevekkül ḳılsun,* **tevekkül ḳılganlar** "I put my trust in Allah, and let those who put their trust in Him rely on Him" (**HKT 234a/4,** 1993: 174).
(2) *taŋrı sewer* **tevekkül ḳılganlarnı** "Allah loves those who trust" (**TIEM 73 53v/15,** 2004: 49).
(3) *taŋrı süwer* **tevekkül ḳılganlarnı** "Allah loves those who trust" (**KT Özb. 132a/5=A: 159,** 2010: 264).

As can be seen, the terms are in the structure of Ar. + Tr. as a one-to-one equivalent of Arabic *mütevekkil* and Persian *tevekkül konend*.

In the Verb Category

In the study, a total of 6 terms were identified in the verb category in the testimony of Islamic-Turkish texts. The terms that we come across in the concept area of 'tevekkül etmek' are as follows:

1. **köŋül ba-** **<Ar.** تَوَكّلْ: تُكْلَانَ 'to set one's heart on, to believe, to trust, to persevere' (Kök, 2004: 476; Boeschoten, 2020: 174; Ünlü, 2012a: 896).

The term is the Turkish equivalent of the Arabic expression تَوَكّلْ: تُكْلَانَ 'tevekkül etmek'. The expression can be seen in the example of *taŋrı üze* **köŋül badımız** "We trusted in Allah, we believed wholeheartedly" (Kök, 2004: 115) in TIEM 121r/4, one of the Islamic-Turkish texts.

Also, in the example in KB 3446 *kelir bolsa dünya* **köŋül bamasa**, *barır erse aġrıp ḳaşın tügmese* "When he comes into the world, if he does not set his heart on it; when he does not frown in pain and goes away" (Arat, 1947: 347), the meaning of 'setting one's heart on' the world is in question.

2. **köŋül baġla-** **<Ar.** تَوَكّلْ: تُكْلَانَ 'to show perseverance' (Ata, 2004: 489; Boeschoten, 2022: 174)

The term is a literal Turkish translation of Arabic *murābetā't* and Persian *kārzār kerden/kardan* (Ata, 2004: 489). Moreover, according to Eckmann, the expression *köŋül baġla-* also has the Arabic equivalent *rabaṭa* (1976: 169). The expression has rich examples especially in Karakhanid and Chagatai Turkish:

(1) *sabr ḳılıŋ* **köŋül baġlaŋ** *korkuŋlar Taŋrıda* "Be patient, show perseverance and fear Allah!" (**RKT, 25/29a2=3: 200,** 2004: 489).
(2) **köŋül** *'ālem öyüge* **baġlama** *köp* "Do not trust the world too much!" (**BV 532/6,** 1988: 434).
(3) *èski 'ālemġa* **köŋül** *köp* **baġlama** "Do not trust in this outdated world!" (**FK 295/6,** 1989: 275).

When the sampled texts are analysed, it is seen that only in text (1) the verb *köŋül baġla-* is used in a religious context, while in the remaining two texts the expression is used in a worldly sense.

3.   **köŋül tüz- <Ar.** تَوَكَّلَ: تَوَكُّلْ **'**(God) set one's heart on'

The term is the Turkish equivalent of the Arabic expression تَوَكَّلَ: تَوَكُّلْ 'to have tawakkul'. The expression has the following witnesses in Islamic-Turkish texts.

(1)   *çıġayḳa üledi üküş neŋ tawar,* **köŋül tüzdi** *rabḳa ḳamuġdın sıŋar* "He gave countless sustenance to the poor and destitute, and trusted and relied on Allah in every way." (**KB 1768,** 1947: 196).

(2)   **köŋül tüzdi** *èlig kör anda naru buḍunḳa bèrü turdı eḍgü törü* "Ilig trusted him. He gave the people good honour." (**KB 3093,** 1947: 317).

In sentence (1), this expression, which is the literal Turkish equivalent, evokes the idea of relying on Allah and trusting in Him, whereas in sentence (2), the expression *anda naru* 'towards Him' indirectly means 'relying on Allah and trusting in Him'.

4.   **köŋül ur- <Ar.** تَوَكَّلَ: تَوَكُّلْ **'**to trust; to rely on, to rely on, to rely on God, to leave one's work to God' (Kök, 2004: 476; Ata, 2004: 489; Boeschoten, 2022: 175, Ünlü, 2012a: 896).

The term is the Turkish equivalent of the Arabic expression تَوَكَّلَ: تَوَكُّلْ 'trust in God'. For the Arabic and Persian equivalents of the word, we can give the expressions *tevekkül* (Ar.) and *i'timād kerden, tekye kerden* (Ata, 2004: 489). Moreover, according to Eckmann, the expression *köŋül ur-* also has the Arabic equivalent of *vakala* (1976: 169). The expression has rich examples in Islamic-Turkish texts.

(1)   *anlar üze belgüleri artar olarḳa kèrtgünmek iḍileri üze* **köŋül ururlar** "Upon them, the insignia increases. They put their trust in Allah in believing." (**KÖK TİEM 73 131v/6,** 2004: 216).

(2)   *ḳorḳuŋlar taŋrıḳa taŋrı üze* **köŋül ursun** *kèrtgünügliler* "Fear Allah. Those who believe in Allah, trust in Allah!" (**KÖK TİEM 73 81v/2,** 2004: 76).

(3)   *ol anıŋ üze* **köŋül urdum** *ol turur uluġ taḫt iḍisi* "I put my trust in Him, God is the owner of the throne of glory." (**KÖK TİEM 152v/7,** 2004: 147).

(4)   *taŋrı belgüleri birle taŋrıḳa* **köŋül urdum** "I trusted in Him with the signs of Allah." (KÖK TİEM 152v/7, 2004: 153).

(5)   *men* **köŋül urdum** *taŋrı üze meniŋ iḍim silerniŋ idiŋizler* "I have put my trust in God, my Lord is your Lord" (**KÖK TİEM 167v/8,** 2004: 161).

(6)   *kim kèrtgündiler iḍileri üze köŋül ururlar* "That they believed and put their trust in Allah" (**KÖK TİEM 167v/8,** 2004: 199).

(7)   *anlar kim serindiler iḍileri üze* **köŋül urdılar** "That they were patient and put their trust in Allah" (**RKT 30/50b3=16: 42,** 2004: 489).

(8)   *taŋrı üze* **köŋül ursun** *mü'minler* "Let the believers put their trust in Allah." (**RKT 27/26A1=5:11,** 2004: 489).

(9)   *anıŋ üze* **köŋül urdumız** "We put our trust in Allah." (**ÜNLÜ TİEM 417r/7,** 2004: 242).

For other examples of the expression see. **TIEM 265r/2, →TIEM 273r/6, →TIEM 279v/6, →TIEM 293v/2, →TIEM 256v/6, →TIEM 73 413v/3**.

As can be seen, the examples from Islamic-Turkish texts indicate that the expression *köŋül ur-* takes the place-direction suffix +A (*üz+e*) and the orientation suffix +KA (*taŋrıḳa*) and points to the conceptual field of 'trusting'.

5. **tevekkül èyle- <Ar.** تَوَكُّلْ: كَانَالْكُتْ 'leaving the work to God and accepting fate' (Ünlü, 2013: 1119; Boeschoten, 2022: 322).

The term is the Turkish equivalent of the Arabic expression تَوَكُّلْ: كَانَالْكُتْ 'tevekkül etmek'. For the Arabic and Persian equivalents of the word, we can give the expressions *tawakkul* (Ar.) and *i'timād kerden, tekye kerden* (Ata, 2004: 489). The expression is seen in BV 438/6, a Chagatai Turkic work, in the example of **tevekkül èyle** *vü kir 'ışḳ yolıġa iy şeyḫ* "O sheikh, trust in God love path!" (Türkay, 1988: 309). The expression is in the conceptual field of 'tevekkül etmek' as Ar. + Tr. structure.

6. **tevekkül ḳıl- <Ar.** تَوَكُّلْ: كَانَالْكُتْ 'to trust, to rely on God, to leave one's work to God; to trust and rely' (Ata, 2004: 676; Kök, 2004: 604, Ünlü, 2012a: 896, 963, Ünlü, 2012b: 588; Ünlü, 2013: 1119).

The term is the Turkish equivalent of the Arabic expression تَوَكُّلْ: كَانَالْكُتْ 'tevekkül etmek'. For the Arabic and Persian equivalents of the word, we can give the expressions *vakala* (Ar.) and *i'timād kerden, tekye kerden, tawakkul kardan* (Eckmann, 1976: 279; Ata, 2004: 489). The expression, as an Ar. + Tr. structure, is included in the conceptual field of 'tevekkül etmek'. The expression has rich examples in Islamic-Turkish texts.

(1) *ol taŋrıġa mu'minlar **tevekkül** ḳılsun, tèdi erse* "When he said, 'Let the believers put their trust in God" (**NF Text 344/4**, 2014: 239).

(2) *tevekkül ne bolur imām Aḥmed rahimehumullah aydı **tevekkül** taŋrı teālāḳa i'timād ḳılmaḳ bolur* "When asked what tawakkul is, Imam Ahmad (r.a) said: Tawakkul is trusting in Allah" (**NF Text 225/5-6,** 2014: 155).

(3) *saŋa **tevekkül** ḳılu sendin isti'ānat tileyü çıkmak kerek erdiler bilmediler* "They did not know that it was necessary to turn to You in trust and supplication" (**NF Text 72/15,** 2014: 53).

(4) *taŋrı üze **tevekkül** ḳılıŋ-a mü'minler* "O believers, put your trust in Allah." (**RKT 38/6b1=58: 10,** 2004: 676).

(5) *taḳı taŋrı üze **tevekkül** ḳılsun mü'minler* "Also, let the believers put their trust in Allah" (**KÖK TİEM 73 50r/2,** 2004: 45).

(6) *yüz ewürgil anlardın taḳı **tevekkül** ḳılgıl taŋrı üze* "Turn away from them and put your trust in Allah!" (**HKT 88b/3,** 1993: 64).

(7) *ḫudāyḳa **tevekkül** ḳılıp cümle mübārizlerdin burun ḫaṣmḳa ḥamle ḳılıp* "Putting your trust in Allah and lashing out at the enemy before all sides" (**GT 16/7,** 2011: 128).

(8) *ṣabr tevessüli birle temām **tevekkül** ḳıla bilmes mén* "I cannot make a tawakkul full of patience." (**GT 59/9,** 2011: 150).

(9) *taḳı taŋrı üze **tevekkül** ḳılsun mü'minler* "Also, if you believe, put your trust in Allah!" (**KT Özb. 122b/3=A: 122,** 2010: 259).

(10) ***tevekkül ḳılġıl*** *taŋrı üze ḥaḳîḳat üze taŋrı süwer tevekkül ḳılġanlarnı* "Put your trust in Allah! Allah loves those who put their trust in Him." (**KT Özb. 132a/5: A: 159,** 2010: 264).

As can be seen, when we look at the examples from Islamic-Turkish texts, it is clear that in all of them, trust and reliance on God is emphasised.

CONCLUSION

In the testimony of Islamic-Turkish texts, 13 terms were identified within the concept field of 'tawakkul'. These terms follow a sequence that includes mainly the Qur'an translations of the early Qarakhanid period and other Islamic texts such as KB, NF, MM etc.

In the study, the expressions that are predominantly preferred in the conceptual field of 'tevekkül, tevekkül etmek, tevekkül eden' are Turkish terms. When the terms in this semantic category are analysed, it is seen that Turkish terms in the conceptual field of 'tevekkül, tevekkül etmek, tevekkül eden' have numerical superiority over borrowed words.

In the study, there are 6 terms (*köŋül urgan, köŋül uruglılar, köŋül ba-, köŋül baġla-, köŋül tüz-, köŋül ur-*) which are the products of direct literal Turkish translation. Although these terms correspond to the Arabic concept, they can also be considered as the equivalents of the Persian translation. Because strong interpretations that Turkish Qur'an translations were made from Persian have been expressed by many researchers in the field of Turkology (Aysu Ata, Janos Eckmann, Osman Fikri Sertkaya, Mustafa Argunşah, Emek Üşenmez etc.).

In the study, there are 2 borrowed words (*mütevekkil, tevekkül*) directly within the concept area of 'tevekkül, tevekkül etmek, tevekkül eden'. These terms directly fulfil the meaning and structure existing in Arabic. The study also includes terms arising from the combination of Arabic, Persian and Turkish words. In the study, there are 4 words in the Arabic+Turkish category (*tevekkül kılmak*→Ar. + Tr.; *tevekkül kılgan*→Ar. + Tr.; *tevekkül èyle-*→Ar. + Tr.; *tevekkül kıl-*→Ar. + Tr.). Although these compounds are mainly transferred from the noun category to the verb category with the Turkish verbs *kıl-* and *èyle-*, they are also transferred from the verb category to the noun category with the moulding effect of the adjective-verb suffix -gAn.

In the study, there is also the term bi-niyāzlık with the combination of Arabic+Persian+Turkish elements. This term is composed of the Arabic prefix *bi-*, the Persian word *niyāz* and the Turkish suffix +lXk.

On the basis of the sources used in the study, when we look at the status of the Turkish terms in the concept area of 'tevekkül' in the following periods, it is seen that the Turkish terms have melted in the face of the Arabic word *tevekkül* since Harezm Turkish, and the elements belonging to the Karakhanid period have left their use to the Ar. word *tevekkül* since this period. For this reason, the second branch of Turkish religious vocabulary, the Islamic-Turkish vocabulary, has an important power in the use of Turkish terms, especially with the Qur'an translations in the Karakhanids period. This can be seen as the traces of the tradition of 'deriving and using terms' inherited from the Buddhist Uighurs.

REFERENCES

Abik, A. D. (1993). *Ali Şir Nevayi'nin risaleleri tarih-i hükema ve enbiya, tarih-i mülük-i Acem, münşeat, metin, gramatikal indeks sözlük* [Unpublished PhD Thesis]. Ankara Üniversitesi Sosyal Bilimler Enstitüsü.

Arat, R. R. (1947). *Kutadgu bilig I: metin*. Millî Eğitim Basımevi.

Ata, A. (2004). *Karahanlı Türkçesinde ilk Kur'an tercümesi (Rylands nüshası, giriş-metin-notlar-dizin)*. Türk Dil Kurumu Yayınları.

Aybakan, B. (2006). Küreselleşme sürecinde İslamî değerler. *Marife*, *6*(3), 397–412.

Berbercan, M.T. (2011). *Çağatayca Gülistan Tercümesi, gramer-metin-dizin* [PhD Thesis]. İstanbul Üniversitesi.

Boeschoten, H. A. (2022). *Dictionary of early middle Turkic*. Brill.

Çağbayır, Y. (2007). *Yazıtlarından günümüze Türkiye Türkçesinin söz varlığı ötüken Türkçe sözlük*. Ötüken Yayınevi.

Çağrıcı, M. (2012). Tevekkül. TDV İslam ansiklopedisi, 41(1-2).

Çengelci, T. (2013). Okul ortamında değerler eğitimi konusunda öğretmen ve öğrenci görüşleri. *Değerler Eğitimi Dergisi*, *11*, 33–56.

Devellioğlu, F. (2006). *Osmanlıca-Türkçe ansiklopedik lûgat. Eski ve yeni harflerle*. Aydın Kitabevi Yayınları.

Eckmann, J. (1976). *Middle Turkic glosses of the Rylands interlinear Koran translation*. Akademiai Kiado.

Eckmann, J., Tezcan, S., Zülfikar, H., & Ata, A. (2014). *Nehcü'l-ferâdîs, uştmaḫlarnıng açuq yolı Maḥmūd bin 'Alî*. Türk Dil Kurumu Yayınları.

Emiroğlu, B. (2017). Değerler eğitiminin gençlerin sağlıklı sosyalleşmelerine etkisi. *International Journal of Eurasian Education And Culture*, *2*, 115–126.

Geyer, A. L., & Baumeister, R. F. (2013). Din, ahlak ve öz-denetim: değerler, erdemler ve kötü alışkanlıklar. In Din ve Maneviyat Psikolojisi: Yeni Yaklaşımlar ve Uygulama Alanları (pp. 241-291). Phoenix yayınları.

Gül, R. (2013). *Bir değer eğitimi olarak ilköğretim döneminde doğruluk eğitimi* [Unpublished Master Thesis]. Hitit Üniversitesi.

Güngör, R. (1995). *Ahlak psikolojisi ve sosyal ahlak*. Ötüken Neşriyat.

Karaman, F. (1996). Tevekkül inancı üzerine bir inceleme. *Fırat Üniversitesi İlahiyat Fakültesi Dergisi*, *1*, 67–92.

Karamanlıoğlu, A. F. (2006). *Şeyh Şeref Hâce, Mu'înü'l-Mürîd, transkripsiyonlu metin-dizin-tıpkıbasım*. Beşir Kitabevi.

Karataş, K. & Baloğlu, M. (2019). Tevekkülün psikolojik yansımaları. *Çukurova Üniversitesi İlahiyat Fakültesi Dergisi*, *19*(1), 110-118.

Kaya, Ö. (1989). *Ali Şir Nevâyî fevayidü'l-kiber (inceleme-metin-dizin)* [Unpublished PhD Thesis]. Ankara Üniversitesi.

Kirschenbaum, H. (1994). *100 Ways to enhance values and morality in schools and youth settings.* Allyn & Bacon, Old Tappan.

Kök, A. (2004). *Karahanlı Türkçesi satır-arası Kur'an tercümesi (TİEM 73 1v-235v/2) giriş inceleme-metin-dizin* [PhD thesis]. Ankara Üniversitesi Sosyal Bilimler Enstitüsü.

Önder, M., & Bulut, H. (2014). Temel dinî değerler ve değerler eğitimi. *Erzincan Üniversitesi Sosyal Bilimler Enstitüsü Dergisi, 6*(1), 15–32.

Özön, M. N. (1988). *Küçük Osmanlıca-Türkçe sözlük.* İnkılap Yayınevi.

Püsküllüoğlu, A. (1977). *Osmanlıca-Türkçe sözlük.* Bilgi Yayınevi.

Sağol, G. (1993). *Harezm Türkçesi satır arası Kur'an tercümesi, giriş-metin-sözlük I* [PhD Thesis]. Marmara Üniversitesi.

Şahin, M. (2018). *Dini bir değer olarak tevekkül yöneliminin psikolojik sebep ve sonuçları üzerine araştırma* [Unpublished PhD Thesis]. Uludağ Üniversitesi Sosyal Bilimler Enstitüsü.

Solmaz, R. (2006). *Din eğitimi açısından Kur'an ve sünnette tevekkül kavramı* [Unpublished Master Thesis]. Marmara Üniversitesi.

Türkay, K. (1988). *Ali Şir Nevayi bedayiul-vasat (inceleme-metin-dizin)* [Unpublished PhD Thesis]. Ankara Üniversitesi Sosyal Bilimler Enstitüsü.

Turner, T. N. (1999). *Essentials of elementary social studies.* Allyn and Bacon.

Ulusoy, K. (2010). Değer eğitimi: Davranışçı ve yapılandırmacı yaklaşıma göre hazırlanan tarih programlarında değer aktarımı. *Trakya Üniversitesi Sosyal Bilimler Dergisi, 12*(1), 32–51.

Ünlü, S. (2004). *Karahanlı Türkçesi satır–arası Kur'an tercümesi (TİEM 73, 235v/3–450r/7)* [PhD Thesis]. Hacettepe Üniversitesi.

Ünlü, S. (2012a). *Karahanlı Türkçesi sözlüğü.* Eğitim Yayınevi.

Ünlü, S. (2012b). *Harezm–Altınordu Türkçesi sözlüğü.* Eğitim Yayınevi.

Ünlü, S. (2013). *Çağatay Türkçesi sözlüğü.* Eğitim Yayınevi.

Üşenmez, E. (2010). *Eski Kur'an tercümelerinden Özbekistan nüshası üzerinde dil incelemesi (giriş-inceleme-metin-sözlük-ekler dizini)* [PhD Thesis]. İstanbul Üniversitesi.

KEY TERMS AND DEFINITIONS

Arabic: A language spoken in Western Asia and North Africa.
Buddha: The holy man (563–483 BC) on whose life and teachings Buddhism is based.

Buddhism: A religion that originally comes from South Asia, and teaches that personal spiritual improvement will lead to escape from human suffering.

Manichaeism: Dualistic religious movement founded in Persia in the 3rd century CE by Mani, who was known as the "Apostle of Light" and supreme "Illuminator."

Persian: Belonging to or relating to Iran, its people, or its language.

Proxy: A term denoting either a person who is authorized to stand in place of another or the legal instrument by which the authority is conferred.

Qur'an: The sacred scripture of Islam.

Socialisation: Yhe process of training people or animals to behave in a way that others in the group think is suitable.

Tawhid: It refers to the nature of that God—that he is a unity, not composed, not made up of parts, but simple and uncompounded.

Chapter 15
Introducing English as a Second Language to the Algerian Primary Schools

Leila Soudani
Ibn Khaldoun University, Tiaret, Algeria

Meriem Chafaa
Ibn Khaldoun University, Tiaret, Algeria

Moulkheir Selmani
Ibn Khaldoun University, Tiaret, Algeria

ABSTRACT

The Algerian educational system of today is different from that of years ago; more approaches are included, more teaching techniques are combined, and the emphasis on language learning has grown. Primary, middle, and high schools offer classes in Arabic, French, and Tamazight. It would be vital to incorporate English into primary schools in light of the government's plan to designate it as a second language in addition to French. This produces a generation that can advance in linguistic proficiency. Of course, switching from French to English, a language that has been used as a second language for hundreds of years, is difficult. The most important weapon for change is education. Such a change obviously meets numerous hurdles and difficulties; for instance, there needs to be an adequate number of teachers and instructors who can spread the language at all levels. This chapter focuses on the methods, requirements, and challenges of introducing English to the Algerian primary school and the potential obstacles that policymakers and educators may face when teaching English.

INTRODUCTION

All facets of life, including education, are impacted by today's changing world. People's needs and aspirations change as the socioeconomic and political order shifts, bringing new difficulties. One of the

DOI: 10.4018/978-1-6684-9295-6.ch015

most significant indicators of a nation's development is changes in how foreign languages are taught, which can occur over time and in different nations. Significant foreign language teaching and learning changes were observed in Algeria and many other nations (Alhuzay, 2015). Since Algeria's independence, planning for foreign languages has been a hot topic. According to their status and the parameters of Algeria's language policy, Algerian educators define foreign languages in the context of education. To replace French in the educational system, English was one of these languages introduced into Algerian primary schools in 1993. However, this project was abandoned in its early stages for various reasons (Marouf, 2017).

The English language is widely spoken worldwide; it has developed into an international lingua franca. Many countries have encouraged its use in society or schools (Crystal, 2003; Phillipson, 2008). This movement, known as globalization, has prompted Algerian decision-makers to reevaluate their current language policies to meet the needs of the Algerian people in learning this essential language and reintroducing English in primary schools (Manseur, 2020). The present chapter investigates the process of teaching and learning English as a foreign language at Algerian Primary schools. It focuses on the prerequisites, the instructional strategies, and any potential difficulties faced by decision-makers and specialists in education when integrating English instruction into Algerian primary schools. This investigation provides some proposed recommendations and strategies and identifies some pedagogical considerations that should be considered for future implementation success.

LINGUISTIC PROFILE OF ALGERIA

Algeria has a very intriguing linguistic environment. From independence in 1962 and for years, this country was 'officially' monolingual, with classical Arabic as the official and national language. However, this did not prevent the social presence of other languages. The latter have long 'fought' for their survival. They remain present in the Algerian cultural heritage. Modern Standard Arabic (MSA), Algerian Arabic (AA), Tamazight, and French are the official languages of Algeria today, which all have a significant impact (Rouabah, 2022).

ARABIC

In terms of both speaker count and floor space, it is the most extensive. It would typically be structured in a continuum of registers (language varieties), ranging from the most standardized register to the least standardized, in Algeria and the rest of the Arab world. First is fusha (or classical) Arabic (CA), used in the Koran. Speaking specifically among religious men, it is distinguished by a complex grammatical structure, followed by standard or modern Arabic (MSA), a proper language of intercommunication between all Arabic-speaking nations; then comes the "dialect of the cultivated" or the Arabic used by educated people, and finally comes the register whose acquisition and use are the most spontaneous, or what is commonly referred to as the dialects or speeches that are distributed in all nations in local and regional variants (Boudjedra, 1992/1994).

ALGERIAN ARABIC

The third definition of "Arabic" refers to an Algerian language (or various languages). Algerian in the sense that more than one language is present. It is a simplified form of classical Arabic called "darija" a colloquial language. In addition, because 80–85% of Algerians speak Algerian Arabic, it is regarded as their first language. Due to this language's straightforward structure, particularly at the phonological and syntactic levels, Algerians choose it as their first language. They defined Algerian levels, focusing primarily on phonological and Arabic. Formerly a ministerial delegate to the universities.

Despite requests to make Algerian Arabic the primary language of instruction and daily communication, MSA has maintained its position so far (Dabène, 1981).

This vernacular (Algerian Arabic) enables the separation of Algeria's rural dialects from its urban dialects (particularly those of Algiers, Constantine, Jijel, Nedroma, and Tlemcen) and the emergence of four main dialect regions: the East around Constantine, Algiers and its hinterland, Orania, and finally the South, which itself experiences significant dialectal diversity from East to West from the Saharan Atlas to the borders of the Hoggar.

The vocabulary of Algerian Arabic is rich in words adapted from other languages with which Algerians had contact throughout history. Words borrowed from Latin, Spanish, Turkish, and numerous other languages. Present-day still exists. Despite this, after 132 years of physical and intellectual colonization, French linguistic traces remain the defining feature of Algerian Arabic (Marouf, 2017).

TAMAZIGHT

The Maghreb, or rather the Berber-speaking region of Africa that stretches from Egypt to Morocco and from Algeria to Niger, is made up of the most recent varieties of the Berber language, which are an extension of the earliest varieties still spoken there. The mother tongue of a portion of the population speaks these Amazigh dialects, as they are now known, which make up the oldest linguistic foundation of this area (El Aissati, 1993).

Aurès, Djur-dura (Kabylie), Gouraya, Hoggar, and Mzab, as well as a few islands strewn throughout the nation, are some of the areas where these dialects have retreated and sought refuge in response to the Islamization and Arabization of the Maghreb. This geographic extension matches an astonishing diversity that sometimes hinders communication. The four most prevalent Amazigh dialects in Algeria are Kabyle or Taqbaylit (Kabylia), Chaoui or Tachaouit (Aurès), Mzabi (Mzab), and Targui or Tamachek of the Tuaregs of the Great South (Hoggar and Tassili) (Taleb Ibrahimi, 2004; Milroy, 2001).

However, since the 1970s, we have been observing initiatives to reassess these dialects and the Berber culture connected to the sometimes violent, sometimes sly demand for recognition of Berber distinctiveness. Since the Berber Spring events of 1980, the founding of the Berber Cultural Movement (MCB), and the fierce suppression of any expression of Algerian diversity - and, in reality, of any free expression - the culturalist claim has been fueled by the democratic deficit of the Algerian power and maintained the pressure manifested during the 1994–1995 school year by the boycott of the school that resulted in the decision taken in May 1995 to introduce Tamazig (Benrabah, 2013; Taleb Ibrahimi, 2004).

According to the Algerian Constitution, "the fundamental constituent parts of Algerians identity…are Islam, Arabism, and Amazighsm" (1996), the term "Amazighsm" was first used to describe a component of Algerian identity. This formal recognition prompted Berbers to request the inclusion of Tamazight in the educational system. By 2002, Tamazight had been added as the second national language to Article 3 of the constitution. The national center for Tamazight Language Planning was established by order of the state of Algeria.

Despite these restrictions made by the Algerian government, Tamazight still has a small population in the Tamzgha. Since no clear decision has been made regarding whether the Roman or the Arabic systems would be preferable for the writing of Tamazight, its gravitation is seen as an obstacle to its advancement. A language must undoubtedly have both a written and a spoken form to be acknowledged (Djaout, 1993).

FRENCH

With almost 16 million residents, Algeria is the second-largest francophone nation in the world; one in two Algerians speak French (Rapport de l'OIF, 2006-2007).

Even though the Algerian elite was nonexistent throughout the colonial era, the 132 years of French colonization have left their mark on entire generations of Algerians, mainly through education. After India gained independence in 1962 and made attendance at school a requirement for everyone, language learning saw a boom. This latter played a crucial role in teaching all languages, including French. French was the official language of Algeria at the time in the fields of education, administration, the environment, and the economy, due to the growth and dissemination of education (Boubakour, 2008; Maamri, 2009).

The French language is now more prevalent in the Algerian linguistic scene. Even though French is only taught as a foreign language in schools today due to a policy of Arabization, it is still widely used in higher education. Even though humanities courses are being taught in Arabic, university instruction is still conducted in French. This includes medical and engineering sciences as well as nearly all post-graduate fields. The majority of media outlets (radio, daily newspapers, weekly magazines, Etc.) are published in French; for instance, half of the Algerian press is still published in French and has a much larger audience than Arabic-language media (Benrabah, 1999; Taleb Ibrahimi, 2004).

EDUCATIONAL POLICIES AND LANGUAGE SYSTEM IN ALGERIA

Algerian leaders decided to reassert the nation's identity through assimilation upon independence immediately. Assimilation strives to homogenize the Algerian community by ensuring everyone speaks Standard Arabic and engages in the same behaviors, ideas, and educational experiences. The most common pattern for assimilation includes language. Like many other recently decolonized nations, Algeria prioritizes education as the most crucial industry for ensuring the socialization and order the ruling elite seeks to establish. The Algerian government implemented a linguistic policy regarded as the most significant in Algerian history to rid the country of the colonizer's language and educational framework (Benrabah, 2007).

Arabization began in October 1962, intending to make Standard Arabic the official tongue of the Algerians. Arabic would be taught in French-speaking elementary schools, according to Ahmad Ben Bella, the first president of the Democratic and Popular Republic of Algeria. However, during the initial time of independence from colonialism, there were many challenges, and this approach ran into significant challenges due to the unhappiness of French speakers (Berri, 1973).

Due to a paucity of Arabic-speaking teachers, 1962–1965 were characterized by ambiguity regarding implementation. However, in 1962 and 1964, the government added seven and 10 hours of Arabic to the curriculum, respectively. The lack of teachers was made up for by recruiting 1,000 teachers from Egypt and Syria, even though they lacked Arabic language proficiency and had no experience teaching foreign languages. With the military coup in 1965, the actual process of Arabization started. Assuming charge of the administration, Houari Boumedian shared the same philosophy as his predecessor and saw the improvement of Arabic as a crucial objective (Benrabah, 2004).

Ahmad Taleb Ibrahimi, Minister of Education, began the introduction of Arabization into the educational system from 1965 to 1970. His acceptance of the value of the French cultural tradition did not conflict with his acceptance of the necessity of Arabic as one of the crucial steps in rehabilitating Algerian individuality (Kouicem, 2019; Marouf, 2017).

Throughout the first phase, Arabic and French were taught side by side, marked by bilingual instruction. The teaching of French as a (foreign language) topic started in the third year, but it was not until 1974 that the entire primary school level had been wholly Arabized. Most of the secondary school's humanities courses were Arabized that same year. However, Arabization was still a problem at the university level because students had to learn French after twelve years of studying Arabic as their primary language of instruction. The shortcomings in the Algerian educational system were caused by this circumstance (Benrabah, 2004; Gorden, 1978).

Instead of using the colonial-era educational framework, a new one was to be implemented in September 1976. The government established the "Ecole Fondamentale": Fundamental School, a six-year elementary school program and a three-year middle school program that used Arabic as the teaching medium. French-Arabic bilingualism in education ended due to this reform, successfully implemented in 1978). Following the establishment of the Fundamental School 20 years ago, the Algerian government and a sizeable portion of the populace have recognized the need for new educational reforms. The Algerian educational system is doomed to failure, from President Boudiaf to Bouteflika to countless academics and educational experts. As a result, the Bouteflika administration decided to restructure the educational system (Moulay, 2017; Taleb Ibrahimi, 1995).

On May 13, 2000, a commission for the reform was established and given the initials CNRSE. The government began implementing the recommendations this commission recommended in September 2003. The outdated French structure, which consists of three levels, has taken the place of foundational education today:

1. Five rather than six years are spent in primary school, and pupils receive a certificate of primary education upon completion.
2. Middle school is a four-year program that culminates in issuing a certificate of middle education. The latter enables the pupils to enroll in secondary schools.
3. Three-year secondary school: Pupils can study literature or science at this level (Marouf, 2017).

The LMD system has replaced the previous one at the university level. All Algerian universities were required to adopt this method that year (2010), despite the challenges this presented for professors and students due to several poorly taken into-account aspects of the new university restructuring, such as syllabus creation. The country's shifting philosophies are reflected in Algeria's educational policies.

Algerian education continues to raise doubts about its quality and sufficiency, from the French educational system to the Foundation school to the current system. Despite criticism of the educational system, Algeria lowered its illiteracy rate from 90% in 1960 to 40% in 1990. There is compulsory and free education for all Algerians, regardless of socioeconomic background or linguistic group. The fact that the vast majority of teachers are graduates of only Algerian-run schools is another noteworthy accomplishment regarding the country's educational system (Lakhal-Ayat, 2008; Mami, 2013; Miliani, 2010).

LANGUAGES IN THE EDUCATIONAL SYSTEM

French has always retained a significant non-official status in the Algerian linguistic situation compared to other languages like Spanish or German due to historical and political causes that have already been stated. However, the post-independence program of Arabization altered this standing, and the French no longer enjoyed the privileged position it did after independence when it was widely utilized in government, academia, and the media. The Algerians' sentiments about the French have changed in favor of Arabic (Modern Standard Arabic), notwithstanding the shortcomings and difficulties of the Arabization policy. However, things are changing, especially in this contemporary age where globalization mandates English as a universal tongue and a key to intercultural communication. The value of English is recognized by Algeria and other nations that seek to be open and have successful ties with different peoples (Benrabah, 2007, Kouicem, 2019; Marouf, 2017).

Therefore, French was transferred from being taught in the second year of middle school to the first year due to the late changes, specifically those of 2004. It was, therefore, given the status of a second language. Additionally, there is a growing demand from people to learn English. This underlying factor promotes English language and culture instruction in private schools nationwide (Miliani, 2000).

German, Spanish, and Italian are examples of foreign languages. However, they have a different significance in Algeria than in French and English. They are covered in secondary education. In their second year, students might select one of these minority languages. For those just starting in these minority languages, departments at the university level offer license degrees (the equivalent of a bachelor's degree in the anglophone educational systems). The Algerian society just encountered a brand-new obstacle. Threats of English invasion are present for both French and Tamazight (as a national language). The only way to end this dispute is to allow Algerians to choose between these three rival languages. Tamazight, French, and English were to be included in the new national curriculum at various levels (Marouf, 2017).

TEACHING ENGLISH AS A FOREIGN LANGUAGE IN ALGERIA

According to Slimani (2016), in Algeria, the general objectives of teaching and learning English as a foreign language state that the learner should achieve communication in its various forms, aspects, and dimensions; four main categories of objectives can be mentioned:

- Socio-cultural objectives;
- Humanistic objectives;
- Educational objectives;
- Academic objectives.

REASONS FOR LEARNING ENGLISH

English is the business, scientific, and technological language. As a result, acquiring such a language is the ultimate objective of any country seeking progress, and our country is no exception. Although English is the second most popular foreign language behind French in Algeria, it has gained popularity due to its importance in international communication.

Furthermore (Caroll,1969) mentioned that time is an essential variable in language learning based on measurable accomplishment in formal educational contexts, indicating that time is the most critical variable in language learning. Similarly, according to Burstall et al. (1974), the achievement of skills in a foreign language is proportional to time spent in the formal study of that language. Furthermore, Lightbown&Spada (1993) argued that younger learners in a formal context in the target language generally have more time to dedicate to learning the language. Fluent citizens in foreign languages, mainly English, enhance competitiveness overseas, facilitate international communication, and protect political interests.

EARLY START FOR LEARNING ENGLISH

When the decision whether to teach a foreign language or not is debated, some educators begin with the assumption that age is more important than other parameters. The concept of 'younger is better' is claimed. Several research initiatives have been conducted to investigate this subject. Studies carried out by Burstallet al (1974) have shown, research has shown that youngsters who begin learning a language before the age of adolescence are more likely to have native-like pronunciation. Several experts, including Penfield & Roberts (1959), including Birdsong & Mollis (2001), have shown that ability is attributed to physiological changes in the maturing brain as a child enters puberty. According to Penfield & Roberts (1959), a child's brain is more plastic than an adult's, and before the age of 9, "A child is a specialist in learning to speak; he can learn 2-3 languages as quickly as one. However, for learning languages, the brain progressively becomes stiff and rigid during the age span of 9-12 (Penfield & Roberts,1959).

Penfield (1959) indicates that a child's cerebral flexibility leads to higher abilities, particularly in acquiring language units. As a result, he urged for the teaching of a foreign language at a young age in school. He shares a similar point of view. Lenneberg (1967), based on research into the physical development of the child's brain and neurophysiology, argued that biological factors influence the innate language learning process, which occurs between the ages of 2 and puberty. This period of age is called the Critical Period. Birdsong & Mollis (2001) defined it as "The period during which an organism displays a heightened sensitivity to certain environmental stimuli; typically, there is an abrupt onset... followed by a gradual offset, or decline which is asymptotic".

In addition, Nash(1997) indicated that the potential to acquire a second language is greatest between the ages of birth and six, and the probability of learning the language remains high throughout elementary school; he stated, " It is clear that foreign language should be taught in elementary school, if not before,"(Nash,1997)a more recent study of Birdsong &Mollis (2001), combined with study of Johnson & Newport (1989); The effect of age on language proficiency attainment revealed that younger learners gained more competence than adults.

In light of the research cited above, various theoretical approaches and particular studies agree that there is a potential advantage to an early start of foreign language learning. Thus, the suggestion to start learning earlier is encouraged.

INTRODUCING ENGLISH AS A SECOND LANGUAGE
TO THE ALGERIAN PRIMARY SCHOOL

Since 1993 and during the effort to improve foreign language teaching at an early age, primary school pupils have had the opportunity of choosing between French and English as compulsory. The program was experienced only in some primary schools but stopped because the vast majority of parents chose French over English.

Algerian children returned to school Wednesday, Sept. 21, 2022, for the first time since the president directed that schools teach English instead of French as a second language alongside Arabic. The government says the move is a modernization effort. On Wednesday, third graders returning to primary school in Algeria will be taught English and French as a foreign language when the new academic year begins.

Various surveys and studies have been conducted to investigate the impact of introducing English in Algerian primary schools. In a more recent study in 2020, one questionnaire was distributed to third-grade young learners in Hassiba Ben Bou Ali Elementary School Chabaat el LehamAinTemouchent town. Also, another questionnaire was designed for parents to learn about their opinions on teaching English in Algerian primary schools. Questionnaires have been analyzed for young learners to determine the evidence of their prior knowledge about English and to see how much pupils are motivated by the concept; through the analysis of data, pupil's answers revealed that most of the pupils in the third primary grade agreed with the introduction of an English course. Furthermore, analysis of parent questionnaires revealed that parents are entirely satisfied with introducing English courses in Algerian primary schools (Guendouze & Bentrari,2020).

According to Guendouze and Bentrari (2020), the findings from the questionnaires of young learners and their parents have provided us with a thorough understanding of the issue of English is going to be the dominant foreign language in Algerian elementary schools.

As a whole, the results show that the majority of young learners of the third-grade "Hassiba Ben Bou Ali" elementary school agreed with the replacement of French with English in primary schools. In light of the results collected from the pupil's questionnaire, they agreed with introducing English courses in Algerian primary schools (Guendouze & Bentrari, 2020).

The questionnaire revealed that parents' attitudes about English in Algerian primary schools were favorable; they agreed with introducing English courses early. Sharing the same point of view, Benzoubir and Bourouina (2020) revealed that most participants agreed on the need to add English in Algerian primary schools throughout the questionnaires.

Many parents want English to replace French as the second language as the national language in Algeria. Because many courses are taught to primary school learners, the primary school program was heavily emphasized. Manseur and Negadi's (2019) study found that most Algerian parents support their children's early exposure to English and promote its learning at the primary school level, as they strongly agree.

Early English study in primary schools in Algeria is encouraged by many parents, as the language has infiltrated multiple sectors and has become a priority in fields such as communication, trade, tourism, and education.

Figure 1. The child's priority is selecting a language
Source: Guendouze and Bentrari (2020)

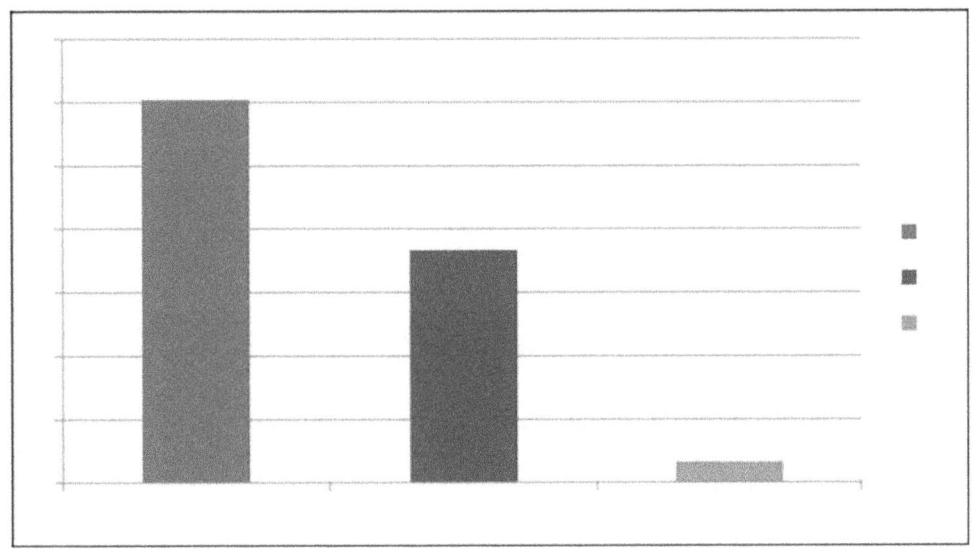

Figure 2. Parents' attitudes toward implementing English in primary schools
Source: Benzoubir and Bourouina (2020)

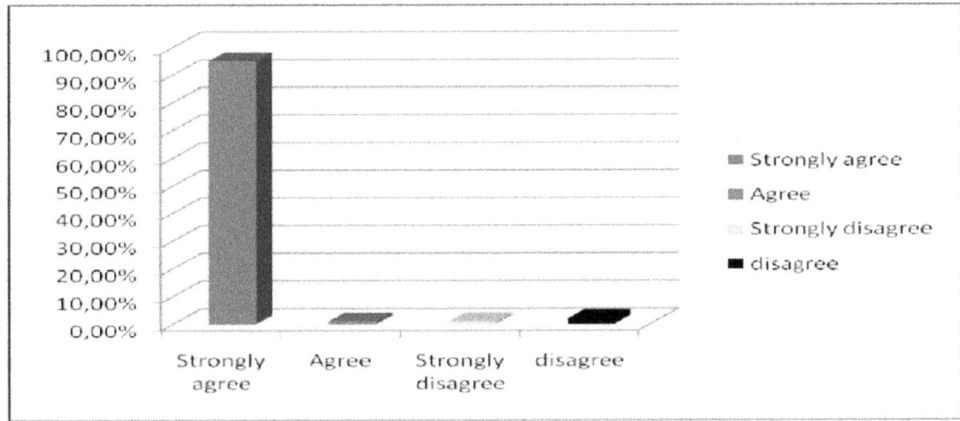

CHALLENGES IN TEACHING ENGLISH IN PRIMARY SCHOOLS

Teaching English in primary schools is difficult since teaching children differs from teaching adult learners. It also has many challenges (Copland et al., 2014; Hadke & Naidu, 2014; Wei-pei, 2008). The problems are in terms of internal and external factors. The internal factor refers to pedagogy and motivation. The external factor includes textbooks, learning resources, and teachers' level of English. (Cahyati&Madya, 2018). The first internal factor problem is pedagogy competency, which deals with the proper application of teaching methodologies. Several innovative learning methodologies, such as Communicative Language Teaching (CLT), have been developed. Task-Based Learning and Teaching

(CBLT), Language instruction, and learning have similar elements. However, teachers may need help introducing those strategies for several reasons (Copland et al., 2014). Furthermore, pupils' progress should be constantly evaluated. It causes some difficulty because the assessment is required to determine how well the pupils understand the lesson. (Hadke& Naidu, 2014).

Textbooks are the most critical challenge of external factors. Books are unavailable in several counties (Hadke& Naidu, 2014).

Figure 3. The 3rd year primary English book in Algeria
Source: https://eddirasa.com/wp-content/uploads/2022/09/book-english-3ap.pdf

Textbooks serve a crucial function in assisting students in acquiring English knowledge. The materials needed to be more frequently fragmented and inadequately illustrated in the selected textbooks available at the school. (Wei-pei, 2008). It is also known that the availability of relevant materials can help teachers prepare activities for use in teaching-learning activities. Regarding this, the textbook lesson must be adapted based on the pupil's requirements and skills and is designed. In terms of source, children need to be explained concretely through demonstrations. They need something tangible rather than theories (Copland et al.,2014). They require media to help them in learning the instruction. However, most schools do not have sufficient teaching aids (Hadke& Naidu, 2014).NextThe English competence of the teachers can have an impact on their teaching. In other words, teachers with low proficiency are indicated to need more self-confidence, find difficulties interacting with young learners, and understand the materials slowly (Copland et al., 2014).

These difficulties raise significant worries about the general quality of English instruction in primary schools. As a result, offering adequate training for English instructors in primary schools might assist them in dealing with the diverse characteristics of their pupils.

RECOMMENDATIONS AND PEDAGOGICAL IMPLICATIONS

The Algerian education system needs more linguistic material in educational establishments. This shortage is specific to the country but varies from region to region. The closer you get to small towns, the greater the shortage. It will therefore be essential to provide the necessary materials to create a favorable learning environment and improve performance.

A study should be devoted to material availability, suitability, and efficacy in primary school. The choice of materials is a complex procedure that necessitates more investigation. The provision of critical resources needs to be improved in Algeria, particularly regarding technology-related equipment, which is frequently expensive and challenging to supply for the entire nation. Additionally, there is debate over whether the materials are appropriate for children because, in some circumstances, they may need to be more productive and focused. Testing the effectiveness of the primary teaching materials would demonstrate their success in the teaching-learning process and offer improved language-learning solutions.

Reduce the number of pupils in classes, as very high numbers can make it difficult to control the class and hamper teaching due to noise and lack of concentration on the part of learners.

Using and communicating in English at the end of the session and outside the classroom will be best, as recent linguistic theories confirm the importance of language exposure in improving English.

The possibility of obliging children to abstain from using their mother language in class, as pupils tend to use their mother language instead of the target language. This can lead to linguistic interference and hamper learning productivity.

According to Piaget's theory (1958) of child development, teaching young learners must always involve tangible concepts that the kid can understand through their five senses because toddlers are unable to understand abstract concepts.

It will be best to teach the English language daily for 45 to 60 minutes with various fun activities that should be presented to avoid leading children to inhibition and refusal to learn.

Encourage teaching the English language through touch, sight, smell, hearing, and taste, an active learning strategy that helps pupils acquire the language in less time.

Introducing new strategies to help children learn English quickly, such as dialogues with foreigners, interacting with things in their real life, trips and field trips (visiting national landmarks), simulating a real-life situation in context, roleplay, drawing, writing, creating stories, and coloring.

Encourage pedagogy through experience, an effective strategy for better target language acquisition. Children prefer being involved and using their five senses, which makes it suitable for young learners.

Encourage pedagogy through experience, an effective strategy for better target language acquisition. Children prefer being involved and using their five senses, which makes it suitable for young learners.

It encourages Montessori pedagogy to teach English. Montessori is very effective in children's education; it is employed throughout Europe, and Montessori-only schools were created in the USA. Recent studies on how it is used in language learning found that it is a welcoming, enjoyable approach to learning as long as the right environment and qualified teachers are available.

Reviewing primary school English language teaching programs, which should place more emphasis on speaking and listening than writing and reading as a first step to making language learning easier, especially for children of that age. Additionally, communication tasks rather than grammatical ones should be the focus, and visual aids, games, imitations, and songs should all be used.

The English textbooks used in primary schools in Algeria in the 1990s must be included in further research because they give an overview of the applied English in those schools and a previous experiment that has to be developed into success.

Since there is neither a paper copy of the textbooks in the archives nor a digital repository of old textbooks, they are challenging to locate. In order to determine an elaborated edition of a new English textbook for elementary schools in Algeria, future research must identify, examine, and compare the English textbooks of that era with the most recent ones to determine contrasts and similarities.

Following the process of creating a syllabus, a Ph.D. student should focus his study on implementing and evaluating the created syllabus. It is recommended to apply the syllabus by a postgraduate for the task is complicated and lengthy for under grades in terms of time, funding, and experience.

To develop the professional competence of English teachers, they should receive training as soon as they are recruited and then periodically during their teaching career. Training can be provided online. Particular professional development pages for English teachers can be set up on social media, and online discussion forums and blogs can also be created.

Teachers and parents can encourage the kids to listen to mobile audiobooks to help them improve their listening and speaking, listening and reading, and listening and writing abilities. They can engage in collaborative reading activities in small groups in the classroom, where they can read multicultural children's short stories and fiction.

English teachers must encourage children to use mobile apps to expand their vocabulary. They can pick up names for different things, including animals, fruits, vegetables, clothes, body parts, rooms in a house, and modes of transportation. They can use the applications to learn the definitions and pronunciation of new words.

Parental concerns and choices should be considered and should play an influential role in education language policy in Algeria.

CONCLUSION

The concept of introducing English in Algerian primary schools is still a challenging one that requires more research. English is preferred over French as a foreign language in Algeria due to its linguistic and cultural context, shown in the widespread use of the language across various sectors.

Following several searches, introducing English to the primary sector has many challenges regarding teacher training or dealing with young children. This process is also made possible by the fact that young children can learn new languages, as is the case with learning French. The introduction of English to elementary schools can be accomplished despite various obstacles with perseverance and hard work.

The process is undoubtedly a complex task to do. Therefore, more complicated efforts must be built to fulfill the needed goals. Effectively, many procedures are expected, and several moves are taken. The challenges are significant, and the requirements are possible to manage. Getting to the desired outcomes, though, requires a long journey. The government and educators should work together to accomplish many aims and open new avenues for Algerian schools. Teachers must undergo extensive training because they are instructing a sensitive group of students who cannot study independently.

Parents are significant agents in the formulation of language education policies. Therefore, it is exciting to consider their attitudes during the formulation process in order to ensure successful implementation.

Finally, young learners should receive an early language education in English due to the demands on the language in our current times, especially from an economic and technological point of view.

REFERENCES

Alkhunazy, S. (2015). Introducing English as a second language to early primary school curriculum in - Saudi Arabia. *Arab World English Journal*, 6(2), 365–371. doi:10.24093/awej/vol6no2.28

Benrabah, M. (1999). *Langue et Pouvoir en Algérie*. Editions Seguier.

Benrabah, M. (2004). La question linguistique. In Y. Beiaskri & C. Chaulet-Achour (Eds.), *l'Epreuve d'une Decennie* (pp. 83–108). Paris-Mediterraneen.

Benrabah, M. (2007). Language in education planning in Algeria: Historical development and current issues. *Language Policy*, 6(2), 225–252. doi:10.100710993-007-9046-7

Benrabah, M. (2013). *Language Conict in Algeria: From Colonialism to Post-Independence*. Multilingual Matters. doi:10.21832/9781847699657

Benzoubir, F., & Bourouina, L. (2020). The implementation of English as a second foreign language in Algerian primary schools between acceptance and refusal. University of Ibn Khaldoun.

Berri, Y. (1973). Algérie: La Révolution en Arabe. *Jeune Afrique (Paris, France)*, (639), 18.

Birdsong, D., & Molis, M. (2001). On the evidence for maturational constraints in second-language acquisition. *Journal of Memory and Language, 44*(2), 235-249.

Boubakour,S. (2011). Etudier le Francais ...Quelle Histoire! *Le francais en Afrique – revue de reseau des observatoires du Francais contemporain en Afrique, 23*, 51-68.

Boudjerda, R. (1992/1994). *Le FIS de la haine*. Editions Denoël.

Burstall, C., Jamieson, M., Cohen, N. F. E. R., & Hargreaves, M. (1974). *Primary French in the balance*. NFER.

Cahyati, P. M., S. (2019). Teaching English in primary schools: Benefits and challenges. In *3rd International Conference on Current Issues in Education (ICCIE 2018)*. Atlantis Press. 10.2991/iccie-18.2019.68

Carroll, J.B. (1969). Psychological and educational research into second language teaching to young children. *Languages and the young school child*, 56-68.

Copland, F., Garton, S., & Burns, A. (2014). Challenges in teaching English to young learners: Global perspectives and local realities. *TESOL Quarterly*, 48(4), 738–762. doi:10.1002/tesq.148

Crystal, D. (2003). *English as a global language*. Cambridge University Press. doi:10.1017/CBO9780511486999

Dabene, L. (dir.). (1981). *Langues et Migrations*. Publications de l'université de Grenoble III.

Djaout, T. (1993). Des acquis? *Ruptures, 15*.

El Aissati, A. (1993). Berber in Morocco and Algeria: Revival or Decay? *AILA Review*, *10*, 88–109. https://varlyproject-blog.cdn.ampproject.org/v/s/varlyproject.blog/teaching-english-inalgeria/amp/?amp_js_v=a6&_gsa=1&usqp=mq331AQHKAFQArABIA

Gordon, D. C. (1978). *The French National Language and National Identity*. Mouton Publishers.

Guendouze, L. Y., & Bentrari, Y. (2020). *Introducing English course in Algerian Primary school: Case of the third –Grade in primary schools in AinTemouchent (Hassiba Ben Bou Ali)* [Master dissertation].

Johnson, J. S., & Newport, E. L. (1989). Critical period effects in second language learning: The influence of maturational state on the acquisition of English as a second language. *Cognitive Psychology*, *21*(1), 60–99. doi:10.1016/0010-0285(89)90003-0 PMID:2920538

Kouicem, K. (2019). Exploring English in education policy in Algeria: Obstacles to its Promotion. *Ichkalat Journal, 8*(4), 573-592.

Lakhal, A., & Benmati, K. (2008). *Is the Algerian educational system weakening? An investigation of the high school curricula and their adequacy with the other curricula. Mentouri University Constantine*. University Curricula.

Lenneberg, E. H. (1967). *Biological foundations of language*. Wiley.

Lightbown, P. M., & Spada, N. (2021). *How languages are learned* (5th ed.). Oxford University Press.

Maamri, M. R. (2009). The Syndrome of the French Language in Algeria. *The International Journal of the Arts in Society*, *3*(3), 77–89.

Manseur, R., & Negadi, M. N. (2019). Parents' attitudes towards exposing their children to English in Algerian Primary Education. *International Journal of English Linguistics*, *9*(4), 145. doi:10.5539/ijel.v9n4p145

Mansour, R. (2020). *Introducing the English language in The Algerian Primary Schools: Teachers, parents, and pupils' attitudes*. University of Tlemcen.

Marouf, N. (2017). English in Algerian primary schools between necessity and contingency. *Journal Al Nassr, 4*(1), 4-15.

Miliani, M. (2010). Between enduring hardships and fleeting ideals. *Mediterranean Journal of Educational Studies*, *15*(2), 65–76.

Milroy, J. (2001). Language ideologies and the consequences of standardization. *Journal of Sociolinguistics*, *5*(4), 530–555. doi:10.1111/1467-9481.00163

Nash, J. M. (1997). Fertile minds. *Time*, *149*(5), 48–56. PMID:10169172

Penfield, W., & Robert, L. (1959). *Speech and Brain\x= req-\Mechanisms*. Academic Press.

Phillipson, R. (2008). Lingua Franca or Lingua Frankensteinia? English in European integration and globalization. *World Englishes*, *27*(2), 250–267. doi:10.1111/j.1467-971X.2008.00555.x

Rapport de l'OIF, Le français dans le monde, 2006-2007.

Rouabah, S. (2022). Multilingualism in Algeria: Educational policies, language practices, and challenges. *Journal of the British Academy*, *10*(4), 21–40. doi:10.5871/jba/010s4.021

Slimani, S. (2016). Teaching English as a foreign language in Algeria. *Revue des Sciences*, *44*, 33–44. doi:10.37136/1003-000-044-041

Taleb Ibrahimi, K. (1995). *Les Algériens et Leurs Langues*. Les Editions EL Hikma.

Wang, W. P. (2008). *Teaching English to young learners in Taiwan: Issues relating to teaching, teacher education, teaching materials and teacher perspectives* [Doctoral dissertation]. The University of Waikato.

KEY TERMS AND DEFINITIONS

Algerian Arabic (AA): Is a dialect derived from the form of Arabic spoken in Algeria. It belongs to the Maghrebi Arabic language.

Critical Period: Is an ethological term that refers to a fixed and crucial time during the early development of an organism when it can learn things essential to survival as language learning.

Foreign Language: Any language not native to a particular region or person. Foreign language instruction is often required or strongly encouraged in primary and secondary education.

LMD System: The LMD is an acronym for Licence, Master, and Doctorate. The LMD system represents a set of changes and innovations introduced in higher education consisting of an organization into three levels of training system: the License (bachelor), Master, and Doctorate.

Modern Standard Arabic (MSA): Is the direct result of modern Arabic and a standardized language version. It is the type of Arabic used in universities, Arabic language schools, audiovisual and written media, and other formal contexts.

National Language: A language officially designated as the language of a nation or country, usually for cultural and ethnic reasons. Such a language may or may not be the official language of the country in question (that is, used in its government and administration).

School Child: A child aged 6-7 to 18 years old studying in a general education institution (secondary school).

Chapter 16

Kindness as a Social Bond and the Education for the Future:
Guidelines From a Psycho–Social Survey

Monica Mastrantonio
Justus Liebig, Germany

ABSTRACT

In the survey Imaginable Futures conducted worldwide in the year of 2022, which had 311 responders across the globe, kindness was mentioned as the one core skill for the future. Together with the importance of education for peace, mental health, and the development of survival skills in case of disasters, kindness is listed as the core skill to social bonds. Children school education and school curriculums are mostly based on content acquisition, whereas research data points to what the new generations will need in the near future. Kindness is connected to happiness, well-being, empathy, and sociability, and it can generate physical benefits, like low blood pressure. However, how can these skills be integrated in the school curriculum? How prepared are the teachers to implement this new acquisition? This research concludes that kindness and hope should be far and firstly implemented as key educational figures at this critical time of Anthropocene.

INTRODUCTION

Kindness is a genuine concern, care, and consideration for another person's wellness and well-being. As kindness encompasses acts of compassion, empathy, generosity, and respect, it also strengthens social bonds, triggering positive emotions such as joy, gratitude, and happiness. Within this cycle of kindness, social connections, and sense of belonging, the future will certainly be brighter and more welcoming (Curry, 2020)

The cultivation of kindness and empathy has become imperative for building better resilient societies in our interconnected and digital world. Kindness has been taken for granted across many generations, potentially because it was passing from one generation to the next. With so many challenges and ruptures,

DOI: 10.4018/978-1-6684-9295-6.ch016

this essential skill is now at bay due to a variety of reasons from an extremely egocentric social-media based society to the period of lockdown that strengthen isolation. Therefore, Kindness Studies are highly relevant in today's world due to an increasingly interconnected and complex global society (Post, 2018)

The exploration and understanding of kindness have become crucial for promoting positive social interactions, well-being, and community development. Here are some key reasons why Kindness Studies are pertinent nowadays. Kindness has been shown to have significant positive effects on mental health, reducing stress, anxiety, and depression. In the face of rising mental health challenges worldwide, research on the psychological benefits of kindness is essential to develop effective interventions and support systems (Post, 2018). Also, acts of kindness foster a sense of social connection, trust, and cooperation among individuals and communities. In a diverse and often polarized world, understanding the role of kindness in promoting social cohesion and harmony is critical for addressing societal challenges and building inclusive societies (Seppälä, 2018).

Kindness education has gained prominence as an important aspect of character development in schools and educational institutions. Research in this field helps identify effective approaches to teach and cultivate kindness in young people, shaping them into compassionate and empathetic citizens (Nelson, K..; Shouse, R. C., 2019).

Workplace and Organizational Culture show that kindness in the workplace has been linked to higher job satisfaction, improved employee well-being, and increased organizational productivity. As organizations recognize the significance of positive work environments, Kindness Studies offer insights into fostering kindness and compassion in the workplace. Moreover, understanding the role of kindness in addressing social issues, such as prejudice, discrimination, and conflict, can lead to more effective interventions and initiatives. Kindness can be a powerful tool for promoting understanding and empathy across diverse groups. (Keltner, D.; Marsh, J., 2018). As technology continues to shape human interactions, the study of kindness in virtual spaces, social media, and online communities becomes increasingly relevant. Understanding the role of kindness in promoting pro-social behaviours and collective action is vital for achieving sustainable development goals.

The field of Kindness Studies for the future is new and has an interdisciplinary nature allowing researchers to explore kindness from various angles, making it a valuable area of study for creating positive societal change that is requested to foresee the new generations humanity aims. Rooted in compassion, empathy, and goodwill, acts of kindness contribute to positive social interactions, well-being, and the creation of harmonious communities. The study of kindness, known as "Kindness Studies," is an emerging interdisciplinary field that seeks to explore, understand, and promote acts of kindness, their psychological and physiological effects, and their impact on individual and societal well-being.

Kindness Studies draws on various disciplines, including psychology, sociology, neuroscience, anthropology, philosophy, and education, to examine the multifaceted nature of kindness and its significance in different contexts. The field delves into the cognitive processes, emotions, and motivations that underlie acts of kindness, investigating how individuals perceive kindness, how they choose to be kind, and the factors that influence these decisions.

Researchers in this field utilize a variety of methodologies, including laboratory experiments, field studies, surveys, and qualitative analyses, to explore the intricate nature of kindness and its far-reaching effects. What are the psychological and physiological benefits of receiving or performing acts of kindness? Can kindness be cultivated and taught? If so, what are the most effective methods for promoting kindness in educational settings and beyond? What role does culture and social norms play in shaping kindness behaviours and attitudes? How can acts of kindness be utilized to address social issues, such as prejudice, discrimination, and conflict?

The cultivation of kindness and empathy has become imperative for building better resilient societies and human relations in a totally interconnected world. Kindness has been taken for granted across many generations through history, potentially because it was passing from one generation to the next. With so many changes and ruptures going on, this essential skill for the future of humanity seems to be now at bay.

As a social bond, kindness has the potential to bridge worlds, include communities, and promote well-beingness (Mathers, 2016). Recognized as having an immense transformative power to well-being, the fact is that a smile can bright anyone's day. Kindness, from a scientific perspective, can be defined as the pro-social behaviour characterized by acts of compassion, empathy, generosity, and concern for the well-being of others. It involves intentional actions or gestures aimed at promoting the welfare and happiness of individuals or communities (Lyubomirsky, Layous, 2013).

The scientific definition of kindness encompasses intentional acts of compassion, empathy, and generosity toward others, with research indicating positive effects on well-being, relationships, physical health, and overall happiness (Piff, et al, 2015).

Numerous scientific studies have explored the effects of kindness on both the giver and the recipient, shedding light on its psychological, physiological, and social benefits. These studies provide empirical evidence supporting the notion that kindness contributes to positive outcomes in various domains of life (Otake, et al, 2006).

One notable reference is a study published in the journal Psychological Bulletin in 2018, titled "The Science of Kindness." The researchers conducted a meta-analysis of over 200 studies, examining the effects of kindness on well-being, relationships, and physical health. They found consistent and significant associations between acts of kindness and enhanced subjective well-being, improved relationship satisfaction, and even improvements in markers of physical health, such as lower blood pressure (Curry, 2018; Hui, 2020).

The profound impact of kindness on the overall well-being and mental health as acts of kindness do stimulate the release of hormones, such as oxytocin and endorphins, which can contribute to feelings of happiness, reduced stress, and improved immune function. Moreover, engaging in kind acts increases one's self-esteem, self-worth, and life satisfaction. These positive effects do not only benefit individuals, but also have an effect on communities and societies.

Additionally, research in the field of social neuroscience has revealed that engaging in acts of kindness activates brain regions associated with reward, empathy, and positive emotions. These neural responses indicate that kindness is not only beneficial for the recipients but also rewarding and fulfilling for the individuals performing the kind acts (Post, 2005).

This way, kindness plays a vital role in fostering social cohesion, which is essential for the functioning of any society. Humans are social beings, and it is this that encourages individuals to recognize and appreciate the humanity in others, leading to trust and cooperation. Thus, the education of the future citizen should go far beyond the transmission of knowledge and skills; but aim to cultivate empathy, compassion, and create positive change (Malti, et al, 2009).

At the same time, the future may also bring many challenges and difficulties, like the rise on anxiety levels, emergence questionings, existential concerns, feelings of hopelessness. Resilience, kindness, new forms of being become imperial for mentally healthy individuals (Weissberg; Cascarino, 2013). Future-orientation and sustainable practices are think-tank core skills for a new education that puts mankind and its survival at the centre of the world (Dovidio, et al, 2006).

This means educating for the future needs to be at the centre of our projects and planning. Together with it, training for teachers and related professionals is imperative, with a whole new role to schools worldwide. To boost sociability, hope, empathy by providing individuals with a sense of Anthropocene purpose and SDG's meaning to construct an equal and bright future for all requires a new sociability, a sociability that takes kindness as school syllabus (Eisenberg, Mussen, 1989; Knafo, Plomin, 2006).

However, excessive worry about the future can lead to anxiety, uncertainties, stress. All of this can deeply affect mental wellness. For instance, anticipatory anxiety, characterized by excessive worry about future events, can significantly impact mental health (Durlak et al, 2011). This way, providing the new generations with the abilities to deal with these sort of challenges is not only important to avoid mental occurrences, but it should be highlighted and pursued in the promotion of heath living.

Moreover, the field of positive psychology, pioneered by psychologists such as Martin Seligman[1], Director of the Positive Centre at Penn University, who has extensively studied the concept of kindness and its impact on overall happiness, and many other scientific data worldwide have already proved the benefits of engaging on positiveness. Apart from its critics as too much positivity can be toxic, or un-beneficial, positive reinforcement does promote self-confidence and self-worth. As Positive Psychology became the area of Psychology that emphasizes the cultivation of virtues, kindness, well-being, and social relations, it should be wise to promote these, than later having to treat the symptoms of these gaps.

Nevertheless, the skills needed to educate the citizens for the future are not static, and keep changing all the time, even more, in a globalized-techno society. Therefore, there is new demand and new challenges at the actual context. Now, new skills and needs are challenging us on how we are all preparing the new generations in a world that is under constant change and threat. The Imaginable Future Survey intended to cover this gap on what people were expecting the future to be and if they felt they were prepared for it.

The aim of this chapter is to present kindness as the one core skill for the future of human cohesion and social bond and to promote its education for the new generation in all school curriculums across the globe. The answers from the Imaginable Future Survey applied worldwide will be presented and discussed below.

This survey highlighted a series of crucial aspects towards the futures humanity wishes to accomplish and how imperative it is that it starts with core human skills such as kindness.

Imaginable Futures Survey

The Imaginable Futures Survey had forty questions with multiple-choice and open questions. It was designed and applied to anonymous people in all different parts of the globe through the internet. It had 313 participants.

As the goal of this study was to focus on the Globalized Future rather than on its local aspects, cultural variations, or pinch personal and specific demographic details of the responders, other personal data was not even inquired. The main goal was to capture this multi-faceted and imbricated Future thinking and Future imagining and how comfortable or anxious people felt towards the future they that they were expecting to be like.

Imaginable Futures was understood as a composition of foresight, expectations, scenarios, visions, which crosses one's thinking and relations when dealing with the future both internally and externally. This relation with the future is not only cognitive, but emotional, social, historical, sensorial. For all of the above, the survey had a variety of questions, which inquired about how someone feels about the future, the impact of the future on health and wellness, and enquiries about what each person would about the future, or how they thought they could get ready for it.

The answers to the questions were either multiple choice or open. This article will focus on the open answers and tabulate them according to quantitative and qualitative textual analysis. The survey was developed in Google Forms, and shared worldwide through a call and a link All collected data was anonymous. The Survey was shared through social media (Instagram, Facebook, and Twitter), plus what's app messages, and reshared by some groups and individuals. The spontaneous method of gathering responders was effective as it provided a wide participation from all continents and age groups. The possibility to access the results of the survey and receive a follow-up of its application also generated positive feedback.

The Imaginable Future Survey was fully developed in English, and responders filled it in English. Afterwards, results were automatically generated by Excel Table for figures and quantitative results, with the respective percentages. The open questions were also tabulated using Textual Analyzer Webtool[2], which extracted meaning from the open responses.

The whole procedure and research choices met its objectives and goals and followed the standards of Open Science, together with anonymous treatment for personal data. There were responders from all continents and all age groups as stated in the Figures below.

Figure 1. Age group of the 312 participants

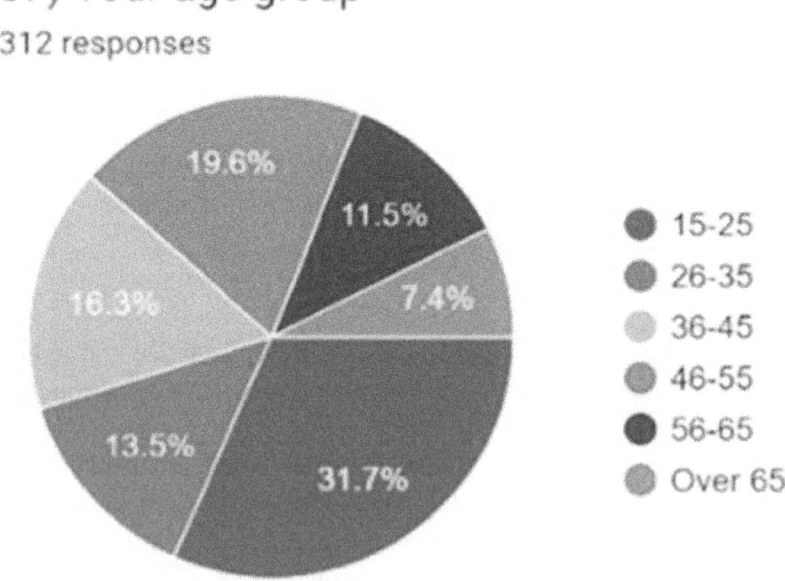

Figure 1 shows that there were 32.2% responders between 15-25, followed by 19.5% who were 56-65, 15.6% who were from the age group 36-45.

Next Figure 2 will show the continent of each participant (Figure 2).

Figure 2. Continent of the 312 participants

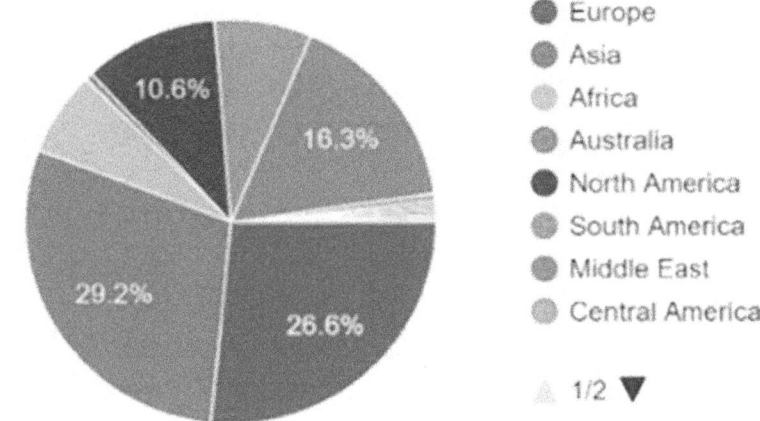

The data shows that there were 29% responders from Asia, followed by 26.4% from Europe, and 16.6% from Middle East, and 10.7% were from North America. As it can be seen in the Figure, all continents were represented. The diversity in the age groups and continents were important as the objective as not to address a particular country or age-group in specific, but to understand the globalized idea of the future that is disseminated through medias and interactions. Despite cultural differences, there is an enormous conversion of experiences that promote the unification of narratives and answers towards the future.

The Figure below shows the topics which were involved in future thinking, which occupies their thinking from very often to always.

The figure above shows that these topics, 1) a better tomorrow, 2) improvement, 3) climate change, 4) accomplishments, 5) war, are the most prevalent topics when thinking about the future. By looking at the figure above, climate change is the topic which appears the most frequently throughout the answer-data. Natural disasters are also mentioned in several responses, often in conjunction with climate change.

Another very important cited topic is war, frequently in relation to climate change or as a crisis in itself. Crisis is mentioned multiple times, both related to a global crisis or an individual one, whereas pandemic crisis is also mentioned.

The next related theme is retirement and leisure time. This shows responders are really looking forward to a time out of work. Retirement is mentioned in a number of responses, often alongside topics like leisure time and a better tomorrow. Furthermore, accomplishments appears in several responses, often associated with a better tomorrow and improvement.

Apocalypse and collapse are also mentioned in a few responses. From planet overconsumption to lack of physical reality sense, together with uncertainty, chaos, civil unrest. All in all, there are more challenging aspects than soothing ones.

Next figure inquiries about the emotions related to the future as it can be seen in Figure 4.

Figure 3. Topics involved in future thinking

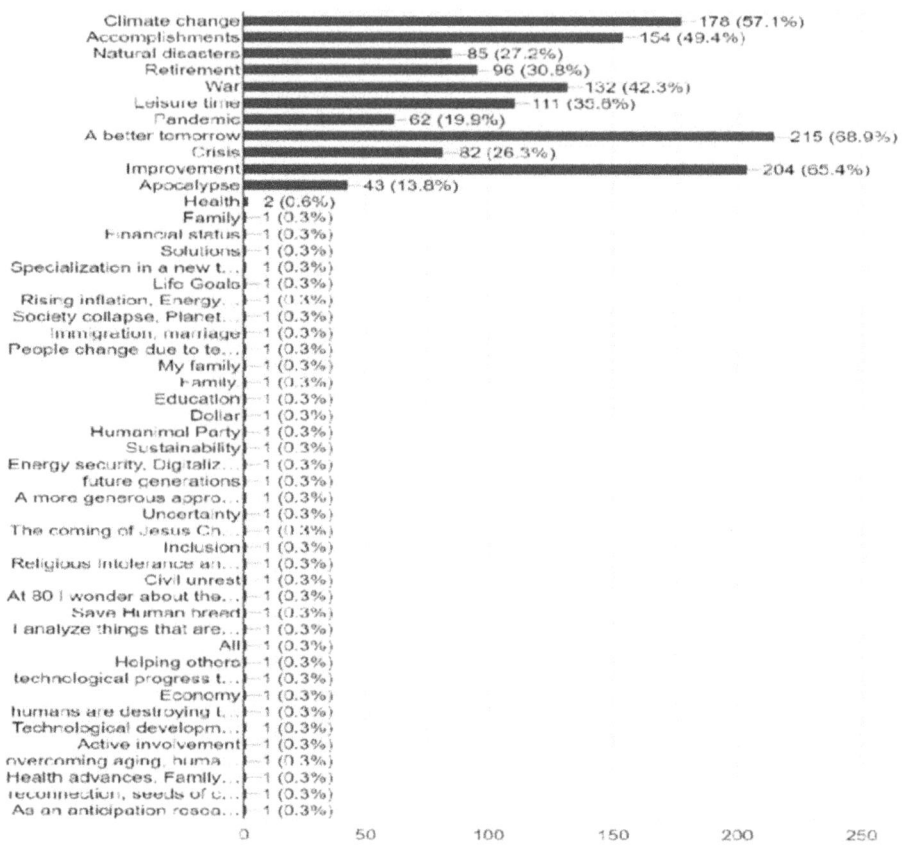

7) When you think about the future, which of these topics are involved. You can tick more than one.
312 responses

This way, the emotions related to the future are interesting with 181 mentions, followed by happiness with 173 mentions. Then, tension is mentioned with 127 answers, apprehension with 89 answers, sadness with 88 responses, calmness with 85 answers, controlled with 61 mentions, control and uncontrol with 71 responders each. Other options received 1 answer only.

This data suggests a range of emotions associated with thinking about the future, including positive emotions like happiness, calmness, relaxation, and interesting, as well as negative ones like sadness, tension, and apprehension. Some individuals also mentioned feelings of control or lack of control. Although there are attribution of positive and negative factors, it is possible that this attribution vary on what they relate to. For instance, negative aspects can be related to climate crisis, meanwhile calmness and other positive factors are related to a desire rather than a condition of the future. Each response is unique, but at the same time, imbricated in a series of factors relating both to the individual and the social.

Next is Figure 3, which corresponds to question 24, where it was inquired about what the future could bring.

Figure 4. Feelings involved in future thinking

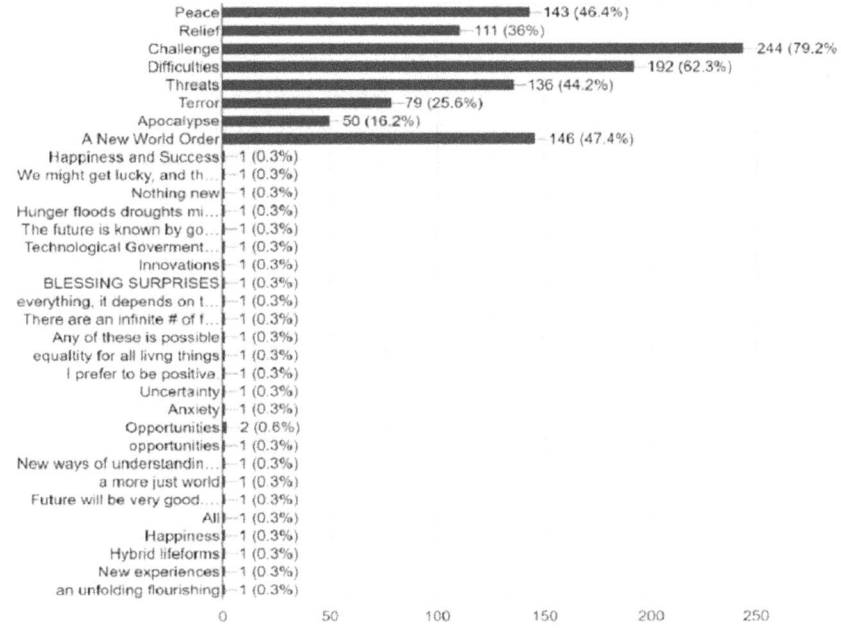

8) When you think about the future, which of these feelings are involved. You can tick more than one.

311 responses

Happiness	173 (55.6%)
Sadness	88 (28.3%)
Calmenss	85 (27.3%)
Tension	127 (40.8%)
Relaxation	81 (26%)
Aprehension	89 (28.6%)
Control	71 (22.8%)
Uncontrol	71 (22.8%)
Interesting	181 (58.2%)
Boring	12 (3.9%)
hope	2 (0.6%)
Rage	1 (0.3%)
Worry	1 (0.3%)
Anxious	1 (0.3%)
fear	1 (0.3%)
Absence of purpose, abse...	1 (0.3%)
Anxiety	1 (0.3%)
Suprise. Joy	1 (0.3%)
Expectation, Uncertainty	1 (0.3%)
Urgent optimism	1 (0.3%)
exitement	1 (0.3%)
Hopeful	1 (0.3%)
Son	1 (0.3%)
Adventure , Possibilities	1 (0.3%)
hopefulness	1 (0.3%)
It will be time of goodness	1 (0.3%)
All	1 (0.3%)
Excitement	2 (0.6%)
Opportunity	1 (0.3%)
Planning. Is that a "feeling	1 (0.3%)
passion, creativity, evolva...	1 (0.3%)

Figure 5. Aspects that the future can bring

24) The future can bring...(You can choose more than one option).

308 responses

Peace	143 (46.4%)
Relief	111 (36%)
Challenge	244 (79.2%)
Difficulties	192 (62.3%)
Threats	136 (44.2%)
Terror	79 (25.6%)
Apocalypse	50 (16.2%)
A New World Order	146 (47.4%)
Happiness and Success	1 (0.3%)
We might get lucky, and th...	1 (0.3%)
Nothing new	1 (0.3%)
Hunger floods droughts mi...	1 (0.3%)
The future is known by go...	1 (0.3%)
Technological Goverment...	1 (0.3%)
Innovations	1 (0.3%)
BLESSING SURPRISES	1 (0.3%)
everything, it depends on t...	1 (0.3%)
There are an infinite # of f...	1 (0.3%)
Any of these is possible	1 (0.3%)
equaltity for all livng things	1 (0.3%)
I prefer to be positive.	1 (0.3%)
Uncertainty	1 (0.3%)
Anxiety	1 (0.3%)
Opportunities	2 (0.6%)
opportunities	1 (0.3%)
New ways of understandin...	1 (0.3%)
a more just world	1 (0.3%)
Future will be very good....	1 (0.3%)
All	1 (0.3%)
Happiness	1 (0.3%)
Hybrid lifeforms	1 (0.3%)
New experiences	1 (0.3%)
an unfolding flourishing	1 (0.3%)

Based on the given options, it seems that the future can bring a variety of possibilities and outcomes. These aspects range from challenge (244 answers), difficulties (192), a new world order (146), peace with 143, and relief with 111 answers, followed by terror and apocalypse.

Again, it is possible that the desired outcome does not correspond to the realistic reality in which challenges and conflicts are so present. A new world order can also lead to different interpretations, and it may refer to a significant shift in global power structures and governance. For sure challenges, obstacles, and hardships are included in the future, but are people ready and skilled to overcome them? Aspects such as social, economic, or environmental issues can have a great impact and influence on what people desire for their own future.

Threats imply potential dangers or risks that can emerge in the future. These threats might be related to security, climate change, pandemics, or other factors that pose significant and demand solutions. There are threats also related to terror, which is noted as extreme fear and violence. This indicates the possibility of increased security threats or acts of terrorism, and war crisis.

Hunger, floods, droughts, migration, despair...these words highlight some of the potential negative consequences that could happen in the future, such as food shortages, natural disasters, mass migration, and emotional distress. On the other hand, relief indicates a sense of comfort or alleviation from difficulties, suggesting that the future could bring relief from current problems. Happiness and success suggest positive outcomes and achievements in the future, indicating a sense of fulfilment and well-being.

The answers mention the potential impact of advanced technologies on governance and the possibility of new forms of government or governance structures as well as future uncertainty, which implies in a lack of predictability or clarity about the future, indicating that there may be unexpected developments or outcomes.

Next, Figure 6 presents the courses and training necessary for being future ready.

By analysing the figure above, we can observe several recurring themes such as mental health with 216 responders, Sustainable practices with 201 answers, kindness with 194 responders. Survival skills, future forecasting, first aid knowledge came next with over a hundred responses. The term positive futurism is particularly interesting to designate a positive approach towards the future, and potentially, it can be very much well-aligned with Positive Psychology.

The interesting mention of kindness as a top response shows the gap that there is in the education process nowadays and where it should be directed to. Kindness is indeed a popular topic, highlighting a desire for personal and interpersonal growth. This may involve cultivating empathy, compassion, and sociability, leading to the construction of a harmonious and empathetic society.

Some of the other least mentioned topics were mental health, indicating a growing recognition of the importance of psychological well-being and the desire to build resilience, and promote mental wellness. The acquisition of training in first aid skill practice to help in emergency situations, can be explored through artificial intelligence, promoting basic training, and leveraging social cohesion. Future forecasting indicates a desire to understand and anticipate future developments and trends, which and if, translated to Future Literacy can be so much more explored.

War skills are also mentioned, suggesting an interest in historical or military knowledge, together with equality and social justice, internet privacy and safeguarding personal information in the digital era. Altruism is also being mentioned as the cultivation of collective responsibility together with spirituality and religious thinking. The diversity of interests highlights the multifaceted nature of individual learning, needs and aspirations.

Figure 6. Courses and training for the future

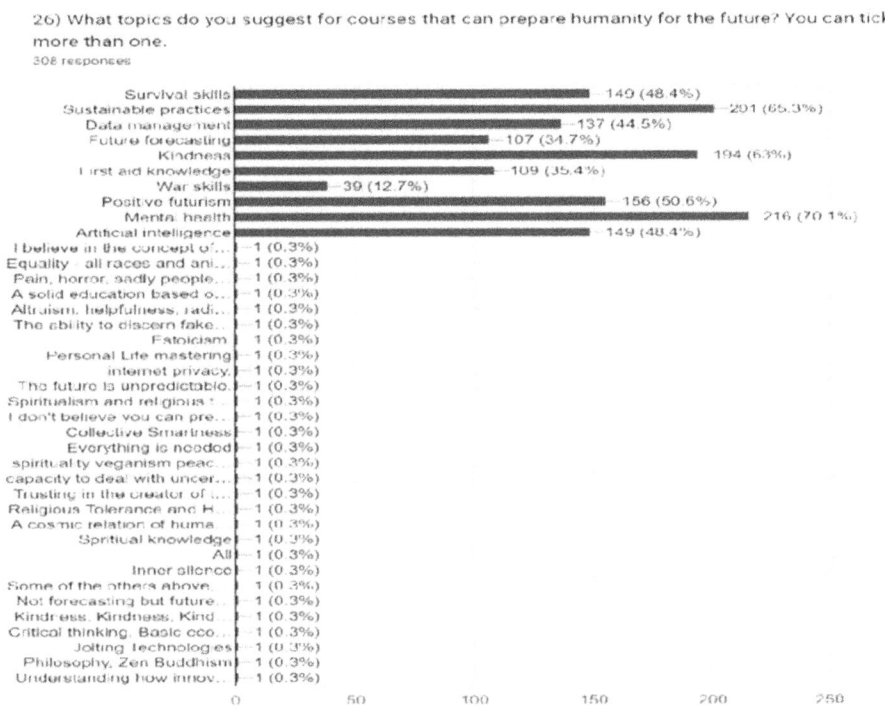

Figure 7. How humans will be in the future

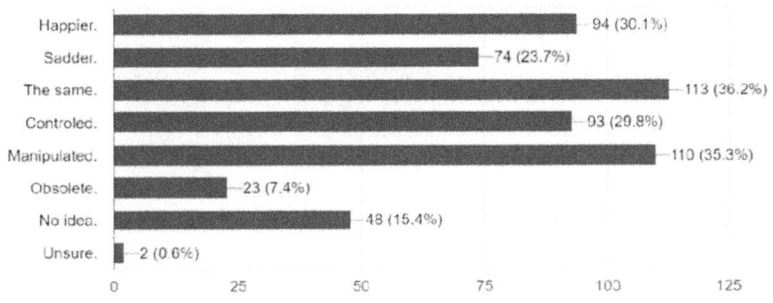

The next figure shows the completion of the sentence as what humans will be like in the next ten years. Answers were completely free and shown below,

Looking at the above figure, the results show the same with the most responses 36.20%, followed by manipulated with 35.50%, then happier with 30.10% and controlled with 29.80%, sadder with 23.70%, and no idea had 15.40% of the choices, followed by obsolete with 7.40% and unsure with 0.60%.

By comparing the results above, it is possible to notice a greater presence of answers which foresee a sadder, controlled and manipulated human being in the future. This can impact other aspects of one's life, from mental health to hope for the future. Also, aspects that relate to emotional and social intelligence are not mentioned, but the consequences of a rather controlled society.

Tables 1 and 2, along with Figure 8, refers to what the imagination (image) of the future for the participants was. So, they described in a few sentences what the year 2050 would look like.

Figure 8 shows the word density for this question, and it was generated by Data Analyzer Tool.

Table 1. Word density for image of the future

Word	freq	%
Will	271	8.15
Technology	51	1.53
People	50	1.50
World	44	1.32
Life	41	1.23
Future	33	0.99
Think	32	0.96
Change	24	0.72
Climate	19	0.57
Same	18	0.54

Table 2. Phrase density for the image of the future

Phrase	freq
will be	128
we will	35
it will	30
be more	29
will be more	25
I think	22
the future	21
it will be	21
the world	21
of the	20

Figure 8. Data visualization of what the future will be like

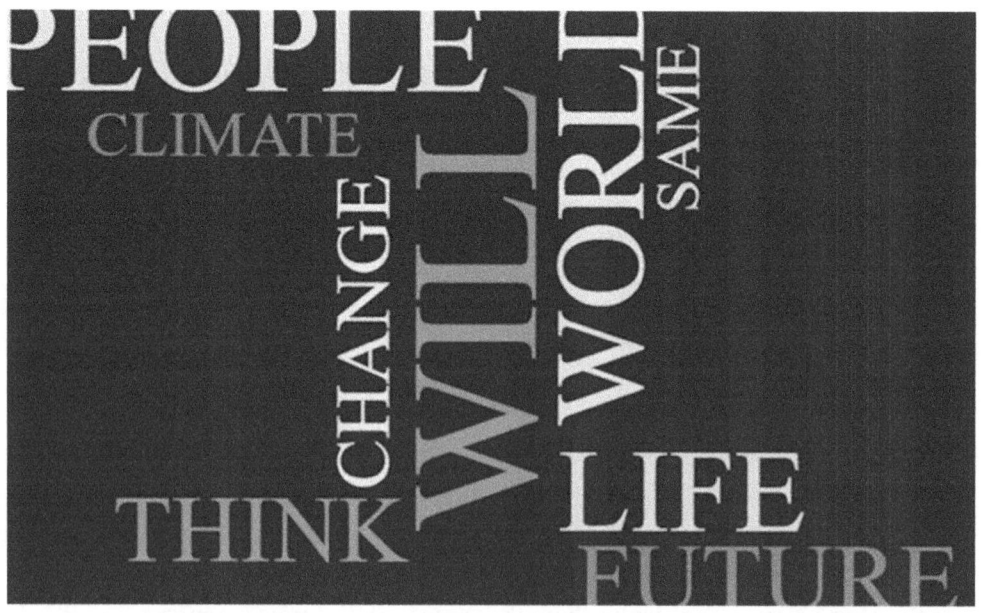

Word Cloud is a powerful data visualization tool, made by a collection of words and symbols depicted in different sizes and colours. The bigger and bolder a word appears, the more often it is mentioned within a given text and the more relevant it is. This format is useful for forming a summary by quickly identifying the prominent ideas, and this can be seen in Figure 8.

From the figures above, it is possible to understand that the future is a lot based on our own will, it involves thinking – climate – change, people, think, life; otherwise the world will continue the same. It is interesting to see how the visualization of the data from responders can be summed up in a picture that uncovers the meaning of the global future, which demands actions from everyone. Even further, it is possible to connect and make sense of these words listed in the picture. The future can change according to our will, that involves people, climate, change; if nothing is done, the world will remain the same.

Figure 9. Responsibility to construct the future

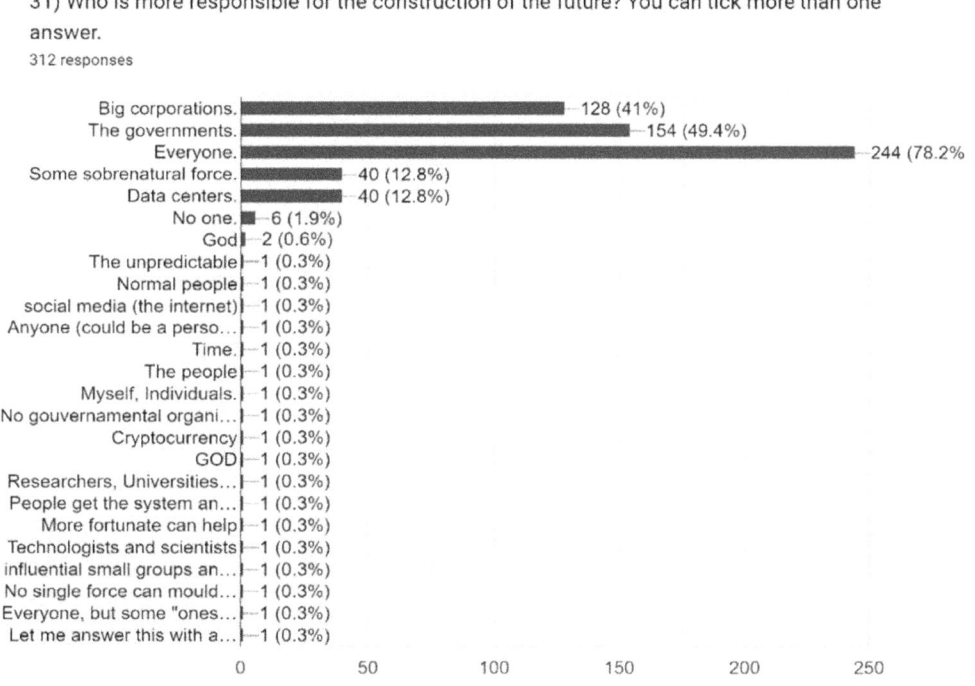

Figure 9 shows who is involved in constructing the future and it is important to point how clear the responders were on mentioning with 78.20% that everyone is responsible for the future, followed by the government with 49.40% and big corporations with 41%. This is very explicit in showing what shares hold the highest responsibilities. It is crucial to note that everyone is responsible to construct the positive futures which are aimed. Therefore, every single human being is implicated to promote the necessary changes so everyone can have better futures.

The selected answers of the survey to compose this article do show that there are many skills that need to be urgently addressed by educators worldwide. Humanity seems not to be prepared for the future and the view of it, although bearing many possibilities, is still encapsulated in controlled by uneven relationships. N0ew educational systems, curriculum and methods are necessary to tackle the challenges mentioned by the figure above.

Kindness is directly linked to positive social interactions and the development of healthy relationships, leading to a deeper understanding of diverse viewpoints and sense of social responsibility. By engaging in acts of kindness, children learn to recognize and manage their emotions effectively, leading to improved self-control, conflict resolution, and overall emotional well-being as stated in the cited references.

The results of this research foresee that it is urgent to reimagine education and pursue new skills and activities that are going to be needed in the future. It is, thus, urgent to review school curriculums and explore new demands and connections to the education of future citizens. By using research data from the Imaginable Futures survey, some issues become central in preparing the new generations for the future, and by all means, kindness is one of them. There will continue to be war and hopeless if kindness and connections are not reinforced and praised from young age, and competitions continue to rape human bonds.

However, many questions arise. How do we prepare to integrating kindness into the school curriculum? What is required to build approaches that goes beyond occasional random acts of kindness? How do we promote kindness within the school educational system? How do we create pathways to kindness measure? How do we train teachers for all of these?

To effectively promote kindness among students, educators, and policymakers, a set of changes is required and that is part of the discussion and importance of pursuing kindness as the core skill that brings humans together that is followed by item 3 below.

DISCUSSION AND CONCLUSION

Kindness, as a social bond, has the power to transform individuals and societies by fostering social cohesion, enhancing well-being, and promoting inclusive communities. By recognizing its significance, educational institutions can reimagine their role in nurturing the citizens of the future in a novel way. In order to integrate kindness in the school curriculum and prioritize social and emotional learning, educators can equip students - with the necessary tools - to navigate an interconnected world based on ethical and wellness principles.

Empathy, compassion, and the commitment to create positiveness can be a key-change in order to promote hope and social justice. Embracing kindness as a fundamental value in education can contribute to the development of a more just, equitable, and harmonious society. Nevertheless, a lot more is needed in order to implement that.

Educators play a vital role in fostering kindness and empathy in students. They can employ various strategies such as modelling kind behavior, facilitate discussions on kindness and its impact, and incorporate storytelling and literature that emphasize kindness. Cultivating empathy requires exposure to diverse perspectives and experiences, promoting dialogue, and encouraging active listening. By creating a safe and supportive learning environment, educators can nurture students' emotional intelligence and social competence, empowering them to become compassionate, kind, and responsible citizens.

Thus, to educate the citizen for the future means to integrate kindness from the beginning of the school curriculum system – at the age of six and beyond. By incorporating kindness to other contents such as core subjects, like literature, or mathematics, will help students to better understand the real-world implications of a future that needs being kind more than ever. Additionally, opportunities for service-learning projects, community engagement, and inclusive classroom environments can contribute to the development of more empathetic and emotional-intelligent individuals. All of that can surely be exploited through AI in a variety of ways. After all, to imagine a future where human relationships are kind-based is also to create a brave new world.

All of this can be achieved by a set of resources. For instance, by incorporating Social-Emotional Learning (SEL) Programs that explicitly teach empathy, compassion, and kindness. These programs can be integrated into daily classroom activities and focus on developing students' emotional intelligence, conflict resolution skills, and pro-social behaviours. Research has shown that SEL interventions can lead to improvements in social behaviour and academic performance (Durlak, et al, 2011).

To create a school environment that values and celebrates kindness can be achieved through recognition of kind acts, establishing peer support networks, and fostering a sense of community and belonging. Schools can organize kindness-themed events, assemblies, or campaigns to raise awareness and promote a culture of kindness. It shall also be necessary to infuse kindness-related themes and activities into the various subjects, such as literature, history, and science. This interdisciplinary approach can help students understand the historical and cultural significance of kindness and its relevance in a diversity of contexts.

Students can also be incentivized to engage in volunteering activities within their communities that directly involve acts of kindness. These experiences can help students develop empathy and a sense of responsibility towards others (Schreier & Schonert-Reichl, 2019).

Teachers and instructors may deeply benefit from professional development that emphasizes the importance of modelling kindness in their interactions with students and colleagues. Teachers can serve as powerful role models for students, demonstrating the value of empathy and compassion in daily interactions.

Technology cannot be left out, and for example, digital platforms can be used to highlight and share stories of kindness, encourage online discussions on empathy, and facilitate peer support networks. New assessment tools to measure students' kindness and pro-social behaviours need to be developed and can work out as trackers for the effectiveness of kindness initiatives and help to identify areas for improvement.

Some of the topics that can be introduced and integrate this new educational system are,

- Futuristic Thinking: to encourage children to imagine and explore different future scenarios.
- Emerging Technologies: to introduce children to emerging technologies like artificial intelligence, robotics, and virtual reality and discuss their impact on future society.
- Sustainability: to highlight the significance of sustainable practices and environmental stewardship for a better future.
- Global Awareness: to discuss global issues, cultural diversity, and the importance of collaboration in a globalized world.

On top of all that, kindness and these co-related topics will require new methods of teaching like, curriculum integration, Project-Based Learning, Future-Oriented Skills Development, engaging resources, new syllabus from books, to games, and online platforms.

For all of the above, some of the benefits of adding kindness in children's education can be 1) enhanced preparedness, 2) increased motivation, 3) sense of belonging, 4) emotional intelligence, 5) diversity of career paths and opportunities, 6) cohesion in humanity.

CONCLUSION

It is now crucial that parents, educators, and policymakers join forces to create a supportive environment for children's education within the very near future. To encourage partnerships with local businesses, governments, and organizations is a first step in creating needed real-world experiences. It is within the answers of this survey that brings insights, answers, and suggestions. Naturally, these are challenging times, but together with it, lies great opportunities. To create healthy bongs among human beings may be by far one of the greatest ones that humanity has never achieved. It is high time that it should be part of everyone's education as well as happiness (Salzberg, 1995), and even mindfulness (Nelson, Shouse, 2019).

This would also mean to achieve something we have never achieved as humanity, an education for happiness (Froh; Bono, 2019).

"Kindness in words creates confidence. Kindness in thinking creates profoundness. Kindness in giving creates love." - Lao Tzu. This quote is attributed to Lao Tzu, an ancient Chinese philosopher and the reputed author of the Tao Te Ching, a foundational text of Taoism. While specific references to Lao Tzu's original writings can be challenging due to the historical nature of the texts, this quote has been widely attributed to him and is celebrated for its timeless wisdom on the transformative power of kindness.

REFERENCES

Curry, O. S. (Ed.). (2020). *The Oxford Handbook of Compassion Science*. Oxford University Press.

Dovidio, J. F., Piliavin, J. A., Schroeder, D. A., & Penner, L. A. (2006). *The Social Psychology of Prosocial Behavior*. Psychology Press.

Durlak, J. A., Weissberg, R. P., Dymnicki, A. B., Taylor, R. D., & Schellinger, K. B. (2011). The impact of enhancing students' social and emotional learning: A meta-analysis of school-based universal interventions. *Child Development*, *82*(1), 405–432. doi:10.1111/j.1467-8624.2010.01564.x PMID:21291449

Eisenberg, N., & Mussen, P. H. (1989). *The Roots of Prosocial Behavior in Children*. Cambridge University Press. doi:10.1017/CBO9780511571121

Froh, J. J., & Bono, G. (Eds.). (2019). *The Oxford Handbook of Happiness*. Oxford University Press.

Keltner, D., & Marsh, J. (Eds.). (2018). *The Compassionate Instinct: The Science of Human Goodness*. W. W. Norton & Company.

Knafo, A., & Plomin, R. (2006). Prosocial Behavior from Early to Middle Childhood: Genetic and Environmental Influences on Stability and Change. *Developmental Psychology*, *42*(5), 771–786. doi:10.1037/0012-1649.42.5.771 PMID:16953685

Lyubomirsky, S., Dickerhoof, R., Boehm, J. K., & Sheldon, K. M. (2011). Becoming happier takes both a will and a proper way: An experimental longitudinal intervention to boost well-being. *Emotion (Washington, D.C.)*, *11*(2), 391–402. doi:10.1037/a0022575 PMID:21500907

Lyubomirsky, S., & Layous, K. (2013). How do simple positive activities increase well-being? *Current Directions in Psychological Science*, *22*(1), 57–62. doi:10.1177/0963721412469809

Malti, T., Gummerum, M., Keller, M., & Chaparro, M. P. (2009). The Development of Emoral Emotions and Decision-Making from Adolescence to Early Adulthood: A 6-Year Longitudinal Study. *Journal of Personality and Social Psychology*, *96*(4), 970–987.

Mathers, N. (2016, July). Compassion and the science of kindness: Harvard Davis Lecture 2015. *The British Journal of General Practice*, *66*(648), e525–e527. doi:10.3399/bjgp16X686041 PMID:27364679

Nel, P. W., Finchilescu, G., & Breetzke, G. D. (2017). Bullying, kindness, and school satisfaction in South Africa. *Journal of Psychology in Africa*, *27*(4), 335–339.

Nelson, K., & Shouse, R. C. (Eds.). (2019). *Handbook of Mindfulness and Self-Regulation*. Springer.

Noddings, N. (2013). *Caring: A relational approach to ethics and moral education*. University of California Press.

Otake, K., Shimai, S., Tanaka-Matsumi, J., Otsui, K., & Fredrickson, B. L. (2006). Happy people become happier through kindness: A counting kindnesses intervention. *Journal of Happiness Studies*, *7*(3), 361–375. doi:10.100710902-005-3650-z PMID:17356687

Piff, P. K., Dietze, P., Feinberg, M., Stancato, D. M., & Keltner, D. (2015). Awe, the small self, and prosocial behavior. *Journal of Personality and Social Psychology*, *108*(6), 883–899. doi:10.1037/pspi0000018 PMID:25984788

Post, S. G. (2005). Altruism, happiness, and health: It's good to be good. *International Journal of Behavioral Medicine*, *12*(2), 66–77. doi:10.120715327558ijbm1202_4 PMID:15901215

Post, S. G. (2018). *The Science of Compassion: A Modern Approach for Cultivating Empathy, Love, and Connection*. New Harbinger Publications.

Salzberg, S. (1995). *Loving-Kindness: The Revolutionary Art of Happiness*. Shambhala Publications.

Schreier, H. M., & Schonert-Reichl, K. A. (2019). Volunteers as Positive Youth Development Promoters: A Review of the Correlates, Benefits, and Potential Mechanisms of Youth Volunteering. *Child Development Perspectives*, *13*(1), 17–22.

Seppälä, E. M., Simon-Thomas, E., Brown, S. L., Worline, M. C., Cameron, C. D., & Doty, J. R. (2018). *The Oxford Handbook of Compassion Science*. Oxford University Press.

Weissberg, R. P., & Cascarino, J. (2013). Academic learning + social-emotional learning = national priority. *Phi Delta Kappan*, *94*(8), 62–65.

KEY TERMS AND DEFINITIONS

Education for the Future: Education for the Future is a dynamic and forward-looking approach that equips students with adaptable skills, critical thinking, and creativity, preparing them to thrive in an ever-changing and technologically advanced world. It emphasizes collaboration, problem-solving, and a deep understanding of global challenges to foster responsible global citizenship and sustainable development.

Kindness: Kindness is the quality of being considerate, compassionate, and altruistic, demonstrating genuine care and empathy towards others, often resulting in positive actions and behaviors that promote well-being and harmony. It is a fundamental aspect of human interaction that fosters a sense of connection and support in diverse social contexts.

School Child: A child aged from 6-7 to 18 years old who is studying in a general education institution (secondary school).

Social Bond: A social bond refers to the emotional and interpersonal connection between individuals or groups, characterized by feelings of trust, mutual support, and shared identity, leading to the formation of cohesive social relationships and communities. It plays a vital role in maintaining social stability and fostering cooperation among members of a society.

Social Psychology: Social Psychology is the scientific study of how individuals' thoughts, feelings, and behaviors are influenced by the presence and actions of others, exploring topics such as attitudes, group dynamics, and social cognition. It examines the impact of social interactions and societal factors on human behavior and mental processes.

ENDNOTES

[1]   https://ppc.sas.upenn.edu/people/martin-ep-seligman

[2]   https://www.webtools.services/text-analyzer

Chapter 17
Countering Children's Depression as an Aspect of Social and Spiritual Security of Modern Society

Tamara Stanislavovna Olenich

https://orcid.org/0000-0002-1212-9181

Don State Tehnical University, Russia

Margarita Vasilievna Finko

Don State Technical University, Russia

ABSTRACT

The chapter examines the peculiarities of the problem of depression among school children in the context of ensuring social and spiritual security. The chapter describes the problem of depression and its most negative consequence, suicide, and the reasons that push children to these social actions, among which the authors have identified the following: the social hierarchy of postmodern society, apathy and indifference of parents, the activities of religious cults and "death groups." The activities of death groups are one of the main causes that lead to a violation of social security and have an impact on the younger generation, committing children to suicide. The mechanism of work of such groups, basic techniques, and mechanisms of their work are described. The authors conduct a sociological study in local secondary schools located in the Don region to identify the level of depression among school children. The authors propose a number of educational innovations and other methods aimed at identifying and preventing depression in the younger generation.

DOI: 10.4018/978-1-6684-9295-6.ch017

INTRODUCTION

The culture of postmodern has brought youth a new type of culture and moral and ethical values that make influence on traditional culture, contributing to the spread of such a threat to national security, including a religious one, such as suicide among children and youth. Of particular concern is the spiritual state of modern children, the blurring and instability of their moral and value orientations, which leads to the extremely negative social consequences. The problem of depression and as a possible consequence – suicide is global characteristic and problem for social security for many countries of the world as well as for Russia. Therefore, in the chapter the case of how Russian state and society manage this problem, find ways for its solutions as well as effective mechanisms of children's adaptation in the modern society are presented.

Russia's National Security Strategy defines the very complex concept of "traditional Russian spiritual and moral values". In the Decree of the President of the Russian Federation of December 31, 2015 N 683 "On the National Security Strategy of the Russian Federation" in Clause 11 of the Strategy it is said about the following spiritual and moral values: history of Russia, freedom and independence of Russia, humanism, interethnic peace and harmony, unity of cultures the multinational people of the Russian Federation, respect for family and confessional traditions, patriotism (Decree of the President of the Russian Federation of December, 2015). In the new version of the National Security Strategy adopted July 2, 2021 it is also specified that "At present, the cohesion of Russian society is strengthening, civic consciousness is strengthening, awareness of the need to protect traditional spiritual and moral values is growing, the social activity of citizens is increasing, their involvement in solving the most urgent problems of local and state importance" (Decree of the President of the Russian Federation, 2021).

At the same time, the interpretation of these values and the mechanisms for their protection depend on the position of the government and top officials of the country used to pay attention to the need to protect spiritual and moral security, for example, working out special culturological course for the school curriculum, which would improve the spiritual and moral culture of school children.

Nevertheless, threats to modern spiritual security exist, for the most part, they are identified, but in this chapter the main attention is given to such an urgent problem as markers of depression of children, the reasons that contribute to an increase in the number of those who have depression and which has a potential to be escalated up to the radical form of suicides in order to propose mechanisms to resist this process, which are contained in the philosophical system of traditional confessions.

This chapter is aimed at studying the characteristics of depressions in the modern school children's environment in order to develop effective means of combating and preventing mortality in this age group by spreading traditional values and providing educational innovations. The analysis of the psychological and emotional state of the school children was carried out on the basis of a study conducted at the secondary schools of the region in 2021.

The authors examine the potential of culturological means to ensure spiritual security and the prevention of depressions among children. To achieve the aim of the study, the authors determined the level of a few indicators within school children: anxiety, depression, aggressiveness and a tendency to addictive behavior. The last two indicators were considered as a factor of influence of postmodern culture, destruction of spiritual and moral values. The indicators of the methodology that determine the level of anxiety were interpreted to identify school children who potentially fall into the risk group - subclinical and clinical anxiety.

LITERATURE REVIEW

School children is a dynamic social group, it reacts to the slightest changes in the life of society, can both reject the traditions of society and give impetus to their development. Group boundaries are usually associated with the age of 15-35 years. But there are studies where the authors indicate the boundaries of 14-40 years (Nesmeyanov, Olenich, & Plotnikov, 2016).

Among modern children, there are some trends and prospects for the general orientation of prospective social development, one of which is its religiosity, the degree of familiarization with religious values and the system that affects the experience and behaviour of young people. The cultural identity of modern children is undergoing changes in connection with the rapid changes in the socio-cultural environment, which a person does not have time to realize. In this case, an identity crisis can take on a massive character, giving birth to "lost generations" (Olenich, 2019). The social space of many modern societies is becoming more multidimensional in the system of social hierarchy, where new parameters of social groups appear. For example, especially striking examples of such changes are the socialization processes of youth sector (Kwiek, 2003). During the period of receiving basic (primary) education in an educational institution, a stratification of school children occurs, determined by the difference in their family income, professions of their parents, etc. (Lee, 2015).

Some reputable experts note the desire of children and adolescents to commit suicide during the period of modern changes, the destruction of traditional values and the spread of postmodern culture. In the definition given by classical psychiatry, "suicide is a voluntary, deliberate taking of one's own life. Suicide can happen as a result of mental illness, or it can be caused by problems in life" (Rakhimkulova & Rozanov, 2013). There are many factors that influence the theoretical risk of suicide: low social status; bad relationship with family, friends; dependence on alcohol, drugs, etc.

A feature of teenage suicide is that the child perceives suicide not as a "departure", but as an entrance into something as a kind of journey beyond consciousness. For a child, everything is as if for fun: "I will close my eyes - I am not there". After all, suicide is often a kind of call for help, a desire to draw attention to oneself. Children have no real desire to die. The idea of death is either completely absent, distorted or infantile. 6-7-year-olds consider death as "another existence". It seems to them that after death life will begin a new, only without the difficulties that they could not cope with. Therefore, children do not experience fear of suicide.

When they try to understand what death is, everything becomes too scary and frightening for them and especially for their parents. Parents regulate the situation by cutting off conversations. Having decided that it is too early for a child to know about such things, he or she is not able to understand yet. Thus, the parents avoid their responsibility and difficult conversations. A child who asks a question and does not receive an answer to it begins to be even more afraid, coming up with his/her own explanations. The child is unable to cope with his/her feelings. The end result is emotional trauma.

The number of teenagers who have depression and who may potentially do suicide is increasing in the world, even in prosperous and stable countries. The reasons are different: these are unsuccessful attempts to cope with problems in school and family, with peers. Parents often do not understand their children, impose their opinion on them. By their actions they exert serious emotional pressure on the still unformed psyche of the child. At school, the situation is exacerbated by enormous workload and fatigue (Zalewska, 2019). And these facts are about children and youth from the whole families. If we consider orphan houses, during the first three years after leaving the orphanage, out of 14,000 graduates of children's state institutions, 5,000 end up in the dock, 3,000 become homeless, 1,500 commit suicides, and only 4,500 adapt to normal life (Bayer & Pavlov, 2013).

A report by Sergei Korotkikh, an employee of the Main Directorate of Criminalistics of the Investigative Committee of Russia, on the discussion platform "The Right of the Child to Safety", provides quite alarming statistics: the number of suicide attempts among minors increased from 1,094 in 2014 to 1,633 in 2016. Moreover, in the first quarter of 2017, 823 such attempts were registered, that is, more than half of the total number recorded for the entire previous year. During suicide attempts in 2014, 737 adolescents died, and in 2017 692. The report notes an increase in the number of suicides that have occurred under the influence of the media: from 22 cases in 2014 to 105 in 2017 (Alarming statistics on child and adolescent suicides released, 2018).

Children's Ombudsman Anna Kuznetsova again raised the topic of children's suicides. Anna Kuznetsova calls one of the main reasons for suicide the activities of "death groups" in social networks. "From 2011 to 2015, the number of suicides in the country has steadily decreased by 10% per year. But in 2016, there is a sharp increase of 57% - 720 suicides. One of the main reasons for this situation is the avalanche spread of "groups of death" in social networks" - said Anna Kuznetsova during a conference call "On the prevention of suicides among minors" in the Ministry of Emergencies.

COVID 2019 has become one more factor to influence the children and youth. As the authors of the paper "Adaptation of Young People in Conditions of Self-Isolation in COVID-19 in the Perspectives of Educational Technologies and Sport Spirituality" claimed: "The spread of coronavirus infection by the nature of the threat and the psychological consequences that it causes can be defined as a psychotraumatic situation characterized by several distinctive features; the sources of stressful experiences are: firstly, the very fact of the existence of a potential danger of infection with coronavirus; secondly, media coverage of these events; thirdly, the economic consequences of the epidemic affecting the entire population (reduction of wages, job loss, etc.); fourthly, changes in the habitual way of life (staying for a long time in a confined space, reducing social activity, switching to home study/work, etc.) in connection with health-preserving measures" (Olenich, Terarakelyants, Shestopalova, & Biryukov, 2020).

It is necessary to mention the fact that there are factors that force children to suffer from the depression and commit suicide. Children and adolescents are influenced by external factors. Adults have a formed psyche, worldview, life goals and opinions. Unfortunately, in a society where there is an element of cultural blurring, it is practically impossible to give clear moral guidelines, although earlier this social role was fully performed by the Orthodox Church.

Of course, one of the reasons for the significant increase in depression and suicide among children and adolescents has become the spread of the so-called death groups, which choose precisely children and adolescents as their social base. An adult, having learned about such groups, will not even be interested in them. A teenager, having learned that his or her peers are dying, immediately begins to measure his or her strength with them and think about whether he or she could pass this "game". The desire to become socially successful and significant for peers becomes the reason that the teenager wants to be the only survivor (Galitsyna, 2017).

Sergei Korotkikh, an employee of the Main Directorate of Criminalistics of the Investigative Committee of Russia, confirms the influence of the Internet among the causes of suicide: "The targeted provocative influence using the Internet was confirmed in two cases in 2015 and already in 173 cases in the first six months of 2017. The prevalence of "death groups" has increased significantly. Until 2014, such groups were not known and were not registered at all, then in 2015 the victims` membership in such groups was confirmed twice, in 2016 - 20 times, and in the first half of 2017, membership in the "death groups" was confirmed 287 times" (Alarming statistics on child and adolescent suicides released, 2018). An alarming symptom that testifies to the spread among adolescents of cultural trends close to the cult of death and suicide is the spread of some symbolism. "The number of suicides has increased tenfold (from two in 2014 to 74 in the first half of 2017), with cuts, tattoos, drawings of whales, dolphins, butterflies, unicorns, jellyfish, various symbols and abbreviations typical for suicidal themes" (Alarming statistics on child and adolescent suicides released, 2018).

Such groups are being established as a pyramid: there is a group administrator who manages a set of curators who directly influence the teenagers. The experts who investigate the activities of the death groups have found a special document – a contract in which there was a special rate for the curator stated to show his/her work performance – number of children who committed to suicide. Moreover, it was written in detail how much each member of the community could be assessed, so for schoolchildren who are athletes or school leaders the curator gets more scores. In case of forcing a teenager to commit a suicide, the administrator pays the curator 25% of the cost of the "human soul", if the teenager refuses to do this, then the curator must reimburse the administrator up to 70%. This is shocking, and it is completely unclear how a psychologically healthy person can agree to such a scheme.

The peculiarity of the spread of "death groups" - specialized groups in social networks, is that - there is no active opposition to this trend in society and no understanding of the characteristics and mechanisms of their activity. Because the cultural and spiritual tradition on a macrosocial scale was interrupted by a period of "lack of spirituality" or "ideological vacuum", and at this time, traditional values are forced to coexist with the spread of various new cults, new religious trends, social groups, etc. do not lend themselves to reasonable restrictions. As a result, there is an immediate threat, on the one hand, to traditional values and their dissemination in society, which leads to a fascination with new, brighter ideas, and on the other hand, cultural diversity affects "immature minds" and leads to the tragic consequences in the certain social groups. All of this is a direct threat to the religious security.

Information about "death groups" is sparse: it is known that they are closed organizations with limited membership, which quickly emerge and quickly disappear, with minimal access to information about their creators. In their work, representatives of such groups use the practice of destructive cults, technologies of manipulation and intimidation, which are very effective in the youth environment. There are general tendencies in the work of such groups, for example, the technique of performing 50 tasks, which is aimed at zombifying and breaking the psyche of a teenager to make him an obedient puppet (Galitsyna, 2017). It is worth considering a list of those that can be found on the Internet, and it becomes clear that all the tasks of such groups have one thing in common: a special language of hints and symbols. This is the essence of any programming - a programmed person regards the most harmless hints as a call to action.

Death group curators use classic techniques that are applied in prisons and concentration camps, for example, the technique of getting up early or "04:20 a.m.". If a person gets up for 40 days at 04:20 a.m., within a month, his or her brain simply does not rest, since the phase of REM sleep is disrupted, when the brain recovers, which leads to a loss of the skill of criticality and analysis of what is happening (Galitsyna, 2017). Another, classic method to influence the psyche is overloading a person with information. Children are given not only tasks but overloaded with negative information to create a negative emotional background. They are forced to watch long-term videos of negative content, scenes of death, the violence of a person against himself/herself, reports of real suicides. Group members actively listen to psychedelic music (the most common music groups are PF, Twisted Mind, Beatroots, etc.). The peculiarity of such music is that it drives the mind of a teenager into a depressive trance.

In addition to sound effects, there are systems of visual effects: each "death" group has a logo. "Most often this is the symbolism of the gods - a child, thinking that he/she is a part of something important, ritual and accessible to the elect, perceives the logo as a tatem, which gives him/her power and impunity, subject to the instructions". Images of knives, blades, razors, scars, cuts and drops of blood on a white background - these pictures teach children to think about death and suffering.

Another technique is the use of special verbal characters. In the posts of such groups, there are many words with the letter "S" ("S" – smert', in English "death"). This is a stress word technique: words like death, suicide, fear, etc. are hidden between other words that begin with the letter "S". Thus, a child quickly gets used to losses, which in fact should have scared him/her: this becomes the norm.

Death calls are veiled behind beautiful philosophical verses. For example, "At 4:20 a.m. the whales will not wake up, the dawn will not wait for them in a quiet house. Stars from the sky will spill onto the rooftops. Are you playing with me? - I'm waiting for an answer". The hashtag contains symbolic words, for example, "#morekits", "# quiet house", "# dead souls", "# nya, bye", etc. - these are the logos of suicide groups. The hashtags f57, f58, d28, etc. are also common (Bebchuk, 2017).

Such a technique is used as a gradual complication of tasks, which was noticed by the parents who, in an attempt to save the children themselves, under false names, communicate with the curators and joined the game. "When specific tasks were sent to us under the fake page, we already realized that this is far from being a game. Children are brought down exactly step by step, at first it is simple: "Draw something on your hand", then it gets more complicated, it gets more complicated, then: "Go up to the top floor", then: "Go up to the roof". Next task: "Come to the edge of the roof". Next task: "Sit on the edge of the roof with your legs dangling" (Bebchuk, 2017). Thus, gradually the adolescent is led to ir- reversible and dangerous actions.

When a child goes through a part of the tasks aimed at breaking the psyche, i.e. the following tasks are a protest to parents. If a child tries to resist, they begin to threaten him or her with reprisals against relatives and friends. Then the mechanism of processing consciousness includes the most terrible stage: to form the absence of fear of death. "The child's psyche is tuned to the inevitability of this event, so the child commits suicide simply because of fear, because of the feeling of panic. At the level of biochem- istry, this is a panic attack" (Rakhimkulova & Rozanov, 2013).

Psychologists and law enforcement officers are engaged in the study of "death groups". The results of the work led to the fact that open access to groups promoting the cult of death on social networks was confirmed. Among them, the Vkontakte and Instagram networks are especially popular.

The reasons for the interest in "death groups" may be associated with an interest in the culture of postmodernism, which, as a new ideological basis, requires the loosening of the foundations of the ideal, as evidenced by the following factors: "Firstly, the idea of the absence of invariant basic truths for ob- jects of different classes (about the inadequacy of ideas about uniform criteria of truth concerning any statements); secondly, the idea of mosaicism, heterogeneity of modern objects of knowledge; thirdly, the idea of changing the tactics of choosing a baseline; finally, fourthly, the idea of the priority of the individual over the whole" (Abramova, 1989).

Now there is a process of formation of a systemic impact of "groups of death" on children who have turned out to be unprotected and, which is much more alarming, defenseless. It should be noted that the goals of the work, organizers and funding of "groups of death" are poorly understood. Certain public cases were covered in the press, but not detailed to avoid the "groups of death" Werther effect", however, this does not solve the problem of opposing the values of "groups of death" and the cultural identity of children, their interest in the cult of death.

It is worthwhile noting that in modern society, many methods and forms to fight against depression are being worked out. For example, the idea of sport spirituality, which means "is aimed at realizing the importance of a healthy lifestyle in life and a person's worldview, openness and desire for cooperation with many sports organizations and associations, and, consequently, the attention of the clergy to this area and the training of specialized personnel" (Biryukov, 2019). This idea of sport spirituality is evidence-based and it can be potential tool to overcome depression and problem of teenage suicides. (Olenich, Terarakelyants, Shestopalova, & Biryukov, 2020).

Nevertheless, above mentioned background makes it an interesting research question – to investigate the current psychological state of the children based on case study of the school children measuring how they react on the today's reality. The more ambitious goals are to work out useful tools and methods, psychological or spiritual, to apply working with the school children.

METHODOLOGY

The research is aimed to study the characteristics of depressions of the current school children to develop the effective means of combating depressive states, preventing mortality in this age group and working out effective tools for social adaptation for them. The research is based on case study method: the school children of the region were surveyed to measure the social and psychological climate and values.

The research hypothesis is that school children (7-15) are vulnerable and unprotected under the influence of depressive ideas taken during the quarantine period and self-isolation in the conditions of disturbing Internet content, when the old algorithms of life are being lost, which leads to persistent feelings "that the earth is slipping from under one's feet" to suggest the ways how to improve the situation and to guarantee the psychological balance within the them.

In order to develop a comfortable educational space, increase the efficiency of educational, educational work and the quality of support for the psychological adaptation of school children, prevention of negative phenomena in their learning environment, we used to organize a survey to test schoolchildren aged from 7 to 16-17 years old. This special psychological testing was conducted online within the schoolchildren who live and study in the secondary schools of Rostov in 2021. 7679 schoolchildren took part in the study.

The study was carried out using specialized, professional psychodiagnostic technique aimed at a point study of "problem areas": hospital scale of anxiety and depression (HADS) eveloped in 1983 (Zigmond & Snaith, 1983). Interpretation of the results on the hospital scale of anxiety and depression: The level of depression and anxiety is assessed independently of each other. For this, a separate scoring is conducted for questions assessing the level of depression and for assessing the degree of anxiety. Also to deepen the analysis 2 others are used as additional indicators: aggressiveness test (Questionnaire worked out by L.G.Pochebut). The technique was developed by L.G. Pochebut on the basis of the Bass-Darki questionnaire, well-known and widely used both in domestic psychological practice and abroad. The technique allows to differentiate such types of aggressive behaviour as verbal, physical, objective, emotional aggression, as well as self-aggression. Aggressiveness is considered by the author as a manifestation of maladjustment and intolerance. The second supportive methodic was questionnaire "Drug addiction risk group". The technique was developed in 1995-1996. Doctor of Psychology B. I. Khasan and candidate of psychological sciences Yu. A. Tyumeneva.

RESULTS

According to the Hospital Anxiety and Depression Scale (HADS), anxiety is an emotional response to anticipation of a threat or danger in the future. Today, when society, including prayer, lives in conditions of heightened uncertainty, fear for its future, the forced reduction of social contacts, the transition of learning and social life to online formats, a state of anxiety appears in many people and is generally an adequate response to an inadequate situation.

However, anxiety becomes pathological when a person either overestimates the strength of a future threat or overreacts to it.

Depressive state can be called a passing bad state of health, i.e. frustration, fatigue, discouragement, and feelings of sadness that occur in normal life. Depressive mood in some cases can be a normal temporary reaction to life events, such as the loss of a loved one or a habitual way of life.

However, severe forms of the depressive state are characterized by the so-called "depressive triad": decreased mood, mental retardation and motor retardation.

Depression (from Lat. Deprimo "to press (down), to suppress") is a mental disorder, the main signs of which are a low mood and a decrease or loss of the ability to have the pleasure (anhedonia). The following symptoms are usually present: low self-esteem, inadequate feelings of guilt, pessimism, impaired concentration, fatigue or lack of energy, sleep and appetite disorders, and suicidal tendencies.

According to the Hospital Anxiety and Depression Scale (HADS), school children were identified as "risk groups" with high (subclinical) and pathologically high (clinical) levels of anxiety and depression.

Table 1. Survey results

Number of People	Risk Group on HADS	Standard
Σ	1973	4363
%	31,1%	68,9%

Table 2.

	Anxiety		Depression		Anxiety+ Depression		Standard
	Subclinical	Clinical	Subclinical	Clinical	Subclinical	Clinical (Full or Mixed)	
Number of people	731	342	324	74	187	315	
Σ	1073		398		502		4363
%	16.9%		6.3%		7.9%		68.9%

31.1% (1973 people) of the schoolchildren who passed the test were included in the "risk group" according to the Hospital scale of anxiety and depression: 16.9% (1073 people) children have anxiety.

Moreover, 731 persons have subclinically expressed anxiety. This is the level of severity of emotional instability, anxiety, with which a psychologist can work (without involving medication).

And 342 people have clinically expressed anxiety, an anxious personality disorder, the level at which it is necessary to consult a psychiatrist for drug treatment.

6.3% (398 people) school children have a depressive state.

Moreover, 324 persons have subclinically pronounced depression, the level with which a psychologist can work (without medication).

74 children have clinically pronounced depression, depressive personality disorder, the level at which it is necessary to consult a psychiatrist for differential diagnosis and, if necessary, prescribe drug treatment.

7.9% (502 persons) of school children have the anxiety-depressive state.

Moreover, 187 persons have subclinically expressed simultaneously anxiety and depression. This is the level of severity of emotional instability, anxiety and depression that a psychologist can work with (without resorting to drug therapy).

And 315 people, who expressed at the same time anxiety and depression (anxiety- depressive personality disorder) were observed. There may be a complete (anxiety and depression are simultaneously expressed clinically) or mixed type (anxiety is clinically expressed, and depression is subclinically expressed, or vice versa, anxiety is subclinically expressed, and depression is clinical). In any case, with such an anxious- depressive disorder, a person should consult a psychiatrist for further differentiation of the state of health and drug treatment.

Table 3. Survey results, 1 course

	Anxiety		Depression		Anxiety and Depression		Standard
	Subclinical	**Clinical**	**Subclinical**	**Clinical**	**Subclinical**	**Clinical**	
Number of people	487	251	218	49			
Σ	738		267		317		2826
%	17.8%		6.4%		7.4%		
	1323						68.1%
	31.9%						

The results of the school children according to the indicators of HADS test are similar to the overall results for the entire sample of test-takers (see Table 3).

The results of the aggressiveness test showed that 12.8% of school children (874 people) have physical aggression, i.e. tend to express their aggression towards another person with the use of physical force. These persons are characterized by an active-aggressive type of response to stressful factors, and their reaction can be instantaneous and occur with the intention of causing direct damage or injury to another person. They are a source of tension and conflict; it is difficult for them to get along in a team because of frequent conflicts. During them they can show inappropriate emotional reactions, react rudely and aggressively. Moreover, 1.7% (118 people), in addition to physical aggression, also demonstrate verbal, objective, emotional aggression, as well as self-aggression. This type of aggressive behaviour leads to intolerance towards the people around and manifestations of maladjustment in the social environment, the educational team, when interacting with others.

The obtained results make it necessary to note that the emotional state is a dynamic characteristic. A person's emotional well-being is influenced by both negative external and internal factors. Last years are characterized with a high level of tension (a situation of a sudden threat to health, COVID limitations, high level of social uncertainty and unpredictability, loss of financial stability, etc.). External tension entails negative internal changes, which is reflected in a decrease in the level of mood, an experience of general anxiety, a decrease in vitality, and a shift in the prospects for the future. But over time, adaptation to external and internal factors arising under their influence can occur, and a return to the optimal level of emotional well-being.

The results of the research showed those schoolchildren who were included in strong emotional experiences in September - October and were emotionally exhausted. Having started working with some of them, we noted the positive dynamics of their emotional state, however, some of them still experience severe anxiety and/or depression, and therefore need individual psychodiagnostics, individual work with a psychologist, as well as doctors' consultations for differential diagnosis, and possible medication.

Thus, the identified "risk groups" according to the criterion of subclinical and clinical anxiety should become a zone of increased attention to their emotional state, educational and social activity and the involvement of these children from, first of all, curators, teachers, civic activists or parents (legal representatives). The curators of the groups need to ensure that the representatives of these groups and their parents are informed about the need to receive psychological counselling based on the test results.

CONCLUSION

Based on the results of the study, it is possible to confirm the hypothesis of the study, namely, that schoolchildren have an unstable emotional state and are extremely vulnerable in the face of any psychoemotional pressure.

The task of the school, primary and secondary education is to educate and prepare children for life in society. Parents, relatives, elders and teachers should be equally active participants in this ongoing process. We ought to care how to help our children become happier and more successful, develop their abilities and prepare them for the future they choose. It is also important for us to know what to do ourselves: to manage the challenges in our careers and families, to overcome our worries, anxiety and depression.

Therefore, one possible and most optimal solution would be to promote the traditional values among the children. The existing mechanisms of psychological self-defense of the population and the search for holistic spiritual guidelines lead to the fact that a part of Russian school children adheres to Orthodox values, even without having stable religious traditions in their families. At the same time, this group is real and can defend their values in opposition to the postmodernism. This statement is proved by the results of the survey hold within another social group, children of the senior school age. The sociological study was conducted on the territory of the Rostov region to clarify the attitude of the schoolchildren of the Rostov region towards the Russian Orthodox Church. As part of the study, 200 respondents aged 15 to 17 were interviewed, of which 38% consider themselves believers, and more than half of the respondents agree that worldview values are important for the spiritual development and psychological well-being (Nesmeyanov, Olenich, & Plotnikov, 2016). Orthodoxy is wary of destructive cults, condemns suicidal manifestations, considering human life invaluable. Suicide is considered by the Orthodox Church as a grave sin, leading to the death of the soul and the grief of those close to them.

The obtained results make it possible to conclude the primacy of religious security in the system of ensuring the national security of the country. Religious security should become the centre of the national security of society because it acts as a buffer for all negative trends, one way or another related to the spiritual sphere, confessional and spiritual culture.

Also based on the obtained results, the primacy of religious security in the system of ensuring the national security of the country can be concluded. Religious security should become the centre of the national security of society because it acts as a buffer for all negative trends, one way or another related to the spiritual sphere, confessional and spiritual culture as it is in the countries of the EU (Tryma & Salnikova, 2020).

Surely, it is impossible to resist the problem of suicides and the spread of "death groups" only with the help of law enforcement measures; effective cultural identifiers and behavioral models that mentally protect society from such manifestations of postmodern culture are necessary to work out. The religious security of Russia in this context is interconnected with Orthodoxy, which can and should act as a kind of guardian of the cultural and civilizational development of society, give impetus to vital spiritual interests and needs of the individual. A partial solution to the problem of suicides is possible in this value system, where human life is an absolute priority, and any encroachment on it is prohibited. In this particular case, we are talking about the mutually beneficial coincidence of public interests and needs, and the prevailing religious norms of behaviour within the framework of traditional confessions.

Reflecting on the problem of children's suicide associated with the activities of "death groups" and the search for cultural identification in the context of combining essentially different evolutionary paradigms, it is necessary to see the sources of crisis phenomena that have emerged in the spiritual development of the society, and the ways to counter these crises.

It seems right to create conditions for the formation of a civic identity in the younger generation, active and responsible positions in solving local problems of socio-economic development of Russian territories; implement social projects and individual rural tourism educational trajectories that can be effective tools for adaptation, especially for the schoolchildren who are at risk.

RECOMMENDATIONS

To acquaint the management of all educational institutions, teachers and tutors, school mentors with the results of the testing and provide them with the recommendations for the prevention of maladaptive behaviour of schoolchildren who are in the risk groups.

Invite the teachers and tutors, school mentors to the Psychological Support Center at university to familiarize them with the socio-psychological portrait of each schoolchild of the "death group" who has passed the test, subject to their responsibility for not disclosing the information received. Give recommendations to the teachers and tutors, school mentors on the specifics of pedagogical interaction with this category of schoolchildren.

To offer advisory and methodological assistance to the tutors and school mentors on enhancing cultural and educational work with study groups, contributing to the rallying of educational teams, helping schoolchildren in choosing healthy life guidelines through the development of their value-semantic and emotional-volitional spheres, their introduction to the spiritual and moral, traditional values, the promotion of physical culture and sports, a healthy lifestyle, to promote the maximum involvement of schoolchildren in the cultural, volunteer, sports, labour creative activities.

Activists of the local NGOs should strengthen the campaigning of their activities and the involvement in their ranks of schoolchildren who are not involved in educational and social activities, as well as to develop, conduct and encourage activities that develop socially significant values of young people, active life position.

Psychologists of the specialized centers have to conduct regularly full-time or online group training sessions within the framework of the "Psychological Club" or other organizational forms for schoolchildren to relieve emotional stress and anxiety, search for psychological resources to solve problem situations, develop self-help skills in stress, conflict-free communication, self-regulation and internal control, increasing general psychological adaptability and competence. The training sessions must be conducted on a voluntary and confidential basis.

To introduce new innovations: social projects and individual educational trajectories on religious tourism, rural (town and village) tourism which can be effective tools for adaptation, especially for the schoolchildren who are in risk groups. Efficient results received from such innovative educational tool as tourism are described in monograph "Global Development of Religious Tourism" in 2020 (Alaverdov & Waseem Bari, 2020). In the Russian provinces, there are cities that are unique and form the basis of national traditions and culture. Unlike big cities and regional centers, small cities have preserved their ecological, cultural and architectural resources and natural landscapes. One of the trends in the development of tourism in many countries of the world is acquiring the development of rural tourism (or neighborhood tourism) - the organization of trips over short distances for residents of large cities, which allows small cities to establish themselves as an important element of rural tourism.

Best practices and successful experience of other educational institutions make it possible to recommend to establish special centers which can provide psychological assistance and adaptation at schools during the academic year, even within online format, conduct individual consultation and mentorship for those children who are in risk groups, face-to-face or online, to establish mass and individual psychologicstual correctional classes with school children who have difficulties in personal development, a tendency to aggressive, depressive, self-destructive behavior, a state of actual stress, conflict, strong emotional stress, etc. Targeted corrective work will be carried out on the principles of voluntariness and confidentiality.

REFERENCES

Abramova, N. T. (1989). The boundaries of the fundamentalist ideal and a new image of science. *Philosophy of Science*, (11), 39–50.

Alaverdov, E., & Waseem Bari, M. (Eds.). (2020). *Global Development of Religious Tourism*. IGI Global. doi:10.4018/978-1-7998-5792-1

All-Russian Parental Resistance. (2018). *Alarming statistics on child and adolescent suicides released*. Retrieved 17 10, 2018, from All-Russian parental resistance: https://rvs.su/novosti/2018/obnarodovana-trevozhnaya-statistika-po-detskim-i- podrostkovym-suicidam#&hcq=UILOdnr/

Bayer, E. A., & Pavlov, I. B. (2013). *Pedagogical system of formation of vitality of orphans by means of physical culture and sports in the conditions of an orphanage*. Rostov- on-Don: FGBOU VPO "KGUFKSiT".

Bebchuk, M. A. (Ed.). (2017). *Sukharev readings. Suicidal behavior of children and adolescents: an effective preventive environment*. G.E. Sukhareva DZM. Retrieved from http://www.npc-pzdp.ru/nauka/konf_2017.pdf

Biryukov, I. (2019). Sports spirituality as a subject of theological and philosophical consideration. *Servis+, 4*. Retrieved from: https://cyberleninka.ru/article/n/sportivnaya-duhovnost-kak-predmet-teologo-filosofskogo-rassmotreniya.

Galitsyna, A. M. (2017). "Groups of death" as a means of manipulating consciousness. *Development of Social Sciences by Russian Students, (4)*, 30-34.

Garant.ru. Information and Legal Portal. (2021). *Decree of the President of the Russian Federation of July 2, 2021 No. 400 "On the National Security Strategy of the Russian Federation"*. Retrieved 07 10, 2021, from Garant.ru - Information and legal portal: https://www.garant.ru/hotlaw/federal/1472577/

Kwiek, M. (2003). The Social functions of the university in the context of the changing State. *Market Relations*, 2-31.

Lee, D., & Profeli, E. (2015). Youths' socialization to work and school within the family. *International Journal for Educational and Vocational Guidance, 15*(2), 145–162. doi:10.100710775-015-9302-x PMID:26101556

Nesmeyanov, E. E., Olenich, T. S., & Plotnikov, S. A. (2016). *Interethnic relations in the Rostov region: history, current state, regulation practices and prospects. Materials of the scientific and practical conference. In "Attitude of young people to Orthodoxy" in the aspect of analyzing the problem of interethnic relations in the south of Russia, in the Rostov region*. DSTU.

Olenich, T., Terarakelyants, V., Shestopalova, O., & Biryukov, I. (2020). E3S Web of Conferences 210 - Innovative Technologies in Science and Education (ITSE- 2020). *Sport Spirituality as an Educational Innovation, 210.* . doi:10.1051/e3sconf/202021017006

Olenich, T. S. (2019). The problem of suicide in the context of religious security. In Interdisciplinary problems of international relations in a global context (pp. 125- 134). Rostov-on-Don: Rostov State Economic University "RINH".

Rakhimkulova, A. S., & Rozanov, V. A. (2013). Suicidality and risk appetite in adolescents: A biopsychosocial synthesis. *Suicidology, 4*(2), 7–25.

Rossiyskaya Gazeta. *(2015). Decree of the President of the Russian Federation of December 31, 2015 N 683 "On the National Security Strategy of the Russian Federation"*. Retrieved 01 10, 2021, from: Rossiyskaya Gazeta: https://rg.ru/2015/12/31/nac-bezopasnost-site-dok.html

Tryma, K., & Salnikova, N. (2020). The Influence of Religion on Political Parties of the European Union. In M. W. Bari & E. Alaverdov (Eds.), *Global Development of Religious Tourism* (pp. 98–112). IGI Global. doi:10.4018/978-1-7998-5792-1

Zalewska, J. (2019). Practice Theory Revisited: How Flexible Meta-habit Complements Habitus. *Polish Sociological Review, 205*, 65–84.

Zigmond, A. S., & Snaith, R. P. (1983). 06). The Hospital Anxiety and Depression Scale. *Acta Psychiatrica Scandinavica, 67*(6), 361–370. doi:10.1111/j.1600-0447.1983.tb09716.x PMID:6880820

KEY TERMS AND DEFINITIONS

Death Group: A group in social networks created for a game, played by children and adolescents and the final goal of which is to commit suicide.

Depression: Rapid mood changes and long-term emotional reactions to problems in everyday life.

Innovation: A new tool, method or technology that provides a qualitative increase in the efficiency of processes or products.

Rural Tourism: The organization of trips over short distances for residents of large cities, which allows small cities to establish themselves as an important element of neighborhood.

School Child: A child aged from 6-7 to 18 years old who is studying in a general education institution (secondary school).

Social Security: A set of measures to protect the interests of the country and the people in the social sphere, the development of social structure and relations in society, the system of life support and socialization of people.

Spiritual Security: The system of relations between the subjects of social life, which provides favorable conditions for spiritual life and healthy spiritual development.

Sport Spirituality: An educational innovation manifested itself as a set of specific communicative techniques associated with mental processes of individual (cognitive and emotional-volitional), such as thinking, memory, attention, feelings, which in the process of sports activities were aimed at developing interest in a healthy lifestyle and adherence to social rules in the process of physical education and sports.

Suicide: A voluntary, deliberate taking of one's own life which can happen as a result of mental illness, or it can be caused by problems in life.

Chapter 18
Value Education in Elementary Ages

Hamiyet Sayan
Mudanya University, Turkey

ABSTRACT

Value education is the teaching and learning of values as empathy, respect, responsibility, etc. in schools. It aims to feed moral development and ethical advances to array students and equip them with the skills to navigate complex social situation. As an important part of education, value education is interested in developing moral values and ethics of the students. It also helps these students develop understanding and evaluating of the importance of these values like respect, honesty, empathy, and the like. They understand how to manage and live satisfactory quality lives.

INTRODUCTION AND BACKGROUND

Value education is the teaching and learning values such as empathy, respect, responsibility, Etc., in schools. It aims to feed moral development and ethical advancement to array students and equip them with the skills to navigate complex social situations.

Educators want all children to be ***educated*** for life, giving them productive and fulfilling lives. All children have the right to a safe, inclusive, and quality ***education***.

As an essential part of education, value education is interested in developing the moral values and ethics of the students. It also helps the students understand and evaluate the importance of values like respect, honesty, empathy, Etc. They know to manage and live a satisfactory quality of life.

Nowadays, developing values is not a critical aspect of education anymore. Education has prioritized winning exams, getting employed, and being empowered. However, as human beings, all are responsible for educating students about these global values. We all be aware of to develop the student's actual values, and we must develop them with the help of education. So we can design our school programs and estimate the role of these values in creating the needed human beings. We can enrich our school programs with the necessary values and teaching strategies. Understanding life and its meaning and its remarkable stories is essential for students. They are stressed so strongly to raise future human beings.

DOI: 10.4018/978-1-6684-9295-6.ch018

Tyree, Vance, and Mcjunkin (1997) mentioned that nowadays, children are in a complicated situation and composite values mass of the world. In the case of this world, children require guidance and help to learn and choose the values they need to learn, especially moral values like responsibility and respect.

To realize this aim is difficult, but as Srivastava said, "Teacher Training Institutes also have to play their part sincerely." Here is a symbiotic relationship between the curriculum of schools and the teacher education curriculum. Till the teachers being prepared are not practicing these values, they can never instill them in their students. Their curricular and co-curricular activities must be restructured in this reference (Stravia,2013).

FUTURE RESEARCH AND DIRECTIONS

This study has potential limitations. All the researches and projects are different, and compiling them under the same topic is complex. The subject varies on how you handle it and the cultural differences. When the world comes to the same point regarding the values of their benefits, it may be generalized. We are still writing about putting them nearer.

VALUE EDUCATION IN ELEMENTARY AGES

Value education is a central part of education. It gives particular importance to that aspect and tries to construct moral and ethical values in the students. The main aim of it is to have the students understand and give great importance to them. Value education differs for different developmental ages. All of us know that value education is necessary for elementary students. Research also concluded that it is required to teach values to elementary students. Value education creates a positive effect on the behaviors of children and improves moral development. In elementary education, children are in the concrete operations period, so value education must be suitable for this age to educate children on the ethical and social side.

Values as a Concept

In the literature, values are defined as everything from everlasting ideas to concrete change actions. They also can be explained as the standard for deciding the degrees of beauty, goodness, worth, or beauty.

Rokeach (1973) said, "Values are impressively full of thoughts about objects, ideas, behavior, Etc. That guide behavior but do not necessarily require it." That definition is related to the value of somebody. In other words, value is what is accepted as 'important' by a person or an organization. Examples may include freedom, courage, honesty, innovation, Etc. Value expresses the degree of importance of action or everything. According to Halstead (1996), values are defined as things that are considered "good," such as beauty, truth, love, honesty, and commitment.

The concept of value can be indicated as personal or social. If the values are related to the individual being, it is called personal value. Examples of personal values, freedom, self-respect, life quality, Etc, can be counted. If it is essential for the other's well-being, it can be called social value, such as national security, peace, equality, justice, Etc. Values help in determining what actions are best to take. Values are the beliefs and action potential of an individual or a social group about what is essential that motivate people to act one way or another. "Equal rights for all," "merit above all else," "dignity of labor," Etc, are representatives of social values. Values have a primary effect on individual behavior and attitude.

On the other hand, valuing is considered an act of judgment, an expression of feeling, or the acquisition of an attachment to a set of principles. Values can be covered as a constructive part of affecting the system. When the values are built, they become a base for input selections, feelings, and thoughts and a basement for affecting and regulating the system. Aydın and Akyol (2012) said that "values aim to reveal the best side of the person and provide him to achieve humane perfection by developing his personality entirely." They also noted that values enhance relations and commitment between individuals. According to them, "Value means the desire for a desirable thing and the humane attitude about events." (Aydın & Akyol, 2012).

Values have different sides, which are individual, social, and cultural. In societies, all aspects are based on moral values. Humane values are similar and shared with all cultures besides society's values. Humans are social beings, so they have significant needs and necessities to survive and live a social life. Because of an important reason, values are compulsory, and to commit them is also. Tezcan explains that (1993) values and beliefs must be harmonious with society. As Durkheim said, "moral education" is consulted on what needs to be done to achieve them'' (Bütev & Dolgun, 2018).

Values and Ethics

The most crucial difference between values and ethics is explained like that; values drive what is essential, and ethics drive what is right. Values are the best, the most right, and the most eligible for the ideals of someone or a group; ethics is all about concerns about how to take the right action. Values motivate morals, while ethics limit them. People tend to adopt the values of the society that they a grow up in. They also near to believe that those values are "right." Culture is the reason for this tending. Values can be defined as those things that someone values. In other words, values are considered valued or necessary by someone or a group. These can be counted as respect, courage, honesty, freedom, Etc.

Types of Values

Values can be classified into many different groups. At first, value as a concept can be explained as personal and social. If something is essential for individual well-being, it is personal value. For example, self-respect, freedom, life quality, Etc. If it is crucial for the other's well-being, it is the social values, such as national security, peace, equality, justice, Etc.

On the other side, values can be classified as the following: ■ Personal values: They are the values we take for ourselves and constitute an essential part of our values. We can see them in individuals' attitudes, beliefs, and actions. Examples of personal values that can be counted are honesty, loyalty, openness, Etc. ■ Social values: These values prioritize social well-being more than the individual. These values include justice, equality, liberty, freedom, Etc. These values must be taught at young ages.

- Political values: These are ideological beliefs to put the organization or the country of our own in the best position. Examples are Political values, democracy, and civic responsibility.
- Economic values: These values are related to money and property ownership. Those values include taxes, the balance of supply and demand, and so on.
- Religious values: Religious values are spiritual and include beliefs and living qualities.

Values vary among individuals and cultures, and time. We know that honesty, goodness, humility Etc form a group of values called Moral Values. There are other types of values, like Geniousity, Beauty, Power, Etc. However, moral values are rated highest among all natural values. Values can be classified as moral values, social values, spiritual values, intellectual values, economic values, political values, Etc.

Another classification of the values is innate or acquired values. Firstly, intrinsic values are inborn, like peace, love, happiness, compassion, and mercilessness. More values can be counted as respect, tolerance, responsibility and humility, honesty, Etc. On the other hand, acquired values are related to "place of birth" or "place of growth." Its also influenced by the environment, traditions, customs, and culture.

No matter how values are classified, the need to be learned and taught is known. For this reason, the concept of value education and the issue of where and how this education should be is gaining importance. For this reason, the education of values in schools is carried out through programs.

Value Education

Value education can be defined as a process in which people try to give and share moral values. According to Powney and others (1995), it is an activity that can take place in any human organization.

Value education is the emphasis on the development of the personality of individuals to shape their future. It aims to develop values for the future of individual and social well-being. It is necessary for struggling with difficult situations quickly. It shapes the children so they get ready to change conditions while fulfilling their social, moral, and democratic duties efficiently. So it became an essential role of education to develop values through their benefits, physical and emotional. Values also teach social skills, religious tolerance, brotherhood, and patriotism. Value education has gained more importance in 21 th century.

On the other hand, value education encourages the individual in society to improve the reflection on the solutions in various forms, the exploration of possibilities, the dependences of responsibilities, the preference of the values, and the orientation of the attitudes and behaviors (Taylor, 1994).

Value education is a central part of education. It gives particular importance to that aspect and tries to construct moral and ethical values in the students. The main aim of it is to have the students understand and give great importance to them. Those values, such as honesty, responsibility, respect, compassion, and others, can be essential for leading, building, and fulfilling a meaningful life (2023, https://ishiksha. net>value-education)

According to John Dewey (1966), "Value education means primarily to a prize to esteem to appraise, holding it dear and also the act of passing judgment upon the nature and amount of its value as compared with something else (Heilborn, 2019). " Durkheim states that social unity is bound to moral unity. It can be said that the "collective conscious" concept of Durkheim also includes education (Coser,2010). Firstly education aims for people who form societies to be beneficial and compatible with their community, and then society will favor the individuals appropriately and efficiently to the individuals. Education is also an efficient process for moral and social unity. According to Tan, "People need to be stimulated or forced to actualize their social roles (1990). Education is one of the practical processes and organizations for this societal role. Through that process, all people can learn essential value judgments. Aslan says, ''The function of the educational establishments is both to transfer the values of the society and to raise individuals that are qualitative of meeting the ideals and expectations of the society towards future (2019). '' Halstead states that (1996) values have a central importance for both the educational theory and the implementation activities.

Teaching value is affected by society. Family, community, and schools have a significant effect on replacing values for the new generations. Of course, a family has the first and strong effect. Parents, their children, and the older generation of the family are at the center of socialization. Children observe their parents or older and have the same behavior. The effect of the family is more vital and broader in the early years. When children are adolescents, they are also under the impact of their environment, friends and groups, and the media. Then, when they became older again family effect became stronger. There is another effect of values on people, and that is socioeconomic status.

Value Education in Different Child Development Stages

Value learning is a complicated process of acquiring personal values as motivational goals and principles that guide behavior (Schwartz, 1992). Values are also realized on the socialization side and represent various stable personal characteristics. As explained above, learning value is affected by many variables, such as school, family, friends, school context, and personal experience. Values are learned throughout life. In early childhood, learning values are affected by the interpersonal identification process with the parents. The behavior of the parents towards each other and their relationship and interaction style affect the children's core values explicitly or implicitly. Parents may tell children what is right and wrong, but the children never behave like they said. Because they are human beings and have their gender as boys learn how to behave as boys, and girls learn how to behave as girls.

A big question is where the child can start to develop a moral and values system (Kaya, 2012, 9). Which is a period Kaya says between the ages of 6 and 12 means the Second Period of Childhood values. It would be more effective for the values education to be given at this early age. Buzzelli (1992) says that many early educators thought that the moral development consciousness leaned toward Piaget and Kohlberg's cognitive development theory and Freud's psychoanalytic theory.

Value education differs for different developmental ages. All of us know that value education is necessary for elementary students. Research also concluded that it is required to teach values to elementary students. Value education creates a positive effect on the behaviors of children and improves moral development. In elementary education, children are in the concrete operations period, so value education must be suitable for this age to educate children on the ethical and social side. Researchers put forward some ways to do this importantly. For scanning, some of the values necessary for students are designated by the Scans Report (Wetzel, 1992).

Behavioral experts and educators obtained a list of essential values necessary for the life success of children and youth. They are honesty, autonomy, benevolence, integrity, compassion, courage, courtesy, responsibility, trustworthiness, and truthfulness. There are also other lists of educators and experts who have developed and listed the following values. For example, The Josephson Institute of Ethics developed the following list: respect, responsibility, trustworthiness, caring, justice and fairness, and civic virtue and citizenship (1996). Another example is the list of The Council for Global Education (1997). Their value set includes compassion, courtesy, critical inquiry, due process, equality of opportunity, freedom of thought and action, human worth and dignity, integrity, justice, knowledge, loyalty, objectivity, order, patriotism, rational consent, reasoned argument, respect for other's rights, responsibility, responsible citizenship, the rule of law, tolerance, and truth, Etc.

Educators and experts must discuss and develop the core value list which must be taught at elementary schools. This list can be created with the effort of all curriculum stakeholders. If this is done once, the next step would be to decide how these values can be taught. Huitt's research is "Survey of Desired

Values, Virtues, and Attributes." A preliminary study shows considerable overlap in beliefs among preservice and practicing educators (Huitt, 2003).

Halstead and Taylor have researched (2000) about learning and teaching values and education of the values. They listed and examined in experimental teaching of values. The values are here: self-control, patience, respect, justice, friendship, honesty, love, responsibility, patriotism, and helpfulness.

Importance and Benefits of Teaching Values in Elementary Schools

Value education is how students are taught to develop necessary values. It helps them to become good persons and responsible citizens. There are many benefits of value education in elementary schools. They guide the children to select suitable and wrong, and it also helps them to develop their characters. It also teaches them how to make good choices in life and be responsible for their actions. They learn to respect other people. They also help the students to be valuable individuals in society. Value education develops children's character, including kindness, honesty, the right choice, self-confidence, raising the right choice skills, a strong personality, reacting against injustice, and responsibility for others. In character development, moral values help too much helpful. The Ministry of National Education (MEB) plans a value education program for elementary schools in Turkey. There is an example of the program prepared in Malatya. The values are designed like that: helpfulness and solidarity, cleanliness, truthfulness, honesty, tolerance, and love are seen as respect, patience, family and community, and justice and responsibility. This ranking and decision-making may differ. However, it may be possible to highlight more abstract values and add different necessary values (2018).

This example is a work that has been carried out. Sub-concepts and their teaching have also been tried to be specified in the program. It can be viewed as a framework that can be customized according to the needs. For example, values such as healthy living and environmental protection should be of primary importance for children during primary school and in terms of realizing future and social responsibilities. Values that may differ from society to society and region to region under the influence of various factors can be prioritized by comparing them with the universality measure and the need (www.meb.gov.tr).

Value education must be given to children at the age of childhood. So that children can find the right way to follow. They can obey the rules of the society with the help of them. For that reason, the elementary curriculum is essential to give the children critical values at a crucial age for their future social life. Halstead and Taylor (2000) have researched learning and teaching values and education of the values. These values are here: self-control, patience, respect, justice, friendship, honesty, love, responsibility, patriotism, and helpfulness.

Teaching moral values means building the children's character and their social life. Moral values also guide wrong and right, and they can vary from person to person and in the culture in which people are raised. Moral values must be taught in elementary schools. They can be a part of the curriculum of the school. Besides curriculum, teachers have significant roles in teaching moral values, too. Moral values prepare children for social life and develop their emotional bits of intelligence as they are connected to problem-solving and other cognitive skills (Saphiro, 1999). Sari (2013) emphasizes the importance of teaching moral values to students. It is vital to raise moral values at elementary school even before it. Early ages and childhood are suitable for building to have them along their life.

Values Children Learn at Elementary Ages

Teaching values in elementary school is also fundamental. Constructing moral values needs to be careful, and it is essential for people's character, so they need to be taught carefully at the childhood stage of their life. At the age of childhood, value education must be given to children so that children can find the right way to follow with the help of education. They can differentiate right and wrong easily and have the necessary emotional argument to decide to take action. They can obey the rules of the society with the help of them. For that reason, the elementary curriculum is essential to give the children critical values at a crucial age for their future social life.

Moral values must be taught in elementary schools. Teaching moral values means building the children's character and their social life. Moral values also guide wrong and right, and they can vary from person to person and in the culture in which people are raised. To succeed in this attempt, value education must be a part of the school's curriculum. Besides curriculum, teachers have prominent roles in teaching moral values, too. Moral values prepare children for social life and develop their emotional bits of intelligence as they are connected to problem-solving and other cognitive skills (Saphiro, 1999). Sari emphasizes the importance of teaching moral values to students (2013). Even before, in early childhood, giving some fundamental values is suitable to have them throughout their life. As we can see, the benefits of teaching values in elementary schools are worth struggling with.

Behavioral experts and educators created a list of essential values necessary for the life success of students and youth. They are honesty, autonomy, benevolence, integrity, compassion, courage, courtesy, responsibility, trustworthiness, and truthfulness. There are also other lists of educators and experts that have developed. For example, The Josephson Institute of Ethics developed the following list: respect, responsibility, trustworthiness, caring, justice and fairness, and civic virtue and citizenship (The Character Education Partnership, Inc., 1996). Another example is the list of The Council for Global Education (1997). Their value set includes compassion, courtesy, critical inquiry, due process, equality of opportunity, freedom of thought and action, human worth and dignity, integrity, justice, knowledge, loyalty, objectivity, order, patriotism, rational consent, reasoned argument, respect for other's rights, responsibility, responsible citizenship, the rule of law, tolerance, and truth, Etc.

Educators and experts must discuss and develop the core value list which must be taught at elementary schools. This list can be created with the effort of all curriculum stakeholders. If this is done once, the next step would be to decide how these values can be taught. Huitt's research is called "Survey of Desired Values, Virtues, and Attributes." A preliminary study shows considerable overlap in beliefs among preservice and practicing educators (Huitt, 2003, https://www.edpsycinteractive.org/topics/affect/values.html)

There are some core values generally parent love for the kids to have. However, it needs to be clarified how we teach those values. Educators suggest ways of giving these values and having the children internalize them as they grow up. Generally, parents want to instill big-picture values in their kids as they grow and explore the world around them. In the beginning, this goal can be seen as complicated and complex. When we are teaching values of honesty and respect, children feel fear of achieving these tasks.

Nevertheless, it can be taught quickly, and children achieve it in small amounts. We can put some central values many parents are eager to teach their children and educators recommend. Here are some central values we all like to see children have them.

In the study of Espinoza and Fernandez (2022), the frequency of values can count in this line. Values most promoted in primary school because of the word frequency and values can count in the line below;

1. generosity
2. respect
3. responsibility
4. charity
5. joy
6. honesty

They are also grouped by domains of the values mentioned in primary education.

1) generosity, kindness, charity, solidarity, empathy, conviviality, community, friendship, companionship, friendliness, friendliness, cordiality, justice, obedience, trust, piety, forgiveness, gratitude, respect, honesty, sincerity, integrity, modesty, chastity
2) responsibility, orderliness, commitment, perseverance, effort, courage, punctuality, self-control, self-regulation, self-esteem, excellence, temperance, patience, humility, optimism, cheerfulness
3) faith, hope, charity
4) truth, prudence, and intelligence.

On the other hand, different values are recommended to teach at elementary stages. Honesty, responsibility, respect, love, consideration, perseverance, courage, justice, and happiness are commonly mentioned values. There are similar values or can be grouped in the same group, but their names differ. For example, patience is identical to perseverance. Other values can be taught at elementary schools. They are justice, responsibility, respect, love, happiness, manners, patriotism, self-control, friendship, charity, helpfulness, Etc.

Parents must be conscientious about their behaviors in the early years to be models for their children. The children typically learn from their experiences. Here are some experienced ways to use teaching values to children.

Honesty

When acquiring values, kids typically learn from what they experience. This means that to develop a truthful disposition in your child, your best tactic is to model honesty as much as possible.

According to psychotherapists, modeling is the most effective method for teaching values to children, and no way can be compared to this issue. If children see their parents dealing with people honestly, that is the best lesson for the child, they say. Even telling the truth is difficult; we must consider its worth to the children. That means you teaching the value of honesty.

Accountability

A significant value for a child is accountability for learning. Because this value finds roots and lays the foundation of the child's future acts in daily life.

Parents must be aware that children are recording their behavior of rule-breaking. When they become the owners of their actions free of parents' guidance, kids know ahead of time that if there are rules that they break, there will be consequences.

Even though the foundation of accountability begins with the parent-child relationship, its test starts at school age. So this value is an essential issue for elementary schools. Teaching values is more complex than setting the expectation of right and wrong because more than teaching is needed. Case schools must teach them how to solve problems according to their values.

Children feel in a complex situation against concepts like moral reasoning and an ethical dilemma that contradicts the family's values. As the children grow up and mature or rise to the class level, they become understanding of reasoning. Accountability behind their values helps them face peer pressure and more complex problems.

Curiosity

Why is this the most popular question for parents and teachers? It is necessary to feed that curiosity.

Educators and parents feed the curiosity. Curiosity is essential for understanding values and life in a significant context.

Educators and parents can ponder some critical questions in the children's life and must have ways to approach these why questions in their tracks. While teaching this, life experiences can be explained in a different freeway.

Respect

As a primary value, learning respect is vital to guide children when they begin school and in the classroom. Children need it for simple tasks such as waiting one's turn to speak and following their teacher's directions. It is also required for complex tasks like understanding the world and context that differ from theirs.

At elementary ages, children are eager to listen to others' views. They can discuss religious concepts at that stage. What situations allow us to watch the children's world and teach related values? Some can think religiously, others look atheistic, and some are willing to explore the questions.

In school classrooms, children can listen to each other, And many kept saying, Every child has their way of thinking, and it is interesting to hear how other children think.

To teach respect during the discussion in the classroom, outside of it, educators have many opportunities while the children grow. Parents and educators want children to learn some central values. The most important one is respect. If children have respect for others, they will live a good life and appreciate the issues suitably. This would develop the children and their thinking skills.

Empathy

Empathy is the ability to understand other people and communicate with them easily. This value is another primary value that children need the help of it to connect with others in their lives. If they have empathy, they can feel others' feelings and their view of them.

Teaching empathy may sometimes require a concrete approach. Playtime can be a good opportunity for teaching it. Playtime offers a child a social setting to explore their context and feel their sense of self and how they interact with others.

When the children get older and make friends, empathy becomes more critical. Then beyond building relationships with others, this value helps to avoid conflict as children can think about another side of the discussion and think about the solution. Children then begin to feel more powerful in the situation and interactions they act in some kind or another. They have a positive effect with the support of this value.

Determination

Generally, a determination needs to be understood as if it is being adventurous. Determination is the ability of children to encounter situations with the resolve to try their best, even if they feel nervous or afraid.

If teachers and parents do everything they can to help their children succeed, they can also learn unintentionally and get the lesson when they struggle.

Communication

As educators or parents, open communication is another significant value to instill in children. So the child can express their wants, thoughts, needs, and concerns freely. They also produce solutions or productive ways for the situations. This approach ensures a successful relationship, too.

The Ministry of National Education plans a value education program for elementary schools in Turkey. There is an example of the program prepared in Malatya. The values are designed: helpfulness and solidarity, cleanliness, truthfulness and honesty, tolerance, respect, patience, family and community love, justice, and responsibility. This ranking and decision-making may differ. Although it may be possible to highlight more abstract values and add different values needed, this work has been carried out. Sub-concepts and their teaching have also been tried to be specified in the program. It can be viewed as a framework that can be customized according to the needs. For example, values such as healthy living and environmental protection should be of primary importance for children during primary school and in terms of realizing future and social responsibilities.

Values that may differ from society to society and region to region under the influence of various factors can be prioritized by comparing them with the universality and need measures.

Implementing Value Teaching in Elementary School

Value education can be carried out in different ways, such as experimental, direct instruction, and modeling. Some successful curricula give students value successfully (Akanksha, 2013). Value education as an activity can take place everywhere by individuals or groups. This kind of education is more suitable at any time, place, or form. While giving value education, educators must decide about specific values to teach first. These values are taught in formal schools at the stage of elementary, middle, and high schools.

However, whatever method, strategy, and technique is used, it is only a moral ideal to bring all students to an excellent character. Even the best character or character education shows a convergence to this ideal. For this reason, educators are often responsible for providing a healthy ethical environment for students rather than whether they can achieve their moral development.

Values can be taught everywhere. Value education is affected by culture and context. So in different countries, the value of education has various factors and must have different approaches to teaching.

Nowadays, schools and national education institutions try to give value education with their curriculum. Value education is how students are taught to develop moral values. The effect of this education makes the children responsible citizens when they become adults. We can count many advantages of value education given at elementary schools. This education shows the right way to select the right way. Education instills the students to choose right and wrong. It also builds their character and makes it suitable. More, values education teaches children how to make their future good choices and build a good life for society and individuals. It guides people on how to be responsible for their actions and also how they can make the right choice in daily life. They learn to respect other people. Again it also helps the students to be good people and valuable individuals in society. Value education develops children's character, including kindness, honesty, the right choice, self-confidence-raising, proper choice skills, strong personality, reacting against injustice, and responsibility for others.

How is Value Education Taught in Elementary Schools

In the early years and at elementary ages, open conversation is always an effective way to teach values. Even adolescents like to talk about more philosophical concepts. This relationship gives the children openness and mutuality and makes them feel respected. Moreover, the child may be shy, but this kind of communication allows them to succeed practically in their social context. Even they can go beyond, and this experiment positively supports their personality. Then they can easily explain their feelings and needs and construct a positive relationship.

There are different approaches to value education. Value education is a crucial attempt and must be planned and observed. Superka, Ahrens, & Hedstrom (1976) state that there are five basic approaches to values education. They are inculcation, moral development, analysis, value clarification, and action learning.

Inculcation

Value education can be thought of as a process of students learning and internalizing, even admitting the values as beliefs. Some educators view valuing as an inculcation process and a socially accepted standard in the education process. In contrast, others recognize it as a natural ordering system of universal design: a universal natural system or the rules of God. If educators view it like social standards, they use the process of value education to inculcate all the practices of social valuing at school. They teach values as the means of culture and social institutions, and the students corporate with them, learn, and internalize them. Talcott and Parsons (1951) believe that society's needs and goals should transcend and even define the needs and goals of individuals. Some say personal freedom and happiness are more important than social beliefs. Individual freedom, justice, Etc, are absolute values that should be considered. Both social and personal values must be in a good balance.

The materials developed by the Georgia Department of Education (1997), the work of William Bennett (e.g., 1993), and The Character Education Institute (CEI) also promote inculcation.

Moral Development has a special care for the educators to teach because moral consciousness develops in special order stages. This approach is based on the work of Lawrence Kohlberg (1969, 1984). Kohlberg states six steps and twenty-five moral concepts. These values are fairness, justice, equity, and human dignity; other values (social, personal, and aesthetic) are usually not considered. It is admitted that children develop moral values in unique and standard stages related to their developmental stages. If a child is in a low setting, he can comprehend the situation in their moral location. -Educators must enhance the students' moral levels.

Analysis

This approach to value education ideas stems from social science educators' suggestions. It was supposed to be rational thinking and reasoning. Education must help the students with logical thinking and follow scientific questioning while relating to values. So valuing includes the cognitive processes and developmental dilemmas presented in the moral development approach. The methods of this approach for teaching values are at the center of group study or individual problems. Teaching methods can be group discussions, social issues of individuals or groups, field research, Etc. These are techniques widely used in social studies instruction. According to this approach, teaching will be individual or group-centered activity trying to find solutions to problems.

Values Clarification

This approach is based on individual participation in the process, self-actualization, deciding the choice and reacting according to their values. This approach was created by Rogers, Maslow, and other humanistic psychologists' effects on education. Education must help the students to use rational thinking and the emotional senses in actual behavior, including value. Values clarification is based predominately on the work of Raths, Harmin & Simon (1978), Simon & Kirschenbaum (1973), and Simon, Howe & Kirschenbaum (1972).

There is another guideline describing the process of value clarification formulated as the following:

- choosing (from the alternatives);
  -free choosing;
- prizing one's choice;
- affirming one's choice;
- acting upon one's choice; and
- repeatedly acting over time (Simon,1972).

Action Learning

This approach needs to be a more potent form of social studies that teaches values through social life rather than the classroom. Educators emphasize social life experiences to teach values.

However, many kinds of recent programs demonstrated the effectiveness of the techniques advocated by this approach (Solomon,1992). Huitt presented the efficacy of this approach and its methods of problem-solving/decision-making model (1992).

At the end of discussing the approaches for value education, every system has different aims and different points of view. All have the perspective of human nature, all have purposes, and all have ways to implement. If it is necessary to give examples, the inculcation approach has a basic view of human nature as a reactive organism. The analysis and values clarification approaches view the human being as primarily active. The moral development approach views human nature as going back and forth between active and reactive, whereas the action learning approach views human nature as interactive.

How to Teach Important Values to the Elementary Students

The most important values to teach elementary students are here; teaching them carefully and earlier is better.:

Honesty

Being a model for teaching honesty is the best way to teach it. Children are conscientious and capture cues easily. If they observe that you are lying, they can accept that lying is normal. Honesty can be taught by telling the bad of lying and the importance of honesty. If they act honestly, you can praise their behavior and give reinforcement. Try to explain the consequences of lies and the truth.

Kindness

Being kind is another value to teach your students. If they learn kindness, they have successful interactions with other people. With this, value modeling is essential too. Teaching kindness and manners is simple and suitable for preparing early. Even a newborn and babies, and also children at early ages, can learn from your action and will imitate you.

Courage

Teaching courage to children is to have them meet some challenging situations. It has become more important nowadays, and parents and educators let them meet the fear and struggle to develop courage. They need courage in their positions and battle with anxiety. Children must stand up and conquer challenging situations. Children will have difficulty establishing courage if parents and educators do everything for them. Moreover, if you always protect your children, they can not develop the courage needed for complex situations. This situation will support the children to win self-confidence.

Justice

Teaching justice is very important and helps children to differentiate right and wrong. They also learn to explain their feeling and the results of their behaviors. They can tell their mistakes, apologize, and learn how to define and correct the situation. Teaching them to set a wrong action helps them develop. Having the children set up ways of building justice.

Happiness

Happiness may be the ultimate value to teach children. Happiness is essential in human life, so education must build this value. Modeling is again the way to teach this value. Educators must be cheerful and optimistic in communication with the children when they are wrong. So the students will learn to be cheerful although the dire situation and try to correct them. Then they can live a positive and thankful life and overcome their daily problems.

Responsibility

Responsibility is another significant value to teach the students. We all be in anticipation about the persons. Education is the responsible side of raising these people. Grown-up people be dependable, keep their word, and be accountable. If the students have not learned about responsibility, it will be easier for the schools to teach them responsibility. The earlier you can teach, the more accessible learning will be. Nowadays people must be more responsible than before, because of wars in the world and the environment keeping. Teaching responsibility can be prepared at home first. Teachers may ask if they tidy their room at home, talk to students about it, and give them some related homework.

Respect

One of the most important values to teach at school is respect. İt must also be begun to teach at early ages. Respect includes different points. Respect is generally understood as if to respect the elders, but it is not only for them. Schools must teach to respect everybody and everything without being indiscriminate of the nation, age, religion, Etc. If schools make the students instill respect, they will be kind and helpful for a peaceful life. It can be succeeded by education.

Love

Children constantly need to be loved, which is a natural basic need. They are also genuine lovers and give much love around. So parents and teachers must meet this need because they need to get enough love to continue to deliver for a long time and finish it. Teachers and parents frequently repeat to show or tell about meeting the children's love needs. This action must include different and creative ways. They also explain their love to all others.

Consideration

It is also necessary to teach children to care for others and be kind to them. This value is a social skill that improves others' emotions and lives. Teaching this value can start with giving emotional help to others. For example, it can be talking about the problems and ways of helping unhealthy people, disabled and depressed ones to feel better. In these ways, children can learn to think about other people and consider them.

Perseverance

Teaching children to be perseverant is another critical issue. This starts with praising and rewarding them for showing or trying the behavior. It is necessary to reinforce this for every child. Another crucial point is giving courage to the children for the challenging behavior of the value. Courage them to try hard work to do.

Evaluation of Value Education

An important subprocess of value education is the evaluation of the education process. Educators can understand if the students internalized the values of the program and the society. Educators try to achieve these goals in every subject and the integrated structure at every opportunity. Different ways are used to ensure these goals individuals internalize them. The end goal of the combined form of social maturity. All approaches to the process are used to teach the values. Not only is a system not enough to teach, but also a teaching method. So teachers can concentrate on different subjects and inculcate values to the students. Every teacher and every issue will have to act as a means to achieve this end. Every teacher has to emphasize the values at every opportunity and stress the soul of the values. Different approaches can be integrated. Treating the child first as a human being, teaching more values around a core value, and teaching value as the curricular subject. They are good role models, leading with love and working with the community.

Students should be encouraged to use their Heads, Heart, and Hands. So activities that make them use their head can be designed by the teachers. Puzzles and riddles can be used as activities. Solving creative problems, role-playing, dramatization, discussions, and debates can be the methods. For using the heart, activities can be music, games, Etc.; for the hands, activities can be; drawing, illustrations and coloring, poster making, making models and collages, craft work, Etc. Value Education has been a part of the curriculum, but making exams to evaluate learning can be something other than a memory test. There have to be some actual activities that can realize the values and evaluate them. They are the values of love, care, sacrifice, equality, Etc. They discussed different methods of assessing the effectiveness of value education programs, such as surveys, observations, and behavioral measures.

Presenting examples of evaluation studies conducted on value education programs in different countries such as Evaluating the Impacts of Value Education: Some Case Studies Amardeep Singh International Journal of Educational Planning & Administration Volume 1, Number 1 (2011), pp. 1-8. Research India Publications http://www.ripublication.com/ijepa.htm

Nowadays, the need for value education must be addressed. We are all surrounded by a consuming and aggressive social environment, and the change is rapid. All systems have a significant difference, and in need of the evolution of value, systems cause negative impacts, mainly in the more impressionable young minds, unless and until they have something robust to anchor upon. Here, the inculcation of values among the students can play a critical role by shielding them from all such influences.

Some analyses explain that value education programs affect the student's academic performance because they explicitly put the value education programs into practice.

There are different approaches and curricula to teach values in the countries. For example; in Australia, value education helps students understand and apply values such as care and compassion; doing your best; fair go; freedom; honesty and trustworthiness; integrity; respect; responsibility and understanding; tolerance and inclusion Etc. (Values education, 2010). On the other hand, in Singapore, value education is designed as a specific part of the civics curriculum just before the university (MOE, 2010). This attempt aims to develop daily social life quality with the help of programs in which students play active roles. Indian national policy on education also changed (1986-1992), an integrated program with critical values for the society (UGC, 2010).

With a project in Australia, trying to test and measure the effects of values education and the school medium and the students. The analysis reported strong links between value education practices and positive learning outcomes. After this effect of the project in Australia, The Ministry of Education put forward a comprehensive project to see the impacts of value education programs on the environment.

The educational curriculum in Turkey is to nurture individuals to become environmentally friendly and literate (Ministry of National Education, 2018). According to the final report, there was little deviation in the coincidence of effects. These effects matched those targeted in the study and were summarised under the ancillary research questions (Impacts of Value Education, 2009). The consequences of this project put the answer to the question affirmatively. The question was, ''Can the impact of values education on teaching and school ethos, as well as student achievement and behavior, be tested empirically and observed reliably?'' The results have demonstrated the centrality of values education to create a stimulating teaching environment, thereby enhancing quality teaching. Measurement and evaluation of values in education are influenced by many factors, as well as it is a difficult and complex process to perform simultaneously. However, although there is a line share, many techniques can be used.

Although various factors complicate measuring and evaluating values education, many measurement and evaluation techniques can be used to understand whether values education is effective. Researchers should give space to different evaluation methods that will support the measurement and evaluation techniques they will use, considering all other possible factors. The more diverse the number of techniques used in measurement and evaluation, the healthier the data obtained will be (Arcan and Demirel, 2008). For this reason, it will be helpful for employees who want to make measurements and evaluations in the field of values education to get more reliable results by applying different methods and techniques, not limited to one way and technique. Measurement and evaluation techniques can be used in values education in the early years of education and elementary education. They can be like the following:

- observation technique,
  -the wish list technique,
  -"What would you do if it were you?" technique,
  -the technique of verifying the selection,
  -according to whom am I, what technique,
  -picture cards test of values,
- role-playing technique,
  -completion technique,
  -scoring technique of internatives,
- artistic activities at home,
  -outside, alone technique,
- peer evaluation, parental evaluation, teacher evaluation,
- I am self-evaluating this technique,
  -contrasting questions technique of discussion,
  -what I feel" technique,
  -the technique of making a wish,
  -the sacrifice technique,
  -decision making technique (for appropriate behavior),
  -case study technique,
  -the brainstorming technique,

-interview,
-question-answer technique,
-portfolio,
-projects,
-self-questioning technique,
-exams,
-attitude scale,
-the scale of moral distancing,
-the scale of justice,

However, whatever method, strategy, and technique is used, it is only a moral ideal to bring all students to an excellent character. Even the best character or character education shows a convergence to this ideal. For this reason, educators are often responsible for providing a healthy ethical environment for students rather than whether they can achieve their moral development. However, applied research on the effectiveness of values education practices points to positive results. In the report of UNESCO, the results of more than forty-character education projects implemented by the United States Department of Education between 1995 and 2006 show that student behavior, staff competence, and school culture have improved due to the practice. After 1995, the method of "value of the week" in schools in Alabama; concluded that the program implemented by the Character Development Project in K-6 schools is effective in the professional development of teachers and provides a significant improvement of 52% in the behavioral development of students. Studies on the effectiveness of character education programs in Turkey have also determined that these programs improve students' scientific values, truth and peace values, and increase academic success (Berkowitz & Bier, 2004). Approaches in values education are not independent of each other at the extremes. Utilizing different aspects of more than one approach in the same educational environment is considered an element that increases the efficiency of values education. Various studies conducted in this direction have shown that holistic approaches are more effective in values education, even though one-way methods and studies sometimes give positive results.

CONCLUSION

As Meydan (2014) mentioned, due to the destruction of nature and various forms of life and; the erosion of fundamental human values, we are faced with the production and consumption frenzy caused by our irresponsible, insatiable greed. To prevent the disasters caused by our current humanity paradigm, we must bring values to the fore in every aspect of education. Values education can be seen as one of the responsibility areas of the school for individual, social, and educational reasons, as explained.

The importance of value education in elementary ages and schools and the need for continued research and development of effective programs are rising. Every education is a value education in a sense.' Aims and methods of curriculum and instruction are inseparably linked with values.'' (Seshadri, 2005). Value education has become a nonignorable part of schools' curricula worldwide. Schools have designed their curriculum to develop the students' characters. Moreover, the wrong use of technology and the internet threatened human and natural contact (Aksoy & Akpınar, 2012; Turgut & Yılmaz, 2010). Most people lost their environmental sensitivity.

Related to the vital example, there are rising degrees of value needs. Teaching values to your children today will determine how they will behave when they become adults. It is the responsibility of the parents and education. Education provides moral values to children as early as possible, although some say there is no need at early ages. Ethics can be learned later, but teaching from childhood the sense of fairness, honesty, and other good values will help them follow in their life as they grow, and it will stay with them forever. The first stage of value education begins at home. Children absorb everything they see, hear, and touch in their environment. So we must be so careful that some are watching us to do the same. So make sure to set a good atmosphere at home and school.

Everybody may have differing views on teaching values in schools. Some say teaching values at schools is unnecessary because students will not apply them after school. So it does not work in real life after graduating. Some other educators think value-based education improves students' performance and positively develops character. By the effect of values, education constructs the life and world that will be better for human existence. Education for teaching values to children can be applied using different approaches, including direct instruction, modeling, and experiential learning. Effective programs often combine these methods and involve a whole-school process that engages teachers, parents, and the wider community. Cultural and contextual factors may impact the effectiveness of value education policies and programs in the countries. However, research suggests that value education can be taught everywhere with suitable implementation in local contexts. Evaluation of value education programs can be conducted using different methods such as surveys, observations, and behavioral measurements. Practical evaluation involves the identification of clear learning objectives, the use of appropriate measures, and ongoing monitoring and adjustment of the program.

REFERENCES

Aksoy, Y., & Akpınar, A. (2012). Research about public green area use and green area demand in İstanbul Fatih district. Istanbul Commerce University Journal of Science, 20, 81-96. http://dergipark.org.tr/en/download/article-file/199585

Asha Thokchom (2012). Reflection on teaching today and tomorrow: An assessment of Manipur. Voice of Research, 1(3).

Aydın, M. Z., & **Akyol** Gürler, Ş. (2012). Okulda değerler eğitimi. Nobel Yayıncılık

Berkowitz, M. W., & Bier, M. C. (2007). *What works in character education: A research-driven guide for educators*. Character Education Partnership.

Buzelli, C. A., & Johnston, B. (2002). *The moral dimensions of teaching: Language, power, and culture in classroom interaction*. RoutledgeFalmer.

Bütev, Ö., & Dolgun, I. (2018). *Values Education*. Current Academic Studies in Education Sciences.

Claude, R. (Nd.). Methodologies for Human Rights Education. A Project of the Independent Commission on Human Rights Education. http://www.pdhre.org/materials/methodologies.html (Adults, Teacher Educator)

Coser, A. L. (2010). Masters of sociological thought: Ideas in Historical and social context (2nd ed.). https://www.researchgate.net/publication/342009010_The_Theoretical_Approaches_of_Durkheim_Parsons_and_Luhmann_Intratraditional_Differences_Interdependencies_and_Contradictions

Espinosa, F. V., & Jorge López, J. González (2023). Virtues and values education in schools: A study in an international sample. Journal of Beliefs & Values, DOI: To link to this article: https://doi.org/10.1080/13617672.2022.2158018 doi:10.1080/13617672.2022.2158018

Gair, M. (2014). Values education: What, how, why, and what next. *Education in Science*, *4*(4), 269–278.

Georgia Department of Education (1997), The materials developed by the work of William Bennett (e.g., 1993) and The Character Education Institute (CEI).

Gürler, Ş. (2012). Okulda değerler eğitimi yöntemler, etkinlikler, kaynaklar. Nobel Yayıncılık https://www.researchgate.net/publication/330245310_Values_Education#fullTextFileContent

Halstead, J. M., & Taylor, M. J. (2010). Learning and teaching about values: A review of recent research. About learning and teaching values and education of the values. Cambridge Journal of Education 30(2): DOI: doi:10.1080/713657146

Heilbronn, R. (2019). John Dewey and Moral Education.The Encyclopedia of Educational Philosophy and Theory. Springer: Editor Michael Peters.

Huitt, W. (2003). "Survey of Desired Values, Virtues, and Attributes." A preliminary study shows considerable overlap in beliefs among preservice and practicing educators. https://www.edpsycinteractive.org/topics/affect/values.html

Lickona, T. (1991). *Educating for character: How our schools can teach respect and responsibility.* Bantam.

Meydan, H. (2014). An evaluation of the role of values education in school and values education approaches. *Journal of Theology Faculty of Bülent Ecevit University*, *1*(1), 93–108.

Millî Eğitim Bakanlığı [MEB] (2017). https://ttkb.meb.gov.tr/meb_iys_dosyalar/2017_07/18160003_basin_aciklamasilamasi-program.pdf s.24

MOE. (2010). Revised Pre-University Civics Syllabus. http://www.moe.gov.sg/education/syllabuses/aesthetics-health-and-moraleducation/files/civics-pre-university-2007.pdf

Narvaez, D., & Lapsley, D. K. (2005). The psychological foundations of everyday morality and moral expertise. In J. L. Bermudez, A. Marcel, & N. Eilan (Eds.), *The body and the self* (pp. 37–61). MIT Press.

Nucci, L. P., & Narvaez, D. (Eds.). (2008). *Handbook of moral and character education*. Routledge.

Nucci, L. P. (2006). *Education in the moral domain*. Cambridge University Press.

Pal, R. (2015). Teaching values in schools: A critical review of the literature. *Journal of Moral Education*, *44*(4), 399–416.

Pranati, P. (2000). *Responsiveness of teacher education curriculum towards human rights education in India* (Vol. VIII). Human Rights Education in Asian Schools.

Rokeach, M. (1973). *The nature of human values*. The Free Press.

Thi, Q., & Nguyen, N. (2017). CLASSROOM-BASED VALUES EDUCATION IN VIETNAM: IMPLE-MENTATION AND ISSUES. https://www.researchgate.net/publication/318283165

Saphiro, D. A. (1999). Teaching ethics from the ınside-out: Some strategies for developing moral reasoning skills in middle-school students. **(ERIC Number:** ED447040)

Sari, N. (2013). The importance of teaching moral values to the students. *Journal of English and Education, 1*(1).

Seshadri, S. (2005). An approach to value orientation of teachers' education. Journal of Value Education, NCERT

Simon, S. B., Howe, L. W., & Krischenbaum, H. (1978). Values clarification: A handbook of practical strategies for teachers and students. A & W Visual Library.

Singh, A. (2011). Evaluating the impacts of value education: Some case studies. *International Journal of Educational Planning and Administration, 1*(1). http://www.ripublication.com/ijepa.htm

Stravia, (2013). *The Voice of Research*, 2(3), December 2013.

Superka, Ahrens, & Hedstrom (1976). Values Education. Values education sourcebook. CO: Social Science Education Consortium.

Sushma, G., & Daya, P. (Nd.). "Education for Values in Schools – A Framework" Department of Educational Psychology and Foundations of Education, National Council of Educational Research and Training. Education for Values in Schools A Framework - PDF Free Download, docplayer.net

Tan, M. (1990). Eğitim sosyolojisinde değişik yaklaşımlar: İşlevselci paradigma ve çatışmacı paradigma. *Ankara Üniversitesi Eğitim Bilimleri Fakültesi Dergisi, 2*, 557–571.

Tezcan, M. (1993). Eğitim sosyolojisinde çağdaş kuramlar ve Türkiye, Ankara Üniversitesi Eğitim Bilimleri Fakültesi Yayınları, No:170. http://kitaplar.ankara.edu.tr/dosyalar/pdf/083.pdf

Tyree, C., Vance, M., & McJunkin, M. (1997). Teaching values to promote a more caring world: A Moral dilemma for the 21st century. Journal For A Just and Caring Education, 3(2), 215-226. https://www.researchgate.net/publication/330245310_Values_Education#fullTextFileContent

UGC. (2010). "National Policy on Education 1986: As modified in 1992." http://education.nic.in/policy/npe86-mod92.pdf (Accessed on 05.08.2010).

UNESCO. (2015). *Global citizenship education: Topics and learning objectives*. United Nations Educational, Scientific and Cultural Organization.

U.S.A. Department of Education. Partnership in character education state plot projects (1995-2001): Lessons Learned, Washington, D.C. https://files.eric.ed.gov

Values Education for Australian Schooling. (2010). http://www.curriculum.edu.au/values/

ADDITIONAL READING

Flowers, N., M. Bernbaum; K. R. Palmer; J. Tolman (2000). The Human Rights Education Handbook: Effective Practices for Learning, Action, and Change. A publication of the human rights resource center and the Stanley Foundation

Krishnaswamy, J. (2016). *Value Education.Book 4, with a section on Yoga*. Viva Education.

KEY TERMS AND DEFINITIONS

Education: The discipline concerned with teaching and learning methods in schools or school-like environments.

Elementary Age: Elementary education is for eight years. The children under elementary schooling cater to the age group of 6-13 years, from classes I-VIII.

Value: Values are our standards and principles for judging worth. They are the criteria by which we believe 'things' (people. objects, ideas, actions, and situations) to be good, worthwhile, desirable, or, on the other hand, evil, worthless, and despicable.

Value Education: Values education is a term used to name several things, and much academic controversy surrounds it. Some regard it as all aspects of the process by which teachers (and other adults) transmit values to pupils. The ideas, customs, and social behavior of a society. Values education helps individuals to develop their values, which ensures personal and social development.

Value Evaluation: Value evaluation is a process that helps determine the worth of something. It can be used to determine the value of a company, a product, or an idea. Value evaluation is so critical that it is often used in business decisions.

Chapter 19
Examples of Activities That Can Be Used for Value Transfer in a Primary School 4th Grade Social Studies Course

Süleyman Temur
(iD) https://orcid.org/0000-0002-5203-6553
Mustafa Kemal University, Turkey

ABSTRACT

Values play a key role in order to exist in social life practices and to ensure the continuity of culture. As a matter of fact, values are a system of beliefs consisting of the experiences of the individual through socialization. In this context, in the study, sample activities were presented in the worksheets supported by nine values in the 4th grade social studies curriculum (SSLC). Literary genres such as epics, stories, poems, proverbs, quotations, comics, and biography were used in the worksheets. As a matter of fact, it is known that the use of literary works in the learning and teaching process serves permanent learning. For this reason, literary works were used in the worksheets prepared on value transfer in the study. Literary works appear as a reflector and transmitter of culture. These works are seen as important works in reflecting the social life, social relations, moral, and religious values of the period. This is important in order to ensure that values are internalized correctly. In this context, it is thought that the study will guide educators.

INTRODUCTION

One of the most important functions of education systems is to raise individuals who have internalized social values and built their actions in line with these values. For this reason, it is necessary to critically reevaluate the extent to which our values integrated into curricula are realized (Kan, 2010). In line with this, education programs are essential in reaching the desired level of remote-targeted education systems. Although primary education programs have a standard value concept system for all courses,

DOI: 10.4018/978-1-6684-9295-6.ch019

the most significant task in terms of value transfer to raise influential citizens falls on the social studies course (Yaşar & Çengelci, 2012). *Social studies course* is an interdisciplinary course that enables the individual to exist in social life practices to raise effective citizenship (Öztürk & Deveci, 2011). One of these disciplines related to the social studies course is literature. The relationship between social studies and literature was first mentioned in the 2005 Social Studies Curriculum; then, it was again emphasized in the revised curriculum in 2018. Under the title of matters to be considered in the 2018 Social Studies Curriculum (SSLC), It is stated as "Social studies lesson should be supported with literary products by making use of genres such as legend, epic, tale, proverb, folk tale, folk song, and poetry" (MEB, 2018: 10). For this reason, literary works are one of the essential tools that serve the realization of the target acquisitions. Literary works are written in one of the literary genres and have artistic value (Türk Dil Kurumu, 2011:754). Şimşek (2015), on the other hand, defined literary products as works written or designed with an artistic purpose and having aesthetic concerns. In other words, literary products are a part of literature, a way of self-expression. In addition, children can visualize the events and phenomena conveyed in literary works in their minds, which helps them gain historical empathy skills (Seyis, 2021; Turfanda, 2022). Öztürk, Coşkun-Keskin, and Otluoğlu (2012) and Mindivanlı, Küçük, and Aktaş (2012) stated that literary works could be used as teaching materials in social studies courses as well as in many programs in the education system. "The ability to use Turkish correctly, beautifully, and effectively" in the 2018 SBDÖP is included in the field of literary products in social studies teaching. For this skill, which facilitates students' daily life, there are stages in the program, such as listening, speaking, and reading (Öztürk, 2018). Frederick (2007), on the other hand, stated that the use of literary works in the social studies course is essential to reach the course's goals. Literary works increase children's academic success (Er & Kaymakcı, 2016; Yeşilbursa & Sabancı, 2015), gain an empathetic perspective (Akyol, 2011, Seyis, 2021), critical and questioning thinking (Beldağ & Aktaş, 2016), correct Turkish, in using beautifully and effectively (Yıldırım, 2017), making abstract subjects more understandable by concretizing (Kaymakcı, 2013), providing motivation (Tokcan, 2016) and developing a positive attitude towards the lesson (İbret, Karasu-Avcı, Karabıyık, Güleş, & Demirci, 2017; Öztaş, 2018) are essential. In addition, McCall (2010) emphasized that through literary works, children can have the opportunity to evaluate similarities and differences with a critical perspective by making comparisons between the present and the past.

In addition, using activities in value transfer will serve permanent learning. According to Northwiev Public Schools, for values education to reach its goals, many activities and materials should be developed to internalize values by students (Act., Dilmaç, 1999:22).

Gündüz (2018) stated that the activities to be designed about the values that are thought to be gained by the students in the classroom;

1. Enabling children to be actively involved in the process
2. With motivational qualities
3. Bringing diversity to teaching
4. Having drawn attention to qualities
5. Appealing to many senses and
6. She stated that it should be designed to address individual differences.

In line with the abovementioned issues, presenting concrete experiences with different activities that can be used in value transfer plays an important role. One of the materials that serve this purpose is worksheets. Worksheets are multifunctional teaching material that can be used at every stage of the course (Çetintaş, 2019, Kaymakcı, 2010; Temur, 2023; Yanmaz, 2017). In addition, in many studies, worksheets are a critical teaching material in terms of gaining both cognitive and affective, and kinesthetic skills (Karataş, Cengiz, and Çalışkan, 2018; Arıkan and Açıkgöz, 2019; Çetintaş, 2019; Keskin, 2019; Özer, 2019; İnan and Erkus, 2022; Konca, 2022) expressed. Many activity areas ("interpretation, inference based on the text, answering open-ended questions, selecting and marking, filling in the blanks, creating, drawing, painting, pasting," Etc.) are used in the worksheets. Kaymakcı (2012) stated that many literary products are used in the worksheets in the social studies guidebooks. Temur (2023) said that many literary products are used in the worksheets in the social studies textbooks, which serves for permanent learning.

USE OF LITERARY PRODUCTS IN SOCIAL STUDIES LESSON

Social studies course aims to bring national and universal values to individuals. To achieve this goal, teaching materials that appeal to many sense organs should be used in the learning and teaching process. One of these teaching materials is literary products (Küçük, Gedik & Akkuş, 2014). Using literary creations in education and teaching helps children develop a multidimensional perspective and empathy skills (Beldağ & Aktaş, 2016). In addition, one of the effective ways of designing different learning environments and making the learning process interesting for students is to teach the lesson with activities supported by literary products (Kurttekin, 2013). Because literary products enrich the individual's vocabulary, increase the sense of excitement, develop the sense of humor, help children love the lesson and school, and contribute to the socialization of the individual (Cartledge & Kiarige, 2001).

Gaining values at the primary education level is critical to internalizing values (Akkaya, 2014). For this reason, it is vital to use literary products that can attract children's attention in primary education and save the lesson from being boring by entertaining while teaching. It is thought that children in the period of abstract thinking will internalize values better through literary products such as fairy tales and stories (Yaldız, 2006).

Because literary products are essential course material that provides permanence by presenting concrete experiences.

Literary products help to discover and learn about life (Beldağ & Aktaş, 2016). This is a prerequisite for the socialization of individuals. The social studies course is essential to the individual's socialization. In this respect, there is a close connection between literary products and social studies courses (Harmanşa, 2017). Using literary products in the Social Studies course helps children realize the relationships between today's problems and the problems experienced in the past and to understand the cultural differences between the past and the present (Kapan, 2019). Social studies course aims to raise individuals with problem-solving skills depending on changing conditions (Yaşar & Çengelci, 2012). In addition, it is known that literary products have essential effects on sensory learning (Otluoğlu, 2001). For this reason, it is vital to use literary creations in the social studies course (Öztürk et al., 2014). Especially the short stories, fairy tales, and instructional texts used in the social studies lesson increase the interest and motivation of the students towards the lesson (Er, Ünal & Gürel, 2016).

One of the essential everyday purposes of literary products is to gain knowledge, skills, attitudes, and values necessary for educating people (Kaymakcı, 2013). In this context, literary works are essential teaching materials that should be used to raise influential citizens in the social studies course (Oruç, 2009; Demir & Akengin, 2014). The use of literary products is not just a case of literature courses. Because in the social studies course, which aims to gain knowledge, skills, attitudes, and values to raise responsible and influential citizens in primary education, it is vital to use literary products because they contain human information. Many researchers have stated that different literary products such as epic, legend, novel, poetry, and biography should be used in social studies lessons (Downey, 1986; Crabtree & Raviteh, 1988; Hartoonson & Laughlin, 1989; cited by Kaymakcı, 2013).

In light of this information, the benefits of using literary products in social studies lessons can be listed as follows: Literary creations:

1. It increases the success of the students in the course
2. It enriches students' conceptual repository
3. It contributes to transferring national and universal values and students' internalization of these values.
4. Contributes to students' effective learning
5. It enables students to be sensitive and active towards social problems.
6. Helps children gain empathy skills and respect differences (Mildivanlı vd., 2012; Kaymakcı, 2013; Kaya ve Ekici, 2015; Ünlü ve Ay, 2017; Değirmenci Toraman, 2018).

Another usage area of literary works is value transfer. Literary works contribute to the development of the individual's affective field competencies, both in the transfer of cultural values and in addressing emotions (Sevinç, 2018). Literary works are important course material that serves this purpose. Because children meet and discover many new values through literary works. Again, thanks to the heroes and events in these texts, children can see the values and internalize them by passing them through mental filters. In this context, to achieve these gains, it is necessary to use literary works suitable for the child's level in the learning and teaching processes (Eryılmaz & Çengelci Köse, 2018). In addition, literary texts play an important role in gaining national and universal values (Tokcan, 2016; Beldağ & Aktaş, 2016; Seyis, 2021) because the heroes presented through literary works constitute role models for children, which is essential in value transfer (Ceran, 2015). Because heroes who are role models facilitate the internalization of values (Berkowitz, 2011). Sucu (2012) also stated that children who enter the world of literary works will understand that individuals' differences should be respected, which will help them gain tolerance.

Since literary products have a quality that appeals to all age groups, they are used in value transfer (Kapan, 2019). Literary products play a crucial role in transferring values to future generations. Because the author reflects the values of her society in her work masterfully, and the reader learns these values by reading and integrating them into her life (Tekşan, 2012). Öztürk and Otluoğlu (2012) also stated that literary products are one of the easiest and most effective tools that can be used in the classroom environment in transferring cultural values. Bohlin also stated that using literary products in character education is vital. According to him, children establish similarities with their lives through the characters in literary products, activating their imaginations (Karatay, 2011).

Using literary products in learning and teaching processes is essential for individuals to learn the values of their society and use them in social life practices. Literary products allow individuals to get to know themselves, their environment, and the world (Öztürk, 2007; Demirci, 2022). Kan (2010) stated that explaining different cultures and lives to children through literary products is essential in transferring values. Erol (2012) also stated that literary works share the cultural values of the past to future generations.

One of the most essential benefits of literary products is to gain the value of sensitivity. Through literary products, it is easier for students to have common sense and empathy toward different events and people. Moreover, literary works contribute to the individual's ability to see her development and change by entering different experiences (Değirmenci Toraman, 2018). Kaymakcı (2013), on the other hand, stated that literary works are models for children with the case studies they contain. He also stated that literary products are crucial in transferring national and universal values to children. Moreover, literary products are essential in overcoming this situation by raising awareness about negative emotions and behaviors such as prejudice, jealousy, stereotype, anger, and hatred.

Table 1. In this context, literary products that can be used in social studies are presented in

Myth	Lament
Epic	Anecdote
Fairytale	Almanac
Proverb	Atlas
Story	Fable
Folk poems	Daily
Historical novels	Educational comics
Travel article	Cartoons
Joke	Mania
Biography	Lullabies
Monograph	Nursery rhymes
Oration	Essay
Moment	Puzzle
Letter	Travelogue

(Kaymakcı, 2013; Akengin ve Demir, 2014; Tokcan, 2016; Topkaya ve Şimşek, 2017; Ulu Kalın, 2017).

It is clearly stated that literary products should be used in the social studies curriculum (MEB, 2018). It is essential how our values, which constitute the perspective of the social studies course curriculum, are given in literary products.

Under the heading of matters to be considered in the Social Studies Curriculum: The social studies lesson should be supported with literary products using genres such as legend, epic, fairy tale, proverb, folk tale, folk song, and poetry. Literary products such as novels, historical novels, stories, memoirs, travel writings, and anecdotes should be encouraged (MEB, 2018, p.10) specified as.

In addition, it was stated that literary products should be used to explain many acquisitions.

Table 2.

Acquisitions	Explanations
SB.4.3.5. It makes inferences about the landforms and population characteristics of the place where it lives and its surroundings.	Literary products such as poems, stories, and epics are used while processing this achievement.
SB.4.2.4. Understands the importance of the National Struggle based on the lives of the heroes of the National Struggle.	The outcome is handled in the context of teaching biography.
SB.6.2.1. He makes inferences about the geographical, political, economic, and cultural characteristics of the first Turkish states established in Central Asia.	Epic, inscription, and other sources are used.
SB.7.2.5. Gives examples of Ottoman culture, art, and aesthetics.	Examples from the travel books of domestic and foreign travelers are included.

VALUE CONCEPT

Values are defined in many ways Values, Bakaç (2013), as all of the common beliefs, attitudes, and ideas that are considered correct and beneficial by the majority of the society for the society to continue its existence, Şekerci and Merter (2018), as a measure of valuable and desirable attitudes of people towards the community they live in, Akto (2016), as any righteousness, obligation, and truth that is considered suitable or desirable, NCSS (1989), as the standards by which individual behavior and group behavior are judged, Collins (1991), as the standards, beliefs, and attitudes accepted by the individual and society, Kuş (2016) defined it as the standards we use to evaluate human behavior. In the Social Studies Course Curriculum, values are defined as "our heritage that has reached today by distilling from the national and spiritual resources of our society and that we will transfer to our future" (MEB, 2018, p.4).

Values are shared ideas, goals, fundamental moral principles, or beliefs that are accepted as valid and necessary by the majority of its members. In addition, values are defined as motives that center the individual's well-being with a unifying effect and direct this point of view to behavior (Özgüven, 1994; MEB, 2005a). Values have a guiding influence on culture. The development process of civilization shapes it. In this respect, values form the basis of culture (Gündüz, 2018). Because values draw the scheme of socially acceptable behavior and guide individuals (Fichter, 1990; cited in Özensel, 2003, p.231-232). Values prevent disapproved behaviors, provide social control and increase solidarity (Özensel, 2003).

Fichter (2019) expressed the functions of values as follows.

1.   It helps the individual in how she should behave in society interaction.
2.   Shows the ideal ways of thinking and acting in society.
3.   It provides social control.
4.   It leads individuals to obey the rules.
5.   It provides social unity, togetherness, and solidarity. (Act., Şahin, 2022).

The Role of Social Studies Lesson in Value Education

In a world that is changing and developing daily, giving our children the correct value of education is essential values education is needed, especially to have a place in social life and establish healthy relationships (Kuş, 2016). One of the aims of values education is to help children socialize by enabling them to develop a healthy and balanced personality. Moreover, the values that shape our attitudes and behaviors have an essential function to have a place in social life. Furthermore, values are the first step in encouraging responsibility (Akto, 2016).

Social studies, aiming to raise influential citizens, is the most critical lesson in bringing values education to children. Because social studies course is a course in which the knowledge, skills, values, and attitudes necessary for primary school students to adapt to the ever-changing and developing world are developed (Sever, 2015, p.6). Doğanay (2002) expressed social studies as a course that raises individuals with democratic values. Humanities, literature, performing arts, and visual arts are essential to the social studies course (Simpson, 2009). Social studies is a field of study that combines social and human sciences to develop citizenship competencies (Savage & Amstrong, 1996, p.9). In this context, it can be said that the social studies course aims to raise individuals who internalize national, spiritual, and universal values. This shows that social studies course plays a crucial role in gaining value for children. Because the social studies course adds richness to values education with its interdisciplinary structure. A correct character and values education is needed to raise influential citizens. As children learn the values of our democratic system, they must also learn about the differences in every aspect of life in a democratic society (Engle & Ochoa, 1988). In this context, social studies course aims to gain knowledge, skills, attitudes, and values by providing information about universal and national values and primary social institutions (Bilenen, 2019).

Social studies course aims to lead individuals to active citizenship and to gain social values to individuals. More is needed for children to understand the content. Children should use their knowledge and skills to improve their environment and world (NCSS, 2008; Tay & Demir, 2016). The ultimate aim of the social studies course is to serve the development of individuals' decision-making and problem-solving skills (Barth, 1991; Barth & Demirtaş, 1997).

It is vital to ensure children's development in the practical sense in the education and training process. Because human is an emotional beings and maintaining its existence with strong emotional characteristics makes it easier to integrate into the changing world. This is only possible with a correct value transfer process (Kurtdede Fidan, 2013). Aydın and Akyol Gürler (2014) also stated that values shape the actions of individuals and contribute to the individual's socialization. In addition, values help society to maintain a strong continuity by providing social unity and solidarity (Ceviz, 2021). This shows that the power of the existence of society has a positive correlation with values. To this end; In the 2018 Social Studies Curriculum (SSLC); Being "justice, giving importance to family unity, independence, peace, being scientific, industriousness, solidarity, sensitivity, honesty, aesthetics, equality, freedom, respect, love, responsibility, savings, patriotism and benevolence" (MEB, 2018, p. 9) 18 values are included. In this context, the most significant task in transferring value falls to the social studies course (Yıldız, 2021; Keskin, 2020; Özel, 2022) because the social studies course desires to raise individuals with internalized values in line with the aim of active citizenship (Temur & Topkaya, 2023; Temur & Çakmak, 2023). Our values in 2018 SSLC are: "The sum of the principles that form the perspective of the curriculum. Its roots are in our traditions and our past; its trunk and branches are fed from these roots and extend to our present and future" (MEB, 2018: 4). In light of this information, when the literature is examined, proverbs (Sönmez, 2014), fairy tales (Arıcı & Bayındır, 2015), newspapers (Ünlüer & Yaşar, 2012), oral literature products (Yangıl & Kerimoğlu, 2014), legends (Topçu & Kaymakçı, 2018), idioms (Mindivanlı, Küçük & Aktaş, 2012), and biographies (Er & Şahin, 2012) Studies have been conducted on its use in education. Again, there are many studies on the necessity of using literary works in value transfer (Kolaç

& Özer, 2018; Cüceloğlu, 2018; Karatay, 2011; Eryılmaz & Çengelci Köse, 2018; Özpek, 2020; İbret, Karasu-Avcı, Karabıyık, Güleş & Demirci, 2017). ; Veziroğlu, 2020; Yıldız, 2021).

In addition, the perspective of the Social Studies Curriculum is expressed as follows: "The main purpose of our education system is to raise individuals with knowledge, skills, and behaviors integrated with our values and competencies" (MEB, 2018, p.4).

Figure 1. Worksheet 1

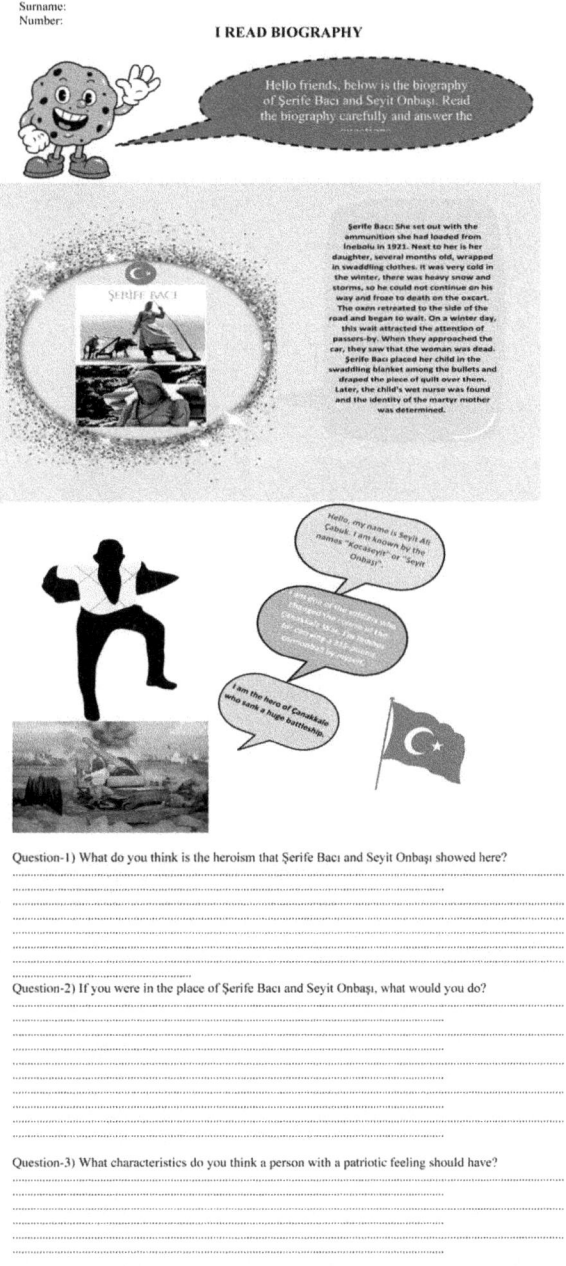

Again, values are expressed in the curriculum: "The roots of our values are in our traditions and our past, and their trunk and branches are fed from these roots and reach our present and future. Our values, which constitute our basic human characteristics, are the source of the power and power that enables us to take action in the routine flow of our lives and in coping with the problems we encounter" (MEB, 2018, p.4).

Figure 2. Worksheet 2

Question-1) What do we gain from respecting differences?

....
....
....

Question-2) Write a quatrain on the subject of respect for differences.

....
....

In light of this information, nine values aimed to be acquired by children in the 4th grade Social Studies Curriculum (SSLC) are presented below through sample activities prepared with worksheets supported by literary works.

Figure 3. Worksheet 3

Figure 4. Worksheet 4

Name:
Surname:
Number:

I INTERPRET THE EPIC

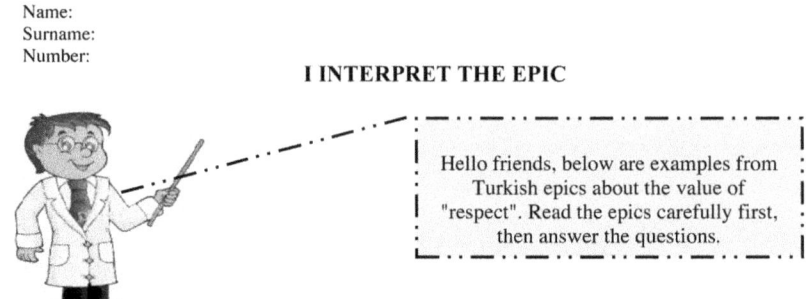

Hello friends, below are examples from Turkish epics about the value of "respect". Read the epics carefully first, then answer the questions.

Respect: The feeling of love that causes to be careful, attentive, measured towards someone or something.

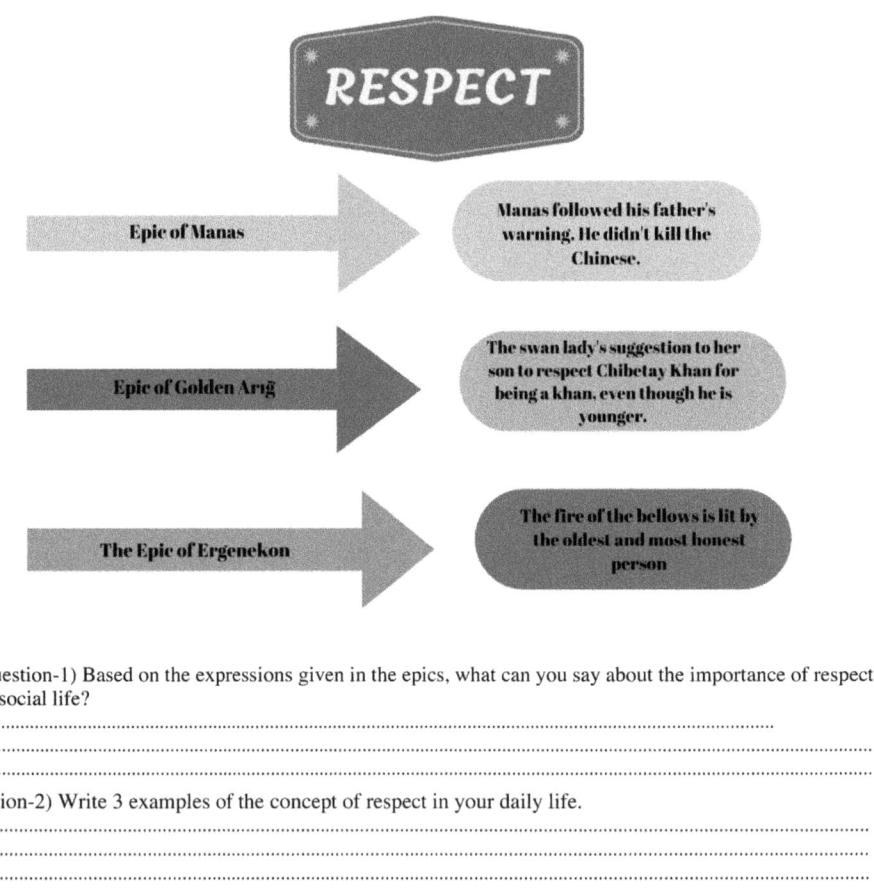

Question-1) Based on the expressions given in the epics, what can you say about the importance of respect in social life?

....
....
....

Question-2) Write 3 examples of the concept of respect in your daily life.

....
....
....
....

Figure 5. Worksheet 5

Question- 1) If you were Ezgi's mother, what would you say to Ezgi about the situation in the rest of the story? Write your thoughts in the blank spaces in the story.

Question-2) What dangers await us in the future if we do not use water sparingly?
Question-3) In what other areas can savings be made in daily life?
....
....
....

CONCLUSION

Values are one of the essential tools that carry society to the future. The individual exists in social life practices through values. A society devoid of values is unthinkable, and societies exist with their values. In this context, education is the most significant task of gaining importance. For this reason, curricula are designed with an understanding of adding value. Although there is a common goal of achieving value for each course, the most significant task falls on the social studies course, which aims to raise active citizens. The social studies course's structure seeks to provide the necessary knowledge, skills, and attitudes to ensure that the individual exists in social life practices. In addition, it was stated in the 2018 SBDÖP as "Our values have been distilled from the national and spiritual resources of our society and have reached today and are our heritage that we will transfer to our future" (MEB, 2018, p.4). As can be understood from this definition, the social studies course plays a crucial role in value transfer. Because social studies is seen as a value education lesson (Kabapınar, 2019). The social studies course, which has an interdisciplinary structure, has rich content regarding value teaching (Sağlam & Genç, 2015). Because it is essential in terms of including historical subjects, bringing life stories and different cultural elements, and conveying good values simultaneously. Because social studies course aims to raise democratic individuals and to get social values to individuals (Poyraz, 2022). Therefore, social studies teaching, especially at the primary level, is essential in gaining and teaching values to individuals best and most effectively (Kaya, 2021).

Figure 6. Worksheet 6

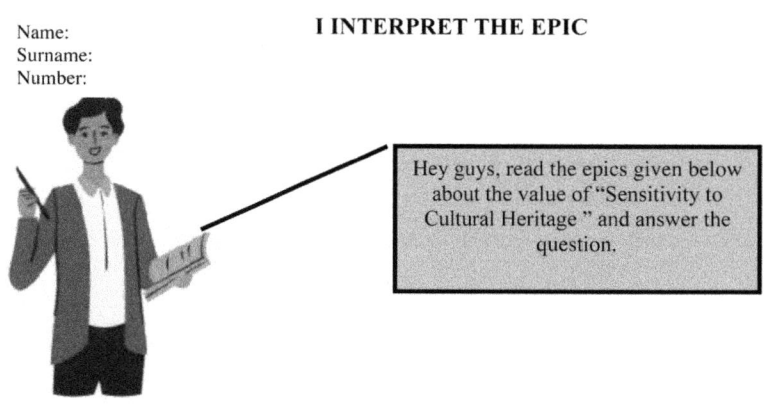

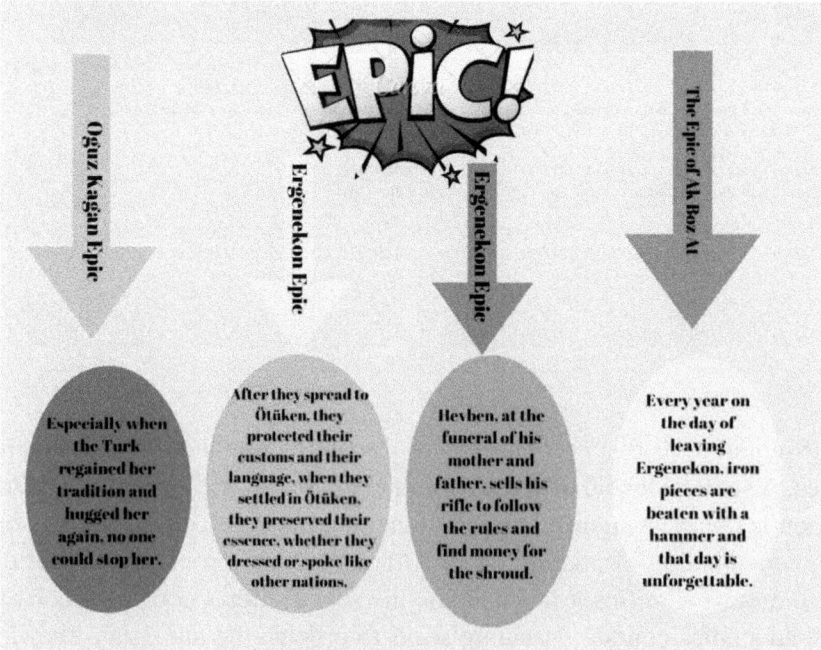

Question- 1) Write down your thoughts on the importance of cultural heritage based on the epics given on the subject of Sensitivity to Cultural Heritage.

....
....
....

Figure 7. Worksheet 7

Name:
Surname:
Number:

Hi guys, I'm Penqui. The words of the Göktürk (Orhun) Inscriptions are given below. Fill in the blanks using the definitions given. Good luck to you all.

I FILL IN THE BLANKS

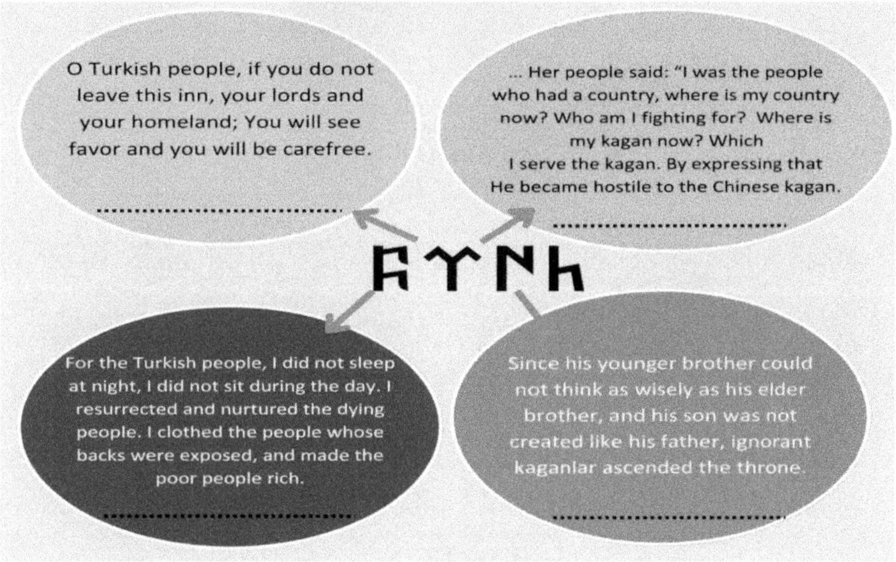

O Turkish people, if you do not leave this inn, your lords and your homeland; You will see favor and you will be carefree.

....

... Her people said: "I was the people who had a country, where is my country now? Who am I fighting for? Where is my kagan now? Which I serve the kagan. By expressing that He became hostile to the Chinese kagan.

....

For the Turkish people, I did not sleep at night, I did not sit during the day. I resurrected and nurtured the dying people. I clothed the people whose backs were exposed, and made the poor people rich.

....

Since his younger brother could not think as wisely as his elder brother, and his son was not created like his father, ignorant kaganlar ascended the throne.

....

CONCEPTS

Patriotism: "An individual's love and devotion to her country."

İndependence: "A free person who can regulate her behavior, attitude and initiatives without the influence of any power."

Responsibility: "The state of being accountable when necessary for a job that a person has undertaken, had to do, or has done."

Scientificity: "Creativity, curiosity, skepticism, open-mindedness, rationality, objectivity, scientific ethics and consistency."

Figure 8. Worksheet 8

Name:
Surname:
Number:

I READ THE PROVERBS

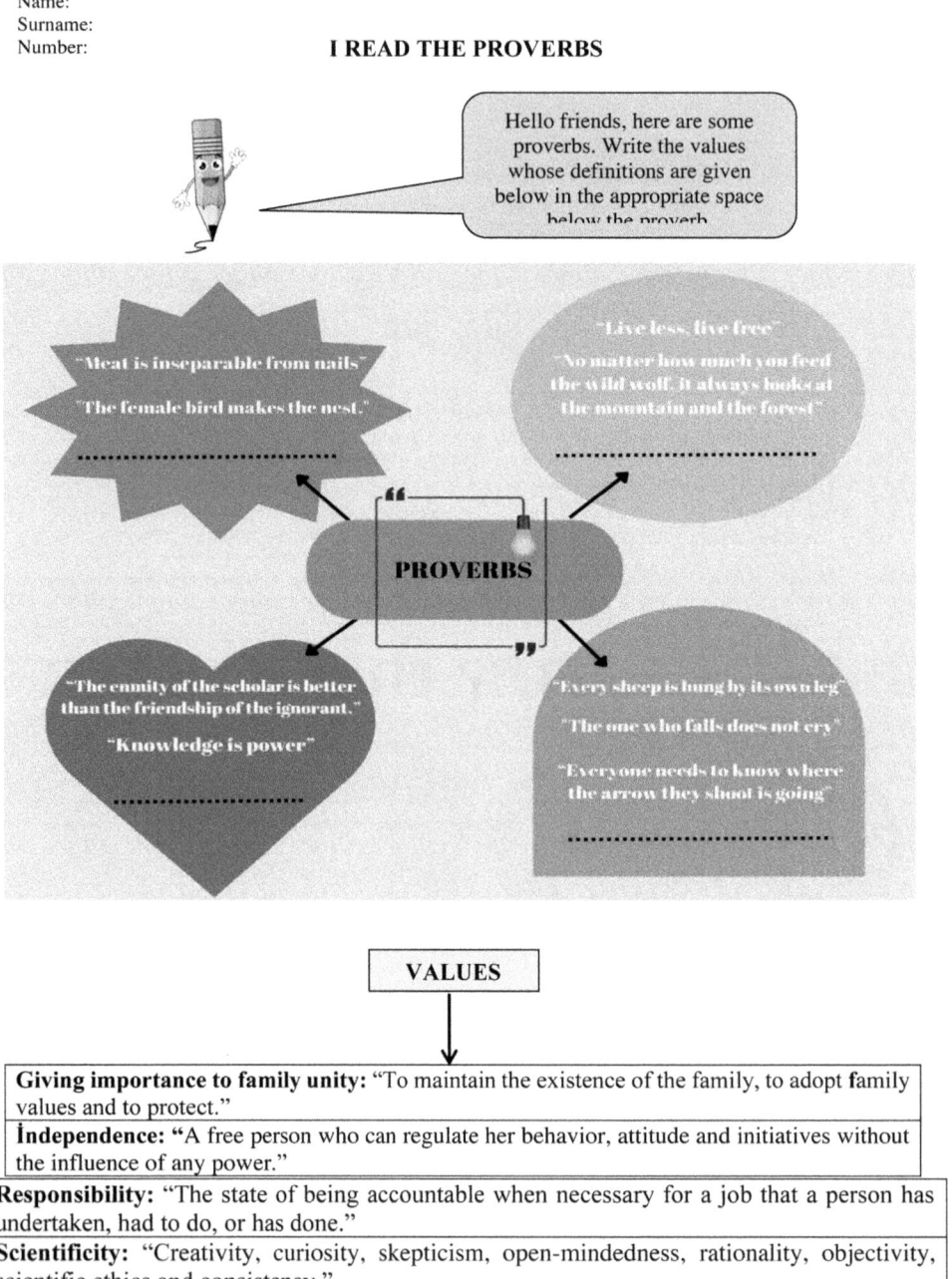

VALUES

Giving importance to family unity: "To maintain the existence of the family, to adopt family values and to protect."

İndependence: "A free person who can regulate her behavior, attitude and initiatives without the influence of any power."

Responsibility: "The state of being accountable when necessary for a job that a person has undertaken, had to do, or has done."

Scientificity: "Creativity, curiosity, skepticism, open-mindedness, rationality, objectivity, scientific ethics and consistency."

Figure 9. Worksheet 9

Name:
Surname:
Number:

I READ COMICS

Question-1) Based on the concise words given above, give a name to the comic?
....

Question-2) In your opinion, what qualities should a person who loves her country have?
....
....

Figure 10. Worksheet 10

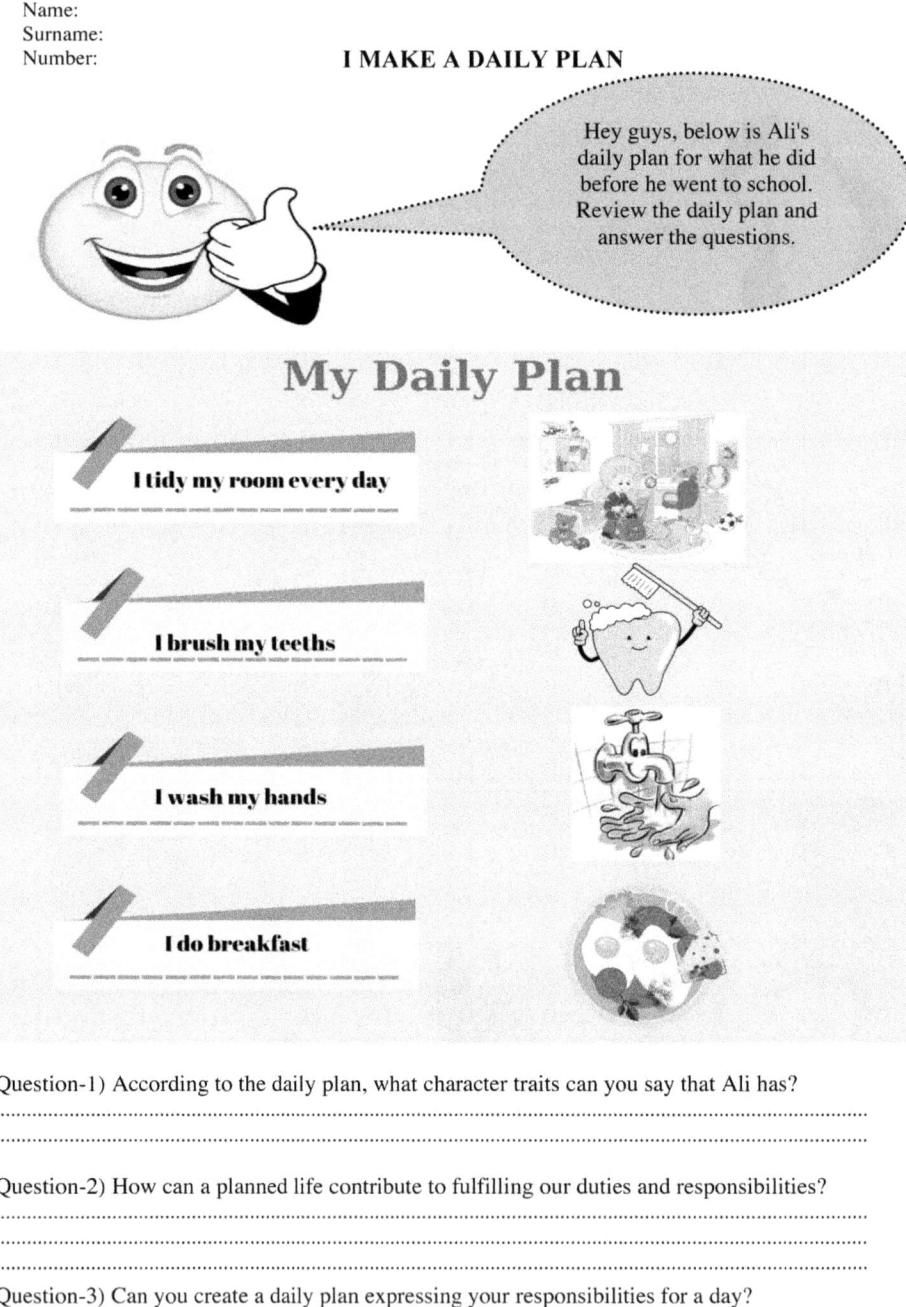

Name:
Surname:
Number:

I MAKE A DAILY PLAN

Hey guys, below is Ali's daily plan for what he did before he went to school. Review the daily plan and answer the questions.

Question-1) According to the daily plan, what character traits can you say that Ali has?
....
....

Question-2) How can a planned life contribute to fulfilling our duties and responsibilities?
....
....
....

Question-3) Can you create a daily plan expressing your responsibilities for a day?
....
....

Figure 11. Worksheet 11

Name:
Surname:
Number:

I'm READING EPIC

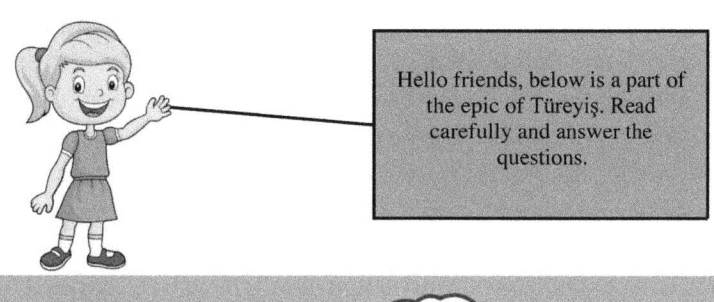

Question-1) Write down your thoughts about the importance of family unity according to the epic.

....
....
....

Question-2) What are your thoughts on the importance of love and respect for family unity?

....

Conversely, teachers should design a teaching environment that will serve the process by using various teaching materials while introducing values to children. Worksheets and literary works are some of these tools. Literary works are an essential source that guides future generations at the point of cultural transmission. Because literary works, besides carrying the traces of the period, also have a crucial function in terms of value transfer. Because literary works offer essential content for the individual to internalize social values. Literary works contain concrete examples of transferring values such as "respect, responsibility, sensitivity to cultural heritage, independence, patriotism, being scientific and giving importance to family unity" in the 4th grade SSLC. Designing literary works by integrating them into worksheets and thus transferring values to children through activities will serve permanent learning by adding diversity to the knowledge and teaching process. Undeniably, activity-oriented studies have a significant impact, especially in acquiring affective domain competencies. On the other hand, worksheets are essential course material in transferring values to children, as they contain many activities. Worksheets, documents containing explanatory information about the actions applied to the students in the teaching of the subject in line with the learning outcome (Anderson, 1995), teaching materials that can be designed in different ways (Ellington & Race, 1993), unfinished activities that contain gaps and that we expect the children to fill (Reece & Walker, 1997) is defined as. Based on these definitions, it is seen that worksheets are an essential tool that provides activity-based and effective participation. In this context, worksheets help to internalize values in terms of providing concrete experiences. In addition, Kaymakcı (2012) and Temur (2023) concluded that there are many fields of activity in the worksheets in their studies. Among these activity areas, it can be said that activities such as "open-ended questions, writing texts, creating, drawing, painting, oral history, object analysis" serve high-level thinking skills. In this context, it is thought that the study will guide educators.

SUGGESTIONS

1. Different teaching materials should be used to gain value in education. This is important in the internalization of values.
2. Teachers, administrators, and parents should cooperate to bring children values.
3. Children should be allowed to realize their values.
4. Literary products used in value transfer should be simplified under children's level.

REFERENCES

Açık, İ. (2020). *İlkokul 4. sınıf sosyal bilgiler dersinde kültürel mirasa duyarlılık ve vatanseverlik değerlerinin biyografilerle öğretimi* [Yayımlanmamış yüksek lisans tezi]. Zonguldak Bülent Ecevit Üniversitesi, Zonguldak, Türkiye.

Akbaş, O. (2008). Değerler eğitimi akımlarına genel bir bakış. *Değerler Eğitimi Dergisi*, 6(16), 9–27.

Aksoy, Ö. A. (1998). *Atasözleri ve deyimler sözlüğü I-II*. İnkılâp Kitabevi.

Akto, A. (2016). *Değer algısı*. İlim Dallarının Düşünce Temellerini Araştırma Enstitüsü Yayınları.

Akyol, Y. (2011). *İlköğretim 7. sınıf sosyal bilgiler dersinde Türk tarihinde yolculuk ünitesinin çocuk edebiyatı ile ilişkilendirilmesinin öğrencilerin empati becerilerine (eğilimlerine) etkisi* [Yayımlanmamış yüksek lisans tezi]. Celal Bayar Üniversitesi Manisa, Türkiye.

Akyol, Y. (2011). *İlköğretim 7.sınıf sosyal bilgiler dersinde 'Türk Tarihinde Yolculuk' ünitesinin çocuk edebiyatı ile ilişkilendirilmesinin öğrencilerin empati becerilerine (eğilimlerine) etkisi* [Yayımlanmamış yüksek lisans tezi]. Celal Bayar Üniversitesi, Manisa, Türkiye.

Altunsoy, Y. (2019). *Sosyal bilgiler dersinde duygu ve düşüncelere saygı değerinin etkinlik temelli öğretiminin öğrencilerin saygı eğilimine etkisi* [Yayımlanmamış yüksek lisans tezi]. Atatürk Üniversitesi, Erzurum, Türkiye.

Anderson, A. (1995). Creative use of worksheets: Lessons my daughter taught me. *Teaching Children Mathematics, 2*(2), 72–79.

Arıcı, A. F. ve Bayındır, N. (2015). Masalların öğretim aracı olarak kullanılması üzerine bir araştırma. *Dil ve Edebiyat Eğitimi Dergisi, 15*, 106–119.

Arslan, E. (2014). *Ortaokul 7. sınıf sosyal bilgiler dersinde hikâye anlatım yönteminin akademik başarıya etkisi* [Yayımlanmamış yüksek lisans tezi]. Gaziantep Üniversitesi, Gaziantep, Türkiye.

Aytaş, G. (2006). Edebi türlerden yararlanma. *Milli Eğitim, 34*(169), 261–276.

Bakaç, E. (2013). Toplumsal değerlere yönelik algı ölçeği: Geçerlik ve güvenirlik çalışması. *Eğitim ve Öğretim Araştırmaları Dergisi, 2*(4), 303–309.

Barth, J. L., & Demirtaş, A. (1997). *İlköğretim sosyal bilgiler öğretimi*. YÖK/Dünya Bankası Yayınları.

Barth, J. L. (1991). *Elementary and junior high/middle school social studies curriculum, activites, and material* (3rd ed.). University Press of America, Inc.

Bayırlı, H. (2018). *Hayat bilgisi bağlamında değerler eğitimi* [Yayımlanmamış yüksek lisans tezi]. Sakarya Üniversitesi, Sakarya, Türkiye.

Beldağ, A., & Aktaş, E. (2016). Sosyal bilgiler öğretiminde edebî eser kullanımı: Nitel bir çalışma. *Erzincan Üniversitesi Eğitim Fakültesi Dergisi, 18*(2), 953–981.

Berkowitz, M. W. (2011). What Works in Values Education. *International Journal of Educational Research, (50)*, 153–158.

Bilgili, A. S. (2019). *Sosyal bilgilerin temelleri (9. Baskı)*. Pegem Akademi.

Bütün Kar, E. (2018). Sosyal bilgiler öğretiminde kanıt ve edebi eserlerin kullanımı. İçinde H. Çalışkan & B. Kılcan (Eds.), Sosyal bilgiler öğretimi (s.283-310). Lisans Yayıncılık.

Cartledge, G. ve Kiarie, M. W. (2001). Through literature for children and adolescents. *Teaching Exceptional Children, 34*(2), 40–47.

Ceran, D. (2015). Çocuklara rol model olması bakımından milli mücadele kahramanları ve edebi eserlere yansıması: "Kurtuluş kahramanları" kitap dizisi örneği. *Tarihi Okul Dergisi, 8*(24), 135–157.

Çetintaş, E. (2019). *Sosyal bilgiler öğretiminde farklılaştırılmış çalışma yapraklarının kullanımı: Bir eylem araştırması* [Yayımlanmamış yüksek lisans tezi]. Erciyes Üniversitesi, Kayseri, Türkiye.

Çetintaş, E. (2019). *Sosyal bilgiler öğretiminde farklılaştırılmış çalışma yapraklarının kullanımı: Bir eylem araştırması* [Yayımlanmamış yüksek lisans tezi]. Erciyes Üniversitesi, Kayseri, Türkiye.

Çiftçi, T. (2011). *Sosyal bilgiler öğretiminde tarihî romanların kullanımının öğrencilerin akademik başarısı üzerine etkisi* [Yayımlanmamış yüksek lisans tezi]. Gazi Üniversitesi, Ankara, Türkiye.

Değirmenci Toraman, K. (2018). *Sözlü ve yazılı edebi ürünlerin sosyal bilgiler dersi öğretiminde akademik başarı, tutum ve kalıcılığa etkisi* [Yayımlanmamış yüksek lisans tezi]. Bolu Abant İzzet Baysal Üniversitesi, Bolu, Türkiye.

Demir, S. B., & Akengin, H. (2014). *Hikayelerle sosyal bilgiler öğretimi*. Pegem Akademi.

Demir, S. B. (2011). *Sosyal bilgiler öğretim programına göre tasarlanmış hikâyelerin etkililiği* [Yayımlanmamış doktora tezi]. Marmara Üniversitesi, İstanbul, Türkiye.

Demirci, M. (2022). *Sosyal bilgiler kitaplarında verilen edebi ürünlerin öğretmen görüşlerine göre incelenmesi* [Yayımlanmamış yüksek lisans tezi]. Yıldız Teknik Üniversitesi, İstanbul, Türkiye.

Dilmaç, B. (1999). *İlköğretim öğrencilerine insani değerler eğitimi verilmesi ve ahlaki olgunluk ölçeği ile eğitimin sınanması* [Yayımlanmamış yüksek lisans tezi]. Marmara Üniversitesi, İstanbul, Türkiye.

Doğanay, A. (2002). Sosyal bilgiler öğretimi. İçinde C. Öztürk ve D. Dilek (Eds.). Hayat bilgisi ve sosyal bilgiler öğretimi (s. 15-46). Pegem Akademi.

Duran, F. (2019). *6. sınıf matematik dersi ondalık sayılar konusunun aktif öğrenme teknikleri ile öğretiminin öğrenci başarısına ve kalıcılığa etkisi* [Yayımlanmamış yüksek lisans tezi]. Erciyes Üniversitesi, Kayseri, Türkiye.

Ellington, P. & Race, H. (1993). *Producing teaching materials: A handbook for teachers and trainers*. Nichols/Gp Publishing.

Engle, S. H., & Ochoa, A. S. (1988). *Education for democratic citizenship: Decision making in the social studies*. Teachers College Press.

Er, H. ve Kaymakcı, S. (2016, Mayıs). *Sosyal bilgiler öğretmenlerinin derslerinde edebi ürün kullanma durumlarının değerlendirilmesi: Bartın örneği* [Bildiri sunumu]. 15. Uluslararası Sınıf Öğretmenliği Eğitimi Sempozyumu, Muğla, Türkiye.

Er, H. ve Şahin, M. (2012). Sosyal bilgiler dersinde "biyografi" kullanımına ilişkin öğrenci görüşleri. *Türk Eğitim Bilimleri Dergisi, 10*(1), 75–96.

Er, H., & Ünal, F. ve Gürel D. (2016). Sosyal bilgiler dersinde değer aktarımı açısından Sadî Şirazî'nin "Bostan" ve "Gülistan" isimli eserinin incelenmesi. *Erzincan Üniversitesi Eğitim Fakültesi Dergisi, 18*(1), 225–242.

Eren, Ü. (2003). *Atasözleri ve deyimler sözlüğü*. Cemre Yayıncılık.

Ergin, M. (2016). Orhun Abideleri (49. baskı). Boğaziçi.

Eryılmaz, Ö. ve Çengelci Köse, T. (2018). Sosyal bilgilerde edebi ürünler ve değerler eğitimi: Küçük Prens örneği. *Batı Anadolu Eğitim Bilimleri Dergisi, 9*(1), 65–79.

Fredericks, A. D. (2007). *Much more social studies through children's literature: A collaborative approach.* Teacher Ideas Press.

Gevenç, S. (2014). *Sosyal bilgiler öğretiminde fıkraların kullanımı* [Yayımlanmamış yüksek lisans tezi]. Niğde Üniversitesi, Niğde, Türkiye.

Gündüz, M. (2018). Sosyal bilgilerde değerler eğitimi. İçinde H. Çalışkan & B. Kılcan (Eds.), Sosyal bilgiler öğretimi (s.165-190). Lisans Yayıncılık.

Gündüz, M. (2018). Sosyal bilgilerde değerler eğitimi. İçinde H. Çalışkan ve B. Kılcan (Eds.), Sosyal bilgiler öğretimi (s. 165-190). Lisans Yayıncılık.

Harmanşa, T. (2017). *4. sınıf sosyal bilgiler dersinde dürüstlük değerini kazandırmada edebi ürünlerin kullanımı* [Yayımlanmamış yüksek lisans tezi]. Recep Tayyip Erdoğan Üniversitesi, Rize, Türkiye.

İbret, B. Ü., Karasu-Avcı, E., Karabıyık, Ş., Güleş, M., & Demirci, M. (2017). Sosyal bilgiler öğretmenlerinin görüşlerine göre değerlerin öğretiminde edebi ürünlerin kullanımı. *Uluslararası Türk Eğitim Bilimleri Dergisi, 9*(5), 104–124.

İl, İ. (2018). *Aktif öğrenme yönteminin 5. sınıf öğrencilerinin sözlü iletişim becerilerine (konuşma-dinleme) etkisi ve öğrencilerin aktif öğrenme uygulamalarına ilişkin görüşleri* [Yayımlanmamış yüksek lisans tezi]. Van Yüzüncü Yıl Üniversitesi, Van, Türkiye.

İnan, C., & Ve Erkuş, S. (2022). Çoklu zeka kuramına dayalı hazırlanan çalışma yapraklarının ortaokul 6. Sınıf öğrencilerinin matematik başarılarına ve tutumlarına etkisi. *Uluslararası Eğitim Bilimleri Dergisi, 9*(30), 111–154.

İnce, M. (2021). *Sosyal bilgiler öğretmen adaylarının vatanseverlik değeri ve vatanseverlik eğitimi hakkındaki görüşleri* [Yayımlanmamış yüksek lisans tezi]. Akdeniz Üniversitesi, Antalya, Türkiye.

Kabapınar, Y. (2019). *Kuramdan uygulamaya hayat bilgisi ve sosyal bilgiler öğretimi.* Pegem Akademi Yayıncılık.

Kan, Ç. (2010). Sosyal bilgiler dersi ve değerler eğitimi. *Milli Eğitim,* (187), 138-145.

Kan, Ç. (2010). Sosyal Bilgiler dersi ve değerler eğitimi. *Milli Eğitim Dergisi, 187,* 138–145.

Kapan, A. (2019). *6.sınıf sosyal bilgiler ders kitabında önerilen edebi ürünlerin öğrenme alanlarında yer alan değerler açısından incelenmesi* [Yayımlanmamış yüksek lisans tezi]. Tokat Gaziosmanpaşa Üniversitesi, Tokat, Türkiye.

Karataş, Ö. F., Cengiz, C., & Ve Çalışkan, B. (2018). İşbirliğine dayalı ve çalışma yaprakları ile desteklenmiş öğrenme ortamında gerçekleştirilen öğretimin öğrencilerin akademik başarıları üzerine etkisi. [ADEDER]. *Araştırma ve Deneyim Dergisi, 3*(1), 1–16.

Karataş, T. N. (2023). *Sınıf öğretmeni adayları için aktif öğrenme temelli çocuk hakları eğitimi* [Yayımlanmamış yüksek lisans tezi]. Gaziantep Üniversitesi, Gaziantep, Türkiye.

Karatay, H. (2011). Karakter eğitiminde edebi eserlerin kullanımı. *Turkish Studies*, *6*(1), 1398–1412.

Karatay, H. (2011). Karakter eğitiminde edebi eserlerin kullanımı. *Turkish Studies - International Periodical for The Languages. Literature and History of Turkish or Turkic*, *6*(1), 1398–1412.

Kaya, E. ve Ekiçi, M. (2015). Sosyal bilgiler öğretiminde gezi yazılarından yararlanma: Gülten Dayıoğlu'nun gezi yazıları örneği. [TSA]. *Türkiye Sosyal Araştırmalar Dergisi*, *19*(1), 87–114.

Kaya, F. (2021). *İlköğretim öğrencilerinin sosyal bilgiler ile insan hakları yurttaşlık ve demokrasi derslerindeki değerlere ilişkin tutumları* [Yayımlanmamış yüksek lisans tezi]. Erzincan Binali Yıldırım Üniversitesi, Erzincan, Türkiye.

Kaymakcı, S. (2010). *Sosyal bilgiler öğretiminde çalışma yaprakları kullanımının öğrencilerin akademik başarılarına ve derse karşı tutumlarına etkisi* [Yayımlanmamış doktora tezi]. Gazi Üniversitesi, Ankara, Türkiye.

Kaymakcı, S. (2010). *Sosyal bilgiler öğretiminde çalışma yaprakları kullanımının öğrencilerin akademik başarılarına ve derse karşı tutumlarına etkisi* [Yayımlanmamış doktora tezi]. Gazi Üniversitesi, Ankara, Türkiye.

Kaymakcı, S. (2012). Sosyal bilgiler öğretim programı kılavuz kitaplarında çalışma yaprakları. *Fırat Üniversitesi Sosyal Bilimler Dergisi*, *22*(2), 169–176.

Kaymakcı, S. (2013). Sosyal bilgiler ders kitaplarında sözlü ve yazılı edebî türlerin kullanım durumu. *Dicle Üniversitesi Ziya Gökalp Eğitim Fakültesi Dergisi*, *20*, 230–255.

Kaymakcı, S. (2013). Sosyal bilgiler ders kitaplarında sözlü ve yazılı edebî türlerin kullanım durumu. *Dicle Üniversitesi Ziya Gökalp Eğitim Fakültesi Dergisi*, (20), 230-255.

Keskin, S. (2019). *Çalışma yapraklarıyla ortaokul 8. sınıflarda üçgenler konusunun öğretiminin akademik başarıya etkisinin incelenmesi* [Yayımlanmamış doktora tezi]. Atatürk Üniversitesi, Erzurum, Türkiye.

Kılınç, F. (2015). *Okul öncesi ve ilkokul döneminde değerler eğitimi*. Eğiten Kitap Yayınları.

Kolaç, E., & Özer, H. (2018). Sosyal bilgiler öğretiminde edebî ürünlerin kullanımı ve değer aktarımındaki katkılarına yönelik öğretmen adaylarının görüşleri. *Uluslararası Türkçe Edebiyat Kültür Eğitim Dergisi*, *7*(4), 2629–2655.

Konca, M. (2022). *Çalışma yapraklarıyla destekli etkinliklerin fen bilimleri dersi 7. sınıf öğrencilerinin hücre ve bölünmeler ünitesini öğrenmelerine etkisinin incelenmesi* [Yayımlanmamış yüksek lisans tezi]. Kastamonu Üniversitesi, Kastamonu, Türkiye.

Kurtdede Fidan, N. (2013). Sosyal bilgiler dersinde değerler eğitimi: Nitel bir araştırma. *The International Journal of Social Sciences (Islamabad)*, *6*(3), 361–388.

Kurttekin, F. (2013). *MEB tarafından tavsiye edilen 100 temel eserden popüler olan on kitap örneğinde dinî ve ahlâkî değerler* [Yayımlanmamış yüksek lisans tezi]. Uludağ Üniversitesi, Bursa, Türkiye.

Kuş, Z. (2016). Demokratik vatandaşlık. İçinde B. Tay ve S. B. Beşir (Eds.), Sosyal bilgiler öğretimi: ilkeler ve uygulamalar (s. 196-208). Anı Yayıncılık.

McCall, A. L. (2010). Teaching powerful social studies ideas through literature Circles. *Social Studies*, *101*(4), 152–159.

MEB. (2005). *İlköğretim sosyal bilgiler dersi 4-5. sınıflar öğretim programı (taslak basım)*. MEB Yayınevi.

MEB. (2018). *Sosyal bilgiler dersi öğretim programı (ilkokul ve ortaokul 4, 5, 6 ve 7. sınıflar)*. TTKB. http://mufredat.meb.gov.tr/ProgramDetay.aspx?PID=354

Milli Eğitim Bakanlığı (MEB). (2005). İlköğretim sosyal bilgiler dersi 6–7.sınıflar öğretim programı ve kılavuzu (taslak basım). Ankara: Millî Eğitim Bakanlığı Talim ve Terbiye Kurulu Başkanlığı, Devlet Kitapları Müdürlüğü.

Milli Eğitim Bakanlığı (MEB). (2018). *Sosyal bilgiler dersi öğretim programı (ilkokul ve ortaokul 4, 5, 6 ve 7. sınıflar)*. TTKB. http://mufredat.meb.gov.tr/ProgramDetay.aspx?PID=354

Mindivanlı, E., & Küçük, B. ve Aktaş, E. (2012). Sosyal bilgiler dersinde değerlerin aktarımında atasözleri ve deyimlerin kullanımı. *Eğitim ve Öğretim Araştırmaları Dergisi*, *1*(3), 93–101.

National Council for the Social Studies Task Force on Early Childhood/Elementary Social Studies. (1989). Social studies for early childhood and elementary school children preparing for the 21st century. *Social Education*, *53*, 14–23.

National Council for the Social Studies Task Force on Scope and Sequence. (1989). In search of a scope and sequence for social studies: Report of the National Council for the Social Studies Task Force on Scope and Sequence. *Social Education*, *53*, 375–387.

National Council for the Social Studies. (2008). A vision of powerful teaching and learning in the social studies: Building influential citizens. *Social Education*, *72*, 277–280.

Nurses, S. (2014). *6. sınıf sosyal bilgiler dersinde yer alan 'Türkiye'de iklim bölgeleri' konusunun öğretiminde görsel materyalleri kullanmanın öğrenci başarısına etkileri* [Yayımlanmamış yüksek lisans tezi]. Atatürk Üniversitesi, Erzurum, Türkiye.

O'Neill, H. (2016). *Başarının Yol Haritası Aktif Öğrenme (Etkili Öğrenci)*. Siyah Beyaz Yayınları.

Onay, İ. (2020). *Sorumluluk değeri etkinliklerinin ilkokul 4. sınıf öğrencilerinin sorumluluk kazanım düzeylerine etkisi* [Yayımlanmamış yüksek lisans tezi]. Ondokuz Mayıs Üniversitesi, Samsun, Türkiye.

Orkun, H. N. (1994). *Eski Türk yazıtları*. Türk Dil Kurumu.

Oruç, Ş. (2009). Sosyal bilgiler 6. sınıf ders kitaplarında edebi ürünler. *Türkiye sosyal Araştırmalar Dergisi,* (2), 10-24.

Oruç, Ş. ve Erdem, R. (2010). Sosyal bilgiler öğretiminde biyografi kullanımının öğrencilerin sosyal bilgiler dersine ilişkin tutumlarına etkisi. *Selçuk Üniversitesi Ahmet Keleşoğlu Eğitim Fakültesi Dergisi*, *30*, 215–229.

Oruç, Ş. ve Ulusoy, K. (2008). Sosyal Bilgiler Öğretimi Alanında Yapılan Tez Çalışmaları. Selçuk Üniversitesi *Ahmet Keleşoğlu Eğitim Fakültesi Dergisi*, (26), 121-138.

Özel, N. (2022). *İlkokul hayat bilgisi ve sosyal bilgiler ders kitaplarında 10 kök değer bağlamında değerler eğitiminin incelenmesi* [Yayımlanmamış yüksek lisans tezi]. Amasya Üniversitesi, Amasya, Türkiye.

Özel, N. (2022). *İlkokul hayat bilgisi ve sosyal bilgiler ders kitaplarında 10 kök değer bağlamında değerler eğitiminin incelenmesi* [Yayımlanmamış yüksek lisans tezi]. Amasya Üniversitesi, Amasya, Türkiye.

Özensel, E. (2003). Sosyolojik bir olgu olarak değer. *Değerler Eğitimi Dergisi, 1*(3), 217–239.

Özer, Y. (2019). *Çoklu zekâ kuramına dayalı hazırlanan çalışma yapraklarının ortaokul 6. sınıf öğrencilerinin matematik başarılarına ve tutumlarına etkisinin incelenme*si [Yayımlanmamış yüksek lisans tezi]. Dicle Üniversitesi, Diyarbakır, Türkiye.

Özgüven, İ. E. (1994). *Psikolojik testler.* Yeni Doğuş Matbaası.

Özpek, M. (2020). T*arihi romanların sosyal bilgiler ile Türkiye Cumhuriyeti İnkılap Tarihi ve Atatürkçülük dersi öğretiminde kullanılması üzerine bir inceleme* [Yayımlanmamış yüksek lisans tezi]. İnönü Üniversitesi, Malatya, Türkiye.

Öztaş, S. (2018). Tarih derslerinde bir öğretim materyali: Edebî ürünler. *Rumelide Dil ve Edebiyat Araştırmaları Dergisi, 11*(11), 27–41.

Öztürk, Ç. (2007). Coğrafya öğretiminde edebi metinlerin kullanımı. *On Dokuz Mayıs Üniversitesi Eğitim Fakültesi Dergisi,* 24, 70-78.

Öztürk, C. (Editör). (2012). *Sosyal bilgiler öğretimi demokratik vatandaşlık eğitimi.* Pegem.

Öztürk, C. ve Deveci, H. (2011). Farklı ülkelerin sosyal bilgiler öğretim programlarının değerlendirilmesi. İçinde C. Öztürk (Ed.), Farklı ülkelerin sosyal bilgiler öğretim programları (s. 1-41). Ankara: Pegem Akademi Yayınları.

Öztürk, C. ve Otluoğlu, R. (2002). Sosyal bilgiler öğretiminde yazılı edebiyat ürünlerini ders aracı olarak kullanmanın duyuşsal davranış özelliklerini kazanmaya etkisi. *Atatürk Eğitim Fakültesi Eğitim Bilimleri Dergisi, 15*, 173–18.

Öztürk, C., Keskin, S. C., & Otluoğlu, R. (2012). *Sosyal bilgiler öğretiminde edebî ürünler ve yazılı materyaller (5. Baskı).* Pegem.

Öztürk, T. (2018). Sosyal bilgilerde beceri eğitimi. İçinde H. Çalışkan & B. Kılcan (Eds.), Sosyal bilgiler öğretimi (s. 191-218). Lisans Yayıncılık.

Poyraz, K. (2022). *Metin Özdamarlar'ın çocuk kitaplarının sosyal bilgiler öğretim programında yer alan değerler açısından incelenmesi* [Yayımlanmamış yüksek lisans tezi]. Niğde Ömer Halis Üniversitesi, Niğde, Türkiye.

Reece, I., & Walker, S. (1997). *Teaching, training, and learning: A practical guide.* Business Education.

Sağlam, E. ve Genç, S.Z. (2015). İlkokul 4. sınıf sosyal bilgiler programında belirlenen değerlerin kazanım düzeyleri. *Uluslararası Türkçe Edebiyat Kültür Eğitim Dergisi, 4*(4), 1708–1728.

Sağlamgöncü, A. (2022). *Sosyal bilgiler dersinde güncel olay öğretiminde aktif öğrenme tekniklerinin kullanılması: Bir eylem araştırması* [Yayımlanmamış doktora tezi]. Anadolu Üniversitesi, Eskişehir, Türkiye.

Savage, T. V., & Amstrong, D. G. (1996). *Effective teaching in elementary education* (10th ed.). Prentice-Hall, Inc.

Seçkin Uygur, H. (2022). *Millî mücadele konulu romanların sosyal bilgiler öğretim programındaki değerler açısından analizi* [Yayımlanmamış yüksek lisans tezi]. İnönü Üniversitesi, Malatya, Türkiye.

Şentürk, M. (2020). *Sosyal bilgiler dersinde eğitici çizgi roman ve eğitici çizgi film kullanımının öğrencilerin, tutum, motivasyon ve akademik başarılarına etkileri* [Yayımlanmamış doktora tezi]. Atatürk Üniversitesi, Erzurum, Türkiye.

Sever, R. (2015). *Sosyal bilgiler öğretimine giriş. İçinde sosyal bilgiler öğretimi.* Nobel Akademik Yayıncılık.

Sevinç, A. (2018). *5. sınıf sosyal bilgiler dersinde yazılı edebi ürün kullanımına yönelik öğretmen ve öğrenci görüşleri* [Yayımlanmamış yüksek lisans tezi]. Fırat Üniversitesi, Elâzığ, Türkiye.

Seyis, Z. (2021). *Sosyal bilgiler derslerinde edebi ürünler aracılığıyla kadın tarihi öğretimi: materyal tasarımı örnekleri* [Yayımlanmamış yüksek lisans tezi]. Sinop Üniversitesi, Sinop, Türkiye.

Simpson, M. (2009). Social studies 2.0: Thinking, connecting, and creating technology [special issue]. *Social Education, 73*(3).

Şimşek, A. (2015). Sosyal bilgiler dersinde bir öğretim materyali olarak edebi ürünler. İçinde M. Safran (Ed.), Sosyal bilgiler öğretimi (s. 389-412). Pegem A

Sönmez, Ö. F. (2014). Atasözlerinin Sosyal Bilgiler programındaki değerler açısından incelenmesi. *Journal of World of Turks, 6*(2), 101–115.

Sucu, A. Ö. (2012). *Mesnevilerin edebiyat eğitiminde değer aktarım aracı olarak kullanılması* [Yayımlanmamış yüksek lisans tezi]. Gazi Üniversitesi, Ankara, Türkiye.

Suna, Y. (2019). *Aktif öğrenme yaklaşımının 7. sınıf matematik dersi rasyonel sayılar konusunun öğretimine etkisinin akademik başarı, tutum ve kalıcılık düzeyleri bağlamında incelenmesi* [Yayımlanmamış yüksek lisans tezi]. Tokat Gaziosmanpaşa Üniversitesi, Tokat, Türkiye.

Tekşan, K. (2012). Türkçe dersi değerler eğitiminde Kutadgu Bilig'in kullanımı. *Ahi Evran Üniversitesi Kırşehir Eğitim Fakültesi Dergisi, 13*(3), 1–17.

Temur, S., & Çakmak, M. (2023). Ortaokul öğrencilerinin özgürlük kavramına ilişkin algılarının sinektik tekniğiyle incelenmesi. *Academia Eğitim Araştırmaları Dergisi, 8*(1), 39–59. doi:10.53506/egitim.1226780

Temur, S., & Topkaya, Y. (2023). 2018 sosyal bilgiler dersi öğretim programının müze kullanımı bakımından incelenmesi. Kırıkkale Üniversitesi Sosyal Bilimler Dergisi, 13(1), 281-307. https://dergipark.org.tr/tr/pub/kusbd/issue/75703/1195574

Temur, S. (2023). Sosyal bilgiler ders kitaplarında çalışma yapraklarının kullanımı. *International Journal of New Approaches in Social Studies, 7*(1), 15–47. https://doi.org/110.38015/sbyy.126077

Tokcan, H. (2016). Sosyal bilgiler ve edebiyat. İçinde Halil Tokcan (Ed.), Sosyal bilgilerde sözlü ve yazılı edebiyat incelemeleri (s.1-24). Pegem A.

Tokcan, H. (2020). *Sosyal bilgilerde sözlü ve yazılı edebiyat incelemeleri.* Salmat Basım Yayıncılık.

Topçu, E., & Kaymakcı, S. (2018). Sosyal bilgiler öğretiminde menkıbelerin kullanılma durumuna ilişkin öğretmen görüşleri. *Erzincan Üniversitesi Eğitim Fakültesi Dergisi, 20*(1), 281–305.

Topkaya, Y. (2016). Doğal çevreye duyarlılık değerinin aktarılmasında kavram karikatürleri ile eğitici çizgi romanların etkililiğinin karşılaştırılması. *Mustafa Kemal Üniversitesi Sosyal Bilimler Enstitüsü Dergisi, 13* (34), 0-0.

Topkaya, Y., & Şimşek, U. (2017). Görsel bir öğretim materyali: Eğitici çizgi roman. İçinde R. Turan, & H. Akdağ (Eds.), Sosyal bilgiler öğretiminde yeni yaklaşımlar III (s. 201-220). Pegem Akademi.

Tuncel, G. (2018). Sosyal bilgiler dersinde "doğal çevreye duyarlılık" değerinin geliştirilmesinde alternatif çevreci uygulamalar. *International Journal of Geography and Geography Education*, (38), 91-103. DOI: doi:10.32003/iggei.440890

Tuncer, T., & Altunay, B. (2010). *Doğrudan öğretim modelinde kavram öğretimi.* Kök Yayıncılık.

Turan, R., & Ulusoy, K. (2016). *Farklı yönleriyle değerler eğitimi.* Pegem Akademi.

Turfanda, S. (2022). *Millî mücadele dönemi edebi eserlerin sosyal bilgiler programındaki değerlere göre incelenmesi* [Yayımlanmamış yüksek lisans tezi]. Aydın Adnan Menderes Üniversitesi, Aydın, Türkiye.

Türk Dil Kurumu (TDK). (2011). *Tük dil kurumu sözlüğü.* Türk Dil Kurumu Yayınları.

Ulu Kalın, Ö., & Koçoğlu, E. (2017). Sosyal bilgiler öğretmen adaylarının bağımsızlık değerine karşı metaforik algıları. *Ahi Evran Üniversitesi Kırşehir Eğitim Fakültesi Dergisi, 18*(2), 419–434.

Ünlü, İ. ve Ay, A. (2017). Hikâyelerle sosyal bilgiler öğretimi. İçinde Sever, R., Aydın, M. ve Koçoğlu, E. (Eds.), Alternatif yaklaşımlarla sosyal bilgiler eğitimi (187-210). Pegem Akademi Yayıncılık.

Ünlüer, G. ve Yaşar, Ş. (2012). Sosyal Bilgiler dersinde gazete kullanımına ilişkin öğrenci görüşleri. *Eskişehir Osmangazi Üniversitesi Sosyal Bilimler Dergisi, 13*(1), 43–57.

Usta, E. (2015). Öğretmen adaylarının öğretim materyalleri geliştirme süreçlerinin görsel ve mesaj tasarımı ilkeleri açısından incelenmesi. *Gazi Eğitim Bilimleri Dergisi, 1*(1), 1–14.

Uzunöz, A., Aktepe, V. ve Özağaçhanlı, Z. (2020). Sosyal bilgiler öğretmen adaylarının tasarruf değerine ilişkin metaforik algıları. *Nevşehir Hacı Bektaş Veli Üniversitesi SBE Dergisi, 10*(1), 36-51.

Veziroğlu, B. B. (2020). *Sosyal bilgiler dersinde Orhun Abidelerinin değer kazanımına etkisi* [Yayımlanmamış yüksek lisans tezi]. Ağrı İbrahim Çeçen Üniversitesi, Ağrı, Türkiye.

Yalçın, Ali, (2021). *5. sınıf sosyal bilgiler dersinde uygulanan sorumluluk temelli etkinliklerin öğrencilere sorumluluk değerini kazandırmadaki etkisi* [Yayımlanmamış yüksek lisans tezi]. Bursa Uludağ Üniversitesi, Bursa, Türkiye.

Yaldız, H. T. (2006). *Masalların çocuk eğitimi açısından incelenmesi (Sarayönü örneği)* [Yayımlanmamış yüksek lisans tezi]. Selçuk Üniversitesi, Konya, Türkiye.

Yangıl, M. K. ve Kerimoğlu, C. (2014). Bilmecelerin eğitimdeki yeri ve önemi. *Eğitim Bilimleri Araştırmaları Dergisi, 4*(2), 341–354.

Yanmaz, D. (2017). *Doğa tarihi müzesinde rehber hazırlama ve çalışma yapraklarıile öğretimin öğrencilerin akademik başarı ve fen öğrenimine yönelik motivasyonları üzerine etkisi* [Yayımlanmamış yüksek lisans tezi]. Sıtkı Kocaman Üniversitesi, Muğla, Türkiye.

Yanmaz, D. (2017). *Doğa tarihi müzesinde rehber hazırlama ve çalışma yapraklarıile öğretimin öğrencilerin akademik başarı ve fen öğrenimine yönelik motivasyonları üzerine etkisi* [Yayımlanmamış yüksek lisans tezi]. Sıtkı Kocaman Üniversitesi, Muğla, Türkiye.

Yaşar, Ş. ve Çengelci, T. (2012). Sosyal bilgiler dersinde değerler eğitimine ilişkin bir durum çalışması. *Uluslararası Avrasya Sosyal Bilimler Dergisi, 3*(9), 1–23.

Yaşar, Ş., & Çengelci, T. (2012). Sosyal bilgiler dersinde değerler eğitimine ilişkin bir durum çalışması. *Uluslararası Avrasya Sosyal Bilimler Dergisi, 3*(9), 1–23.

Yaylı, B. (2020). *Sevgi değerinin kazanılmasında yaratıcı drama kullanımının sınıf öğretmeni adaylarının görüşlerine yansımaları* [Yayımlanmamış yüksek lisans tezi]. Recep Tayyip Erdoğan Üniversitesi, Rize, Türkiye.

Yeşilbursa, C. C., & Sabancı, O. (2015). Sosyal bilgiler öğretmen adaylarının sosyal bilgiler öğretiminde edebi ürünlerin kullanımına yönelik görüşleri. *Mehmet Akif Ersoy Üniversitesi Eğitim Fakültesi Dergisi, 1*(36), 19–33.

Yıldırım, M. (2017). *Sosyal bilgiler öğretmenlerinin derslerinde edebi ürün kullanma durumları (Erzurum örneği)* [Yayımlanmamış yüksek lisans tezi]. Atatürk Üniversitesi, Erzurum, Türkiye.

Yıldız, A. (2021). *Orhun Yazıtlarındaki sosyal bilgiler dersi değerleri ve bu değerlere yönelik değer eğitimi etkinliklerinin oluşturulması* [Yayımlanmamış yüksek lisans tezi]. Trabzon Üniversitesi, Trabzon, Türkiye.

Yurtbaşı, M. (2012). *Sınıflandırılmış atasözleri sözlüğü*. Excellence Publishing Yayıncılık.

KEY TERMS AND DEFINITIONS

Active Citizenship: Having the necessary knowledge, skills, and attitudes to enable individuals to participate actively in social life practices.

Activity: All activities performed at a particular place and time for a move, action, or behavior to achieve its purpose.

Education: It is a planned and programmed process for individuals' personal and social development.

Epic: They are long verse works with national character, formed by kneading the historical events of nations with legendary and mythological elements.

Literary Products: Each of the works is written in one of the literary genres and has aesthetic value.

Proverb: A word of advice that has been said based on long trials and observations and has become popular with the public.

Social Studies: It is a course that emerges by integrating the data obtained from social sciences to the developmental levels of children in line to raise influential citizens.

Teaching Materials: The teacher offers students all the tools and materials in different environments during the learning and teaching.

Value: It is the system of beliefs brought about by the mind and the system of thought brought by the mind which distinguishes the individual from other living species.

Worksheets: Worksheets are multifunctional teaching material that can be used at every stage of the course.

Compilation of References

(2016). Friendship. InLonge, J. L. (Ed.), *Gale virtual reference library: The Gale encyclopedia of psychology* (3rd ed.). Gale. Credo Reference.

Abik, A. D. (1993). *Ali Şir Nevayi'nin risaleleri tarih-i hükema ve enbiya, tarih-i mülük-i Acem, münşeat, metin, gramatikal indeks sözlük* [Unpublished PhD Thesis]. Ankara Üniversitesi Sosyal Bilimler Enstitüsü.

Abramova, N. T. (1989). The boundaries of the fundamentalist ideal and a new image of science. *Philosophy of Science*, (11), 39–50.

Abu-Nimer, M. (2000). A framework for non-violence and peacebuilding in Islam. *The Journal of Law and Religion*, *15*(1/2), 217–265. doi:10.2307/1051519

Abusaleh, K., & Haque, N. (2022). *The Impact of the COVID-19 Outbreak on Primary Education in Bangladesh.* doi:10.4018/978-1-7998-8402-6.ch016

Acat, M. B., & Aslan, M. (2011). Okulların karakter eğitimi yetkinliği ölçeği (OKEYÖ). *Değerler Eğitimi Dergisi, 9*(21), 7-27. https://dergipark.org.tr/en/pub/ded/issue/29179/312453

Açık, İ. (2020). *İlkokul 4. sınıf sosyal bilgiler dersinde kültürel mirasa duyarlılık ve vatanseverlik değerlerinin biyografilerle öğretimi* [Yayımlanmamış yüksek lisans tezi]. Zonguldak Bülent Ecevit Üniversitesi, Zonguldak, Türkiye.

Acosta, M. (2017). Estrategias didácticas para educar en valores. *Revista Educación en Valores*, *2*(8), 59–60.

Adela Kohan, S. (2013). *Escribir es para niños. Todas las claves para escribir lo que los niños quieren leer.* Ediciones Alba.

Adem, M. (1982). *Kalkınma Planlarında Eğitimimizin Hedefleri ve Finansmanı.* Sevinç Publishing.

Adipat, S., Laksana, K., Busayanan, K., Asawasowan, A. & Adipat, B. (2021). Engaging students in the learning process with game-based learning. *Journal of Technology in Education, 4*(3), 542-552. . doi:10.46328/ijte.169

Africa, S., Psychology, O., Science, P., Hoel, H., Zapf, D., Psychology, O., Cooper, C. L., Psychology, O., & Activities, E. (2003). *Bullying and Emotional Abuse in the Workplace.* Academic Press.

Agervold, M., & Mikkelsen, E. G. (2006). *Relationships between bullying, psychosocial work environment, and individual stress reactions.* doi:10.1080/02678370412331319794

Ahmmed, M., & Mullick, J. (2014). Implementing inclusive education in primary schools in Bangladesh: Recommended strategies. *Educational Research for Policy and Practice*, *13*(2), 167–180. Advance online publication. doi:10.100710671-013-9156-2

Akan, Y. (2021). An analysis of the impact of the values education class over the university students' levels of acquisition of moral maturity and human values. *International Journal of Psychology and Educational Studies*, 8(2), 38–50. doi:10.52380/ijpes.2021.8.2.294

Akbaş, O. (2008). Değer eğitimi akımlarına genel bir bakış. *Değerler Eğitimi Dergisi*, 6(16), 9–27.

Akbaş, O. (2008). Değerler eğitimi akımlarına genel bir bakış. *Değerler Eğitimi Dergisi*, 6(16), 9–27.

Akbaş, O. (2008). Sosyal bilgilerde değerler ve öğretimi [Values and teaching in social studies]. In B. Tay & A. Öcal (Eds.), *Sosyal bilgiler öğretimi* [Social studies teaching] (pp. 335–360). Pegem Akademi.

Akşin, S. (1989). *Türkiye Tarihi 4, Çağdaş Türkiye 1908- 1980*. Cem Publishing.

Aksoy, Y., & Akpınar, A. (2012). Research about public green area use and green area demand in İstanbul Fatih district. Istanbul Commerce University Journal of Science, 20, 81-96. http://dergipark.org.tr/en/download/article-file/199585

Aksoy, Ö. A. (1998). *Atasözleri ve deyimler sözlüğü I-II*. İnkılâp Kitabevi.

Aktepe, V., & Yel, S. (2019). Describing the value judgments of primary teachers. *Turkish Journal of Educational Sciences*, 7(3), 607–622. doi:10.29329/ijpe.2019.203.19

Akto, A. (2016). *Değer algısı*. İlim Dallarının Düşünce Temellerini Araştırma Enstitüsü Yayınları.

Akyol, Y. (2011). *İlköğretim 7.sınıf sosyal bilgiler dersinde 'Türk Tarihinde Yolculuk' ünitesinin çocuk edebiyatı ile ilişkilendirilmesinin öğrencilerin empati becerilerine (eğilimlerine) etkisi* [Yayımlanmamış yüksek lisans tezi]. Celal Bayar Üniversitesi, Manisa, Türkiye.

Akyol, Y. (2011). *İlköğretim 7. sınıf sosyal bilgiler dersinde Türk tarihinde yolculuk ünitesinin çocuk edebiyatı ile ilişkilendirilmesinin öğrencilerin empati becerilerine (eğilimlerine) etkisi* [Yayımlanmamış yüksek lisans tezi]. Celal Bayar Üniversitesi Manisa, Türkiye.

Akyüz, Y. (2013). *Türk Eğitim Tarihi M.Ö. 1000- M.S. 2013*. Pegem Akademi Publishing.

Alam, M. J., & Islam, S. R. (2021a). Discrete Primary Education Curriculum in Bangladesh. doi:10.4018/978-1-7998-7271-9.ch036

Alaverdov, E., & Waseem Bari, M. (Eds.). (2020). *Global Development of Religious Tourism*. IGI Global. doi:10.4018/978-1-7998-5792-1

Albizuri, I. E., Samaniego, C. M., & Torrientes, E. Q. (2018). Desarrollo de los valores en las instituciones educativas. *El Mensajero*.

Alkhunazy, S. (2015). Introducing English as a second language to early primary school curriculum in - Saudi Arabia. *Arab World English Journal*, 6(2), 365–371. doi:10.24093/awej/vol6no2.28

Allan, J. (2018). *An analysis of Daniel Kahneman's Thinking, fast and slow*. Taylor & Francis.

All-Russian Parental Resistance. (2018). *Alarming statistics on child and adolescent suicides released*. Retrieved 17 10, 2018, from All-Russian parental resistance: https://rvs.su/novosti/2018/obnarodovana-trevozhnaya-statistika-po-detskim-i- podrostkovym-suicidam#&hcq=UILOdnr/

Alonso, J. M. (2018). *La educación en valores en la institución escolar: Planteamiento y programación*. Editorial Plaza y Valdés.

Altunsoy, Y. (2019). *Sosyal bilgiler dersinde duygu ve düşüncelere saygı değerinin etkinlik temelli öğretiminin öğrencilerin saygı eğilimine etkisi* [Yayımlanmamış yüksek lisans tezi]. Atatürk Üniversitesi, Erzurum, Türkiye.

Alutu, A. N. G., & Adubale, A. A. (2020). Effective character education for undergraduates students: A case study of the University of Benin. *International Journal of Educational Research*, 7(1), 120–128.

Alvarez, M. J., & Kemmelmeier, M. (2017). Free speech as a cultural value in the United States. *Journal of Social and Political Psychology*, 5(2), 707–735. doi:10.5964/jspp.v5i2.590

Ambia, S. J. M. U., & Rahman, M. (2021). Challenges in Primary Level Inclusive Education in Bangladesh. *International Journal for Innovation Education and Research*, 9(11), 14–20. Advance online publication. doi:10.31686/ijier.vol9.iss11.3453

Amin, A., Zubaedi, Z., Siregar, A., & Alimni, A. (2021). The Relationship of Education on Healthy Living Values of Multicultural Islamic Perspective with Healthy Lifestyle Behavior of Junior High School Students in Bengkulu, Indonesia. doi:10.21203/rs.3.rs-895737/v1

Anaut, L. (2012). *Valores escolares y educación para la ciudadanía*. Editorial Graó.

Anderson, A. (1995). Creative use of worksheets: Lessons my daughter taught me. *Teaching Children Mathematics*, 2(2), 72–79.

Aneja, N. (2021). The importance of value education in the present education system. *International Journal of Social Science and Humanities Research*, 2(3), 230–243.

Anggara, N., & Negara, C. K. (2022). Health Education on Personal Hygiene of Students. *Journal of Education*, 1(1).

Anjum, A., & Shoukat, A. (2013). Workplace Bullying: Prevalence and Risk Groups in a Pakistani Sample. *Journal of Public Administration and Governance*, 3(2), 226. doi:10.5296/jpag.v3i2.3985

Aquino, K., & Thau, S. (2009). Workplace Victimization: Aggression from the Target's Perspective. *Annual Review of Psychology*, 60(1), 717–741. Advance online publication. doi:10.1146/annurev.psych.60.110707.163703 PMID:19035831

Arat, R. R. (1947). *Kutadgu bilig I: metin*. Millî Eğitim Basımevi.

Arıcı, A. F. ve Bayındır, N. (2015). Masalların öğretim aracı olarak kullanılması üzerine bir araştırma. *Dil ve Edebiyat Eğitimi Dergisi*, 15, 106–119.

Arjoranta, J. (2019). How to define games and why we need to. *The Computer Games Journal*, 8(1), 109–120. doi:10.100740869-019-00080-6

Arseneault, L., Bowes, L., & Shakoor, S. (2013). *Bullying victimization in youths and mental health problems : 'Much ado about nothing'?* doi:10.1017/S0033291709991383

Arslan, E. (2014). *Ortaokul 7. sınıf sosyal bilgiler dersinde hikâye anlatım yönteminin akademik başarıya etkisi* [Yayımlanmamış yüksek lisans tezi]. Gaziantep Üniversitesi, Gaziantep, Türkiye.

Arthur, J., Harrison, T., & Taylor, E. (2015). *Building Character through Youth Social Action*. Research report. University of Birmingham, Jubilee Centre for Character and Virtues. https://www.jubileecentre.ac.uk/userfiles/jubileecentre/pdf/Research%20Reports/Building_Character_Through_Youth_Social_Action.pdf

Arthur, J. (2011). Personal character and tomorrow's citizens: Student expectations of their teachers. *International Journal of Educational Research*, 50(3), 184–189. doi:10.1016/j.ijer.2011.07.001

Arthur, J., Kristjánsson, K., Harrison, T., Sanderse, W., & Wright, D. (2017). *Teaching character and virtue in schools*. Routledge. doi:10.4324/9781315695013

Arthur, J., Kristjánsson, K., Walker, D. I., Sanderse, W., Jones, C., Thoma, S., Curren, R., & Roberts, M. (2015). *Character education in UK schools research report.* University of Birmingham Jubilee Centre for Character and Virtues. https://www.jubileecentre.ac.uk/userfiles/jubileecentre/pdf/Research%20Reports/Character_Education_in_UK_Schools.pdf

Arufe Graldés, V. (2021). La educación en valores en el aula de educación física. ¿Mito o Realidad? *Revista digital de Educación física, 9.*

Asha Thokchom (2012). Reflection on teaching today and tomorrow: An assessment of Manipur. Voice of Research, 1(3).

Aslanargun, E. (2007). Criticisms of modern educational administration and educated post-modern management. *Journal of Educational Administration in Theory and Practice, 50,* 195–212.

Aspin, D. N. (2007). The ontology of values and values education. In D. N. Aspin & J. D. Chapman (Eds.), *Values education and lifelong learning: Principles, policies, programs* (pp. 27–35). Springer. doi:10.1007/978-1-4020-6184-4_1

Assadullayev, E. (2018). Bureaucratic tradition of China: Confucianism and legalism. *Journal of Civilization Studies, 3*(6), 133–148. https://dergipark.org.tr/tr/download/article-file/612819

Ata, A. (2004). *Karahanlı Türkçesinde ilk Kur'an tercümesi (Rylands nüshası, giriş-metin-notlar-dizin).* Türk Dil Kurumu Yayınları.

Ateş, T. (2007). *Türk Devrim Tarihi.* Bilgi University Publishing.

Aybakan, B. (2006). Küreselleşme sürecinde İslamî değerler. *Marife, 6*(3), 397–412.

Aydın, M. Z., & **Akyol** Gürler, Ş. (2012). Okulda değerler eğitimi. Nobel Yayıncılık

Aydın, M. Z., & Akyol Gürler, Ş. (2014). *Okulda değerler eğitimi.* Nobel.

Aytaş, G. (2006). Edebi türlerden yararlanma. *Milli Eğitim, 34*(169), 261–276.

Baader, M. (2001). On the theory and practice of the just community approach in moral education. In E. Liebau (Ed.), *The formation of the subject. Contributions to the pedagogy of participation* (pp. 159–193). Juventa.

Baccarini, E. (2018). Art, moral understanding, radical changes. Empirical Evidence and Philosophy, 69, 40-53. doi:10.4000/estetica.3666

Backes, E. P., & Bonnie, R. J. (2019). *The Promise of Adolescence: Realizing Opportunity for All Youth.* Academic Press.

Bakaç, E. (2013). Toplumsal değerlere yönelik algı ölçeği: Geçerlik ve güvenirlik çalışması. *Eğitim ve Öğretim Araştırmaları Dergisi, 2*(4), 303–309.

Balakrishnan, V. (2010). The Development of Moral Education in Malaysia. Journal of Educators & Education / Jurnal Pendidik dan Pendidikan, 25, 89-101.

Bandura, A. (1977). *Social learning theory.* Prentice Hall.

Bandura, A. (1997). *Self-efficacy: The exercise of control.* W H Freeman.

Banks, T. (2018). Creating positive learning environments: Antecedent strategies for managing the classroom environment and student behavior. *Creative Education, 5*(7), 519–524. doi:10.4236/ce.2014.57061

Barth, J. L. (1991). *Elementary and junior high/middle school social studies curriculum, activites, and material* (3rd ed.). University Press of America, Inc.

Barth, J. L., & Demirtaş, A. (1997). *İlköğretim sosyal bilgiler öğretimi.* YÖK/Dünya Bankası Yayınları.

Bayer, E. A., & Pavlov, I. B. (2013). *Pedagogical system of formation of vitality of orphans by means of physical culture and sports in the conditions of an orphanage.* Rostov- on-Don: FGBOU VPO "KGUFKSiT".

Bayer, A. (1997). *Muhtaç Olduğumuz Kudret Atatürk.* Aykırı Sanat Publishing.

Bayırlı, H. (2018). *Hayat bilgisi bağlamında değerler eğitimi* [Yayımlanmamış yüksek lisans tezi]. Sakarya Üniversitesi, Sakarya, Türkiye.

Bebchuk, M. A. (Ed.). (2017). *Sukharev readings. Suicidal behavior of children and adolescents: an effective preventive environment.* G.E. Sukhareva DZM. Retrieved from http://www.npc-pzdp.ru/nauka/konf_2017.pdf

Bektaş, Ö., & Zabun, E. (2019). Vatandaşlık eğitiminde değerler karşılaştırması: Türkiye ve Fransa [Comparison of values in citizenship education: Turkey and France]. *Değerler Eğitimi Dergisi, 17*(37), 247-289. doi:10.34234/ded.512221

Beldağ, A., & Aktaş, E. (2016). Sosyal bilgiler öğretiminde edebî eser kullanımı: Nitel bir çalışma. *Erzincan Üniversitesi Eğitim Fakültesi Dergisi, 18*(2), 953–981.

Bellibaş, M. Ş. (2018). Sistematik derleme çalışmalarında betimsel içerik analizi. In K. Beycioğlu, N. Özer, & Y. Kondakçı (Eds.), *Eğitim yönetiminde araştırma* (pp. 511–529). Pegem Akademi.

Benítez Grande-Caballero, L. J. (2019). *Actividades y recursos para educar en valores.* PPC.

Benrabah, M. (1999). *Langue et Pouvoir en Algérie.* Editions Seguier.

Benrabah, M. (2004). La question linguistique. In Y. Beiaskri & C. Chaulet-Achour (Eds.), *l'Epreuve d'une Decennie* (pp. 83–108). Paris-Mediterraneen.

Benrabah, M. (2007). Language in education planning in Algeria: Historical development and current issues. *Language Policy, 6*(2), 225–252. doi:10.100710993-007-9046-7

Benrabah, M. (2013). *Language Conict in Algeria: From Colonialism to Post-Independence.* Multilingual Matters. doi:10.21832/9781847699657

Benzoubir, F., & Bourouina, L. (2020). The implementation of English as a second foreign language in Algerian primary schools between acceptance and refusal. University of Ibn Khaldoun.

Berbercan, M.T. (2011). *Çağatayca Gülistan Tercümesi, gramer-metin-dizin* [PhD Thesis]. İstanbul Üniversitesi.

Berkowitz, D. (2021). Oral storytelling: Building community through dialogue, engagement, and problem solving. *NAEYC Young Children, 2*(3), 36–41.

Berkowitz, M. W. (1981). A critical appraisal of the 'plus-one' convention in moral education. [Allyn and Bacon.]. *Phi Delta Kappan,* ●●●, 488–489.

Berkowitz, M. W. (2011). What Works in Values Education. *International Journal of Educational Research,* (50), 153–158.

Berkowitz, M. W. (2011). What works in values education? *International Journal of Educational Research, 50*(3), 153–158. doi:10.1016/j.ijer.2011.07.003

Berkowitz, M. W., & Bier, M. C. (2007). *What works in character education: A research-driven guide for educators.* Character Education Partnership.

Berkowitz, M. W., & Bustamante, A. (2013). Using research to set priorities for character education in schools: A global perspective. *KEDI Journal of Educational Policy, 10*(3), 7–20.

Bernal, G., & García, M. (2020). Storytelling: A key to speaking fluently in English. *Cuadernos de Lingüística Hispánica*, *15*, 151–162.

Berri, Y. (1973). Algérie: La Révolution en Arabe. *Jeune Afrique (Paris, France)*, (639), 18.

Bertsch, A. (2009). *Exploring perceptions of values in US managers: interstate cross-cultural differences and similarities within the USA*. University of Reading.

Best Sale. (2019, January 11). *Rubbish bins for recycling different types of waste garbage*. IStock. https://www.istockphoto.com/en/vector/rubbish-bins-for-recycling-different-types-of-waste-garbage-containers-vector-gm1092504754-293138771?phrase=recycle

Bilgili, A. S. (2019). *Sosyal bilgilerin temelleri (9. Baskı)*. Pegem Akademi.

Birdsong, D., & Molis, M. (2001). On the evidence for maturational constraints in second-language acquisition. *Journal of Memory and Language, 44*(2), 235-249.

Birkmann, J. (2006). Indicators and criteria for measuring vulnerability: Theoretical bases and requirements. *Measuring Vulnerability to Natural Hazards: Towards Disaster Resilient Societies*, 55–77.

Biryukov, I. (2019). Sports spirituality as a subject of theological and philosophical consideration. *Servis+, 4*. Retrieved from: https://cyberleninka.ru/article/n/sportivnaya-duhovnost-kak-predmet-teologo-filosofskogo-rassmotreniya.

Blase, J., & Blase, J. (2011). *The mistreated teacher : a national study*. doi:10.1108/09578230810869257

Boeschoten, H. A. (2022). *Dictionary of early middle Turkic*. Brill.

Bones, G. N. (2010). *The six pillars of character in 21st-century Newbery award books* [Doctoral dissertation, Liberty University]. ProQuest Dissertataion Publishing. https://www.proquest.com/docview/743818398

Borum, R., Cornell, D. G., Modzeleski, W., & Jimerson, S. R. (2015). *What Can Be Done About School Shootings? A Review of the Evidence. February 2010*. doi:10.3102/0013189X09357620

Bosworth, K., & Judkins, M. (2014). *Tapping Into the Power of School Climate to Prevent Bullying : One Application of School-wide Positive Behavior Interventions and Supports*. doi:10.1080/00405841.2014.947224

Boubakour,S. (2011). Etudier le Francais ...Quelle Histoire! *Le francais en Afrique – revue de reseau des observatoires du Francais contemporain en Afrique, 23*, 51-68.

Boud, D., Keogh, R., & Walker, D. (1985). *Promoting Reflection in Learning: A Model. Reflection: Turning Reflection into Learning*. Routledge.

Boudjerda, R. (1992/1994). *Le FIS de la haine*. Editions Denoël.

Bożek, A., Nowak, P. F., & Blukacz, M. (2020). The Relationship Between Spirituality, Health-Related Behavior, and Psychological Well-Being. *Frontiers in Psychology, 11*, 1997. Advance online publication. doi:10.3389/fpsyg.2020.01997 PMID:32922340

Brackett, M. A., Reyes, R., Rivers, M., Elbertson, N., & Salovey, P. (2011). Classroom emotional climate, teacher affiliation, and student conduct. *Journal of Classroom Interaction, 45*(1), 27-36. https://www.jstor.org/stable/23870549

Branch, S., Ramsay, S., & Barker, M. (2013). Workplace bullying, mobbing, and general harassment: A review. *International Journal of Management Reviews*, *15*(3), 280–299. doi:10.1111/j.1468-2370.2012.00339.x

Brighouse, H., Ladd, H. F., Loeb, S., & Swift, A. (2015). Educational goods and values: A framework for decision-makers. *Theory and Research in Education*, *14*(1), 3–25. doi:10.1177/1477878515620887

Broadbent, C., & Boyle, M. (2014). Promoting positive education, resilience, and student well-being through values education—*The European Journal of Social & Behavioral Sciences*.

Bröder, J., Okan, O., Bauer, U., Bruland, D., Schlupp, S., Bollweg, T. M., Saboga-Nunes, L., Bond, E., Sørensen, K., Bitzer, E. M., Jordan, S., Domanska, O., Firnges, C., Carvalho, G. S., Bittlingmayer, U. H., Levin-Zamir, D., Pelikan, J., Sahrai, D., Lenz, A., ... Pinheiro, P. (2017). Health literacy in childhood and youth: A systematic review of definitions and models. *BMC Public Health*, *17*(1), 361. doi:10.118612889-017-4267-y PMID:28441934

Brown, H., Woods, A., Hirst, E., & Heck, D. (2016). *The public construction of values in education*. Australian Association for Research in Education.

Buchanan, J., Pressick-Kilborn, K., & Maher, D. (2019). Promoting environmental education for primary school-aged students using digital technologies. *Eurasia Journal of Mathematics, Science and Technology Education*, *15*(2). Advance online publication. doi:10.29333/ejmste/100639

Buonomo, I., Fiorilli, C., Romano, L., & Benevene, P. (2020). The Roles of Work-Life Conflict and Gender in the Relationship between Workplace Bullying and Personal Burnout. A Study on Italian School Principals. *International Journal of Environmental Research and Public Health*, *17*(23), 1–17. doi:10.3390/ijerph17238745 PMID:33255556

Burkhardt, J. (1999). Scientific values and moral education in the teaching of science. *Perspectives on Science*, *7*(1), 87–110. doi:10.1162/posc.1999.7.1.87

Burstall, C., Jamieson, M., Cohen, N. F. E. R., & Hargreaves, M. (1974). *Primary French in the balance*. NFER.

Bütev, Ö., & Dolgun, I. (2018). *Values Education*. Current Academic Studies in Education Sciences.

Bütün Kar, E. (2018). Sosyal bilgiler öğretiminde kanıt ve edebi eserlerin kullanımı. İçinde H. Çalışkan & B. Kılcan (Eds.), Sosyal bilgiler öğretimi (s.283-310). Lisans Yayıncılık.

Buxarrais, M. R., & Martínez Martín, M. (2019). Educación en valores y educación emocional: Propuestas para la acción pedagógica. *Teoría de la Educación*, *10*(2), 263–275. doi:10.14201/eks.7519

Buzelli, C. A., & Johnston, B. (2002). *The moral dimensions of teaching: Language, power, and culture in classroom interaction*. RoutledgeFalmer.

Bylieva, D. & Sastre, M. (2018). Classification of Educational Games according to their complexity and the player's skills. *The European Proceedings of Social & Behavioural Sciences*, 438-446. Doi:10154058epshs.2018.12.02.47

Cabedo-Mas, A., Nethsinghe, R., & Forrest, D. (2017). The role of the arts in education for peacebuilding, diversity, and intercultural understanding: A comparative study of educational policies in Australia and Spain. *International Journal of Education & the Arts*, *18*(11).

Çağbayır, Y. (2007). *Yazıtlarından günümüze Türkiye Türkçesinin söz varlığı ötüken Türkçe sözlük*. Ötüken Yayınevi.

Çağrıcı, M. (2012). Tevekkül. TDV İslam ansiklopedisi, 41(1-2).

Cahyati, P. M., S. (2019). Teaching English in primary schools: Benefits and challenges. In *3rd International Conference on Current Issues in Education (ICCIE 2018)*. Atlantis Press. 10.2991/iccie-18.2019.68

Camps, V., García, J., Gil, R., & Ruiz, J. (2018). *Educar en valores: Un reto educativo actual*. Servicio de Publicaciones de la Universidad de Deusto.

Cannon, T., Davis, I., & Wisner, B. (2003). *At Risk: Natural Hazards, People's Vulnerability and Disasters*. Taylor & Francis.

Carr, D. (2006). The moral roots of citizenship: Reconciling principle and character in citizenship education. *Journal of Moral Education, 35*(4), 443–456. doi:10.1080/03057240601012212

Carreras, L., Eijo, P., Estany, A., Gómez, M. T., Guich, R., Mir, V., Ojeda, F., Planas, T., & Serrats, M. G. (2018). *Cómo educar en valores.* Ediciones Narcea.

Carroll, J.B. (1969). Psychological and educational research into second language teaching to young children. *Languages and the young school child,* 56-68.

Cartledge, G. ve Kiarie, M. W. (2001). Through literature for children and adolescents. *Teaching Exceptional Children, 34*(2), 40–47.

Cass, A. L., Holt, E. W., Criss, S., Hunt, E. R., & Reed, R. (2020). Health-Related Priorities, Perceptions, and Values of University Students: Implications for Wellness Education. *American Journal of Health Education, 52*(1), 37–47. doi:10.1080/19325037.2020.1844103

Cavioni, V., Grazzani, I., & Ornaghi, V. (2020). *Mental health promotion in schools: A comprehensive theoretical framework.* Academic Press.

CDC. (2022a). *Children's Oral Health.* Centers for Disease Control and Prevention. Retrieved 17/06/2023 from https://www.cdc.gov/oralhealth/basics/childrens-oral-health/index.html

CDC. (2022b). *Health Benefits of Physical Activity for Children.* Centers for Disease Control and Prevention. https://www.cdc.gov/physicalactivity/basics/adults/health-benefits-of-physical-activity-for-children.html

CDC. (2023a). *Dental Sealants Can Improve Students' Oral Health.* Centers for Disease Control and Prevention. Retrieved 15 June from https://www.cdc.gov/healthyschools/features/dental_health.htm

CDC. (2023b). *Healthy Eating Learning Opportunities and Nutrition Education.* Centers for Disease Control and Prevention. Retrieved 15 June from https://www.cdc.gov/healthyschools/nutrition/school_nutrition_education.htm

CDC. (2023c). *What Works In Schools: Sexual Health Education.* Centers for Disease Control and Prevention. Retrieved 15 June from https://www.cdc.gov/healthyyouth/whatworks/what-works-sexual-health-education.htm#:~:text=What%20is%20sexual%20health%20education,(STI)%20and%20unintended%20pregnancy

Çelik Yılmaz, Ç., & Argon, T. (2020). Prejudice, discrimination, and alienation in educational environments. In S. Polat & G. Günçavdı (Eds.), *Empowering multiculturalism and peacebuilding in schools* (pp. 35–60). IGI Global. doi:10.4018/978-1-7998-2827-3.ch002

Çengelci, T. (2013). Okul ortamında değerler eğitimi konusunda öğretmen ve öğrenci görüşleri. *Değerler Eğitimi Dergisi, 11,* 33–56.

Cepni, A. B., Hatem, C., Ledoux, T. A., & Johnston, C. A. (2021). The Importance of Health Values Among Health Care Providers. *American Journal of Lifestyle Medicine, 15*(3), 224–226. doi:10.1177/1559827621992271 PMID:34025310

Ceran, D. (2015). Çocuklara rol model olması bakımından milli mücadele kahramanları ve edebi eserlere yansıması: "Kurtuluş kahramanları" kitap dizisi örneği. *Tarihi Okul Dergisi, 8*(24), 135–157.

Çetin, N., & Balanuye, Ç. (2015). Değerler ve eğitim ilişkisi üzerine. *Kaygı. Bursa Uludağ Üniversitesi Fen-Edebiyat Fakültesi Felsefe Dergisi,* (24), 191–203.

Çetintaş, E. (2019). *Sosyal bilgiler öğretiminde farklılaştırılmış çalışma yapraklarının kullanımı: Bir eylem araştırması* [Yayımlanmamış yüksek lisans tezi]. Erciyes Üniversitesi, Kayseri, Türkiye.

Cheng, A., & Fleischmann, K. R. (2010). Developing a meta-inventory of human values. *Proceedings of the American Society for Information Science and Technology, 47*(1), 1–10.

Chowdhury, M. (2016). Emphasizing morals, values, ethics, and character education in science education and science teaching. *The Malaysian Online Journal of Educational Science, 4*(2), 1–16.

Çiftçi, T. (2011). *Sosyal bilgiler öğretiminde tarihî romanların kullanımının öğrencilerin akademik başarısı üzerine etkisi* [Yayımlanmamış yüksek lisans tezi]. Gazi Üniversitesi, Ankara, Türkiye.

Claude, R. (Nd.). Methodologies for Human Rights Education. A Project of the Independent Commission on Human Rights Education. http://www.pdhre.org/materials/methodologies.html (Adults, Teacher Educator)

Clement, N. (2009). Perspectives from research and practice in values education. In T. Lovat & R. Tomey (Eds.), *Values education and quality teaching the double helix effect* (pp. 13–25). Springer Dordrecht. doi:10.1007/978-1-4020-9962-5_2

Cogan, J. J., & Derricot, R. (1998). *Citizenship for the 21st Century: an international perspective on education.* Cogan Page.

Colby, A., & Kohlberg, L. (1987). The Measurement of Moral Judgement, Volume 2, Standard Issue Scoring Manual. Cambridge University Press.

Colby, A. (2014). Fostering The Moral and Civic Development of College Students. In L. Nucci, D. Narvaez, & T. Krettenauer (Eds.), *Handbook of Moral and Character Education* (pp. 368–385). Routledge.

Collie, J., & Slater, S. (2012). *Literature in the Language Classroom: A resource book of ideas and activities.* Cambridge University Press.

Colomer, J., Serra, T., Cañabate, D., & Bubnys, R. (2020). Reflective learning in higher education: Active methodologies for transformative practices. *Sustainability (Basel), 12*(3827), 3827. doi:10.3390u12093827

Committee, N. H. (1998). *The social, cultural and economic determinants of health in New Zealand: action to improve health.* National Advisory Committee on Health and Disability.

Contreras, O. R. (2007). Incorporating values into the English classroom. *HOW, 14*, 11-26. https://www.redalyc.org/pdf/4994/499450713002.pdf

Copland, F., Garton, S., & Burns, A. (2014). Challenges in teaching English to young learners: Global perspectives and local realities. *TESOL Quarterly, 48*(4), 738–762. doi:10.1002/tesq.148

Corominas, F. (2012). *Educar hoy.* Editorial Palabra.

Cortina, A. (2020). *La educación y los valores.* Biblioteca Nueva.

Cortina, K. S., Arel, S., & Smith-Darden, J. P. (2017). School belonging in different cultures: The effects of individualism and power distance. *Frontiers in Education, 2*, 56. Advance online publication. doi:10.3389/feduc.2017.00056

Coser, A. L. (2010). Masters of sociological thought: Ideas in Historical and social context (2nd ed.). https://www.researchgate.net/publication/342009010_The_Theoretical_Approaches_of_Durkheim_Parsons_and_Luhmann_Intra-traditional_Differences_Interdependencies_and_Contradictions

Cowan, R. L. (2012). *It's Complicated: Defining Workplace Bullying From the Human Resource Professional's Perspective.* doi:10.1177/0893318912439474

Creative Images. (2022, February 24). *Little boy throwing ice cream wrap or plastic rubbish in the park.* IStock. https://www.istockphoto.com/en/vector/little-boy-throwing-plastic-rubbish-in-the-park-gm1372454528-441554339?phrase=littering

CRED. (2023). *Disasters Year in Review 2022.* https://www.cred.be/publications

Cruz, P. D., Noronha, E., & Editors, S. T. (2021). *Special Topics and Particular Occupations*. Professions, and Sectors. doi:10.1007/978-981-10-5308-5

Crystal, D. (2003). *English as a global language*. Cambridge University Press. doi:10.1017/CBO9780511486999

Cunningham, L. R. (2022). *Intra-Racial Bullying Among African American Female Students in Middle School From*. Academic Press.

Curry, O. S. (Ed.). (2020). *The Oxford Handbook of Compassion Science*. Oxford University Press.

Dabene, L. (dir.). (1981). *Langues et Migrations*. Publications de l'université de Grenoble III.

Daniel, A. K. (2012). *Storytelling across the Primary classroom*. Routledge.

Davis, H., Waycott, J., & Schleser, M. (2019). Digital storytelling. In Managing Complexity and Creating Innovation through Design (pp.15–24). doi:10.4324/9780429022746-3

Değirmenci Toraman, K. (2018). *Sözlü ve yazılı edebi ürünlerin sosyal bilgiler dersi öğretiminde akademik başarı, tutum ve kalıcılığa etkisi* [Yayımlanmamış yüksek lisans tezi]. Bolu Abant İzzet Baysal Üniversitesi, Bolu, Türkiye.

Değirmenci, Y., Kuzey, M., & Yetişensoy, O. (2019). Sosyal bilgiler ders kitaplarında afet bilinci ve eğitimi. *E-Kafkas Journal of Educational Research*, 6(2), 33–46.

Demir, S. B. (2011). *Sosyal bilgiler öğretim programına göre tasarlanmış hikâyelerin etkililiği* [Yayımlanmamış doktora tezi]. Marmara Üniversitesi, İstanbul, Türkiye.

Demirci, M. (2022). *Sosyal bilgiler kitaplarında verilen edebi ürünlerin öğretmen görüşlerine göre incelenmesi* [Yayımlanmamış yüksek lisans tezi]. Yıldız Teknik Üniversitesi, İstanbul, Türkiye.

Demircioğlu, A. (2020). İbn Sina ve Gazali'nin bazı değer kavramları yönünden karşılaştırılması [Comparison of Avicenna and Ghazali for some value concepts]. *OPUS–Uluslararası Toplum Araştırmaları Dergisi*, 16(28), 1562–1584. doi:10.26466/opus.684445

Demir, S. B., & Akengin, H. (2014). *Hikayelerle sosyal bilgiler öğretimi*. Pegem Akademi.

Denham, S. A., & Brown, C. (2010). "Plays nice with others": Social–emotional learning and academic success. *Early Education and Development*, 21(5), 652–680. doi:10.1080/10409289.2010.497450

Detjen, J. (2012). *Constitutional values: Which values determine the Basic Law?* Federal Agency for Civic Education.

Devellioğlu, F. (2006). *Osmanlıca-Türkçe ansiklopedik lûgat. Eski ve yeni harflerle*. Aydın Kitabevi Yayınları.

Dewey, J. (2008). *Okul ve toplum. Eğitim klasikleri dizisi-1*. Pegem Akademi.

Dewey, J. (1933). *How we think: A restatement of the relation of reflective thinking to the educative process*. D.C. Heath & Co Publishers.

Dewey, J. (1938). *Experience and education*. Collier Books.

Díaz Torres, J.M. & Rodríguez Gómez, J.M. (2018). La educación en valores como estrategia de desarrollo y consolidación personal moral. *Estudios sobre educación*, 15, 159-169. doi:10.15581/004.15.23441

Díaz, C. (2015). *Educar en valores: Guía para padres y maestros*. Editorial Trillas.

Dicher, C., & Dichera, D. (2017). Gamifying education: What is known, what is believed, and what remains uncertain. *International Journal of Educational Technology in Higher Education*, 14(1), 1–9. doi:10.118641239-017-0042-5

Dilmaç, B. (1999). *İlköğretim öğrencilerine insani değerler eğitimi verilmesi ve ahlaki olgunluk ölçeği ile eğitimin sınanması* [Yayımlanmamış yüksek lisans tezi]. Marmara Üniversitesi, İstanbul, Türkiye.

Dimitra, K., Kousris, K., Zafeiriou, C., & Tzafilkas, K. (2020). Types of Game-Based Learning in Education. *The European Educational Researcher*, *3*(2), 87–100. doi:10.31757/euer.324

Ding, L. (2019). Applying gamification to asynchronous online discussions: A mixed methods study. *Computers in Human Behavior*, *91*, 1–11. doi:10.1016/j.chb.2018.09.022

Djaout, T. (1993). Des acquis? *Ruptures, 15*.

Doğanay, A. (2002). Sosyal bilgiler öğretimi. İçinde C. Öztürk ve D. Dilek (Eds.). Hayat bilgisi ve sosyal bilgiler öğretimi (s. 15-46). Pegem Akademi.

DoggieMonkey. (2016, November 1). *Vector illustration of shopping plastic bags with groceries products*. IStock. https://www.istockphoto.com/en/vector/grocery-shopping-gm618221966-107518513?phrase=plastic+bag

Domingo, M. G., & Garganté, A. B. (2016). Exploring the use of educational technology in primary education: Teachers' perception of mobile technology learning impacts and applications' use in the classroom. *Computers in Human Behavior*, *56*, 21–28. Advance online publication. doi:10.1016/j.chb.2015.11.023

Domitrovich, C. E. (2010). *Integrated models of school-based prevention: logic and theory*. https://doi.org/ doi:10.1002/pits

Donegan, R. (2012). Bullying and Cyberbullying: History, Statistics, Law, Prevention and Analysis. *The Elon Journal of Undergraduate Research in Communications*, *3*(1), 33–42.

Dönmez, Ö., & Uyanık, G. (2022). Farklı Ülkelerde Değerler Eğitimi ve Değer Eğitimi Programlarından Örnekler. *Temel Eğitim Araştırmaları Dergisi*, *2*(1), 74–88. doi:10.55008/te-ad.1099697

Döring, A. K., Blauensteiner, A., Aryus, K., Drögekamp, L., & Bilsky, W. (2010). Assessing values early on: The picture-based value survey for children (PBVS–C). *Journal of Personality Assessment*, *92*(5), 439–448.

Dovidio, J. F., Piliavin, J. A., Schroeder, D. A., & Penner, L. A. (2006). *The Social Psychology of Prosocial Behavior*. Psychology Press.

Du Val d'Epremesnil, D. (2021). Integrating life in education: An Indian perspective. *Religious Education (Chicago, Ill.)*, *116*(3), 239–251. doi:10.1080/00344087.2021.1892996

Dülger, İ. (2012). *Cumhuriyet Döneminde Türk Toplumu*. Yeni Türkiye Publishing.

Dunlop, F. (2005). Democratic values and the foundations of political education. J. M. Halstead & M. J. Taylor (Eds.), Values in education and education in values (pp.66–76). Taylor & Francis.

Dunst, C. J., Simkus, A., & Hamby, D. W. (2012). Children's story retelling for teachers and pupils. *CELL Reviews*, *5*(2), 1–14.

Duran, F. (2019). *6. sınıf matematik dersi ondalık sayılar konusunun aktif öğrenme teknikleri ile öğretiminin öğrenci başarısına ve kalıcılığa etkisi* [Yayımlanmamış yüksek lisans tezi]. Erciyes Üniversitesi, Kayseri, Türkiye.

Durlak, J. A., Weissberg, R. P., Dymnicki, A. B., Taylor, R. D., & Schellinger, K. B. (2011). The impact of enhancing students' social and emotional learning: A meta-analysis of school-based universal interventions. *Child Development*, *82*(1), 405–432. doi:10.1111/j.1467-8624.2010.01564.x PMID:21291449

Duverger, M. (2020). *Introduction to the social sciences (RLE Social Theory)*. Routledge. doi:10.4324/9781003074458

Eckmann, J., Tezcan, S., Zülfikar, H., & Ata, A. (2014). *Nehcü'l-ferâdîs, uştmaḫlarnıng açuq yolı Maḥmūd bin ʿAlî*. Türk Dil Kurumu Yayınları.

Eckmann, J. (1976). *Middle Turkic glosses of the Rylands interlinear Koran translation*. Akademiai Kiado.

Edelstein, W., & Krettenauer, T. (2014). Citizenship and democracy education in a diverse Europe. In L. Nucci, D. Narvaez, & T. Krettenauer (Eds.), *Handbook of moral and character education* (pp. 386–400). Routledge.

Edgington, L. (1993). *Report of the task force on educational values and implementation of teaching values in Arizona Schools*. Arizona Department of Education.

Education Bureau, The Government of Hong Kong Special Administrative Region of the People's Republic of China. (2022). *Values Education*. https://www.edb.gov.hk/en/curriculum-development/4-key-tasks/moral-civic/index.html

Einarsen, S., Aasland, M. S., & Skogstad, A. (2007). Destructive leadership behavior: A definition and conceptual model. *The Leadership Quarterly*, *18*(3), 207–216. doi:10.1016/j.leaqua.2007.03.002

Eisenberg, N., & Mussen, P. H. (1989). *The Roots of Prosocial Behavior in Children*. Cambridge University Press. doi:10.1017/CBO9780511571121

Ekşi, H. (2003). Temel insani değerlerin kazandırılmasında bir yaklaşım: karakter eğitimi programları. *Değerler Eğitimi Dergisi, 1*(1), 79-96. https://dergipark.org.tr/en/pub/ded/issue/29200/312609

Ekşi, H., & Katılmış, H. (2011). *Karakter eğitimi el kitabı* [Handbook of character education]. Nobel.

El Aissati, A. (1993). Berber in Morocco and Algeria: Revival or Decay? *AILA Review*, *10*, 88–109. https://varlyproject-blog.cdn.ampproject.org/v/s/varlyproject.blog/teaching-english-inalgeria/amp/?amp_js_v=a6&_gsa=1&usqp=mq331AQHKAFQArABIA

Elexpuru Albizuri, I., & Medrano Samaniego, C. (2022). *Desarrollo de los valores en las instituciones educativas*. Ediciones Mensajero.

Ellington, P. & Race, H. (1993). *Producing teaching materials: A handbook for teachers and trainers*. Nichols/Gp Publishing.

Ellington, L. (1990). Dominant values in Japanese education. *Comparative Education Review*, *34*(3), 405–410. doi:10.1086/446958

Ellis, G., & Brewster, J. (2014). *Tell it again: The storytelling handbook for Primary English Language Teachers*. British Council.

Elmira, U., Abay, D., Shaimahanovna, D. A., Erzhenbaikyzy, M. A., Aigul, A., & Rabikha, K. (2022). The importance of game technology in primary education. *World Journal on Educational Technology: Current Issues*, *14*(4), 996–1004. Advance online publication. doi:10.18844/wjet.v14i4.7652

Emiroğlu, B. (2017). Değerler eğitiminin gençlerin sağlıklı sosyalleşmelerine etkisi. *International Journal of Eurasian Education And Culture*, *2*, 115–126.

Engle, S. H., & Ochoa, A. S. (1988). *Education for democratic citizenship: Decision making in the social studies*. Teachers College Press.

Er, H. ve Kaymakcı, S. (2016, Mayıs). *Sosyal bilgiler öğretmenlerinin derslerinde edebi ürün kullanma durumlarının değerlendirilmesi: Bartın örneği* [Bildiri sunumu]. 15. Uluslararası Sınıf Öğretmenliği Eğitimi Sempozyumu, Muğla, Türkiye.

Eren, Ü. (2003). *Atasözleri ve deyimler sözlüğü*. Cemre Yayıncılık.

Ergin, M. (2016). Orhun Abideleri (49. baskı). Boğaziçi.

Er, H. ve Şahin, M. (2012). Sosyal bilgiler dersinde "biyografi" kullanımına ilişkin öğrenci görüşleri. *Türk Eğitim Bilimleri Dergisi, 10*(1), 75–96.

Er, H., & Ünal, F. ve Gürel D. (2016). Sosyal bilgiler dersinde değer aktarımı açısından Sadî Şirazî'nin "Bostan" ve "Gülistan" isimli eserinin incelenmesi. *Erzincan Üniversitesi Eğitim Fakültesi Dergisi, 18*(1), 225–242.

Erinç, S. (1995). *Resmin eleştirisi üzerine*. Hil Yayınları.

Ermat, B., & Ermat, K. (1943). *Yurt Bilgisi Dersleri Grade V*. Milli Eğitim Publishing.

Ermat, B., & Ermat, K. (1945). *Yurt Bilgisi Dersleri Grade IV*. Milli Eğitim Publishing.

Eroğlu, S. E. (2012). Values: Great challenge for the construction of social structure with social institutions. *Journal of Human Sciences, 9*(2), 82–90.

Ersoy, A. F. (2016). Sosyal bilgiler dersi ve vatandaşlık eğitimi [Social studies course and citizenship education]. In R. Turan & T. Yıldırım (Eds.), *Sosyal bilgilerin temelleri* [Foundations of social studies] (pp. 143–164). Anı Publishing.

Eryılmaz, Ö. ve Çengelci Köse, T. (2018). Sosyal bilgilerde edebi ürünler ve değerler eğitimi: Küçük Prens örneği. *Batı Anadolu Eğitim Bilimleri Dergisi, 9*(1), 65–79.

Escámez, J., García, R., Pérez, C., & Llopis, A. (2017). *El aprendizaje de valores y actitudes: Teoría y práctica*. Octaedro.

Espelage, D. L. (2014). *Ecological Theory : Preventing Youth Bullying, Aggression, and Victimization*. doi:10.1080/00405841.2014.947216

Espelage, D. L., Ph, D., Low, S., Ph, D., & Polanin, J. R. (2013). The Impact of a Middle School Program to Reduce Aggression, Victimization, and Sexual Violence. *The Journal of Adolescent Health, 53*(2), 180–186. doi:10.1016/j.jadohealth.2013.02.021 PMID:23643338

Espelage, D. L., & Swearer, S. M. (2019). *Research on School Bullying and Victimization: What Have We Learned and Where Do We Go From Here?* Academic Press. doi:10.1080/00313831.2012.725099

Espinosa, F. V., & Jorge López, J. González (2023). Virtues and values education in schools: A study in an international sample. Journal of Beliefs & Values, DOI: To link to this article: https://doi.org/10.1080/13617672.2022.2158018 doi: 10.1080/13617672.2022.2158018

Ethics. (2015). *Lehrplan Ethik, bildungsgang Realschule Jahrgangsstufen* 5-10. Hessisches Kulturministerium.

Ethicunterricht. (2008). Zur Situation des Ethikunterrichts in der Bundesrepublik Deutschland. Kultusministerkonferenz vom. *Eric, 51*(3), 6-11.

Etta, E. E., Esowe, D. D., & Asukwo, O. O. (2016). African communalism and globalization. *African Research Review, 10*(3), 302–316. doi:10.4314/afrrev.v10i3.20

Eyuboğlu, İ. Z. (1981). *Atatürk'ten Özdeyişler*. Uygarlık Publishing.

Fazel, M., Hoagwood, K., Stephan, S., & Ford, T. (2014). Mental health interventions in schools in high-income countries. *The Lancet. Psychiatry, 1*(5), 377–387. doi:10.1016/S2215-0366(14)70312-8 PMID:26114092

Fernández-Batanero, J. M., Montenegro-Rueda, M., & Fernández-Cerero, J. (2022). Are primary education teachers trained for the use of the technology with disabled students? *Research and Practice in Technology Enhanced Learning*, *17*(1), 19. Advance online publication. doi:10.118641039-022-00195-x

Ferreira Pinto, C., & Soares, H. (2012). Using children's literature in ELT: A story-based approach. *Sensos*, *2*, 23–39.

Forghani, N., Keshtiaray, N., & Yousefy, A. (2015). A critical examination of postmodernism based on religious and moral values education. *International Education Studies*, *8*(9). Advance online publication. doi:10.5539/ies.v8n9p98

Franz, M. (2010). *The main thing is value creation. Experiencing and developing values with children, manual for value education in kindergarten and after-school care*. Don Bosco.

Fredericks, A. D. (2007). *Much more social studies through children's literature: A collaborative approach*. Teacher Ideas Press.

Frobel, W., Grafe, N., Meigen, C., Vogel, M., Hiemisch, A., Kiess, W., & Poulain, T. (2022). Substance use in childhood and adolescence and its associations with quality of life and behavioral strengths and difficulties. *BMC Public Health*, *22*(1), 275. doi:10.118612889-022-12586-2 PMID:35144574

Froh, J. J., & Bono, G. (Eds.). (2019). *The Oxford Handbook of Happiness*. Oxford University Press.

Gage, N. A., Prykanowski, D. A., & Larson, A. (2014). *School Climate and Bullying Victimization : A Latent Class Growth Model Analysis*. Academic Press.

Gair, M. (2014). Values education: What, how, why, and what next. *Education in Science*, *4*(4), 269–278.

Galitsyna, A. M. (2017). "Groups of death" as a means of manipulating consciousness. *Development of Social Sciences by Russian Students,* (4), 30-34.

Gamage, K. A. A., Dehideniya, D., & Ekanayake, S. Y. (2021). The Role of Personal Values in Learning Approaches and Student Achievements. *Behavioral Sciences (Basel, Switzerland)*, *11*(7), 102. Advance online publication. doi:10.3390/bs11070102 PMID:34356719

Ganguli, H. C., Mehrotra, G. P., & Mehlinger, H. D. (1981). Values, moral education, and social studies. In H. D. Mehlinger (Ed.), *UNESCO handbook for the teaching of social studies*. UNESCO.

Garant.ru. Information and Legal Portal. (2021). *Decree of the President of the Russian Federation of July 2, 2021 No. 400 "On the National Security Strategy of the Russian Federation"*. Retrieved 07 10, 2021, from Garant.ru - Information and legal portal: https://www.garant.ru/hotlaw/federal/1472577/

García Campos, V. (2018). Escuela de Valores. *Revista Digital Enfoques Educativos*, *16*, 60–70.

Gaut, B. (2009). *Art, emotion, and ethics*. Oxford University Press.

Genç, S. (2018). Görsel sanatlar eğitiminde kök değerler. *Turkish Studies Educational Sciences, 13*(11), 543-560.

Genç, S. (2019). Görsel sanatlar eğitimi neden önemlidir? In Güzel sanatlar eğitimi araştırmaları. Akademisyen kitabevi.

Georgia Department of Education (1997), The materials developed by the work of William Bennett (e.g., 1993) and The Character Education Institute (CEI).

German Red Cross. (2014). *Working aid for the project "Value formation in families." Basics a value-sensitive family formation*. http://www.Wertebildunginfamilien.de/wp-content/uploads/2014/12/Arbeitshilfe_Wertebildung.pdf

Gervilla, E. (2012). Educadores del future, valores de hoy. *Revista de educación de la Universidad de Granada, 15*, 7-25.

Gevenç, S. (2014). *Sosyal bilgiler öğretiminde fıkraların kullanımı* [Yayımlanmamış yüksek lisans tezi]. Niğde Üniversitesi, Niğde, Türkiye.

Geyer, A. L., & Baumeister, R. F. (2013). Din, ahlak ve öz-denetim: değerler, erdemler ve kötü alışkanlıklar. In Din ve Maneviyat Psikolojisi: Yeni Yaklaşımlar ve Uygulama Alanları (pp. 241-291). Phoenix yayınları.

Ghosn, I. (2012). Four good reasons to use literature in primary school ELT. *ELT Journal, 56,* 2.

Giesecke, H. (2004). What can the school contribute to value education? In S. Gruehn, G. Kluchert, & T. Koinzer (eds.), What makes schools? School, teaching and value education: Theoretical, historical, empirical. Achim Leschinsky on his 60th birthday (pp. 235-246). Beltz. 17

Giorgi, G., Leon-Perez, J. M., & Arenas, A. (2015). Are Bullying Behaviors Tolerated in Some Cultures? Evidence for a Curvilinear Relationship Between Workplace Bullying and Job Satisfaction Among Italian Workers. *Journal of Business Ethics, 131*(1), 227–237. doi:10.100710551-014-2266-9

Glambek, M., Skogstad, A., & Einarsen, S. (2015). *Take it or leave a five-year prospective study of workplace bullying and indicators of expulsion in working life.* Academic Press.

Glambek, M., Matthiesen, S. B., Hetland, J., & Einarsen, S. (2014). Workplace bullying as an antecedent to job insecurity and intention to leave: A 6-month prospective study. *Human Resource Management Journal, 24*(3), 255–268. doi:10.1111/1748-8583.12035

Glanz, K., Rimer, B. K., & Viswanath, K. (2008). *Health behavior and health education: Theory, research, and practice* (4th ed.). Jossey-Bass.

Gökaydın, N. (1998). *Eğitimde tasarım ve görsel algı.* Millî eğitim basımevi.

Goloğlu, M. (2011). *Devrimler ve Tepkileri, Türkiye Cumhuriyeti Tarihi I (1924- 1930).* Türkiye İş Bankası Kültür Publishing.

Gölpınarlı, A. (2007). *Muallim Abdülbaki Gölpınarlı, Yurt Bilgisi Atatürk Dönemi Ders Kitabı.* Kaynak Publishing.

Gonzalez, P., & Birnbaum-Weitzman, O. (2020). Sociocultural. In M. D. Gellman (Ed.), *Encyclopedia of Behavioral Medicine* (pp. 2105–2107). Springer International Publishing. doi:10.1007/978-3-030-39903-0_1511

Goodboy, A. K., Martin, M. M., Brown, E., Goodboy, A. K., Martin, M. M., Bullying, E. B., Goodboy, A. K., Martin, M. M., & Brown, E. (2016). *Bullying on the school bus : deleterious effects on public school bus drivers.* doi:10.1080/00909882.2016.1225161

Gordon, D. C. (1978). *The French National Language and National Identity.* Mouton Publishers.

Gozcu, E. & Caganaga, L. (2021). The importance of using games in ELF classrooms. *Cypriot Journal of Educational Science, 11*(3), 126-135.

Grace, L. (2019). *Doing things with games: Social impact through play.* Routledge. doi:10.1201/9780429429880

Grube, J. W., Rokeach, M., & Getzlaf, S. B. (1990). Adolescents value images of smokers, ex-smokers, and nonsmokers. *Addictive Behaviors, 15*(1), 81–88. doi:10.1016/0306-4603(90)90010-U PMID:2316415

Grugeon, E., & Gardner, P. (2010). *The art of storytelling for teachers and pupils.* David Fulton Publishing.

Guendouze, L. Y., & Bentrari, Y. (2020). *Introducing English course in Algerian Primary school: Case of the third – Grade in primary schools in AinTemouchent (Hassiba Ben Bou Ali)* [Master dissertation].

Gül, R. (2013). *Bir değer eğitimi olarak ilköğretim döneminde doğruluk eğitimi* [Unpublished Master Thesis]. Hitit Üniversitesi.

Gumbus, A., & Meglich, P. (2012). Lean and Mean: Workplace Culture and the Prevention of Workplace Bullying. *Journal of Applied Business and Economics*, *13*(5), 11–20. http://search.proquest.com.library.capella.edu/docview/1315304221

Gümüş, S. (2018). Nitel araştırmaların sistematik derlenmesi. In K. Beycioğlu, N. Özer, & Y. Kondakçı (Eds.), *Eğitim yönetiminde araştırma* (pp. 533–550). Pegem Akademi.

Gündüz, M. (2018). Sosyal bilgilerde değerler eğitimi. İçinde H. Çalışkan & B. Kılcan (Eds.), Sosyal bilgiler öğretimi (s.165-190). Lisans Yayıncılık.

Gündüz, M. (2018). Sosyal bilgilerde değerler eğitimi. İçinde H. Çalışkan ve B. Kılcan (Eds.), Sosyal bilgiler öğretimi (s. 165-190). Lisans Yayıncılık.

Güngör, R. (1995). *Ahlak psikolojisi ve sosyal ahlak*. Ötüken Neşriyat.

Gupta, R., Bakhshi, A., & Einarsen, S. (2017). Investigating Workplace Bullying in India: Psychometric Properties, Validity, and Cutoff Scores of Negative Acts Questionnaire–Revised. *SAGE Open*, *7*(2). Advance online publication. doi:10.1177/2158244017715674

Gürler, Ş. (2012). Okulda değerler eğitimi yöntemler, etkinlikler, kaynaklar. Nobel Yayıncılık https://www.researchgate.net/publication/330245310_Values_Education#fullTextFileContent

Güven, S. (1999). *Toplum bilim*. Ezgi kitapevi.

Hall, S. E. (2018). Kimlik [Identity]. In Değerler eğitimi ansiklopedisi [Moral education/A Handbook] (pp. 320–322). EDAM.

Halstead, J. M. (1996). Values in education and education in values. In Values in education and education in values. Routledge Falmer.

Halstead, J. M. (1996). Values and values education in schools. In J. M. Halstead & M. J. Taylor (Eds.), *Values in education and education in values* (pp. 3–14). The Falmer Press.

Halstead, J. M. (2018). Değerler eğitimi [Value Education]. In *Değerler eğitimi ansiklopedisi* [Moral Education/A Handbook] (pp. 151-152). EDAM.

Halstead, J. M. (2019). Ahlak eğitimi ve yurttaşlık eğitimi [Moral education and civic education]. In R. Bailey, R. Barrow, D. Carr, & C. McCarthy (Eds.), *Eğitim felsefesi kılavuzu* [The SAGE Handbook of philisophy of education] (pp. 249–264). Pegem Akademi.

Halstead, J. M., & Taylor, J. M. (2000). Learning and teaching about values: A review of recent research. *Cambridge Journal of Education*, *30*(2), 169–202. doi:10.1080/713657146

Halstead, J. M., & Taylor, M. J. (2000). *The Development of Values, Attitudes and Personel Qualities*. National Foundation for Educational Research.

Hamada, T., Shimizu, M., & Ebihara, T. (2021). Good patriotism, social consideration, environmental problem cognition, and pro-environmental attitudes and behaviors: A cross-sectional study of Chinese attitudes. *SN Applied Sciences*, *3*(3), 361. Advance online publication. doi:10.100742452-021-04358-1

Hanel, P. H., Wolfradt, U., Wolf, L. J., Coelho, G. L. H., & Maio, G. R. (2020). Well-being as a function of person-country fit in human values. *Nature Communications*, *11*(1), 5150. doi:10.103841467-020-18831-9 PMID:33051452

Hang, Z., Bekker, T., Markopoulos, P., & Brok, P. D. (2020). Children's reflection-in-action during collaborative design-based learning. In The challenges of the digital transformation in education: Proceedings of the 21st international conference on interactive, collaborative learning (ICL2018)-Volume 1 (pp. 790-800). Springer International Publishing.

Haque, F. (2013). Education for Sustainable Development: An Evaluation of the New Curriculum of the Formal Primary Education in Bangladesh. *European Scientific Journal, 1*, 1857–7881.

Harmanşa, T. (2017). *4. sınıf sosyal bilgiler dersinde dürüstlük değerini kazandırmada edebi ürünlerin kullanımı* [Yayımlanmamış yüksek lisans tezi]. Recep Tayyip Erdoğan Üniversitesi, Rize, Türkiye.

Hauge, L. J., & Skogstad, A. (2010). *Personality and Social Sciences The relative impact of workplace bullying as a social stressor at work.* doi:10.1111/j.1467-9450.2010.00813.x

Hauge, L. J., Skogstad, A., & Einarsen, S. (2009). *Work & Stress : An International Journal of Work, Health & Organisations Individual and situational predictors of workplace bullying : Why do perpetrators engage in the bullying of others ?* doi:10.1080/02678370903395568

Havilland, W., Prins, H., Walrath, D. & Mcbride, B. (2008). *Kültürel antropoloji.* Kaknüs yayınları.

Haydon, G. (2021). *Enseñar valores: un nuevo enfoque.* Ediciones Morata.

Heathfield, D. (2014). *Storytelling with our students.* Delta Publishing.

Heilbronn, R. (2019). John Dewey and Moral Education.The Encyclopedia of Educational Philosophy and Theory. Springer: Editor Michael Peters.

Hills, A. (2009). Moral testimony and moral epistemology. *Ethics, 120*(1), 94–127. doi:10.1086/648610

Hinduja, S., Patchin, J. W., Justice, C., & Atlantic, F. (2010). *Archives of Suicide Research Bullying, Cyberbullying.* doi:10.1080/13811118.2010.494133

Hmelo, C. E., & Lin, X. (2000). Becoming self-directed learners: Strategy development in problem-based learning. In D. H. Evensen & C. E. Hmelo (Eds.), *Problem-based learning: A research perspective on learning interactions* (pp. 227–250). Lawrence Erlbaum Associates Publishers.

Hoel, H., & Cooper, C. L. (2010). *The experience of bullying in Great Britain : The impact of organizational status.* doi:10.1080/13594320143000780

Hoge, J. D. (2002). Character education, citizenship education, and the social studies. *Social Studies, 93*(3), 103–108. doi:10.1080/00377990209599891

Horton, P. (2019). The bullied boy: Masculinity, embodiment, and the gendered social-ecology of Vietnamese school bullying. *Gender and Education, 31*(3), 394–407. doi:10.1080/09540253.2018.1458076

Hovdelien, O. (2015). Education and common values in a multicultural society – The Norwegian Case. *Journal of Intercultural Studies (Melbourne, Vic.), 36*(3), 306–319. doi:10.1080/07256868.2015.1029887

Howard, S. (2006). What is Waldorf early childhood education? Waldorf Early Childhood Education Association.

Howard, R. W. (2018). Demokratik değerler [Democratic values]. In *Değerler eğitimi ansiklopedisi* [Moral education/A Handbook] (pp. 157–159). EDAM.

Huah, G. L., Soon, S. T., Tan, J. P. S., Muthukrishnan, P., Revati, R., & Rosalind, A. (2022). A study on children's perceptions of their moral values using an online picture-based values survey. *Computer Assisted Language Learning, 23*(4), 240–262.

Huff, M. J. (2022). *Storytelling with puppets, props, and playful tales*. Curriculum Corporation.

Hughson, T. A., & Wood, B. E. (2022). The OECD Learning Compass 2030 and the future of disciplinary learning: A Bernsteinian critique. *Journal of Education Policy, 37*(4), 634–654.

Huitt, W. (2003). "Survey of Desired Values, Virtues, and Attributes." A preliminary study shows considerable overlap in beliefs among preservice and practicing educators. https://www.edpsycinteractive.org/topics/affect/values.html

Hunt, T. C., & Mullins, M. M. (2018). Giriş [Introduction]. In Değerler eğitimi ansiklopedisi [Moral Education/A Handbook] (pp. vi-xxvi). EDAM.

Hurtado, S., Alvarez, C. I., Guillermo-Wann, C., Cuellar, M., & Arellano, L. (2018). *A model for diverse learning environments*. Springer.

İbret, B. Ü., Karasu-Avcı, E., Karabıyık, Ş., Güleş, M., & Demirci, M. (2017). Sosyal bilgiler öğretmenlerinin görüşlerine göre değerlerin öğretiminde edebi ürünlerin kullanımı. *Uluslararası Türk Eğitim Bilimleri Dergisi, 9*(5), 104–124.

İl, İ. (2018). *Aktif öğrenme yönteminin 5. sınıf öğrencilerinin sözlü iletişim becerilerine (konuşma-dinleme) etkisi ve öğrencilerin aktif öğrenme uygulamalarına ilişkin görüşleri* [Yayımlanmamış yüksek lisans tezi]. Van Yüzüncü Yıl Üniversitesi, Van, Türkiye.

Ilyabolotov. (2019, January 28). *Trash can full of garbage bin filled with waste*. IStock. https://www.istockphoto.com/en/vector/trash-can-full-gm1125611454-295978809?phrase=rubbish+bin

İnan, C., & Ve Erkuş, S. (2022). Çoklu zeka kuramına dayalı hazırlanan çalışma yapraklarının ortaokul 6. Sınıf öğrencilerinin matematik başarılarına ve tutumlarına etkisi. *Uluslararası Eğitim Bilimleri Dergisi, 9*(30), 111–154.

İnce, M. (2021). *Sosyal bilgiler öğretmen adaylarının vatanseverlik değeri ve vatanseverlik eğitimi hakkındaki görüşleri* [Yayımlanmamış yüksek lisans tezi]. Akdeniz Üniversitesi, Antalya, Türkiye.

İnce, B. (2012). Citizenship education in Turkey: Inclusive or exclusive. *Oxford Review of Education, 38*(2), 115–131. doi:10.1080/03054985.2011.651314

Inglehart, R. (2016). Mapping global values. *Comparative Sociology, 5*(2), 115–136. doi:10.1163/156913306778667401

İşisağ, K. U. (2010). The acceptance and recognition of cultural diversity in foreign language teaching. *Gazi Akademik Bakış, 4*(7), 251-260. https://dergipark.org.tr/en/pub/gav/issue/6524/86512

Islam, M. (2019). Quality of Primary Education Management System of Bangladesh: A Case Study on Jhenaidaj Upazila Education Office. *International Journal for Research in Applied Science and Engineering Technology, 7*(2), 78–96. Advance online publication. doi:10.22214/ijraset.2019.2014

Islam, T., Rashel, A., Lim, Y. T., & Sang-Gyun, N. (2019). The role of management and monitoring in achieving quality primary education at char area in Bangladesh. *International Journal of Learning. Teaching and Educational Research, 18*(7), 245–260. Advance online publication. doi:10.26803/ijlter.18.7.16

Janelle, M. (2023). *Teaching Values to Students in Health Education*. Project School Welness, PSW. Retrieved 12 June from https://www.projectschoolwellness.com/teaching-values-to-students-in-health-education/

Janelle, T. (2023). *Understanding Sexual Values and the Fundamental Role Values Play in Raising Sexually Healthy Children*. Western Oregon University. Retrieved 19 April from https://wou.edu/health/resources/student-health-101/spiritual-wellness/personal-values/

Jessiman, P., Kidger, J., Spencer, L., Simpson, E. G., Kaluzeviciute, G., Burn, A. M., Leonard, N., & Limmer, M. (2022). School culture and student mental health : A qualitative study in UK secondary schools. *BMC Public Health*, *22*(1), 1–18. doi:10.118612889-022-13034-x PMID:35351062

Johann, A., & Martinez, S. (2016). *Managing workplace violence with Evidence-Based Interventions*. Academic Press.

Johnson, J. S., & Newport, E. L. (1989). Critical period effects in second language learning: The influence of maturational state on the acquisition of English as a second language. *Cognitive Psychology*, *21*(1), 60–99. doi:10.1016/0010-0285(89)90003-0 PMID:2920538

Kabapınar, Y. (2019). *Kuramdan uygulamaya hayat bilgisi ve sosyal bilgiler öğretimi*. Pegem Akademi Yayıncılık.

KajaNi. (2021, August 15). *Big dump with of trash and rubbish waste recycling in city landfill*. IStock. https://www.istockphoto.com/en/vector/pile-of-garbage-isolated-on-white-background-gm1334125608-416372596?phrase=rubbish

Kallestad, J. H. (2010). Changes in School Climate in a Long-Term Perspective. *Scandinavian Journal of Educational Research*, *54*(1), 1–14. doi:10.1080/00313830903488429

Kan, Ç. (2010). Sosyal bilgiler dersi ve değerler eğitimi. *Milli Eğitim*, (187), 138-145.

Kan, Ç. (2010). Sosyal Bilgiler dersi ve değerler eğitimi. *Milli Eğitim Dergisi*, *187*, 138–145.

KanKhem. (2019, March 12). *Vector illustration of happy kids riding bicycles in the park*. IStock. https://www.istockphoto.com/en/vector/vector-illustration-of-happy-kids-riding-bicycles-in-the-park-gm1135282671-301961955?phrase=bicycle+cycling+child

Kapan, A. (2019). *6.sınıf sosyal bilgiler ders kitabında önerilen edebi ürünlerin öğrenme alanlarında yer alan değerler açısından incelenmesi* [Yayımlanmamış yüksek lisans tezi]. Tokat Gaziosmanpaşa Üniversitesi, Tokat, Türkiye.

Kappes, M. S., Keiler, M., von Elverfeldt, K., & Glade, T. (2012). Challenges of analyzing multi-hazard risk: A review. In Natural Hazards (Vol. 64, Issue 2, pp. 1925–1958). doi:10.100711069-012-0294-2

Karakoc, B., Eryilmaz, K., Ozpolat, E. T., & Yildirim, I. (2022). The effect of game-based learning on student achievement: A meta-analysis study. *Technology. Knowledge and Learning*, *27*(1), 1–16. doi:10.100710758-020-09471-5

Karaman, B., Er, H., & Karadeniz, O. (2022). Teaching with educational games in social studies: A teacher's perspective. *The Turkish Online Journal of Educational Technology*, *21*(1), 124–137.

Karaman, F. (1996). Tevekkül inancı üzerine bir inceleme. *Fırat Üniversitesi İlahiyat Fakültesi Dergisi*, *1*, 67–92.

Karamanlıoğlu, A. F. (2006). *Şeyh Şeref Hâce, Mu'înü'l-Mürîd, transkripsiyonlu metin-dizin-tıpkıbasım*. Beşir Kitabevi.

Karasu Avcı, E., Faiz, M., & Turan, S. (2020). Etkili vatandaşlık eğitiminde değerler eğitimi: Sosyal bilgiler öğretmenlerinin düşünceleri. *Değerler Eğitimi Dergisi*, *18*(39), 263–296. doi:10.34234/ded.655916

Karataş, K. & Baloğlu, M. (2019). Tevekkülün psikolojik yansımaları. *Çukurova Üniversitesi İlahiyat Fakültesi Dergisi*, *19*(1), 110-118.

Karataş, T. N. (2023). *Sınıf öğretmeni adayları için aktif öğrenme temelli çocuk hakları eğitimi* [Yayımlanmamış yüksek lisans tezi]. Gaziantep Üniversitesi, Gaziantep, Türkiye.

Karataş, Ö. F., Cengiz, C., & Ve Çalışkan, B. (2018). İşbirliğine dayalı ve çalışma yaprakları ile desteklenmiş öğrenme ortamında gerçekleştirilen öğretimin öğrencilerin akademik başarıları üzerine etkisi. [ADEDER]. *Araştırma ve Deneyim Dergisi*, *3*(1), 1–16.

Karatay, H. (2011). Karakter eğitiminde edebi eserlerin kullanımı. *Turkish Studies - International Periodical for The Languages. Literature and History of Turkish or Turkic, 6*(1), 1398–1412.

Karatay, H. (2011). Karakter eğitiminde edebi eserlerin kullanımı. *Turkish Studies, 6*(1), 1398–1412.

Karatay, H. (2011). Transfer values in the Turkish and Western Children's literacy work Character education in Turkey. *Educational Research Review, 6*(6), 472–480.

Kaya, F. (2021). *İlköğretim öğrencilerinin sosyal bilgiler ile insan hakları yurttaşlık ve demokrasi derslerindeki değerlere ilişkin tutumları* [Yayımlanmamış yüksek lisans tezi]. Erzincan Binali Yıldırım Üniversitesi, Erzincan, Türkiye.

Kaya, Ö. (1989). *Ali Şir Nevâyî fevayidü'l-kiber (inceleme-metin-dizin)* [Unpublished PhD Thesis]. Ankara Üniversitesi.

Kaya, E. ve Ekiçi, M. (2015). Sosyal bilgiler öğretiminde gezi yazılarından yararlanma: Gülten Dayıoğlu'nun gezi yazıları örneği. [TSA]. *Türkiye Sosyal Araştırmalar Dergisi, 19*(1), 87–114.

Kayır, A. (2011). Cinsellik ve Cinsel Eğitim. In *Gria Reklam Ltd.Şti.: Turkey Family Health and Planning Foundation.* CETAD.

Kaymakcan, R., & Meydan, H. (2010). Democratic citizenship and religious education: New approaches and an evaluation in the context of DKAB courses in Turkey. İnönü University. *Journal of Theology Faculty., 1*(1), 29–53.

Kaymakcan, R., & Meydan, H. (2014). *Ahlak, değerler ve eğitimi* [Morals, values and education]. DEM.

Kaymakcı, S. (2010). *Sosyal bilgiler öğretiminde çalışma yaprakları kullanımının öğrencilerin akademik başarılarına ve derse karşı tutumlarına etkisi* [Yayımlanmamış doktora tezi]. Gazi Üniversitesi, Ankara, Türkiye.

Kaymakcı, S. (2013). Sosyal bilgiler ders kitaplarında sözlü ve yazılı edebî türlerin kullanım durumu. *Dicle Üniversitesi Ziya Gökalp Eğitim Fakültesi Dergisi,* (20), 230-255.

Kaymakcı, S. (2012). Sosyal bilgiler öğretim programı kılavuz kitaplarında çalışma yaprakları. *Fırat Üniversitesi Sosyal Bilimler Dergisi, 22*(2), 169–176.

Kaymakcı, S. (2013). Sosyal bilgiler ders kitaplarında sözlü ve yazılı edebî türlerin kullanım durumu. *Dicle Üniversitesi Ziya Gökalp Eğitim Fakültesi Dergisi, 20,* 230–255.

Kekic, D., & Milenkovic, M. (2015). *Disaster risk reduction through education.* https://www.researchgate.net/publication/309728178_Disaster_risk_reduction_through_education

Kelly, G. A. (1955). *A theory of personality: The psychology of personal constructs.* Norton.

Keltner, D., & Marsh, J. (Eds.). (2018). *The Compassionate Instinct: The Science of Human Goodness.* W. W. Norton & Company.

Keskin, S. (2019). *Çalışma yapraklarıyla ortaokul 8.sınıflarda üçgenler konusunun öğretiminin akademik başarıya etkisinin incelenmesi* [Yayımlanmamış doktora tezi]. Atatürk Üniversitesi, Erzurum, Türkiye.

Kılıç, A. (2007). *Fedakâr Eş- Fedakâr Yurttaş, Yurttaşlık Bilgisi ve Yurttaş Eğitimi 1970- 1990.* Kitap Publishing.

Kılınç, F. (2015). *Okul öncesi ve ilkokul döneminde değerler eğitimi.* Eğiten Kitap Yayınları.

Kırıkkaya, E. B., Ünver, A. O., & Çakın, O. (2011). Teachers views on the topic of disaster education at the field on elementary science and technology curriculum. *Necatibey Eğitim Fakültesi Elektronik Fen ve Matematik Eğitimi Dergisi, 5*(1), 24–42.

Kırışoğlu, O. (1991). *Sanatta eğitimi.* Demircioğlu matbaası.

Kirmizi, F. S. (2014). 4. sınıf Türkçe ders kitabı metinlerinde yer alan değerler. *Değerler Eğitimi Dergisi, 12*(27), 217–259.

Kirschenbaum, H. (2000). From values clarification to character education: A personal journey. *Journal of Humanistic Counseling. Education & Development, 39*(1), 4-1.

Kirschenbaum, H. (1994). *100 Ways to enhance values and morality in schools and youth settings.* Allyn & Bacon, Old Tappan.

Kirschenbaum, H. (1994). *100 ways to enhance values and morality in schools and youth settings.* Allyn and Bacon.

Knafo, A., & Plomin, R. (2006). Prosocial Behavior from Early to Middle Childhood: Genetic and Environmental Influences on Stability and Change. *Developmental Psychology, 42*(5), 771–786. doi:10.1037/0012-1649.42.5.771 PMID:16953685

Knafo, A., & Schwartz, S. H. (2004). Identity status and parent-child value congruence in adolescence. *British Journal of Developmental Psychology, 22*(3), 439–458. doi:10.1348/0261510041552765

Kocayiğit, A., & Sağnak, M. (2012). İlköğretim okullarında etik iklimin çeşitli değişkenler açısından incelenmesi. *Değerler Eğitimi Dergisi, 10*(23), 183-197. https://dergipark.org.tr/en/pub/ded/issue/29177/312444

Kohlberg, L. (1964). Development of moral character and moral ideology. *Review of child development research, 1,* 381-431.

Kök, A. (2004). *Karahanlı Türkçesi satır-arası Kur'an tercümesi (TİEM 73 1v-235v/2) giriş inceleme-metin-dizin* [PhD thesis]. Ankara Üniversitesi Sosyal Bilimler Enstitüsü.

Kolaç, E., & Özer, H. (2018). Sosyal bilgiler öğretiminde edebî ürünlerin kullanımı ve değer aktarımındaki katkılarına yönelik öğretmen adaylarının görüşleri. *Uluslararası Türkçe Edebiyat Kültür Eğitim Dergisi, 7*(4), 2629–2655.

Kołczyńska, M. (2020). Democratic values, education, and political trust. *International Journal of Comparative Sociology, 61*(1), 3–26. doi:10.1177/0020715220909881

Konca, M. (2022). *Çalışma yapraklarıyla destekli etkinliklerin fen bilimleri dersi 7. sınıf öğrencilerinin hücre ve bölünmeler ünitesini öğrenmelerine etkisinin incelenmesi* [Yayımlanmamış yüksek lisans tezi]. Kastamonu Üniversitesi, Kastamonu, Türkiye.

Kopp, B., Niedermeier, S., & Mandl, H. (2014). *Actual practical value education in Germany* (Conference Paper), ICERI 2014 (17th-19th November 2014), Seville, Spain.

Kouicem, K. (2019). Exploring English in education policy in Algeria: Obstacles to its Promotion. *Ichkalat Journal, 8*(4), 573-592.

Köylü, M. (2013). *Küresel ahlak eğitimi* [Global moral education]. DEM.

Kucan, L., & Beck, I. L. (1997). Thinking aloud and reading comprehension research: Inquiry, instruction, and social interaction. *Review of Educational Research, 67*(3), 271–299.

Kucher, T. (2021). Principles and best practices of designing digital game-based learning environments. *International Journal of Technology in Education and Science, 5*(2), 213-223. . doi:10.46328/ijtes.190

Kula, S. S. (2021). Mind games with the views of classroom teachers. *International Journal of Research in Education and Science, 7*(3), 747–766. doi:10.46328/ijres.1471

Kulig, J. C. (2023). *Values In Health Education.* Encyclopedia of Public Health. Retrieved 15 June from https://www.encyclopedia.com/education/encyclopedias-almanacs-transcripts-and-maps/values-health-education

Kurtdede Fidan, N. (2013). Sosyal bilgiler dersinde değerler eğitimi: Nitel bir araştırma. *The International Journal of Social Sciences (Islamabad), 6*(3), 361–388.

Kurttekin, F. (2013). *MEB tarafından tavsiye edilen 100 temel eserden popüler olan on kitap örneğinde dinî ve ahlâkî değerler* [Yayımlanmamış yüksek lisans tezi]. Uludağ Üniversitesi, Bursa, Türkiye.

Kuş, Z. (2016). Demokratik vatandaşlık. İçinde B. Tay ve S. B. Beşir (Eds.), Sosyal bilgiler öğretimi: ilkeler ve uygulamalar (s. 196-208). Anı Yayıncılık.

Kwiek, M. (2003). The Social functions of the university in the context of the changing State. *Market Relations*, 2-31.

Lakhal, A., & Benmati, K. (2008). *Is the Algerian educational system weakening? An investigation of the high school curricula and their adequacy with the other curricula. Mentouri University Constantine.* University Curricula.

Lave, J., & Wenger, E. (1991). *Situated learning: Legitimate peripheral participation.* Cambridge University Press.

Lee, D., & Profeli, E. (2015). Youths' socialization to work and school within the family. *International Journal for Educational and Vocational Guidance*, *15*(2), 145–162. doi:10.100710775-015-9302-x PMID:26101556

Lee, J.-S., Lee, C.-K., & Choi, Y. (2010). Examining the role of emotional and functional values in festival evaluation. *Journal of Travel Research*, *50*(6), 685–696. doi:10.1177/0047287510385465

Lemba, J. (2020, August 13). *Paper sheets pile for paperwork and office routine: Heap of white papers.* IStock. https://www.istockphoto.com/en/vector/paper-sheets-pile-gm1266139919-371087003?phrase=paper+pile

Lenneberg, E. H. (1967). *Biological foundations of language.* Wiley.

Leymann, H. (1996). The content and development of mobbing at work. *European Journal of Work and Organizational Psychology*, *5*(2), 165–184. doi:10.1080/13594329608414853

Lickona, T. (1991). *Educating for Character: How our schools can teach respect and responsibility.* Bantam House. https://liu.se/en/research/values-education

Lickona, Th. (1989). *How to raise good children! The moral development of the child from Birth through adolescence and what you can do to help.*

Lickona, T. (1991). *Educating for character: How our schools can teach respect and responsibility.* Bantam.

Lickona, T. (1993). The return of character education. *Educational Leadership*, *51*(3), 6–11.

Lightbown, P. M., & Spada, N. (2021). *How languages are learned* (5th ed.). Oxford University Press.

Li, N., Zhang, L., Xiao, G., Chen, Z. J., & Lu, Q. (2020). Effects of organizational commitment, job satisfaction, and workplace violence on turnover intention of emergency nurses: A cross-sectional study. *International Journal of Nursing Practice*, *26*(6), 1–9. doi:10.1111/ijn.12854 PMID:32529786

Lind, G. (2009), Morality is teachable. Munich: Oldenbourg. Lind, G. (2011). Moral education. In: E. Zierer & K. Kiel (eds.). Basic knowledge of lesson design (p. 39-50). Schneider.

Lind, G. (2012). The method of dilemma discussion. In F. Brüggen, W. Sander, & Ch. Igelbrink (Hrsg.), Basic texts on judgment formation (judgment formation, vol. 2).

Lin, G. (2009). Higher education research methodology-literature method. *International Education Studies*, *2*(4), 179–181. doi:10.5539/ies.v2n4p179

Liu, H., Yu, S., Cottrell, L., Lunn, S., Deveaux, L., Brathwaite, N. V., Marshall, S., Li, X., & Stanton, B. (2007). Personal values and involvement in problem behaviors among Bahamian early adolescents: A cross-sectional study. *BMC Public Health*, *7*(1), 135. doi:10.1186/1471-2458-7-135 PMID:17605792

López Díaz, C. (2019). *El valor de los cuentos como parte de la educación en valores*. Central Sindical Independiente y de Funcionarios.

López, R. (2021). *Educar en valores*. Adice Ediciones.

Louis, K. S. (2023). Democratic Schools, Democratic Communities. *Leadership and Policy in Schools*, *2*(2), 93–108. doi:10.1076/lpos.2.2.93.15544

Lovat, T., & Clement, N. (2018). The pedagogical imperative of values education. *Journal of Beliefs & Values*, *29*(3), 273–285. doi:10.1080/13617670802465821

Luik, P., & Taimalu, M. (2021). Predicting the intention to use technology in education among student teachers: A path analysis. *Education Sciences*, *11*(9), 1–14. doi:10.3390/educsci11090564

Lutgen-Sandvik, P., Tracy, S. J., & Alberts, J. K. (2007). Burned by bullying in the American workplace: Prevalence, perception, degree, and impact. *Journal of Management Studies*, *44*(6), 837–862. doi:10.1111/j.1467-6486.2007.00715.x

Lyubomirsky, S., Dickerhoof, R., Boehm, J. K., & Sheldon, K. M. (2011). Becoming happier takes both a will and a proper way: An experimental longitudinal intervention to boost well-being. *Emotion (Washington, D.C.)*, *11*(2), 391–402. doi:10.1037/a0022575 PMID:21500907

Lyubomirsky, S., & Layous, K. (2013). How do simple positive activities increase well-being? *Current Directions in Psychological Science*, *22*(1), 57–62. doi:10.1177/0963721412469809

Maamri, M. R. (2009). The Syndrome of the French Language in Algeria. *The International Journal of the Arts in Society*, *3*(3), 77–89.

Malti, T., Gummerum, M., Keller, M., & Chaparro, M. P. (2009). The Development of Emoral Emotions and Decision-Making from Adolescence to Early Adulthood: A 6-Year Longitudinal Study. *Journal of Personality and Social Psychology*, *96*(4), 970–987.

Mandl, H. (2016), Mint and Values - Formation of Values in Experimental Lessons. Interview with the Siemens Foundation. https://www.siemens-stiftung.org/de/projects/mint-und- values/insight/

Mango, A. (2004). *Atatürk Modern Türkiye'nin Kurucusu*. Remzi Publishing.

Manseur, R., & Negadi, M. N. (2019). Parents' attitudes towards exposing their children to English in Algerian Primary Education. *International Journal of English Linguistics*, *9*(4), 145. doi:10.5539/ijel.v9n4p145

Mansour, R. (2020). *Introducing the English language in The Algerian Primary Schools: Teachers, parents, and pupils' attitudes*. University of Tlemcen.

Marouf, N. (2017). English in Algerian primary schools between necessity and contingency. *Journal Al Nassr*, *4*(1), 4-15.

Marples, R. (2017). Art, knowledge and moral understanding. *Ethics and Education, 12*(2), 243-258. doi:10.1080/17449642.2017.1323425

Martínez Martin, M., & Hoyos Vásquez, G. (2014). *Educar en valores es crear condiciones. ¿Qué significa educar en valores hoy?* Octaedro.

Matanle, P. (2011). The Great East Japan Earthquake, tsunami, and nuclear meltdown: Towards the (re) construction of a safe, sustainable, and compassionate society in Japan's shrinking regions. *Local Environment*, *16*(9), 823–847. doi:10.1080/13549839.2011.607160

367

Mathers, N. (2016, July). Compassion and the science of kindness: Harvard Davis Lecture 2015. *The British Journal of General Practice*, *66*(648), e525–e527. doi:10.3399/bjgp16X686041 PMID:27364679

Mathur, S. R., & Corley, K. M. (2014). Bringing ethics into the classroom: Making a case for frameworks, multiple perspectives and narrative sharing. *International Education Studies*, *7*(9). Advance online publication. doi:10.5539/ies. v7n9p136

Matvienko1, O. V., Kudina, V. V., & Kuzmina, S. A. (2022). *Values education and teaching zest for life: Japanese experience and New Ukrainian school reform*. 8th International Conference on Higher Education Advances (HEAd'22), Valencia, Spain. http://dx.doi.org/ doi:10.4995/HEAd22.2022.14626

McCall, A. L. (2010). Teaching powerful social studies ideas through literature Circles. *Social Studies*, *101*(4), 152–159.

McGuire, J. (2001). *What works in correctional intervention? Evidence and practical implications Offender rehabilitation in practice: Implementing and evaluating effective programs*. Academic Press.

McLaughlin, T. H. (1992). Citizenship, diversity and education: A philosophical perspective. *Journal of Moral Education*, *21*(3), 235–250. doi:10.1080/0305724920210307

MEB. (2005). *İlköğretim sosyal bilgiler dersi 4-5. sınıflar öğretim programı (taslak basım)*. MEB Yayınevi.

MEB. (2018). *Sosyal bilgiler dersi öğretim programı (ilkokul ve ortaokul 4, 5, 6 ve 7. sınıflar)*. TTKB. http://mufredat. meb.gov.tr/ProgramDetay.aspx?PID=354

Meehan, Z. M., Hubbard, J. A., Bookhout, M. K., Swift, L. E., Docimo, M., & Grassetti, S. N. (2023). School Absenteeism and In-class Avoidant Behaviors Mediate the Link Between Peer Victimization and Academic Outcomes. *School Mental Health*, *2010*(2), 519–527. Advance online publication. doi:10.100712310-023-09566-1

Meier, M. (2008). *Cyber Bullying: Overview and Strategies for School Counsellors, Guidance Officers, and All School Personnel*. Academic Press.

MentalHelp. (2023). *Self-Identity and Values*. Supermind Platforms, Inc. Retrieved 15 June from https://www.mentalhelp. net/adolescent-development/self-identity-and-values/

Mercin, L., & Diksoy, İ. (2017). Değerler eğitiminde görsel sanatların yeri. In Ö. Demirel & S. Dinçer (Eds.), *Küreselleşen dünyada eğitim*. Pegem Akademi. doi:10.14527/9786053188407.20

Merriam, S. B. (2013). *Qualitative research* (S. Turan, Trans.). Nobel Publishing.

Meydan, H. (2014). An evaluation of the role of values education in school and values education approaches. *Journal of Theology Faculty of Bülent Ecevit University*, *1*(1), 93–108.

Michaelis, U. J. (1988). *Social studies for children (A guide to basic instruction)*. Prentice Hall Inc.

Miliani, M. (2010). Between enduring hardships and fleeting ideals. *Mediterranean Journal of Educational Studies*, *15*(2), 65–76.

Milli Eğitim Bakanlığı (MEB). (2005). İlköğretim sosyal bilgiler dersi 6–7.sınıflar öğretim programı ve kılavuzu (taslak basım). Ankara: Millî Eğitim Bakanlığı Talim ve Terbiye Kurulu Başkanlığı, Devlet Kitapları Müdürlüğü.

Milli Eğitim Bakanlığı (MEB). (2018). *Sosyal bilgiler dersi öğretim programı (ilkokul ve ortaokul 4, 5, 6 ve 7. sınıflar)*. TTKB. http://mufredat.meb.gov.tr/ProgramDetay.aspx?PID=354

Millî Eğitim Bakanlığı [MEB] (2017). **Error! Hyperlink reference not valid.** https://ttkb.meb.gov.tr/meb_iys_dosyalar/2017_07/18160003_basin_aciklamasilamasi-program.pdf s.24

Millî Eğitim Bakanlığı. (2013). *İlkokul ve ortaokul görsel sanatlar dersi öğretim programı.* Millî Eğitim Bakanlığı yayınları. http://www.eryamansanat.com/pluginfile.php/334/mod_resource/content/2/ilkokul%20ve%20ortaokul%20 g%C3%B6rsel%20sanatlar%20ders%20program%C4%B1.pdf

Milroy, J. (2001). Language ideologies and the consequences of standardization. *Journal of Sociolinguistics, 5*(4), 530–555. doi:10.1111/1467-9481.00163

Mindivanlı, E., & Küçük, B. ve Aktaş, E. (2012). Sosyal bilgiler dersinde değerlerin aktarımında atasözleri ve deyimlerin kullanımı. *Eğitim ve Öğretim Araştırmaları Dergisi, 1*(3), 93–101.

Mintz, S. (2018). *What are values?* Ethics Sage. Retrieved 15 June from https://www.ethicssage.com/2018/08/what-are-values.html

MOE. (2010). Revised Pre-University Civics Syllabus. http://www.moe.gov.sg/education/syllabuses/aesthetics-health-and-moraleducation/files/civics-pre-university-2007.pdf

Molina Prieto, R. (2018). *Los cuentos ayudan a crecer.* Central Sindical Independiente y de Funcionarios.

Moltudal, S. H., Krumsvik, R. J., & Høydal, K. L. (2022). Adaptive Learning Technology in Primary Education: Implications for Professional Teacher Knowledge and Classroom Management. *Frontiers in Education, 7*, 830536. Advance online publication. doi:10.3389/feduc.2022.830536

Monia, S. H. (2020). Towards a normative legal mechanism of a unitary primary education in bangladesh. *Education. Sustainability Science, 3*(2), 65–68. Advance online publication. doi:10.26480/ess.02.2020.65.68

Morgan, J., & Rinvolucri, M. (2014). *Using stories in the language classroom.* Cambridge University Press.

Mosley, A. & Baltazar, E. (n.d.). *An introduction to logic: from everyday life to formal systems.* Smith College.

Moss, P. and Urban, M. (2010). *Democracy and experimentation: Two fundamental values for education.* Bertelsmann Stiftung, 1-96

Mourao, S. (2019). *Using stories in the Primary classroom.* APAC.

Mullins, M. M. (2018). Vatandaşlık eğitimi [Citizenship education]. In *Değerler eğitimi ansiklopedisi* [Moral education/A Handbook] (pp. 500–502). EDAM.

Multrus, U. (2008), Values education in schools - An overview of current concepts. In the Bavarian State Ministry for Education and Culture (ed.), Values make you strong. Values Education Practice Guide (1st Edition, pp. 22-37). Brigg Pedagogy.

Mumcu, A. (1992). *Tarih Açısından Türk Devrimi'nin Temelleri ve Gelişimi.* İnkılap Publishing.

Muthukrishnan, P., & Huah, G. L. (2023). A study on children's understandings of values through reflective practices using a values-based reflection framework (VBRF). In Reimagining Innovation in Education and Social Sciences (pp. 295-304). Routledge. doi:10.1201/9781003366683-36

Muttaqin, M., Raharjo, T., & Masturi, M. (2018). The implementation of main values of character education reinforcement in elementary school. *Journal of Primary Education, 7*(1), 103–112. doi:10.15294/jpe.v7i1.22766

Myers, D. G. (2011). *Social psychology* (10th ed.). McGraw Hill Companies, Inc.

Narvaez, D., & Lapsley, D. K. (2005). The psychological foundations of everyday morality and moral expertise. In J. L. Bermudez, A. Marcel, & N. Eilan (Eds.), *The body and the self* (pp. 37–61). MIT Press.

Nash, J. M. (1997). Fertile minds. *Time, 149*(5), 48–56. PMID:10169172

National Council for the Social Studies Task Force on Early Childhood/Elementary Social Studies. (1989). Social studies for early childhood and elementary school children preparing for the 21st century. *Social Education*, *53*, 14–23.

National Council for the Social Studies Task Force on Scope and Sequence. (1989). In search of a scope and sequence for social studies: Report of the National Council for the Social Studies Task Force on Scope and Sequence. *Social Education*, *53*, 375–387.

National Council for the Social Studies. (2008). A vision of powerful teaching and learning in the social studies: Building influential citizens. *Social Education*, *72*, 277–280.

Naurath, E. (2013). Appreciation as a basic pedagogical attitude for the formation of values. In E. Naurath, M. Blasberg-Kuhnke, E. Gläser, R. Mokrosch, & S. Müller-Using (Eds.), *How values are formed. Interdisciplinary and subject-specific value formation* (pp. 29–42). Goettingen University Press Osnabrück., doi:10.14220/9783737001304.29

Naurath, E., Blasberg-Kuhnke, M., Gläser, E., Mokrosch, R., & Müller-Using, S. (Eds.). (2013). *How values are created. Interdisciplinary and subject-specific values*. Goettingen University Press.

Naylor, D. T., & Diem, R. (1987). *Elementary and middle school social studies*. Random House.

Nel, P. W., Finchilescu, G., & Breetzke, G. D. (2017). Bullying, kindness, and school satisfaction in South Africa. *Journal of Psychology in Africa*, *27*(4), 335–339.

Nelson, K., & Shouse, R. C. (Eds.). (2019). *Handbook of Mindfulness and Self-Regulation*. Springer.

Nesmeyanov, E. E., Olenich, T. S., & Plotnikov, S. A. (2016). *Interethnic relations in the Rostov region: history, current state, regulation practices and prospects. Materials of the scientific and practical conference. In "Attitude of young people to Orthodoxy" in the aspect of analyzing the problem of interethnic relations in the south of Russia, in the Rostov region*. DSTU.

Nguyen, D. T. N., Teo, S. T. T., Grover, S. L., Phong, N., & Grover, S. L. (2017). Psychological safety climate and workplace bullying in Vietnams public sector. *Public Management Review*, *00*(00), 1–22. doi:10.1080/14719037.2016.1272712

Niedhammer, I., David, S., & Degioanni, S. (2006). *Association between workplace bullying and depressive symptoms in the French working population*. doi:10.1016/j.jpsychores.2006.03.051

Nielsen-Bohlman, L., Panzer, A. M., & Kindig, D. A. (2004). Health Literacy: A Prescription to End Confusion. National Academies Press. doi:10.17226/10883

Noddings, N. (2013). *Caring: A relational approach to ethics and moral education*. University of California Press.

Nowack, D., & Schoderer, S. (2020). *The role of values for social cohesion: theoretical explication and empirical exploration*. Deutsches Institut für Entwicklungspolitik., . doi:10.23661/dp6.2020

Nucci, L. P. (2006). *Education in the moral domain*. Cambridge University Press.

Nucci, L. P., & Narvaez, D. (Eds.). (2008). *Handbook of moral and character education*. Routledge.

Nunner-Winkler, G. (2007). Understanding Morals - Developments in Childhood. In D. Horster (ed.), Moral Development of Children and Adolescents (pp. 51-76). Wiesbaden: Publishing house for social sciences.

Nunner-Winkler, G. (2009). Processes of moral learning and unlearning. *Journal of Education*, *55*(2), 528–548.

Nurse Key, F. (2017). *Concepts and values in health promotion*. Retrieved 15 June from https://nursekey.com/concepts-and-values-in-health-promotion/

Nurses, S. (2014). *6. sınıf sosyal bilgiler dersinde yer alan 'Türkiye'de iklim bölgeleri' konusunun öğretiminde görsel materyalleri kullanmanın öğrenci başarısına etkileri* [Yayımlanmamış yüksek lisans tezi]. Atatürk Üniversitesi, Erzurum, Türkiye.

Nzıadam, L. (2020). Education in a democratic and multicultural Nigerian State: an assessment. *Afro Eurasian Studies, 9*(2), 102-112. https://do.org/10.33722/afes.1099684

O'Connell, M. E., Boat, T., & Warner, K. E. (2009). *Risk and Protective Factors for Youth.* youth.Gov. Retrieved 3 June from https://youth.gov/youth-topics/youth-mental-health/risk-and-protective-factors-youth

O'Driscoll, M. P., Cooper-Thomas, H. D., Bentley, T., Catley, B. E., Gardner, D. H., & Trenberth, L. (2011). Workplace bullying in new zealand: A survey of employee perceptions and attitudes. *Asia Pacific Journal of Human Resources, 49*(4), 390–408. doi:10.1177/1038411111422140

O'Neill, H. (2016). *Başarının Yol Haritası Aktif Öğrenme (Etkili Öğrenci).* Siyah Beyaz Yayınları.

Obaydullah, H. M. A. and Dr. A. K. M. (2019). Inclusive Practice and Barriers in the Primary Education of Bangladesh. *International Journal of Advance Research and Innovative Ideas in Education, 5*(4).

OECD. (2009). *Creating effective teaching and learning environments: first results from TALIS.* https://www.oecd.org/education/school/43023606.pdf

OECD. (2018). *The future of education and skills: Education 2030.* OECD Publishing. https://www.oecd.org/education/2030-project/

Ogieurvil. (2018, March 6). *Funny and cute tap water - vector.* IStock. https://www.istockphoto.com/en/vector/cute-tap-water-gm927423546-254420819?phrase=water+tap

Olenich, T. S. (2019). The problem of suicide in the context of religious security. In Interdisciplinary problems of international relations in a global context (pp. 125- 134). Rostov-on-Don: Rostov State Economic University "RINH".

Olenich, T., Terarakelyants, V., Shestopalova, O., & Biryukov, I. (2020). E3S Web of Conferences 210 - Innovative Technologies in Science and Education (ITSE- 2020). *Sport Spirituality as an Educational Innovation, 210.* . doi:10.1051/e3sconf/202021017006

Olweus, D. (1994). Bullying at school: Basic facts and an effective intervention program. *Promotion & Education, 1*(4), 27–31.

Olweus, D. A. (2014). *Bullying in schools : facts and intervention.* Academic Press.

Onay, İ. (2020). *Sorumluluk değeri etkinliklerinin ilkokul 4. sınıf öğrencilerinin sorumluluk kazanım düzeylerine etkisi* [Yayımlanmamış yüksek lisans tezi]. Ondokuz Mayıs Üniversitesi, Samsun, Türkiye.

Önder, M., & Bulut, H. (2014). Temel dinî değerler ve değerler eğitimi. *Erzincan Üniversitesi Sosyal Bilimler Enstitüsü Dergisi, 6*(1), 15–32.

Orkun, H. N. (1994). *Eski Türk yazıtları.* Türk Dil Kurumu.

Ortega Ruiz, P., & Hernández Prados, M. (2018). Lectura, narración y experiencia en la educación en valores. *Revista iberoamericana de educación, 45*, 1-5.

Ortega Ruiz, P., & Mínguez Vallejos, R. (2021). *Los valores en la educación.* Editorial Ariel.

Oruç, Ş. (2009). Sosyal bilgiler 6. sınıf ders kitaplarında edebi ürünler. *Türkiye sosyal Araştırmalar Dergisi,* (2), 10-24.

Oruç, Ş. ve Ulusoy, K. (2008). Sosyal Bilgiler Öğretimi Alanında Yapılan Tez Çalışmaları. Selçuk Üniversitesi *Ahmet Keleşoğlu Eğitim Fakültesi Dergisi*, (26), 121-138.

Oruç, Ş. ve Erdem, R. (2010). Sosyal bilgiler öğretiminde biyografi kullanımının öğrencilerin sosyal bilgiler dersine ilişkin tutumlarına etkisi. *Selçuk Üniversitesi Ahmet Keleşoğlu Eğitim Fakültesi Dergisi, 30*, 215–229.

Oser, A. D., & Patry, J.-L. (Eds.), *Effective and Responsible Teaching* (pp. 109–125). Jossey Bass.

Oser, F. (1986). Moral education and value education: The discourse perspective. In M. C. Wittwock (Ed.), *Handbuch der Lehrforschung* (pp. 917–941). Macmillan.

Oser, F. (1992). *Morality in professional action: A discourse approach for teaching*. In FK.

Oser, F. (2005). Negative knowledge and morality. *Journal of Education, 49*, 171–181.

Oser, F., & Spychiger, M. (2005). *Learning is painful. On the theory of negative knowledge and the practice of error culture*. Beltz.

Otake, K., Shimai, S., Tanaka-Matsumi, J., Otsui, K., & Fredrickson, B. L. (2006). Happy people become happier through kindness: A counting kindnesses intervention. *Journal of Happiness Studies, 7*(3), 361–375. doi:10.100710902-005-3650-z PMID:17356687

Oysterman, D. (2018). *Psychology of Values*. Elsevier.

Özcan, S. (2023). Opinions of classroom teachers on values education in primary school curriculum. *Journal for the Education of Gifted Young Scientists, 11*(2), 129–136. doi:10.17478/jegys.1300101

Özdenk, S., Demir Özdenk, G., Özcebe, L. H., & Üner, S. (2019). Bir üniversitenin 4. sınıf öğrencilerinin sağlık okuryazarlığı ve ilişkili bazı faktörlerin incelenmesi. *Mersin Üniversitesi Saglik Bilimleri Dergisi, 12*(1), 48–59. doi:10.26559/mersinsbd.412666

Özel, N. (2022). *İlkokul hayat bilgisi ve sosyal bilgiler ders kitaplarında 10 kök değer bağlamında değerler eğitiminin incelenmesi* [Yayımlanmamış yüksek lisans tezi]. Amasya Üniversitesi, Amasya, Türkiye.

Özen, F. (2022). Kültürlerarası farklılaşma, eğitim ve öğrenme. In M. Güçlü (Ed.), *Eğitim antropolojisi* (pp. 80–96). Pegem Akademi.

Özen, F., & Çakır, R. (2021). İlkokulda öğretmenin sorumlulukları [Teacher's responsibilities in primary school]. In I. Korkmaz (Ed.), *İlkokulda öğretim: Öğretmen el kitabı* [Teaching in primary school: Teacher's handbook] (pp. 587–610). Pegem Akademi.

Özensel, E. (2003). Sosyolojik bir olgu olarak değer. *Değerler Eğitimi Dergisi, 1*(3), 217–239.

Özer, Y. (2019). *Çoklu zekâ kuramına dayalı hazırlanan çalışma yapraklarının ortaokul 6. sınıf öğrencilerinin matematik başarılarına ve tutumlarına etkisinin incelenm*esi [Yayımlanmamış yüksek lisans tezi]. Dicle Üniversitesi, Diyarbakır, Türkiye.

Özerdim, S. N. (1976). *Bilinmiyen Atatürk*. Varlık Publishing.

Özgen, G. (2021). *Kuşaklararası annelik bağlamında ehil annelik: Orta çocukluk döneminde çocuğu olan annelerin annelik süreçleri ve deneyimleri üzerine bir araştırma* [Expertise in motherhood in the context of intergenerational transmisson of motherhood: A study on the motherhood processes and experiences of mothers with children in the middle childhood] [Unpublished doctoral dissertation]. Marmara Üniversitesi Eğitim Bilimleri Enstitüsü, İstanbul.

Özgüven, İ. E. (1994). *Psikolojik testler*. Yeni Doğuş Matbaası.

Özkan, R. (2011). Toplumsal yapı, değerler ve eğitim ilişkisi. *Kastamonu Eğitim Fakültesi Dergisi, 9*(1), 333-344. https://dergipark.org.tr/tr/pub/kefdergi/issue/49053/625844

Özön, M. N. (1988). *Küçük Osmanlıca-Türkçe sözlük*. İnkılap Yayınevi.

Özpek, M. (2020). T*arihi romanların sosyal bilgiler ile Türkiye Cumhuriyeti İnkılap Tarihi ve Atatürkçülük dersi öğretiminde kullanılması üzerine bir inceleme* [Yayımlanmamış yüksek lisans tezi]. İnönü Üniversitesi, Malatya, Türkiye.

Öztaş, S. (2018). Tarih derslerinde bir öğretim materyali: Edebî ürünler. *Rumelide Dil ve Edebiyat Araştırmaları Dergisi, 11*(11), 27–41.

Özteke-Kozan, H. İ. (2021). İlkokul öğrencisinin gelişim özellikleri [Developmental characteristics of primary school students]. In I. Korkmaz (Ed.), *İlkokulda öğretim: Öğretmen el kitabı* [Teaching in primary school: teacher's handbook] (pp. 17–39). Pegem Akademi.

Öztürk, Ç. (2007). Coğrafya öğretiminde edebi metinlerin kullanımı. *On Dokuz Mayıs Üniversitesi Eğitim Fakültesi Dergisi, 24*, 70-78.

Öztürk, C. (Editör). (2012). *Sosyal bilgiler öğretimi demokratik vatandaşlık eğitimi*. Pegem.

Öztürk, C. ve Deveci, H. (2011). Farklı ülkelerin sosyal bilgiler öğretim programlarının değerlendirilmesi. İçinde C. Öztürk (Ed.), Farklı ülkelerin sosyal bilgiler öğretim programları (s. 1-41). Ankara: Pegem Akademi Yayınları.

Öztürk, T. (2018). Sosyal bilgilerde beceri eğitimi. İçinde H. Çalışkan & B. Kılcan (Eds.), Sosyal bilgiler öğretimi (s. 191-218). Lisans Yayıncılık.

Öztürk, C. ve Otluoğlu, R. (2002). Sosyal bilgiler öğretiminde yazılı edebiyat ürünlerini ders aracı olarak kullanmanın duyuşsal davranış özelliklerini kazanmaya etkisi. *Atatürk Eğitim Fakültesi Eğitim Bilimleri Dergisi, 15*, 173–18.

Öztürk, C., Keskin, S. C., & Otluoğlu, R. (2012). *Sosyal bilgiler öğretiminde edebî ürünler ve yazılı materyaller (5. Baskı)*. Pegem.

Öztürk, F., Ferah Özcan, A., Çimen, S., Ozkan, A., & Balkaş, S. R. (2016). Cross-cultural comparative research on values education: The case of Germany, Sweden, South Korea, and Malaysia. *Journal of Academic Social Research, 4*(30), 629–649.

Paker, E. B., & Akça, İ. (2010). *Türkiye'de Ordu, Devlet ve Güvenlik Siyaseti*. İstanbul Bilgi University Publishing.

Pal, R. (2015). Teaching values in schools: A critical review of the literature. *Journal of Moral Education, 44*(4), 399–416.

Panev, V. (2020). Theoretical basis and models for developing students' values in Primary Education. *International Journal of Cognitive Research in Science, Engineering, and Education, 8*(1), 81–91. doi:10.5937/IJCRSEE2001081P

Papathoma-Köhle, M., Kappes, M., Keiler, M., & Glade, T. (2011). Physical vulnerability assessment for alpine hazards: State of the art and future needs. In Natural Hazards (Vol. 58, Issue 2, pp. 645–680). doi:10.100711069-010-9632-4

Parker, W. C. (2014). Citizenship education in the United States: Regime type, foundational questions, and classroom practice. In L. Nucci, D. Narvaez, & T. Krettenauer (Eds.), *Handbook of moral and character education* (pp. 347–367). Routledge.

Park, J. H., & Ono, M. (2017). Effects of workplace bullying on work engagement and health : The mediating role of job insecurity. *International Journal of Human Resource Management, 5192*(22), 1–24. doi:10.1080/09585192.2016.1155164

Parra, J. M. (2018). Educación en valores y su práctica en el aula. *Revista Tendencias Pedagógicas, 8*, 69–71.

Patil, V. K., & Patil, K. D. (2021). Traditional Indian education values and new national education policy adopted by India. *Journal of Education*, *203*(1), 242–245. doi:10.1177/00220574211016404

Patry, J.-L. (2007). VaKE introduction and theoretical background. In K. Tirri (Ed.), *Values and Foundations in Gifted Education* (pp. 157–169). Peter Lang.

Patry, J.-L., Weinberger, A., Weyringer, S., & Nussbaumer, M. (2012). Combination of values and knowledge transfer. In B. J. Irby, G. Brown, R. Lara-Alecio, & S. Jackson (Eds.), *The Handbook of Educational Theories* (pp. 563–577). Publishing in the Information Age.

Patry, J.-L., Weyringer, S., Aichinger, K., & Weinberger, A. (2016). Integration work with immigrant youth with VaKE (Values and Knowledge Education). *International Educational Dialogues: Past and Present*, *3*(3), 123–139.

Pekcan, G., Şanlıer, N., & Baş, M. (2019). *The Turkish Dietary Guidelines*. M. o. H. o. Turkey.

Penfield, W., & Robert, L. (1959). *Speech and Brain\x= req-\Mechanisms*. Academic Press.

Pérez Pico, A. M., Mingorance Álvarez, E., Villar Rodríguez, J., & Mayordomo Acevedo, R. (2022). Differences in Hygiene Habits among Children Aged 8 to 11 Years by Type of Schooling. *Children (Basel, Switzerland)*, *9*(2), 129. Advance online publication. doi:10.3390/children9020129 PMID:35204850

Pescaroli, G., & Alexander, D. (2015). A definition of cascading disasters and cascading effects: Going beyond the "toppling dominos" metaphor. *Planet@ Risk, 3*(1), 58–67.

Petovarga. (2022, January 13). *Renewable energy power distribution with family house residence*. IStock. https://www.istockphoto.com/en/vector/power-distribution-transmission-of-renewable-solar-electricity-energy-grid-with-gm1364369919-435602009?phrase=electricity+tower

Phillipson, R. (2008). Lingua Franca or Lingua Frankensteinia? English in European integration and globalization. *World Englishes*, *27*(2), 250–267. doi:10.1111/j.1467-971X.2008.00555.x

Piaget, J. (1977). The role of action in the development of thinking. In W. F. Overton & J. M. Gallagher (Eds.), *Knowledge and development*. Springer.

Piaget, J. (1985). *The equilibration of cognitive structures: The central problem of intellectual development*. University of Chicago Press.

Piaget, J. (1986). *The child's moral judgment*. Necklace. (Original work published 1932)

Piaget, J., & Inhelder, B. (1969). *The psychology of the child*. Basic Books.

Piff, P. K., Dietze, P., Feinberg, M., Stancato, D. M., & Keltner, D. (2015). Awe, the small self, and prosocial behavior. *Journal of Personality and Social Psychology*, *108*(6), 883–899. doi:10.1037/pspi0000018 PMID:25984788

Piliavin, J. A., & Charng, H.-W. (1990). Altruism: A review of recent theory and research. *Annual Review of Sociology*, *16*(1), 27–65. doi:10.1146/annurev.so.16.080190.000331

Pinto-Llorente, A. M., & Sánchez-Gómez, M. C. (2020). Perceptions and attitudes of future primary education teachers on technology and inclusive education: A mixed methods research. *Journal of Information Technology Research*, *13*(3), 37–57. Advance online publication. doi:10.4018/JITR.2020070103

Pommeranz, A., Detweiler, C., Wiggers, P., & Jonker, C. M. (2011, July). Self-reflection on personal values to support value-sensitive design. In *Proceedings of HCI 2011 The 25th BCS Conference on Human-Computer Interaction 25* (pp. 491-496).

Post, S. G. (2005). Altruism, happiness, and health: It's good to be good. *International Journal of Behavioral Medicine*, *12*(2), 66–77. doi:10.120715327558ijbm1202_4 PMID:15901215

Post, S. G. (2018). *The Science of Compassion: A Modern Approach for Cultivating Empathy, Love, and Connection*. New Harbinger Publications.

Poyraz, K. (2022). *Metin Özdamarlar'ın çocuk kitaplarının sosyal bilgiler öğretim programında yer alan değerler açısından incelenmesi* [Yayımlanmamış yüksek lisans tezi]. Niğde Ömer Halis Üniversitesi, Niğde, Türkiye.

Pranati, P. (2000). *Responsiveness of teacher education curriculum towards human rights education in India* (Vol. VIII). Human Rights Education in Asian Schools.

Pulimeno, M., Piscitelli, P., Colazzo, S., Colao, A., & Miani, A. (2020). School is an ideal setting to promote health and well-being among young people. *Health Promotion Perspectives*, *10*(4), 316–324. doi:10.34172/hpp.2020.50 PMID:33312927

Puni, A., Mohammed, I., & Asamoah, E. (2018). Transformational leadership and job satisfaction: The moderating effect of contingent reward. *Leadership and Organization Development Journal*, *39*(4), 522–537. doi:10.1108/LODJ-11-2017-0358

Püsküllüoğlu, A. (1977). *Osmanlıca-Türkçe sözlük*. Bilgi Yayınevi.

Rakhimkulova, A. S., & Rozanov, V. A. (2013). Suicidality and risk appetite in adolescents: A biopsychosocial synthesis. *Suicidology*, *4*(2), 7–25.

Rapport de l'OIF, Le français dans le monde, 2006-2007.

Raths, L. E., Harmin, M., & Simon, S.B. (1966). *Values and teaching: working with values in the classroom*. Charles E. Merrill Books Inc.

Ratnawat, R. G. (2018). *Understanding values and their role in human life*. Retrieved 11 June from https://www.hrkatha.com/opinion/understanding-values-and-their-role-in-human-life/

Ray, B., & Seely, C. (2018). *Fluency through TPR Storytelling: Achieving natural language acquisition in school*. Command Performance Language Institute.

Reece, I., & Walker, S. (1997). *Teaching, training, and learning: A practical guide*. Business Education.

Reiner, R. C. Jr, Olsen, H. E., Ikeda, C. T., Echko, M. M., Ballestreros, K. E., Manguerra, H., Martopullo, I., Millear, A., Shields, C., Smith, A., Strub, B., Abebe, M., Abebe, Z., Adhena, B. M., Adhikari, T. B., Akibu, M., Al-Raddadi, R. M., Alvis-Guzman, N., Antonio, C. A. T., ... Kassebaum, N. J. (2019). Diseases, Injuries, and Risk Factors in Child and Adolescent Health, 1990 to 2017: Findings From the Global Burden of Diseases, Injuries, and Risk Factors 2017 Study. *JAMA Pediatrics*, *173*(6), e190337. doi:10.1001/jamapediatrics.2019.0337 PMID:31034019

Religionsunterricht. (2014) *Kern-curriculum für die Schulformen des Sekundarbereichs I schuljahrgange 5-10, Islamische Religion*. Niedersachsisches Kultusministerium.

Religionunterricht. (2009) *Kerncurriculum für das Gymnasium Schuljahrgange 5-10*, Evangelische Religion. Niedersachsisches Kultusministerium.

Renstrom, M., Ferri, M., & Mandil, A. (2017). Substance use prevention: Evidence-based intervention. *Eastern Mediterranean Health Journal*, *23*(3), 198–205. doi:10.26719/2017.23.3.198 PMID:28493267

Retnasari, L., Hidayah, Y., & Prasetyo, D. (2021). Reinforcement of character education based on school culture to enhance elementary school students' citizenship character. *Jurnal Ilmiah Sekolah Dasar*, *5*(2), 351–358. doi:10.23887/jisd.v5i2.38072

Riemer, H. L. (2011). *Role models and role models. About the change in values and the chances of its rediscovery.* Dr. Köster.

Ritchie, H., & Hoser, M. (2020). *Natural Disasters.* https://ourworldindata.org/naturaldisasters

Ritchie, L. (2018). Opening the curriculum through open educational practices: International experience. *Open Praxis,* *10*(2), 201–208. doi:10.5944/openpraxis.10.2.821

Robb, B. (1998). What are the values of education-and so what? *The Journal of Values Education, 1,* 1-11.

Robert, F. (2018). Impact of Workplace Bullying on Job Performance and Job Stress. *Journal of Management Info, 5*(3), 12–15. doi:10.31580/jmi.v5i3.123

Roberts, J. (2015). *Local action on health inequalities: improving health literacy.* https://assets.publishing.service.gov.uk/government/uploads/system/uploads/attachment_data/file/460710/4b_Health_Literacy-Briefing.pdf

Rohaan, E. J., Taconis, R., & Jochems, W. M. G. (2010). Reviewing the relations between teachers' knowledge and pupils' attitude in the field of primary technology education. In International Journal of Technology and Design Education (Vol. 20, Issue 1). doi:10.100710798-008-9055-7

Rohaan, E. J., Taconis, R., & Jochems, W. M. G. (2009). Measuring teachers' pedagogical content knowledge in primary technology education. *Research in Science & Technological Education, 27*(3), 327–338. Advance online publication. doi:10.1080/02635140903162652

Rokeach, M. (1973). *The nature of human values.* The free press.

Rona, T. E. (1940). *Yurt Bilgisi Dersleri Grade V, İlkokul Kitapları.* Maarif Matbaası Publishing.

Rossiyskaya Gazeta. *(2015). Decree of the President of the Russian Federation of December 31, 2015 N 683 "On the National Security Strategy of the Russian Federation".* Retrieved 01 10, 2021, from: Rossiyskaya Gazeta: https://rg.ru/2015/12/31/nac-bezopasnost-site-dok.html

Rouabah, S. (2022). Multilingualism in Algeria: Educational policies, language practices, and challenges. *Journal of the British Academy, 10*(4), 21–40. doi:10.5871/jba/010s4.021

Roy, G. (2017). Competency-Based Assessment in Primary Education in Bangladesh - A Review. SSRN *Electronic Journal.* doi:10.2139/ssrn.2899109

Rush, D. D., Shelden, M. L., & Raab, M. (2008). A framework for reflective questioning when using a coaching interaction style. *CASEtools, 4*(1), 1-7. https://fipp.ncdhhs.gov/wp-content/uploads/casetools_vol4_no1.pdf

Sabancı, O., & Altıkulaç, A. (2020). Values and value education according to students of education faculty. *International Journal of Education Technology and Scientific Researches, 13*(13), 1881–1932. doi:10.35826/ijetsar.273

Sáez López, J. M., Sevillano García, M. L., & Pascual Sevillano, M. A. (2019). Aplicación del juego ubicuo con realidad aumentada en Educación Primaria. *Comunicar, 61,* 71–82. doi:10.3916/C61-2019-06

Sagiv, L., Roccas, S., Cieciuch, J., & Schwartz, S. H. (2017). Personal values in human life. *Nature Human Behaviour, 1*(9), 630–639. doi:10.103841562-017-0185-3 PMID:31024134

Sağlam, E. ve Genç, S.Z. (2015). İlkokul 4. sınıf sosyal bilgiler programında belirlenen değerlerin kazanım düzeyleri. *Uluslararası Türkçe Edebiyat Kültür Eğitim Dergisi, 4*(4), 1708–1728.

Sağlamgöncü, A. (2022). *Sosyal bilgiler dersinde güncel olay öğretiminde aktif öğrenme tekniklerinin kullanılması: Bir eylem araştırması* [Yayımlanmamış doktora tezi]. Anadolu Üniversitesi, Eskişehir, Türkiye.

Saglam, M. (1999). *Education systems of European countries*. Anadolu University Press.

Sağol, G. (1993). *Harezm Türkçesi satır arası Kur'an tercümesi, giriş-metin-sözlük I* [PhD Thesis]. Marmara Üniversitesi.

Şahin, M. (2018). *Dini bir değer olarak tevekkül yöneliminin psikolojik sebep ve sonuçları üzerine araştırma* [Unpublished PhD Thesis]. Uludağ Üniversitesi Sosyal Bilimler Enstitüsü.

Sahin, Ü. (2019). Values and values education as perceived by primary school teacher candidates. *International Journal of Progressive Education*, *15*(3), 74–90.

Sahin, U. (2019). Values and Values Education as Perceived by Primary School Teacher Candidates. *International Journal of Progressive Education*, *15*(3), 74–90. doi:10.29329/ijpe.2019.193.6

Salam, S. (2018). Visual-art education for character development. *Advances in Social Science, Education, and Humanities Research*. Vol. 255. *1st International Conference on Arts and Design Education (ICADE 2018)*, 315-319.

Salmivalli, C., & Poskiparta, E. (2012). *Making bullying prevention a priority in Finnish schools: The KiVa anti-bullying program*. https://doi.org/ doi:10.1002/yd

Salzberg, S. (1995). *Loving-Kindness: The Revolutionary Art of Happiness*. Shambhala Publications.

Saphiro, D. A. (1999). Teaching ethics from the inside-out: Some strategies for developing moral reasoning skills in middle-school students. **(ERIC Number:** ED447040)

Sari, N. (2013). The importance of teaching moral values to the students. *Journal of English and Education*, *1*(1).

Satriani, I. (2019). Storytelling in teaching literacy: Benefits and challenges. English Review. *Journal of English Education*, *8*(1), 113–120. doi:10.25134/erjee.v8i1.1924

Saunders, P., Huynh, A., & Goodman-Delahunty, J. (2007). Defining workplace bullying behavior, professionals lay definitions of workplace bullying. *International Journal of Law and Psychiatry*, *30*(4–5), 340–354. doi:10.1016/j.ijlp.2007.06.007 PMID:17692375

Savage, T. V., & Amstrong, D. G. (1996). *Effective teaching in elementary education* (10th ed.). Prentice-Hall, Inc.

Scandinavian, S. (2016). Workplace bullying and sickness absence : a systematic review and meta-analysis of the research literature. *Scandinavian Journal of Work, Environment & Heal, 42*.

Scholarly Community Encyclopedia. (n.d.). *Value (ethics)*. https://encyclopedia.pub/entry/28294

Schön, D. (1987). *Educating the reflective practitioner*. Jossey-Bass.

Schön, D. A. (1983). *The reflective practitioner: How professionals think in actions*. Basic Book.

Schrader, D. E. (2018). Ahlaki gelişim [Moral development]. In *Değerler eğitimi ansiklopedisi* [Moral education/A Handbook] (pp. 26-28). EDAM.

Schreier, H. M., & Schonert-Reichl, K. A. (2019). Volunteers as Positive Youth Development Promoters: A Review of the Correlates, Benefits, and Potential Mechanisms of Youth Volunteering. *Child Development Perspectives*, *13*(1), 17–22.

Schubarth, W. (2010), The return of values." The debate about new values and the chances of value formation, In W. Schubarth, K. Speck and H. von Lynen Berg (eds.), Value formation in youth work, school, and community. Balance sheet and outlook (pp. 21-42). VS publishing house for social sciences.

Schubarth, W., Speck, K. & Lynen Berg, H. von (2010). *Value formation in youth work, school, and community: balance and perspectives*. VS publishing house for social sciences.

Schuck, S. (2016). Enhancing teacher education in primary mathematics with mobile technologies. *The Australian Journal of Teacher Education, 41*(3), 126–139. Advance online publication. doi:10.14221/ajte.2016v41n3.8

Schulte, P. A., Guerin, R. J., Schill, A. L., Bhattacharya, A., Cunningham, T. R., Pandalai, S. P., Eggerth, D., & Stephenson, C. M. (2015). Considerations for incorporating "well-being" in public policy for workers and workplaces. *American Journal of Public Health, 105*(8), e31–e44. doi:10.2105/AJPH.2015.302616 PMID:26066933

Schwartz, S. H. (1992). Universals in the content and structure of values: Theoretical advances and empirical tests in 20 countries. In Advances in experimental social psychology, 25, 1-65. Academic Press.

Schwartz, M. J. (2018). Ahlak eğitiminde öğretmenin rolü [The role of the teacher in moral education]. In *Değerler eğitimi ansiklopedisi* [Moral education/A Handbook] (pp. 11-13). EDAM.

Schwartz, S. H. (1992). Universals in the content and structure of values: Theoretical advances and empirical tests in 20 countries. *Advances in Experimental Social Psychology, 25*, 1–65. doi:10.1016/S0065-2601(08)60281-6

Schwartz, S. H. (2012). An overview of the Schwartz theory of core values. *Online Readings in Psychology and Culture, 2*(1). http://scholarworks.gvsu.edu/orpc/vol2/iss1/11

Schwartz, S. H. (2012). An overview of the Schwartz Theory of the Basic Values. *Online Readings in Psychology and Culture, 2*(1), 1–12. doi:10.9707/2307-0919.1116

Seçkin Uygur, H. (2022). *Millî mücadele konulu romanların sosyal bilgiler öğretim programındaki değerler açısından analizi* [Yayımlanmamış yüksek lisans tezi]. İnönü Üniversitesi, Malatya, Türkiye.

Seifert, A., & Zentner, S. (2010). *Service Learning – Learning through engagement: Method, quality, examples, and selected focal points*. Freudenberg Foundation.

Şentürk, M. (2020). *Sosyal bilgiler dersinde eğitici çizgi roman ve eğitici çizgi film kullanımının öğrencilerin, tutum, motivasyon ve akademik başarılarına etkileri* [Yayımlanmamış doktora tezi]. Atatürk Üniversitesi, Erzurum, Türkiye.

Seshadri, S. (2005). An approach to value orientation of teachers' education. Journal of Value Education, NCERT

Sever, R. (2015). *Sosyal bilgiler öğretimine giriş. İçinde sosyal bilgiler öğretimi*. Nobel Akademik Yayıncılık.

Sevinç, A. (2018). *5. sınıf sosyal bilgiler dersinde yazılı edebi ürün kullanımına yönelik öğretmen ve öğrenci görüşleri* [Yayımlanmamış yüksek lisans tezi]. Fırat Üniversitesi, Elâzığ, Türkiye.

Seyis, Z. (2021). *Sosyal bilgiler derslerinde edebi ürünler aracılığıyla kadın tarihi öğretimi: materyal tasarımı örnekleri* [Yayımlanmamış yüksek lisans tezi]. Sinop Üniversitesi, Sinop, Türkiye.

Shaw, R., Shiwaku, K., & Takeuchi, Y. (2011). *Disaster education*. Emerald Group Publishing. doi:10.1108/S2040-7262(2011)7

Sherrow, H. M., & Ph.D. (2014). *The Origins of Bullying*. Academic Press.

Shohel, M. M. C., & Howes, A. J. (2011). Models of Education for Sustainable Development and Nonformal Primary Education in Bangladesh. *Journal of Education for Sustainable Development, 5*(1), 129–139. Advance online publication. doi:10.1177/097340821000500115

Short, R., Case, G., & McKenzie, K. (2018). The long-term impact of a whole school approach of restorative practice: The views of secondary school teachers. *Pastoral Care in Education, 36*(4), 313–324. doi:10.1080/02643944.2018.1528625

Silcock, P., & Duncan, D. (2001). Values acquisition and values education: Some proposals. *British Journal of Educational Studies, 49*(3), 242–259. doi:10.1111/1467-8527.t01-1-00174

Simon, S. B., Howe, L. W., & Krischenbaum, H. (1978). Values clarification: A handbook of practical strategies for teachers and students. A & W Visual Library.

Simpson, M. (2009). Social studies 2.0: Thinking, connecting, and creating technology [special issue]. *Social Education, 73*(3).

Şimşek, A. (2015). Sosyal bilgiler dersinde bir öğretim materyali olarak edebi ürünler. İçinde M. Safran (Ed.), Sosyal bilgiler öğretimi (s. 389-412). Pegem A

Simsek, C. L. (2007). Children's Ideas about Earthquakes. *International Journal of Environmental and Science Education, 2*(1), 14–19.

Şimşir, B. N. (2006). *Atatürk ve Cumhuriyet.* İleri Publishing.

Sinclair, J. (Chief Ed.) (1990). Value. In Collins Cobuild English Language Dictionary (5th ed.). William Collins Sons & Co Ltd.

Singh, A. (2011). Evaluating the impacts of value education: Some case studies. *International Journal of Educational Planning and Administration, 1*(1). http://www.ripublication.com/ijepa.htm

Slimani, S. (2016). Teaching English as a foreign language in Algeria. *Revue des Sciences, 44*, 33–44. doi:10.37136/1003-000-044-041

Sloan, L., Matyók, T., Schmitz, C., & Short, G. (2010). A story to tell: Bullying and mobbing in the workplace. *International Journal of Business and Social Science, 1*(3), 87–98.

Smith, P. K., & Brain, P. (2000). *Bullying in Schools : Lessons From Two Decades of Research.* Academic Press.

Smith, P. K., Smith, C., & Osborn, R. (2008). *Educational Psychology in Practice : Theory, research, and Practice in Educational Psychology A content analysis of school anti-bullying policies : Progress and limitations.* doi:10.1080/02667360701661165

Smorgorzewska, J. (2014). Developing children's language creativity through telling stories: An experimental study. *Thinking Skills and Creativity, 13*, 20–31. doi:10.1016/j.tsc.2014.02.005

Sokol, N., Bussey, K., & Rapee, R. M. (2016). Teachers' perspectives on effective responses to overt bullying. *British Educational Research Journal, 42*(5), 851–870. doi:10.1002/berj.3237

Solmaz, R. (2006). *Din eğitimi açısından Kur'an ve sünnette tevekkül kavramı* [Unpublished Master Thesis]. Marmara Üniversitesi.

Sommers, C. (2013). *Primary education in rural Bangladesh: Degrees of access, choice and participation of the poorest.* ESP Working Paper Special Series on the Privatisation in Education Research Initiative, No. 52.

Sönmez, Ö. F. (2014). Atasözlerinin Sosyal Bilgiler programındaki değerler açısından incelenmesi. *Journal of World of Turks, 6*(2), 101–115.

Sørensen, K., & Paakkari, L. (2023). *Guide to Health Literacy Contributing to Trust Building and Equitable Access to Healthcare.* Academic Press.

Speck, K. (2010). *Value formation and participation of children and young people.*

Speck, K. (2010). Value formation and participation of children and young people. In: W. Schubarth, K. Speck and H. von Lynen Berg (eds.), Value formation in youth work, school, and community: Balance sheet and perspectives (pp. 61-90). VS publishing house for social sciences.

Standup, J. (2005). *Value formation: Introduction to the most important concepts of value formation*. Beltz.

Standup, J. (2005). *Werte-Erziehung*. Beltz Verlag.

Straughan, R. (1999). *Can we teach children to be good? Basic issues in moral, personal, and social education*. Open university press.

Stravia, (2013). *The Voice of Research*, 2(3), December 2013.

Sucu, A. Ö. (2012). *Mesnevilerin edebiyat eğitiminde değer aktarım aracı olarak kullanılması* [Yayımlanmamış yüksek lisans tezi]. Gazi Üniversitesi, Ankara, Türkiye.

Suherman, A. (2018). Implementing character education values in integrated physical education subject in elementary school. *SHS Web of Conferences, 42*, 45. https://doi.org/10.1051hsconf/20184200045

Suna, Y. (2019). *Aktif öğrenme yaklaşımının 7. sınıf matematik dersi rasyonel sayılar konusunun öğretimine etkisinin akademik başarı, tutum ve kalıcılık düzeyleri bağlamında incelenmesi* [Yayımlanmamış yüksek lisans tezi]. Tokat Gaziosmanpaşa Üniversitesi, Tokat, Türkiye.

Sunal, C. Y., & Haas, M. E. (2011). *Social studies for the elementary and middle grades. A constructivist approach*. Pearson.

Sünney, F. H. (2019). Eğitim felsefesi ve hedefleri yönünden karakter ve değer eğitimi. In M. Kağan & N. Yılmaz (Eds.), *Karakter ve değer eğitimi* (pp. 175–186). Pegem Akademi. doi:10.14527/9786050370133.10

Sun, P. Y. (2016). *Using drama and theatre to promote literacy development*. ERIC.

Superka, Ahrens, & Hedstrom (1976). Values Education. Values education sourcebook. CO: Social Science Education Consortium.

Surendranath, R., & Lavanya, M. (2021). *Value Education*. Charulatha Publications.

Sushma, G., & Daya, P. (Nd.). "Education for Values in Schools – A Framework" Department of Educational Psychology and Foundations of Education, National Council of Educational Research and Training. Education for Values in Schools A Framework - PDF Free Download, docplayer.net

Suwalska, A. (2021). Values and their influence on learning in primary education in Finland selected aspects. *Roczniki Pedagogiczne, 13*(2), 141–154. doi:10.18290/rped21132.10

Swearer, S. M., Espelage, D. L., Vaillancourt, T., Hymel, S., Swearer, S. M., Espelage, D. L., Vaillancourt, T., & Hymel, S. (2010). What Can Be Done About School Bullying? *Educational Researcher, 39*(1), 38–47. Advance online publication. doi:10.3102/0013189X09357622

Syafii, L., Kusnawan, W., & Syukroni, A. (2020). Enhancing listening skills using games. *International Journal on Studies in Education, 2*(2), 78–107. doi:10.46328/ijonse.21

Taleb Ibrahimi, K. (1995). *Les Algériens et Leurs Langues*. Les Editions EL Hikma.

Tan, M. (1990). Eğitim sosyolojisinde değişik yaklaşımlar: İşlevselci paradigma ve çatışmacı paradigma. *Ankara Üniversitesi Eğitim Bilimleri Fakültesi Dergisi, 2*, 557–571.

Tawfik, G. M., Dila, K. A. S., Mohamed, M. Y. F., Tam, D. N. H., Kien, N. D., Ahmed, A. M., & Huy, N. T. (2019). A step-by-step guide for conducting a systematic review and meta-analysis with simulation data. *Tropical Medicine and Health, 47*(1), 46. doi:10.118641182-019-0165-6 PMID:31388330

Taylor, M. (1994). *Values education in Europe: A comparative overview of a survey of 26 countries in 1993*. Scottish Consultative Council on the Curriculum for Cidree/UNESCO.

TDK. (2023). *TDK (Turkish Language Institution)*. https://sozluk.gov.tr/

Tekşan, K. (2012). Türkçe dersi değerler eğitiminde Kutadgu Bilig'in kullanımı. *Ahi Evran Üniversitesi Kırşehir Eğitim Fakültesi Dergisi*, *13*(3), 1–17.

Temur, S., & Topkaya, Y. (2023). 2018 sosyal bilgiler dersi öğretim programının müze kullanımı bakımından incelenmesi. Kırıkkale Üniversitesi Sosyal Bilimler Dergisi, 13(1), 281-307. https://dergipark.org.tr/tr/pub/kusbd/issue/75703/1195574

Temur, S. (2023). Sosyal bilgiler ders kitaplarında çalışma yapraklarının kullanımı. *International Journal of New Approaches in Social Studies*, *7*(1), 15–47. https://doi.org/110.38015/sbyy.126077

Temur, S., & Çakmak, M. (2023). Ortaokul öğrencilerinin özgürlük kavramına ilişkin algılarının sinektik tekniğiyle incelenmesi. *Academia Eğitim Araştırmaları Dergisi*, *8*(1), 39–59. doi:10.53506/egitim.1226780

Tezcan, M. (1993). Eğitim sosyolojisinde çağdaş kuramlar ve Türkiye, Ankara Üniversitesi Eğitim Bilimleri Fakültesi Yayınları, No:170. http://kitaplar.ankara.edu.tr/dosyalar/pdf/083.pdf

Tezcan, N. (1994). *Atatürk'ün Yazdığı Yurttaşlık Bilgileri*. Çağdaş Publishing.

The Commission. (1926). Tebliğler Dergisi. *Maarif Vekâleti Tebliğler Mecmuası*, 1.

The Commission. (1930). *1930 İlkmektep Müfredat Programı*. Türkiye Cumhuriyeti Maarif Vekâleti Devlet Publishing.

The Commission. (1933). *Yurt Bilgisi İlkmektep Kitapları: Grade IV*. Devlet Publishing.

The Commission. (1933). *Yurt Bilgisi İlkmektep Kitapları: Grade V*. Türk Kitapçılığı Limited Company.

The Commission. (1979). *Ulusal Eğitim Politikamız*. Türk Eğitim Derneği Publishing.

The Commission. (1986). *Atatürk Haftası Armağanı 10 Kasım 1986*. Genelkurmay Askeri Tarih ve Stratejik Etüt Başkanlığı Publishing.

The Commission. (1997). *Atatürk'ün Söylev ve Demeçleri I- III*. Türk Tarih Kurumu Publishing.

The Commission. (1998). *75. Yılda Tebaa'dan Yurttaş'a Doğru*. Tarih Vakfı Publishing.

The Commission. (1998). *Devrimci Cumhuriyetin Eğitim Politikaları*. Kaynak Publishing.

The Commission. (2002). *Türkler Ansiklopedisi*, 17.

The Commission. (2003). *Atatürk Haftası Armağanı 10 Kasım 2003*. Genelkurmay Askeri Tarih ve Stratejik Etüt Başkanlığı Publishing.

Thi, Q., & Nguyen, N. (2017). CLASSROOM-BASED VALUES EDUCATION IN VIETNAM: IMPLEMENTATION AND ISSUES. https://www.researchgate.net/publication/318283165

Thornberg, R. (2018). The lack of professional knowledge in values education. *Teaching and Teacher Education*, *24*(7), 1791–1798. doi:10.1016/j.tate.2008.04.004

Tillman, D. (2000). *Living values activities for young adults*. Health Communications Inc.

Tinker, V. (2016). Peace education as a post-conflict peacebuilding tool. *All Azimuth: A Journal of Foreign Policy and Peace, 5*, 27-42. https://doi.org/ doi:10.20991/allazimuth.167339

Titus, D. N. (1994). *Values education in American secondary schools*. Paper presented at the Kutztown University Education Conference.

Tokcan, H. (2016). Sosyal bilgiler ve edebiyat. İçinde Halil Tokcan (Ed.), Sosyal bilgilerde sözlü ve yazılı edebiyat incelemeleri (s.1-24). Pegem A.

Tokcan, H. (2020). *Sosyal bilgilerde sözlü ve yazılı edebiyat incelemeleri.* Salmat Basım Yayıncılık.

Topçu, E., & Kaymakcı, S. (2018). Sosyal bilgiler öğretiminde menkıbelerin kullanılma durumuna ilişkin öğretmen görüşleri. *Erzincan Üniversitesi Eğitim Fakültesi Dergisi, 20*(1), 281–305.

Topkaya, Y. (2016). Doğal çevreye duyarlılık değerinin aktarılmasında kavram karikatürleri ile eğitici çizgi romanların etkiliğinin karşılaştırılması. *Mustafa Kemal Üniversitesi Sosyal Bilimler Enstitüsü Dergisi, 13* (34), 0-0.

Topkaya, Y., & Şimşek, U. (2017). Görsel bir öğretim materyali: Eğitici çizgi roman. İçinde R. Turan, & H. Akdağ (Eds.), Sosyal bilgiler öğretiminde yeni yaklaşımlar III (s. 201-220). Pegem Akademi.

Torani, S., Majd, P. M., Maroufi, S. S., Dowlati, M., & Sheikhi, R. A. (2019). The importance of education on disasters and emergencies: A review article. *Journal of Education and Health Promotion*, 8. PMID:31143802

Tosun, Y. (2021). *Sınıf öğretmenlerinin değerler eğitimini zorlaştıran faktörlere ilişkin görüşleri ve değerler eğitimine yönelik uygulamaları.* Van Yüzüncü Yıl Üniversitesi Eğitim Bilimleri Enstitüsü / Eğitim Bilimleri Ana Bilim Dalı / Eğitim Programları ve Öğretim Bilim Dalı.

Touriñán, J. M. (2015). Educación en valores, educación intercultural y formación para la convivencia pacífica. *Revista Galega do Ensino*, 47.

Tranfield, D., Denyer, D., & Smart, P. (2003). Towards a methodology for developing evidence-informed management knowledge by means of systematic review. *British Journal of Management, 14*(3), 207–222. doi:10.1111/1467-8551.00375

Trasobares, P., & Valdivieso, L. (2019). *Aprendizaje del inglés a través del juego en Educación Primaria.* Servicio de Publicaciones de la Universidad de Valladolid.

Trujillo Trujillo, J. A. (2020). La Educación en Valores. *Cuadernos de Educación y Desarrollo, 2*, 14.

Ttofi, M. M., & Farrington, D. P. (2011). *Effectiveness of school-based programs to reduce bullying : a systematic and meta-analytic review.* doi:10.1007/s11292-010-9109-1

Tuncel, G. (2018). Sosyal bilgiler dersinde "doğal çevreye duyarlılık" değerinin geliştirilmesinde alternatif çevreci uygulamalar. *International Journal of Geography and Geography Education*, (38), 91-103. Doi:10.32003/iggei.440890

Tuncer, T., & Altunay, B. (2010). *Doğrudan öğretim modelinde kavram öğretimi.* Kök Yayıncılık.

Turan, İ. (2002). *İsmet İnönü Eğitim- Öğretim Üzerine.* Türk Eğitim Derneği İnönü Vakfı.

Turan, R., & Ulusoy, K. (2016). *Farklı yönleriyle değerler eğitimi.* Pegem Akademi.

Turfanda, S. (2022). *Millî mücadele dönemi edebi eserlerin sosyal bilgiler programındaki değerlere göre incelenmesi* [Yayımlanmamış yüksek lisans tezi]. Aydın Adnan Menderes Üniversitesi, Aydın, Türkiye.

Türk Dil Kurumu (TDK). (2011). *Tük dil kurumu sözlüğü.* Türk Dil Kurumu Yayınları.

Türkay, K. (1988). *Ali Şir Nevayi bedayiul-vasat (inceleme-metin-dizin)* [Unpublished PhD Thesis]. Ankara Üniversitesi Sosyal Bilimler Enstitüsü.

Turkbal, A. (2003). *Scientific research methods and writing techniques.*

Turkish Ministry of Education. (2018). *İngilizce dersi öğretim programı: İlkokul ve ortaokul 2, 3, 4, 5, 6, 7 ve 8. sınıflar* [English language curriculum: Primary and secondary school years 2, 3, 4, 5, 6, 7 and 8]. http://mufredat.meb.gov.tr/Dosyalar/201812411191321-%C4%B0NG%C4%B0L%C4%B0ZCE%20%C3%96%C4%9ERET%C4%B0M%20PRO-GRAMI%20Klas%C3%B6r%C3%BC.pdf

Turkish Ministry of National Education. (2015). *Sosyal bilgiler dersi 4, 5, 6 ve 7. sınıflar öğretim programı.* Ankara: Milli Eğitim Basımevi. http://mufredat.meb.gov.tr/Dosyalar/201812103847686-SosyalBilgilerÖğretimProgramı.pdf

Turkish Ministry of National Education. (2018). *Hayat Bilgisi Dersi Öğretim Programı.* http://mufredat.meb.gov.tr/Dosyalar/2018122171428547-hayatbilgisiöğretimprogrami.pdf

Turkish Republic Strategy and Budget Presidency. (2023). *Kahramanmaras and Hatay earthquake report.* https://www.sbb.gov.tr/2023-kahramanmaras-ve-hatay-depremleri-raporu/

Turner, T. N. (1999). *Essentials of elementary social studies.* Allyn and Bacon.

Tutti-frutti. (2019, September 23). *Ceiling lamp light bulb shine.* IStock. https://www.istockphoto.com/en/vector/ceiling-lamp-light-bulb-shine-bright-business-background-for-your-text-vector-gm1176531164-328058114?phrase=lamp

Tyree, C., Vance, M., & McJunkin, M. (1997). Teaching values to promote a more caring world: A Moral dilemma for the 21st century. Journal For A Just and Caring Education, 3(2), 215-226. https://www.researchgate.net/publication/330245310_Values_Education#fullTextFileContent

U.S.A. Department of Education. Partnership in character education state plot projects (1995-2001): Lessons Learned, Washington, D.C. https://files.eric.ed.gov

UGC. (2010). "National Policy on Education 1986: As modified in 1992." http://education.nic.in/policy/npe86-mod92.pdf (Accessed on 05.08.2010).

Ulfatin, N., & Mukhadis, A. (2017). Personal values and social skills student MTS and its development in curriculum and school program. *Advances in Economics, 45*, 218-222. https://doi.org/https://doi.org/10.2991/coema-17.2017.39

Ulu Kalın, Ö., & Koçoğlu, E. (2017). Sosyal bilgiler öğretmen adaylarının bağımsızlık değerine karşı metaforik algıları. *Ahi Evran Üniversitesi Kırşehir Eğitim Fakültesi Dergisi, 18*(2), 419–434.

Ulusoy, K. (2010). Değer eğitimi: Davranışçı ve yapılandırmacı yaklaşıma göre hazırlanan tarih programlarında değer aktarımı. *Trakya Üniversitesi Sosyal Bilimler Dergisi, 12*(1), 32–51.

Ulusoy, K., & Arslan, A. (2014). Değerli bir kavram olarak "değer ve değerler eğitimi". In R. Turan & K. Ulusoy (Eds.), *Farklı yönleri ile değerler eğitimi* (pp. 1–16). Pegem Akademi. doi:10.14527/9786053648222.01

UN. (2020). *UNODC/WHO International Standards on Drug Use Prevention.* Retrieved 12 June from https://www.unodc.org/unodc/en/prevention/prevention-standards.html

UNESCO. (2015). *Education 2030 Incheon Declaration.* WHO, UNICEF, UNESCO. Retrieved 10 June from https://uis.unesco.org/sites/default/files/documents/education-2030-incheon-framework-for-action-implementation-of-sdg4-2016-en_2.pdf

UNESCO. (2015). *Global citizenship education: Topics and learning objectives.* United Nations Educational, Scientific and Cultural Organization.

UNICEF. (2014) *Geolino UNICEF Children's Values Monitor.* https://www.unicef.de/blob/56990/a121cfd7c7acbdc2f-4b97cbcdf0cc716/geolino-unicef-child Values Monitor-2014-data.pdf

UNICEF. (2021). *Nutrition in Middle Childhood and Adolescence.* UNICEF. Retrieved 11 June from https://www.unicef.org/nutrition/middle-childhood-and-adolescence

UNICEF. (2022). *Promoting and protecting mental health in schools and learning environments.* https://healtheducation-resources.unesco.org/library/documents/five-essential-pillars-promoting-and-protecting-mental-health-and-psychosocial

UNISDR. (2009). *2009 UNISDR Terminology on Disaster Risk Reduction. International Stratergy for Disaster Reduction.* ISDR.

United Kingdom Department for Education. (2017). *Developing character skills in schools qualitative case Studies final report - August 2017.* https://assets.publishing.service.gov.uk/government/uploads/system/uploads/attachment_data/file/634712/Developing_Character_skills-Case_study_report.pdf

Ünlü, İ. ve Ay, A. (2017). Hikâyelerle sosyal bilgiler öğretimi. İçinde Sever, R., Aydın, M. ve Koçoğlu, E. (Eds.), Alternatif yaklaşımlarla sosyal bilgiler eğitimi (187-210). Pegem Akademi Yayıncılık.

Ünlü, S. (2004). *Karahanlı Türkçesi satır–arası Kur'an tercümesi (TİEM 73, 235v/3–450r/7)* [PhD Thesis]. Hacettepe Üniversitesi.

Ünlüer, G. ve Yaşar, Ş. (2012). Sosyal Bilgiler dersinde gazete kullanımına ilişkin öğrenci görüşleri. *Eskişehir Osmangazi Üniversitesi Sosyal Bilimler Dergisi, 13*(1), 43–57.

Ünlü, S. (2012a). *Karahanlı Türkçesi sözlüğü.* Eğitim Yayınevi.

Ünlü, S. (2012b). *Harezm–Altınordu Türkçesi sözlüğü.* Eğitim Yayınevi.

Ünlü, S. (2013). *Çağatay Türkçesi sözlüğü.* Eğitim Yayınevi.

Ünver, E. (2011). *Görsel sanatlar ve eğitimi üzerine.* Detay yayıncılık.

Üşenmez, E. (2010). *Eski Kur'an tercümelerinden Özbekistan nüshası üzerinde dil incelemesi (giriş-inceleme-metin-sözlük-ekler dizini)* [PhD Thesis]. İstanbul Üniversitesi.

Usta, E. (2015). Öğretmen adaylarının öğretim materyalleri geliştirme süreçlerinin görsel ve mesaj tasarımı ilkeleri açısından incelenmesi. *Gazi Eğitim Bilimleri Dergisi, 1*(1), 1–14.

Üstel, F. (2004). *Makbul Vatandaşın Peşinde, II. Meşrutiyet'ten Bugüne Vatandaşlık Eğitimi.* İletişim Publishing.

Uzunöz, A., Aktepe, V. ve Özağaçhanlı, Z. (2020). Sosyal bilgiler öğretmen adaylarının tasarruf değerine ilişkin metaforik algıları. *Nevşehir Hacı Bektaş Veli Üniversitesi SBE Dergisi, 10*(1), 36-51.

Valkanova, Y., Jackson, A., & Watts, D. M. (2004). Enhancing self-reflection in children: The use of digital video in the primary science classroom. Journal of eLiteracy, 1, 42-55.

Values Education for Australian Schooling. (2010). http://www.curriculum.edu.au/values/

Vamos, S., Okan, O., Sentell, T., & Rootman, I. (2020). Making a Case for "Education for Health Literacy": An International Perspective. *International Journal of Environmental Research and Public Health, 17*(4), 1436. Advance online publication. doi:10.3390/ijerph17041436 PMID:32102271

van Delden, J. J. M., & van der Graaf, R. (2021). Social Value. In A. Ganguli-Mitra, A. Sorbie, C. McMillan, E. Dove, E. Postan, G. Laurie, & N. Sethi (Eds.), *The Cambridge Handbook of Health Research Regulation* (pp. 46–55). Cambridge University Press. doi:10.1017/9781108620024.007

Venimo. (2017, November 26). *Vector set of icons and illustrations in flat linear style - nature.* IStock. https://www.istockphoto.com/en/vector/nature-landscapes-with-green-trees-gm879289876-245119756?phrase=trees+and+forest

Venimo. (2019, October 23). *Vector illustration in flat simple style - greenhouse with plants.* IStock. https://www.istockphoto.com/en/vector/vector-illustration-in-flat-simple-style-greenhouse-with-plants-gm1182830958-332306487?phrase=plants+indoor

Verlag, L. I. T. Lind, G. (2015). Favorable learning environments for moral competence development. A multiple intervention study with 3,000 students in a higher education context. *International Journal of University Teaching and Faculty Development. (4)*4. https://www.novapublishers.com/catalog/product_info.php?products_id=53411

Veugelers, W. (2011). The moral and the political in global citizenship: Appreciating differences in education. *Globalisation, Societies and Education, 9*(3-4), 3–4, 473–485. doi:10.1080/14767724.2011.605329

Veugelers, W., & Vedder, P. (2003). Values in teaching. *Teachers and Teaching, 9*(4), 377–389. doi:10.1080/1354060032000097262

Veziroğlu, B. B. (2020). *Sosyal bilgiler dersinde Orhun Abidelerinin değer kazanımına etkisi* [Yayımlanmamış yüksek lisans tezi]. Ağrı İbrahim Çeçen Üniversitesi, Ağrı, Türkiye.

Volpe, G., & Gori, M. (2019). Multisensory interactive technologies for primary education: From science to technology. *Frontiers in Psychology, 10,* 1076. Advance online publication. doi:10.3389/fpsyg.2019.01076 PMID:31316410

Von Suchodoletz, A., & Hepach, R. (2021). Cultural values shape the expression of self-evaluative social emotions. *Scientific Reports, 11*(1), 13169. doi:10.103841598-021-92652-8 PMID:34162979

Vossekuil, Fein, Reddy, & Borum. (2002). *The Final Report And Findings Of The Safe School Initiative : Implications For The Prevention Of School Attacks In Of The Safe School Initiative.* https://static1.squarespace.com/static/55674542e4b074aad07152ba/t/5733a5f8c2ea51ad0fa1f82a/1463002617464/ssi_final_report.pdf

Vygotsky, L. S. (1977). *Mind in Society: The development of higher psychological processes.* Harvard University Press.

Waasdorp, T. E., Fu, R., Perepezko, A. L., Bradshaw, C. P., Evian, T., Fu, R., Perepezko, A. L., & Bradshaw, C. P. (2021). The role of bullying-related policies : Understanding how school staff respond to bullying situations The role of bullying-related policies . *European Journal of Developmental Psychology, 00*(00), 1–16. doi:10.1080/17405629.2021.1889503 PMID:34899942

Walker, L. J. (1986). Cognitive processes in moral development. In G. L. Sapp (Ed.), *Handbook of moral development* (pp. 109–145). Religious Education Press.

Wang, W. P. (2008). *Teaching English to young learners in Taiwan: Issues relating to teaching, teacher education, teaching materials and teacher perspectives* [Doctoral dissertation]. The University of Waikato.

Weinberger, A., Patry, J.-L., & Weyringer, S. (2016). Improving professional practice through hands-on research: VaKE (Values and Knowledge Education) in university teacher education. *Professions and Learning, 9*(1), 63–84.

Weissberg, R. P., & Cascarino, J. (2013). Academic learning + social-emotional learning = national priority. *Phi Delta Kappan, 94*(8), 62–65.

Wells, C. (1971). *İnsan ve dünyası.* Remzi kitabevi.

Wetherill, R. R., Neal, D. J., & Fromme, K. (2010). Parents, peers, and sexual values influence sexual behavior during the transition to college. *Archives of Sexual Behavior, 39*(3), 682–694. doi:10.100710508-009-9476-8 PMID:19291385

WFP. (2020). *The global and strategic role of WFP in school health and nutrition.* W. F. Pro.

WHO. (2003). *Oral health promotion: an essential element of a health-promoting school* (1727-2335). https://apps.who.int/iris/handle/10665/70207C

WHO. (2010). *A healthy lifestyle - WHO recommendations*. Regional Office For Europe. https://www.who.int/europe/news-room/fact-sheets/item/a-healthy-lifestyle---who-recommendations

WHO. (2017). *Determinants of health*. World Health Organization. Retrieved 13 June from https://www.who.int/news-room/questions-and-answers/item/determinants-of-health

WHO. (2019). *Translating community research into global policy reform for national action*. https://www.who.int/publications/i/item/9789241515627

WHO. (2020a). *Guidelines on mental health promotive and preventive interventions for adolescents: Helping adolescents thrive*. W. H. Organization. https://www.who.int/publications/i/item/9789240011854

WHO. (2020b). *WHO guidelines on physical activity and sedentary behavior* (Geneva: World Health Organization, Issue. https://apps.who.int/iris/handle/10665/336656

WHO. (2022a). *Global status report on physical activity 2022*. W. H. Organization. https://apps.who.int/iris/handle/10665/363607

WHO. (2022b). *Mental disorders*. World Health Organization. Retrieved 10 June from https://www.who.int/news-room/fact-sheets/mental-disorders

WHO. (2022c). *Physical activity*. World Health Organization. Retrieved 11 June from https://www.who.int/news-room/fact-sheets/detail/physical-activity

WHO. (2022d). *Promoting physical activity through schools: policy brief*. W. H. Organization. https://www.who.int/publications/i/item/9789240049567

WHO. (2023). *WHO Coronavirus (COVID-19) Dashboard*. https://covid19.who.int/

WHO. (2023a). *Constitution*. World Health Organization. Retrieved 1 June from https://www.who.int/about/governance/constitution

WHO. (2023b). *Improving health literacy*. World Health Organization. Retrieved 9 June from https://www.who.int/activities/improving-health-literacy

WHO. (2023c). *The mandate for health literacy*. World Health Organization. Retrieved 10 June from https://www.who.int/teams/health-promotion/enhanced-wellbeing/ninth-global-conference/health-literacy

Wiselia, D., Tanusetiawana, R., & Purnomoa, F. (2019). Simulation Game as a Reference to Smart City Management. *Procedia Computer Science, 116*, 468–475. doi:10.1016/j.procs.2017.10.053

Yalçın, Ali, (2021). *5. sınıf sosyal bilgiler dersinde uygulanan sorumluluk temelli etkinliklerin öğrencilere sorumluluk değerini kazandırmadaki etkisi* [Yayımlanmamış yüksek lisans tezi]. Bursa Uludağ Üniversitesi, Bursa, Türkiye.

Yalçın, A. (1985). *Cumhuriyetin İlk Yıllarında Eğitim Durumumuz*. Belgelerle Türk Tarihi Dün/ Bugün/ Yarın.

Yaldız, H. T. (2006). *Masalların çocuk eğitimi açısından incelenmesi (Sarayönü örneği)* [Yayımlanmamış yüksek lisans tezi]. Selçuk Üniversitesi, Konya, Türkiye.

Yangıl, M. K. ve Kerimoğlu, C. (2014). Bilmecelerin eğitimdeki yeri ve önemi. *Eğitim Bilimleri Araştırmaları Dergisi, 4*(2), 341–354.

Yanmaz, D. (2017). *Doğa tarihi müzesinde rehber hazırlama ve çalışma yapraklarıile öğretimin öğrencilerin akademik başarı ve fen öğrenimine yönelik motivasyonları üzerine etkisi* [Yayımlanmamış yüksek lisans tezi]. Sıtkı Kocaman Üniversitesi, Muğla, Türkiye.

Yap, S. F. (2014). Beliefs, values, ethics and moral reasoning in socio-scientific education. *Issues in Educational Research*, *24*(3), 299–319.

Yaşar, Ş. ve Çengelci, T. (2012). Sosyal bilgiler dersinde değerler eğitimine ilişkin bir durum çalışması. *Uluslararası Avrasya Sosyal Bilimler Dergisi*, *3*(9), 1–23.

Yasmin, S., & Rumi, M. A. (2020). Impact of pre-primary education on children in Bangladesh: A study on government primary schools in Sylhet City. *American Journal of Educational Research*, *8*(5).

Yaylı, B. (2020). *Sevgi değerinin kazanılmasında yaratıcı drama kullanımının sınıf öğretmeni adaylarının görüşlerine yansımaları* [Yayımlanmamış yüksek lisans tezi]. Recep Tayyip Erdoğan Üniversitesi, Rize, Türkiye.

Yazicioglu, T., & Aktepe, V. (2022). Identifying the values to be acquired by the students in inclusive classrooms based on the views of the classroom teachers. *International Journal of Progressive Education*, *18*(1), 52–64. doi:10.29329/ijpe.2022.426.4

Yeşilbursa, C. C., & Sabancı, O. (2015). Sosyal bilgiler öğretmen adaylarının sosyal bilgiler öğretiminde edebi ürünlerin kullanımına yönelik görüşleri. *Mehmet Akif Ersoy Üniversitesi Eğitim Fakültesi Dergisi*, *1*(36), 19–33.

Yetkin, S. K. (1972). *Estetik doctrine*. Bilgi Yayınevi.

Yıldırım, M. (2017). *Sosyal bilgiler öğretmenlerinin derslerinde edebi ürün kullanma durumları (Erzurum örneği)* [Yayımlanmamış yüksek lisans tezi]. Atatürk Üniversitesi, Erzurum, Türkiye.

Yıldız, A. (2021). *Orhun Yazıtlarındaki sosyal bilgiler dersi değerleri ve bu değerlere yönelik değer eğitimi etkinliklerinin oluşturulması* [Yayımlanmamış yüksek lisans tezi]. Trabzon Üniversitesi, Trabzon, Türkiye.

Yolageldili, G., & Arikan, A. (2021). Effectiveness of using games in teaching grammar to young learners. *Elementary Education Online*, *10*(1), 219–229.

Younan, B., & Younan, B. (2018). *A systematic review of bullying definitions : how definition and format affect study outcome*. doi:10.1108/JACPR-02-2018-0347

Young, R., & West, P. (2010). Do 'good values' lead to 'good' health behaviors? Longitudinal associations between young people's values and later substance use. *BMC Public Health*, *10*(1), 165. doi:10.1186/1471-2458-10-165 PMID:20346109

Yücel, H. A. (1994). *Hasan Ali Yücel, Türkiye'de Orta Öğretim*. Kültür ve Turizm Bakanlığı Publishing.

Yudkin, D. A., Gantman, A. P., Hofmann, W., & Quoidbach, J. (2021). Binding moral values gain importance in the presence of close others. *Nature Communications*, *12*(1), 2718. Advance online publication. doi:10.103841467-021-22566-6 PMID:33976160

Yunus, M., & Shahana, S. (2018). New Evidence on Outcomes of Primary Education Stipend Programme in Bangladesh. *Bangladesh Development Studies*, *41*(4).

Yurtbaşı, M. (2012). *Sınıflandırılmış atasözleri sözlüğü*. Excellence Publishing Yayıncılık.

Yussen, S. R. (1985). *The growth of reflection in children*. Academic Press.

Zalewska, J. (2019). Practice Theory Revisited: How Flexible Meta-habit Complements Habitus. *Polish Sociological Review*, *205*, 65–84.

Zelazo, P. D. (2000). Self-reflection and the development of consciously controlled processing. Children's reasoning and the mind, 169-189.

Zhelanov, D. V., Palamar, B. I., Gruzieva, T. S., Zhelanova, V. V., Leontieva, I. V., & Yepikhina, M. A. (2021). Value-Motivational Component of a Healthy Lifestyle of Modern University Students: The Real State and Logic of Formation. *Wiadomosci Lekarskie (Warsaw, Poland)*, *74*(5), 1079–1085. doi:10.36740/WLek202105106 PMID:34090268

Zheng, R., & Gardner, M. K. (2017). *Handbook of Research on Serious Games for Educational Application.* IGI Publishing. doi:10.4018/978-1-5225-0513-6

Zierer, K. (2010). *School value education.* Schneider.

Zigmond, A. S., & Snaith, R. P. (1983). 06). The Hospital Anxiety and Depression Scale. *Acta Psychiatrica Scandinavica*, *67*(6), 361–370. doi:10.1111/j.1600-0447.1983.tb09716.x PMID:6880820

Znaniecki, F. (1927). The object matter of sociology. *American Journal of Sociology*, *32*(4), 529–584. doi:10.1086/214184

Zych, I. (2021). *Childhood Risk and Protective Factors as Predictors of Adolescent Bullying Roles.* Academic Press.

About the Contributors

Aytekin Demircioğlu is a Professor at Kastamonu University Faculty of Humanities and Social Sciences. Study fields include Philosophy and Related Sciences Education.

* * *

Berke Andic is a lecturer of English for Academic Purposes, working at the American University of the Middle East (AUM), Kuwait, as part of the Liberal Arts Department. Having graduated with a B. Ed. in English Language Teaching from Yeditepe University, she obtained her Master's degree from the University of Oxford in Applied Linguistics and Second Language Acquisition in 2015. After this, she taught as a kindergarten and primary school teacher in Turkey. In 2017, she moved to Kuwait and started working as a lecturer in the English Preparatory Program at AUM. A year later she transferred to the Writing Center and has since been a consultant, guiding students on their academic writing journeys. Along with this, she has taught English for Academic Purposes, Communication, and Research and Technology courses within the Liberal Arts Department. Growing up in the United Kingdom, she is a Turkish-English bilingual, which fuels her research interest in linguistics and bilingualism. Her further research interests include teaching English as a second language, cross-linguistic influence, syntax-grammar, academic writing, and learning strategies.

Faiza Baig is a determined and ambitious individual pursuing her passion for knowledge and excellence in the field of Business Administration, with a focus on research areas such as benevolent leadership, self-efficacy, autonomy, task performance, contextual performance, bullying, and workplace bullying. Currently, she is immersed in the journey of obtaining her PhD in Business Administration, where she combines her strong analytical skills with her innate leadership abilities to explore and contribute to these important areas of study. Faiza's drive, resilience, and commitment are the pillars of her success as she works towards completing her PhD and advancing knowledge in the field of Business Administration. Through her research and expertise, she aims to empower future generations with valuable insights, foster positive work environments, and contribute to the well-being and success of individuals and organizations.

Md Ikhtiar Uddin Bhuiyan is an Associate Professor in the Department of Government and Politics at Jahangirnagar University, Dhaka, Bangladesh. In addition, he is working as Students Welfare Advisor in the Department of Government and Politics. In addition with academic rules he is serving as an Advisor of Transparency International of Bangladesh(TIB)- Yes Group, Jahangirnagar University. Moreover, he is playing pivotal role to eliminate food adulteration in the position of advisor in Youth Consumers

Forum. Mr. Ikhtiar is an academic with a proven track record both in teaching and research on issues of international relations and public policy issues which are central to meet social challenges. His publications prove his commitment to investigate social issues. Mr. Ikhtiar joined the department in 2016 as a lecturer. Since joining as a lecturer, he has been actively involved in research, teaching and administrative activities with sincerity and dedication. Prior to joining in the department, he worked in Bangladesh Civil Service (BCS) since 2014 and before joining in BCS, he also served in the Customs Department as a Customs Officer. In addition, he also worked in the Ministry of Information, Communication and Technology (ICT) as a protocol officer. Moreover, he worked in the Investment Corporation of Bangladesh as a senior officer. In 2018, Mr. Ikhtiar went to Japan for his advanced level second Master degree on Public Policy and returned in September 2019 after successfully completing his Master degree from National Graduate Institute for Policy Studies (GRIPS), Tokyo, Japan.

Okan Çoban completed his undergraduate education in the Department of Classroom Education at the Faculty of Education, Gazi University. He started his duty as a Classroom Teacher in 2000. He completed his Master's degree in 2005 and his Doctorate Education in 2016. In 2018, he served as the Minister's Advisor at the Ministry of National Education, as the Head of the Department in the Directorate General of Higher Education and Foreign Education in 2019, and as the Minister's Advisor at the Ministry of National Education between 2020 and August 2021. His field of work is social studies education.

Gülcan Demir, Assistant Professor, works as a faculty member at the Vocational School of Health Services, Sinop University.

Margarita Finko graduated from Rostov State Pedagogical Institute in 1986. The academic degree of PhD in Philosophy was awarded in 2005. She received in 2008 the academic title of processor in the Department of Philosophy, Cultural Studies and Philosophy of Science. She had more than 70 publications. In the center of scientific interests: philosophy of education, Russian philosophy, psychology of personality, sociology of youth. At various times she took part in academic programs: USA, Medford, Massachusetts, Tufts University; Denmark, Alborg, University of Alborg; Poland. Warsaw, Warsaw University. She had the title of "Honorary Worker of Higher Professional Education of the Russian Federation". Finko Margarita is a member of the editorial board of the journal "Economic and Humanitarian Research of Regions."

Isabel María Garcia Conesa has a degree in English Studies from the University of Alicante and a PhD from the National University of Distance Education (UNED). She is currently working as a full time lecturer at the Centro Universitario de la Defensa in San Javier (Spain). She has been awarded a scholarship by the Franklin Institute (University of Alcala de Henares, Spain) and the Radcliffe Institute for Advanced Study (Harvard University, USA), where she conducted a pre-doctoral research stay in the year 2012. Among her main lines of research, we can highlight the role of different women in literature and culture of the United States in contrast to Francophone writers with publication in Spanish journals like Revista Estudios Humanísticos (University of León), Tonos Digital (University of Murcia), Dossiers Feministes (University Jaime I), Prisma Social, Raudem (University of Almeria), Camino Real (University of Alcala de Henres), or Nomadas (University Complutense of Madrid). She also focuses on the study of the history of the teaching of English and gender studies with publications in journals such as Revista Feminismo (University of Alicante) or even Quaderns Digitals.

Ferah İzgi, after completing her undergraduate education, completed her master's degree in psychological counseling and guidance and clinical psychology. She is currently doing her doctorate in psychological counseling and guidance. She worked in the field of pedagogy both in the administrative and professional fields for a long time. She also received advanced training in family counseling, relationship, individual, sexual, psychodynamic, short-term solution-oriented, psychodynamic, transfer-oriented, filial therapy, mindfulness, self-compassionate awareness. She also received software development engineering tester training from the USA and self-coaching training from the UK. She published two books on values education written in 4 different languages and two books on child education. She is currently continuing her academic studies in Germany.

Antonio Juan Rubio has a degree in English Studies from the University of Murcia and a PhD from the National University of Distance Education (UNED) with the positive accreditation by the ANECA body, being given the Extraordinary Doctorate Award. He is currently working as a professor at the University of Granada. He has been awarded a scholarship by University College (Cork, Ireland), the Franklin Institute (University of Alcala de Henares, Spain) and the Radcliffe Institute for Advanced Study (Harvard University, USA), where he conducted a pre-doctoral research visit in the year 2012. He is currently a member of the scientific committee of several national and international journals as well as a member of the editorial board of several international journals. He also belongs to the organizing and scientific committee of several conferences organized by the Athens Institute for Education and Research (Greece). Among his main lines of research we can emphasize the following aspects: cultural studies in the United States; gender issues associated with the role of women in the Anglo-American literature; or the teaching practice and process of English.

Seda Liman Turan was born in Ankara in 1982. She graduated from Gazi University, Faculty of Education, Department of Painting Education, which she started in 2000, in 2004 as the second in the Faculty of Education and the first in the Department. She started her graduate education in the same year. She worked as a Visual Design Specialist at a private publishing house for a long time. She prepared illustrations and photographic images for many textbooks written in various fields. She started her doctoral studies at Gazi University in 2009 with her thesis titled "Evaluation of the Effect of Metaphysics and Psychoanalysis on Modernism and Post-Art" in 2012. She participated in many national and international group exhibitions. She started her academic career at KTU Fatih Education Faculty Painting Education Department in 2010 and continues within the scope of Trabzon University.

Monica Mastrantonio has a Ph.D. in Social Psychology, with over twenty years of practice as a psychologist and educator. She is now a post-doctoral researcher at the University Justus Liebig, Giessen, Germany. Her research interests are within the SDG's goals and equality, future narrative studies, and critical thinking.

Md Meshkat Mollik is a dynamic researcher and writer hailing from the vibrant nation of Bangladesh. As a devoted student of Government and Politics at Jahangirnagar University, he has embarked on an intellectual journey that has shaped his multifaceted expertise. His pioneering research papers shed light on the far-reaching consequences of the global health crisis, offering valuable insights into the socioeconomic challenges faced by individuals and communities during these unprecedented times. In addition to his exploration of contemporary issues, Md Meshkat Mollik also ventured into the realm of international relations. His profound understanding of the complex dynamics between nations led him to delve into the historic and ongoing relationship between Bangladesh and India. Through his meticulous analysis and thought-provoking reflections, he unravelled the intricacies of the fifty-year-long journey, offering a fresh perspective on the evolving ties between these neighboring countries.

Priyadarshini Muthukrishnan is a research enthusiast and passionate about to explore new areas of educational research. Her research is focused on teacher education and professional development. Her recent research interests are e-learning, growth mindset teaching practices, postgraduate students' graduation on time and eye-tracking research.

Turgay Öntaş completed his undergraduate education in the Department of Social Studies Education at the Faculty of Education, Sivas Cumhuriyet University in 2007. He obtained his master's degree in March 2010 at the Institute of Social Sciences, Hacettepe University, and his doctoral degree in November 2014 in the field of Classroom Education at the Institute of Educational Sciences, Gazi University. Between 2008-2010, he worked at the Ministry of Labor and Social Security, at the Maya Private Schools between 2010-2015, and at Zonguldak Bülent Ecevit University between 2015-2020. In 2020, he transferred to Tekirdağ Namık Kemal University. He served as the Minister's Advisor at the Ministry of National Education from 2018 to 2021. ÖNTAŞ, who received the title of Associate Professor in January 2021, is currently working as a faculty member at Tekirdağ Namık Kemal University. His fields of study include social studies education and teacher training.

Lütfiye Hilal Özcebe is a faculty member at the Department of Public Health, Faculty of Medicine, Hacettepe University.

Fatmanur Özen earned her undergraduate degree in Physics Education from the Middle East Technical University Faculty of Education. She completed her master's and doctoral degrees in Education Management Inspection Planning and Economics at Ankara University Education Sciences Institute. Her research interests include accountability in education, the impact of positive psychology (ethical climate, organizational happiness, virtue, restorative justice) on organizational behaviors in educational institutions, and fairness in education (multicultural education, gender equality). Özen has published articles and book chapters on these topics in national and international journals.

Esra Savaş is employed as an teacher at Boyabat Mevlana Vocational and Technical Anatolian High School.

Irum Shahzadi is a lecturer in Lyallpur Business School at Government College University, Faisalabad, Punjab, Pakistan. She holds her degree in Management and has more than 10 years of teaching. She is a Ph.D. scholar and young researcher. She has immense research interests in the areas of employees' workplace deviant behaviors.

Saziye Yaman is an Associate Professor of English in the Liberal Arts Department at American University of the Middle East in Kuwait since 2015. She taught various Academic writing and English communication courses in the Liberal Arts department. She was appointed as the Head of Foundation Program between 2016-2018, and later she initiated and acted as the head of the Writing Center at AUM for 3 years. She taught ELT Methodology and various TEFL and ESL courses at Cukurova University and Mersin University at B.A., M.A., and Ph.D. levels for over two decades in Turkey. She is the founder of the Foreign Languages Department, English Language and Literature Department, ELT Department, the Institute of Educational Sciences at Mersin University, where she worked for 25 years. She has been to several Erasmus universities to deliver lectures. She has served as the ELT Program Chair at Mersin University about 11 years and made numerous contributions to the university Boards, faculty journals and research committees, councils as well as in recruitment, Bologna and accreditation process. She supervised many MA Theses in ELT, taught in PhD in English Language Teaching programs, and contributed to various MA and PhD theses defense juries. Her research interests span both TEFL and ESL theories in In-service/Teacher Education. Much of her work has been on improving the understanding Reflection and Feedback in Education, Action Research, Learning Strategies, Professional Development, Academic Writing and Teacher Education. Her research focuses on constructivism, the use of technology in language classes, teachers' professional learning, language teachers' beliefs and perceptions. Dr. Yaman currently lives in Kuwait where she has been involved in both teaching and research.

Index

Milton Keynes UK
Ingram Content Group UK Ltd.
UKHW050630301023
431584UK00012B/577